PRAISE FOR *THE MIGHTY EIGHTH*

"No one does oral history better than Gerald Astor . . . here the men of the mightiest air force ever built tell their story in their own words—of trials, tribulations, triumphs, terror, and tedium."
—Stephen Ambrose, author of *Band of Brothers*

"Bold, brawny, epic in scope . . . Astor captures the fire and passion of these tens of thousands of U.S. airmen who flew through the inferno that was the bomber war over Europe." —Stephen Coonts, author of *The Red Horseman*

"[Astor's] many interviews of American airmen turn up some fascinating anecdotes, catching the grim realities of air combat in a way that more conventional strategic histories cannot . . . Revealing and vivid personal sketches of the quiet heroes in a unit that suffered more lives lost than the entire Marine Corps in WWII." —*Kirkus Reviews*

"The first-person testimony of these courageous men is invaluable in terms of understanding both the process of protracted war and its effect on the human spirit. Their anecdotes are fascinating . . . Excelling in weaving these stories into a broader analysis of the Eighth's role in the air war with Germany, Astor demonstrates once again that he's one of the most accomplished oral historians at work today." —*Publishers Weekly*

"Astor stitches together about a hundred eyewitness experiences of the combat, linking them with a workmanlike narrative of the battle's course. Here he presents the saga, frequently disastrous, of American daylight bombing against Germany . . . Riveting vignettes of dogfights and destruction."
—*Booklist*

"Gerald Astor has proven himself a master. Here, World War II is brought to life through the hammer blows of their airborne triumphs and fears. This book should be of interest to anyone who fought that war—or any war—in the air, and those who want to understand what combat was like for the airmen and their leaders." —J. Robert Moskin, author of *American Statecraft*

T0200748

ALSO BY GERALD ASTOR

THE
MIGHTY EIGHTH

The Air War in Europe
as Told by the Men Who Fought It

GERALD ASTOR

CALIBER

Dutton Caliber
An imprint of Penguin Random House LLC
375 Hudson Street
New York, New York 10014

ISBN: 978-0-425-28157-4

PUBLISHING HISTORY
Dutton hardcover edition / June 1997
Dell mass-market edition / November 1998
Berkley Caliber trade paperback edition / September 2015
Dutton Caliber trade paperback edition: 2018

Interior text design by Kelly Lipovich.

Printed in the United States of America

For those who flew and those who backed them up on the ground, and for Sonia who has been so supportive and given me wings.

CONTENTS

ACKNOWLEDGMENTS

I am foremost indebted to all of those, listed under Roll Call, who graciously shared with me their diaries, accounts, journals, letters home and especially those whom I interviewed. Magda Salvesen allowed me to use portions of the manuscript written by her late husband, Jon Schueler, and also supplied me with a copy of Billy Southworth's diary. Don Lopez at the National Air and Space Museum in Washington, D.C., supplied me with names and information. I was also aided by Dr. Walton S. Moody, historian of the Department of the Air Force, and Yvonne Kinkaid, the librarian who made available material from the USAF library at Bolling Field, Washington, D.C.; John Correll, editor of *Air Force* magazine, and Pearlie M. Draughn, research librarian of *Air Force*, provided counsel and reprints. Lois Harrington of the American Air Power Heritage Museum in Midland, Texas, supplied me with copies of oral histories from a number of Air Corps veterans. The United States Army Military History Library at Carlisle, Pennsylvania, was as usual helpful through its archives and Dr. Richard J. Sommers.

A number of people put me in touch with additional sources. These include: Mary Beth Barnard, director of history and archives at the Mighty Eighth Air Force Heritage Center, Jim Hill, editor of the *Eighth Air Force* newsletter, Ralph Rosensteel of the 92nd Bomb Group Association, Harry Alsaker of the 97th Bomb Group Reunion Association, Jim Clements of the 44th Bomb Group Association, Harry Crosby of the 100th Bomb Group Association, Lt. Col. Robert D. Elliott, USAF Ret., of the 92nd Bomb Group Association, Col. C. V. Glines, USAF Ret., and an authority on the Air Force, John Gray who served with Eighth Air Force Headquarters during World War II. George Hruska, editor of the 385th Bomb Group newsletter, Ollie Joiner of the 364th Fighter Group Association and Aida Kaye of the Eighth Air Force Historical Society, Edward Kueppers Jr. of the Eighth Air Force Historical Society, C. Will Lundy of the 2nd Air Division Association, Eric Nord Gilbertson, a World War II aviation buff, and Matt Clark, a former colleague in magazine journalism.

PREFACE

Rummaging through the attic of World War II in search of oral and eye-witness history one realizes that the amount of material about what was then the U.S. Army Air Corps far exceeds the collections of any other military branch. There are several reasons for this volume of information. Because the roles of pilot, navigator and bombardier, the officer component and close to half of the flight personnel required a high level of intelligence, technical knowledge and book learning, the Air Corps initially demanded a minimum of two years of college, and when it ran out of qualified candidates required applicants to pass entrance examinations. Several of the enlisted men's positions, the flight engineer and radio operator slots, also involved an ability to acquire information and skill. The kinds of intelligence tests given then, and to a considerable extent today, were partially based upon reading and comprehension of the English language. Under these circumstances it is not surprising to find that a large number of the flight crews had a learned or innate ability to communicate.

The fact that all of those who flew combat were volunteers suggests that these were men with some outgoing, assertive aspect to their personalities. Whatever motivated them to fly—infatuation with the notion of flight, the glamour that went with wings pinned to the uniform breast, an aversion to the life of a foot soldier—they made a choice rather than having their kind of service chosen for them.

Perhaps most influential was the kind of war they lived. If they survived a mission, they came home to a bed, hot food, showers and clean clothes. They had a place that was their own, if not a room, at least a bunk with a foot locker and some other space in which to keep personal items. Airmen usually had a respite between their encounters with the enemy, a night at the minimum or even several days, which gave them an opportunity to keep a diary or journal. Ground troops while in combat toted only what they needed to survive and even if pulled off the front line, their lodgings would only consist of a tent without the amenities that would enable them to preserve a personal log. For that matter, foot soldiers were strictly enjoined against carrying a diary or account of their experiences because if they were captured or fell on the field of battle, the information could be highly useful to enemy intelligence. Airmen could leave any documents about their doings back in their quarters, safe even if they were shot down.

Because the airmen jotted down their experiences so soon after the fact, there is perhaps less of a susceptibility to the distortions of memory that influence accounts well after the experience. On the other hand, even the freshest recall of things does not eliminate the possibility of self-serving descriptions. And just as eyewitnesses to an event often see things differently, so too did airmen able to view the action only from their own vantage point differ with one another.

Within the limitations of a single book it wasn't possible to cover every unit of the Mighty Eighth and that organization was only one of several involved in the European campaign. That being said, I believe the history of the Eighth Air Force as presented by those who served as sources for this book gives a true picture of what the battle for the skies was like.

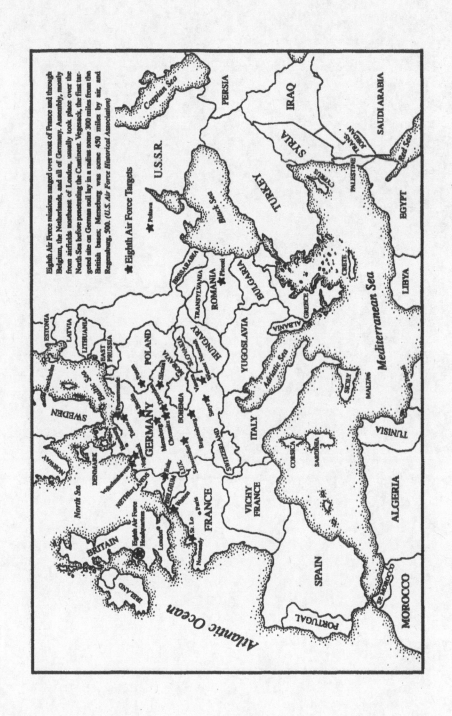

★ Eighth Air Force Targets

Eighth Air Force missions ranged over most of France and through Belgium, the Netherlands, and all of Germany. Assembly, mostly from airfields northeast of London, usually took place over the North Sea before penetrating the Continent. Wopenack, the first target site on German soil lay in radius some 300 miles from the British bases; Merseburg was some 450 miles by air, and Regensburg, 500. (U.S. Air Force Historical Association)

1

THE MIGHTY EIGHTH IS BORN

Within twenty-four hours after the first bombs from carrier-based Japanese airplanes exploded at Pearl Harbor, the United States entered a world-wide war in which the flying machine, largely a bit player previously, assumed an ever larger role. But, on December 7, 1941, what would become the single largest component of the American aerial arms, the Eighth Air Force, which carried the heaviest portion of war in the skies to Germany, did not even exist on paper. For that matter, the entire U.S. Air Force hardly deserved the name, so deficient was it in terms of numbers of combat aircraft performance capability and qualified airmen compared to enemy forces.

The Japanese Mitsubishi Zero or Zeke fighters in the South Pacific flew faster, higher and farther than any comparable aircraft in the American arsenal. In Europe, the German Messerschmitt 109 and 110 and the Focke Wulf 190s could outperform the P-39s and P-40s, the best U.S. Air Corps fighters. Only the biggest bombers, the four-engine B-17 Flying Fortress and the B-24 Liberator, surpassed what the enemy operated, but this reflected more the Axis powers' decision to employ smaller bombers than any deficiency of design or production on their part.

The inventory of all types of planes available to the handful of air crews was small; U.S. factories had yet to move into high gear and much of what was produced had been committed to Allies already engaged in combat. What had been accomplished during the two years and three months from the onset of the war in Europe to the entry of the United States was a series of plans that would eventually help shape the use of American military assets. During what were officially labeled United States–British Staff

Conversations of March 27, 1941, and became known as ABC-1, the participants settled on a number of policies including, "U.S. Army air bombardment units [would] operate offensively in collaboration with the Royal Air Force, primarily against German Military Power at its source." In the immediate aftermath of the devastation wrought against the U.S. fleet and the rapid onslaught of the Japanese against the Asiatic outposts of the Allies, President Franklin D. Roosevelt and his associates, in accord with such agreements as ABC-1 and various elaborations of the overall War Plan Orange series, had agreed that execution of the war against Germany held first priority.

In preparation for the mandates of ABC-1, before December 7, 1941, an American military mission occupied offices in London. But even before then, in recognition of the ties with Great Britain and the inevitability of a confrontation with Adolf Hitler's Nazi Germany, a stream of U.S. observers made their way to England to watch the RAF fight the Battle of Britain against German fighters and bombers during the summer of 1940. They also scouted potential bases for American contingents and managed lend-lease deals that included American-built planes such as A-20 light bombers dubbed "Bostons" by the RAF.

The advent of war almost instantly changed the nomenclature from the limited title of "mission" to U.S. Army Forces in the British Isles (USAFBI), and the label presaged the establishment of a significant presence of men and machines. As chief of the Army Air Forces, Lt. Gen. Henry (Hap) Arnold secured approval from the War Department to activate an air force as part of USAFBI. He chose Maj. Gen. Carl Spaatz, a World War I combat pilot, respected tactician, strategist and administrator to head the outfit and nominated Brig. Gen. Ira Eaker to run the bomber command. Even before Spaatz and Eaker could begin to mobilize the airplanes to carry out the task, they encountered fierce opposition from the brass in charge of all U.S. Army efforts in England. The traditional resistance of ground commanders to grant any autonomy to the air forces succumbed only through the intervention of Army chief of staff Gen. George C. Marshall. The vehicle tapped for Spaatz and Eaker was the Eighth Air Force, activated in January 1942.

While the newly formed outfit initially consisted of a medium bombardment group, two pursuit groups (the designations of fighters or interceptors were not yet in vogue) and auxiliary units, other priorities reduced the Eighth to a bare skeletal form as the Japanese advanced in the Pacific. The original bomber group committed to the Eighth joined Lt. Col. James H. Doolittle to train for his mission against Tokyo. Other aircraft allotted to the Eighth were siphoned away to participate in the critical anti-submarine warfare off the U.S. coast and for other responsibilities.

In February of 1942, Ira Eaker took up station in England as the head of the Eighth Bomber Command, but the parent organization was not in residence until May 11, 1942, when the first contingent of thirty-nine officers and 384 enlisted men set foot on British soil. Eaker, at the time all too aware of what little material strength he brought with him, rose to speak to an assembly of RAF guests at an early June ceremony at the newly opened High Wycombe headquarters. "We won't do much talking until we've done more fighting. We hope that when we leave you'll be glad we came. Thank you."

Eaker's twenty-three words could hardly offend the host country as they implicitly recognized that six months after the declaration of war, the American contribution to the air war effort in Europe had been only money and goods while British fliers continued to pay a bloody price. But while the British approved the gracious note, furious discord marked the opinions and policies of the two Allies even before they joined forces to fight.

With less than thirty years' presence in the fields of combat, aerial warfare had never generated a consensus on its conduct. In 1907, a scant four years after the Wright brothers successfully demonstrated a twelve-second, 120-foot flight at Kitty Hawk, North Carolina, the U.S. Army created the Aeronautical Division as a wholly controlled subsidiary of the Signal Corps. The premise for this arrangement lay in the belief that the basic role of the airplane would be as a more mobile reconnaissance tool, an improvement on the balloon-borne observer who had appeared overhead as early as the French Revolution and later in the Civil War. In 1910, nineteen-year-old U.S. Military Academy plebe Carl Spaatz gazed skyward and saw aviation pioneer Glenn Curtiss win a $10,000 prize as the first to fly all the way down the Hudson River from Albany to New York City, passing West Point en route. Spaatz instantly decided to make a career in the fledgling Aeronautical Service.

During World War I, while experts tinkered with such basic problems as reducing the fatality rate in accidents below that incurred during battle, and preventing machine guns from shooting off propeller blades, the air arm, renamed the Aviation Section, remained a Signal Corps fief until 1918 when American Expeditionary Force commander, Gen. John J. Pershing, removed Signal Corps control and President Woodrow Wilson officially proclaimed the Air Service as an organization within the Army. The military mission had slowly begun to evolve from solely scouting to a more active role in warfare. The European combatants all sought to develop aircraft that themselves served as weapons. The initial idea of inflicting damage on the foe's observation planes soon led to a battle for control of the air. Machine guns enabled fliers to strafe ground forces, and the addition of bombs provided the opportunity to hammer troop concentrations, artillery positions and even lines of transportation. The top Allied commanders had even begun to think of striking at cities or factories; although in some circles there was great reluctance to the notion of dropping high explosives on civilian areas. Occasionally, German airplanes and long range artillery did hit some populated sections, and their dirigibles struck London.

As the possible roles for an air force evolved, individuals who would play major parts in World War II surfaced. Carl Spaatz, already a rising star in the Air Service and involved in training Americans at a French installation wangled a tour as a combat pilot where he flew a Spad (U.S. design and production of planes during World War I was limited to manufacturing engines). In a brief period of three weeks he knocked down a trio of enemy Fokkers but also suffered the indignity of being shot out of the skies by the foe. He was able to walk away from his wrecked plane. Two key members of the Eighth, Ira Eaker and Jimmy Doolittle, both earned their wings in 1918 but neither saw action. However, the most important Air Service figure to achieve prominence was Billy Mitchell.

During World War I, Pershing, who had employed airplanes and airmen like Spaatz when he pursued Pancho Villa, the Mexican revolutionary—bandit in American eyes—across the border, relied on Mitchell to oversee his air arm. Mitchell, who only qualified as an aviator in 1916, gradually assumed the enthusiasm of a convert. At first, somewhat cautiously following the script that dictated a subservient role for airplanes, he showed a talent for innovation. He developed techniques for more effective offensive use of the airplane, massing his assets for an attack in October that led an analyst for the Associated Press to write: "This navy of the air is to be expanded until no part of Germany is safe from the rain of bombs. It is a thing apart from the fighting, observation and bombing squadrons attached to the various army corps. The work of the independent force is bombing munitions works, factories, cities and other important centers far behind the German lines. It has been promised that eventually Berlin itself will know what an air raid means, and the whole great project is a direct answer to the German air attacks on helpless and unfortified British, French, and Belgian cities."

Mitchell even petitioned Pershing to assign an infantry division to the Air Service which would load up aircraft with parachute-equipped soldiers and drop them behind the enemy lines. The 1918 November armistice aborted all plans for raids on cities and the employment of airborne troops but Mitchell emerged from the war with a prophet's zeal. He talked of a need for an independent air force, one that while supporting the ground efforts, would have its own agenda and control its destiny.

Mitchell believed in the airplane as an offensive weapon limited only by the capabilities of the machine, the location of bases, the weather and the strength of the enemy in the air. Discounting the role of antiaircraft guns, he argued there was no defense against aviation other than another air force. It naturally followed that the first responsibility of the fliers would be to obtain supremacy of the skies. Once that was achieved, planes could freely attack enemy ground troops, transportation, supply dumps and communications. Initially, Mitchell limited the offensive actions to these, but subsequently he admitted to another possibility. "We must expect . . . to have the enemy attempt to destroy any or all of our combatant or *industrial* [my italics] forces—his attacks being entirely controlled by the dictates of strategy, and the means of bringing the war to a quick conclusion. It may be at times the best strategy to damage and destroy property, and to kill and disable an enemy's forces and resources at points far removed from the field of battle of either armies or navies." Without using the word, Mitchell in 1921 had made the civilian a potential target. Four years later he flatly declared that bombers would smash "centers of production of all kinds, means of transportation, agricultural areas, ports and shipping, . . . they will destroy the means of making war."

Convinced by his experience with bombs dropped upon troops being marshaled in the rear of the front lines, Mitchell now argued that the airplane had superseded ships as the best means to defend the U.S. He persuaded congressmen, anxious to find a less expensive way to protect the national interest, to order a test of his theory. Near the mouth of the Chesapeake in 1921, navy fliers destroyed a captured German U-boat sitting on the water's surface. Then Mitchell's contingent of eight biplanes, at a speed of ninety miles per hour and an altitude of 8,000 feet, sank the anchored former German battleship *Oestfriesland,* the cruiser *Frankfurt* and a destroyer within thirty minutes.

While the results might appear conclusive they were hardly accepted by vested or even impartial interests. Sitting targets which offered no opposition to the bombers hardly replicated what might be expected in a real attack. But even more deadly to Mitchell's cause, the ground commanders who dominated the Army stoutly resisted any attempt to obtain independence for the airmen and their missions. An equally adamant Navy establishment saw Mitchell's proposals as usurping its position. Advocates of a stronger and more independent air force hoped a second demonstration off Cape Hatteras in 1923 would convince the policy makers. A galaxy of top brass from the navy and army as well as a contingent of reporters gathered to observe an assault upon a pair of 16,000-ton battleships. The *Virginia* and the *New Jersey,* already obsolescent in World War I, served as the targets. Samuel Taylor Moore, a former AEF balloon officer and newsman with a rooting interest in the fortunes of airmen, recalled the dismay among the aviation-minded when Pershing interrupted a briefing by Maj. Gen. Mason Patrick, chief of the Air Service. Patrick had hardly begun his remarks about the controversy over the vulnerability of armed ships to attack from the sky when Pershing undercut him. "What General Patrick is telling you is that his Air Service is having some target practice." Good soldier Patrick stopped his talk, saluted and concluded, "Yes, the Air Service is having target practice."

Eight planes, each bearing a pair of 600-pound bombs set upon the *New Jersey.* They scored four hits that left the aged vessel with a slight list. A second assault from an altitude of 6,000 feet with one-ton bombs registered a couple of near misses and increased the list but the battleship remained afloat. The *Virginia,* however, capsized after being blasted by a flight at 3,000 feet while Mitchell himself led a final raid on the *New Jersey.* One aircraft, making two runs over the ship pinpointed its explosives perfectly. The battlewagon heaved and bucked in a flash of fire and smoke before heading for the bottom of the bay.

The event failed to persuade anyone of consequence. Admirals scoffed that ships under way could have maneuvered out of harm's way and perhaps destroyed the planes with their guns. The army generals similarly dismissed the affair as a stunt without implications for the airpower role. Mitchell turned Jeremiah, preaching his gospel to the public when officialdom refused to heed. Inevitably that led to the prophet's doom, in this case a court-martial that forced him to resign from the Army.

The prophet may have been silenced, but followers, albeit more circumspect in their utterances, remained. The controversy continued to simmer until a committee named by President Calvin Coolidge studied the matter. Chaired by Dwight W. Morrow (his daughter would marry Charles Lindbergh), the results of the inquiry were some minor revisions in the status of the Air Service, promises of more adequate funding, increases in strength and the designation as the Army Air Corps.

During the 1930s, the subject of independence occasionally reared its head only to have it chopped off by panels and committees. With that avenue blocked, the Air Corps planners sought to define a mission and create the tools to carry it out. Aside from Mitchell, the other thinker who influenced the development of airpower was an Italian named Giulio Douhet. During the early 1920s, Douhet, a more classical military scholar than Mitchell or another air-war proponent, Hugh Trenchard of the Royal Flying Corps, expounded the theme that modern war involved an entire society, "the soldier carrying his rifle, the woman loading shells in a factory, the farmer growing his wheat, the scientist experimenting in his laboratory." His was a concept of strategic bombing, rather than tactical support for the ground forces. Douhet believed the rain of explosives would not only halt wartime production, but that the terror it wrought would annihilate the will to oppose. "How could a country go on living and working, oppressed by the nightmare of imminent destruction and death?" His was a war without mercy, "tragic," he admitted, "one in which morality or civilized behavior had no place," and even included the use of poison gas on the noncombatants. Douhet scoffed at distinctions between the killing of soldiers or civilians. He consoled the appalled by arguing such a conflict would end swiftly, perhaps with less bloodshed over the long run than such horrors as inflicted in World War I.

Like Mitchell, Douhet argued that the airplane, if properly employed, could quickly eliminate the capacity of the enemy to wage war. Inevitably, the followers of Mitchell and Douhet saw the bomber as the weapon of choice. The accepted philosophy among this school of warfare was stated by RAF commander Hugh Trenchard who issued a statement, "It is not necessary . . . for an air force, in order to defeat the enemy nation, to defeat its armed forces first. Air power can dispense with that intermediate step, can pass over the enemy, navies and armies, and penetrate the air defenses and directly attack the centers of production, transportation and communications from which the enemy war effort is maintained." Trenchard explained that domination of the skies would naturally lead to a direct offensive against the foe's vital centers. Harold George (subsequently commander of the U.S. Air Transport Command), as a member of the Air Corps Tactical School faculty in 1935 declared, "The spectacle of huge air forces meeting in the air is the figment of imagination of the uninitiated." Ground force proponents may have continued to believe the only way to win lay in physically conquering enemy armies and occupying the land, but to airmen their attitudes only confirmed their ignorance of what modern war would be about.

The pursuit or interceptor, the fighter plane in later parlance, was not an offensive weapon useful against the strategic centers delineated by Douhet. Its major function lay in fending off attacks by enemy bombers and defensive efforts, but would not produce victory outright. Influential aviators like Carl Spaatz, who had cut his combat teeth in pursuit ships during World War I, now wholeheartedly focused on the bombers. Not only did they bear the means to obliterate the vital organs of an enemy, but the very nature of the beast, its size and payload forced the development of engines with innovations like superchargers, variable pitch propellers that gave it the capacity for speed and sustained flight at high altitudes, going far beyond the state-of-the-art fighters. As early as 1931 Spaatz wrote to a colleague, "Normally, at low altitudes, i.e., altitudes below 15,000 feet, penetration of attack and bombardment [aircraft formations] into enemy territory will be shallow unless protected by pursuit. At altitudes above 15,000 feet observation from the ground becomes difficult, and above 20,000 feet bombardment airplanes can make deep penetrations without pursuit protection." He was willing to grant that the former object of his affection still had a role as a weapon for ground support.

During the 1930s, an Air Corps study team pondered the proper specifications for a genuine escort for bombers and decided that under the existing state of military aeronautics the requirements defeated the performance characteristics of a genuine fighter. A later board that included Eaker and Col. Frank Hunter, the first chief of fighter command when the Eighth Air Force began operations in England, reached a similar conclusion. The authors covered their backsides with a remark about the feasibility of continuing a search for an escort able to travel the distance while providing fighter quality. Neither British nor German aeronautical designers and engineers of the period between World War I and World War II could discover how to build an airplane capable of accompanying bombers without being vulnerable in itself. During the Battle of Britain in 1940, the RAF dined heartily on the German two-engine escorts which possessed the range but not the speed or maneuverability to cope with the defenders' Spitfires and Hurricanes. Likewise, when the RAF sought to chaperone its heavyweights with Typhoons and Tornadoes they too could not compete with German fighters.

In 1932, the bombsight invented by C. L. Norden, originally for the Navy, won adoption by the Air Corps. Its accuracy encouraged U.S. strategists further toward a critical decision, the emphasis on high altitude, daylight bombing. Spaatz had predicated his ideas partially on the limits of the human eye and optical instruments of the day. He knew nothing of radar that could locate aircraft over distance, through darkness and cloud cover. Nor did he foresee that designers could create fighters able to reach levels far above 20,000 feet. It is also true that later he tempered his initial remarks with cautionary comments that indicated bombers might still be vulnerable to fighters under certain circumstances. At first, Spaatz did not include the goal of strategic attacks upon an enemy's populated areas and their means of production as espoused by both Mitchell and Douhet, but instead theorized that airpower would concentrate upon combined operations with the ground forces.

The mélange of ideas on airpower, its components and its mission influenced the kinds of aircraft manufactured by the U.S. as World War II approached. The essential stance of America during the 1920s and 30s was a defensive, isolationist one. With a country 3,000 miles long, 1,500 miles wide, an airplane capable of traveling great distances that could be based anywhere in the States and still hit attackers at the shoreline seemed attractive to the Air Corps. The big bomber would also serve to protect far-off interests, the Philippines, Hawaii and Alaska. It was regarded as the main aerial tool and its development became the top priority for the Air Corps and civilian industry.

In 1933–34, Boeing designed and built the first B-17. Although the performance of the prototype four-engine bomber bowled over the Air Corps with its first flights in 1935, a crash of the original model briefly dampened enthusiasm and limited orders. But the major obstacle to a fleet of B-17s was possible duplication of the Navy's role. Advocates of seapower and budget-oriented bureaucrats lobbied against aerial dreadnaughts as usurping the Navy's function with an excessively expensive tool. Medium, short-range land bombers could back up carrier strikes with torpedo bombers launched at any adversary that approached American shores. Only after Nazi Germany devoured both Czechoslovakia and Austria, did Franklin Roosevelt and his advisors agree to modest increases in the B-17 fleet.

The B-17B, standard in 1941, packed just five flexible .30 caliber machine guns, lacked a belly turret and tail gunner, and possessed little protective armor. It hardly lived up to the publicity that labeled it a "Flying Fortress." But by the end of World War II the addition of twelve or even thirteen .50 caliber machine guns plus steel padding in vulnerable areas, power-driven turrets, gunners to the rear and below and bulletproof windshields lent some credence to the name.

The B-24 Liberator, the other U.S. heavyweight of the American war in Europe also sprang from Roosevelt's intervention on behalf of airpower. Invited to develop a prototype, Consolidated Aircraft Company took on the job of creating a four-engine bomber with higher speed and a greater payload than the B-17. In its original design, the Liberator also lacked firepower, power-operated turrets and sufficient protection for the crew. Nevertheless the planes began to roll off the assembly line by early 1941. Toward the close of that year as the smoke and fire engulfed Pearl Harbor, the heavy bomber armada counted slightly fewer than 300 inadequately weaponed or armor-protected planes.

The two modern fighter planes with which the Air Corps entered the war reflect the preoccupation with the long-range bomber. The intelligence on which the top brass and civilian leaders based their criteria for performance was abysmal, leading to such absurdities as a General Headquarters Air Force statement, ". . . the airplane design had reached the point where a large airplane could be made to go as fast as a small one and that the defensive armament of the large plane was more than a match for the small plane." Only six months off lay the Battle of Britain, where the RAF and Luftwaffe fighters engaged in furious dogfights exceeding any speed, height or firepower that the best U.S. bombers could achieve. In addition, the American fighters of the day were built on the premise of coastal defense. No high-altitude heavy bombers could be expected to assault the continent, and for low-level strafing and bombing runs the P-39s and P-40s would be effective.

The P-39 Airacobra, a sleek ship on the ground, maneuvered poorly, climbed slowly and not high enough. During the war, however, P-39s were gratefully accepted by the Soviet Army which valued them for their use against enemy ground troops and installations. The P-40 Warhawk, a considerable improvement, nevertheless took too much time reaching upper altitudes, and was at a considerable disadvantage against the tighter turning capability of enemy planes like the Japanese Zero. The Airacobra and Warhawk were already obsolescent by the time they fired their first shots in anger. Improvements began with the P-38, the Lockheed twin engine whose turbosuperchargers enabled it to operate at great speed even in the rarefied atmosphere. The P-38 Lightnings, able to act as fighter bombers and blessed with good range, rolled off assembly lines slowly, starting in 1939. They would become the first effective U.S.-built escort for the Eighth Air Force.

By 1940, in spite of the nonsense spewed in the official GHQ paper, the Air Corps realized it needed something better if it was to compete with the enemy fighters. In May 1941, the XP-47B left the ground. Subsequently, Ira Eaker himself test flew the plane and endorsed it heartily, but not until 1943 did engineers get the bugs out of the Thunderbolt making it fit for combat. As an escort and fighter bomber it would serve valiantly for the Eighth Air Force and other American outfits around the world.

At the same time as aeronautical designers and engineers conceived and built the P-47, North American Aviation, under contract to the RAF for a new fighter, created the P-51 Mustang. An instant hit with the client who declared it, "the best American fighter that has reached this country," the P-51, with the addition of the British Merlin 61 engine, would become the favorite fighter of the Eighth Air Force because its speed, high-altitude capability and range, enhanced through extra fuel tanks, enabled it to accompany the Forts and Liberators wherever they went.

The Air Corps also contracted for light and medium bombers, two-engine aircraft—the A-20, B-25 and B-26. Except for a very brief period, these planes were not part of the Mighty Eighth's inventory, but since the simpler machines were available and required fewer crewmen they went to war in Europe before their bigger brethren.

Just as the designers and manufacturers of warplanes slowly moved to build implements that would be appropriate for the demands of combat in the 1940s, so too did the future leaders of the Air Corps develop their skills and understanding of what would be required. Arnold, Spaatz and Eaker all began their march to prominence during World War I. Other key people of what eventually became known as "the Mighty Eighth" embarked on their march to the command path slightly later.

Arnold, a 1909 West Point grad, actually learned to fly from the Wright brothers in Dayton, Ohio, before he completed his instruction at the Army school set up at College Park, Maryland. The flimsy, experimental machines of the day imperiled even the best of the aviators. In 1912, according to one biography, with more than a thousand successful flights behind him, Arnold barely survived a terrifying stall and dive towards the ground from which he managed to pull out only at the last moment. Supposedly he told a fellow officer, "A man doesn't face death twice," and he refused to fly again for four years.

A staff officer during World War I, Arnold, then a rising star of the Air Service, stoutly supported Billy Mitchell. The wrath of the War Department against the Mitchell entourage almost consigned Arnold's career to a black hole, but he successfully navigated his way back from an obscure post until he soared to the top of the heap. He admitted he lacked patience or tolerance and demanded the utmost of subordinates.

Spaatz, an outspoken adherent of the Mitchell philosophy and the need for a separate air force, escaped serious disciplinary action for his comments, largely because as a mere major he seemed less of a target than the likes of Mitchell and Arnold. Frustrated by the rejection of the new ideas on airpower, Spaatz busied himself with improving the limited assets of what was now the Army Air Corps. During this period, Spaatz investigated and promulgated new tactical notions. He contributed to improvements of air-to-ground communications. He sought engines that would enable his branch to win air races against Navy entries. He influenced designs on drawing boards, and although he did not ignore the need for pursuit ships, his input was most notable in connection with long-range bombers. By 1939 he had advanced to chief of the Plans Division for the Air Corps and perhaps enlightened by the punishment meted out to Mitchell had become known as a team player, a fellow who could be counted upon to follow orders and almost equally important, one who measured his words carefully.

Ira Eaker, five years younger than Spaatz and destined to become Spaatz's deputy and lead the Mighty Eighth in its earliest and darkest period, missed an opportunity for combat in World War I but he too endorsed the Mitchell program. Less outspoken than many of his contemporaries, Eaker, in his post as an executive officer to an assistant secretary of war, with the blessing of Maj. Gen. Mason Patrick, chief of the Air Service, funneled useful documents to support Mitchell's case. When the case for an independent, stronger outfit collapsed, Eaker escaped opprobrium.

A scholar of law at Columbia and of journalism at the University of Southern California while in uniform, Eaker also piloted goodwill flights to Central America, occupied the cockpit during a world-record 150-hour endurance flight featuring midair refueling in 1929, and in 1936 became the first pilot ever to fly coast-to-coast strictly on instruments. Recognized for his skillful handling of political powers and as an artful propagandist for the Air Corps, he gained the confidence of both Spaatz and Arnold and when the latter tapped the former to open up shop in England, Spaatz chose Eaker as his second in command.

James H. Doolittle, born in 1896, as was Eaker, spent most of his boyhood in Nome, Alaska, amid the hurly-burly of the turn-of-the-century gold rush. Bantam-sized, he compensated by learning how to fight off bigger kids and developed an adventurous thirst that led him to building gliders, boxing as an amateur and performing gymnastics. At the University of California he studied engineering, but after President Woodrow Wilson declared war on Germany in 1917 he enlisted as a private in the neonate flying service. Doolittle earned his wings and a lieutenant's commission but never reached France and aerial combat.

Choosing to stick with the service, Doolittle researched gunnery, taught flying and indulged his lust for risks by performing spectacular acrobatics at air shows. He also learned what he could about aircraft engines, frames and fuel. To help encourage public support for the Army in the air, he set a record for a cross-country flight, set new marks for speed and still furthered his education with a master's degree from MIT. Curtiss Aircraft borrowed him to sell its new P-1 fighter in South America where Doolittle distinguished himself by his cocktail consumption and a night of tumbling and gymnastics on a balcony. When a ledge cracked, Doolittle fell two stories, fracturing both ankles.

Determined not to disappoint the Army and Curtiss because of his rash behavior, Doolittle performed in an air show with casts on both legs. Special clips rigged by a mechanic allowed him to keep his feet on the rudder pedals as he outflew the German competition in a gunless dogfight. He then continued to demonstrate the P-1 with his legs in splints all the while. He burnished his reputation even further through exploits as a test pilot demonstrating instrument flight while a hood totally obscured his vision.

But in 1930, the thirty-four-year-old Doolittle, still a lieutenant in the promotion-starved military establishment, resigned for a private aviation post. He entered various competitions and won trophies and prizes for speed races but after several crashes and near disasters, family man Doolittle quit the sport. Instead he promoted the development of 100-octane gas which the bigger, faster planes would need. Traveling around the world on behalf of U.S. aircraft manufacturers, Doolittle visited Germany and was horrified by the nascent Nazi airpower, an obvious violation of the Versailles Treaty signed after World War I. Doolittle informed Hap Arnold of what he had seen and then, in 1940, he resigned his civilian job to be a major on active duty. Following the attack by the Japanese, Arnold summoned Doolittle to Washington to head special projects.

Curtis LeMay, a mechanic's son, was a twelve-year-old schoolboy in Columbus, Ohio, when World War I ended. He graduated from Ohio State in 1928 and enlisted as a flying cadet. A serious student of strategy and a qualified engineer, LeMay originally flew fighters before taking on the exploration of the new B-24 Liberator bombers. His long-distance, over-the-water flights marked the plane and the pilot as promising. Transferred to the 305th Bomb Group, a B-17 organization as the shooting war began for America, LeMay quickly familiarized himself with the aircraft as the group prepared for duty with the Eighth Air Force.

Whatever their backgrounds, the men who would lead the Mighty Eighth all accepted an essential aspect of combat command, a willingness to order men to kill and be killed. Air Corps officers in general are believed to have been psychologically more prepared for the casualties of war, since even in peacetime there was a much higher number of deaths due to accidents than befell those in the infantry, field artillery or other outfits. "I won't say you get callous," said Eaker, "but you get realistic." He remarked to an interviewer of the necessity to be "trained and inured" if one was to carry out the tasks. LeMay said one in his position could not "meditate on the process of death" nor "mope around about the deaths he has caused personally by deed or impersonally in the act of command."

For Carl Spaatz, a tour with the U.S. military mission during the Battle of Britain, opened his eyes to some of the weaknesses of the Air Corps. He quickly realized that the effectiveness of the British radar system, crude as it was, detected aircraft long before they could be seen. He understood that the protection of invisibility through distance, darkness or cloud cover no longer pertained. His talks with RAF pilots and commanders revealed the weakness of the German bombers which were restricted in distance, too lightly armed to defend themselves, flew too low and maintained level flight, all adding up to a recipe for disaster. He also learned that the limited range of the German fighter escorts allowed the Spitfires and Hurricanes to decoy enemy planes into expending their fuel, forcing them to leave the scene of battle. That allowed others access to the bombers. Since enemy fighters appeared able to reach the altitude of the B-17 and B-24, Spaatz recognized that the heavyweights needed rear firepower to ward off attacks from behind and armor plate to shield personnel and vital organs of the aircraft. He also accepted that escort fighters would be desirable but the solution of how to load enough fuel on the small, lightweight aircraft without destroying their maneuverability and speed remained a problem.

Spaatz and his associates remained committed to their notion of daylight bombing from high altitudes. Only the U.S. possessed the Norden sight which the strategists believed guaranteed effective delivery. In the spring of 1941, having weathered the Battle of Britain and now intent on carrying the death and destruction to the enemy, the British welcomed about twenty B-17s delivered under lend-lease to the RAF. After training and some modifications to incorporate the local control system, a trio of Forts headed for Wilhelmshaven on July 8. The raid was a fiasco; the bombs dropped from 30,000 feet missed the target and the machine guns froze up when German fighters attacked. Subsequent missions against shipping and other objectives produced dismal results, almost half the sorties aborted, only a couple of planes reached primary targets; eight of the twenty B-17s were lost or grounded for repairs. Not a single enemy fighter had been knocked down.

British enthusiasm for the B-17 and its daylight operations vanished. The Americans noted their allies insisted on operating at well over 30,000 feet, excessive even for the high-altitude bomber, leading to overloads on the oxygen systems, a freeze-up of weapons and reduction in airspeed, lessening ability to defend against enemy fighters. Finally, the RAF relied on the Sperry bombsight, considered quite inferior to the Norden. But, unconvinced by the arguments of the Americans, when B-24s were delivered the RAF shunted them away from strategic-bomb operations and into antisubmarine patrols.

The failure to convert the British to the potential of the heavy bombers for their designed purpose dogged Ira Eaker almost immediately. Not only did the ally clamor for immediate deeds by the Americans but they insisted the proposed approach would be a disaster. Not too subtly the British suggested that all American aircraft come under RAF control. No one in America, certainly not Chief of Staff George C. Marshall, or Hap Arnold as boss of the Air Corps could stomach that. Spaatz and Eaker would have to prove to the British that daylight, precision bombing could work.

2

OPENING SALVO

As the American representatives of the Air Corps in Europe, Spaatz and Eaker wrestled with their British counterparts over two prickly issues: daylight raids and area bombing. The Allied commanders all agreed on the need for a strategic bombing campaign. Aerial assaults on centers of production and transportation, economic pressure upon neutrals, hit and run operations by commandos, sabotage by people in occupied lands and the murderous war between the Soviets and Germans could bleed the Axis powers sufficiently to provide optimum conditions for a direct frontal assault by ground troops in the West. In fact, the RAF publicly wondered if intensive bombing might even obviate any need to invade the Continent.

The two American generals faced an uphill battle to win favor for their daylight precision bombing campaign. Having seen RAF fighters smash German bombers during daylight forays and then experiencing the loss of fifteen two-engine Vickers Wellingtons from a total of twenty-four during an early daytime foray against Germans and after the failure of the B-17 experiment, the RAF insisted that only under the shroud of darkness could strategic bombing successfully hammer the enemy. The policy makers, aware that night attacks sacrificed precision, introduced the notion of "area" bombing. Destruction in the vicinity of a strategic site, while perhaps not inflicting all the desired damage on the target, would destroy the surrounding neighborhood, which included workers. Psychological as well as physical injury would result; the ideas of Douhet rendered real. The approach dictated the design of British aircraft; bombers with great range, oversize loads and because of the presumed protection by darkness against opposition, less armament and fewer crewmen. Because of their nocturnal rounds, the Lancasters and Stirlings sallied forth without fighter escort; indeed the British made no effort to extend the short range of the otherwise superb Spitfire. At the end of May and beginning of June, just before the first of the Eighth Air Force elements arrived, the RAF scrounged aircraft from training and noncombat commands to mount Operation Millennium, the first thousand-plane saturation raid upon Cologne. More than two-thirds of the attackers consisted of two-engine planes with no margin for error if they were to return to base. The bombs killed 469, wounded more than 5,000 and destroyed 45,000 homes. Subsequently similar assaults blasted Bremen and the Ruhr with widespread havoc but relatively little effect on the German war effort, other than to stimulate production of fighters. From a propaganda viewpoint, however, the attacks seriously wounded Luftwaffe chief Hermann Goering, who had boasted in 1939, "My name is not Goering. If any enemy aircraft is ever seen over Germany, you can call me Meyer." (An anti-Semitic reference.)

The Air Corps predicated its faith in the daylight approach on the ability of the Norden sight to pinpoint targets and for the Forts and Liberators to fly high enough and fast enough to defeat efforts to stop them. Theorists denigrated area bombing as a wasteful dispersion of resources. The British-convened Butt Committee, charged with an investigation of the effectiveness of the RAF by the War Cabinet Secretariat, statistically analyzed night bombing through the use of photography. The results were discouraging. The averages indicated only one of three attacking aircraft over Europe came within five miles of the target, with the best achievements registered for France but a severe drop to one in ten for areas like the German Ruhr. Some of the nighttime missions struck the wrong cities or dummy versions erected by the Germans in empty fields. To enhance accuracy British scientists developed a pair of radar-based systems, first the Gee and later the H2S which aided navigators to locate targets. Gee was supposed to locate an airplane precisely enough to bomb within a tenth of a mile of the target. In practice it was less accurate; its range limited and over German territory the enemy successfully jammed it. H2S used its beams to indicate ground features, giving airmen a rough picture of the territory below with readings that distinguished water, open fields and built-up areas. Both of these tools would be adopted by the U.S. airmen operating from the United Kingdom.

The Americans argued that precision could take out key elements in the enemy war effort, rendering him weak if not helpless more quickly than area bombing could. The Air Corps stance also reflected reluctance to the inevitable slaughter of noncombatants by area bombing. Even the Japanese at Pearl Harbor had concentrated on military targets. However, Italian airmen bombed and strafed Ethiopian citizens in 1935, the Germans struck at the town of Guernica in Spain while supporting the rebels under Gen. Francisco Franco and then hurled death and destruction upon Polish cities before finally battering Coventry and London. These actions provoked outrage about such barbaric disregard for life. But, as the RAF commenced its nighttime area bombing, wreaking havoc among civilians, the Allies muted the talk about victims. But initially, American officials could argue their approach as more humane. As World War II stretched over the years, daylight bombing eventually spared relatively few civilians in Europe and when B-29s began massive raids on the Japanese home islands the net effect was the same as the area bombing practiced by the British.

Serious weaknesses afflicted the initial American plan. The exaggerated and legendary belief that the Norden bombsight was accurate enough to drop a bomb in a pickle barrel not only overstated the capacity of the instrument but it included no recognition of its effectiveness under combat conditions with exploding antiaircraft shells, enemy fighters with guns and cannons careening through formations. Furthermore, the Messerschmitts and Focke Wulfs could reach altitudes above those favored by the B-17s or B-24s and flew hundreds of miles faster than any bomber. Spaatz, having witnessed the Battle of Britain, undoubtedly realized the potential for interception, but he hoped that extra armor and greater firepower would rebalance the equation in the Air Corps' favor. He also counted on the newer American fighters which might provide more extended escort service than what previously existed.

Well before Pearl Harbor, a small number of Americans participated in the air war. These were volunteers who enlisted either in the RAF or the Royal Canadian Air Force and initially received assignment to regular RAF squadrons but who later formed the American Eagle Squadrons. James Goodson, a nineteen-year-old student at the University of Toronto visited Europe in the summer of 1939. "I was advised by the U.S. embassy to get on the first boat for home as war was imminent," recalled Goodson. He had the bad luck to sail on the *Athenia,* which was torpedoed off the Hebrides a day after the declarations of war that began World War II. "When the *Athenia* went down around 4:00 A.M., I was picked up from a lifeboat by a Norwegian tanker. We were taken to the nearest neutral port, Galway [Ireland]. From there I made my way to Belfast and then Glasgow. I had stayed on board the *Athenia* trying to help some other people to escape. I went down into the bowels of the ship to aid some others and there were bodies, women and children floating around. That changed my attitude to the seriousness of the war. I desperately wanted to get into it and was convinced that America would join in sooner or later. Most Americans at the time were determined we should stay neutral. They didn't want to repeat the experience of the first world war where the country did not get much out of it. But I had the motivation of anger, revenge, a feeling of great sympathy for England because my mother was English and I had aunts and uncles there.

"I found an RAF recruiting station and immediately asked if any American could join. No one seemed to know at first if I could but later was told I could but would probably lose my American citizenship when I swore allegiance to the King of England. I told the recruiters that if the king needed my allegiance, he had it. The question of pay arose and I think the fellow said it was seven shillings and six pence a day [less than $2.00]. I was heartbroken. I said, 'I've lost everything I have. I don't think I can afford it.' The fellow said, 'No, no, no. We pay *you* seven and six.'

"I remember thinking, 'These lovable fools. They could have had me for nothing.' To be able to fly a Spitfire and be paid for it was just beyond my wildest dreams. England was not set up to train the large number of airmen required. It made sense to train people in Canada where there was plenty of room, no danger of interference from the enemy. The Commonwealth Empire Air Training Scheme was set up in a remarkably short space of time. I was sent back to Canada and joined the programs with thousands of Commonwealth young men. Our greatest fear was not that we would crash but be washed out. Less than 10 percent were accepted as pilots. My instructor felt I should be washed out. I went up for a test flight with an RAF officer who got in the back cockpit and told me to go through the paces, acrobatics, loops, rolls and when we were very low, he cut off the ignition and told me to make a forced landing. At the very last moment, he switched it back on and instead of washing me out, said, 'Son, I've got news for you. You're a fighter pilot.' In no time at all, a stream of pretty well trained airmen were arriving in England for their final instruction and entry into squadrons.

"There was a tremendous spirit in all the RAF squadrons. I joined 43rd Squadron, the Fighting Cocks. Our wing commander was the famous Douglas Bader. [He continued to fly fighters even after he lost both legs when shot down during the Battle of Britain.] The RAF method of training and carrying on, the strange mixture of discipline and lack of it was a marvelous element. The spirit and morale were tremendous. I had joined 43 when the Battle of Britain was supposed to be over but we never noticed when it ended; pilots continued to be shot down. Everybody was supposedly discouraged and on the verge of a nervous breakdown but I remember none of that, or anyone being anything but keen. We all fought to get on missions. Above all, there was the laughter; it was a great game and it was always fun. The more desperate side of the situation, that if we felt it, we never never showed. Later, when they formed the Eagle Squadrons we carried that spirit over from the RAF.

"I started with the Hurricane, the plane that won the Battle of Britain, for relatively few Spitfires were available. Most of us initially were not all that happy to leave the Hurricane to fly a Spitfire. My first attempt to attack in a Spit, I got on the tail of a 109. Being used to the steady old Hurricane, I pushed the firing button and because the stick was so sensitive in a Spitfire, the nose immediately went down. The Hurricane was a very good gun platform, very reliable, very steady and took a lot of punishment. I had flown one that got shot up and flames were coming out. I thought I'd better bail out over the Channel and got out on the wing. The Hurricane started to sideslip and I saw the flames were not as bad as I had thought. I climbed back into the cockpit and took it home and landed. That would have been impossible with a Spitfire, but it had remarkable maneuverability. You hardly had to move the stick at all to go into a loop, roll or anything else. It was a delightful plane to fly; we had a love affair with the Spit, just as the Germans did with the 109 although the 190 actually was superior. You didn't aim your guns, or the plane, you aimed yourself. If you wanted to look behind you, you just skewed the plane around. You didn't turn your neck so much. If I dropped my cigarette lighter on the floor, I didn't reach down but simply rolled the plane over and caught the lighter as it dropped into my hand. It was like pulling on a very tight pair of jeans. You became part of the plane."

Goodson and the other U.S. volunteers, as members of the RAF, did not qualify as Americans carrying the Stars and Stripes into the air war. British officialdom and the local press forcefully criticized both the absence of U.S. forces and the American ideas. Implicit in the ongoing controversy were questions of command and control. Spaatz, Eaker and Hap Arnold all feared that if they converted themselves into warriors of the night, they would become subservient to the RAF's bomber chief, Sir Arthur Harris, surrendering the limited independence wrested from the U.S. Army hierarchy. Furthermore, the B-17s and B-24s would require substantial changes to adapt for different work. The engine exhausts for the Forts, for example, spurted flames, making the aircraft obvious to any night marauders or even antiaircraft gunners. Crews also would need considerable retraining.

The initial reticence displayed by Eaker at that first luncheon did not mollify a growing impatience with the pace of the American combat effort. Winston Churchill himself constantly nagged U.S. leaders to put their planes in the air, their bombs on targets. It was not simply an attempt to relieve his forces from carrying the weight of the war. The British Empire, already shrunken by the Japanese in the Far East, was losing more ground in North Africa to the German Afrika Korps. There was genuine worry that Germans would shortly overwhelm the Soviet Union unless the Allies applied pressure that diverted the enemy and strengthened Red Army resolution. There was even talk of an invasion late in 1942 or early '43, preposterous and most certainly doomed to a devastating loss since the British Army was still recovering from its mauling at Dunkirk and there was a lack of trained, properly equipped U.S. troops. The United States fortunes were near bottom, with the Japanese having swept over the Philippines, Wake, Guam and lands formerly held by the Allies.

Toward the end of May 1942, with Operation Millennium, which signaled the beginning of saturation bombing, a few days off a small number of Americans already could claim to have met the enemy. These were three Eagle Squadrons, a collection of pre–Pearl Harbor volunteers who manned Spitfires for the RAF but they would not operate under the Stars and Stripes until transferred to the 4th Fighter Group several months later. Meanwhile, the first home-breds, ground echelons for the 97th Bombardment Group, a B-17 outfit and the 1st and 31st Fighter Groups with P-38s and P-39s, respectively, expected to sail from New York early in June, arriving a few days after the combat aircraft, with their crews and pilots, ferried themselves across the Atlantic.

Everything bound for Europe suddenly appeared in jeopardy. Naval intelligence warned of the Japanese fleet headed for Midway Island, the vital Pacific outpost. The Japanese also extended their conquests by seizing a pair of Aleutian islands off Alaska, erroneously raising fear of an attack on the mainland. Both the 1st Fighter Group and the 97th Bombardment Group reversed course and tracked toward the West Coast, prepared to reinforce the defenders of Midway. The 31st Fighter Group, whose pilots were to have depended upon the 97th's B-17 navigators to lead them over the Atlantic, now boarded ships for England.

Within a few days of the alert that halted the movement of bombers and fighters to Europe, U.S. Navy dive bombers and torpedo planes demolished or damaged enemy vessels off Midway in a coup that sank Japanese hopes for control of the seas. Nevertheless, Midway had delayed the scheduled deployment of American airpower. Midway notwithstanding, British command from Churchill on down continued to press the Americans, including Maj. Gen. Dwight D. Eisenhower who had assumed command of the European theater of operations United States Army (ETOUSA) to do something. In North Africa, Afrika Korps commander Erwin Rommel threatened the Suez Canal while across Egypt, the British and Australians barely hung on in front of Alexandria. On July 2, the Nazi juggernaut smashed into Sevastopol, completing the conquest of the Crimea. German radio sneered at talk of an American airpower debut.

The Nazis seemed to have better intelligence than Washington. Hap Arnold, to placate the British prime minister had told him on May 30, 1942, "We will be fighting with you on July 4th." At the moment he made his rash promise, Arnold believed the 97th would have trained for a month over England and be ready to commence operations. Eaker and Spaatz had precious little with which to work. When word reached Eaker, he reportedly remarked, "Someone must have confused the 4th of July with April Fool's Day."

To fulfill their boss's order, Spaatz and Eaker desperately turned to the one unit actually on hand, the 15th Bombardment Squadron. Far from a heavy bomber outfit, the 15th originally intended to employ night fighters and flew twin-engine Douglas A-20s, four-man light bombers which the British called Bostons. The aircraft used by the 15th actually belonged to the RAF and carried the British insignia. One crew flying with the RAF 226 Squadron, with Capt. Charles Kegelman as pilot, had been the first to bomb occupied Europe during the June 29 raid on a marshaling yard at Hazebrouck.

With the 15th was Bill Odell, a Chicago youth born in 1915, who entered the army under the Thomason Act, a reserve officer program established at his college, Washington University in St. Louis. "As an ROTC graduate," says Odell, "I was fully aware of world events—Franco's Spanish war, Japanese moves in Asia, and German (Nazi) military aggression in Europe. My feelings were concern about German intentions and U.S. reaction to them."

Odell put in a year at Fort Sheridan, Illinois, in an antiaircraft artillery regiment and then applied for pilot training. His reasons included the romance of flying and the silver wings, as well as his experience with ground forces. "Having endured four maneuvers during which Air Corps units were involved, I saw no torrential rain, shin-deep mud, well-digger's butt temperatures, impenetrable woods and thickets, inadequate maps, missed meals and sleep up where the Air Corps were. The hazardous duty pay was a windfall. There were few classmates who had increased their income by 50 percent in two years to $187.50 a month since graduation. The number one grad in our engineering class, a Mensa-type Phi Beta Kappa had been offered the highest salary of $138.

"At the time, the Air Corps was not looking for bombardiers or navigators. These aircrew positions were filled by active duty enlisted men selected from the ranks and trained by the unit to which they were assigned. Pilot training, dictated by Air Corps GHQ, established minimum hours and required instruction in flying, gunnery (air and ground), navigation, instrument, formation, night and aerobatics (commensurate with the type of aircraft). Four hundred flying hours were allotted per pilot per year for the program. Additional flying time was allowed for three or four maneuvers or special assignments each year.

"The 15th Squadron, as an old-line combat unit, received the best prewar training and support GHQ could furnish. We flew the Curtiss-Wright A-18, a twin-engine, two-man (pilot and gunner) attack aircraft that was fine to fly but already obsolete in 1939. We had nothing better in my squadron until May 1941, when we got the A-20, a first-class war machine used extensively through the war by U.S., British, French and Russians."

Odell and his fellow members of the 15th reached England in mid-May of 1942 and the crewmen were assigned to RAF outfits that flew Bostons. "These were front-line, operational units doing battle almost every day. Every day was packed with learning opportunities. We covered the essentials of survival in combat; aircraft identification, communications procedures, ditching techniques, discussions of all phases of aircraft operation and combat flying. RAF senior pilots even admitted that Americans were better suited by far for flying mainly because of their innate technical bent. Young, teenage Englishmen had little mechanical aptitude. Few had previous contact with mechanical apparatus above the bicycle level. Those taught to drive vehicles had scant knowledge of what made them run. Post-1940, mass-produced American pilots had twice as much flight training than post-1940 British lads who had to be rushed through the program because of the need for replacements."

Another member of the 15th was Marshall Draper, who had enlisted in 1941 as a twenty-three-year-old dropout from UCLA. "I ran out of money for college and applied for pilot training in hope of saving enough to finish school." But instead of becoming a pilot, the Air Corps taught Draper the bombardier trade. Draper shuffled through several outfits, learning to use the Norden while at a B-24 base in Florida and then on B-17s with the 97th Bomb Group before joining the 15th Bomb Squadron.

"I was impressed by the beauty of the English countryside," says Draper, "but since my family lived in Hong Kong, a British crown colony, for about three years, and I attended English schools there, I was accustomed to the habits and mannerisms of the English. The spirit [of the first Americans in England] was willing but the supplies were meager. The German submarine campaign was in full swing and confusion reigned. I had an abbreviated course in the Royal Air Force navigation system and did a little practice bombing."

As July 4 approached, Odell kept his diary informed. He lost some sleep on June 29 as the Germans struck in the dark. On the following day he noted, "The afternoon was devoted to individual bombing, from low altitudes. Each of us dropped four bombs from seventy-five feet on a range. In the evening, Keg [Charles Kegelman], Crabtree, Loehrle and myself took two RAF men to the local cinema."

On July 2, while at Swanton, he went off on another preparatory exercise, "We're practising for a 4th of July show somewhere over Germany [as yet the crews did not know their target]. We expect to make an American low-level attack on fighter airdromes during daylight. Gen. Spaatz and Eaker arrived and Keg talked to them. They wanted us to put on a 'circus' without fighter escort. Just shows how much our brass hats know or how they value the cost of men's lives.

"Captain _____ and Lt. _____ were killed at Molesworth yesterday. Coming back from an altitude chamber test, they spun in from 400 feet and every indication shows the controls must have locked. Have to keep this quiet here—it might be bad for the boys to know."

The following day, says Odell, "Crabbie and I flew low-level on a simulated attack of a cement plant. A flight sergeant, leading, learned little except the British don't look out for their wingmen. If you don't keep an eye ahead, the leader will fly you through a tree—as long as he misses. In the afternoon my crew went out to a sunken ship off the coast and bombed and machine gunned the part sticking up out of the water. Back home after a successful mission."

The promised July 4th event brought out Spaatz, Eaker and Eisenhower who met the crews going on the sortie. They shook hands with everyone. "It was obvious they had been told it was not going to be a 'piece of cake.' Their faces were somber, if not grim. Then to dinner and the food did some good."

The planned U.S. Independence Day affair, endorsed by President Roosevelt as a highly appropriate date for actual entrance into the shooting war, met almost none of the concepts behind the Eighth Air Force. Instead of a huge armada of heavy bombers soaring far above the clouds penetrating deep into enemy territory while relying on the precision of the Norden sight, a dozen RAF Bostons, with six U.S. crews combined with an equal number of Britons raided four enemy airfields in Holland at low level. British bomber command had balked at a high-level excursion because the Spitfires ordinarily assigned as escort on such raids were already committed to other operations. And while the civilian leaders may have relished the effort by the U.S. Air Corps, the senior RAF Command recognized the operation as more show biz than strategy.

Bombardier Draper recalls, "Our assigned target was De Kooy, a Luftwaffe base on the northern tip of Holland. The flight was led by an RAF pilot with Capt. Charles Kegelman and 2nd Lt. F. A. Loehrle, both U.S. pilots, flying the wings. I was the bombardier-navigator in Loehrle's plane. Just before takeoff, the RAF officer who normally flew in this plane, handed me a one-inch by two-inch piece of armor plate and a steel infantryman's hat and said, 'Be sure you put the plate under your feet and wear the hat.' I have been told that this practice was vigorously discouraged later because of the added weight in heavy bombers with a larger crew. Nevertheless it probably saved my life since I was the point man of our plane. (The A-20 positioned the bombardier/navigator in its plexiglass nose.)

"The flight took off, formed up, and we headed east at a height of about fifty feet above the water toward Holland. About ten miles from the target we passed a couple of small boats which appeared to be fishing craft but were picket boats, called 'squealers' by the RAF, whose function was to alert the shore-based antiaircraft defenses, as we soon discovered.

"A few moments later, we were approaching a sea wall on the shore when heavy flak opened up. Tracers were going by and above the plane on both sides of my head like flaming grapefruit. This kind of situation concentrates the mind wonderfully, and everything went into slow motion. I could not see why we weren't getting hit but we cleared the sea wall and I felt the plane lift as we let the bombs go. We immediately turned left to get out, and came face to face with a flak battery. [The German word for antiaircraft was *Fliegerabwehrkanone* which U.S. fliers shortened to flak. The British usually used 'ack-ack,' a World War I term.] The four wing guns were firing but we were so close the fire was converging beyond the battery. I glanced at the airspeed indicator which registered 285 mph and suddenly realized the battery gunner was shooting directly at me. We were getting ripped right up the middle as we passed over, about two feet above the gunner's head. We were fifteen feet off the ground at this point. That was my last memory of the attack."

In his diary for Saturday, July 4, Odell scribbled, "Up at 5:15 and had a cup of coffee in the mess hall. Then to the operations room and turned in papers and got packet for combat flight (concentrated food, water purifier, compass and French, Dutch and German money).

"Had no trouble but was a bit anxious on the takeoff. After getting in the air, we settled down and flew right on the trees to the coast. We went close to the water. Felt a bit uneasy because there was a cloudless sky but no fighters appeared. Found land ahead and could spot the landmark of the lighthouse a long way off."

As he cleared the coast of Holland, Odell checked out his people over the intercom to see if they were all right. "My bombardier, Lt. Leslie Birleson answered, 'If blood stinks, I've been shot.'"

In the diary, Odell reports, "Swung over the edge of the coast even lower than the leader and stayed right on the grass. I opened the bomb doors, yelled to Birleson and then it started. I fired all the guns for all I was worth and Birly dropped the bombs. I saw the hangar but that wasn't my dish. I saw Germans running all over the place but I put most of my shots over their heads." Two gunners on RAF Bostons manned single, flexible machine guns from the rear, upper and lower positions. Affixed to the fuselage also were two pairs of .303 caliber machine guns located on the lower port and starboard sides of the ship. A pilot like Odell could fire all four in unison by depressing a single trigger on his control column. He aimed through a ring and cross-hair sight, pointing his aircraft at either enemy fighters or ground objectives.

As the raiders zoomed over the airfield, dumping bombs and spraying machine gun bullets, the defenders fired back. "Our bombs were okay," Odell noted, "but I thought we would crash any moment for I never flew so recklessly in my life. The next moment we were flashing past the coast and out to sea—the water behind us boiling from the bullets dropping into it all around. I kicked and pulled and jerked from side to side. Didn't look at the airspeed—was trying to miss the waves. Over the target we were doing 265 but shortly after I opened it up a bit.

"'Digger' [another pilot] claims he shot his guns into a formation of men lined up for inspection. His bombs hit well before they should have. 'Elkie' was a bit behind but he got rid of his load. He got a broken radio antenna and a mashed-in wing edge. I picked up a hole just above the pilot's step and a badly knocked-up bomb door. We zigged and zagged until three miles out and then closed up waiting for fighters. None came. We reached the coast and were the first ones home.

"All came back except Loehrle, Lynn and a Britisher (Henning). Loehrle was hit by a heavy shell and hit the ground right in the middle of the airdrome. 'He flew into a million pieces' one of the rear gunners said. And I owed him one pound ten shillings. I feel like a thief! Lynn was following before the flight hit the target but never came away from it. His wife is to have a baby in November. He really wasn't cut out for this game. At breakfast he was salting his food, trying to hold the salt spoon steady, yet throwing salt all over his shoulders. I hope he didn't crash. Henning was shot down by an ME-109 that took off just ahead of him. He tried to get it but it turned, got behind him and set one motor on fire. He crashed into the sea. Keg got his right prop and nose section shot off by heavy stuff right over the target. His wing dropped, hit the ground and he managed to right it and come home on one motor."

While a gunner said he saw Loehrle's bomber crash onto the tarmac, Draper, the bombardier on the fallen A-20, says, "I woke up lying on my back on the bottom of the North Sea in about twenty feet of water, very confused about where I was or what I was doing there. I thought I was dead and kept waiting in the gray gloom for something to happen. Then I thought, maybe I better look for someone. I sat up and saw my breath bubbling up through the water and finally realized I was submerged.

"When I surfaced I was opposite a small beach under the sea wall and on about a sixty-degree tangent with the tail of the A-20 protruding from the water, which was all that was visible of the plane. Various subsequent reports had us crashing in flames, or disintegrating, but I saw no smoke or signs of fire associated with the plane and no debris. However, for me to be vectored nearly sideways to the plane, which appeared pointed to the west, I must have been subjected to a very powerful force.

"I swam ashore, walked a few feet from the water's edge, and sat down, overcome suddenly with an enormous fatigue. Somehow I had been taken right out of my parachute harness and flotation vest and my uniform was ripped to shreds. Also, I was bleeding from an assortment of places.

"A path led up from the beach to the sea wall and I could see several soldiers at the top of the path but they made no effort to come down. So I sat and rested for a time. After a while, my mental tiles had clattered back into place, and it occurred to me that I might be better off starting up the path than sitting on the beach bleeding like a stabbed hog. I got to my feet with some difficulty, trudged across the little beach and started up the rather steep path. To my astonishment, the soldiers came rushing down the path and grabbed me by the arms. They were mumbling 'minen,' 'minen,' as if to excuse some perceived lack of hospitality in not coming to my assistance. The beach had been mined, presumably by the Dutch before the Germans got there. The next thing I remember I was lying on a table in what appeared to be a first-aid room. The cast had changed from the Wehrmacht to three Luftwaffe types, one of whom was holding my eyelid up and looking at my eye with a little flashlight. He straightened up, turned off the flashlight and announced to the room at large, 'Shock.' Then he asked me, 'Have you lost many blood?' I corrected him, 'That's much blood. You mean much blood. I don't know.'

"I was still functioning in an offset mode. I did notice that my clothes had been removed and I could see my shoes lying on another table. The rubber heels had been torn off—shoe heels were a common hiding place for escape materials. I thought, 'That must have been a big disappointment.' I was already acquiring a *Kriegsgefangener* [POW in German which those incarcerated shortened to 'kriegie'] mindset." In fact, Draper qualified as the very first U.S. Air Corps prisoner in Europe.

The July 4th event was celebrated in newspapers and Kegelman received a Distinguished Flying Cross. But overall, the affair was a fiasco. The tactics had no relation to the concept of strategic bombing. The three Bostons shot down represented a 25 percent loss; an insupportable rate of casualties. The bodies of the other three men with Draper were recovered. Furthermore, most of the aircraft that made their way home needed considerable repairs from the shot and shell inflicted by flak gunners and enemy fighters. (One researcher, George Pames, claims that Eisenhower was so dismayed he "never again permitted men of his command to engage in needless combat to satisfy American pride or produce media events for propaganda purposes.")

In spite of the obvious deficiencies of the adventure, the 15th remained the only operational American squadron, even if it used aircraft decorated with the markings of the RAF. Odell went on a second strike. This time half a dozen planes all crewed by U.S. airmen, struck at an airfield at Abbeville/Drucat near the French coast. Having learned an agonizing lesson about ground fire from the previous effort at an extremely low altitude, the planes approached at medium altitude, about 6,500 feet according to Odell. "About four miles from Abbeville, began to see flak burst on our level and off to the left and behind. Continued mild evasive action and bombed target. Dove away through fringe of cloud and kept going down and weaving. The coast seemed a long way off and a couple of flak bursts came uncomfortably close, throwing the ship about and damaging one of the formation.

"Returned at low level with about fifty fighters weaving all around. We were flying into the sun and low dark clouds. On sighting the sharp lines of the English coast with the deep shadows, the cliff and clouds east, it struck me as being very quiet, beautiful and a bit poetic. It reminded me of a Grant Wood painting and I found myself saying, 'Perhaps I will learn to like England after all.'

"We arrived okay and answered all the questions and returned to the mess and after drinking four Scotches (though not too happy) I signed my name on the ceiling. [An RAF tradition required men who come back from their first 'op' to climb on a table and chair and autograph the ceiling.] Birly made the mistake of going to bed and was brought down clad in shorts and made to sign too—followed by a baptism of beer. More beer was thrown, so I saw it was time to get out, which a few of us did—and so to bed." For some reason, Odell and the others inscribed their signatures after what was their second operation.

While Odell and his comrades toasted themselves and fulfilled the ritual, their erstwhile companion, Marshall Draper, had embarked on his career as a *Kriegie*. "The Luftwaffe people had set about plastering me up with paper bandages because I was getting their table pretty messy. Eventually I was loaded into a car and taken to a hospital in Amsterdam where I was sewed up and some metal fragments taken out of my leg. I eventually ended up at a hospital in Oberursel, after ten days in Amsterdam. I spent another three weeks in Oberursel and nearly lost the leg. The trip there was a nightmare. I was accompanied by two RAF officers, a Canadian pilot and a Polish tail-gunner, both severely injured. The Polish officer had .30 caliber bullets through both thighs and he hemorrhaged and hallucinated throughout the trip. Among the three of us we had two good legs and at the time it seemed as though we were doomed to spend our remaining lives in the German railroad system, a consequence of very heavy RAF raids on Cologne and Essen which screwed up the system." Patched up, Draper began the process leading to incarceration in a prison camp.

Immediately after its July 12 mission, the 15th stood down while receiving its own A-20s, installing new equipment and putting the planes into operational condition. Nearly two months would pass before the 15th saw combat again but in its place newcomers now carried the war to the Continent.

3

ENTER THE HEAVYWEIGHTS

The 15th Bomb Squadron's valiant but insignificant achievements only increased the pressure for the debut of the four-engine, heavyweight bombers upon which the entire daylight strategic bombing program of the Eighth Air Force was predicated. Furthermore, the American commanders wanted control over the fighter escorts and while RAF efforts on their behalf would be welcome, Spaatz and Eaker always planned that the Eighth would field its own.

By the second week in June, after a decisive defeat of the Japanese Navy destroyed several carriers, the 97th Bomb Group resumed its path toward England. It was too late for the fighters who had also been diverted. Their pilots were already on the high seas with their P-39s to follow. The trip by the 97th to the United Kingdom was almost akin to the earliest voyages against the uncharted Atlantic 450 years earlier, although Columbus at least knew enough to sail through the southern climes rather than the shorter and much less forgiving North Atlantic.

The 97th's itinerary began with the B-17s headed to Presque Isle, Maine. After a pause in Goose Bay, Labrador, the flights scheduled stopovers at Bluie West 1 or Bluie West 8, a pair of outposts in Greenland, then to Reykjavik, Iceland, before touchdown on United Kingdom soil at Prestwick, Scotland.

Because of the changes of plans almost overnight occasioned by the threat at Midway, neither ground crews nor supplies could keep up with the Forts. When the 97th landed at Presque Isle the crews lacked changes of clothes and mechanics to service the aircraft. The fliers themselves performed the necessary work. Presque Isle offered not even the basic amenities. The men often slept in their planes.

A large flight of B-17s took off from Maine on June 26, and set down at Goose Bay late in the afternoon without incident. But when they soared into the skies three hours later, the weather worsened. The group tried to find Bluie 1, but after a warning from the area weather station, eleven ships returned to Goose Bay, having been airborne almost fourteen hours. Four planes were missing but one, piloted by Lt. Fred Dallas, successfully located Bluie 8 on the coast, north of the Arctic Circle.

My Gal Sal, piloted by Lt. Ralf Stinson, wandered through the frigid murk until fuel ran low. Stinson chose to land on an icecap but the glare of sun on ice and snow deceived depth perception. He ordered the crew to dump luggage and used the baggage strewn over the landscape as guidelines. *My Gal Sal*, wheels up, slid and bounced over the ice but everyone crawled from the wreckage under his own power. Fortunately for them, the commander at Bluie West 8 was Bernt Balchen, the renowned Norwegian polar explorer. With Dallas at the controls, Balchen navigated towards an emergency signal from the downed aircraft. Dallas and Balchen dropped emergency supplies, including a bottle of whiskey and a case of condoms stowed on the plane as a joke by Dallas.

"I thought I was being funny," said Dallas later. "I was going to drop him condoms on the icecap because he needs them. Stinson told me, 'You think that's funny but those condoms saved my life, my whole damn crew's lives. We took the prop off an engine so we could run the generator and keep a battery going so we could operate a radio. But we needed an aerial so we blew up these condoms, tied a wire to them and put them up. We had enough condoms so that when they blew away, we could put up another aerial and by that means we could communicate with BW 8.'"

Homing in on the radio signals, Balchen and an associate flew a small plane to a frozen lake about twelve miles away. They skied through the snow, then led the entire crew back to the lake where they were removed in twos and threes over a period of days on the small aircraft, even as the ice pack thawed and started to break apart, threatening to maroon them forever.

Another Fortress splashed into a fjord in the vicinity of Bluie West 3, a radio station. Alerted by the radio outpost, a Coast Guard cutter gathered up the entire crew from life rafts. A third B-17 also lost its bearings and when its fuel petered out, the pilot chose to land near an Eskimo village. The ships struck a cliff that tore off the ball turret and then boulders chopped off the wings and propellers. But everyone survived until the ubiquitous Balchen arrived in a Navy PBY to rescue them.

The first ship from the 97th actually cleared the Atlantic on July 1. The remainder straggled in twenty-six days after the migration began. They had lost five aircraft but no personnel.

The 97th struggled to acclimate themselves to their new home under demanding conditions. As they sought to absorb what information they could from RAF advisors, coped with the frequently poor flying weather and attempted to master the art of tight formation flying, the 15th Bombardment Squadron continued to practice with its new aircraft while awaiting orders to resume their lightweight but deadly campaign.

On July 24, after a visit to London, Bill Odell returned to the Molesworth base just in time for another evening of free liquor and hamburgers with female guests. "Went to bed at 12:15," noted Odell, "but the officers' quarters was as bad as a brothel with women giggling or screaming. Had trouble getting to sleep."

On the following day, as "the only one capable," Odell flew a guest RAF man back to his field at Swanton Morely, "fooled around getting back, flying formation with everyone in the sky. Back at the base and out over the channel for a look around. On getting down, I found Stevens [Sgt. John P.] my gunner shot through the head and quite dead. My association with Sergeant Stevens was strictly crew business. I knew nothing about his personal life, or any back-home family troubles, if any. There was stress of combat, and it did not take me long after the first few missions to realize aircrew members on a one-pilot aircraft had lower odds of survival in combat than the multipilot planes—thus more stress." A considerable number of people would develop the condition listed as "combat neurosis," "battle fatigue" or "flak happy" as the war continued.

Among those who straggled into Scotland was Walt Kelly, a twenty-three-year-old tavern keeper's son from Norristown, Pennsylvania. "I had a Bachelor of Science in electrical engineering and I always wanted to fly. I had flown with barnstorming friends of my father. It wasn't a matter of comfort, pay or my career, but that I fiercely wanted to help defeat Hitler. After I enlisted, my father from behind his bar would shout, 'My boy will be the greatest pilot that ever flew for the Army Air Corps.'

"I volunteered for a B-17 assignment in response to a bulletin-board notice in order to get out of flying the O-52, a turkey! I was fortunate to get over 90 hours in the B-17 in April 1942, and learned to fly tight formations from more experienced flight leaders. I became a cocky and confident pilot, and always keen to learn more and to demonstrate my skills.

THE MIGHTY EIGHTH | 33

"When we got to England, the facilities and conditions were A-OK but we did have problems keeping the planes flying. The RAF told us we would get our butts blown off if we persisted with daylight bombing. We were told that the Luftwaffe was highly skilled and that their 88s were very accurate, both of which were confirmed later.

"For our part we were ready for action and wanted to prove ourselves in combat. We were impatient for the big day to come. We didn't have to wait long. August 17, 1942, turned out to be a beautiful sunlit day— one of a very few since our arrival in the United Kingdom. Our very first combat briefing was full of detail about the Messerschmitt 109 and the Focke Wulf 190 fighters, our escort (RAF) and specifics about the marshaling yards at Rouen, France, our target.

"It was cause for celebration, for finally we were gonna get it done or fail desperately in trying, as many, especially the RAF Bomber Command, predicted. We in the 342nd Squadron of the 97th were confident. We just wanted to be let loose to punish Hitler and the Luftwaffe."

On this uncharacteristically bright, clear day, in fact, the lead element of the twelve B-17s spotted Rouen ten minutes before turning into its bomb run. "I can see the target. I can see the target," exulted Lt. Frank R. Beadle, the bombardier in *Butcher Shop,* flown by Maj. Paul W. Tibbetts who just shy of three years later would pilot the *Enola Gay* over Hiroshima. Also on *Butcher Shop,* in the copilot seat, group commander Col. Frank Armstrong, on hearing Beadle's cry, snapped over the intercom, "Yes, you damn fool and the Germans can see you too."

Only temporarily chastened, Beadle switched open the bomb bay doors and as he cut loose the ordnance, sang through the intercom, "I don't want to set the world on fire . . ." Walt Kelly in *Heidi Ho* describes the experience, "It was a cakewalk. We saw little opposition and it seemed to me like a realistic practice mission like one we had flown in recent days. We were cocky when we took off and more so when we landed. There was lots of hoopla and queries from the press. Several planes buzzed the runway before landing [a stunt forbidden but often unchallenged as on this occasion]."

From a ringside seat in the lead plane of the second flight, Ira Eaker observed what his tiny air force wrought. He was pleased enough to announce, "A great pall of smoke and sand was left over the railroad tracks." Armstrong chimed in, "We ruined Rouen," hardly descriptive of the actual minimal damage done. Rail traffic was disrupted only temporarily and no serious impact upon the German war effort occurred.

Perhaps delighted at any addition to the efforts of his forces, Air

Marshal Sir Arthur T. Harris, chief of British Bomber Command sent a message, "Congratulations from all ranks of Bomber Command on the highly successful completion of the first all-American raid by the big fellows on German-occupied territory in Europe. Yankee Doodle went to town and can stick yet another well-deserved feather in his cap."

The debut of the U.S. heavy bombers prompted an outpouring of self-congratulatory declarations. In Washington, Hap Arnold wrote a memorandum for the attention of Gen. George C. Marshall, chief of staff, and to the attention of Navy head Adm. Ernest J. King and Adm. William Leahy, an adviser to the president. "The attack on Rouen," claimed Arnold, "again verifies the soundness of our policy of the precision bombing of strategic objectives rather than the mass (blitz) bombing of large, city-size areas." In fact, the attack of August 17 proved little as the 97th encountered limited opposition, most of which was met by the RAF Spitfires. The Germans may also have been misled by two diversionary flights of B-17s.

The euphoria dissipated rapidly. "We weren't wiped out as the British predicted," says Kelly. "But this to them was just a token raid in which the Germans were taken by surprise. Early claims of enemy fighters shot down dwindled to one as gunners were pressed for confirmation of kills. High-altitude, precision, daylight bombing would have to be proven over deeper and more difficult missions. We still had to prove we could hold our own in aerial combat over Continental Europe."

Eaker also recognized some deficiencies. He felt the crews showed a lack of discipline, almost nonchalance about combat. He was concerned at what he perceived was loose rather than tight formation flying. He also called for added drill in the use of oxygen, advocated lengthening the hoses to give men more freedom to move and for improvements in the masks which were clumsy and tended to freeze up.

THE 97th had opened for business just in time to participate in the Allied assault in force on the French port of Dieppe. A full infantry division of Canadians along with British commandos and a few American Rangers struck at the Continent from landing craft in the early hours of August 19. While half a dozen of their number carried out a diversionary thrust, the 97th dispatched twenty-two B-17s towards the Abbeville/Drucat airdrome, home to bevies of yellow-nosed Focke Wulf fighters. Two of the marauders turned back because of mechanical problems but the remainder dumped a mixed bag of 149 general purpose and incendiary explosives on the target. The British high command reported sixteen enemy planes either damaged or destroyed, the airfield ceased operations totally for two hours and its controllers shut down until the evening. While Air Marshal Sir Trafford Leigh-Mallory said "the raid on Abbeville undoubtedly struck a heavy blow at the German fighter organization at a very critical moment during the operations," the Dieppe venture was a disaster for the foot soldiers who retreated with enormous casualties; perhaps half the attack force was lost.

The assault on Dieppe primarily was to test the Continental defenses and at the same time tempt the Luftwaffe to commit planes against Spitfires flown by both the RAF and the American 31st Fighter Group. The latter had expected to cross the Atlantic in their P-39 Airacobras chaperoned by the B-17s of the 97th which would provide navigation data. However, the flap over Midway that detoured the B-17s forced the 31st personnel to travel to England by ship with their P-39s to follow. Once in the United Kingdom, however, with their P-39s still awaiting shipment, the pilots of the outfit climbed into the cockpits of Spitfires.

Frank Hill, a New Jersey high school grad in 1937 who had belonged to a club that owned a glider, was among those learning the ways of the British plane. A former plumber's helper, a student of aeronautical engineering by mail and in night school, Hill passed a two-year college equivalency test in 1940 and earned his wings in November of that year. Initially assigned to P-40 Warhawks, Hill then worked with the Airacobra.

"The Spitfire was really a welcomed airplane," says Hill. "After only a few flights, we were unanimous in our praise for it and thankful not to have the P-39. The Spitfire was an easy plane to fly and to maneuver. Our mechanics were quick to adapt to the engine and armament. In less than thirty days, we were ready to go."

To ease the 31st into combat, it flew what Hill calls "indoctrination"—sightseeing—missions along the coast of France. Mostly these were practice "rodeos," maneuvers designed to entice enemy aircraft to put in an appearance. On July 26 during a sweep that carried him over occupied France, Lt. Col. Albert Clark, an unlucky member of the 31st, bailed out after engine failure to become the first fighter pilot from the Eighth Air Force to be taken prisoner.

Hill and the 31st participated in the August 19 action over Dieppe. "We had been over Dieppe only a few minutes when the RAF operations center that was controlling all the fighters [the Eighth Air Force still relied on some British facilities, particularly during joint efforts] reported that a dozen or so enemy aircraft were approaching Dieppe from the direction of the big German airdrome at Abbeville. A few minutes later, a number of aircraft arrived above us, at about 12,000 feet and immediately rolled over and commenced an attack on my flight." Hill on this venture led a unit of four ships.

"I wanted to keep my flight together and avoid giving away the advantage. As the Germans attacked, their formation broke up into pairs. I turned up toward them and flew at them head-on as they came down. This made it hard for the German pilots to keep their sights on us, and it forced them to attack us head-on.

"One pair of FWs came in real close, and that gave us an opportunity to fire our guns directly into them. On this pass, my number four airplane, piloted by Lt. D. K. Smith, received a burst of cannon fire through its left wing. It left an eight-inch hole on top and took out about two feet on the underside of the wing.

"After about three minutes of trying to keep my flight from being hit—by constantly breaking and turning into the Germans—I found myself in position to get a good shot at one of the Focke Wulfs, so I fired all four .303 caliber Browning machine guns and both Hispano 20 mm cannon at it. The German swung out to my left and I got in another good three-second burst of cannon and machine-gun fire. I fired into his left side at a forty-five-degree angle from about 300 yards down to about 200 feet. The Focke Wulf started pouring black smoke. He rolled over and went straight down.

"I followed the smoking FW down to about 3,000 feet, but at that point I had to pull out because the ack-ack coming from the ground was really intense and I didn't want to lose any of my planes to ground fire. The last I saw of the Focke Wulf it was about 1,000 feet over the Channel. It was still smoking and still in a steep dive.

"We climbed back to 8,000 feet. It was quiet for a few minutes, and then more Focke Wulfs came down. We headed up and kept breaking into them. As my wingman and I turned into them, making it harder for them to track us in their sights and forcing them to come at us head-on, my second element was given an opportunity to fire on them. This was our first combat and we didn't know much else to do except turn into them and fire as best we could. We were fighting defensively, but we had a chance to hit them as they came down to hit us.

"It was constant look-see-turn for about thirty-five minutes. Then we started to get low on fuel. I had run out of cannon ammunition by then. I don't think I did much damage after I hit the first Focke Wulf. I made one last attack on another Focke Wulf from above and behind. I don't think I hit him. If I did, I didn't damage him very much.

"I was getting ready to turn for home when my element leader, Lt. Robert 'Buck' Ingraham called, 'Snackbar Blue-three going down.' I thought he was going down after something but then I saw him bail out at about 7,000 feet. As Buck approached the water, I saw two boats heading toward him. I thought he was going to be picked up okay. I later found out that these were German E-boats and he was a prisoner for the rest of the war.

"When we got back to Kenley [the 31st airfield] we refueled and had the airplanes ready to go in about ten minutes. We picked up another pilot to fill in for Buck Ingraham and D. K. Smith got another airplane. [All units ordinarily included extra pilots and crew as well as reserve aircraft.] I was wearing a leather jacket and when I landed after the first mission, I discovered that it was soaking wet from sweat.

"B flight flew four missions that day, and we had quite a time. I fired my machine guns and cannon on each mission. We learned a lot. Flying and firing on each mission was quite an indoctrination to fighting."

As Hill's account indicates, short distance to the action enabled the limited-range Spits to go to work, return, refuel, rearm and sortie again. That ability enabled the Spitfire to dominate the Battle of Britain. The same advantage, however, would accrue to the German interceptors when the Eighth Air Force began to penetrate deep into the Continent. In addition, as Hill implies, there was no substitute for learning on the job. Because no one could confirm that the German fighter he last saw smoking in a steep dive actually crashed, he only received credit for a "probable." Lt. Samuel Junkin of the 31st was named the first of the Army Air Corps in Europe to score a kill, although Junkin himself was severely wounded and shot down during the same action.

FOR the 97th Bomb Group, the risk increased sharply with a fourth mission aimed at Rotterdam. Delayed by an abort and some mechanical failures, the Forts arrived sixteen minutes late for a rendezvous with fighters. In sight of the Dutch coast, the Spitfires reluctantly peeled away to go back to base and they were almost instantly replaced by hordes of enemy fighters.

Aboard *Johnny Reb*, waist gunner Sgt. John H. Hughes advised the cockpit crew that the Spitfires were gone. As the enemy swarmed up through the clouds, Hughes and his mates fired their .50s. Tail gunner Sgt. Adam R. Jenkins waited until the leading attacker came in range. "I kept watching them bear down, but I had a finger on the trigger of each gun. I knew I had the 'tail-end Charlie' position and I couldn't let them babies sneak up on our formation. The Nazis seemed to be trying to gauge our speed, finally they got the same altitude as ours and were right in my sights. I let them get within 300 yards or so. Then I figured, Adam, it's time to let go. I had never seen anything like what happened then, only in the movies. That Nazi's wings came plumb off, busted into bits and he just burst into a big flame and went trailing down to the clouds."

In his excitement, Hughes developed an ice lump in the mouth of his oxygen mask, forcing him to hold it in one hand while he fired a gun with the other, gasping for air at the same time. The top turret weapons, manned by Sgt. Roy Allen, jammed after one burst. In the nose, navigator Lt. Harold Spire let loose at a plane crossing ahead when cannon shells tore through the windshield. Shrapnel and plexiglass splinters fatally wounded copilot Lt. Donald A. Walter and seriously injured pilot Lt. Richard Starks who called for help. Bombardier Ewart Sconiers and Allen pushed into the cockpit, removed the body of the dead man and started first aid for Starks.

Sconiers took the copilot seat and tried to recall what he had learned before washing out of flight school, while Starks gave him instructions. Despite the loss of two engines, Sconiers and Starks managed to bring *Johnny Reb* to an emergency landing at an RAF base. The 97th now counted one KIA and five WIA.

On September 6, the 97th lost its first airplane to enemy fire and the first operation for the 92nd Bomb Group cost it one B-17. En route to hammer the Avions Potez aircraft factory at Meaulte close to the French coast, escorted by Eagle Squadron Spitfires (planes were crewed by Americans who had volunteered for the RAF before Pearl Harbor) the B-17s barged into flocks of interceptors. Apparently, the seemingly reticent enemy had only been analyzing the American bomber procedures and developing a tactical approach. Charles Travinek, a radio operator and waist gunner says, "Midway over the water all hell broke loose. Goering's Abbeville Kids were waiting for us with 200-plus Luftwaffe fighter planes, ME-109s and FW-190s. And they stayed with us, constantly firing away until our planes were crippled while fighting our way through direct hits over the target.

"Three of our engines were shot out as we dropped our bomb load over Meaulte. The fourth engine was feathered. Our vertical stabilizer was shot out as was the oxygen and intercom. Our plane began making spasmodic drops of 500 feet to 1,000 feet in altitude. We hit the ceiling with each sudden drop along with the unsecured equipment. Then we rapidly dropped with the flying objects to the plane's rubber walkway." The ship was observed gliding down with three fighters in hot pursuit while four parachutes blossomed near the target area.

In a crash landing, the right wing tore off and the ball turret smashed through the tail on impact. "Bill Warren, the ball-turret gunner," says Travinek, "was the only crew member not seriously hurt—just a gash on his head. He dragged Bill Peltier, tail gunner, away from the plane to safety but was unable to get [William] Dunbar, [Thomas] Matson or the [radio operator] and [me] out because they were wrapped up in the metal of the bomb bay tanks and the radio room.

"Warren then went to the nose of the plane looking for injured officers. When he found none, Warren realized they must have bailed out. Instead, he found Paul Drain, bombardier, trapped in the cockpit with a broken leg. He got Drain out and over by Peltier, Matson, Dunbar and [I] managed to extricate ourselves from the twisted wreckage and crawl to safety should the plane have exploded."

According to tail-gunner Peltier, "No bailout alarm was sounded. Whether due to pilot failure, or the electrical system being damaged by shell fire is open to debate. Anyway, four of them jumped, pilot, copilot, navigator and the engineers. Six of us were left behind, four gunners, bombardier, radio operator. The plane was in a steep glide, pretty close to the ground, when the bombardier [Drain] managed to straighten it out a little. We crash-landed in a wheat field. I've never explained the miracle of how all six of us survived that crash."

A band of French Maquis, guerrilla fighters, reached the scene an hour or so after they came to earth. Recalls Travinek, "When they saw the shape we were in they explained that they couldn't take hospital cases which would have slowed them up in their work. Warren and the French officer destroyed the bombsight. Warren also gave him five submachine guns with about 5,000 rounds of ammunition and Colt .45 automatics."

The French freedom fighters slipped away as German soldiers located the wreck and the survivors three hours later. The troops transported the wounded to hospitals for medical treatment before the entire bunch headed for the stalags. Officially, the reports on the first Fortress shot down listed nine men as MIA. But in fact there were ten. S. Sgt. William Dunbar, an armament chief in the ground crew wanted to get an idea of a combat mission. He had approached the crew led by pilot Lt. Clarence Lipsky and asked to go along. Qualified as a .50 caliber gunner, he was welcomed aboard and stationed at one of the waist positions. Under these circumstances, his presence went unrecorded and he may have been carried as AWOL for the three years he endured as a *kriegie*. Dunbar was by no means the last ground crewman to volunteer for combat missions although the regulations expressly forbade such guests.

THE 15th Bomb Squadron had resumed its strikes on September 5. Odell, with his bombardier off in London, stood by as a reserve. On the following day he joined a concerted effort after a briefing on the target, Abbeville. "I led the second box [a formation of aircraft]. Met the fighters, mostly American Spitfires [from the 31st] and cruised across the channel at sea level until I thought sure we were going in low-level. The visibility was remarkable. We climbed and had a very peculiar bomb run. Brown told me to open the bomb doors and no sooner were they opened than Brown said the bombs were gone. We turned, diving away and not until we were almost to the coast did any flak appear. It was way off and I saw only a few bursts at all. The trip home was uneventful except we were a bit off course."

On the following morning, Odell was awakened and summoned to appear before Wing with squadron commander Maj. John Griffith. "It seems we had missed the target—by about twenty miles! Thank goodness I couldn't be blamed. I gave my ideas about where we bombed and it turned out to be a dummy airdrome near Dieppe."

Odell recalls the hearing before a board of five U.S. officers and an RAF wing commander, all of whom were senior to the squadron commander and Odell. "Griffith was grilled sharply. From the beginning, the tone of the questions made it apparent that no excuse would be accepted for his flying on a heading that would cause him to lead the twelve-plane formation to a dummy airdrome instead of Abbeville.

"When Griffith proposed the most likely fault was a miscalibrated compass, he was then blamed additionally for failing to oversee required instrument maintenance and compass checks in the squadron aircraft. I squirmed a lot, watching Griffith take the heat. The senior board member made it clear that the Eighth Air Force could not condone the failure of any aircraft to locate its assigned target. Such a gross error smacked of poor training, sloppy navigation and inept squadron commanders unable to lead and accomplish a simple mission. That kind of conduct was not acceptable and contrary to the standards being set by what would be the mightiest air armada ever assembled [although at the time an infant in arms] which boasted of unerring 'pickle-barrel' bombing accuracy.

"When the ordeal seemed close to a conclusion, I was asked to describe the mission, and had to admit that about midway across the channel, Lt. Cecil Brown, my bombardier, advised me over the intercom that he thought we were off course. My cockpit compass reading did not correspond to the plotted course, but only enough to believe Griffith deviated momentarily and he would make a correction. I added that flying under fifty feet at midchannel, no land was in sight to check our position visually to verify we were off course.

"When I hesitated after being asked why I didn't advise Griffith of the situation Maj. James Beckwith, supported by the RAF wing commander, came to my defense on that crucial question. They noted I had acted properly, having no other choice but to follow established operational procedure by maintaining radio silence. Not to do so would alert enemy defenses; the formation would come under attack and I, more than anyone present, knew the consequences."

Griffith was relieved of his command and Odell believes he got a raw deal. "He made an error, but as it turned out, making an example of him did nothing to prevent the same situation from occurring time and again. Post-war strategic bombing survey studies cite numerous instances, particularly after the Germans began emphasizing camouflage and dispersal of industrial facilities, of flawed Eighth Air Force bombing missions launched at or lured into attacking simulated targets. Even worse, the review reveals surprisingly numerous samples of poor bombing accuracy. Large formations massing hundreds of bombers missed clearly identified assigned objectives by up to two miles.

"These errors were not made public by the Eighth Air Force during the war. Censorship was the shield, justifiable for intelligence and morale purposes. [Reading] the Strategic Bombing Surveys, I did not run across any case of disciplinary action meted out to squadron, group or wing commanders to equal the brusque way Griffith was stripped of his command, curtailing his career opportunities from that time on." Actually, the unfortunate Griffith eventually earned the silver leaf of a lieutenant colonel in command of a B-29 squadron. He and his crew were lost during one of the firestorm raids upon Tokyo in 1945.

In any event, the role of lighter bombers as part of the Eighth Air Force began to phase out. The 15th Bomb Squadron bade farewell to England with an assault on the port of LeHavre on October 2, before departing to North Africa. There Odell and his companions became members of the newly formed Twelfth Air Force in support of Torch, the American and British campaign to oust the Axis from the top rim of the dark continent. Their boss was Maj. Gen. Jimmy Doolittle, newly decorated with the Congressional Medal of Honor for the April 1942, carrier-based attack by B-25s, appropriately named Mitchells, upon Tokyo.

Meanwhile two more B-17 outfits, the 92nd and 301st had begun operations against the enemy. The 97th with Walt Kelly continued its runs. "It did not take long before an opportunity [came] to prove we could hold our own in aerial combat over continental Europe," according to Kelly. On September 6 and 7, "We smashed our way through heavy Luftwaffe opposition to bomb targets in France and Holland, knocking off seventy-seven Nazi fighters in the two sweeps." Officially, the totals for all three of the Bomb Groups were sixteen kills, twenty-nine probables and twenty-two damaged.

Mishaps as much as enemy action dogged the early forays. On September 26, RAF Spitfires including the American volunteers of Eagle Squadron 133 set out to accompany the 97th Bomb Group to a Focke Wulf plant at Morlaix on the northern coast of the Brest peninsula. Weather officers at the briefings for fighters and bombers advised of a thirty-five-mile headwind en route when in fact a 100-mile-an-hour *tailwind* blew. With the customary clouds blanking out the ground, navigators on the B-17s relied on dead reckoning and in turn, their escort depended upon them for a proper course.

The 97th's ships never spotted the assigned target and thanks to the tailwind, outran their escorts and traveled as far as the base of the Pyrenees that separate France from Spain. When they finally reversed course and headed home the bombers met the Spits from the 133rd and both contingents contended with gale-force headwinds. Without landmarks to identify, and still unaware of the navigation errors due to the faulty weather intelligence, the Spitfires broke through the overcast while 3,000 feet up and soon saw a shoreline. Eagle Squadron pilot Bob Smith said, "What we didn't know was that this was the south coast of the Brittany peninsula, not the south coast of England. The low altitude made it impossible to see enough of the region to identify it. Someone said, 'There's a city off to starboard.' That city should have been Southampton, or Plymouth or Portsmouth . . . it was Brest—wall-to-wall antiaircraft guns and odd fighter bases here and there.

"No self-respecting fighter squadron is going to fly over a friendly city in a loose unimpressive formation . . . no way. Tighten it up! Wing to wing! That's what we did—close formation over Brest at about 2,500 feet. What a target! Those German gunners must have had a hundred casualties, stepping on one another, trying to get off the first shot."

The highly capable flak gunners knocked down a dozen Spitfires, killing five with the remainder, including Bob Smith, rounded up and hauled off to the stalags. None of the highflying B-17s incurred any damage.

JIM Goodson, the survivor of the *Athenia* sinking, had not immediately switched from the RAF after Pearl Harbor. But in the summer of 1942, he remembered, "I got a call from Charles O. Douglas of Fighter Command who said, 'Before, we invited you to join the Eagle Squadrons. Now I'm ordering you to report to the 133 Eagle Squadron of the RAF tomorrow morning.' I turned up at Debdem [the airdrome], walked into the officers' barracks to find every room empty. There were half-finished letters, toothbrushes, shaving mugs, but no pilots. Every single one who had gone out with the 133 on a mission had been shot down. No planes returned. This brought the war home very sharply. We had the job of reforming the 133 Eagle Squadron virtually over night, which was accomplished by bringing in pilots from RAF squadrons.

"The ground crew was all British and they were wonderful people with great dedication. I became close friends with my mechanic and I remember when I came back from a mission, he'd say, 'How did we go?' I would say, 'We got two' or 'We got one' [Goodson became an ace]. It was always a team effort. We both had our names on the plane; it was our plane.

"We also had an agreement. At one time, when we were flying several missions a day, I tried to help the mechanics out at night. Because they had to work almost through the night in order to keep the planes flying, I tried to do my bit. Finally, Bob said to me, 'Major, can we make a deal? I'll promise not to fly the plane if you promise not to help me work on the engine.'"

Paul Ellington wound up with an Eagle Squadron because of a discipline breach. He had held an ROTC commission in the cavalry but decided he would rather fly than ride. Having completed college he enlisted in the Air Corps in 1940. "After I checked out on the P-35 and P-36 [the obsolete fighters upon which men of his era cut their teeth], I got caught hedgehopping and doing low flying. That spelled the end of my flying career with the Air Corps. I was told I could go to bombardier school or navigator school. But I wasn't through piloting. I looked up a representative of the Clayton Knight Committee; they represented the RAF in the U.S. It was illegal then to recruit American citizens for service in a foreign nation's military and the committee barely qualified as legal but everyone in the Air Corps knew they were looking for people whom they could polish up a bit and send to England.

"I accepted an honorable discharge from the Air Corps for 'flying deficiency' and took a refresher course at Spartan Aircraft. I did a lot of cross-country but I had learned my lesson about hedgehopping. In early December of 1941, I reported to the RAF at Ottawa in Canada. We shipped out of Halifax for England just around the time of Pearl Harbor. When we arrived at Liverpool the antisubmarine boom was already up for the night so we sat out in the water. We saw the German planes make a raid. When we went ashore the next morning, we were in the middle of the rubble and fire and I thought, 'My God, what am I getting into?'"

Sworn into the Royal Air Force and named a pilot officer, Ellington began operational training. "Near the Firth of Forth, above Edinburgh, we met the Spitfire. It was wonderful. After a few days of skull practice, you strapped it on and took off. They were lovely aircraft, very forgiving. I kinda left my stomach back on the runway the first time I took off even though what we flew were old war wearies, Spit 2s. We had about six weeks of instruction from seasoned combat pilots. I was then posted to the 121 Squadron and as the new kid on the block did a lot of convoy patrol, getting flight time to become familiar with the aircraft. We started to do some escort but we couldn't go in too deep. We were limited to about two and a half hours of flying time."

4

FRESH BLOOD

By the end of August 1942, the escort service provided by the 31st Fighter Group in Spitfires was bolstered temporarily by the 1st Fighter Group manning P-38 Lightnings, the U.S.-built twin-engine, double-boomed aircraft blessed with speed and greater range. As the first fighter unit to cross the Atlantic under its own power, the group, like its bomber predecessors, encountered serious problems. In mid-July six P-38s, confounded by the weather and misled by directional broadcasts from German radio, had no recourse but to land on the icecap of eastern Greenland. The Lightnings' wreckage couldn't be salvaged but the fliers all survived. With time the accident rate during passage to England via the North Atlantic route would fall drastically and by January 1943, 920 planes had attempted the crossing with a loss rate of 5.2 percent, far below the anticipated 10 percent.

The 1st Fighter Group, which went operational at the end of August, started full-scale sweeps in mid-September but it too left Europe for North Africa in November. In preparation for this departure and its P-38s, in late September the Eighth Air Force incorporated the American pilots of the Eagle Squadron into the newly activated 4th Fighter Group. Spitfires continued to be their aircraft.

On October 9, the Americans mounted their most impressive show yet. "Against Lille and other objectives," says Walt Kelly, "we sent 110 of our own bombers, twenty-seven of which were B-24s. We downed fifty-six enemy fighters with twenty-six more probables. Our escort was credited with only five. Four bombers failed to return to the UK, three B-17s and one B-24 with one crew picked up in the channel. We had now provided ample evidence of who was to be boss of daytime air over western Europe. This action was against some of Goering's most experienced pilots—some German aces had more than 300 kills [after three years of war including duty on the Soviet front]. Our squadron morale was very high. We considered our flying and bombing skills to be the very best and were particularly proud of our tight formation flying."

Kelly's declaration of victory may have been premature but the thrust at Lille presaged the style that would become a hallmark of the Eighth Air Force. Eaker put up 108 bombers, the first occasion in which a raid exceeded the century mark, but unfortunately a total of twenty-nine B-17s and B-24s turned back. The Forts included those from the 301st and then the 92nd Bomb Groups, the most recent newcomers, who had entered combat in September. After three missions including Lille, the latter stood down from the shooting war to train replacement crews.

For their inauguration into combat that October 9, twenty-four brand-new B-17Fs, designated as the 306th Bomb Group, warmed up their engines at the Thurleigh field for the trip to Lille and their first mission. In the command seat of one of the 368th Squadron's planes was a twenty-two-year-old native of Boise, Idaho, Lt. John Regan. "My grandfather was a successful miner and my father inherited a considerable amount of money so we had no particular problems during the Depression," says Regan. "I had heard Hitler speak and it became obvious to me that we were going to be involved in World War II. I had two years of college and initially tried to enlist in the Navy but failed the eye test. After doing exercises prescribed by a doctor, I was able to enter the Air Corps in 1941. I didn't want to enter the draft, preferring to choose my own career in the military. The idea of silver wings, extra pay did not influence me. In my younger years my father and I went on an old Ford trimotor and since I wanted to get into the Air Corps I took flying lessons at the Ryan Aeronautical Academy in San Diego. I already had a private pilot's license. When I graduated from flying school in March 1942, several of my class were assigned to Wendover Field in Utah. While I was there, I met General LeMay, then a lieutenant colonel and the executive officer of our bomb group. I used to play poker with him in the evenings. He talked to us about leadership and I remember him saying that commanding generals have no friends. They can't afford to have them." LeMay soon left the 306th to take command of the new-born 305th Bomb Group.

The 306th, like so many newly activated organizations, had set up shop in a barren wasteland, marked by runways, stark barracks and tents with much of their personnel and machines still on paper. The aircraft arrived more slowly than those who expected to use them. "I started with the B-18," says Regan, "and when we saw our first B-17 it was a great thing. I became an instructor pilot in the B-17 after only six and a half hours of flying time."

Regan flew one of the first of the 306th Forts from Wendover to Maine, then to Gander, Newfoundland, before the final leg to Prestwick and the hop to the base at Thurleigh. "We had not been told about flak and German fighters because the people with us hadn't any experience in combat. After I finished my tour and rotated home I directed flying operations at a B-17 school to train replacement crews in combat. These people did not understand how fortunate they were that they had people teaching them flying who could explain what combat was like and what could be expected of them when they got to England. We found that if a crew could get through the first five missions, their chances of survival were almost double. Those first missions, you were looking around, not sure what to do, nobody telling you what to expect, it was difficult to absorb what was going on. We lost a lot of people because they didn't know instinctively what moves to make, what to do and how to follow.

"The first mission of our group was against a factory in the city of Lille, not a very deep penetration but one that required us to be in formation. I had been a football player in high school and college and the feeling was the same. I was really excited. This was what I trained for. I was over here to fly combat. Boy, I was young, eager, ready to go.

"When we crossed the coast, we didn't have fighter escort. We climbed to altitude, went toward our target and we started getting attacked by fighters and the ground antiaircraft was shooting at us. I thought, 'My God! Those people are serious.' From that point on, combat was never thrilling to me. It was a job that had to be done and a job that turned out to be extremely tough. I imagine the rest of my crew felt very much like I did.

"After we departed the target, I lost my No. 2 engine which suffered some minor damage from flak. We had to drop back from the formation and were attacked by about twenty to twenty-five yellow-nosed ME-109s, Goering's own airplanes. Fortunately for me at the time, the Germans didn't know how to attack the B-17, which was still an airplane with which they were not familiar. They stood out, forming an echelon on my left side and they would peel off and try to attack us from that side. They just were not successful. When they did this, I would pull up so I would get the prop wash from the airplanes that were much farther ahead of me and these people would have to fly through it. I would then go from one side to another to keep them from attacking us well."

Regan belonged to the 368th Squadron of the 306th, and then-Maj. James W. Wilson led a brother outfit, the 423rd Squadron. A U.S. Military Academy graduate in 1939, Wilson, a Wyoming native, says "I went to West Point so I could learn to fly. I hated the Army and if I couldn't have gotten into flight school I would have quit." Upon graduation and receipt of his wings, Wilson met his first B-17 at March Field, California, in 1940. "It was a very early version," says Wilson, "without much of the equipment and armament of the later models." Subsequently, after he appeared on the roster of the 306th, Wilson had enough hours in a Fort to become squadron commander of the fourth unit in the bomb group. On this first mission, says Wilson, "We came home intact and we thought we were great. We hadn't gotten shot up in our particular squadron; we felt we were great warriors." Actually, flak damaged an engine on Wilson's plane and as it rolled down the runway at the end of the mission, the propeller fell off.

Another first for Lille was the B-24s mentioned by Kelly. They came from the 93rd Bomb Group and among the new crews was Luther Cox, the twenty-four-year-old son of a Baltimore executive who had worked his way up the ladder at a chemical company. Lu Cox, with a B.S. diploma in hand and a year of teaching science and math says, "I could clearly see the handwriting on the wall. We were going to be at war with the Germans. I didn't realize until Pearl Harbor Day that first we'd be at war with Japan.

"I enlisted in the Army Air Corps pilot training program and in late May 1941, arrived at the flying school at Muskogee, Oklahoma. It was basically run by the civilian Spartan School of Aeronautics. I opted for army flying rather than naval or the role of a ground pounder since I had completed several years of Civilian Military Training Corps at Fort Meade, Maryland, with a machine gun unit. I definitely knew I didn't want to be in the mud or snow with artillery coming in on my machine gun nest. I had no comprehension of aerial combat so like any bushy-tailed, young American I decided I wanted wings. I had never flown before. However, as a kid I did see army barnstorming fliers put on demonstrations. I was always building models, out of blocks of wood.

"I chose navigation after I washed out of flying school. This was a great disappointment. About 80 percent of my class washed out. We

were a very select group of young men, both from a physical and educational standpoint. When I took my prepilot physical there were seventeen of us and only three qualified. My only explanation for such an
extraordinarily high failure rate was that since we were not yet at war
and having limited numbers of aircraft they were told to hold back on
how many passed. I was told, for example, that I was 'too mechanical.'
Much later I got to pilot a B-24 and found there was a large amount of
mechanical flying in such a large and stable aircraft." Many officers in
the nose of the B-24 were taught to fly by each aircraft commander. This
paid off handsomely in Europe when a number of pilots were wounded
and a bombardier or navigator could take over.

In April 1942, Cox reported to Barksdale Field, Shreveport, Louisiana, where the 93rd Bomb Group was forming. As navigator for the
Liberator *Shoot Luke,* Cox says the work at Barksdale involved very
limited preparation for combat. "The main emphasis was on formation
flying. No aerial-gunner work. No instructions on strategic or tactical
bombing. We had absolutely no idea how much weather flying we could
get involved in when we were sent over to England." The name of the
plane derived from the oft heard cry in innumerable barracks crap games,
"Shoot, Luke, you're faded." On the nose of *Shoot Luke* a painter
depicted a hillbilly leaning against a tree while holding a long rifle.

On September 9, Cox and *Shoot Luke* learned just how difficult
conditions could be. "My very first severe weather experience was as
navigator in the lead aircraft as our ship led a squadron across the North
Atlantic. Couldn't see the ocean or the stars. Ordered to maintain radio
silence all the way. This gave me but one method of navigation—dead
reckoning based upon a given wind at takeoff base. We passed through
terrible weather and had absolutely no idea of what kind of true winds
we experienced. It was one solid wall of clouds, seemingly from the ocean
floor up. We immediately started climbing, hoping to get above the
weather. As we climbed higher and higher, we rapidly began to pick up
ice on the wings. Major Baker [the squadron commander flying with
Shoot Luke] wisely pointed the nose downward and took us down to
about 2,000 feet. However, we were still in the midst of all that weather,
flying blind, on instruments. Not until about six hours on instruments
did we break into a clear sky. I got a celestial course line off the sun and
using that plus my dead-reckoning data gave a slight change of heading
to get us to our first stop, Prestwick. We were one of the first crews to
land. Throughout the next several days our other aircraft began to arrive,

with one exception. Lieutenant Henshaw and his crew of ten simply disappeared off the face of the earth. One can only assume that they were heavily iced up in that bad weather and spun into the sea, or else his altimeter was off and he could have flown her right into the ocean."

Cox's pilot, John Murphy, recalled a normal takeoff and heading out to sea. "The wing ships made a beautiful picture against the flaming red of the sunset. Shortly after dark we began to hit bad weather. We tried to climb above it. As we went up, the thermometer went down and at about 12,000 feet we began to pick up some ice on the wings and props. The ice flying off the props and hitting the fuselage sounded like gun fire. The navigator [Cox] became ill and his oxygen system had frozen up, so between administering first aid to him—he was almost frozen— and worrying about our course and the weather, it was anything but a dull trip."

From Prestwick the crews of the 93rd moved to their home field, Alconbury. Nearly a month elapsed as the Liberator crews familiarized themselves with formation flying at high altitudes, firing guns at extreme low temperatures, learning to work in the bulky flight clothes.

Cox recalls the morning of his and *Shoot Luke*'s first mission—the raid on Lille. "After breakfast we all went into the briefing room which was dimly lighted. The hustle and bustle of crewmen entering and finding their seats together was overpowered by the undertone of conversation that hung above the fliers. The lights on the stage in front of us came on and flooded the walls upon which hung some air-navigation charts. The fact that it was ice cold in the room didn't seem to be recognized, so intense was everybody to hear what the target will be. Throughout every mission ever flown, I am certain that the most important words offered from the briefing stage was, 'Gentlemen, the target for today is . . .' In that tense atmosphere we could clearly see our target and the course we were to take in and coming out. It was very important to be aware in great detail of your position at all times while over enemy territory for although you might not be the lead aircraft, all that had to happen was for you to have to drop out of the formation and then you would hear the voice of the pilot asking for a heading back to England and our base.

"As all the planes warmed up their engines it seemed as though the entire base had turned out to watch this great moment in the history of the 93rd Bomb Group. We were lined up in snake fashion waiting for the signal from the control tower. At ten o'clock sharp, KK [Maj. Keith Compton, operations officer] pointed his Very pistol skywards and fired a flare, signaling number one aircraft, the lead ship, to take off. One ship after another staggered down the runway which seemed so short, and finally lifted off the ground, each just barely clearing the perimeter fence.

"Finally it became our turn to line up and take off. Earlier, back when we were in our parking space, Murph [pilot John Murphy] had run each engine up to its fullest rpm, checking the array of instruments before him very carefully. Our faithful ground-crew chief stood by each engine in turn with a fire extinguisher, as Murph cranked up each one, waiting for the right speed of prop rotation and compression before he would energize the starter. Starting these huge engines could be anxious moments as each engine seemed to stubbornly defy being kicked in. They seemed to come to life with a grunt, a puff of smoke and then that roar as she caught. The aircraft shuddered each time this happened.

"Now, at the beginning of the runway and with a crew at a peak of anticipation and excitement, Murph locked all four throttles and gradually moved them forward, as those four mighty engines began to come to life and roar, both Murph and [Frank] Lown [copilot] pushed as hard as they could on the brakes trying to hold *Shoot Luke* down. Finally, with the air frame of the plane fairly jumping up and down, they released the brakes and she seemed to leap forth as she charged down the runway. Carrying twelve 500-pound demolition bombs and 2,500 gallons of fuel, the gross weight of the aircraft was over 70,000 pounds. Murph held her on the runway as long as he could in order to get her moving faster and faster until at almost the last moment he eased back on the wheel and she staggered off into the sky. He quickly called for wheels up and Lown flicked the switch to bring them up. This greatly reduced drag and *Shoot Luke* took to the air like a huge bird."

For Cox's flight to Lille, operations decreed a bombing altitude of 22,000 feet. As soon as he saw the coast of France, Cox alerted all gunners to watch for enemy planes. "Our lead navigator brought us in too close to Dunkerque and they threw everything at us but the kitchen sink. One of the very first planes to cross the coast of France received a direct hit in its bomb bay. Their plane seemed to disintegrate in midair. It wasn't until months later that I discovered that Captain Simpson and Nick Cox were the only two members of the crew to survive such a mighty explosion. One can only surmise that the force of the blast blew their aircraft apart and they fell free. The same concussion evidently opened their parachute packs. They survived practically unscathed."

Even as he witnessed his group's first loss in combat, Cox himself nearly became a casualty. As the plane approached the target, enemy fighters started to appear and, with bombardier Ed Janic, Cox manned a machine gun in the B-24 nose. Suddenly he fell unconscious on the floor of the nose. Janic saw what happened and immediately put a walk-about bottle of oxygen to Cox's face.

According to Murphy, "The bombardier called to say the navigator was sick and that it was suicide to go into combat with him in that condition. We had a hurried talk over the interphone and then saw there was nothing to do but turn *Luke* around and go home. It almost broke the hearts of the crew when they headed back for England [the bombs were dumped] and saw the rest of the group continuing into enemy territory. When the other ships and crews returned they told of flak like huge clouds and fighters in swarms, some of the ships had been shot to hell, but *Luke* was so far a virgin."

After *Shoot Luke* returned to base the flight surgeon hospitalized navigator Luther Cox for tests. "I felt very bad about being the cause of aborting our first mission, which we had looked forward to with great excitement and anticipation. The crew, like myself, at the time didn't have the slightest idea of why I fell out. Later, I learned the problem was a faulty oxygen mask. We had never been made aware of the physical, mental and visual conditions that the body and mind runs through from the onset of oxygen deprivation until loss of consciousness. This was not a rare occasion in high-altitude flying, particularly using such inefficient equipment as we had. In subsequent missions I recall pulling the plug from the bottom of my oxygen mask and then having to crush the ice in it, letting the water flow out so I could get the proper amount of oxygen." Pronounced fit for duty, Cox shifted to the role of navigator for another 93rd Liberator, *Double Trouble,* as his slot on *Shoot Luke* had been filled.

The discrepancy in the eyewitness reports of Luther Cox and Ramsay Potts, aboard another B-24, on what happened to the aircraft piloted by Simpson exemplifies the difficulty in sorting out who did what unto whom and the results. As vexing as it is to determine which version is correct, there is no guarantee of the truth in the final Air Force summaries of actions. The personal accounts of those involved frequently vary from the official statements and the latter are almost equally suspect in their accuracy.

Ramsay Potts, a former college instructor in economics, commissioned and awarded his wings four days after Pearl Harbor, piloted one of the B-24s that continued on to Lille. "I was flying element lead, a twenty-four-plane formation," says Potts. "It seemed to me that we had no sooner formed up and turned towards France than we were over there. This was due to a 100-knot tailwind at 23,000 feet. We were supposed to have fighter escort but we never saw them. Very shortly after we penetrated the coast of France, we ran into some FW-190s and they attacked from different directions. It seemed to me most of the attacks were coming in from the rear. I had a tail gunner who was a pretty good man but shortly after the first attack, I couldn't contact him on the intercom radio. I thought perhaps he had been hit. I sent the engineer back to find out. He reported the man was in a state of shock, not from being hit, just from fright and he had frozen up. He wasn't firing his guns; he wasn't talking to anybody on the intercom.

"Then my left wing man got hit and his airplane caught on fire. I got a report nine chutes were seen. This, coming on the heels of the problem with the tail gunner, was another sort of psychological shock, because the man flying the plane on my left was my closest friend in the squadron and a very able fellow named Simpson.

"We overshot the Initial Point to turn into the bomb run because of the very high wind at our altitude. As a consequence we actually made a very poor bomb run. We were subjected to severe fighter attacks during that time. We dropped our bombs and later learned we had not hit the target.

"We turned and now were going back against that wind. Until this time it seemed as if we had been flying for a very short time. Now I kept looking down at the French landscape and it seemed to me we were hardly moving. Minute after minute rolled by and it was an interminable amount of time throughout which we were catching sporadic fighter attacks. There had been flak over the target which, since this was our first time, was a little nerve-wracking.

"Finally we got home and we had two airplanes make crash landings on the field and they tore off their landing gears and one lost its wings. Then we got news that another one had crash-landed on the beach. We knew Simpson had been lost. Altogether I felt it was a pretty tough operation.

"I went back to my quarters after the interrogation and was trying to light the small potbellied stove we had with some sort of cinders that passed as a form of charcoal. I was so cold. I think it was not only because it was damp and chilly but also I suppose I was experiencing a kind of shock reaction from this mission plus evidence of fear. I don't remember throughout the whole rest of the war ever again feeling as fearful about going on missions as I did right after this first one. I couldn't get warm.

I put on all kinds of sweaters and heavy jackets and even wrapped a big tartan blanket around myself while I tried to get the fire going.

"It was a typical early mission and later there were ones that were really tougher. But I never felt as badly afterwards as this time. My friend Simpson and the copilot and about five other members of the crew were captured by the Germans. Two of the members of the crew were killed and one was unaccounted for, a tech sergeant named Cox [no kin to Luther].

"The sergeant was from my home state and I knew of him as a very fine NCO, highly qualified as a mechanic and quite serious about drilling himself in all of the things that a person would have to do in an emergency. He worked hard on knowing and remembering what to do in the event of being shot down, in terms of evading capture. A year and a half later, I received a call from Eighth Air Force headquarters and they said, 'We'd like to bring somebody up to see you. We can't tell you his name but we want you to talk to this man.'

"We set up a time and they brought in Sergeant Cox who had evaded capture, had joined the Maquis and worked with them until they finally got him across the border to Spain. He was then handed over to the American Air Force. He told me that after being shot down he had made his way to a French farmhouse. An old man and a couple of girls there were very suspicious of him when they discovered him in the barn. They couldn't speak English but they finally brought someone who could. This man accused Cox of being a German plant. Cox pulled from his pocket a clipping of an English newspaper but the interrogator said we'll have to talk with someone else.

"Another man came around and asked Cox, 'Where are you from?' Cox told him he was from Tennessee. The man said that was a coincidence, one of the few Americans I know is from Tennessee. 'His name is Ramsay Potts. I played tennis against him at Forest Hills [New York].'

"Cox said, 'I got very excited and told him, "He's my squadron operations officer. He was flying on this mission."' That convinced the French and they accepted him." Cox may well have been the first member of the Eighth Air Force to succeed as an "evadee."

ON Sunday, December 7, 1941, W. J. "Red" Komarek, after a radio flash about the attack on Pearl Harbor, left his home in the Yorkville section of New York City. "I went to Sol's candy store and met some of the guys and pieced together the whole story and its significance. 'This gotta be war,' I said feeling grown-up. I was eighteen and had a month's basic infantry in the Civilian Military Training Camp in July 1940. Feeling a cocky patriotism, I announced that I was enlisting."

His parents agreed to give their permission provided he waited until after the Christmas holiday. Komarek first sought the Navy but when he couldn't pass their eye exam walked a half a block to the Army recruiting station and signed up for the Air Corps. Initially Komarek asked for the radio operator's course but when too many applied, he gladly dropped out in favor of gunnery school.

Conditions at the gunnery instruction field were less than ideal. "The pilots were staff sergeants who thought they were going to gunnery school, not to ferry aerial gunners," recalls Komarek. "We had no helmets and no intercom with the pilots and flew in AT-6s and O-47s. You sat with your back physically separated from the pilot and your .30 caliber machine gun was stowed in front of you on a tracking swivel. The instructions amounted to the pilot telling you to fire when in position with the tow target, that is when he waggled his wings, and to stop firing when he waggled his wings again.

"He said at no time should you release your seat belt. On the first flight you learned you can't substitute a handkerchief tied on your head for a helmet, you can't reach a stowed machine gun without releasing your seat belt to get the gun to the quarter position against the wind, you had to struggle like hell against the slipstream to clamp the gun down for firing at the tow target."

Komarek was assigned to the 93rd Bomb Group equipped with B-24s and became a tail gunner for a Liberator named *Globe Trotter*. The outfit, activated March 1, 1942, commenced training crews with flights out of Fort Myers, Florida, combining this phase of preparation with antisubmarine patrols over the Gulf of Mexico. After four months of this work, Komarek along with other airmen sailed to England on a troopship. The B-24s practiced for their encounters with the enemy in mock combat with RAF Spitfires. "The Spits barreled in and we tracked in our sights and pretended leading and firing. Although the turret was equipped and fitted for gun cameras, they were not available to us. We had no way to evaluate our effectiveness." Nor did he relish the high-altitude flights. "I was cold and my seat seemed tiny and we appeared to go slow. I had to get used to adjusting oxygen for altitude and the heat suit. The door of the turret was a real obstacle. I never seemed to get enough heat in the suit and the electric gloves were worthless. I was getting the impression that we should know these things by osmosis. If it weren't for the bull sessions with other combat men, we would have had a helluva time."

On the 93rd's maiden mission to Lille, Komarek says, "Seeing my first flak burst I called the Skipper. Imitating John Wayne, I said, 'It looks like they're shooting at us but the bursts are low and behind.' No sooner said and big black bursts with a whoosh and pebbles hitting the window sounds seemed to be all around us. I quickly forgot John Wayne. They found us and I had better imitate a tail gunner. I didn't see any fighter escort but a fighter was diving down on us. I watched fascinated as he dove below and disappeared. I didn't fire! Why? Buck fever? Then there was another. I tracked him firing short bursts. I wasn't leading him enough. My tracers were arching away from his tail. I led the next, firing short bursts when suddenly my sight was filled with a B-24, our left wing ship. I stopped firing momentarily. Did I stop in time or did I put a couple of fifties in its nose? I strained to see if there was any damage.

"I kept squeezing the green balloon on my oxygen mask. We were told to do this to prevent your saliva from freezing the vent, since this was a constant-flow system, the green bag would burst with the vent clogged. My green balloon was growing larger. What the hell am I doing here anyway? I should be back in high school."

The tail gunner on *Globe Trotter* gaped at the sights and coped with his own problems. "God Almighty, what is that! A 24 trailing smoke . . . going down. I see chutes, one . . . two . . . three . . . watch for fighters . . . short bursts. The balloon on my mask is now twice as large. Pull the feed line off the intake and stick the hose in your mouth. I don't feel so good. Then it had to happen, biting down on a hose with pressure building, the hose spewed out of my mouth. Where did it go? Grab it from the turret valve and trace it down to the end. Am I seeing purple dots? Put the hose back in your mouth . . . don't bite down on it. Look for fighters . . . There they are, twin booms, they're P-38s and Spits, just like the cavalry. What a sight! I had a seat on the fifty-yard line watching our fighters roaring in to attack. A fighter was going down . . . for every German there was a Spit or 38 on its tail . . . An intercom check from the pilot . . . all okay, thank God, nobody got hit. I got through the mission, oxygen trouble and all."

ALMOST two weeks later, the 97th Bomb Group, on its final assignment for the Eighth Air Force before transferring to the North Africa–based Twelfth, reeled from punishment meted out over the Lorient U-boat bases. The tally showed three aircraft shot down with thirty airmen missing, six planes damaged, five crewmen wounded. Worse, even direct hits with five one-ton bombs made no dent in the submarine pens. A navigator who saw the explosives fall dead on target reported, "They bounced off those massive concrete U-boat shelters like Ping-Pong balls."

Walt Kelly survived the Lorient debacle but the new place of business challenged even the most optimistic. "We were to be led to North Africa to participate in Torch by Jimmy Doolittle, the newly designated commander of the Twelfth. On November 6 we took off for Gibraltar. It was a long flight without incident except for a skirmish by Lt. John Summers's plane with some JU-88s. Some crew members were wounded but the plane made it into Gibraltar. After several days we flew on to Africa where the ground forces were still in the midst of skirmishes with the Vichy French who were supporting the Germans.

"Amid sniper fire and bare base conditions, we struggled to load bombs and refuel the planes from five-gallon cans. Some were hopelessly bogged down in the mud at Tafauri and couldn't operate. The turf field was a soggy mess. We offloaded the bombs and managed to fly out to Biskra, an oasis resort on the edge of the Sahara. We went from mud to sand. Every takeoff left a sandstorm behind. Some air crews, mine included, were lucky enough to have rooms at the Palace and other hotels in town." For many, living standards dropped far below what they experienced in England. The flak and enemy fighters remained as dangerous as ever.

The 97th was not the only outfit lost to strategic bombing by the Eighth Air Force during this period. Ramsay Potts took a squadron from the 93rd to a southern RAF base to perform antisubmarine patrol in the Atlantic as part of the preparation for Torch. The British had long advocated use of the B-24s with their extended range for combating U-boats.

"We didn't know anything about any invasion of North Africa," says Potts. "We were trying to locate submarines and use our depth charges to kill them. On a very long patrol down into the Bay of Biscay, we were returning. I'd gotten up out of my seat and looked over the ocean to the left and for just a moment I mistook what I saw for a flight of birds, way off, close to the water. This flock of birds turned out to be twin-engine German ME-210s.

"There were five of them. I jumped back into the pilot's seat and noticed a split in the flight. I was getting reports from the rear gunner and it quickly became apparent that two of them were trying to move ahead of us and two were turning in toward us. One had sort of moved to get into position for an attack at the tail.

"As they started climbing, so did I because we had been below a ragged cloudbed which was maybe 2,500 to 3,000 feet above us. The first airplane came in towards us and as he approached, I turned sharply towards him. He then came right across the top of our airplane. It seemed I could practically reach up and touch him. Our top gunner just split him open and he burst into flames practically atop our airplane. At the same time the waist gunner was claiming that he was firing at another plane making an attack and the tail gunner was firing on a third. The waist gunner claimed he'd shot down his man and so did the tail gunner. Nobody saw the plane coming toward the tail go down except the gunner but one other crewman saw the plane shot down by the man at the waist.

"By the time I completed the maneuvers, I had done about a 270-degree shift, a part circle climbing and getting up and approaching the cloud cover overhead. When I ducked into the clouds we didn't have any attacks from the two ME-210s that had streaked out in front to intercept us.

"I stayed in the cloud cover, set a course that finally brought us to Land's End where we landed in high spirits because we knew we had shot down two airplanes and were claiming three. A message had gone on ahead of us. They knew we had been under attack and that we'd had an engagement. All of our squadron and the RAF permanent party was out there when we landed. They counted 156 .30 caliber holes in the airplane. No vital part had been hit and we felt pretty good. I had not been flying precisely as our operations procedure indicated—it required that planes on patrol fly just below the cloud cover when it was half a mile or more and just above it when it was under half a mile, if one could see through it down on the ocean. I should have been closer to the clouds but the deck had been lifting and I'd been careless and hadn't changed my procedure.

"Instead of congratulating me, the squadron commander said, 'What the hell were you doing, flying so far below the cloud cover?' He was not happy. Instead of being gratified that we had shot down two or three German aircraft, he was angry that I had exposed the plane. The RAF interrogated the intelligence people. They were skeptical. They did not believe one bomber could have an engagement with five fighter aircraft and survive. They questioned my crew for a very long time. Finally, they seemed to get a story that satisfied them. So they gave us two probably destroyed and one possible. Later, through communications intercepts, the coastal command established that we shot down three enemy planes and the RAF considered it quite a feat.

"That evening I was sitting in the mess when an RAF corporal came in with a message for Captain Potts. It was a teletype from Air Chief Marshal Joubert who was head of coastal command. It congratulated me and my crew for a fine performance. He had commended us, so naturally I took it to the squadron commander and said, 'Look at this message from Joubert. Perhaps this will cause you to change your mind a little bit about what happened today.'

"He looked at it and said, 'You know what this proves?' 'No,' I said. 'What does it prove?' He said, 'It proves Air Chief Marshal Joubert doesn't know his ass from third base.'"

The use of B-24s as part of the antisubmarine campaign actually preceded the assignment of Potts and his unit by several months. Bill Topping, a native of a small town near Roanoke, Virginia, with only a high school education and working for the Chesapeake and Ohio Railroad, enlisted in the Air Corps the day after Pearl Harbor. Although flight training required two years of college, he was accepted after he passed an equivalency exam.

"I wanted to be a pilot but they said they needed navigators and bombardiers. If you wash out of those you can go back and try pilot training. I felt I'd be better off as an officer so agreed to bombardier instruction." After he graduated he began a tour with the 19th Antisubmarine Squadron that patrolled the waters around Gander protecting convoys and searching for submarine wolfpacks. "I never saw a German sub but we did see what happened to ships getting torpedoed while in convoys."

When the U.S. Navy assumed responsibility for that sector of the Atlantic, Topping flew to England to perform antisub work in a B-24 off the southeast coast. Attached to the RAF, Topping and the officers lived comfortably in a hotel. "We had tea servings and I had a batman who took care of my clothes and shined my shoes. Next door lived a group of Land Army girls. The missions and techniques were the same as those of the RAF. Stay in cloud cover as much as possible, use radar to indicate someone was out there. In an attack we were to dive down to about fifty feet and as bombardier I was to string out five depth charges. It was hours and hours of boredom, flying the Bay of Biscay, sometimes going to Gibraltar to refuel. I belonged to the whale and ale club, getting a couple of whales we dove on. The British were quite concerned about whales in the Bay of Biscay, always asking how many we saw and in what direction they were headed. But one day, it all came together.

"I spotted the subs, there were three, followed by four all on the surface going towards France probably for supplies, including torpedoes. We broke radio silence and the navigator gave our position. Then we attacked. We dove on them and I tried to string out the depth charges. As we pulled out and swung away from them, we were taking a lot of hits from the subs. We had attacked the first three subs and were getting ready for another depth-charge run when the tail gunner said, 'Nothing came out, no depth charges.'

"I rushed back to the bomb bays and I found out what had happened. We were helpless. We had been shot up so bad on the left side of the bomb bay that the main wiring system along the top left was shredded. There was nothing we could do and we had to stay out of range of shells from the subs which could throw up a lot of lead.

"We waited until other planes came in, the first a British Sunderland. I said, 'Bring me some ammunition from the back.' I had a .50 caliber nose gun and I figured I can at least fire if we attack. We dove and I was shooting at the Germans on the subs who were firing at us and trying to get the Sunderland behind us. I don't know how many I hit; they looked like ten pins in a bowling alley, just being knocked off the sub. The Sunderland dropped some depth charges and the tail gunner told us he had dropped them and was still with us. Six or seven other planes came in and we proceeded to lead, telling them to follow us. They started hitting the other subs. One of the Wellingtons went into the water, losing all but one of the crew. Some Royal Navy sloops showed up. They fanned out, went through throwing their depth charges and firing off their decks. It was a long battle, lasted six hours, but it seemed like all day."

The British air ministry announced the engagement sank three U-boats, but Topping upset his commanding officer. "Back at the base, my CO wanted to know why I didn't drop any depth charges. He was a West Pointer and we did not get along too well. I made the snotty remark, 'I just missed getting the Congressional Medal of Honor.' He asked, 'How come?' I said, 'I should have gone back into the bomb bay, grabbed one of the depth charges and dove out, giving my life.' That comment gave me a lot of trouble, but I deserved it; I was always causing him a lot of headaches." Topping saw no more subs while posted to southeastern England.

On November 7, two more bomb groups, the B-17–equipped 91st and the B-24–manned 44th were committed to operations. Whit Hill, son of a Philadelphia Navy Yard worker and born in 1920, graduated from high school after a curriculum that included math, chemistry, Latin, geography and world history. "But I learned about 'rubbers' from the big boys. After high school—college funds were not available—I moved from one job to another in order to improve my position in life. The jobs included roofers' helper, truck driver, accounting clerk, and apprentice in a metal edge box company.

"As the European war escalated, reports were almost daily in the Philadelphia newspapers. My chums discussed the war situation and girls nearly daily. When the first military draft for twenty-one-year-olds came up in 1940, many local draftees were sent to Fort Dix, New Jersey. They were photographed sleeping in pup tents. That was Boy Scout stuff to me and several of the crowd decided to 'Join the Navy and see the world.' But the Navy recruiting office was closed on Saturday afternoons, the only time we could get there.

"Finally reaching the dangerous old age of twenty-one, a new draft drew my number which they quickly followed up with the famous 'Greetings' [the opening salutation] notice to report. To avoid being drafted and sleeping in tents, I promptly enlisted for three years in the Army Air Corps in September 1941, and was shipped to Sheppard Field, Wichita Falls, Texas. (I never saw any falls.) I was given and passed a battery of tests. Eyeglasses struck me out as a pilot. When asking about attending OCS for a ground position, a sergeant advised he could get me a commission tomorrow by changing my application to the tank corps. My reply was no thanks, I'd rather be a private in the Air Corps.

"Meanwhile, there was a career to decide upon. Having worked around the house with my father and being handy with my hands, I opted for Aircraft Sheet Metal Repair School. On the weekend of December 7, 1941, I managed to be AWOL from Chanute Field, Illinois, and on a boozing spree in Chicago. Hitchhiking back to Chanute on that Sunday morning, I learned about Pearl Harbor from a car radio. With a bit of luck, and the chaos caused by many local patriotic men who wanted to get on the base and enlist, I got to my barracks without incident.

"The comprehensive aircraft sheet metal course covered layout procedures, rivet gun instructions and operation, metallurgy, repairing wrecked fuselage carcasses, metal plating, cable splicing and many other subjects. Following graduation it was off to MacDill Field, Tampa, Florida, to join the 91st Bomb Group. Dutywise there was no sheet-metal work as all repairs were made at the base maintenance shops. Our main employment was fatigue duty, picking up paper. In June 1942, the entire 91st BG shipped out on a troop train to Walla Walla, Washington, for combat training. I assisted 323rd Bomb Squadron aircraft maintenance crews in changing engines, replacing parts such as plugs, magnetos, propellers, wiping up oil, sweeping floors. I finally made sergeant.

"On the 29th of September, we boarded the *Queen Mary* in New York harbor and five days later we were in the Firth of Clyde, Scotland. From Scotland we loaded on a train to Kimbolton. The generous, good-hearted American troops, being loaded with candy bars and gum purchased on the *Queen Mary,* began tossing these prizes out the train windows to the British kids along the route. They soon adopted the famous, 'Any gum, chum?' plea. We later learned that many of these children were injured or killed as they searched along the train tracks for these prizes.

"Kimbolton, a newly built Quonset-hut base with potbelly stoves, outdoor toilets and ablution centers had runways that would not support our B-17s. It would take weeks to correct. Meanwhile, our commanding officer, Lt. Col. Stanley T. Wray, learned of a vacant, permanent RAF aerodrome at Bassingbourn, Royston, Herts. Without a word to anyone, the group moved in overnight. HQ, Eighth AAF was not too pleased, but we stayed there for nearly three years.

"Bassingbourn had permanent barracks with central heat, showers and bathtubs, a consolidated mess hall, officers and NCO clubs, four big hangars that held up to four B-17s at one time. Each of the four squadrons had a sheet-metal crew of seven and a crew chief, myself for the 323rd Squadron. We were in heaven, but only for a moment. Our missions against Hitler began in October 1942, and they were far different than our training flights."

The 44th Bomb Group which eventually bedded down at Shipdham, acted as a diversion on its first two visits to the Continent and then on a third trip cloud cover prevented a bomb drop. Even though the 44th had escaped significant damage from the enemy, its commanders, as well as those in the more experienced 93rd Bomb Group, realized the absence of armor protection endangered the Liberator crews. After the enterprising engineering officers of one B-24 squadron arranged for a local contractor to pave the nose compartment floor with boiler plate, not only adding protection to the navigator and bombardier but apparently also providing better balance to the aircraft, all models began to receive similar modifications. Then, sheet steel plates added to the side of the ships shielded the pilots. In fact, engineers, maintenance workers and factories responding to the complaints, critiques and requests of aircrews, constantly tinkered or changed in varying degrees all of the planes flown by the Eighth Air Force throughout the course of the war.

WEST Pointer, Lt. Howard F. Adams, a twenty-five-year-old, June 1941 graduate of primary flying school, piloted a model B-24D for the 44th in September from Manchester, New Hampshire, to Gander Lake, New-foundland. "A more miserable and bleak place is hard to imagine," he noted in his diary. "No town, no roads, few people, but much wind and bitter cold, too." He cheered up as his ship, *Maisie*, lifted off for the long haul to Prestwick. "Everything went smoothly as our automatic pilot was doing the work now—allowing me to sit and watch the compass and other instruments and making the necessary adjustments to keep us on course. And so passed the night of September 29–30, 1942, until finally it began to grow light to the east. One of the most beautiful and breathtaking sunrises I have ever seen followed. The air was crystal clear and as the sun rose out of the water it painted everything a golden color."

Maisie located Prestwick without difficulty a short time later and within a few days, at another site, the flight crews met up with the ground personnel whom they had not seen for some six weeks. The airdrome for the squadron at Shipdham near Norwich seemed adequate for oper-ations but Adams complained, "The quarters are worse than ever—no running water and poor sanitation facilities. It's very cold at night mak-ing it necessary to use five blankets. Several B-17 pilots, navigators and radio men have been giving us lectures on radio procedure, operations techniques, etc. They have been over France several times on bombing missions with quite a bit of success and only three or four planes lost."

To break the monotony, Adams and several companions rode their bicycles [an essential piece of equipment, for flight crews often housed a mile or more from their aircraft] to a railway station for a train ride to Norwich. "Our first impression of Norwich, a city of about 135,000, was the numerous buildings that had been blasted by bombs or gutted by fire. After searching for several hours for a place to stay, we finally found a shabby hotel of ancient vintage that had rooms of a sort. We then went over to the Royal Hotel for a dinner of filet of sole which was good but not much to get fat on. After strolling the streets a bit, we went to a dance at the Samson and Hercules Inn. Scotch soldiers in their kilts, British soldiers and sailors, W.A.A.F.s and many U.S. officers and men filled the dance hall. Everyone danced the peculiar British windmill sort of dancing."

On October 20, Adams reported, "We flew down to Bovingdon [before heading to a repair installation at Burtonwood] in an effort to fix my plane up with armor plate, more guns. No sooner had we gotten to 500 feet than we were in the soup and so we hedgehopped all the way home to try again the next day. On the 21st we got off early, flew on to Burtonwood where to our dismay, we found out the depot was far too busy fixing up Colonel Roosevelt's B-17s to bother with us." Adams and company then attempted to get the work done at another place but again the weather forced a change; he took refuge at an RAF airfield where the hosts plied him with food and whiskey. After three days of frustration he finally managed to reach a base where *Maisie* received her alterations.

Weather problems continued to dog Adams. After another practice flight he reported, "All went well until we got down to 4,000 feet on our return. Here we split up the formation to go down through the overcast. I immediately found a hole but at 2,000 it closed in again. I searched for another break in the overcast and finally managed to wiggle down to about 500 feet where the visibility was almost nil and so I flew back up to 2,000 feet to search for another field. We flew west and south in a vain attempt to find a clear spot. Finally we saw some mountains sticking above the clouds and so I headed towards them hoping to find it clear there, but no such luck.

"All the while we kept our eyes peeled for an airport, but the visibility was just too poor. Once we saw one but it was under construction and, as I came down to around 200 feet to have a look at it, I just missed the top of a hill and so decided to climb back to a safe altitude. By this time it was around five o'clock and commencing to grow dark. A bit later we came to an inlet on the western coast but were unable to locate ourselves and so quite lost. Again I went down, skimming about 100 feet over the water hoping to find a field near the coast. Finding none we headed back inland again and it was at this time that I saw a church steeple on a level with me 100 or so feet away.

"By now it was really dark and we climbed up through the soup which was thicker than ever. We broke through at about 4,000 feet where it was clear as a crystal. The sun was just dying out in the west. Our radio was quite dead but a searchlight flickering across the sky brought fresh hope. They laid the beam of light along the ground pointing towards the nearest airport as we found out later. We followed its direction and soon came to another light and followed it and then another all pointing in the same direction. Pretty soon we saw three beams intersecting in a point below us and on looking down we saw an airport all lighted up. It was a wonderful sight. As we spiraled down they shot up some yellow rockets to further attract our attention but now the sky was ablaze with searchlights.

"I flew over the field, went on a way and then turned around for a landing. As both of my landing lights were burnt out, I had to come in without any and managed to set her down on the end of the runway.

'Twas a very comfortable feeling to have those wheels safely on the ground again. It was 6:15 P.M. when I cut the engines and black as pitch."

Frequent thick fogs, towering mountains of clouds, capricious winds and sudden shifts from crystal-clear skies to ground-obscuring murk frustrated all Eighth Air Force pilots and navigators. Routine practice flights or trips to other bases could be as dangerous as a mission. The conditions forced innumerable unplanned landings, led to crashes, lost planes and killed crewmen. For bombers shot up during missions with hydraulic and electrical systems out of whack and desperately wounded men aboard, the weather extended the nightmare beyond the zone of combat.

Whit Hill recalls his squadron's first casualty as the 91st and the three other bomb groups still in England, the 44th, 93rd and 306th were dispatched to St. Nazaire. "Bombardier Lieutenant Briglia, born in St. Nazaire, was killed when flak hit him in the chest as he leaned over his bombsight to see where his bombs were falling. The plane made an emergency landing at RAF Exeter and I was one of the crew sent there to make repairs. Working with the RAF personnel was a new experience. We picked up some useful notes on aircraft repair and the use of new tools, particularly the pop rivet gun, used for blind riveting. This was without doubt one of the most important tools for without it, fixing damages to the inaccessible areas of the wing and stablilizers would have been a slow and tedious task.

"Our aircraft were parked in a dispersal area off the base. The B-17s were amongst a beautiful avenue of huge and ancient elm trees that extended about three-quarters of a mile from the Wimpole Hall Estate, then owned by the sister of Rudyard Kipling. It was a magnificent location but without water, electricity or shelter except for a couple of one-hole outhouses.

"When we first arrived on the scene, our equipment was limited by a 'table of authorization' which was inadequate to say the least. We had no aluminum sheets to use for patches, rivet guns or even hand-rivet sets to rivet on patches. In Hangar #1, however, there was an RAF maintenance shop whose most friendly personnel were more than ready to assist us all they could. We 'borrowed' sheets of aluminum and used their machine shop to make hand-rivet sets and other repair equipment.

"One day I was ordered to attend an airframe school at the Eighth Air Force's Burtonwood supply depot. While there, Captain Larson, our engineering officer, appeared and together we reviewed the depot's supply bins. While he distracted the depot guide, I was busy loading up Captain Larson's staff car with much needed but unauthorized equipment such as straight and offset electrical drills, rivet guns, rivet sets, bucking bars, etc. On return we were ready to meet the action. Meanwhile, the group sheet-metal crews had obtained surplus bomb-loading carts and modified them into portable sheet-metal work benches that included electric and air compressors, a floodlight, workbench with vise, storage for sheet metal and parts and room for eight tool boxes used by the sheet-metal crew, all towed by a Jeep assigned to the crew chief like myself.

"At the end of each mission the battle and mechanical damage of each returning aircraft was assessed and time to make necessary repairs was estimated. The planes requiring the least amount of work were the first to be repaired. Then there were many shot-up aircraft. The sheet-metal crews would help each other out. There were times when the sheet-metal crews did not get to bed for 72 hours. None of the men from the ground crew—mechanics, electricians, prop specialists, bomb loaders, sheet-metal repairmen had any set daily working hours. Every day was Monday; it was 'work until you drop' and the password for requested tasks was 'how soon?'"

THE efforts of the first heavyweight bombers, the airmen and their ground support did not impress Winston Churchill, still unconvinced of either the quality of U.S. bombers or the daylight, precision-bombing campaign. In a letter to his air chief marshal, Sir Charles Portal, November 2, Churchill complained, "The number of American Air Force personnel [in England] has risen to about 55,000 . . . So far the results have been pitifully small . . . Far from dropping bombs on Germany, the daylight bombers have not ventured beyond Lille [RAF Lancasters had already paid their disrespects to Berlin and Cologne among other German targets]." The British prime minister expressed frustration with the political currents that defeated what he considered the Allies' best interests. "Considering the American professional interests and high reputation which are engaged in this scheme, and the shock it would be to the American people and to the Administration if the policy proved a glaring failure, we must expect most obstinate perseverance in this method." He gloomily concluded, "for many months ahead large numbers of American air personnel will be here playing very little part in the war."

Oddly enough, Eaker's opposite number in the RAF, Air Marshal Arthur Harris, the bomber chief, was one of the few Britons who approved of the U.S. theory and practice. He wrote to a subordinate commander, "I have never been apprehensive about the ability of the heavy bomber to look after itself in daylight vis-à-vis the fighter. There is not the least doubt in my mind that if we and all the available Americans started daylight attacks against the less heavily defended targets in Germany by big formations of heavy bombers now, we should knock the German fighter force out of the sky in two or three months, by the simple process of shooting them down. . . . It has all along been our experience that whenever the rear gunner, even at night, sees the enemy fighter first, he either destroys it or the fighter refuses to come in and attack."

At the time he made these comments, December 1942, the U.S. Army Air Corps for all of its 55,000 people in the United Kingdom, could never mobilize much more than seventy-five effective bombers for a mission, in contrast to the several hundred from the RAF. Harris, a man with a reputation for deviousness that masked his own implacable ideas, never showed any real willingness to switch his forces from night to day. Furthermore, as he should have known then and certainly was shown shortly, the contest between bombers and fighters was anything but weighted in favor of the heavyweights.

FOR Howard Adams in the 44th it may have seemed as if true to the Churchill prediction, *Maisie* was destined to roam the skies without ever striking a blow. On December 6, three squadrons, the 66th (Adams's outfit), the 67th and 68th headed for Abbeville/Drucat. When the fighter escort missed the rendezvous, the 66th and 67th squadrons aborted the mission but the third member of the group plowed toward the target. Basing his comments on what others related to him, Adams told his diary, "The 68th dropped their bombs and turned for home. On the way back the FW-190s started a series of frontal attacks concentrating on Lieutenant DuBard, the right wing of the lead element of three. They shot out one engine but he managed to stick in formation. About that time a 20 mm burst in the cockpit of Lieutenant Holmes's ship on the left wing, wounding both the pilot and copilot, Lieutenant Ager, causing them to fall out of formation for a while. They poured the coals to her anyhow and got back onto formation. Around this time they got another engine in DuBard's ship and he began to drop away quite rapidly, losing altitude all the while. All at once the 190s swarmed around him, attacking from all angles. The old B-24 went into a lazy spiral down towards the Channel below with the Huns buzzing around it like gnats. The crews in the rest of the 68th watched their doomed brothers until the

B-24 took its final plunge into the Channel where it burst into flames. The whole crew was given up as lost. Though Holmes had one dead engine, he got back safely with the rest of the 68th, thereby earning the DFC for himself."

On December 12, Adams took off as a member of a six-ship party intent on wrecking a popular target, the Luftwaffe installation at Abbeville. A helpful tailwind boosted airspeed across the Channel to 300 miles an hour. But the half-dozen would-be predators ran afoul of an impenetrable blanket of clouds. "Had to turn around and come back," he told his diary "as we cannot bomb France indiscriminately." Two days later, his copilot accidentally taxied *Maisie* off the runway and the B-17 sank hub-deep in mud. The remainder of the day the crew labored to extricate the bogged-down plane.

Finally, on December 20, flocks of B-24s joined by swarms of B-17s launched themselves at Romilly-sur-Seine 150 miles southeast of Paris. Adams led an element of four aircraft. "As we neared the coast we started several huge circles to join in one huge formation all the while test-firing our guns. About a dozen Forts and Libs turned back for various reasons but some seventy Forts and our twelve Liberators headed for France. The planes were stacked up from 20,000 to 23,000 feet and stretching miles to the front—we tagged onto the rear.

"It was bitter cold—way below zero—but in a few minutes we all forgot about that as we were attacked by some German fighters. I closed in behind the first element until we almost touched wing tips, but all of a sudden an FW-190 came down in a screaming dive, shooting at Major Key's ship just ahead of me and passing between him and my ship. This was my first sight of a German plane despite the fact that I have been in England almost three months now. He was so close that I could easily see the pilot and the beautiful yellow and silver markings of the plane. I watched him until he disappeared some five or six thousand feet below us.

"I was too busy to be scared but managed to call the crew on the interphone and told them to keep their eyes peeled for more fighters. My navigator had fired a quick burst on his .50 caliber nose gun at the FW-190 to no avail. It took all my time and energy to keep in tight formation so I did not see Paris as we passed over it. The Germans kept buzzing around us but I didn't see them. One of them dived on Major Key's ship just to my front and fired his 20 mm, which hit one of the gunners square in the head and that was the end of him. I was unaware of this at the time—in fact I didn't even see the plane.

"After what seemed ages, we neared our target. I caught a glimpse of the Seine River winding its way over the apparently peaceful French countryside, but the frequent puffs of smoke around us made it quite plain that we were not wanted. But we kept on our way and soon the red light on my instrument panel told me that our bomb bay doors were open and the time had come for us to deliver the 'bacon.' After interminable minutes, I heard Lieutenant Hannan my bombardier shout, 'Bombs away!' just as I saw the bombs fall from the ship ahead of me. After months of just fooling around, it gave us quite a thrill to see those bombs drop. My radio operator watched them fall and string themselves across the hangars and buildings of the German field 23,000 feet below us.

"We turned to our left and headed on that long journey home and I prayed that our beloved old *Maisie* would not fail us this time. Minutes ticked by like hours! Every once in a while I would catch sight of an FW diving at our huge formation and turning away. Now and again I would hear a short burst from one of our guns and would look over at my tiny copilot, Lieutenant McLeod, huddled underneath his steel helmet. I returned his weak smile and went back to flying which was real work as my fingers were like ice and my oxygen mask was full of water and ice. Every once in a while my plane would rock viciously, and I knew that the flak was getting uncomfortably close.

"The gunners in the rear were having a hell of a time with their oxygen masks and hands freezing but by using several extra masks they got along OK. Being faster than the B-17s, we flew back and forth over the top of them, finally working our way up so we were in the middle of the formation which was lucky as the FWs were concentrating on the front and rear. We continued our running dogfight and after a wee bit, I saw Paris spread out beneath us. The Eiffel Tower stood out like a sore thumb even from our altitude. It was not long before I saw several squadrons of RAF Spitfires cutting capers high above us. The white vapor trails against the blue sky was a beautiful and comfortable sight.

"*Maisie* roared along as faithful as ever but I thought I never would reach the English Channel. Narrow as it is, the Channel seems like a gate which the enemy dares not pass. Soon we started losing altitude very slowly but as we picked up speed, we passed the B-17s and headed for home feeling very happy and gay at our good luck. We chattered over the interphone like silly school boys—everything we said seemed funny though when our radio operator told us there was a wounded man on Major Key's ship we sobered up some. As for us, *Maisie* was unscathed and so was our crew.

"After buzzing the field, I peeled off and landed very cold and tired. We were questioned by the intelligence officers as we sipped hot cups of coffee. Everyone was extremely polite and the air seemed filled with excitement and endless chatter. Questions such as—How many planes did you see? Did you get any? Where did you meet flak? Where did your bombs drop? Did you see any bombers go down? They fired all these questions although we were tired as well as excited. Food and sleep were all we could think about after our five-hour ordeal. So ended our first real raid!"

5

WINTRY DISCONTENTS, CHILLING FEARS

To buttress Torch in North Africa, the British-American high command had dispatched the 93rd, 97th and 301st Bomb Groups along with the 1st, 31st and 82nd Fighter Groups to Tunisia under the command of Doolittle. With the 92nd Bomb Group committed to training, the transfers depleted the thin ranks of warriors and machines available to Eaker. As winter approached he could call only upon the more recent arrivals from the 44th, 303rd, 305th and 306th Bomb Groups, and the only American-flown escorts, the limited-range Spitfires of the 4th Fighter Group.

Capt. Billy Southworth Jr. commanded one of the 303rd's B-17Fs. "The first thing I can remember almost," wrote Southworth in preparation for a proposed magazine piece, "was sitting on a bench with a bunch of ballplayers, big leaguers that played hard and played to win. My father [Billy Southworth Sr.] was one of them. Not a big fellow, but full of scrap and determination. I soon had as much desire to win as he did. At nine I was pulling bats for Rochester [a minor-league baseball team where his father began a managing career], shagging flies during fielding practice, running errands for the ballplayers and sitting in on pregame meetings. It was there and in the field, hunting with Dad, that I learned the meaning of teamwork. Our hunts were organized as a team, each doing his job, taking his shot."

The younger Southworth, whose father now led the St. Louis Cardinals in 1942 to a World Series championship, had shown promise as an outfielder and played for a high minor-league team before enlisting in the Air Corps nearly a year before the Japanese attack. Toward the end of January 1941, at Parks Air College in Illinois, Southworth soloed. After he completed his initial training, Southworth joined the newly activated 303rd. The diary he kept reflects a young man with no shortage of confidence in himself, and indicates the nomadic, uncertain world of bomber crews in the first months of the war. In a June 1942 entry, Southworth noted, "Today had another thrill. The history of our plane hasn't been too good. Got it in the Mojave Desert in foul shape. No. 2 engine falters, so I took her off on three engines to climb slowly over the mountains to March Field [California]. An overcast was over March where peaks extend 1,000 feet upward. We came down, all fellows with full confidence. Visibility only three miles, very hazy, caught a glimpse of the field, turned away in a slow turn and kept our bad engine high. Jim Hudson wished to argue about a technicality on final approach, he was wrong as usual. Sergeant Means who has been with me for about two and a half months, said, 'You are good, aren't you, sir?' Hell yes, Means. They have confidence in me. Schueler, my navigator, nervous type, but a solid guy, wasn't at all bothered."

The travail with the Fort continued. A subsequent trip to Salt Lake City forced a landing with only two engines and then on a flight to Alamagordo he had barely enough power to reach the runway. The dutiful Means supposedly said, "That was perfect. If you can handle jams like this now, combat will be a cinch. You sure are good." In fact Southworth was skillful enough to coach other pilots new to handling the B-17. Others were not so proficient, and the Southworth diary contains many laconic mentions of companions who had washed out or died in accidents, like Hudson who criticized an earlier Southworth landing.

In addition to comments about the poor condition of the aircraft, the journal frequently notes the efforts of the Cardinals in the pennant race, the failings of superior officers and the romantic entanglements of himself and his associates. Southworth courted and broke an engagement with one woman before pursuing numerous "swell gals." He remarked on navigator Jon Schueler taking "the fatal step" proposing by telephone, and later noted that bombardier Milt Conver also married.

In Michigan, Southworth picked up a B-17 that would carry him to England, with the usual pause at Bangor, Maine. "Had a party last night. We're all confined to the post so the girls came to see us. 'Spook' Hargrove threw a bottle through a window at the end of a BOQ. Lieutenant Mitchell put his hand through another and cut it badly. The boys were high. Colonel Hughes wanted to know who was baying at the moon at 2:20 A.M. Stockton was out with [name deleted by author] who likes to spread her affections about. Seems that all of the girls did.

"Dad paid me a visit. Autographed Reber's and my plane. He's the grandest guy I know. Sure tired of sitting around. I want to go into combat. That's where the real work lies and where things must be accomplished.

"I'll never marry Helene hard as she's trying. Babs proposed persistently to me last night, second date. She's very pretty but wouldn't have her on a silver platter. There's Ann, wealthy in looks but lacks something. Ruth had everything but was too fond of herself. Betty a swell gal but too set in ways and lacks oomph. Cliffy might be a possiblity, sure she cares, haven't known her long enough. I'd like to get into this damn war and return so I can settle down."

On the final day of October, Southworth could scribble notes about the last legs from Newfoundland to a field near Liverpool. "Got off on instruments and was in the soup three-quarters of the trip. It took us ten and a half hours. Dillinger, my copilot, slept most of the way. Means, the sergeant engineer, did likewise while Doughty, radio, and Schueler, navigator, did a bang-up job. Jon missed his ETA by one minute. Land was sighted, all men were alert at their stations ready to fire (save Means, asleep). We were impressed by the jagged shores [Ireland], green hills, hedge fences, beautiful estates, picturesque with ancient moats of King Arthur's time surrounding them. Airports then littered the way to Prestwick."

The 303rd made Molesworth its home and Southworth reported to his diary early in November, "Rained every day since we've been here. These muddy days, a foot deep in places I'll never forget. Cold, wet, and black nights, cold wind stinging your face while your feet just get used to that dead cold feeling. The British are a fine people. Take the bitter with the sweet, defeat and victory without feeling—they hang on, just keep hanging on. They aren't deceiving, love their country and are proud of it. We'll win this war but it will take a long time."

Southworth expressed unhappiness with his superiors. "Lt. Joe Haas got Dumbell [award for a blunder] after Captain Blythe and Major Calloway Snafued a situation worse than Joe. Told Colonel Wallace [group commander] of a desirable landing procedure also the desirable way to fly a formation. It wasn't appreciated nor listened to but I'll wager that they'll adopt it as their own idea . . . God damn!! Flew with Major Calloway's outfit and he snafued as usual. He led a very poor formation and was lost nearly all the time . . . Flew No. 2 with Major Sheridan. Dillinger is the poorest excuse for a copilot that I've ever seen. He went to sleep three times this morning on our flight." The Southworth crew named its B-17 *Bad Check* in the obvious hope that it too would always bounce back. But throughout the war men often flew different aircraft, sharing them with other crews when one was in reserve or taking up another one because of malfunctions or combat damage.

The winds of war blew together an unlikely companion for Southworth in the person of Jon Schueler, the navigator for Southworth's plane. In place of a famous father who brought his boy to the office and even on business trips with the ballclub, Schueler grew up in Milwaukee as the son of a widowed, self-made businessman, a somewhat distant father who struggled through the Depression. After his father remarried, Jon described his relationship with his stepmother, a woman of beauty and frugality, as a series of "battles." He remarked, "When I was in high school, I had to go to bed at eight-thirty and all my clothes—terrible clothes were chosen for me.

"I went out for basketball in high school but I wasn't any good. I went out for track and became a miler, but I was never in any races, because no one else had a miler. I had worked one summer selling ties and shirts and when I graduated they asked me to stay on. That was pretty depressing. Then my stepmother gave me the money to enroll at the University of Wisconsin. I went a little crazy. I joined Alpha Delta Phi, the best drinking house on what may have been the best drinking campus in the country. But it's a good thing I cut loose, because I had been treated like a twelve-year-old at home."

After trying journalism, then economics, and finally obtaining a master's in English, Schueler entered the Bread Loaf School of English in Vermont, waiting on tables to pay for courses in how to write. By September of 1941, the draft loomed over him and Schueler enlisted in the Air Corps. "I tried like hell to think like a soldier. At one time I was appointed platoon leader and overnight lost all my friends because I started acting like a Prussian general. I thought that's what one was supposed to do to win the war, and was quite hurt at all the criticism. Fortunately, I was demoted soon enough."

Astigmatism in one eye eliminated pilot training and Schueler attended navigator classes. "I was so rigid about wanting to do everything right that for a while I was terribly slow at learning. But somewhere along the line I got the sense of it and became a pretty good navigator. One night marching with the platoon to a class, I realized that for a moment that terrible pressure to *do* something wasn't there. All I had to do was move along where the orders took me and I was a free man. In the Air Force all decisions were taken out of one's hands, except for those within the larger framework of the discipline.

"Everyone approved of me for the first time in my life," said Schueler.

"I was one of the boys. I was Uncle Sam's boy wonder. My father, God bless him, was proud. My stepmother couldn't say much. She had always said, 'Well, Jack, I guess you will always be a failure.'"

Schueler was well aware of the differences between him and South-worth. "My pilot was a Jack Armstrong–type named Billy Southworth. Billy and I hated each other's guts. He was the cocky son of a bitch, the pampered son of the manager of the St. Louis Cards. Our backgrounds and personalities couldn't have been more different, except that we were both prima donnas of kinds. Billy was a hard-driving guy, very ambitious and driven to try to be the best. I probably have many of the same drives but they're confused by the complexities of my being, fears of failure, depressions, impulsive responses to the world, inner contradictions. We didn't get on too well at first, particularly after I had messed up on a train-ing flight and he said to me in plain hearing of the crews, 'I don't suppose you know where we are?' One day on a cross-country flight to Chicago we took off in perfect weather but about two hours east of the base we saw a front rising in the distance. From the time we flew into the clouds I navi-gated on dead reckoning. I kept the radio silent. About two hours later we were still in total cloud, silver grayness pressed against the windows, opaquely glowing, holding us mysteriously. We couldn't get out of the stuff. Billy kept calling to ask where we were in a voice that plainly suggested I wouldn't have the faintest idea, and I was getting more and more enraged. I kept working, and the line of the plotting moved steadily along the charts.

"The next thing I knew the plane started flying all over the place. Billy was no longer following my directions, but had decided that we were lost and was trying to pick up the beam. There was nothing for me to do but track him. The line moved crazily over the chart until he picked up a radio beam and turned, headed back toward the base. He'd call up and taunt me once in a while and finally asked me for a position report. I told him we were about one minute east of the little town of C_____ and by the grace of God, in one minute the clouds parted below us and there was the sweetest little town west of the Mississippi. I wish to hell I could remember its name.

"I called Billy on the intercom and said, in as matter of fact a tone as I could manage, 'We are now flying over C_____ and our ETA Boise is at 15:36.' 'Roger,' he said and he didn't say one damned word more for the rest of the trip. When we landed, Jimmy [the copilot] stopped me and took my charts and told me that he wanted to show them to Billy so that he could see what had happened. I didn't wait for the demonstration but walked past Billy without saying a word.

"That night at the officers' club I was sitting at the bar properly brooding when I noticed that Billy was standing next to me. He ordered a drink, and then he said, very quietly, 'That was a great bit of navigating you did this afternoon.' I said, 'Thank you, Billy,' and from that moment he became one of the closest friends I have ever had."

Like Southworth and the other young males in uniform, Schueler also partied enthusiastically when not carrying out his flight duties. "All of us knew we were flirting with death from the moment we saw the planes. It was like the feeling at the beginning of a love affair, when all of the enticement is joy, yet one senses also the excitement of unknown possibilities, sadness, treachery, death. Larry [another bombardier in training] and I had seen the two planes crash on that first day and the image didn't leave our minds. We heard of other crashes through the country by the Air Force grapevine. One night a plane full of classmates didn't return. It had crashed against the side of some high mountain mass. We'd hear death in the night as we'd hunch over our instruments in the droning planes or on the field as we'd listen to the landings. We tried not to think about it. I pretended it was not there."

Indeed, with the country at war, the omnipresent threat to life, the geographical displacement of people, the enormous demands, responsibilities and expectations thrust upon young people, for men and women desperately in search of excitement, almost the only outlet lay in sexuality.

Recalled Schueler of one affair, "When I saw her in Chicago, she didn't blame me once for blanking out, just wondered why I hadn't written. She told me the story with a voice that was full of tension and of pain, but it was like a story of life. She wanted to cry, and maybe did a bit, but I never found a moment's bitterness in her. I saw her then, and every time I stopped in Chicago I would stay with her or she'd come to my hotel. The last times, I was in uniform as a cadet and then as a second lieutenant navigator. [She] and I had an incredible time. Perhaps she was more the hot, wonderful whore this time than before, because we were playing wartime and I was in uniform and cocky as hell, not having been shot at."

Then another interval away, and when Schueler returned to Chicago she was gone. There were boozy nights with prostitutes in Juarez as well as brief encounters aided by his artful companion, Larry. "When the command scheduled a pass, we'd head for town with [him] charging me: 'Now, Schueler, don't dally around. Remember, there is only one point and that is to get in there. You've got to Get In There.' He told me, 'Schueler, quit talking about yourself and don't talk about books and politics and stuff like that. Listen to me.' He was very charming and had a most ingratiating smile and laughing eyes, and was truly interested in the woman he spoke to—while he spoke to her. He'd ask question after question of some young clerk or secretary, his brow creased as he considered the answers. He'd find out that the girl wanted to write or travel or get married or have a child or leave town, and he'd say, 'You can do it, baby. I know you can do it.' When I'd hear those words, I'd know he was almost 'In There.' Even with the whores it wasn't enough and everyone was writing slushy letters and realizing how much in love with the last girls they had known in Boise." In fact, the young woman Schueler proposed to and wed before leaving for England was a Boise resident.

A soldier cut from still another mold, S. Sgt. Bill Fleming, a Jenkins, Kentucky, coal miner's son born in 1924, operated machine guns from the waist of the Southworth plane during its first missions. Says Fleming, "There were eight children in the family, five boys and three girls. We grew up in the Depression and it was very hard but we were a happy family." Two months before Pearl Harbor, Fleming, only seventeen, enlisted in the Air Corps. "I had never even seen a plane on the ground at the time. I thought I would enjoy it. After thirteen weeks of basic training, at Jefferson Barracks in Missouri, I took the test for radio operator's school at Scott Field, Illinois. They taught me to send and receive Morse code, how to work and maintain the radio equipment. Then I went to gunnery school in Florida, training in AT-6s with .30 caliber machine guns mounted in the rear cockpit. We'd fire at sleeves towed by other planes over the Gulf of Mexico.

"After six weeks about thirty-five of us were assigned to the 303rd Bomb Group at Boise, Idaho. Sixteen days later we got off a troop train because when we got to Boise, the group had moved on to Spokane so they sent us there. From Spokane to March Field, California, to Alamagordo, New Mexico, where we finally joined the group. I was assigned to Billy Southworth's crew.

"We only had four planes in our squadron, the old B-17Es. That's all there was to train crews on [nine planes were the basic complement of a squadron]. I enjoyed meeting the fellows. We got along pretty well. Billy Southworth was a very good pilot but he did not associate with his crew very much. He gave you the feeling that socially he was above you.

"In October 1942, at Battle Creek, Michigan, we received our new planes from the factory and flew them to Bangor, then to Gander and finally to Prestwick. Molesworth became our base of operation until the end of the war. None of the crew, myself included, at this time had ever fired a .50 caliber machine gun from a B-17. Most of our training was on .30 calibers out of small planes. We were due for some on-the-job training.

"At Molesworth we had a few practice missions that we were all enthusiastic about. We were so young we didn't realize what we were getting into. Orders came down for us to go November 17 on our first mission, St. Nazaire."

On the eve, an exuberant Southworth declared, "On the morrow, pilots and crews will spring into action all looking forward to a day of 'Success!' We bomb St. Nazaire submarine base, a heavily protected area. It will be our first combat experience. We expect to find opposition without looking too hard. It's not like patrol. Last raid on St. Nazaire, three Forts were lost."

According to Fleming, however, "Success!" was denied because, "Somewhere in the lead lane, the navigator got off course and we missed the entire target. We didn't come close and had to return to base with all of the bombs on board. We weren't allowed to drop them over occupied France. It was a big disappointment. There was no antiaircraft fire or enemy airplanes. Germans flew around us a couple of times wondering who we were. I guess they were as curious about us as we were about them."

A furious Southworth noted, "Major Robinson Snafued, screwed up the mission, clear day and all. I'd hide myself after that." He consoled himself that the error lay in the past and with the knowledge that the 303rd would be in the air the following day. "It'll be a blow to the Axis if we succeed. They may be waiting for us after the first attempt. I fly on the colonel's right wing. He will lead the group. I'll give him all that me and my crew can dish out. They're fine boys."

On the morning of November 18, Southworth said he was awakened at 5:30 A.M., when it was still cold and black. In his diary, he wrote, "Seemed as if I were going on a hunting trip back home. Carefully selected clothes, papers, pencil, oxygen equipment, pistol, etc. Off to eat a quick breakfast, then to the briefing room where we get the dope. The target: La Pallice, French seaport, sub base, workshops, factories. Secondary is Lorient.

"I missed my place in the taxi procession as the wind and takeoff position had changed. All seemed to be taken care of before turning 'em over. Jenkins, a damn good man to be my waist gunner, bombs loaded, crew intact. Twenty minutes before takeoff time I am told the primer is broken. I did all in my power to start them. It worked. Then due to some poor head-work on Lieutenant Robey's part, I lost my spot taxiing. I was mad, damn mad.

"We took off at 10:00. I quickly got into formation and stuck tight—no help from Dillinger [the copilot]. I did all the work that day. We were over an overcast then there was the French coast. Peaceful, pretty country but we had been warned what would come. Approaching Nantes we were hopped by German pursuit and heavy flak. One of the boys said on interphone, 'Here they come, 6 UP.' Guns started to chatter, formation tightened. Bursts of flak came close. We began our evasive action. My arms began to ache, steam and sweat rolled off me. Dillinger sat there, looking out of his window, either scared to death or bored with it all. Flak would bounce our ship now and then. I just bore down harder, just flew tight automatically.

"We began to circle as though we were lost. Jon called up and said we were over St. Nazaire, a big Nazi sub base—good target. An FW dived at the 306 [BG] group formation, then made a feint at us. We were being attacked from the rear. Our outfit downed three of six attacking ME-109s. Fleming and [Waldo] Brandt [tail gunner] sighted thirty FW-190s keeping out of range. We kept on circling. Flak made large bursts above, below to the side, just a few feet from us. We flew through their smoke. Bomb doors finally opened, we were on our run. Flak bursts were intense—bombs away.

"We started ours after the colonel had let his go. They were excellent hits. Ten 500-pounders in each ship, twenty-one of them after Robey turned back. They sure looked good. We then headed out to sea and home. I let Dilly handle the throttles to give one arm a rest. Soon enough he was asleep and we all but passed the colonel up. I was damn mad, hit his heavy flying suit with the back of my hand. The colonel landed at Chelveston, me and Goetz behind. It was the wrong target but a good one. Won't be much good for several months to come."

In fact, the post mortem criticized the 303rd for having struck at St. Nazaire instead of the briefed objective, La Pallice, 100 miles away. Furthermore, the 500-pounders could barely have scratched the concrete walls of the enemy sub base.

ALONG with the 303rd Bomb Group, the 305th led by Curtis LeMay had added its weight to the still slender resources of the Eighth, making its first strike November 23. While junior officers like Southworth expressed satisfaction with their results, LeMay and his fellow senior officers, braced with the data provided by photo reconnaissance intelligence, were aware that the strategic bombing campaign was not inflicting serious damage. Furthermore, having studied the tactics of the U.S. raiders, the enemy was raising the price of each foray.

LeMay decided that better results could only be achieved if the bombers maintained altitude and flew a straight course in the final moments before the drop. Evasive actions in the face of flak, implied in Southworth's descriptions of his first missions, defeated the work of the Norden bombsight and the concept of precision bombing. LeMay subsequently calculated, using an old artillery manual and compensating for the improvements of the German 88, that flak gunners would need to fire 372 rounds in order to guarantee a single hit on a B-17 in level flight. Whether his arithmetic was correct or not, LeMay believed the figures enough to like the odds. On the very first mission of the 305th LeMay announced to his dubious pilots they could take "no evasive action" over the target. He sought to allay their fears by announcing he would fly the lead aircraft. To be sure, the first ship over had a much better chance for survival than the tail-end Charlie, since gunners had time to adjust for range and speed as the flight passed over. But still, the willingness to do what he asked of his subordinates gave him some credence.

American bombers, previously, also broke away from the bombing path when enemy fighters charged. LeMay directed his subordinates not to deviate from course because of the Luftwaffe. His luck and theory stood up in that initial raid; the Eighth Air Force intelligence photos showed that the 305th laid down twice as many bombs on target as any other group and lost no planes. It would take several months before the principles established by LeMay, buttressed by the insights of other commanders, would become gospel for the rest of the Eighth Air Force.

Overall, however, the bombing continued to be erratic, with most of the ordnance missing the aiming point. LeMay also blamed inadequate training of navigators and bombardiers and the difficulty of concentrating upon the target while beset by enemy fighters. He advised his superiors of the need for intensive instruction in navigation and target recognition under poor visibility.

He wrote to his mentor, Gen. Robert S. Olds, "There is a lot of difference between bombing an undefended target and running through a barrage of six-inch shellfire while a swarm of pursuits are working on you." Furthermore, he advised Olds, "On our arrival here our gunners were very poorly trained. [Bill Fleming in the Southworth crew said he and his fellow gunners had never fired a .50 caliber from a B-17 before reaching England.] Most of them had not received enough shooting [instruction], especially at altitude, to even familiarize themselves with their equipment . . . due to weather and missions, the only practice we have had so far is shooting at FW-190s and ME-109s."

While the on-the-job education indicated improving marksmanship, LeMay searched for a way to circle the wagons when facing an attack by fighters. He theorized that the best means for bombers to protect themselves against interceptors lay in a modified staggered formation with the aircraft tightly packed. The arrangement pointed the maximum number of machine guns at would-be marauders. The combat box for a bomb group based upon three squadrons, placed six to nine aircraft in the lead with a similar number as a second echelon 1,000 feet higher and to one side, while the third squadron flew 1,000 feet below the leaders and on the opposite flank. When in proper array, a group could bear as many as 200 .50 caliber machine guns on any interceptor while a wing composed of several group boxes could respond to attack with between 500 and 600 machine guns.

The key for both bombing accuracy and for protection through tight formation flying was discipline; maintaining position no matter what the enemy did, or how difficult climatic conditions. Gunners also needed to control themselves; indiscriminate shooting amid the tightly packed formations could and did result in deadly friendly fire. Other aerial warfare thinkers concocted similar schemes, but LeMay was in a position to put his theories into practice. He personally supervised training runs from the top turret of a B-17. His insistence upon practice runs while other bomb group crews enjoyed a respite from flight duty generated some resentment. But the results achieved by the 305th as a result of LeMay's demands impressed even those who scorned him as "Iron Ass."

Many months later, with all planes expected to follow the leaders and further ensure accuracy, the theorists developed the notions of lead navigators and lead bombardiers, with deputies in a position to take over should the guide abort or be knocked down. Unfortunately, at the time LeMay began to implement his ideas, there were so few units and crews in residence, that opportunities to practice innovations were limited. The closed-in formations, as Southworth experienced, demanded skill, knowledge and concentration. Buffeted by winds, the turbulence of prop wash and the jolts of ack-ack, it was inevitable that a few of the huge aircraft laden with heavy explosives and sluggish to respond at high altitudes would collide, even in the hands of the most capable pilots as the distance between them shortened. With just five full groups on hand, the numbers required for mounting LeMay's wing-size box formation simply did not exist in the winter of 1942–43 and the early months of the following spring.

The ebullience drained from Southworth as the missions continued. His diary refers to drunken brawls among the squadron officers, and his frustration as the 303rd's superiors refused to accept his recommendations for better tactics. Regular crewmen became unfit for duty. He noted his bombardier Milt Conver left *Bad Check* because of chronic ear infections. Respiratory problems felled navigator Jon Schueler. Flight surgeons scrubbed two of the regular gunners for what Southworth listed as "a dose," the GI slang for gonorrhea. The pilot himself sought treatment for a cold and sore throat, a threat to his own readiness.

Nevertheless Southworth was at the controls December 12, for the run at Rouen/Sotteville, the same marshaling yards stung by the first Eighth Air Force heavy-bomber attack in August. "Twenty-one planes were scheduled for takeoff, twenty took to the air. Two were knocked down before reaching target, eight turned back and twelve dropped their bombs, mind you," groused Southworth, "only twelve. Smells like fish.

"Two minutes over the French coast here come the Jerries, attacking in pairs and large numbers. Six of our ships took positions on our right and an even level (piss poor). Another bunch [was] on our left and level—stinks. The Huns bore in. Here come four at me, firing across my nose from one and two o'clock. Our guns, top turret and more guns blasted a steady stream. My window, already cracked, became streaked with cracks at which I became furious at Sergeant Means [top turret] for disobeying orders, firing forward as his zone was rear. The ball turret reported out of order.

"Flickenger received the shots meant for my ship. One engine smoking, he disappeared behind me. Another moved up into his place. Frequent attacks came from the rear. The Spitfires had left us to return home. Continual attacks were made by the yellow nosed FW-190s, often from the nose." Southworth had observed the latest wrinkle in enemy tactics. The Germans had become aware that the front end of the B-17F was the most vulnerable point if attacked head-on at a slightly elevated angle. Only the top turret could then get a clear line of sight. The machine guns installed for use by a bombardier were .30 caliber and could not focus on hostile aircraft directly ahead.

Southworth's complaint about his bomb group maintaining the same altitude was justified. He remarked, "Our Forts were so close and on the same level that [they] seemed to lose effectiveness as the gunners couldn't fire and few turrets could be brought into play. We made a turn for evasive purposes and L slid over, into me, missing by inches. I tried to get Dilly to watch him but he didn't and then again this numbskull slid fifty yards out of his formation and into ours. I skidded out of danger, extremely lucky to avoid a terrible crash. He hit our horizontal stabilizers, putting a damn good dent in it. I'll take a bow for being on the alert and saving our necks there.

"Flickenger, hit with shells, peeled off to the left, one engine afire. Frost down below came up above me, directly atop, not ten yards [off]. I read his ship's nickname *Werewolf.* Unbeknownst to me, two of his crew had bailed out, his bomb bay doors were open, the ship out of control. I saw him slide off to the left; he peeled off into a long spiral, all engines going, men jumping in parachutes. Six or eight got out."

Bad Check managed to dump its cargo in the vicinity of a railroad complex and fought off enemy fighters until Spitfires met the returning bombers. Although they had lost two aircraft with their crews, the surviving pilots buzzed the airdrome before settling in. "There was Schueler to meet us," wrote Southworth. "He's my boy." On the ground the pilot reported relatively minor damage to the planes that completed the mission. He proudly contrasted the effort of the 303rd with that of the 91st assigned to the same target, where only six of its twenty-one aircraft crossed the Channel.

ON January 3, as dawn neared, an exultant Southworth scribbled in his diary, "Will be copilot with Colonel Wallace [Group CO]. We will lead five groups, twenty-one planes each. General [Haywood] Hansell, two-star boy will fly with us." Hansell served as head of Eighth Air Force planning. Southworth blithely remarked on the briefing data, "Smile lady luck. Over flak area of fifty-six heavy guns plus mobile installations of guns. Loads of fighters and loads of fun. Submarine installations and torpedo docks will be 'leveled.' What a red-letter day."

Indeed it was a momentous occasion. Acting as copilot while Wallace sat in the left seat, Southworth maneuvered a different plane than *Bad Check,* one he lists as number 619, to the French coast. In an elliptical and disjointed account he reported, "It seemed to be deadly peaceful. There was no escort. The general seemed to be a good stick. We got on a four-minute bombing run. The colonel thought he heard someone say, 'Bombs away' and he turned off the run a couple of seconds early. He had a fit but cooled down. All going too perfect, then here they came. Four FW-190s from the front. [They] shot two down. Of our first nine ships over the target, four were shot down; they got seven in all. We've now lost nine crews and ships in combat on eight missions.

"The general served sandwiches on the way home. The general said that we had some good Indians on our ship. 'For plain unadulterated guts,' he said, 'you boys have it.' Schueler did a fine job. Was pleased until I found out our losses. Sheridan and Goetz gone. Sure will miss Goetz, one of my best friends. We were all at the club after dinner. Bought Schueler a drink. Then a bunch of us began to flip coins. Loud singing began. More liquor was ordered. At 10:00 we left for Diddington and the nurses. There were loads of us. I was drunk for the first time. Don't remember a thing. Guess we tore things up, running in and out of huts while girls screamed. One walked me around while I staggered. Wow! Got home—said 'Do I live here?' Froze at night, had a cramp."

According to Fleming, the facts of war came stunningly home to him on this, his third mission, after he missed several with the *Bad Check* crew because of illness, including one sudden onset of severe pains en route which earlier had forced Southworth to abort a mission. "By this time we had experienced some antiaircraft fire, but not enough to make you think somebody was trying to kill you. It wasn't that bad. The third mission [for Fleming] to St. Nazaire was the shocker for all of us. Over the target the antiaircraft fire was very heavy and it was hitting the planes; we started to realize somebody was really shooting at us. All of a sudden the plane on our wing, the squadron leader, Major Sheridan's took a direct hit and completely blew up. Pieces of it flew all over our plane, knocked holes in the wings and the stabilizer. It was a terrible shock to see. None of us could believe what had happened. But by the time we got off that target we knew Germany was no playground anymore. When we got back to our field, the ten empty beds from the lost crew made everybody realize what could happen."

Navigator Schueler described the routine of these first forays and his reactions. "We'd be awakened at 2:30 A.M. and we'd dress in the cold of the room and slog outside into the rain and muck and we'd have our breakfast and then we'd go to the briefing room. 'Attention!' We'd pop to and the colonel would stride down the aisle and mount the platform and announce the target. 'St. Nazaire' and we'd groan and laugh at the same time. From then on it was business. We'd be told the time of take-off, the time and place of rendezvous, the point of crossing the channel, the initial point, the target, the procedure and route back. Then we'd go to individual briefings, navigators' briefings, gunners' briefings, pilots' briefings, bombardiers' briefings. All night long the bombs were being loaded and the ground crew was working on the planes. We could hear the engines being revved up.

"As long as the momentum of activity was going, everything would be OK. I felt the excitement, the blood coursing through my veins. I felt the intensity of it. We would start the engines revving and I'd lay out my charts and have everything ready, oxygen mask, parachute. Check all the dials. Computer, pencils, Weems plotter. Milt Conver would be making wisecracks. We could feel the plane being readied, we could feel the vibration of readiness of men moving back and forth at their dials, controls and guns. Everything was OK. We were a team and we knew each other and loved each other. The men were truly noble. The planes themselves were noble.

"The B-17s are scattered around the field and it is seven in the morning, the first dim light of day. The first dim, gray silver light, mists rising from the fields. And then you hear engines starting here and there, some close, a roar, and then rrrrrr-mmmmmm, ready on one, ready on two, contact, ready on three, ready on four. And the four engines of the B-17 slowly throbbing, vibrations increasing, a spitting and grumbling, a lust for the morning air, a waking from the dead, a waking from the night, a waking to life, the life of the new day, of the throb, the heart throb of the plane, four engines beating, four propellers whirling, engines revving, echoing each other across the field.

"The olive-drab B-17s would slowly move, brakes screeching, the ground crew watching, one of them helping to guide the plane around the circle onto the tarmac path to the perimeter track. One after another, lumbering out onto the track and then all of them, single file on each side of the field, two files moving, lumbering slowly toward the takeoff point at the end of the runway. All of them, engines growling and propellers twirling. The nose of the B-17 in the air, the body sloping down to the rear tail wheel, already in an attitude of urgency, of wanting to rise into the gray morning sky. Because of the morning light, because of the vast, flat stretch of the field, the planes looked larger and more powerful than they actually were.

"Men. Each an individual who lived and suffered, who had a woman or women, who sweated, crapped, lusted, who drank and got cold in the damp billets, who tried to light the stoves, who sat around and talked into the night, talking about the raids, and latterly, about the chances for survival. It really was beautiful, beautiful in many, many ways."

In a more prosaic tone, Bill Fleming reminisced, "Some of our equipment bothered us as much as the Germans. Our planes were open [at the waist positions for the machine guns] so the temperatures at 30,000 to 32,000 feet were forty to seventy degrees below zero. We had to dress very heavily. I wore long underwear, and a uniform shirt and pants, an electric suit over that, plus a fur-lined flying suit on top of it. On my feet I wore silk stockings, wool stockings, electric shoes and fur-lined flying boots. My hands had silk gloves, wool gloves, electric gloves, and then the fur-lined flying mitts. You could barely move a finger and you always left one free to work the trigger of the machine gun. We didn't dare unplug the electric suits which were connected to the battery system. Without heat you would freeze to death in a matter of minutes. It was funny to look at the man next to you and see his eyebrows white with frost. There were several severe cases of frostbite. You did not dare fly while you had a cold because if you did, your oxygen mask, which was the old bag-type, would freeze with ice and cut off your oxygen. We lost two gunners out of our squadron that way. One was a ball turret and the other a tail gunner.

"We had to clean our guns after every mission using the solvent carbon tetrachloride. That kept the guns dry because any kind of moisture on them and they would freeze up. Later, of course, in the U.S. factories carbon tetrachloride was banned as a deadly poison. I wonder how many of our guys got sick from it. I remember over Halle, Germany, during one mission when it was so cold that our guns wouldn't fire. Fortunately for us, the Germans couldn't fire theirs either."

The astute if acerbic Southworth expressed his continuing exasperation with his superiors for their refusal to consider more effective formations, "What a bunch of little tin gods. I like the colonel but there sure are a lot of deadbeats running this outfit." He shifted his attention to the other major weakness. "Went down to see how progress, if any, was being made on the new nose-gun mount. We can't get that too soon. It's a sheer waste of men and airplanes to attack without nose guns. Just sit and wait to get shot down." Eighth Air Force tacticians had realized the enemy's approach and they asked for modifications to protect the planes. Subsequently, B-17Gs would come to Europe with a chin turret whose pair of .50 caliber guns significantly improved a Fort's ability to defend itself against those who attacked at twelve o'clock high.

Whatever the formation, maintaining position demanded strenuous effort at the controls. Southworth, an exceptionally skilled pilot, speaking of an excursion to Lille said, "I fought and fought propwash. As we neared the French coast, it was so bad that when I turned one way with all my strength applied, the ship was going the other way towards Buck who was also flying formation propwash. I managed to push my nose down in time to break out of it. I was 200 to 300 yards out of formation and then had to battle my way back in there. This went on for an hour or two, a battle all the way. We'd get out of formation and nearly dive into other ships. The FW-190s didn't bother me. It was the 17's prop-wash. The plane felt loggy and flew like a truck. We saw two B-17Fs ahead of us crash in midair. The tail section came off one, broke in two and damaged the wing of another so that it too spun in."

SUBSEQUENTLY, Bomber Command dispatched the 303rd with the South-worth crew to Lorient and Brest and their severest test yet. "Little happened until we reached the target," said the pilot, "until we reached the target where huge puffs of heavy flak broke in close proximity. It sounded like rain blowing on a tin roof, or a limb cracking, a bolt of lightning. We had passed through a solid bank of haze at 25,000 feet and then it was clear as I have ever seen it over the target. There were about fifty to one hundred fighters in the area. We watched groups of 190s at 30,000 feet. They would peel off, leaving beautiful vapor trails but soon to spell the end for some of my buddies.

"We dropped our bombs and turned off when the fighters attacked. Hagenbuch's engine failed and Colonel Robinson pulled off with another group, Cole and Reber with him. Both squadrons on our side left us, the three of us alone. We were sitting targets when the attacks came. Over the interphone a constant position report came through: 'Nine o'clock, lower six, upper five, two, low five, up three, eleven, low ten, twelve o'clock.' There was continuous shooting. An FW gained position eight to ten miles forward and started a long head-on attack. Upper turret firing felt like someone pounding on my head, a loud noise with heavy vibration. My glass cracked in front of me. I bent my head slightly in case she let go. Our .30 caliber from the nose sounded like a toy or an electric sewing machine. The FW firing lit up like an electric sign. Robey, to my left, was being hit in the fuselage and vertical stabilizer. Looked as if we would crash head-on, so I raised my nose to allow my lower turret to fire back but instead pulled up violently, throwing everyone on the floor as the enemy grazed below me. At that moment, Dillinger pushed my controls forward trying to talk through his oxygen mask and the drone of the engines. I put the ship under control. Robey missed our tail by inches as he peeled off into a dive straight down, many thousands of feet, his tail gunner hanging on, firing both of his weapons.

"Attack positions kept coming in and brief reports of an FW shot down and its clock position were briefly sounded off. We were headed toward Brest, heaviest flak-defended area in that section. We took slight evasive action. Our interphone went out and only the roar of the engines and the bark of the .50s could be heard. FWs were attacking furiously.

"Two miles to our left the 305 Group was moving up. We came within 200 yards of the 305th as flak pounded up in large black puffs. I covered Buck [Glenn Hagenbuch] taking more violent evasive action as the 305th bombs fell. They pulled away from us like [Ernie] Lombardi and [Terry] Moore in a foot race." The former was a Cincinnati catcher known for slow speed afoot and the latter an extremely fleet St. Louis Cardinal outfielder. Unable to gather with the B-17s of the 305th, Southworth and the remnants of the 303rd huddled together hoping to mutually fend off further assaults.

"There were only a few attackers left. We had little ammunition. One waist gunner was out of the same as was the lower turret and the .30 in the nose. Low on gas and with an unpredictable radio, we landed at Exeter. Fleming had shot down two planes and Kirkpatrick shot down one from the ball turret. Upon our arrival at Molesworth, we learned of Reber's tough luck and the others' fate. Hate to lose the lot of them." [The 303rd listed a staggering five aircraft shot down, with fifty airmen MIA. And those that reached the United Kingdom bore one dead and nineteen wounded.]

Fleming's account confirms Southworth's account but in far less detail. "As we were over the target, Lorient, dropping our bombs, we received a hit on one of our engines. We lost the No. 3 engine. We were not able to keep up with close formation of the other bombers. That's what the Germans waited on, for some crew to drop out. They took their turn at us. It was 300 miles back to the base. We finally made it. I received credit for a Focke Wulf 190 shot down. There was a second one but I didn't get credit for that one because other planes were firing on it."

CAPT. John Regan of the 306th Bomb Group was awakened at 3:00 A.M. on January 27, and advised breakfast would be served an hour later with the briefing at 5:00 for a mission against a German target. "This was somewhat routine," recalls Regan. "We had already bombed German targets in occupied Europe—routine that is if one could adjust to the tremendous pressures of combat and the all too often loss of close friends. Frankly, I knew of no one who could truthfully say that any combat mission was just routine.

"I wish it were possible to accurately describe the tension, the emotion that was evident in our thirty-five-man crew huts on those mornings when we were awakened for combat missions. One would have to be present to feel the electricity that filled the air. Some men shouted to relieve tension, others laughed out loud when nothing was really funny and others were silent with their thoughts, probably fixed on coming events or on loved ones. I even knew some who would silently slip outside in the darkness to become ill—they didn't want their buddies to see them. Everyone wanted to appear strong and tough—it is normal, we were all so young—but we had learned that war is hell and that the only romance or glamour associated with it is fiction.

"All was as usual until the 5 A.M. briefing. This took place in our combat operations hut which had become very familiar to all of us. We sat together as combat crews and exchanged small talk while we waited anxious to find out what our target for the day was to be.

"A large map of England and Europe that took up most of the front of the briefing room was covered as usual with a blue cloth so that crews would only find out what the mission of the day would be after the briefing had started. At 5:00 A.M., our commanding officer and the operations briefing officer entered the hut. We came to attention and then sat down. After a few short, opening comments, our commander paused, then said, dramatically, 'Gentlemen, this is it,' and with that drew back the blue cloth covering the map, so we could see it and the telltale ribbon that would show our course to fly and the target for the day.

"Initially, there was a stunned silence and then the room erupted with shouts of exultation and wonderment, as the significance of the mission sank in. Yes, we actually were going to hit the enemy near his heart. The excitement was intense. For a moment, even the fear of combat was forgotten, as exultation reigned. The historic meaning of this event sank in even further when we were told that our group had been selected to lead the mission. I was doubly thrilled as my squadron was to lead the total American bombing effort."

The mission that so galvanized Regan was the Eighth Air Force's first assault upon German turf in the form of the shipyards at Vegesack outside the city of Bremen. The 1st Bomb Wing, composed of the 91st, 303rd, 305th and 306th contributed fifty-five B-17s. The planners had expected the B-24s of the 2nd Bomb Wing—the 44th and 93rd Bomb Groups—to participate but all twenty-seven Liberators returned to base, defeated by the weather and an inability to navigate to the target. But despite the failure to unload their ordnance, the B-24s would endure a terrible pounding from enemy fighters.

Regan remembers, "The rest of the briefing was anticlimactic, as were the preparation of aircraft, the takeoff, the rendezvous with other aircraft and the initial flight to target. As the bombers crossed the coast of Germany and headed for the primary target at Vegesack, it became apparent that the complex to be attacked was covered by low clouds, which made bombing impossible.

"What a dilemma! Over Germany for the first time, all aircraft with a full load of bombs and the ground at the target hidden by low clouds. To return to home bases without bombing would have turned this momentous event into a failed sortie. A choice of action had to be made. The air commander, Col. Frank A. Armstrong Jr. weighed the alternatives and elected to try and bomb the secondary target, the shipyards and docks at Wilhelmshaven.

"As this secondary target was approached there fortunately was a break in the low clouds that allowed the bombardiers to see the target and successfully drop their bombs. Although the size of the bombing effort that day was relatively small, it was a great morale booster for the young Eighth Air Force.

"The Germans had been taken by surprise. They had not anticipated this attack and had probably felt that bombers would not dare penetrate the airspace over their homeland in daylight. There was some antiaircraft fire over the target, but it was not accurate, and a small number of fighters attacked our bombers which attested to the success of the surprise aspect of the mission."

Billy Southworth was on hand. "Awaken at 4:30," he recalled, "sick with sinus headache and bad cold. Told to fly 966 while its pilot, a vet of one raid, sat on the ground. I was tired and sore. Just got 966 ready in time and taxied like a bat out of hell into position, my crew jumping into ship as I pulled on to perimeter track.

"Bad weather again. Hole in the nose making it damn cold. Heater also out and me in scant clothing, a ball cap as a headdress felt good for a change. It was a long trip with a good leader, Colonel Marion. Eleven ships took off and three soon returned [aborted] making a total of eight over the target. It was all that we had in commission. Our first sign of Germany was islands off Holland and an ME-109 looking us over. The land was almost overcast. A convoy below with Germany's last battleship. We were at 25,000 feet, flew over Bremen our primary target. Engaged by flak and fighters. We took violent evasive action all the while, dropped our bombs and fought off attacks with methodical coolness. Our bombs landed the same moment as Colonel Marion's, making us first to bomb

Germany." Actually, the 306th Bomb Group which led the procession towards Wilhelmshaven probably deserves credit for dropping the first of the 265 1,000-pound general-purpose explosives on Germany.

Howard Adams piloted one of the Liberators briefed for the raid. "We took off around 9:30 in the morning and after rendezvousing over the field started our long climb up to 25,000 heading out for the North Sea. Everything went quite well until we reached an altitude of around 17,000 feet where my No. 3 engine began to falter, due to a clogged line to the supercharger, I later found out. I kept on for a way hoping it would settle down but it only grew worse and so finally I peeled out of the formation and headed for home. We were around eighty miles out to sea and so scooted for home as fast as we could go. I turned once and could see the rest of the 44th disappearing in the direction of Germany. Soon we were back over our field, quite disappointed for not being able to go.

"After dinner, I went down to watch the others come in. I noticed that two of our ships were missing. Later I found out that they were my friend and West Point classmate, Lieutenant Sullivan and a Lieutenant Cargile. I learned that as they neared the German border, around thirty enemy fighters came up to meet them, mostly FW-190s and ME-109s. For around a half-hour they were under attack and not being able to find their target, they dropped their bombs on a coastal town. During one of the numerous frontal attacks, the Huns scored a hit on Sully's No. 3 engine, setting it on fire which soon grew in fury as he dropped out of formation. Soon the fire had burnt a large section of the wing away and in no time the right wing folded back along the fuselage and Sully plummeted down for his last landing. The crews in the other planes watched helplessly as his plane disintegrated in the air and fell into the sea like a burning rag. Two men were seen to jump out and float down towards the sea in their parachutes. A third man jumped but his chute trailed out behind him, never seeming to open fully. Their fate is still unknown.

"A little later, another FW-190 came in on a head-on attack aiming at Cargile's plane. Either through accident or design, as he went to turn away, his wing clipped the wing and then the right tail fin of Cargile's B-24, knocking them both off. The FW-190 seemed to fold up and then go into its last dive. With part of his wing gone, the big B-24 dropped away like a fluttering leaf, finally going into a tight spin—its fate sealed. None of the crew were seen to jump. Captain Wilkenson, a very swell fellow and friend, was the navigator in Sullivan's ship.

"As the attack continued, many of our ships were shot up, but no more were knocked down. Captain O'Brien had a waist gunner and bombardier killed and his navigator wounded. Nearly every ship had a hole in it somewhere, Billings having a shell come up through the cabin between him and his copilot." Aside from the two B-24s described by Adams, Curtis LeMay's 305th Bomb Group had a B-17 shot out of the sky. The Americans claimed to have destroyed twenty-two enemy aircraft, probably knocked down fourteen more and damaged thirteen. Captured German records examined after the war indicated a loss of seven aircraft that day.

The critique of the mission, organized by Southworth's former passenger and sandwich purveyor, General Hansell, sounded some ominous themes. "The Combat Wings on this mission did not keep close enough together to give shielding protection, one to the other. Fifty-five aircraft in a formation are not enough aircraft to be able to defend themselves. It is felt that most of our losses were the result of poor formation flying which resulted in aircraft becoming separated and an easy prey to fighters.

"Gunnery must be stressed. Even when a formation brought all its guns to bear on some of the attackers during this mission, the enemy continued to come in firing. Poor visibility at the target made the bombing very difficult. A target as small as this one should only be assigned when the weather is very clear and visibility is good." For all of the theories of LeMay and the high command which agreed with his precepts, the air crews of the Eighth obviously required continued training and a more focused effort.

AS January drew to a close, Southworth recorded a dismal inventory. "We arrived as a complete group on October 31. In three short (or long) months the group has completed some eleven raids and lost over 50 percent of the [organization]. We average about fifteen planes per raid which means that we have lost about 120 percent of our combat equipment and are operating [by using] reserve. We still lack nose guns. Eighty to 90 percent of our losses have been from nose attacks on our squadron. Nine pilots were lost."

A bout of the flu mandated a hospital stay for Southworth. In his absence, *Bad Check*'s usual navigator, Jon Schueler, volunteered to fill in with another crew out to slam St. Nazaire once again. The experience shattered Schueler. Years later, he wrote a surrealist account of what became an extended nightmare. "Billy had been sick and was off flying. I had a cold too, and was off flying but I wasn't in the hospital. We were called upon for a raid and we could only get a few ships out of the group in the air—because of lost ships, because of badly shot-up ships, because of shortage of personnel. Either shot down or sick. Two minutes before St. Nazaire, the squadron is seven ships. At St. Nazaire it is two. This was the raid in which we headed into a steep descent down to the deck from 20,000 feet after dropping our bombs and the pain shot through my head like I had never before imagined."

Savage as the reception was at St. Nazaire, another calamity struck on the voyage home, a headwind at 120 miles per hour. The hapless bombers, reduced to the pace of a tortoise, crawled toward sanctuary while predators stalked them. "I see the clouds, the clouds building up so that we couldn't see the ground, we had no sign of movement, the B-17s standing still and the Focke Wulfs and Messserschmitts coming in to meet them, coming in to knock us out of the sky.

"For a moment, for a long moment, I was not navigating, I was watching the planes falling, the head-on crash of a fighter into a B-17, the exploding, burning, war-torn falling planes, all too often no chutes in sight, the lonely men, held to their seats, to the walls, to the roof of the plane as it twisted and fell, sometimes with machine guns blazing, and a spume of smoke for a long moment. It seemed endless. It seemed as though we would never get home. I was looking out of the window at the endless blue sky and white cloud beneath us. We waited for the Focke Wulfs and the Messerschmitts and we watched the Fortresses fall. Falling Forts. I wanted to hold them. I wanted to go down with them. I wanted to go home. I prayed. I prayed, please God, I'm bored, please don't make this go on and on and on, it's boring, it's ennui. I can't stand this boring repetition, please God, get us out of here and get this over with. I was probably frightened too, although I was seldom scared while actually flying.

"Had I been able to feel the fear, call it that name, I might have been able to feel the rage. Had I been able to feel the rage, I could have poured out the machine gun fire. I could have slammed bullets into the sky, into the waiting Focke Wulf. In combat, I could not feel the fear or the rage and therefore the love, the love and excitement of what I was doing. I was quite cool in combat. I'd always be so goddamned busy with charts, mental averages, counting and noting falling ships. I was a cool cookie. And I lost everything in my cool. I drowned myself in it. I lost my way."

With Southworth temporarily disabled, waist-gunner Fleming made this mission as a crewman for the B-17 piloted by Glenn Hagenbuch. "He told us we would have a general on board that day, Brigadier General LeMay. We were all kind of excited about having a general aboard until LeMay climbed aboard wearing two parachutes, both a chest and a back parachute. I'd like to have had three of them on myself," says Fleming, "but it was unusual to see a man with two. It was the first time we saw anyone with both on. He took his seat behind the pilot and everything went smoothly for a while. Then things got really warm over the target, they were ready for us with those yellow-nosed Messerschmitts and Focke Wulfs and plenty of antiaircraft. They gave us hell when we were dropping those bombs. We wore throat mikes, and understanding what was said over the intercom was hard enough, but if someone got excited, you couldn't understand anything. Right as we were directly over the target, someone started yelling over the intercom, 'Get us out of here! Get us out of here! Get us out of here!' We had a hottempered flight engineer, our top turret gunner, Lucian Means. All of the crew knew who was doing the shouting but none of the officers would do anything. Means finally cuts in and tells the guy to shut up or he'll knock his teeth down his throat. When it's all over the general wanted to know who said it but nobody would say. That's not to knock the general. Hell, we were all scared. What disturbed me and the rest of the crew, even though we laughed and joked about it, was when we picked up a *Stars and Stripes* newspaper and it had an account of him being awarded the Silver Star for leading this group back through enemy flak and fighter fire. Although he did a wonderful job after that and in the Pacific, every time I saw him and looked at that medal on his chest I thought of the St. Nazaire mission."

Upon his return from St. Nazaire, inner demons overwhelmed Schueler. "I started to feel guilty, responsible for every death. I was not sleeping, afraid that I'd make errors and cause the death of many. It could happen—navigation errors, pilot errors. Ending in death. Planes falling, planes shot down. So many were dying and I felt responsible. But I felt more responsible for those who might die. The flight surgeon gave me sleeping pills and talked to the group commander about taking me off combat for a while to rest up. I had lost twenty pounds or more and was skinny as a rail. They needed an operations navigation officer and I was made that.

"We sent out as many planes as we could muster on a mission and instead of being on it myself I was left on the base. At the end of the day I was on the tower, looking to the sky, watching for the returning planes, counting when they appeared. One, two, three, four . . . nine ten eleven twelve . . . twelve . . . twelve . . . there are no others. We look anxiously, scanning the sky. Then the planes are flying in low over the field. Then there is a flare from one and he's moving right down the runway without permission. He's floating down, landing, another flare denoting wounded on board and the ambulance is rushing toward the plane even as it rolls to a stop. The group is badly shot up. One plane is missing."

Transferred to the VIII Bomber Command in High Wycombe, Schueler became increasingly uncomfortable in the almost luxurious surroundings, a private room, "superb food" and an office in an air-conditioned hillside burrow. The meetings and briefings took on the atmosphere of theater. "It was as though I was moving onto a stage, parts to be played until no one could clearly remember the reality. The reality of flight and fear and death, but also the reality of comradeship and effort, and being alive, and meaning, and strength. I felt dead amongst the living. I felt weak, washed out, through." Schueler contracted mumps and collapsed into a depression complicated by a second childhood ailment, chicken pox. He entered a hospital.

Fleming comments on the status of the outfit. "In March of 1943, Lieutenant Schueler and Lieutenant Conver had left our crew. It was nothing against Schueler that he was grounded. All of our nerves were affected. We were now down to only three of the original nine crews in our squadron. No replacements. It wasn't anything to see some guy break down and cry. I felt like doing it myself many, many times."

Subsequently, the waist gunner himself began to fall apart. "Things were not looking good," says Fleming. "I was having blackout spells, running a high temperature. They put me in a hospital. They couldn't find out what it was. After six weeks, a young doctor discovered I had an infection of my inner ear that upset my sense of balance. They treated me and released me. By that time I had completed fourteen missions. We had lost four of our nine crews, and were down to fifty of the original crewmen. There were no replacements available at the time."

6

FALSE SPRING

During the third week of January, Luther Cox, the 93rd Bomb Group navigator who passed out because of oxygen deprivation on the first B-24 mission from England, looked forward to an R & R [Rest and Recuperation] interlude of clean sheets, a soft bed, showers and better food after the transfer from the Eighth at his new base near Ismalia with the Twelfth Air Force. To his dismay, he learned that his crew and ship, *Double Trouble,* was on standby, prepped and ready for a mission if anyone aborted. The target was Sousse, Tunisia, a port city through which passed the supplies for the Afrika Korps.

When one of the planes scheduled to go developed engine trouble, the control tower signaled *Double Trouble* to go on what was Cox's twenty-first mission. In the twelve-plane expedition, composed of four Vee-shaped echelons, *Double Trouble* led the last of these elements, known as Tail-end Charlie and, says Cox, "It was usually the portion of the formation that caught both the most flak over the target as well as the brunt of aerial attack." The combat box designed by LeMay had not been mandated for North Africa.

During the bomb run, Cox reported, "This has got to be the worst flak we have ever experienced. You can feel the chunks of shrapnel piercing the body of our aircraft as it shudders and shakes and wavers. Through it all, Gus [bombardier Gerald Gray], with steel nerves kept his eyes glued upon his bombsight. Whuff, Whuff, Whuff . . . the ship staggers as it is hit very hard. Gus had his hand raised and when he dropped it, I salvoed our load of bombs and called, 'Bombs away!' Gus normally does all of this himself but he promised me that this time I could drop the load.

"As Benny [Capt. Benjamin Riggs] our pilot took over the controls there were three heavy bursts of flak and I was knocked to my knees. They have scored numerous hits on us and we must be hit pretty badly. No. 3 engine seems the hardest hit of the four. Smoke and pieces of metal, gas and oil are flowing out of it. I yelled to Benny to get us the hell out of here, as he wheeled it over and dived out of the murderous box barrage of AAA."

Double Trouble, with two engines shut down and unable to keep up with others in the squadron, began a desperate run to the nearest friendly field at Malta about 100 miles away. Also a subject of attention by the enemy was Cox's former plane *Shoot Luke*. "Nothing much happened over the target," said pilot John Murphy, "but when we headed for home, after dropping our bombs, the fighters attacked. One FW-190 got through the guns of our formation and put a burst into *Luke*—four 20 mm explosive cannon shells and half a dozen machine gun bullets tore into *Luke*'s wing and fuselage. The cannon shells severed eight spars and made two ribs look like a piece of cheesecloth and blew the skin away from the spars and ribs underneath, destroying the airfoil characteristics. One cannon shell lodged in the fuel cells and started them smouldering. Another penetrated the control cabin and blew up, wounding two men badly and damaging the hydraulic system and radio. The badly damaged plane limped into Malta with the wing in very bad shape and three fuel cells smoking."

Shoot Luke had managed to stave off its tormentors and reach Malta. Enemy fighters quickly zeroed in on the more vulnerable *Double Trouble*. In the nose compartment, Cox and the bombardier frantically fired their three .50 caliber machine guns, one pointed directly to the fore and the other pair covering the sides. "It seemed only seconds and Gus and I were pouring all the lead we could through each of our fifties, firing around 1,000 rounds a minute, but they kept coming. Benny called for a heading to the closest land. I gave him a 270-degree heading for the closest point on the Tunisian coast. He immediately turned our mortally wounded ship in a near futile gesture to get his crew over land, or at least a lot closer.

"Our ship is staggering under Benny's mighty attempt to keep her flying but we are losing her. Brrrrrrrr . . . THE BAIL OUT BELL goes off as Captain Riggs orders us to abandon ship before she blows up or crashes. Our altitude is now about 15,000 feet and we are under constant attack. Gus crosses behind me to pull the emergency release that gets rid of the nose-wheel hatches. He yanks the handle and the two doors fall away from the ship. Finding we are still quite high and still driving in a fair degree of control towards the land, we elect to stay and fight off the fighters. Perhaps we can give the other crew members a better chance to bail out. I tried the intercom system but no answer.

"Gus goes back to the wheel opening and yells to me, are you coming? I told him I was and with that he slips out and is gone. I turned my guns at the attacking fighters again and catch one pretty good. Smoke and flames are coming from his plane and it dives straight down. I never saw what happened to it because there was another right behind him, taking his place. I just held the trigger down and let her go without pause. This can burn out a gun barrel, but I knew I'd never have any more use for it again.

"Suddenly the ship lurched into a violent diving bank. I am down on my knees and things are hazy and spinning around. I pull myself along the floor and throw myself out the wheel exit, head first, tucking into a ball. We must be around 500 feet altitude by now because the ship is in a power dive. I hope I haven't stayed too long. All I can feel is the cold air as it rushes by me. I am tumbling end over end and I can neither make out the sky nor the sea. Can't wait any longer . . . must pull the rip cord. I tried to wait a few seconds before pulling the rip cord because I didn't want my chute to get tangled in the ship, but I knew that I didn't have seconds to wait.

"I pulled the rip cord. It was as though I had been struck by a Mack truck when that chute opened. I felt as though every bone in my body had been crushed. I had no feeling in my legs at all. The heavy steel buckle across my chest was forced up over my neck, scraping my neck raw, breaking my front teeth and flattening the bridge of my nose as it forced its way across my face before it came to a stop. Just a few inches more and I would have been out of my chute, so great was the deceleration when that chute opened. I guess I must have been falling over 400 mph when the chute opened. Of course the leg harnesses also did their job on me as they jammed up into my groin.

"A terrific explosion occurred, followed by a heat wave. I felt my body surge momentarily upwards as my ship hit almost directly below me and exploded. We must have had 1,200 to 1,500 gallons of high-octane aviation fuel on board. Then downward again and then with a violent swing backwards, I hit the cold waters of the Mediterranean Sea. I sank like a rock. I had no time to take the necessary precautions of loosening all straps before hitting the water so I could get out of my chute.

"Wearing our life vest under our flight clothes was standard operating procedure. Someone must have figured you'd have to get rid of your clothes for their wet weight would drag you down. But it is also vital so you can pull the little strings that pop the CO_2 bottles. These operational procedures almost cost me my life for I was still sinking, tangled up in the shrouds of my parachute. They were like the tentacles of an octopus. Freeing myself from the harness, I found that the cloth belt around my waist had swollen from the water and I couldn't undo it, so I slipped it down over my waist, legs and feet. I reached under my clothes and pulled the CO_2 release and immediately felt the pressure of the gas as it filled up one side of my life vest.

"Upward I started. I had yet to fight my way out of the entanglements of my parachute which was wrapped all around me. Slowly I went up, up, up. My head and lungs felt as though they would explode if I didn't soon get some air. My head finally broke the surface and I was free of my suit. I quickly gasped a huge breath of air."

Cox called out for other downed airmen but no one replied. He started swimming towards the coast. For what seemed an eternity he swam against a stubborn current and the resistance caused by his Mae West. He realized he could never make it to the beach and when he glimpsed the top of a sail, he feebly stroked towards it before lapsing into unconsciousness. When Cox came to, his head lay in the lap of bombardier Gus Gray. Subsequently, Cox learned that the bombardier himself had been plucked from the sea by Arab fishermen. Gray, seeing Cox floating facedown in the water, dove overboard and rescued him. Ten minutes after Cox came to his senses, a German patrol took the downed aviators into custody. Cox entered the ranks of the *kriegies*.

HAVING been denied the opportunity to participate in the first blow against Germany proper because of mechanical problems, Howard Adams with the 44th Bomb Group had taken off for the railyards at Hamm, Germany, on February 2, only to turn about and return to base as a gunner reported he could not get oxygen. The extreme cold also afflicted others in the flight and the entire squadron canceled its plans.

On February 4, Adams and the 44th Bomb Group tucked in behind several B-17 groups for a second try at Hamm. "It was very cold up there," said Adams, "and one after the other, our ships peeled off and headed for home! The guns were extremely sluggish and the gunners were practically frozen as it was around 45 degrees Centigrade below!

"Soon, Capt. Bill Brandon peeled out and I took over the lead of the second element, sticking close behind Big Bill McCoy. By this time my rudder and elevator controls were frozen so hard that they were useless, but by using my throttles and ailerons, I managed to keep in formation.

Around half an hour later, Lieutenant Miller on McCoy's left wing faded away and so I pulled up into his position. Pretty soon Lieutenant Abernethy peels out and his place is taken by Lieutenant Phillips of the 67th Squadron. So now only three ships out of the original twenty or so are left, and it isn't long before McCoy does a swinging turn to the left and heads for home hell-bent-for-election and by this time we are over Holland, which is very unhealthy territory.

"We streak down through clouds around 1,000 feet per minute at 230 mph, hoping to high heaven we won't meet any enemy fighters. All of a sudden my No. 3 engine starts surging badly, making me yank off the supercharger. A bit later No. 4 roars all the way up to 100 inches of Hg [manifold pressure] pulling *Maisie* out of position. So until we got down to low altitude, I have to fly on two engines. All of us are back safely but we learn later that the B-17s went on to the target, losing five ships in a running fight with the German FW-190s and ME-109s. On landing I found out that most of our twelve machine guns were only firing one shot at a time because of the severe cold."

Fortunate to avoid the fate that befell the B-17s on this last effort, the 44th Bomb Group now paid an exorbitant price over the following two weeks. On February 15, the outfit's twenty-four Liberators crossed the Channel to Dunkirk seeking a ship used by the Germans to pillage Allied merchant vessels.

"Soon our bomb bay doors opened," reported Adams, "and I knew our target was close at hand. The weather was perfect and bombs began to drop like rain. Each ship carried ten 500-pounders. I was so close behind Bill McCoy that I was afraid his bombs would hit my plane. I saw Captain Cullen's ship pull up into a steep climb, fall off on one wing, and go into a vertical dive, its engines still roaring. My navigator watched it and said it continued to dive straight down for 20,000 feet, crashing into the sea at terrific speed. I knew that German antiaircraft guns had made a direct hit on Cullen's plane. Soon after his fatal dive, Capt. Fritz Cramer, a friend and West Point classmate of mine, started drifting off to the right over France. Hit by debris from Cullen's aircraft and possibly flak, he had one engine on fire, one engine dead, and another just windmilling. He was flying on just one engine! Immediately his two wing ships faded out of formation to try to help him home. The rest of us turned around and headed for England. Soon the FW-190s and ME-109s were climbing up after us. They made several attacks on our formation but after we knocked down several of them, they concentrated on Cramer and his wing ships, despite RAF Spitfires who were buzzing all around us doing their best to drive off the Jerry fighters."

Adams could only watch as one of the B-24s that hoped to protect an injured comrade itself absorbed mortal hits that set it afire, exploded the gas tanks and tore off the wing. "The burning ship and most of the crew fell into the sea. Several were seen to jump in their chutes and float down into the cold water of the Channel. The beleaguered Cramer managed to beach his plane on the English shore. Adams consoled himself for the losses, "All evidence showed that our bombs had given the target a good plastering. Faithful old *Maisie* was still unscratched."

On the next day, the 44th again lifted off the airbases, this time to participate in the brutal slugfest over St. Nazaire, the same scene in which Fleming and Schueler participated as part of the 303rd Bomb Group. Adams again aborted after his crew reported the tail turret frozen, the right waist and hatch guns nonoperative, and he discovered his rudder and elevator controls were not functioning. On the trip back, said Adams, his tail gunner called up and informed him that as the 44th had headed out, two B-24s in the squadron behind Adams had collided in midair. Caught in the propwash of the B-17s, they were thrown together. "The wing on Billings's ship broke off and the two ships seemed to fall together, back to back. After a bit they separated, caught on fire and then exploded into a thousand flaming pieces. Four fellows were seen to bail out." Later, search and rescue units located neither wreckage nor survivors.

Adams remarked that within two days five aircraft had been lost and before the week concluded, another close friend, pilot Bill McCoy with a bombardier in the copilot seat crashed during a practice landing, killing both men. An investigation indicated that the entire tail assembly had somehow broken away while the aircraft was several thousand feet off the ground.

The skeletal remains of the 44th could only get eleven ships off the ground for Bremen on February 26. As Adams had implied earlier, the mix with B-17s, slower but able to fly at higher altitudes than the B-24s, jeopardized everyone. According to the plan, the 93rd Bomb Group was to trail behind the 44th. However, during assembly, the 93rd cut in ahead, making the 44th the Tail-end Charlies. The B-17s were assigned to lead while the B-24s behind them would maintain a higher altitude. But on the way to the target, the Forts rose higher than expected. When the Liberators sought to jockey into their position they encountered difficulties maintaining formation in the rarefied atmosphere. Over the North Sea, west of Heligoland Island, droves of German fighters menaced the bombers.

FOR the first time, newsmen who had clamored for an opportunity to accompany planes on missions, were not just in front row seats, but in the midst of the aerial melee. A group of candidates, including reporters from major publications, broadcasters from the wire services, as well as Andy Rooney, then a correspondent for *Stars and Stripes,* attended high-altitude flight and survival courses. Twenty-five-year-old reporter Robert Post completed the instruction and went along as an observer with Howard Adams, chosen to take the newsman because of his proficiency as a pilot. Adams, the point in a three-plane element behind the B-17s and at the lowest echelon of B-24s, hit the propwash from the Forts. His trio immediately dropped a thousand feet and out of the formation. Almost immediately, enemy planes sprang at the stragglers, separated from the protective fire of the pack.

Lt. Robert McPhillamey, pilot of the *Sad Sack,* one of the three, recalled, "They picked me off shortly before we reached the I.P. Two engines were shot out and on fire, the oxygen was shot out and there was a fire in the bomb bay. Controls, elevators, wings, etc., were also badly hit and the plane became inoperable. Under those conditions I gave the order to bail out." McPhillamey and seven of the crew spent the rest of the war as POWs. One man was KIA and another died while a captive.

On board the *Maisie* navigator Wayne Gotke reported, "Our aircraft was under constant fighter attack from the time we reached the island of Texel until we were shot down. We had fought off the planes with very minor damage until we were almost to Oldenburg, then all hell broke loose. We had dropped behind, so I spent most of this time working with position reports, trying to get shortcuts filled into the flight to allow us to gain and catch the rest of the formation. I am reasonably sure no one was injured up to this time except for Sergeant Welsh, the belly gunner who had passed out from lack of oxygen. When we were almost to Oldenburg, fighters hit us from all sides. Sergeant Vogt, the engineer and top turret gunner, shot down the first fighter, and I shot down the next one but not until he had sent 20 mms into the nose and cockpit. Someone, I'm not sure who, was hurt on the flight deck. Bill Hannan, bombardier, was riding in the nose and was uninjured up to this point. He had passed out twice from lack of oxygen. He had a crimped supply hose and I replaced his mask and straightened the hose to bring him back to normal.

"Engines 3 and 4 had been hit and were on fire. I believe the fire spread into the wing tanks and caused the ship to explode. I was working on my guns when all at once it seemed as if someone pushed me from behind, and all went black. I woke up falling through space and I pulled my rip cord, but with no results! I reached back and tore the back off of my chute and quickly pulled as much of the material out as possible until it all opened. My last look at our altimeter in the ship was at 26,000 feet.

"They [the Germans] picked me up after I had sat dangling between two trees about twenty feet in the air for about twenty-five minutes, afraid that if I unbuckled I'd fall. At the first-aid station I saw Sgt. J. Mifflin. Also there was the copilot of the other ship shot down [*Sad Sack*] who said that he saw Captain Adams's leather jacket and it appeared the man had been killed. The Germans had obtained the ship's loading list from that jacket and asked me about a Robert B. Post, the New York *Times* correspondent who was flying with us. I gave them no information whatsoever as my orders were to say nothing in hopes that if men were at large their chances of getting home would be better." In fact, Post did not survive, and only Gotke and Mifflin escaped death, while diarist and West Point graduate Howard Adams perished along with the others.

Along with the 44th, the other five groups in the UK—the 91st, the 93rd reassigned from North Africa back to England, the 303rd, 305th and 306th attempted to fulfill the demands upon the Eighth Air Force despite the constant and tremendous depletion in crewmen and effective airplanes. During March, those units in residence completed nine missions that saw ten bombers shot down with their 100 airmen missing, killed or taken prisoner. With operations averaging an 8 percent casualty rate per outing, few airmen could expect to finish the prescribed twenty-five-mission tour. Churchill, still unconvinced of the U.S. strategy, wrote in a memorandum to Portal, "The real question is not whether the American heavy bombers can penetrate into Germany by day without prohibitive losses, but how often they can do it and what weight of bombs they can discharge for the vast mass of ground personnel and [materiel] involved." With the handful of bomber groups hard pressed to get 100 ships off the ground at a time, the Air Corps, however valiant, contrasted poorly with the 1,000-plane efforts of the RAF. The prime minister's criticisms, and those of others in the Allied command vexed the American leadership. Hap Arnold, from Washington, chivvied Eaker regularly, demanding more planes in the air and fewer excuses for grounded bombers or abandoned efforts.

LUTHER Cox's former crew on *Shoot Luke* was among the ninety-seven that converged on Vegesack on March 18. The U-boat yards had been the primary for the first venture by the Eighth Air Force against territorial Germany, but cloud cover had forced a shift to target Wilhelmshaven. "The trip was uneventful," said pilot John Murphy, "until we reached our altitude about fifty miles off the German coast. From then on we were under constant fighter attack for one hour and forty-five minutes. Our run into the target was a good one (one gunner had already accounted for three fighters) and the bombing results were excellent. We turned away from the target and headed home. The fighters by now were really getting warmed up. At one time a mass attack developed in which about thirty fighters attacked our nine-ship element. One of these hit the No. 4 engine on Frank's ship and blew a large hole in the vertical stabilizer [Frank Lown had been Murphy's copilot]. We saw that Frank was in trouble and told the gunners to keep an eye on him. So far he was still in formation.

"Next, the twin-engine fighters (JU-88s, ME-110s and 210s) took us on. They were slower than the single-engined boys and it was more nerve-wracking as their attacks were more methodical and took longer to complete and break away. Just as you'd think they couldn't shoot any more they'd skid their ship so they could get in a longer burst at us. Finally, these too left and as far as we knew we were on our way home.

"Then Frank's No. 4 engine began to smoke and vibrate very badly, and he had to drop out of formation. We held a hurried conversation on the interphone and all of us voted to go help him home. We left the formation and took a position off his wing—suddenly out of nowhere reared one lonely FW-190. He looked us over and came in on an attack from nine o'clock low with his four cannons and machine guns firing. There was a sudden explosion and I knew we'd been hit by cannon and machine gun fire. I glanced over at George [Black, his copilot] and at first thought he'd been hit. But he soon looked at me and I saw he was OK, even if three slugs had missed his head by less than eighteen inches.

"The fighter had hit us with two cannon shells and about six machine gun slugs, the cannon shells had both hit the rear part of the ship where they had exploded, one fragment going into T. Sgt. Floyd Mabee's eye, and causing him several other painful wounds." Mabee tracked the fighter broadside of his left waist gun and shot him down.

Murphy noted, "S. Sgt. Paul Slankard was in the rear turret when the fighter attacked and as soon as it was over he called up to tell me that he had been hit too. When I asked how bad, he said, 'Pretty bad. I think my leg is broken.'" In fact, the force of the explosion had hurled Slankard upward, his head smashing through the plexiglass and his upper body thrust outside the aircraft. Had his foot not caught in the gun controls below he might have been blasted completely out of the plane.

Said Murphy, "We tried to send someone back to him only to find that the radio operator, the copilot and I were the only men on the ship who hadn't been wounded. When we were finally able to get Paul out of the turret it was only to discover that his left leg had been almost blown off by the cannon shell that penetrated his left buttock and then exploded."

"I tried to crawl back into the turret," said Slankard, "but the winds were too strong. It was like a tug of war with the suction of the slipstream trying to pull me free from the plane. Mabee pulled me back in."

"After the all clear," said Mabee, "I went back to the tail gunner, saw that he was in bad shape. I put my oxygen mask from the emergency oxygen bottle on [Slankard], carried him back to the waist position floor and put sulfa powder on his wound. We couldn't administer a painkiller because [the hypodermics] were frozen."

Bombardier Ed Janic, painfully wounded himself, crawled back to assist Mabee. Unable to stop the bleeding from the wound, the two airmen jammed Slankard's bloody buttocks up against a hole in the fuselage created by one of the cannon shells. The frigid temperatures quickly sealed the broken blood vessels. Janic unsuccessfully tried to thaw the hypodermic needles by holding them in his mouth while Mabee and he massaged the wounded gunner's hands to maintain circulation. The ordeal lasted just shy of three hours before the aircraft made it to England, along with Frank Lown's crippled ship.

"When Frank landed," recalled Murphy, "he came over to each one of us and thanked us for saving his crew from certain destruction. But all of us knew that had the positions been reversed, he would have done exactly as we did." In fact, Eighth Air Force directives frowned on such efforts because the would-be shepherd became endangered once he left the flock.

The immediate diagnosis by doctors upon arrival was that Slankard probably would not survive and certainly would lose his leg. To their surprise he recovered completely and even volunteered to fly missions against Japan, but the war there ended before he could be assigned.

While the crews licked their wounds, mourned their fallen comrades and ground crews frantically repaired battered aircraft, Spaatz, in the face of the opposition from Churchill, sounded an optimistic note, writing to Eaker, "I am just as convinced as ever that the operations of the day bombers, if applied in sufficient force from the United Kingdom, cannot be stopped by any means the enemy now has and your more recent raids should have gone a long way towards demonstrating the fact to the more persistent unbelievers."

After more than a month out of action, Billy Southworth returned to the war for a strike at Lorient. He confided to his diary, "Came closest to being shot down due to poor maintenance and two bad engines. My ground crew has done a poor job for me so am seeking a change here. Our group operations is an interesting room. Our names, ship numbers on one board. It changes when boys are shot down or lose their plane. Replacements come in and so on. Permanent charts had to be made over as we lost one-half of our personnel (air). Lost one of our group at Lorient. He was new, didn't even know him. Head-on attack. He wasn't experienced. His formation flying was poor . . . Too bad.

"We'll have to continue to bomb and bomb without hope of relief for fear we will tell the truth of the fight at home. [Rather than fear of morale problems, the Air Corps kept the men like Southworth on duty because of a lack of planes or crews available to reduce tours.] FW-190s have speed to burn, four 20 mm cannon and four machine guns. In the nose we haven't even one .50 caliber machine gun. Were I not lucky, I'd have been gone long ago."

Some days Southworth occupied a seat in *Bad Check*, frequently he piloted ships designated only by number and in his absence, his original crew had been split up because of sickness. At the end of March Southworth himself was grounded again for an appendectomy.

ALTHOUGH Bomber Command more than halved the number of missions from those of March, April turned into an even crueler month. During the first week's attacks on a Paris factory and the port of Antwerp the Bomber Command listed a total of eight B-17s downed. When the 306th had taken off for Antwerp, John Regan, normally a command pilot, sat in the copilot's seat for Lt. Col. Jim Wilson, while Brig. Gen. Frank Armstrong, just promoted from Group CO to the newly formed 101st Provisional Wing stood behind them.

Armstrong in fact had been the 306th's CO for a bare three months, hastily given the post after a disastrous performance by the group on a December 30 mission to Lorient. Seventeen of the eighteen ships that took off from the Thurleigh home base quit even before they assembled to head for the target. Armstrong brought a firm command and instituted a program of training that inevitably met some resistance. His subordinates soon recognized an improvement in their effectiveness. Moreover, his willingness to participate in raids, including his position in the lead ship for the first Eighth Air Force assault on Wilhelmshaven demonstrated the kind of leadership that persuades people to follow.

It seemed only natural for Armstrong to fly with the 306th in his capacity as head of the new wing that included it. "The flight had been routine," recalled Regan, "until we crossed the Belgian coast toward the target. Then all hell broke loose. This was somewhat surprising. I had thought this mission might be a little easier than most, as we would only be over enemy-occupied territory a short time and not over their homeland.

"The first waves of German fighters attacked us as we crossed the coast and continued to press their attack until we hit the English Channel on our way home. Since we were leading the raid our formation took the brunt of these assaults. I was so damn busy helping to fly that I only vaguely saw and absorbed what was going on around us. I do recall seeing one B-17 go down just after we crossed the coast and others later.

"The last German fighter pretty nearly rammed us head-on and one of his 20 mm cannon shells exploded in the nose of our B-17, hitting a can of .50 caliber ammo and blowing it up. The resulting explosion and shrapnel shattered the leg of our navigator, 'Salty' Saltirnik, slightly wounding me, knocking out the oxygen system in the cockpit and setting part of our hydraulic system on fire. When we were hit I realized quickly that our oxygen system had been knocked out so I grabbed an emergency bottle to share with General Armstrong (we took turns using it). General Armstrong went into the nose of the airplane to assure that the badly wounded Salty was getting oxygen and to tear open his pant leg and pour sulfa on his wounds.

"On one of Armstrong's many trips into the nose I glanced behind me and saw that our hydraulic lines were burning. I struggled out of my seat and with our flight engineer, John Crowther, we fought the fire with our hands until it was out. I was lucky I didn't pass out from lack of oxygen but managed to get to my emergency source to keep me going. I returned to my seat just in time to grab General Armstrong by his gray hair and give him oxygen before he passed out.

"Under these difficult circumstances, we dropped our bombs and headed home. In spite of his pain and severe wounds, Salty propped himself up and gave us headings to fly to our base. As we crossed the

English Channel, RAF Spitfires joined us as escorts to England. Only then did the German fighters break off their attacks.

"We limped back to Thurleigh. Wilson, who had done a superb job of flying, brought us down with no further serious complications. On final [approach] we had fired a red flare showing we had wounded aboard and were met by a medical crew and ambulance. Salty, who had lost a lot of blood, was given four pints of plasma right on the spot before he was taken to the Eighth AF hospital at Paddington. I was treated at the base clinic and released little the worse for wear."

Armstrong, who started out as an observer, soon became an active participant according to his own notes taken during the flight when he had an opportunity. "Made sign language to pilot to be on alert for enemy attackers through the overcast. Pointed out two smoke trails coming out of France high to our left . . . Cursed a FW-190 as it came into our right. Watched the first enemy attack develop ahead of the formation. Pointed out the attackers to the pilot as they became more ferocious and concentrated. Pressed the control column forward as a FW-190 met us head-on. Back-seat driving, and I was sorry about it. FW-190 rolled under wing, missed a collision by a few feet." For a few moments, while one of the pilots was busy elsewhere, Armstrong apparently sat down at the controls.

"Flinched as shell exploded the oxygen and hydraulic system. Looked at pilot and copilot to see how badly they were wounded. Began to feel queer . . . checked oxygen supply—pressure down to 100. Tried to attach oxygen lead to emergency supply bottle. Couldn't get it to fasten, so tore up mask. Copilot [Regan] reached for emergency oxygen bottle. Gave it to him. Asked for a whiff and he gave it to me. Pilot told me that Capt. Robert J. Saltirnik, navigator, had been hit and wanted some assistance. Got another whiff of oxygen from copilot and started to forward compartment.

"Crawled through hydraulic fluid on hands and knees. The navigator had received a severe shrapnel wound in the leg and was bleeding badly. Used oxygen mask connecting hose as tourniquet on navigator's leg. Helped to take navigator's parachute off and stretch him out. Rearranged tourniquet and gave to bombardier to hold (had my own thumb on it). Took navigator's data out of [his] pocket and tried to locate our position on the map. Couldn't get maps straight.

"Crawled back to pilot's compartment to give him compass course on the paper . . . lost information on floor and crawled back for it. Rearranged tourniquet and continued to nose of aircraft. Put on throat mike and headset. Called pilot to inform him he would be forced to land at the first RAF station because the navigator was seriously wounded . . . gave pilot course to fly. Could not locate any field on the ground. Crawled over to navigator and slapped his face. Looked at his eyes. Requested pilot to get down as rapidly as possible as all oxygen for navigator had been used. Sat by navigator feeling his head. Rearranged tourniquet. Held navigator's arm as bombardier tried to give him a hypodermic. Fluid ran out before needle got in. Pilot called to report a fire had started in the cockpit. Just sat until lower altitude was reached. Crawled back to pilot's compartment and notified him I would stand by rear door with fire extinguisher ready." When the aircraft touched down, Armstrong bolted from his seat, ran to the front of the aircraft ready to put out any flames but saw no fire. A Distinguished Flying Cross was awarded to Armstrong with a citation that described him as flying the plane, but except for the one moment when he forgot himself, he was never at the controls.

Said Regan, "I visited Salty at the hospital several times and watched his condition improve markedly. I thought he had it made. However, on my last visit to him April 15, I found him delirious and in great pain. I talked with the head nurse who advised me they were going to take his cast off his damaged leg and treat him further. When it was removed they found that gangrene had set in and had spread through his body. He died on 16 April. Our group had lost a great navigator and a natural leader. I had lost a good friend.

"During the time I was in England, our group lost 113 air crews, perhaps 1,130 men. It was very difficult; one evening I remember meeting a replacement gunner who just came in. I introduced myself, said I am really sorry to get you when you've just arrived but you'll have to fly tomorrow because we need a gunner and you're qualified. He went on the mission the next day and was shot down. I was only twenty-three and had a wonderful adjutant, an older guy named Ed Miazza. He helped me write letters to the families of everyone lost from my squadron. I would write them in longhand, trying to soften the blow, saying how sorry I was that the person had been shot down and that he'd done so much for the squadron.

"We did have people who could no longer take it. They would ask permission to get off flight duty. We'd take their wings, put them on ground mechanical duty. Many would ask then to be put back on flights."

Bill Fleming, the waist gunner for Southworth aboard *Bad Check*, remembers his build-up of stress. "I had taken a spell when I had blackouts and I wondered if combat fatigue was getting to me. I would run a high temperature and black out. They finally sent me to Wilford Hall, a castle converted into a hospital and I stayed there for approximately six weeks. A young doctor discovered I had an infection in my inner ear that upset my sense of balance. They treated it and I returned to my group. At that point I had to have eleven more missions to finish.

"I hated to leave my regular crew; I had been very friendly with Waldo Brandt our tail gunner. We went on many passes together and Jack Belk our belly gunner and Edward Doughty the radio operator. Conver and Schueler too; we always made a lot of jokes about our copilot whose name was John Dillinger. He was a nice guy [Dillinger's actions as a copilot had been unsatisfactory to Southworth].

"I was assigned to a crew with Major Hagenbuch and we flew General Eaker to North Africa and back. He went to Casablanca for a meeting with Churchill and Roosevelt. They were to decide whether to go ahead with a plan to bomb Germany night and day, with the RAF making its raids after dark and the Eighth Air Force during the day. That's when they finally agreed to give us replacement crews. It was a highlight of my life to meet those two gentlemen, Churchill and Roosevelt.

"Our losses originally figured that one out of three would be lucky enough to finish a tour and then it went down to one out of five. One incident disturbed all of us. Lieutenant Stockton had flown on all of the group's missions. Instead of taking passes he'd make the missions. He was on his twenty-fourth, and would have been the first pilot to complete a tour but he was killed. They released the cause of his death as due to a 20 mm cannon shell hitting him, the autopsy report which was never made public, showed a .50 caliber machine gun bullet killed him. This wasn't unusual. I'm sure a lot of people got hit by their own shells; there were so many guns firing in so many directions in such a heavy formation of planes that it was bound to happen. His death upset everybody."

ON April 16, the 93rd and 44th combined in an assault upon Brest. Red Komarek of the 93rd in a Liberator named *Yardbird* noted, "Those familiar ugly black puffs of smoke began appearing in the sky and the Skipper [Capt. Leon Packer] began evasive action. Our pilots made these big-ass birds do more than the book allowed. Packer studied flak patterns and more than once evaded bursts by veering into spent flak avoiding new shells in the pattern spread.

"Scanning the skies, half-standing, I spotted an FW-190 at about 1,000 yards. Sitting down, I lined him up in my sights, mindful of the fact that I wasn't sure to date if I ever really damaged or even hit an enemy ship. All too often my tracers danced around the tails of attacking fighters. Before I got in a burst, I suddenly experienced a blinding shattering blast and was blown backward.

"Little white lights flickered about and I was uncertain as to what was happening. For a moment I was completely disoriented. Gradually I realized my position and found I was lying on the catwalk outside the turret and my feet were up around the controls of the turret. My oxygen mask was up covering my right cheek and eye. My face throbbed and felt wet. Slowly I reached with my right hand and pulled the oxygen mask back into place and glanced at my glove. The glove was wet and red and I felt part of my face was hit. As I sucked in the oxygen, my head cleared and I reacted by pulling myself back into the turret. The wet glove looked bad until I realized it was not all blood but my saliva. Still not completely clear-minded, I stood up straight in the turret. I was able to do this since all the plexiglass had been blown away. My head was in the slipstream [which] was the shock I needed to bring me to and aware of the continuing danger we were in.

"Settling back down, my turret took another hit, this time at my left gun. Bud Wurm [gunner and assistant radio operator] reported later that I was blown out a second time but I have no recollection of this. When returning fire, I did realize my left gun was out and became aware of smoke. I was startled as the bailout bell sounded. I stared at it. I never expected it to ring for real. 'Bail out! Bail out' it seemed to scream.

"I reached for my portable oxygen bottle and glanced out the turret, seeing land, water, and land again and realized we were in a wide spin. I reached up in back of me, grabbing the ammo rail bar and pulled myself out of the turret. Standing outside the turret, oxygen bottle in my hand, I saw a chute blossom open below and to the rear. Then there was another explosion. This time I felt I had been swatted with the flat side of a shovel with a force that buckled me but didn't hurt. I stood up again with a feeling that my left leg had gone to sleep. The wet feeling in my boot reminded me of getting my feet wet with water squishing inside the shoe.

"I looked at Bud who had a pained expression on his face, standing, ready to go. He had taken an armor-piercing slug in his back. The bullet's copper jacket broke up causing lacerations and the steel slug lodged in his back. His back chute prevented the slug from going through him entirely. We looked at each other, waiting for the first to move or to keep each other company in death. The hesitation was to our advantage.

"At that time up front, after an 88 mm shell went through our wing behind No. 3 engine and started a fire and several 20 mm cannon shells hit gas lines in the bomb bay, the situation appeared hopeless. The hits on the gas lines caused air locks which caused the other engines to sputter and lose power. The fire was extinguished in No. 3 engine and the prop was feathered but with the power loss in the other engines made it necessary to abandon ship. Lt. [Parkman] Davis [bombardier] went out the nose wheel hatch and was stuck momentarily until Lt. [Hal] Bilyeu [navigator] pushed him through with his foot on his shoulder. Jack Lang [radio operator] was poised in the open bomb bay ready to jump with Harry Ahlborn [engineer/gunner], Lt. Earl Hurd [copilot] and the Skipper in line.

"The engines came to life, No. 2 sputtering with more power, followed by No. 1 and No. 4. Hearing the miracle, Skipper and Hurd bounced back behind the controls and worked frantically to get the engines going. They did. Harry climbed up to his turret and began firing and Bilyeu returned to the nose machine guns and his shredded map case . . . courtesy of a 20 mm hit. I do not know why the rest of us in the rear knew we no longer had to bail out. Our radio was shot out but we just seemed to know and all of us went back to our positions. [Assistant engineer] Merle Wolf's appeal on intercom for us not to bail out was fruitless as he was talking into a dead mike.

"I could not climb back into the turret due to my leg but I started to operate it standing on the catwalk with half of me in the turret. This did limit the azimuth operation but it was better than nothing. Was there some chivalry early in the war? When we were going down, smoking and with one chute leaving the ship, the fighters seemed to abstain from further attack. Maybe it was to conserve ammo but I like to think there was a quality of mercy shown.

"Once our trouble was overcome, Packer took us down to the deck and we flew just over the water. By now we were far from our formation and on our own. The German fighters, seeing our recovery, dove after us for the kill. Hugging the water made their attack passes difficult as they could easily hit the water even in a shallow dive. There were at least a dozen FW-190s against us, frustrated and angered that we were still flying. They appeared from every angle. Merle Wolf cut loose on an attacker who then got in a few meaningful bursts of cannon fire and there were two hits at the left waist section. Merle went down and seemed to be unconscious. Jimmie Poe stepped in and alternately fired the left and right waist guns. Bud Wurm moved in to help and grabbed one of the waist guns. Ahlborn fired at the attacking fighters coming in head-on, helping Lieutenant Bilyeu who now manned three guns alone.

"From the Germans' view we were dying and they became fearless.

One came so close as to knock off the radio antenna. There were three 20 mm hits on my turret. I think they thought I was out of action. In a sense I was as both my guns were out. Confident we were going down, two 190s flew alongside of us and a third followed in the rear. This one gave me nightmares. He sat there, his wing lighting up as he took pot shots. I charged my guns feverishly. On the verge of panic I screamed, 'Get 'em, Harry, get 'em!' The top turret were the only guns with a chance to get this bastard. I alternately prayed and cursed . . . 'get 'em, Harry!'"

Komarek frantically focused on enabling his weapons to fire by charging them and suddenly they came to life. "The chattering of the gun was blissful relief. The FW slipped up to his right. Still firing, I turned my turret to the left, pinning my head between the turret door opening and the side of the ship. I felt no pain and continued firing. My racing thoughts were for the bastard to get out of there. I wasn't thinking of killing. I was firing to survive. My finger froze on the trigger—to hell with burning out the barrel.

"The FW rose to his right, then stood on his left wing, descending to his left. I kept firing and he crossed in front of me and went down under our ship. I thought I saw pieces and smoke but all I could do was soak in the blessed relief of the moment. He was gone. Harry, about the same time, spotted a fighter coming in and gave him a short burst as he began to pull up and over. Harry fired again and saw his tracers enter the engine, making the FW quiver. It blew up into a cloud of black smoke, flipped over and dove into the water. What had been a cacophony was now strangely silent except for our three engines.

"I turned jubilantly and using the ammo rail for assistance, I made my way to the waist section. Wolf was conscious. Bud Wurm was smiling but looked dazed and Jimmie Poe grinned from ear to ear. I reached these guys I loved. We won. What a bunch."

Leaking copious amounts of fuel from shattered lines, the hydraulic system wrecked, and with holes in the fuselage and wing, *Yardbird* stumbled towards England. The crew jettisoned everything removable, waist windows, guns, ammunition, the toilet, even their throat mikes to gain a precious 800 to 1,000 feet. But the damaged engines began failing as they approached the runway. Alhborn fired flares to signal mechanical trouble and wounded aboard. Except for the pilots the men braced themselves for a crash. "We were roaring at 155 miles per hour," says Komarek. "A rugged hill loomed ahead and Packer tried to pull up. We inched up but hit the hill with our landing gear that miraculously sheared off completely. We bounded through some trees and slammed down on the runway. *Yardbird* screamed as the belly was ripped away by the concrete runway. I squinted out the waist window that was now almost at ground level and was terrified to see the shower of sparks we were creating. Fire and explosion were uppermost in my mind."

Concrete tore out the bottom of the aircraft and the impact twisted Komarek's ankle while jamming his knee into his face. An anchored waist-gun ammunition box broke loose and bashed his head. As the plane crumbled it slid off the runway into a field stacked with portable steel runway construction grids. Dirt poured into the remains of *Yardbird*. When the hulk halted, the ambulatory men scrambled out of the wreckage, reaching in to drag out their more seriously wounded comrades like Komarek and Wurm. Wounded in both legs and his ankle broken, Komarek was carted off to a hospital along with Bud Wurm. His leather jacket had a bullet hole in the armpit and some 20 mm fragment punctures, but none of these touched his skin. He received credit for knocking down an enemy fighter, as did Wolf and Ahlborn. But when he had recovered from his injuries, he was permanently grounded and assigned as an armorer for a B-17 group. "They were a decent bunch, but not like my family the 329th Squadron."

April introduced more P-47s, but that did not change the combat equation for Eighth Air Force. The Thunderbolts on hand were neither numerous enough nor able to travel far enough to accompany more than 100 B-17s launched at Bremen. Appalled operations officers counted sixteen bombers that did not return as the Luftwaffe mounted the stiffest opposition yet. Waves of coordinated FW-190s slashed through the formations, knocking down a great number of Forts from the 91st Bomb Group and John Regan's 306th. "I lost sixty men in a single day," mourned John Regan. "It didn't fill me with hatred against the enemy. I had never liked the Germans but they were doing their job just as we were."

WHIT Hill, the sheet metal crew chief for the 91st recalled, "During the training period prior to departing for the European Theater of Operations, all the enlisted ground and combat crews were randomly assigned to the same barracks. As a result friendships were formed between the ground and flying men. This turned out to be a bad policy for when we entered into actual combat operations and friends turned up wounded, killed or missing, there was great mourning and a crisis in the morale of the ground crews. We ground crews sweated out the return of every aircraft. As a result flight and ground crews were moved to separate quarters. After a while the ground and flight crews were only passing friends, as they met mostly in the early mornings before takeoff on a mission.

"Those days after all the aircraft had departed on a mission there was a quiet pall that hung over the base which lasted until word was out that they were 'coming in.' Those who weren't working grabbed their bicycles and headed for the tower building to watch incoming formations. If they arrived together in a good formation, it was a sign of a successful mission and we were exhilarated. If they straggled in one at a time, indicating a bad mission, anxiety showed on the faces and in the conversations as we watched. It was especially upsetting when an aircraft fired off a 'wounded on board' flare."

After the Bremen mission, six B-17s from the 91st fell to the German defenders and the planes returning to Bassingbourn on April 17 bore one dead man. Unfortunately, the 91st happened to have scheduled a large party that evening with 150 guests expected to celebrate with the 200 officers. The gala went on as planned; the bachanalia that ensued was written off as the reaction of crews to the excessive stress of the day.

REPLACEMENTS trickled in to fill in for the dead and wounded. One such was S. Sgt. Maynard Smith, who crawled into the ball turret of a 306th Bomb Group B-17 for his first mission, St. Nazaire, after his predecessor racked up his twenty-fifth. A small-town Michigan youth, the slightly built Smith was nicknamed "Snuffy" after a popular funny paper figure of the day. This was to be the last mission of the tour for pilot Lt. Lewis P. Johnson Jr. but it was no milk run. Headed for home the ship rocked from German fighter hits. Johnson said, "I knew we had been hit and had a serious problem; the plane was on fire and not flying well." He directed his engineer T. Sgt. William Fahrenhold to check conditions in the rear. When Fahrenhold opened the door to the bomb bay a wall of flames covered the rear wall. With an extinguisher, Fahrenhold doused the fire but beyond lay even more destruction.

Ball gunner Smith heard and felt a tremendous explosion above him. He told Andy Rooney, a correspondent for *Stars and Stripes,* "My interphone and the electrical controls to my turret went out, so I handcranked myself up and crawled out of the turret into the ship. The first thing I saw was a sheet of flame coming out of the radio room and another fire by the tail-wheel section.

"Suddenly, the radio operator came staggering out of the flames. He made a beeline for the gun hatch and dived out. I glanced out and watched him hit the horizontal stabilizer, bounce off and open his chute. By this time the right waist gunner had bailed out over his gun and the left waist gunner was trying to jump but was stuck half in and half out of his gun hatch. I pulled him back into the ship and asked him if the heat was too much for him. All he did was to stare at me and I watched him bail out the rear door. His chute opened okay." The trio chose to abandon the plane even though they were over water.

"The smoke and gas were really thick," Andy Rooney quoted Smith. "I wrapped a sweater around my face so I could breathe, grabbed a fire extinguisher and attacked the fire in the radio room. Glancing over my shoulder at the tail fire, I thought I saw something coming and ran back. It was [Roy H.] Gibson, the tail gunner, painfully crawling back, wounded. He had blood all over him.

"Looking him over, I saw that he had been hit in the back and that it had probably gone through his left lung. I laid him down on his left side so that the wound would not drain into the right lung, gave him a shot of morphine and made him as comfortable as possible before going back to the fires.

"I had just got started in this when that FW came in again. I jumped for one of the waist guns and fired at him. As he swept under us, I turned to the other waist gun and let him have it from the other side. He left us for a while, so I went back to the radio room fire again.

"I got into the room this time and began throwing out burning debris. The fire had burned holes so large in the side of the ship that I just tossed the stuff out through them. Gas from a burning extinguisher was choking me so I went back to the tail fire. I took off my chute so I could move easier. I'm glad I didn't take it off sooner because later I found that it had stopped a .30 caliber bullet.

"I fired another burst with the waist guns, and went back to the radio room with the last of the extinguisher fluid. When that ran out I found a water bottle and a urine can and poured these out. After that I was so mad I urinated on the fire and finally beat on it with my hands and feet until my clothes began to smoulder. That FW came around again and I let him have it. This time he left us for good. The fire was under control, more or less and we were in sight of land."

The pilots managed to stabilize their lurching aircraft, but aircraft commander Johnson realized it was in no condition for any kind of maneuvers in preparation for landing. He brought the ship in smoothly, but as the B-17 rolled along the runway, the joint of wing and fuselage cracked. The plane was declared salvage. Three of the crew were wounded and those who leaped out in chutes were presumed drowned.

Smith's heroics won him a Congressional Medal of Honor. When it came time for the presentation ceremony several months later, according to reporter Rooney, Smith, a less than ideal garrison soldier, was located doing KP for a minor infraction. Secretary of War Henry L. Stimson, visiting the troops in the United Kingdom hung the award around the neck of Smith, hurriedly stuffed into a dress uniform.

FATE plucked Smith from obscurity for a brief moment but the Air Corps glamour attracted Hollywood's leading male movie star, Clark Gable, who flew to England with the 351st Bomb Group in April. At forty-two years of age, Captain Gable was obviously too old for flight training but the Air Corps put his talents to the task of making a training film. "One day," recalled Bill Fleming, "they told us we would have a passenger, an extra waist gunner. When we got into the plane, the man came and it was Clark Gable. It amazed us all. He'd been assigned to make a gunnery training movie and elected to go on three or four missions. We all admired him since he certainly didn't have to go. He had a lot of guts." Another prominent movie figure, James Stewart, would play a more active role with the Eighth Air Force, having risen from the rank of private to command-pilot status. Ronald Reagan was also a member of the Hollywood community who chose the Air Corps, although his service did not include the Eighth.

The appearance of Gable along with the 351st was a faint harbinger of better days ahead, or at least a sharing of the burden. Four bomb groups, the 94th, 95th, 96th and 351st went operational on May 13, and the 92nd reverted from an instructional assignment to combat status a few days later. The 322nd Bomb Group, a B-26 medium bomb group pitched in also and was one of the few organizations of its kind with the Eighth until transferred to the newly formed Ninth Air Force in October.

JIM Goodson and his colleagues from the Eagle Squadrons who had been folded into the 4th Fighter Group, said, "The transition was very gradual. Since they couldn't just take us out of combat, we went down to London in twos to join the Air Corps. We had kept flying Spitfires and were piecing together U.S. uniforms. When Dixie Alexander and I went to London, he had on his RAF uniform and I had a bit of an American one.

"We decided we'd have to have stars on our wings and had trouble trying to draw them in place of the RAF rondelles. Finally, my crew chief, Manny Green, who was Jewish, said he had a Star of David which we could copy. We later found out that wasn't like the Air Force star at all, but our first few missions over Europe were flown under the Star of David."

Goodson's outfit, the 4th Fighter Group, provided escort and occasionally ranged over the Channel for offensive patrols. On March 10, the outfit had actually dispatched fourteen P-47s, the first operational efforts by Thunderbolts. The Spitfire remained the dominant aircraft until April 8 when the 56th and 78th Fighter Groups opened shop and added their P-47s. The switch to the P-47 aroused the same unhappiness expressed by Goodson when he went from Hurricanes to Spitfires. "The Hurricane and Spitfire were designed as defensive planes. During the Battle of Britain, they could outturn the Germans but when the Germans shoved the stick forward and dived for the deck, they couldn't follow. Not only were they slower in the dive, but they had gravity feed carburetors. If you shoved the stick forward, the engines stopped and the enemy was always diving away from you. Still, when we looked at the first Thunderbolt, we thought we were looking at a Stirling bomber. It was an enormous thing after the Spitfire and we were horrified at having to take this unwieldy thing into the air. After I had test flown it, I said to Don Blakeslee, our wing commander, at least this thing will be able to outdive the German fighters. On one of our first missions, I was on Blakeslee's wing and down we went on 109s and 190s, in their standard procedure for evasion, diving for the deck. Sure enough we caught up with them in the dive and were able to shoot them down. 'See, Don, I said it could dive.' 'Well,' he answered, 'it damn well ought to because it sure as hell can't climb.' He already knew about the P-51 Mustang and that's what we really wanted. But the P-47 was more of an offensive weapon than the Spits and the war had changed. With Spitfires, we could only go on fighter sweeps and hope the Germans would come up and fight but they didn't. We used Blenheim bombers and Bostons as bait to force the Germans to come out, but they did not. We couldn't carry the battle to them. During the daylight bombing, we could only escort them a short part of the way. We'd see the 109s and 190s waiting out there and when we left they'd come in and clobber the bombers."

Other Americans retired their Spitfires with slight regrets. As Goodson said, the British fighter was easy to fly and highly capable against all comers but its short range restricted it to basically a defensive weapon, an interceptor of enemy ships but not one able to carry the war tactically to the Germans. In contrast, even the first P-47s could travel farther while holding their own in terms of speed and ability to climb, after modifications. The eight .50s mounted in its wings gushed torrents of destruction in a concentrated area, doing more damage than a pair of 20 mm cannons. While the "Jug," as it was affectionately known, initially made a poor impression on the British who derided the plane when compared to their "race horse" Spitfire, its performance eventually converted many critics. Stubby and imposing on the ground, the P-47 Thunderbolt, thanks to an extremely powerful engine, astounded doubters in the air. Ruggedly built, the new fighters quickly proved to be as resilient as the B-17s, absorbing considerable damage and still managing to make their way home. Later, belly tanks and disposable wing tanks greatly enhanced the ability of the Thunderbolts to escort deep into Germany. They also were adapted to carry bombs, making them highly effective for ground support.

7

THE BUILDUP

The 56th Fighter Group officially debuted on April 8 with a rodeo along the French coast near Dunkirk but nothing of consequence occurred. Among those in the P-47s, an original pilot with the 56th Fighter Group was John McClure, born in 1917, about thirty miles from Columbus, Ohio. "I got interested in aviation as a kid, hanging around airfields. I got a ride with a barnstormer in an old De Havilland [a World War I vintage plane]. It gave me the bug. After I was in college I made application for military training on advice of a friend who'd done it and been commissioned. When I went through the physical I had a problem with my weight and size. I was five feet six, an inch above the minimum height, but the minimum weight was 125 pounds and I was only 110. They sent me home for a diet, to get fat, milkshakes between meals. It didn't work. I gave it up and went back to school, getting my degree in 1939.

"When the draft came out I was in the age bracket to be quite eligible and I drew a nice low number. I enlisted and forwarded my application for flight training and was called in early April 1941. I went to Parks Air College, did my Primary there, then to Randolph Field and with my classmates opened a new base at Victoria, Texas. I was an instructor with a class of students when Pearl Harbor came on. Two days before Christmas about fifteen of us got orders to report to the 56th Fighter Group at Charleston [South Carolina], with the 61st, 62nd and 63rd Squadrons. We started with P-35s, a P-36 and a P-39."

The 56th became a part of the 1st Fighter Command, in defense of New York City, and the squadrons stationed in adjacent areas. After a nodding acquaintance with P-38s, the outfit welcomed the Jugs. Following training with their new equipment, the 56th, in January 1943, boarded the *Queen Elizabeth* and sailed to England, bedding down at the Horsham Saint Faith airdrome.

"We'd started our operations in early April and I was on my seventh mission, the 29th of April," recalled McClure. "It was our first major contact with the enemy. In the mess we had a little confusion and we got separated. I got hit and managed to get back out over the coast. The one set of instructions we had was for heaven's sake don't let 'em get a hold of a Jug. They don't know anything about it and we don't want them to know.

"I got out over the North Sea and I was down to about 400 feet when I bailed out. A German coastal patrol picked me up. In the water like that you lose your sense of time, but from my watch which stopped when I hit the water I determined that I was in the water for about an hour and a half. The Germans shook their heads, 'No way,' because at that time of the year, twenty minutes is about average survival time. I had discovered that my life raft was full of holes and my Mae West had a puncture. I pulled the emergency kit off the raft and proceeded to float. I didn't really have time to be afraid on the way down because there are so many things you have to do, you don't have time to think. And then you suffer from a certain amount of shock. I couldn't move, almost paralyzed, they drug me up over the side of the boat and took me into an island up along the Dutch coast."

Kept overnight in a small room there, his clothes taken away to dry, McClure was issued a skimpy blanket and then taken to a train station for a trip to Amsterdam with a trio of guards. There he was lodged in what had been a prison and thrust into solitary confinement. "It was absolutely black, no light, about six feet long, three or four wide with an iron bench on one side. You lose all concept of time under such circumstances but I later figured out I was there a little over two weeks. I'd get a little piece of *ersatz* bread—half sawdust—and a cup of *ersatz* coffee, twice a day. That was it.

"Periodically, they'd take me up for an interrogation by an officer who spoke very good English. He didn't mince too many words. They asked questions beyond name, rank and serial number, they wanted to know what you were flying, who was your CO, where you were located, what kind of armament does this aircraft have and a lot of technical questions. They seemed particularly interested in organization, who was there and how many. They kept coming back to this. When you didn't go beyond name, rank and serial number, they took to encouraging you with the good old rubber hose. When you didn't answer, they'd say, 'We'll give you a little time to think this over.' This was repeated, every day or so.

"There was another prisoner across the way from me who wanted to be sociable. That kinda made me a little suspicious. He had a British accent and I just clammed up and didn't answer him. To pass the time you start going back over the nightmare. You have to learn that this is not doing you any good, you're just getting in deeper. You have to occupy your mind. Some people would work mathematical problems. I thought about building a house. I laid out the plans for the rooms, how I was going to landscape it. I had the measurements down and how I'd do it.

"They came down at the end of about two weeks and took me for interrogation. The guy told me that if they didn't get some answers out of me, they'd call in the firing squad. They weren't going to fool with me any more and he'd give me a couple of hours to think it over. They pulled me back after some hours and it was almost a repeat of the same thing and then the third time there were three guards with bayonets drawn. They herded me up and out into the courtyard of the prison. About then, here comes a ten-man rifle squad and they lined up just opposite me. They led me down a flight of steps and suddenly turned, took me out the gate, placed me on a train for Frankfurt and *Dulag Luft*.

"I didn't think at the time that my life had just been saved. Your mind gets to a pretty low ebb when you're in solitary. Then when they take you out into the light I thought 'Great, I'm going to get out of this.' But when you see that squad, you think it's a firing squad and that guy wasn't joking. But the thought crossed my mind, 'By God, I'm going to get out of here anyway.' I was quite startled when they took me out of the gate, still in my own uniform, GI trousers, a khaki shirt and my leather flying jacket."

Dulag Luft was the official interrogation center for the German air force. McClure debarked from the train close enough to walk into the compound where his captors shoved him into a slightly larger room in a wooden barracks. He received little food, was not permitted to bathe and a tin can served as his toilet.

According to McClure, the German method of questioning followed a routine. "They left you alone for three or four days. You saw no one and spoke to no one. Then one of their interrogative personnel, in my case a captain probably in his early forties and who spoke excellent English appeared. He asked if you had a chance to shower, and he knows of course the answer is no. 'Oh, that's terrible, you mean you haven't had this or that. Come on let me take you to the officers' dining room and we'll have a cup of coffee,' and he did. Of course the place had been vacated. He asked, 'Have you been outside yet? Will you give me your parole?' Meaning, give your word not to try to escape." McClure demurred. "Then he said, 'In that case you understand I am armed,' and he carried a pistol.

"We sat down and he just wants to be sociable. He asks where you were born, getting information all the time."

ANOTHER member of the 56th Fighter Group was Robert Johnson, a twenty-three-year-old Oklahoma native whose auto-mechanic father passed along to his offspring the knowledge to work with tools. "We made our own toys," said Johnson, "and I worked in a cabinet shop. I was not much into athletics at first. I could box; being little, I had to fight and after a few years guys were arranging fights for me. In the tenth grade I decided to play football; I weighed only about 140 in high school and 145 in college and the guys on the other side were well over 200 pounds. I was very quick to pull out of the line, bounce off the tackle or into the line which let Speck Sanders [a college star] or someone get through the line. I played sixty minutes, offense and defense.

"When I was a kid I wanted to be a cowboy or a railroad engineer. The Rock Island Railroad ran through the town which had a depot, huge roundhouse. The big engines and whistle excited me. But when I was about eight, an air show came to town with three little biplanes. They did acrobatics and right then I decided I wanted to be an army pilot. We had a neighbor who was a lieutenant, a great guy and I was always hanging around him, looking at his goggles and helmet. A barnstorming pilot came through, charging $1.50 a ride. He said if four or five in my Scout troop helped control the mob and get people to come to and from the plane, he would take us for a ride. But at the end of the day it was too late."

Earning $4.50 a week in the cabinet shop, Johnson at fourteen hung out at the airport where he washed planes and spent $1.50 a week for fifteen minutes of flying time. "I got my student pilot's license the day before I was fifteen." He had six or seven hours in flying time when he soloed. "That was one of the biggest thrills of my life. I never really noticed that the instructor wasn't there on the right side until I was off the ground and staring around the field. I remember I looked and gee, I really made a beautiful landing."

A burgeoning interest in the opposite sex, however, temporarily grounded Johnson who used his dollars for dates at the movie houses. He attended Lawton Junior College, readying himself for Oklahoma A and M [now Oklahoma State] but seized an opportunity to renew his fondness for flight through the Civilian Pilot Training Corps. Enlistment in the Army Air Corps followed.

"We had civilian pilot instructors in primary school, mature guys, tough, severe but fair. I flew in open cockpit Stearmans in Sikeston, Missouri. We had several boys freeze their faces, the skin crack just like leather. We tried to fly with a leather mask and goggles but these would steam up. I had a choice on graduation and although I had a desire for fighters, the thing to do was go into bombers, multi-engine planes because of jobs later with the airlines." He graduated from Kelly Field, Texas, as a bomber pilot. "At the end of our training at Kelly Field, we were all given the typical army choice: 'Anything you want, boys, just put it down and you've got it. I put down the nearest thing to fighters I could get, as a bomber pilot. My first choice was the A-20 training in Oklahoma City. I selected that because it was loud, noisy, flew close to the ground. My second choice was A-20s in Seattle and so was my third in Florida. Instead I got P-47s in Connecticut.

"We had to break those airplanes in—a brand-new engine, and the brand-new airplane. We had a lot of accidents; we killed a few boys in training. The P-47s were like big Cadillacs, a super big old Cadillac. It would fly itself. When one landed a Jug," which seemed to come into a field and squat, Johnson said, "it was just like you were approaching a cold toilet seat." Johnson struggled to learn gunnery. "One training technique was for another guy to fly 100 to 200 feet over the water and then we'd come in and shoot at his shadow. It was a matter of a quick burst and than a break because you could be in the water real quick. We did a lot of skeet shooting to teach us how to lead a target. From time to time, they took us to shoot at flying targets. I never did qualify because I could not hit the flags. I learned my combat shooting firing at airplanes."

When the 56th Fighter Group arrived in England, he listened to an RAF pilot who advised, "If a German gets on your tail, don't sit still. Move, shake your airplane, get all over the sky. Don't sit still because then he's got you." He also benefitted from the early leadership which included men who'd flown with the Eagle Squadrons and taught him some tactics.

"The P-47 was a very comfortable airplane—big cockpit, very warm, so we wore our typical woolen OD [olive drab] uniform. We put a silk scarf around our necks inside the shirt collar to keep from cutting our necks on those wool shirts while constantly turning our heads. That was the purpose of the scarf, not flamboyancy. You had to look backwards 90 percent of the time when you were flying.

"As a bomber pilot trainee, I needed instrument flying, navigation, formation flying and night flying—that type of instruction. Thank God we had it because in England you had to walk with your hands in front of you to keep from running into a wall. Many times the weather there was so bad you could not see."

As the newest entry to the war, the Thunderbolt confused the Germans at first. "We got a lot of them because the elliptical wing of a P-47 at first glance looked like a Spitfire if you didn't happen to notice that big, bulky nose. The Germans might fly under us or maybe we would catch them beneath and they'd simply roll over and dive because they could always outdive a Spitfire. We'd roll over, throttle back, slide right up their ass and shoot them down. They were not going to get away from the P-47s straight, level or down. Our guns narrowed around 400 yards until the eight .50s came together in a two-foot-square box.

"You got used to each little squeak and noise in the airplane. You knew almost to a second when one fuel tank was going to be empty. A lot of our crew chiefs were old timers and greatly experienced. We were their guys so we always made a point of putting on a show for them. My crew chief kind of felt I was his son—he was ten years older. They sandpapered and waxed my airplane which gave it a gleam and added five to eight miles of speed per hour. You couldn't stand well on the wing."

Johnson remembered his first operational sortie from England. "It was simply a fighter sweep and it was a little bit unreal—you were anticipating something but you did not know what. We didn't really believe they were shooting to kill over there. We thought it was a big game. All we had done was shoot camera gunnery and then always you would come in and land with the guy you shot at. You could not believe that you were shooting to kill and you were being shot at to kill.

"That first mission, I was flying as [a wingman]. There were forty-eight of us all together, sixteen per squadron, with three squadrons at different levels and we made a sweep at 35,000 feet back to England. We were way up at the top and I was way to the right of everyone else when they made a turn. I was following orders, 'Stay on your leader,' and I was looking around and did not realize they had turned a little bit sharper and really left me. So when I looked back and saw them leaving me, I pulled in the stick and hit my gun trigger. That scared hell out of me; of course there was no one around.

"I had heard about flak and seen two or three airplanes up above us quite a ways back. I wasn't worried about them because they were quite [far off]. I saw all these little white things popping all around me and thought, 'That must be the antiaircraft they are talking about. I wonder where my buddies are.' I looked to the right and out of the corner of my eyes saw something blinking at me. There were two 109s!

"I rolled that thing over and instinctively to the left. [I had been told] never fly a straight line. I started to split-S and then as I got halfway through it, I realized this was enemy country that I was split-S-ing into. So I straightened it up and at a good forty-five-degree angle—[inverted], I was kicking rudders at the same time—upside down. I was really slashing that airplane all over the sky. I had the throttles bent forward; got home a good thirty minutes before anyone else."

Johnson flew a number of missions without engaging the enemy. He, like the other newcomers, continued to discuss the choreography of a dogfight. One evening, Johnson said he raised the question of the opening gambit. After a day on which he saw German fighters pass apparently unobserved by flight leaders, Johnson, mindful of the requirement to maintain position, asked one of the senior individuals, "Suppose I am not the leader but I see an enemy and he is a perfect spot for me to bounce [attack] and there is just not time to do anything but call him in and bounce him. If I call him in and then we [the flight] try to maneuver so that the other planes are in position to bounce him, he is gone. What do you do?

"He said, 'That's a good question.' And that was his answer. But to me it was enough—go get him. Call them in and then go get 'im.

"The next day, June 13, we had the same thing happen. I was number forty-eight-man. Here was [Hub] Zemke leading the whole group. I was on [Paul] Conger's wing, sitting up there on the top and I saw about twelve Focke Wulfs pass under us. I knew someone had to see them. I wasn't the first. I called them in and I said 'Come on, Paul,' and zooom, I went right down through our guys. I pulled up behind the sort of Vee echelon they had.

"I figured I had my answer from the night before—'that is a good question'—and I figured it was up to me to answer. I took it very slow, easy and casual, my airplane was really coming in, overtaking them. The pipper [on the gunsight] was on the crosspiece of the rudder and the elevators. I thought, nice and gentle and then that is not right. I remembered in our camera gunnery, you always put the pipper on the back of the pilot's head. I put it up on his head, calmly checked the needle ball. It was centered and I pulled the trigger.

"My whole airplane vibrated. All this smoke and fire—all this noise. I released it immediately, because I thought I am hit. Then I realized it was my own guns and I saw what had happened to the guy ahead of me. He went all to pieces. This was the leader of that German formation. If I had had any experience at all, I could have gotten one or two more, but as it was, I was rolling out through the sky, having a great time. Then suddenly I realized that it was easy and I should go back and get some more. I ended up alone over there wandering around enemy country—Belgium and that area.

"I got home thirty or forty minutes later than anyone. They weren't sure what happened to me. When I landed, flight commander Jerry Johnson right on through [Francis] Gabreski and Zemke really reamed my butt and rightly so—I was wrong. But after they all chewed me out, they congratulated me on getting my first one. Carl Spaatz himself later offered his compliments along with a bottle of Scotch. I had come home not too long before that by myself on my first mission and now again I was not with [the formation]."

In fact, because of his eagerness which led to going off on his own, Johnson admitted he quickly earned the reputation of a wild man. "Everyone said, 'Don't fly with Johnson, he will kill you.'" Even when not in the cockpit, Johnson personified the stereotypical image of the swaggering fighter pilot. "We were confined to the base one time. It was cold, too cold to get up and put out the lights. I shot them out with my .45. It became a standard joke, fusillades of bullets to put out the lights. One man had a Tommy gun, another a rifle." With rain leaking through the roof holes, higher echelon officers firmly requested less violent means to extinguish the bulbs.

Just shy of three weeks after his first victory, Johnson's career almost came to a crashing halt. "I was so badly shot up that had I been able to get out of the airplane, I would have been a prisoner, or dead or an evadee. I couldn't get out of the airplane. My oxygen had been shot out and flash-flamed my cockpit. That singed the side of my head a little. My wrist bone [a knuckle rammed back into his wrist] was part of the damage that I did to myself trying to fight my way out of the cockpit.

"Loss of oxygen at altitude—you get a little cocky, like I'd had several drinks, maybe a little too much. As you go down, your mind goes into super-high speed. Everything is coming by real fast and very clearly; all the things you've been told flash by real quick. Your intelligence officer had told you that if you have to go down, go down inland pretty deep, because near the coastline the enemy is all over. In my mind I could look down and see them on the coastline three miles deep, just like ants. They weren't there but in my mind they were.

"As time went on, the airplane was still thumping a little bit, so I throttled it back a little bit. It smoothed out somewhat. There was a shell hole in the propeller; that made it uneven. There were also a couple of cylinders shot away. I was thinking quite hard about what I was going to do. I couldn't get out of the airplane; I had tried several times.

"Running through my mind was that I would go south as far as I could, belly it in, crawl out of the airplane, take my hand grenade [fighter planes were equipped with a hand grenade with which to destroy the airplane should the need arise] and explode the airplane and the parachute, then try to make it out through Spain. At the time the record for getting shot down and getting through Spain back to England was about ten days. So sticking in my mind was I'd be back in England in about ten days.

"I proceeded that way for a while then began to think about my wife and my folks. They would be worried about me all of this time, yet I knew I'd be okay. I thought maybe I'd just turn the airplane around and go back home. I was down about to Paris by this time. I'd been hit up around Dieppe. No airplanes were around at this time and that made me very happy.

"This was the one mission on which I had not worn my goggles; I had cracked them the day before, so I'd left them at home. One of the 20 mms had exploded in the left-hand side of my cockpit and knocked out my hydraulic throttle or control. Hydraulic fluid was all over the floor of the airplane and flying around in the air of the open cockpit and getting into my eyes, which were starting to swell. I was flying half the time with my eyes closed and part of the time with my head sticking out of the window, getting air blown into my eyes and the rest of the time just trying to see.

"I had dropped down to about seven or eight thousand feet and my head was beginning to clear. I was heading north, going toward England and I had to cross the Channel. I looked back to the right at about four o'clock and slightly high, and saw a beautiful dappled, blue gray yellow-nose [plane] coming in at me. Black crosses on it. I recognized it of course as a Focke Wulf. I was sitting there, thinking about it as he kept coming right at me.

"I waited for him to move the nose of his airplane forward of my airplane but he kept his nose directly on me, which meant he was taking pictures. Then when he got about fifty yards from me I thought, 'Now what would I do if I was in his shoes. I would stick my guns in the guy's cockpit and blow him out of the sky. That's what that bugger is going to do to me.'

"I turned and went under him real quick and headed again to the north. I didn't know how badly my airplane was banged up and didn't know whether I could fight him or not—so I didn't try. As I went under him, he pulled up, pulled back around, came directly in on my tail and emptied a lot of .30 caliber machine gun shells into me. They all hit me. All I could do was sit back there, leaning against the armor plate and take it." As Johnson turned his head, a bullet nicked the end of his nose. Another passed through the side of the cockpit, split, and half of it pierced the upper part of his right thigh while the rest entered several inches below.

"I held my course. He overshot me and just out of anger, I stuck my head out of the window and hit hard right rudder, and skidded a little bit and fired at him. I got two bullets into his left wingtip. It didn't really hurt him, but he at least knew I still had a little fight. He came back around and got in formation with me. I could have reached out and touched his wingtip. He was sitting in there the way we flew when going through weather.

"He probably saved my life. We went over Dieppe at 4,000 feet, a P-47 and a Focke Wulf in tight formation. So, no antiaircraft. He took me out over the water. He was looking at my airplane up and down. He'd just shake his head. Incidentally, he had black eyes. He shook his head and kind of waved at me, tipped his left hand like a little salute and pulled off. I thought, 'Thank God, he's going home.' Then he pulled in behind me again and emptied the rest of his .30 calibers. It sounded like a goat on a tin roof. This time he didn't make the mistake of overshooting me. He came back in formation with me, stayed with me until I was down to about 1,000 feet over the Channel, then waved his wings and went home.

"I relaxed a little and thought I'd better get ready to put the airplane down in the water or whatever. As I released the throttle, I realized I'd been so tense that I was also gripping the mike button. I was transmitting everything I was saying, everything I'd called the German, the gunfire and everything else. As I released the throttle, my mike popped open again and I heard this beautiful voice, 'Oh I say there, Blue Four, climb if you can, climb if you can. You're getting very faint.'

"I thought, 'Hey, I'm alive and here's a friend talking to me.' All at once I felt greatly elated. Here I was alive and I'd been dead a few minutes before. I then realized the airplane would fly. I zoom-climbed up through some low clouds to about 6,000 feet. I was so cocky and so happy I would have taken the whole German air force on.

"I was directed to an airbase in southern England. I had kicked out my instruments trying to bail out. I had thrown my feet up on the dashboard and leaned back as I tried to yank the canopy open but it was jammed shut. I was brought over the airbase in southern England, but I couldn't see the field when I looked down, partially because my eyes were swollen and partially because it was so well camouflaged. I told the controller I'd just go on up to another base where all my buddies were, at Manston.

"I called Manston and told them I expected to make a gear-up landing because I had no brakes, no hydraulics, no flaps, and I wasn't sure I could get the gear down. I was told if possible to bring the airplane in gear-down because there were a lot of crashed airplanes coming back. I dropped the gear. The doors popped open and the tires were okay. I landed and ground-looped the airplane to stop it—I had no brakes—and backed it in between two British aircraft, just like I'd parked there.

"I crawled out of the airplane and kissed the ground, then got my chute out. I went to the flight surgeon. He doctored my nose. Later, as I was taking my trousers off for a shower, I discovered the two partial bullets in my right leg. I put iodine on the holes thinking that would cure everything." To his enormous satisfaction, Johnson, on return to his home field, heard over the radio a German flier describing how he had seen a P-47 with the number of Johnson's plane going into the water.

"I flew the next day," said Johnson, "flew every day. The bullet wounds in my right thigh began to fester, became infected like two boils. Finally, I couldn't strap the parachute over my right leg. I had to let it hang free while I went on flying. Finally, I couldn't get up on the wing of the airplane anymore so I had to go to our flight surgeon.

"He was quite mad, because I hadn't come to him earlier and I'd let my leg become infected. He was not very gentle as he slashed away at those things, got the poisoning out of them and doctored them. He was the nicest guy in the world, but I could have just hit him to release some of the pain. But I didn't.

"After such an event I had a great deal of confidence in the airplane. I realized how rugged it really was and how much firepower it had. And the pilot had so much protection." But the day of Johnson's adventure, his 56th Fighter Group counted five pilots MIA.

For all the fondness Johnson developed for the P-47, the monster 2,000-horsepower Jug engine, heaving a seven-ton fighter through the sky, gobbled up fuel at a prodigious rate. During these first few months with the P-47s in operation, the bombers continued to go it alone once they penetrated the Continental air.

IN January 1943, Eaker could call on only six bomber groups but by the end of June he commanded thirteen of these plus three fighter groups. However, the statistics for units hid a scarcity of operational strength. The Mighty Eighth could dispatch little more than 200 of the heavyweights. The number fell short of what the strategists on the scene deemed necessary. Eight months earlier Eaker had written Hap Arnold that his people were "absolutely convinced that . . . 300 heavy bombers can attack any target in Germany with less than 4 percent losses." The figure of 300 seems to have been plucked from the air, like a .300 batting average as a magical talisman in baseball, for no evidence supported Eaker or, as became woefully apparent later, the idea that the German defenders would be overwhelmed by 300 or more aircraft.

Furthermore, the top command clung to another deadly misperception. The battles in the early months of spring 1943 persuaded the brass that the strongest German fighter defense lay near the Channel coast, a crust that once pierced opened up the heartland to a more lightly resisted attack. That theory was obliterated within a few weeks with the discovery of an intricate web of German airfields arranged in depth. Furthermore, the Luftwaffe had also developed its own radar and early warning apparatus much like that which helped preserve England in 1940 and any intruders found the defenders ready and waiting. To knock down bombers, the Germans in addition to machine guns and cannons, added rockets, explosives dangling from parachutes, and even tried unsuccessfully to deploy an infantry mortar shell as part of the air-to-air ordnance.

Nevertheless, real relief for the Eighth Bomber Command was in the person and machines of the latest groups to enter battle, the 94th, 95th, 96th and 351st Bomb Groups. In addition the 92nd returned from a May training operation, and in June the appearance of the 100th, 381st and 384th bolstered the outfit.

Archie J. Old Jr., a thirty-seven-year-old Texan, brought his 96th Bomb Group to a base at Grafton Underwood that spring. Fifteen years earlier Old, fresh out of college and a budding civil engineer working at road building, saw a graduating class from Kelly Field pass by during a cross-country flight. One pilot landed in a cornfield near Old and he chatted with the flier. Learning about the life of a cadet, Old abandoned his career in construction and won a commission in 1929. He left the Air Corps but signed up for the reserve. Called to active duty in 1940, Old progressed up the chain of command.

Following activation of the 96th in July 1942, Old became its CO within a month. He faced two major problems immediately; inexperienced pilots and a shortage of aircraft. "I was given thirty-five copilots as airplane commanders but I knew these people [from his earlier work training fliers] better than anyone on earth. Then brand-new guys out of the flying schools would be assigned to us. They were our copilots, brand-new second lieutenants and we got bombardiers, navigators on about the same basis. I sent a fellow by the name of Alexander S. Moffett, a nonpilot, hell of a line officer, up to Salt Lake City to interrogate and pick, as far as possible, every goddamn man. They all came through the personnel replacement center there [including mechanics, cooks, bakers and other ground workers]. Most people just accepted what they gave them. I was getting the best of the crop. He did a superb job.

"At Walla Walla, I had twelve or fifteen airplanes. The one thing you didn't want was an accident. If you had a second one, it didn't make a damn whether it was your fault or not, you were walking down the road [relieved and transferred]. The number one job was to train these crews."

Toward this goal, Old instituted a rigorous regimen based on eight hours in the air, eight hours of schooling, eight hours reserved for sleep. He scheduled airmen to fly on rotating shifts that gave them experience both day and night. To avoid any down time, recalled Old, "If the airplane didn't need any particular maintenance, we would actually change crews with the engines running to save time. We refueled with engines running. It was dangerous as hell, but never did we burn one up. We were getting the maximum amount of flying time, since we had only twelve planes and thirty-five crews who needed to fly. We were flying those damn aircraft twenty hours a day."

The 96th shifted to a new home at Rapid City, South Dakota. "It had never had an airplane on it," said Old. "They had a base commander and they had the support troops but we were the first outfit to come in and the commander was a retread from World War I. I climbed all over him. I was a lieutenant colonel and he was a colonel who reminded me of this fact. I told him 'I don't give a goddamn. What I'm talking about is you have not let us keep our schedule. We can't do it if you have a bunch of goddamn civilians out here with everything going to make sure they get fed over the priority of my crews, my people.' We got nowhere.

"I called Fort George Wright [Washington, and headquarters for the area training command] and said I wanted to talk to Gen. Nathan Forrest, grandson or something of the Civil War's Nathan Bedford Forrest. He was chief of staff there. I told him, 'Forrest, you gave me the job of training this outfit and I cannot do it with the base commander here. He is not the slightest bit cooperative and is not properly supporting me. I can't carry out my mission as long as he is running things.'

"Forrest asked where he was now and I said, 'Right here, I am in his office.' 'Let me talk to him,' said Nate, and he relieved him right then. He was fired. Word got around and that paved the way further down."

When the 96th began operations from Grafton Underwood, Old, like his predecessors and successors quickly learned that no amount of screening guaranteed performance under combat conditions. "I had a bombardier," said Old, "who was the best in the outfit. He could drop them in a barrel. He was as good a bombardier as I have ever seen. I was not on the mission and when they came back, we were anxiously waiting, standing out by the control tower to see how many goddamn airplanes were up there. We knew how many left and we were damn anxious to count the same number back. The lead airplane with this bombardier taxied up on the line and I was up there very anxiously looking at him. He gave this motion [to indicate], right on the button. Good. I knew we could count on him.

"Then we went in and developed the goddamn picture and shit, you couldn't even find the target in the pictures. The son of a bitch was nothing but thumbs. He couldn't stand that damn flak and those fighters. I think I wasted two missions on him and then put him back as a togglier [technician whose bomb release is controlled by a lead bombardier]. Don't give a damn how good he was out there on the practice range. How good was he when he was over there being shot at."

According to Old, common sense taught him that evasive action in the face of flak brought no real protection and it inevitably led to missing the target because the changes in air speed and angle among the bombers in formation significantly altered the direction of ordnance. He strictly insisted on a no-evasive-action policy during the bomb runs, believing the results proved him correct. "If you were a German fighter pilot leading a bunch of fighters out there, you would start looking for the ones split out a little bit, not in line. Every man in my outfit heard me harp all the time, 'Get that goddamn formation in there and keep it there if you are interested in a long life and doing a good job. The tighter the formation is, the better the bomb pattern. And those damn fighters looking at you, if you have a nice, tight, compact formation, they know there is a hell of a lot of guns that can start unloading on them.' The idea would be, 'Don't go for that guy. Look at the outfit yonder that is scattered all over the sky.' I didn't pass this information right on because I knew it would be unwelcome and have to be sold."

The ideas of the 96th CO meshed with the thinking of LeMay who had ascended to the leadership of the Fourth Bombardment Wing, making him Old's superior. "LeMay invited me up invariably after I led a mission," said Old. "We also had critiques on every damn mission where the lead crews would critique a half-dozen missions at a time. We would go over them in detail and discuss the mistakes. One of the things that made LeMay a great leader during the war was that after I had just led a mission yesterday, tonight he had me up at his place for dinner. We had a drink or two and we were talking about that mission. We ate and we talked about that mission. We had an after-dinner drink; we talked about that mission. I'll guarantee you that by the time we got through, he knew as much if not more about that mission than I did. I felt like I had to keep flying missions to stay abreast. That's why I flew a lot until LeMay would ground me. He would say, 'You're flying too much. Let someone else lead a few of them for a while.' Hell, the low group, the low squadron of the low group that was the hotspot. Everybody was always talking about it, so I would go down there and fly it. I would fly the low airplane of the low squadron of the low group. If you wanted to see a lot of fighters, that is where you saw them, particularly the head-on attack which the Germans primarily used." Old believed that he actively participated in seventy-two missions—often riding as an unofficial observer not only with the 96th but also later upon ascension to the top job in the 45th Bombardment Wing.

Along with the shooting war against Germany, the Eighth Air Force engaged in campaigns to win the hearts and minds of both the public and the policy powerhouses. That explains the presence of the likes of Andy Rooney and the unfortunate Robert Post on combat missions. Persuading the British leaders called for more subtle tactics than taking American correspondents along. One of the most influential local writers, Peter Masefield, air correspondent of the prestigious *Sunday Times,* had been a vociferous critic of the Eighth Air Force's approach and efforts. According to Archie Old, "Masefield made no bones about the fact that he thought daylight precision bombing was rather asinine. The Americans didn't know what they were doing. The B-17s could not survive. He was having a hell of an effect on public opinion in Britain."

Old recalled a telephone conversation with Ira Eaker who informed Old he would play host to Masefield in an attempt to convert the writer. "I am sending him down to you and you *will* sell him on daylight precision bombing," said the Eighth Air Force leader.

"General," Old said he responded, "I will do the best I can."

"That will not get it," snapped Eaker. "My directive to you is: *You will sell* Peter Masefield on daylight precision bombing, get him on our side in that damn thing to the extent that *he will* notify the British public about it, period!"

"I determined the only way to do this," remembered Old, "was to be just as frank as hell with him, not try to put on a show for him but let him see day-to-day operations there, exactly how we did it. That way we wouldn't be caught in anything that looked like we were covering up anything." Old allowed Masefield free run of the base, giving him acccess to briefings, the ability to interview any crewmen and even permitted him to bunk in with crews. The correspondent stayed with his story for close to a month. Midway through his sojourn, Masefield confided to Old that he had had his eyes opened and he appreciated the honest handling he received. He even flew a mission with the 96th and his stories in the *Sunday Times* now spoke favorably of the U.S. approach.

LEROY Kuest, from an Odessa, Washington, farm, drove delivery trucks after his high school graduation in 1936. Because an enlistee could pick his branch of service, Kuest volunteered in early 1942 and entered aircraft mechanics school with a postgraduate-type course in the maintenance of B-24s. "We had one training flight in a B-24," said Kuest. "I had flown once on a Stearman, two-place biplane that a barnstormer brought to a Fourth of July celebration at Odessa. He used my father's wheatfield as his base of operations and gave us kids free rides for use of the field."

Upon the award of his mechanic's diploma Kuest joined the 94th Bomb Group. "We were greeted by the CO, Major Saltzman and only then found out we would be in a B-17 group. The major sat on our beds, talked with us and told us we could transfer out if we wished. He was so nice we decided to stay. We had already checked out on four-engine aircraft and while the B-24 is mostly hydraulic and the B-17 electrical, it wasn't much of a change."

The ground crews of the 94th had steamed up Scotland's River Clyde in May. The 94th flew its first mission at the end of the month, then settled into permanent headquarters at an airdrome located in Bury St. Edmunds. By the third mission, Kuest was already noting in his diary, "Two planes were lost from our squadron and nine from the group . . . July 14: Today our ships went to Le Bourget, an air base in France [in the environs of Paris]. We were hard hit and lost three planes, Major Saltzman, Captain Frank, Lieutenant Purdy and crews were lost. Some were seen parachuting to safety. Lieutenant Purdy was hit head-on by a fighter; the pilot presumably dead, between number 2 & 3 engines and fuselage. The fighter just missed Major Saltzman in the lead ship. Nine chutes were seen opening from the major's ship. Some of our crews have returned through the French underground and everyone hopes the same for the major.

"July 16: Today we worked all day and night until eleven o'clock, as someone got the bright idea they wanted 698 to fly. When we finished no pilot was available, so we were rather browned off because of all the hard work for nothing."

Billy Southworth continued to praise some and blame others in his diary as he and those who had come to the 303rd and the United Kingdom with him approached their last missions. He remarked, "Just back from Kiel, where I dropped incendiaries, 4,000 pounds of them, tired as hell and glad to be alive. Fighters greeted us at sea and a continued two-hour battle ensued. Before it was ten minutes old I saw two fighters and three B-17s shot down. The fight out was fierce, ME-110s shooting from the front, side and rear, FW-190s bursting in from head-on. What a day, Cards lost to the Dodgers 1–0. Henderson shot one down at 200 yards."

A few lines later he confided, "An interesting question asked of me. 'Do you feel the same before each mission?' The answer is no. It used to be a big thing like the opening game of the season with the bases loaded, only more so. As we taxied down it was all business. The night before it was on one's mind, anxious to go but sleeping light as a mouse. First over enemy territory seemed like a new world waiting for the big fight to follow. Once it came, I worked harder than ever before and keen as a razor. It's all the same now, except preceded by a sound sleep, mindful of the crew, target position in formation and characteristics of the ship [I am] scheduled to fly. Mind on the new boys on my wing. Are they new? Green? Fly close? Stick in on evasive action? Do they understand their job and their ship? He bears watching or, I can count on him. Today I heard from Dad, the Cards beat Brooklyn. Took pictures of Clark Gable and met him." Toward the end of June, Southworth wrote of a number of farewells as various members of his crew recorded their twenty-fifth mission.

Southworth would complete his final mission July 17. It was an anticlimax. "Took a trip to Hanover and brought bombs back due to an overcast target. Dropped one of my baseballs on Germany and another on the field." He had taken to leaving these souvenirs strewn over Europe, to the undoubted mystification of the inhabitants. Southworth passed up an opportunity to go back to the States when offered a staff job with a promise of higher rank.

DESPERATE as the bomber command was for flight crewmen, they could not at this point extend tours without crushing morale. In the summer of 1943, as the number of missions piled up, so did the bodies. The 306th Bomb Group, for example, which had become operational in October 1942, with thirty-five air crews consisting of 315 men, lost twenty-seven of its crews and only eight completed the full twenty-five-mission tour. KIAs added up to ninety-three and POWS covered another eighty-eight. More than a dozen men died in training accidents and twenty-nine had to be relieved and reassigned. Other groups recorded similarly dire results.

Survival of the Eighth Air Force as a bomber weapon was thus by no means assured as summer approached. Drained of men and aircraft by punishment delivered by the foe and the need to siphon off assets for the Twelfth Air Force operating out of North Africa, the Mighty Eighth hardly offered the prospect of a long life to its members. On May 19, the publicity flacks could trumpet the news of the 91st Bomb Group's *Memphis Belle* as the first bomber to complete a twenty-five-mission tour without losing any of the crew. The feat, to be celebrated with a documentary film and later a fictional movie, only emphasized how fragile was the lifeline. Many crews and several groups had preceded the 91st to Europe ten months earlier and yet only this solitary bunch had completed a tour.

Whether flak struck a particular ship or a marauding fighter's 20 mm guns hit one bomber instead of another depended not only on the enemy's aim but upon a certain amount of chance. Hard luck even struck the 95th Bomb Group, which entered the lists at the same time as the 96th. Two weeks after beginning operations from the Alconbury airdrome, ground crews were loading the planes when a bomb load aboard one ship exploded. The blast killed nineteen men, seriously injured twenty and wrecked four other B-17s parked nearby.

The 95th also had the ill luck to be in an experiment devised by Brig. Gen. Nathan Forrest who had championed Old in his dispute with the South Dakota base commander. Dispatched to England where Eaker intended to name him a commander of the Third Division, an assortment of bomb and fighter groups, Forrest remembered Old offered a critique, saying "I am getting a very different picture of things over here than I thought. I have been on two missions now, and I think it is an absolute crime for us to ever lose a damn airplane to enemy action. There is no excuse for it."

"Hell," recalls Old, "we sort of looked at each other. We were not on those two missions but he must have been out on a couple of milk runs." The confident Forrest proposed a new type of formation for the bombers. Instead of the box at staggered altitudes formulated by LeMay, Forrest drafted a blueprint that flattened the setup, placing the planes wing tip to wing tip. He was convinced that this formation would concentrate fire-power ahead, below, above and to the rear. For two weeks the 95th practiced the new system and when the outfit headed for Kiel, the huge German naval base on the Danish peninsula, Forrest occupied the copilot's seat of the lead airplane. Forrest, concerned with the ongoing problem of machine guns freezing at high altitudes also ordered a different oil for lubrication.

Pilot William Lindley reported, "Landfall was made on the Kiel peninsula and within seconds the Luftwaffe fighters appeared. There were so many more black dots on the horizon, thicker than the gnats around the rear end of a camel. About the time I made the turn from the I.P. toward the target, heavy and accurate flak began bursting among our formation; the fighters pulled in front of us. The flak looked awesome but the FW-190s and ME-109s would put the fear of God in anyone. To see them attack head-on from the twelve o'clock position with their wings flaring and smoking from their machine-gun fire is frightful to say the least. The 109s also fired their cannon located in the nose hub . . . Awesome, particularly when one realized they are firing directly at us.

"For the next fifteen minutes I was in a state of absolute and incredulous shock. Between the exploding flak shells, the burning aircraft going down, excited voices yelling over the radio, and those concentrated and continuous fighter attacks, I spent half the time with my head in my steel helmet ducked down behind the instrument panel. The airplane was on automatic flight-control equipment, being steered by the bombardier. He managed to get the bombs away over the target area."

Lt. Robert Cozens, deputy leader of the group for the mission, said, "I was instructed to keep the nose of my B-17 tucked up under the tail of the lead aircraft. The Forrest formation was subjected to the 'true test' when, just as we completed the bomb run, the formation received a massive diving frontal attack from the German FW-190s and ME-109s. In our position in the formation, as well as that of our wingmen, we were unable to clear any of our guns on the attacking aircraft because of the line of sight through our lead echelon aircraft. Consequently, the lead aircraft was raked with enemy fire from one end to the other and immediately fell out of formation."

A total of sixty bombers from the Fourth Bomb Wing, hewing to Forrest's arrangement, attacked Kiel. "Goddamn," said Old, "the fighters blew him [Forrest] out right ahead of me. They took his whole squadron out at one time." Indeed, the enemy shot down ten ships from the twenty-four effectives of the 95th Bomb Group (with whom Forrest rode as an observer) and rendered one more fit only for the salvage heap. Nor did the other raiders fare much better; the 94th Bomb Group lost nine and Old's outfit another three, a daunting 37 percent casualty rate.

THE Casablanca conference of Churchill and Roosevelt, to which Fleming served on a crew that ferried Ira Eaker, set in motion around-the-clock bombing against the Third Reich's war industry. The massive British assaults upon Ruhr Valley installations hampered production and killed enough civilians to persuade the enemy to deploy increased numbers of fighter aircraft for defenses. At the same time, the Eighth Air Force in pursuit of its precision, daylight approach found itself battered by the FW-190s and ME-109s to nearly unsustainable levels, making deeper penetrations into the Continent extremely risky. The Allied high command decided that continued operations in the face of this formidable resistance demanded a shift in emphasis.

On June 10, 1943, RAF Bomber Commander Air Marshal Arthur Harris and his counterpart, the Eighth Air Force's Ira Eaker, received a directive which said, "It has become essential to check the growth and to reduce the strength of the day and night fighter forces which the enemy can concentrate against us in this theatre . . . first priority in the operation of British and American bombers based in the United Kingdom shall be accorded to the attack of German fighter forces and the industry upon which they depend." Perhaps not a whole-hearted reversal of the theory that winning the war did not require conquest in the skies, the policy, which became known as "Pointblank," called for destruction of aircraft in the air, on the ground and in the manufacturing process—air frames, engines, ball bearings and other components.

Pointblank delineated a series of sites for bombers to visit for sake of the goal. Means to carry out Pointblank against enemy fighters already on the wing, however, remained unavailable since the proposed targets for bombers lay well beyond the range of Allied fighters. Furthermore, to husband the limited number of U.S. bombers, the outriders were forbidden to leave the herd in pursuit of enemy marauders. Frustrated pilots watched coveys of hostile aircraft, lurking in the distance, awaiting the moment when the P-47s or Spitfires would be forced to return to base. Once the shepherds departed, the wolves would fall upon the flock, the Forts and Libs fending for themselves against the savage onslaughts.

In line with the objectives of Pointblank, the 306th Bomb Group headed for Tricqueville, a German air base in France. It was only a short hop across the Channel and James Wilson, although now serving as the group's executive officer, arranged to fly with his old squadron in honor of Capt. Raymond Check, an original pilot under Wilson, for whom this would be his twenty-fifth and final mission. Wilson took the left-hand command seat while Check acted as copilot. The ship's regular copilot, Lt. William Cassedy decided he could profit from a milk run and flew as one of the waist gunners.

The nineteen effectives from the 306th began to unload on the airdrome. Suddenly, a German fighter attacked Wilson and Check's ship from out of the sun. The Americans never saw the enemy, whose shells smashed into the cockpit during the bomb run. The explosion of shrapnel killed Check instantly and seriously wounded Wilson. A flash fire enveloped the cockpit. "Those models of the B-17," says Wilson, "had the oxygen and hydraulic lines side by side, which was not a good idea."

Wilson rang the alarm bell and the bombardier bailed out before any further signal. The engineer, Sgt. James A. Bobbet, descended from his turret and was injured when he grabbed an extinguisher to put out the blaze. According to Wilson, Bobbet laced him with morphine to dull the pain of his wounds and burns while he continued to pilot the aircraft. A history of the 306th states that Cassedy left his waist-gunner post and extricated the body of Check while Wilson, who had been operating the controls with his elbows because the skin from his hands was hanging in long strands, climbed down to the nose of the plane. There the pilot received emergency medical treatment from a flight surgeon who had gone along for the ride.

Patched up for the moment, Wilson went back to his post while Cassedy continued to fly the B-17. With all communications systems out and their flares for signaling distress consumed by the fire, Cassedy headed for the Thurleigh home base where he believed the wounded could get the quickest and best medical attention. To add to the copilot's distress, he was aware that the dead man was to be married to a nurse the next day and she would be at the end of the runway with a welcoming party to greet her fiancé as he completed his combat tour. Cassedy set the plane down against the flow of traffic and pulled off the runway away from the crowd. He was awarded a Distinguished Flying Cross and Wilson received a Distinguished Service Cross for carrying on despite his "excruciating pain." Indeed, the West Pointer endured nine months of hospitalization and treatment both in the United Kingdom and the U.S. before he could return to duty.

ON July 24, the Allies opened a subset of Pointblank, Blitz Week, a series of combined strikes by the RAF and the Eighth Air Force upon a wide ranging series of targets, Norway, Kiel, Hanover, Hamburg, Kassel and Warnemünde. Hamburg indicated one exception to the concentration against aircraft. The port city held shipyards that built and assembled U-boats as well as merchant and naval vesssels. As the Battle of the Atlantic, the threat to the seaborne lifeline from the U.S. to the United Kingdom, continued to rage, submarine pens and production centers stayed on the target list.

The raid by the British upon the port of Hamburg at the beginning of Blitz Week witnessed the first use of chaff, also known as window. Tens of thousands of strips of aluminum foil were released from a plane, which confused ground and air radar into believing a massive 11,000 planes were attacking instead of the actual 740 bombers. The local radar-guided searchlights wandered futilely through the night skies, antiaircraft batteries fired aimlessly. One German night-fighter controller was heard to shout, "I cannot follow any of the hostile; they are very cunning."

The British dumped 2,400 tons of explosives upon Hamburg during the night and when the Americans came the following day, their 350 tons, a fraction of the RAF contribution, nevertheless kept the pressure on the weary firefighters. Successive waves of British planes over the next three days bombarded Hamburg with incendiaries and ignited a firestorm. "The last day that we went," said Southworth's erstwhile gunner Bill Fleming, "you could see the smoke from a hundred miles away. When we flew over the city at 30,000 feet, the smoke was coming up through the formation. On July 26, I was making my fourth trip to Hamburg, flying with Lieutenant Lefevbre on the bomber known as *Flak Wolf*. At 28,000 feet over the target the plane was hit by I do not know what, either antiaircraft or a fighter plane. We went into a diving spin and the pilot rang the bail-out alarm but nobody could jump out because the centrifugal force was holding us. The experience is impossible to describe. Once I couldn't move, I knew there was no way we could come out of that dive and I was going to die. The fear I felt was unbelievable.

As we came down, somehow, even the pilot couldn't say later how he did it, he pulled that plane out of the dive. We started at 28,000 feet and leveled off only at 6,000.

"Once he leveled off, everybody was very quiet. I realized I had a terrific pain in my left leg, a searing pain. I thought I'd been hit by anti-aircraft. I tried to paw along my clothes to see where the hole in my clothes was but couldn't find it. Then it dawned on me. I had wet on myself and shorted out my electric suit and it was burning me from my crotch down to my ankle, resulting in a solid blister all the way down. When we got back I spent two weeks grounded on that account. It wasn't that funny when it happened."

The holocaust at Hamburg reached 1,000 degrees Centigrade, creating a tornado of fire that yanked trees from the ground, burned up asphalt streets, sucked human beings from buildings into its vortex, cremated citizens alive in their bomb shelters. Those who did not succumb to fire died of smoke inhalation or asphyxiation from carbon monoxide. The official figures counted 50,000 dead but no one really knew the amount because the city held vast numbers of slave laborers, displaced persons and foreigners. An estimated 900,000 residents were homeless. When Fleming read an account in the GI newspaper *Stars and Stripes,* he said it disturbed him. "German children and old people were there. Of all my experiences that's the one that continues to bother me, even though I never spoke to my wife about it."

Hamburg cost the RAF 2.8 percent of the dispatched aircraft, eighty-seven of 2,592 sortied. The Mighty Eighth paid a much higher price for Blitz Week, 8.5 percent of its attacking force or eighty-eight aircraft from 1,720 sorties. In real numbers the picture was actually worse as the Eighth could not even muster 200 heavies upon conclusion of Blitz Week. For that matter, the Hamburg effort also exhausted the RAF. According to Dudley Saward, a former RAF group captain and author who visited Albert Speer, Nazi Germany's minister of armaments production after the war, a similar sacking of a half-dozen other German cities immediately on the heels of Hamburg might have actually ended the war. Whether this would have been the case is questionable but in any account the British bombers could not return in force for another two weeks and in markedly fewer numbers.

Over Oschersleben, the Germans scored their first air-to-air rocket hit, blowing up a B-17 from the 385th with such force that two more Forts from the group went down. The most notable first for the Americans during Blitz Week was the use of auxiliary fuel tanks on the Thunderbolts which were previously restricted to about 200 miles from home bases, able only to escort as far as Amsterdam. Frustrated by the apparent inability or unwillingness of the folks back home to produce jettisonable tanks, VIII Fighter Command contracted locally and slung a cardboard version on the P-47s. However, these added a mere sixty miles, leaving the big planes still unprotected when they ventured any significant distance beyond the coastline. The newest B-17s installed "Tokyo" wing tanks that allowed them to travel considerably farther, eventually enabling them to reach anywhere in Germany. Overall, however, Blitz Week may have done more damage to the Eighth Air Force than to the German war effort. When the period ended, the heavyweights basically stood down for nearly two weeks.

8

SUMMER FIRE

In principle Pointblank set a limit to the types of targets which the Allied air arms would strike, but in practice the spectrum of targets widened as almost any kind of industrial or manufacturing site could be related to the enemy air strength. Certainly, the huge oil refining plants located at Ploesti in the heart of Rumania could qualify as vital to the German fighter effort. If this source of petroleum could be eliminated the Nazi war machine would be forced to rely on costly and scarce synthetics extracted from coal. Ploesti lay beyond the arms of even the longest-range RAF bombers in England but the Allied conquest of Rommel in North Africa led to bases at Benghazi, putting the Rumanian oil complex within reach of B-24s equipped with extra fuel tanks.

Strategists plotted a low-level attack that might evade early detection, would conserve fuel for the extended run and enhance bombing marksmanship. Intelligence reports erroneously indicated weak antiaircraft defenses manned by unenthusiastic Rumanians protecting an approach from North Africa. Supposedly, the flak batteries expected any raiders to come from the east, originating in the Soviet Union.

In preparation at the end of May 1943, two B-24 bomb groups in England, the 44th and 93rd, halted their missions for the Eighth Air Force and practiced low-altitude flights and maneuvers. They were joined by the 389th, which had yet to go operational. Within a few weeks all three outfits flew to North Africa, temporarily attached to the Ninth Air Force for a strike at Ploesti.

Ramsay Potts, then a major and squadron leader for the 93rd Bomb

Group recalled, "We were told there was some sort of special mission coming but not what it was. While we were training, the higher echelons were holding their conferences, discussions and arguments. Conditions were not very good. The food was terrible, C rations, maybe some canned fruit salad and it was terribly hot. Sandstorms, frequent high winds during the day forced us to work on the planes at night, after six o'clock and before seven in the morning. The sand blowing in the engines was difficult to deal with. We had a large number of diarrhea cases; everyone lost weight.

"We flew a few missions up into Italy and one long one to the Messerschmitt plant at Wiener Neustadt. Then we settled down to practice low-level runs over some dummy installations in the desert. The planning, training and briefing preparations were quite thorough. We were briefed on our approaches. We had dummy mockups for targets. Everything that we could do within limitations was done. The mission was recognized as being of utmost importance and everyone had a real keenness that it had to be accomplished at any cost.

"We had some RAF bomber pilots who had flown through barrage balloons in Germany and they briefed us on balloons surrounding Ploesti. Operations officers and the command were a little skeptical but we accepted the hazard of the balloons as one of the things you had to go through. We had been briefed on the balloon barrages, the flak defenses, the fighter units and their locations. We had been briefed on the hazards of exploding oil tanks and distillation units. The low-level aspect didn't frighten anybody. Many of us looked forward to this because it was the only way to get the necessary range out of the airplane.

"It was to be a thirteen-hour mission. Even with an extra tank in the bomb bay, you couldn't have done it flying at a high altitude. Five groups were going and attacking seven targets. The 93rd was split into two forces. The main one was to be led by Colonel Baker, the group commander, and the other by our former group commander, Colonel Timberlake who'd just been promoted to brigadier general. He was going to fly in the copilot seat of my airplane. Just prior to the mission, Gen. [Lewis] Brereton [9th Air Force chief] decided there were too many generals going and he told Timberlake not to go. That meant I had to act as commander of the force as well as be the pilot."

The top echelons were aware of how precarious the business could be. Brereton, unscathed despite his stint as MacArthur's Air Corps chief in which the Japanese destroyed half of the entire B-17 fleet in the Philippines on the ground eight or nine hours after word of the events at Pearl Harbor, said, "We expect our losses to be 50 percent, but even though we should lose everything we've sent, hitting the target will be well worth it."

At 4:00 A.M. on August 1, tower controllers fired flares into the dark skies to signify beginning of Operation Tidal Wave, and *Wingo Wango,* the leader for the entire attack rolled down the runway. Like the other planes it was laden with extra fuel and ammunition as well as the maximum bomb tonnage, but it also bore the lead navigator for the attack. Of the 178 Liberators headed for Rumania, one crashed on takeoff killing most of the crew and ten aborted en route. Potts, piloting *Duchess,* recalled, "We formed up and started over the Mediterranean, seven different task forces numbering about 175 planes. We were flying at low altitude, maybe a few thousand feet over the Mediterranean and quite a bit spread out. Looking out, I saw the lead airplane suddenly turn off to the right and then he fell into the water and burst into flames. It was a shock and my radio operator who was pretty callous, stood up and said, 'Look at that fire.' I was so indignant that I turned around and knocked him back into his seat."

Unfortunately, the doomed *Wingo Wango* not only carried the mission lead navigator to his death but also lost its wingman, who dropped down to scout for survivors and drop them rafts. He found none but the time and fuel spent in his fruitless search made it impossible for him to climb back into position. He headed back towards Benghazi, taking with him the deputy route navigator. Other B-24s pulled up into the empty slots but key personnel were now gone.

Undeterred, the B-24s skimmed the water until they crossed the coast where Albania and Greece meet. "We started climbing up to get over the mountains," said Potts, "and ran into a few cumulus clouds. I stayed in close on the heels of the leader of the second group and we wound our way through these clouds, over the mountains and then started to let down to the minimum altitude over the Danube Plain. But the four task forces behind us had disappeared. We didn't know what had happened to them. They vanished while we were passing through those cumulus clouds. We in the first three groups were still together but couldn't see the ones who'd been following."

In *Teggie Ann,* Col. Keith Compton, the Ploesti expedition commander, flanked by Brig. Gen. Uzal Ent, IX Bomber Command boss, anxiously studied the landmarks that delineated the last navigation keys before the final bomb run. The topography, the streams, even the villages and towns looked similar and the leaders became confused. Believing they had reached the final marker, Compton instructed *Teggie Ann*'s pilot to bear right.

"We were all getting keener and keener," recalled Potts. "My navigator and I were coordinating with each other. On the intercom he gave me the time of nine minutes to the Initial Point. Just after he said this, the leader started to turn to the right. I was behind him, a little bit higher and about the same altitude as the number two group which was in echelon off to the left. When both of them turned to the right, I did also, because I couldn't do anything else. I was boxed in. I checked again with the navigator and he said that wasn't the right place. We were still short of the Initial Point. At the same time as we completed the turn, the descent to treetop-level started.

"This was part of the bomb runup to the target. The plan was to do this in line abreast with each task force assigned its own refinery. Within the task force you had elements come across in line in a sequence. The leaders, first over each target, had delayed action bombs in the hope they wouldn't have anything blowing up in front of the planes coming behind in their attack. As we came down to the minimum altitude, we seemed to have made a mistake with the turn and I broke radio silence and talked to the leader."

One of the forceful exponents of a low-level attack, Maj. Norman Appold, piloting one of the B-24s, broke radio silence to shout, "Not here! Not here!" Potts reportedly exclaimed, "Mistake! Mistake!" Other aircraft now chimed in.

Remembered Potts, "He [Compton] said he was aware they had made the wrong turn and now were going to turn back to the left. It was unclear to me exactly what he was going to do at this point, making almost a 180 or perhaps 165 degree turn to go back to the I.P. but he did start his turn. You could see Bucharest up ahead. We had good visibility but we were going along at 210 miles per hour right on the deck with a lot of confusion everywhere. After we made this turn, it was established that the leader was going to the right, coming in on his target by skirting the Ploesti area and coming in at a heading of 180 degrees opposite the one he was supposed to follow."

The first consequence shifted the Liberators to a path directly over the heaviest flak concentrations in the area. As the ground batteries opened up, gunners on the B-24s sprayed the installations with countering fire. The second result of the error on *Teggie Ann* fortunately lengthened the distance between the air armada and the enemy fighter fields, delaying the arrival of hostile interceptors. Because of the deviation, ground spotters issued alarms not only for Ploesti but also Bucharest, thereby confusing the defenders.

"By this time I was coming up and running over some refineries," says Potts, "and we were being shot at by a lot of small antiaircraft weapons on the ground—machine guns, 40 mms and that sort of stuff. We gradually approached our target for an attack on it. Some other planes in my outfit actually dropped their bombs on the refinery we had just passed over. I think they may have been confused, believing maybe this was the target, or else maybe they were hit because quite a few planes in my formation were shot down. They may have simply jettisoned their bombs at the earliest target of opportunity. We made our [prescribed] attack but I don't think more than three airplanes in the unit actually hit the refinery they were supposed to. We had made our drop on the primary target because I had a very good navigator and he knew at all times exactly where we were. Some others had either been hit and felt it necessary to jettison or else did not know where they were because we had come in from a totally unfamiliar direction. There had been no study or planning for a runup from the southerly direction. I had no trouble with the barrage balloons but one plane in my group hit one, partially shearing off his wing. My airplane had been hit several times."

Others fared much worse. A direct hit in the bomb bay of *Euroclydon* ignited an auxiliary tank needed for the return trip. Flames sprouted from the tail and amidship as bodies hurtled free. One chute opened, another did not. The B-24 smashed to earth in flames. *Hell's Wench,* bearing Col. Addison Baker, the 93rd's CO, struck a balloon cable, then absorbed four punishing blows, hit in the nose, wing, wing root and ultimately the cockpit, setting it ablaze. Fire raged in the now mortally struck B-24. To remain in the air and lead to the target, *Hell's Wench* dumped its ordnance, a few minutes before the bomb-release point. The flaming aircraft bore on, passing up an opportunity for a crash landing in wheat fields to aim at an opening between a pair of refinery stacks. Another pilot saw a man tumble out of the nosewheel hatch, his parachute burning as he drifted by so close they could see his burned legs. Whoever was at the controls, by Herculean effort, held the fiery wreck on its course until it fell to earth. Even though several tried to jump at the last moment, no one survived. A third doomed B-24, both wings sheared off, careened toward the ground and another suddenly exploded into a gaseous red fireball.

"While others were dropping on different installations," said Potts, "my target lay right in the middle of the Ploesti defenses. I went through those on the southern side of the refineries and then through the main defenses, passing over the northern side batteries before we finally got through. On the way home, as we were turning at low altitude in the target area, we came abreast of what appeared to be a distillation unit, a cracking plant. My left waist, a young fellow about nineteen years old, let loose with a barrage of .50 caliber machine gun at the unit which suddenly burst into flames. That was sort of a dividend."

As the aircraft waded through the ground fire over the refinery, one of Potts's wingmen, *Jersey Bounce,* already wounded by a Rumanian air force plane, faded toward the ground, only two engines running. The bomber burst into flames as it mixed sparks with leaking gasoline. Five of the crew perished. The others became prisoners.

The task force that included Ramsay Potts had been the first to reach Ploesti and now the other formations roared in to meet a barrage from thoroughly aroused defenders. The wall of enemy fire forced the commanders to cancel the prearranged objectives and signal a targets-of-opportunity attack. That enabled some who surely would have perished to evade destruction but nevertheless dozens of B-24s blew up in midair, blossomed deadly flames and tumbled or dove into the ground for their final spasms of life.

Appalling as the carnage was from antiaircraft fire, the nightmare entered a new phase as enemy fighters arrived on the scene just as the first elements from North Africa completed their runs and fled. A substantial number of the later Americans, battered by the ground batteries, were victimized by the savvy German fliers.

Said Potts, "We came out of the target area, turned left to head home. I regrouped the remaining airplanes in my formation and we started back. It seemed to me I had ten or eleven planes in my formation at that point; I think we had fifteen when we began. We had lost four or five in the target area.

"As we climbed over the mountains coming out of the Danube Plain, we ran into those cumulus clouds again but they seemed thicker. I gave the signal to loosen up the formation to go through them. As we came out of the clouds, my right waist gunner reported that parts of an airplane were falling down through the clouds. One of the best pilots in my squadron, flying with a very good formation pilot on his wing but who always tried to fly a bit too close—I'd warned him about it—flew in very tight, not loosened up enough. When they went into the clouds, the two planes came together. I never got any report on them until after the war I learned that three or four of the crew had survived."

The other wingman for Potts, *Lucky*, limped towards home with a cannon shell hole in the bomb bay tanks, costing it much of the gasoline required to get across the Mediterranean. The pilot chose to gamble with an emergency landing at an airfield on Sicily where he smashed into a row of recently repaired P-40 fighters. Other ships, some with dead and desperately wounded set down at Malta or at emergency strips in Libya.

"When we got home," said Potts, "I believe there were seven airplanes from my formation that landed at the base and some landed elsewhere. A couple went down in Turkey and another was lost. It was a very gloomy base that night."

Of the more than 1,600 airmen who got off the ground for Tidal Wave, more than 300 died, hundreds more were wounded or captured and seventy-nine were interned in Turkey. From the 178 Liberators assigned to the affair, only thirty-three could be listed as fit for duty the following day. It was altogether the worst day in the Air Corps' war so far. Perhaps conscious of the impact upon morale, the authorities conferred four Congressional Medals of Honor (two posthumously) upon individuals; no other mission during World War II brought more than a single such decoration to the men involved. Two subsequent attacks on Ploesti added another pair of Medals of Honor to crewmen (both recipients KIA on scene), bleak testament to the ferocious defenses that surrounded the oil complex.

The fire smoke and destruction observed by the aircrews and shown on reconnaissance photographs taken after August 1 indicated a serious blow to enemy facilities. President Roosevelt apprised Congress of the casualties but declared, "I am certain that the German or Japanese High Commands would cheerfully sacrifice tens of thousands of men to do the same amount of damage to us, if they could." But in fact, Ploesti prior to Tidal Wave functioned at only an estimated 60 percent of capacity. While some installations had been reduced to rubble, the production pace quickly resumed a normal rate. Had the Ninth Air Force the resources, quick followup attacks on Ploesti might well have accomplished the stated goals, but in the summer of 1943 it had borrowed all the Eighth could spare. The Air Corps lacked ships and crews sufficient to recover swiftly after a maximum effort.

Ploesti registered one essential fact with the Air Corps. The surest, most awful route to disaster lay in low-level attacks by its heavyweights. Unfortunately, within a few weeks, an event of almost equally awful magnitude would befall the Eighth Air Force.

THE strategists in England had schemed to implement Pointblank more directly with a twin strike at the Messerschmitt factory in Regensburg and the ball bearing plants at Schweinfurt, both of which lay deep inside Germany. Curtailment of enemy fighter-plane production at an installation that supplied 200 MEs a month was an obvious goal. Schweinfurt churned out 42 percent of the country's ball bearings, the antifriction mechanisms vital to aircraft, tanks, weapons, ships, subs and manufacturing operations. For the first time, the magic figure of 300 heavy bombers would be reached with 376 planes from sixteen bomb groups assigned to the runs.

Actually, the strategists had planned a three-point attack. While the UK-based heavyweights slammed Regensburg and Schweinfurt, groups from North Africa, including those lent to the Ninth Air Force for Ploesti would return to England via Wiener Neustadt, site of a Focke Wulf factory. However, the bomber groups based in England, busy pounding airfields in hopes of suppressing fighter attacks and plagued with the habitual weather problems, postponed their effort. Carl Spaatz, commander of the Ninth, impatient with the delay and prodded by Hap Arnold in the States as well as his RAF colleagues, ordered the strike against Wiener Neustadt for August 13 without waiting for the Eighth to dispatch its aircraft.

Ramsay Potts flying one of the 93rd's B-24s to Wiener Neustadt recalls, "It was another thirteen-hour mission, with no fighter escort like all those flown from North Africa. When you got attacked by enemy fighter planes it was just a question of trying to fight it out. Because of previous strikes at the Wiener Neustadt plant, the Germans knew it was in range of our bombers. Therefore, they increased the flak defenses as well as the enemy fighters in the target area.

"It was very important that we compress our attack time in order to have minimum exposure to flak. I led the third group. As we flew up toward the area, the second group lagged behind and I closed in as much as I could trying to get them to move up. When we finally got to the target area and the second group still hung back, I went ahead and closed in the gap. Finally, we were over the target and I was now number two in sequence rather than number three. That didn't compress the attack as much as I wanted but it helped.

"If you have the maximum amount of planes going through over the target at about the same time, the ground guns can only fire at the lead planes, and by the time they reload, resight and reaim, a number of planes have passed over. The gunners then must pick up someone from the rear. So the number of shots any battery can take at a formation is more limited than if you are spread out, giving them time to set up and take aim on each little element that goes through.

"We came off the target and there was a very severe fighter attack from the rear. It centered on the original number two group which now occupied the third position. If I hadn't closed in, the fighters would have hit us. I didn't know in advance this would happen but the other group had very heavy losses, as much as half their force. I think my group lost only two airplanes.

"We got home and the other group commander, who had survived, was very upset about his losses to severe antiaircraft plus aggressive fighter opposition. He and I had rather strong words about what happened. There was a board convened to analyze whether there was any fault or blame. Finally, they said I'd done the right thing closing in. But for a while that didn't relieve the tension between the other commander and me. After a while when he had thought about it, he realized it was just one of the things that happen in a war. If he had been where he should have, my groups would have caught the heaviest part of the attacks, not his. Later we became friends."

Meanwhile, the script organized the B-17s into a single compact force that would split south of Frankfurt with 230 ships from the First Air Division and attack Schweinfurt before returning to England while the remainder, drawn from the Third Air Division commanded by LeMay (planes in his squad were equipped with Tokyo tanks) continued towards Regensburg, 110 miles southeast. From there they would then fly over Austria and Italy to bases in Algeria. Even on paper the affair dismayed the participants. The crews who attended the predawn briefing on August 17 and saw the maps with the extended ribbons into southern Germany understood what they faced.

On August 17, exactly one year after the very first B-17 paid a call on occupied Europe, the Eighth Air Force gave the go signal. At the scheduled takeoff times a ground fog settled that was so thick it made taxiing aircraft to the runways impossible, halting operations. The dense clouds extending high above the United Kingdom obscured the skies, rendering formation assembly too susceptible to midair collisions. Bomber Command delayed the beginning of the mission to Regensburg for ninety minutes. LeMay, who had insisted that those in his Fourth

Bomb Wing practice instrument takeoffs, advised Bomber Command he believed his outfit could get airborne if he used ground crews with flashlights to guide the aircraft as they taxied to the end of the runways. Bomber Command then uneasily signaled for the start. Any further wait meant the aircraft would be hunting for the unfamiliar Algerian fields as darkness came. LeMay himself scrambled aboard the lead aircraft for the 96th Bomb Group. Archie Old, under orders to stand down, would not make this trip.

The assembly above the overcast skies went off relatively smoothly but an angry LeMay demanded to know where were the missing escorts and the First Bomb Wing (assigned to Schweinfurt). The P-47s, socked in by the weather and without the navigational tools aboard the bombers, never connected with the Fourth Bomb Wing. The Schweinfurt groups, also bowing to the restrictions on visibility, continued to wait for better conditions. Disgusted, LeMay headed for Regensburg without the others. When the First Bomb Wing got off the ground, it was almost four hours late, eliminating any possibility of the two forces entering Germany as a united phalanx or dividing German predators enough to prevent concentration upon either element. In fact, having hammered LeMay's troops advancing on Regensburg, the Luftwaffe had time to refuel and rearm their planes to savage those bound for Schweinfurt.

ONE of the most recent additions to the Eighth Air Force, the 100th Bomb Group, as part of LeMay's contingent, took off from its base at Thorpe Abbotts northeast of London. Operations officer Maj. Jack Kidd, occupying a copilot's seat, led the group which filled the unenviable position of the last outfit in the formation. Born in 1918, Kidd grew up under comfortable circumstances in the suburbs. "While I was living in Winnetka, Illinois, they had these air races on a grass-covered field outside of town. I saw Jimmy Doolittle set a record of 305 miles per hour, going around these pylons set ten miles apart and I was hooked. I told my parents that I wanted to become an airline pilot. As soon as I had two years of college at Oberlin—I majored in business and paid no attention to world affairs—I enlisted in the Air Corps. When I graduated from Kelly Field in 1940, I immediately became an instructor. Then I applied for B-17 training and after thirty days I checked out in the airplane."

In 1942, the Air Corps activated the 100th Bomb Group. "There were five names on the original list," said Kidd, "and mine was one of them. I was now the commander of the 351st Squadron. It is a measure of how fast things were happening. When I enlisted the Air Corps had about 2,000 planes and 50,000 men. At the height of World War II there were 78,000 aircraft and two and a half million people involved. In a period of eighteen months I went from second lieutenant to lieutenant colonel."

The rapidity of expansion inevitably generated turmoil, causing stumbles and bumps in organizations like the 100th in its rush to action. The original CO of the 100th, Darr Alkire, and several of his top associates, expert pilots Bucky Egan and Bucky Cleven, personified the stereotypical airmen. They swaggered, sported 100-mission crush hats and indulged their penchant for good times. Many of the raw crews assigned to the 100th aped their leaders and by January 1943, a series of incidents convinced the top brass of serious disciplinary problems. The hard-drinking group commander departed; others in positions of authority received demotions. Jack Kidd, whose squadron had demonstrated discipline and proficiency, moved up to the post of Group Operations Officer. Still, when the 100th traveled overseas its baggage included a reputation for carousing, a disregard for rules and a lack of conformity to the proper combat practices. The notoriety would later haunt the 100th.

Harry H. Crosby, a navigator for the 100th, commented, "Essentially the 100th had two personalities and they came from our leaders. Alkire and the two Buckys were flamboyant; Bill Veal, Ollie Turner and Jack Kidd were businesslike. Down in the ranks, we had to live with that ambiguity, and Jack Kidd helped us make that adjustment. Jack was our stricter self, our less romantic self, but he was such a great flier and leader that he could get by with it. He did not let us do evasive action on the bomb run. He did not let us lose 500 feet between the I.P. and the target.

"I remember once during a briefing the air crews were acting up and making smartass, ribald remarks. Jack pointed to one and said, 'Stand up.' Jack said, 'You're the kind of person who does not listen. Unless you shape up, you will be the kind of person who does not come back from a mission.' The man sat down and the briefing was quiet."

Like all staff officers, Kidd flew selected missions. On his first one to an airfield near Paris, German fighters dove from on high to attack his formation. "That was the only time I ever saw them come straight down. Usually they went ahead of the unit, turned and then came head-on to limit their exposure to our fire. The fire from our twenty-one-plane formation, about a thousand feet deep and about 300 feet wide, with from ten to thirteen .50 caliber machine guns must have been hair-raising for a German pilot to fly through.

"Somebody else was scheduled to lead that shuttle mission from the 100th [Regensburg] to Africa but at the last minute I was put in as the command pilot to lead our group which was the last and the lowest in the 3rd Division." Some 240 P-47s sought to provide safe conduct for the B-17s as they entered enemy air space. Unfortunately, those assigned to protect the Third Division never caught up with those bound for Regensburg. "The enemy fighters," reported Kidd, "seemed to gang up on us. It took less fuel for them to get up ahead of the group and come on back in. The further ahead they flew, the less fuel they would have. Their fire was murderous."

Harry Crosby, as navigator in Kidd's aircraft, noted the appearance of the first Focke Wulfs over Holland as the fifteen-mile-long fleet of B-17s entered enemy radar screens. "Gaggles of ME-109s and FW-190s came up behind us, paused for an instant and then slid up and under us. Arcs of our .50 caliber tracers and their 20 mm cannon fire scorched the sky. Beams of horror threaded our formation. The tail gunner reported, 'The whole last element in the low squadron went out.'" Crosby wrote in his logbook the names of the crew commanders shot down and counted thirty lost friends from the three aircraft. The lead of the trio had blown up; no chutes. As the opposing aircraft flailed away at one another, both sides scored kills; the ball gunner reported over the intercom that he had counted sixty parachutes in the air at one time, men leaping from bombers and fighters.

In the copilot seat of a 100th B-17 sat Lt. Col. Beirne Lay, a veteran of just four missions but expected to command a bomber group. He was on hand as an observer, charged with drafting a first-hand account of events along with recommendations for improvements in procedures. Based upon what he saw, Lay would later coauthor the screenplay for the film *Twelve O'Clock High,* with Sy Bartlett, another Eighth Air Force staff officer. (Veterans of the air war over Europe consider it the best movie ever made on the subject.)

"At 1017 hrs," said Lay in his official report, "near Woensdrecht [Holland] I saw the first flak blossom out in our vicinity, light and inaccurate. A few minutes later . . . two FW-190s appeared at one o'clock level and whizzed through the formation ahead of us in a frontal attack, nicking two B-17s of the 95th Group in the wings . . . Smoke immediately trailed from both B-17s but they held their stations. As the fighters passed us at a high rate of closure, the guns of our group went into action. The pungent smell of burnt powder filled our cockpit, and the B-17 trembled to the recoil of nose and ball-turret guns. I saw pieces fly off the wing

of one of the fighters before they passed from view. . . . For a few seconds
the interphone was busy with admonitions; 'Lead 'em more' . . . 'short
bursts' . . . 'don't throw rounds away' . . . 'there'll be more along in a
minute.'

"A coordinated attack followed, with the head-on fighters coming in
from slightly above, the nine and three o'clock attackers approaching
from about level, and the rear attackers from slightly below. [Lay's sight-
ings explain the apparent discrepancy between Crosby and Kidd, whose
vantage points differed.] Every gun from every B-17 in our group and the
95th was firing, crisscrossing our patch of the sky with tracers to match
the time-fuse cannon shell puffs that squirted from the wings of the Jerry
single-seaters. I would estimate that 75 percent of our fire was inaccurate,
falling astern of the target—particularly the fire from hand-held guns.
Nevertheless, both sides got hurt in this clash, with two B-17s from our
low squadron and one from the 95th Group falling out of formation on
fire with crews bailing out, and several fighters heading for the deck in
flames or with their pilots lingering behind under dirty yellow parachutes.
Our group leader, Maj. John Kidd, pulled us nearer the 95th Group for
mutual support."

The dismayed Lay looked out his window at two entire squadrons
of interceptors climbing to a parallel position ahead of the 100th, preparing to turn and slash through the formation. Over the interphone he
heard reports of a similar situation building on the other side while down
below more enemy planes rose into the air. Off to one side and out of
range sat an ME-110, there to radio information on the disposition,
route, speed and other vital information on the Americans.

"At the sight of all these fighters, I had the distinct feeling of being
trapped—that the Hun was tipped off, or at least had guessed our destination and was waiting for us." Americans frequently insisted the Germans picked up advance word on missions but more likely, it was the
early-warning radar stations that tipped the Luftwaffe to impending
operations. "No P-47s were visible," continued Lay. "The life expectancy
of the 100th Group suddenly seemed very short, since it had already
appeared that the fighters were passing up the preceding groups, with
the exception of the 95th, to take a cut at us.

"Swinging their yellow noses around in a wide U-turn, the twelve-
ship squadron of ME-109s came in from twelve to two o'clock in pairs
and in fours and the main event was on. A shining silver object sailed
past over our right wing. I recognized it as a main exit door. Seconds

later a dark object came hurtling through the formation, barely missing several props. It was a man, clasping his knees to his head, revolving like a diver in a triple somersault. I didn't see his chute open.

"A B-17 turned gradually out of the formation to the right, maintaining altitude. In a split second, the B-17 completely disappeared in a brilliant explosion, from which the only remains were four small balls of fire, the fuel tanks, which were quickly consumed as they fell earthward.

"Our airplane was endangered by various debris. Emergency hatches, exit doors, prematurely opened parachutes, bodies and assorted fragments of B-17s and Hun fighters breezed past us in the slipstream . . . I watched two fighters explode not far beneath, disappearing in sheets of orange flame, B-17s dropping out in every stage of distress, from engines on fire to control surfaces shot away, friendly and enemy parachutes floating down, and on the green carpet far behind us, numerous funeral pyres of smoke from fallen fighters, marking our trail.

"I watched a B-17 turn slowly to the right with its cockpit a mass of flames. The copilot crawled out of his window, held on with one hand, reached back for his chute, buckled it on, let go and was whisked back into the horizontal stabilizer. I believe the impact killed him. His chute didn't open.

"Our B-17 shook steadily with the fire of its .50s and the air inside was heavy with smoke. It was cold in the cockpit, but when I looked across at Lt. Thomas Murphy, the pilot, and a good one, he had sweat pouring off his forehead and over his oxygen mask. He turned the controls over to me for a while. It was a blessed relief to concentrate on holding station in formation instead of watching those everlasting fighters boring in. It was possible to forget the fighters. Then the top-turret gunner's twin muzzles would pound away a foot above my head, giving a realistic imitation of cannon shells exploding in the cockpit, while I gave an even better imitation of a man jumping six inches out of his seat.

"After we had been under constant attack for a solid hour," continued Lay, "it appeared certain that the 100th Group was faced with annihilation. Seven of our group had been shot down, the sky was still mottled with rising fighters and it was only 1120 hours with target-time still thirty-five minutes away. I doubt if a man in the group visualized the possibility of our getting much further without 100 percent loss. Mentally I had long since accepted the fact of death and that it was simply a question of the next second or the next minute. I learned first-hand that a man can resign himself to the certainty of death without becoming panicky. Our group firepower was reduced 33 percent, ammunition was running low. Our tail guns had to be replenished from another gun station."

Lay detailed the enemy tactics, noting that the fighters employed a frontal approach to the low and lead squadrons while menacing the high element from the rear. He felt that the more experienced of the foe relied on a slower rate of closure that gave them greater accuracy and these veterans seemed able to time their thrusts to moments when the top and ball-turret gunners were occupied with rear and side defensive shooting. Less skilled pilots tended to press their attacks to a mere 250 yards to improve their marksmanship but that set them up as point-blank targets for the Americans.

"Near the I.P. at 1150 hours, one hour and a half after the first of at least 200 individual fighter attacks," said Lay, "the pressure eased off, although hostiles were still in the vicinity. We turned at the I.P. at 1154 hours with fourteen B-17s left in the group, two of which were badly crippled. They dropped out soon after bombing the target and headed for Switzerland . . . Weather over the target, as on the entire trip, was ideal. Flak was negligible. The group got its bombs away promptly on the leader. As we turned and headed for the Alps, I got a grim satisfaction out of seeing a rectangular column of smoke rising straight up from the ME-109 shops, with only one burst over the town of Regensburg."

The copilot observer regarded the trip to Africa as anticlimactic. Only a few fighters ventured to peck at the planes and a single burst of flak greeted them over the Brenner Pass. "At 1815 hours, with red lights showing on all our fuel tanks in my ship, the seven B-17s of the group who were still in formation circled over Bertoux [the Tunisian airfield] and landed in the dust." Miraculously, Lay's ship bore only a few souvenirs of the mission, holes around the tail from flak and 20 mm shells.

Kidd recalled, "We lost seven out of our twenty-one airplanes on that mission. [Official figures say nine.] One of ours belly-landed on a lake in Switzerland and they spent the rest of the year there. The flight to Africa was about twelve hours, quite a number of planes hit the water. We landed at a little dirt field that was hard and smooth. We stayed for a week. At a postmission critique, General LeMay asked me where the rest of my airplanes were. I said, 'They were shot down, sir.' That ended the conversation."

In fact, the totals for the Third Division appalled everyone. Of the 127 "effectives" after nineteen aborted, twenty-four B-17s went down and one more could not be restored. Fifty aircraft needed repairs. Aircraft could be replaced relatively quickly and painlessly as the war plants in the States accelerated into high gear. The human cost of Regensburg was another matter. The aircraft that survived brought back four dead or mortally wounded and nine men who required hospitalization. Two hundred MIA were either dead, in prison camps or enemy hospitals.

IN the wake of Regensburg, as the 100th appeared to incur higher losses than other units, the August 17 raid spawned a legend. In his account Beirne Lay included a vignette: "One B-17 dropped out on fire and put its wheels down while the crew bailed out. Three ME-109s circled it closely, but held their fire, apparently ensuring that no one stayed in the ship to try for home." It was believed by many that wheels-down over enemy territory signaled surrender. In his next sentence Lay said, "I saw Hun fighters hold their fire even when being shot at by a B-17 from which the crew was bailing out."

Some chroniclers may have telescoped the two different incidents. Rumors and stories subsequently claimed that a damaged B-17 from the 100th lowered its gear and then while German aircraft circled it without firing, the bomber suddenly erupted with .50 calibers and knocked down a handful of the would-be protectors. Other German fighter pilots enraged by this treachery promptly sent the offending B-17 into a death spiral. As a consequence, the 100th was allegedly marked for special attention whenever it showed over the Continental skies.

The offending B-17 pilot supposedly was a veteran of the 100th, Robert Knox. Credence for the tale came from Knox's navigator, Ernie Warsaw, after researcher John Miller interviewed him. Warsaw told Miller, the attacks on the aircraft shut down two engines and destroyed the hydraulic system near Cologne. The crew, given a choice between Switzerland and Thorpe Abbotts chose the latter. Warsaw said, "After flying for approximately five to ten minutes at approximately 15,000 feet, a group of Messerschmitts and Focke Wulf fighters were approaching from five o'clock and surprisingly gave no indication of attacking— it was as if they didn't see us. When they came within range, as fire control officer I gave the order to fire."

Warsaw continued, "I shot down three of the attackers and when I followed one of them down I noticed our wheels were down . . . When had that happened? Our intercom was shot up and didn't function . . . It was probable that one of the attacks had severed the electrical system or destroyed the fuse panel on No. 6 bulkhead, causing some malfunction or a short actuating the landing gear mechanism . . . No one had heard Knox saying anything about putting down the wheels—the signal for aerial surrender."

Contradicting the navigator, bombardier Ed Tobin, who occupied the front area with Warsaw, told Miller he did not see the wheels down and added that Knox, intent on reaching safety with only two functioning engines was too good a pilot to increase the drag caused by an extended gear. Still, Warsaw contended that after he finally reached a POW camp and identified his group to the other captives, someone remarked, "Oh, yeah, the Bloody 100th. You were the guys who keep firing after your wheels are down."

Writer Martin Middlebrook pursued the investigation further and identified the three German fliers credited with shooting down the Knox B-17. The report by one of them, Oberleutnant Barte, details how the trio in ME-110 night fighters hunted for crippled bombers. The others in Barte's flight struck first; both fell victims to the .50s on Knox's ship and made emergency landings. "I came around from the front," said Barte "and got off just one short burst. That was all the time there was from the front . . . One wing fell completely off—the right one—and the bomber spun down." (Six in the crew died, including Knox, while Warsaw, Tobin and two others entered stalags.) Significantly, the German fighter pilots interviewed never mentioned wheels being extended nor did they indicate they saw any compatriots being shot down.

Oddly, Middlebrook discovered a B-17 guilty of the actions imputed to Knox. A B-17 from the 390th Group, badly damaged, limped toward Switzerland. As it nosed down with pilot James Regan at the controls, the wheels were lowered, feasible in this instance because the descent maintained flying speed. Two fighters hovered in close proximity presumably serving as an escort. None of the bomber crew could have heard a surrender signal, if one were sounded, because the intercom was destroyed. When an enemy fighter incautiously moved within range, machine guns shot it out of the sky. Its companion then blasted the Regan plane. Six men including Regan perished but Middlebrook confirmed the account with four who survived the crash landing.

As death and destruction piled up in the 100th, airmen invoked the spectre of the Knox plane. Whether or not the incident actually occurred and whether anyone was guilty by design or accident in no way explains what befell the Bloody 100th. Luck of the draw and the disposition of groups in the formation determined whether one received a drubbing or not from flak or fighters. Choice of placement such as Ramsay Potts recounted over Wiener Neustadt was a rarity. The history of an outfit did not enter into the calculations of the flak gunners who used radar to track their often invisible targets far above them. The shell might not have the name of one's crew on it but if destined to explode a wingman laden with bombs and fuel, both planes went down. Enemy fighters selected their quarry for tactical reasons, charging through echelons of bombers in order to scatter them, rendering them less able to support one another. Wounded ships, stragglers, and echelons decimated enough to reduce their fields of covering fire were the most inviting prey. The deadly nature of aerial combat during World War II allowed no room for personal crusades. Finally, with closing speeds near 500 miles per hour, not even the most keen-eyed Luftwaffe pilot could have spotted the 100th's Square "D" insignia from a distance and pursued them.

Those who bedded down in North Africa after Regensburg, however, knew only that they had lived to fight another day, which as Jack Kidd recalled came a week later. "On the way back, we had to refuel our airplanes by hand out of fifty-five-gallon drums, and 2,400 gallons was the capacity, wearing out a lot of pumps and arms. Bombs also had to be loaded. We bombed a Bordeaux submarine base and then landed back at Thorpe Abbotts."

Regensburg was only half of the savagery visited upon the Eighth Air Force on August 17. An even bigger armada of 188 B-17s (a whopping forty-two from those originally dispatched chose to call off their participation for mechanical or other reasons) struck at the ball-bearing center of Schweinfurt. Brig. Robert Williams, a black patch over an eye destroyed by shrapnel during a London raid, commanded the 1st Bomb Wing from one of the 91st Bomb Group ships. The long time interval between the start of this mission and that of LeMay's enabled the enemy fighters to restore themselves sufficiently to greet the day's second stream of B-17s with equal fury. For ninety minutes, from the Belgian coast to the target, in the midst of flak, the MEs and FWs battled the stolid procession of Forts.

More than 424 tons of ordnance exploded amid the ball-bearing factories, seemingly inflicting serious damage. The return from the target eased only near Eupen on the German–Belgian border where squadrons of P-47s appeared to fly shotgun. When back on the ground, the 1st Bomb Wing counted thirty-six B-17s missing with 352 airmen. Three aircraft which crash-landed in England went on the scrap heap and another 118 required the attention of mechanics and sheet-metal workers. The planes that made it to bases carried twelve wounded and three dead.

The maximum effort drained so much strength from the Eighth Air Force that for the following two weeks, the magnitude of missions dropped below 100 bombers per objective.

9

FALL FIASCOS

The first major thrust at the enemy after the twin blows at Regensburg and Schweinfurt was in response to intelligence from the French underground and reconnaissance photos. The site in northeastern France, known as Watten, housed some mysterious excavations and odd-looking structures. It was apparent that whatever the purpose of the installation, the enemy was investing heavily in manpower and materials. In fact, Watten contained the works for launching the first of the V-bombs at England and qualified as a legitimate threat to the Allied military, the British civilians and the war effort in the United Kingdom. Under strict definition, the target fell outside the mandate of Pointblank. But in fact Allied Air Forces, and particularly the British (especially Arthur Harris who continued to believe the German will to continue the war could be crushed along with their loved ones, homes and factories), never confined themselves to facilities directly connected to the battle for the skies.

It was, however, strictly in accord with Pointblank as the newly activated First and Third Bomb Divisions, made up of B-17 groups, including the 100th, scheduled 338 aircraft to attack Stuttgart, a locale featuring avionics and more ball-bearing factories. Well over one-fifth of those dispatched on September 6 aborted while en route because of mechanical failure or were overwhelmed by the miserable weather conditions. Those that assembled in ragged formations and labored on towards the briefed objectives encountered fierce resistance from enemy fighters, then coped with an opaque cloud veil over the target.

Navigator Harry Crosby with the 100th Bomb Group wrote, "We split up and dropped our bombs wherever we could. We got rid of our load over a German airfield at Conches. Other flights bombed Bernay, St. Martin and Evreux . . . One plane left us near Stuttgart and headed for Switzerland. They crash-landed in Lake Constance, the ball-turret operator dead. Most of the crew were badly injured . . . My roommate at Tulare primary flying school, Sumner Reeder, lost his copilot, his head nearly blown off. Reeder dived down to the deck and played hide and seek in the clouds. His navigator, even though he had lost an eye, filled in as a copilot. Our group was hit so badly that our crews landed at whatever landing strip they saw first." At that Crosby could count his outfit lucky that it belonged to Curtis LeMay's Third Bomb Division since LeMay insisted all of his B-17s bear Tokyo tanks. The less fortunate members of the First Bomb Division, operating without the extra fuel, incurred worse injury; twenty ships ditched or crash-landed because they ran out of gas. Luck and the skill of the RAF Air-Sea Rescue teams preserved the lives of all 118 airmen aboard the dozen planes that fell into the cold, turbulent waters.

THE Bloody 100th hemorrhaged again on October 10, while trying to destroy the railroad center at Münster, a gateway vital to Ruhr Valley enterprises. The yards lay in the center of the old walled city and the impact upon civilian workers was obvious. Maj. Bucky Egan insisted on leading the outfit to avenge the downing of his equally flamboyant colleague Bucky Cleven, shot down over Bremen a few days before. At the premission session, Egan recalled, "Miner Shaw's voice [the intelligence officer] drones on that we are going to sock a residential district. At this point I find myself on my feet cheering. Others who have lost close friends in the past few raids join in the cheering, 'cause here is a chance to kill Germans, the spawners of race hatred and minority oppression. It is a dream mission to avenge the death of a buddy." According to author Richard LeStrange, despite the hurrahs, some men "were clearly apprehensive about purposefully bombing civilians, including slave laborers, for the first time."

To the disappointment of those bound for Münster, the P-47s left them some nine minutes from the target when replacements, delayed by ground fog, did not arrive on schedule. In the interim, an estimated 200 enemy aircraft swooped down upon the bombers with the baker's dozen ships of the 100th the center for their attention. In the group's lead, *Mlle. Zig Zag,* Egan at the copilot position, started a slow descent after a rocket apparently smashed into the plane's belly. Flak had already killed a waist gunner and wounded the ball-turret gunner. "It was obvious that we'd had it," remembered Egan. "Brady [Lt. John, the pilot] and I pulled off our oxygen masks to say simultaneously, No. 2 [engine] has quit . . . there goes one . . . and there goes three. No. 4 proceeded to run away." The crew shoved free a pair of wounded in their parachutes and then everyone bailed out.

The slaughter of the 100th went on unabated. A rocket attack destroyed the air worthiness of *El P'sstofo*. Its crew salvoed the bomb load and all ten men floated to the ground under their silk canopies. *Shackrat* exploded in midair and only two men, blown free, lived. In succession or simultaneously, the action was deadly swift, a trail of blazing, exploding and crashing B-17 wreckage. From the Initial Point to the target twelve from the 100th succumbed. Only *Royal Flush*, piloted by Lt. Robert Rosenthal, unloaded over the Münster objective and started towards home, albeit with one engine already out. Savaged en route, *Royal Flush* lost another engine and its oxygen system but managed to stave off the assaults and land at the home field, Thorpe Abbotts.

Two days later, the 100th drew the honor of leading the 13th Combat Wing, composed of three groups, against the submarine pens along the river at Bremen. Jack Kidd, as command pilot for the venture [Ev Blakely piloted the plane and Harry Crosby navigated], says, "The sky was beautifully clear. The technique was to pick an initial point, and at this predesignated spot, to peel off and bomb one group at a time. The flak up ahead, black splatters in the sky got thicker and thicker, an ominous sight. I remember praying the most earnest ones I have ever prayed, watching that flak just before we went in on the bomb run. On the bomb run, the command pilot has absolutely nothing to do. The bombardier is actually flying the airplane through his bombsight and you just sit and watch and wait.

"Just about at bombs-away at 24,000 feet, we were caught in what they called a box-barrage of flak. Sixteen German gunners on 88 mm guns, twenty-five-pound shells, all fired at the same time to fill a cube of air space with shrapnel that broke into bits of half an inch or so. Pretty deadly stuff to airplanes, equipment, engines, people. We were bracketed perfectly. Within seconds almost, nine out of our twenty-one airplanes were in trouble.

"We had a momentary fire on our No. 3 engine. The propeller hub on our No. 4 was hit and all of the oil came out, the shaft broke and we had windmilling props on No. 4 and No. 3. We had 500 miles or so back to the British coast on two engines on one side. It kinda looked like a hopeless situation. We were doing about 100 to 115 miles an hour which was all we could manage and we kept losing altitude. We were all by ourselves. I didn't realize at the time but from Bremen to the Dutch coast, the gunners in back of me were extremely busy. The official report was a claim of twelve, ten shot down by this one airplane. I believe that was a record for a single B-17.

"Crossing the Dutch coast at about 3,000 feet, you could look down and see the muzzles of the guns flashing as we went overhead. We kept losing altitude and it looked like we were going to go into the water for sure. The North Sea in October was rather chilly and our chances of survival weren't very good. We started throwing everything overboard, gun barrels, guns, even the self-erecting bombsight, a $15,000 instrument which at that time seemed like a tremendous lot of money. A B-17 then cost about $250,000, compared to today's B-2 bombers that cost up to $2.4 billion." Harry Crosby recalled dumping spent cartridges swept up from the floor, their .45 pistols, woolen flight clothes, even his jacket with its gold officer's insignia.

"We had to fly at an angle of about fifteen degrees in order to go straight. The compass didn't work that great at this angle. We simply pointed the nose toward the sun which brought us to the English coast. We managed to reach a ceiling of about 1,200 feet and saw a dummy airfield, not a soul on it. We circled it and came in and landed. The pilot was Ev Blakely. We hit the ground; the tail wheel did not come down. With all the potential for fire all the switches were cut. At the instant of contact, the rudder cables snapped. Here we were a projectile traveling at seventy to eighty miles per hour along the ground, absolutely out of control. There were two large oak trees off the runway and we headed directly for them. We peeled off the nose. Someone later counted 800 holes and our life rafts were absolute sieves. We'd never have survived if we'd ditched."

Four of the gunners including one Crosby described as having his "whole lower body smashed and bleeding" required medical help. In fact, the 100th had seven planes shot down with their crews plus Kidd's aircraft which was obviously damaged beyond repair.

Against such ever vicious resistance by the Third Reich, the Mighty Eighth slowly bolstered its combat effectives in terms of bombers and fighters. The 306th Bomb Group welcomed the B-17G models. These latest Forts answered the challenge of the German fighters' head-on tactics with a chin turret, providing machine guns that fired forward. Staggered waist windows enclosed the formerly exposed positions of the gunners amidships, previously constantly menaced by frostbite. Delivered without camouflage paint which never concealed the presence of the bombers, the new ships added a few miles to their speed and the now standard Tokyo tanks extended range considerably.

New fighter groups boosted the ramrod personnel. Among them Robert "Punchy" Powell. "I had my first flight when I was about seven," says Powell, "with a barnstormer flying out of Bluefield, West Virginia. He was giving rides in an open-cockpit aircraft for two dollars. I was so excited that I forgot to get my change for the five dollars I gave him and my Dad was mad as hell when he discovered it." Like so many of the era, the Powell family would regret the error a few years later as the Great Depression struck and the breadwinner, a banker who owned service stations among other investments, lost everything and could only find work as a police sergeant employed by a steel company.

After the attack by the Japanese, the nineteen-year-old Powell, with a high school diploma and a year in college passed the aviation cadet exam. "In Primary, the instructors were civilian pilots, some old, some young, mostly tough and demanding. I remember yelling for joy when I soloed, cleared the telephone lines at the end of the field in my Stearman, then circled the field and brought it in for a landing a tremendous and joyous kick in the ass.

"In Basic we encountered our first military flight instructors and they were much more demanding, less understanding and damned tough to please. Our Advance teachers were much easier to work with, realizing that most of us who had reached that stage would probably get our wings unless we really screwed up. They concentrated on teaching us aerobatics, formation flying, instrument flying and a smattering of air-to-ground and air-to-air gunnery.

"We had an opportunity to state our preference for fighters or multiengine aircraft but I don't think it mattered much. There was no real consistence in the selection except that the great big guys, six feet or over, were almost always sent on to multiengine school. I think the Air Corps' needs at any particular time were the primary criteria for selection. Whatever Uncle wanted, Uncle got.

"I got my wings and commission in January 1943, and went to Cross City, Florida, where they had been training fighter pilots in P-39s. We were the first class in P-47s. With only about thirty-plus hours in the Thunderbolt, we were shipped over to England, fifty of us as replacement pilots in April 1943." At that point, the 4th Fighter Group, already in combat operations, was in the process of transition from Spitfires to P-47s. While the 4th, and subsequently the 56th and 78th took over full responsibility for escort of U.S. bombers, Powell and the other replacements learned more about their trade which included the first opportunity to fire the weapons on a P-47. When the students graduated they were sent to the earlier three fighter groups and the 352nd which became Powell's address.

The 352nd started to make its rounds in September. "Since only a few of our pilots had experienced combat," said Powell, "when we flew our first missions, most of our knowledge of tactics came through on-the-job training. If you survived your early mistakes and learned from them, your chances for survival and success multiplied with each mission. Our debriefings were shared by all and every experience was a learning one, if you paid attention, and most of us did because we knew the consequences if we did not. Most of us believed we had better aircraft, better training and better fighting spirit than the German pilots. Long after the war, however, I told Gen. Adolf Galland [a high-scoring ace and eventually fighter aircraft commander for the Luftwaffe] 'I didn't really learn to fly until the first time one of your fighters got on my ass.' He laughed and said he had the same experience flying during the Spanish Civil War where most of the early German pilots got the opportunity to test themselves in combat."

Some of the replacement fliers, however, benefitted from assignment to the veteran fighter groups. For example, those that went to the 56th Fighter Group spent at least a month under the supervision and instruction of the experienced pilots, who included not only Bob Johnson but also the renowned Hub Zemke and Francis Gabreski.

Like Jim Goodson, Powell lavishes praise upon support staff. "We had excellent ground crews. The maintenance of the aircraft was superb and I never once found fault. I had only two aborts for mechanical reasons in my eighty-three missions and one of these was a defective radio. Just so I could fly my own plane, *The West by Gawd Virginian*, on a mission for which I was scheduled, Bob Lyons my crew chief assisted by others changed my engine during the wee hours the night before. Bob came to wake me early in my Nissen hut to tell me the plane was ready, but needed a couple hours of 'slow timing' [breaking-in an engine] before I could fly it on a mission. I got up and flew it so it would be ready. Less considerate crews would have just let me fly someone else's plane not scheduled for that mission. Also, I recall plugs were required to be changed after a specified number of hours of flying time. Lyons and the other members of my crew somehow managed to secure new plugs for my ship and changed them much more frequently."

Lyons himself, a draftee from Newark, New Jersey, hoped to become a cadet. "I was too tall at six feet, five inches. I had always loved to work on cars. They sent me to the Air Force School in Lincoln, Nebraska, Factory Air Craft School for the P-47, and then in Scotland later, on P-51 engines. I joined the 352nd when it was being formed and we got to England July 4, 1943. The work schedule consisted of inspections—daily preflight and starting and running the ship. Following missions, complaints, if any, from the pilots, were taken care of. After daily inspections there were twenty-five-, fifty- and 100-hour inspections. The more hours, the more complex the inspections. All this was done on the line but if the work got too involved the plane was taken to a Quonset hangar for a crew there to work on it." After the fighters took off, Lyons and the other ground-crew people worked on idle planes while sweating out the return of the mission. "If it was too long, we would check with operations to see how things were going."

For both American fighters and bombers, prospects remained bleak. The unpleasant truth accepted by intelligence experts indicated that while the first assault on Schweinfurt had cut production of ball-bearings by 38 percent the enemy appeared to have repaired much of the damage. The strategists drew up plans for a second raid. Unbeknownst to the bomber command, the enemy was aware that a concentration of works for such a vital item invited attention, and had begun to disperse the production facilities, substituted other kinds of bearings for less critical uses and had begun to purchase the items from Sweden.

Well in advance, the bomb groups began to prepare for Schweinfurt. As a mechanic with the 94th Bomb Group, Leroy Kuest toiled on a B-17 named *Marge H* for the pilot's wife, with five missions to its credit. On September 27, *Marge H* was last sighted disappearing into a cloud bank with a smoking engine after a single enemy fighter had attacked the Fort. "We really had a swell crew," mourned Kuest, "and everyone had a long face when they failed to return." A day later Kuest told his diary, "Nothing more has been heard about our crew as yet. Last night some English Stirlings and Halifaxes which couldn't find their home base because of rain and fog, landed at our base. We serviced them and had an awful time finding the places for everything. They look like big clumsy boxcars or as Mac says, a big dog sitting down on his ass."

Less than a week later, Kuest reported receipt of a brand-new ship, #453 to replace their lost *Marge H*. In the diary he also announced a move to a different barracks. "We are getting new combat crews and must make room for them. We have three original crews left and they have about completed their twenty-five missions." Subsequently he recorded the departure of twenty-two aircraft from the 96th for Bremen. "This was our ship's first one. It really got banged up. A piece of flak hit the pushrod on No. 4 engine. Oil covered the whole wing. We worked all night changing this." On the next day #453 flew another mission and returned with its No. 4 prop feathered after the engine stopped while the B-17 was over the target. Kuest and others in the ground crew worked on the engine and finally changed it. On October 13, he noted, " . . . went up for an hour's slow time . . . just as we were taking off a wire shorted out and we thought surely we would crash." That evening, Kuest and some companions departed from Bury St. Edmunds on a one-week furlough in Scotland. He toured historic sites, dined in hotels, danced with "really beautiful girls" having "a swell time" in "a soldier's paradise."

While he was gone, the mechanical problems with #453 apparently convinced the 94th air crews that the ship was unreliable. When the group would take off for Schweinfurt on October 14, #453 was not part of its caravan. Instead, the plane was lent to the 96th Bomb Group, desperately in need of aircraft.

The 96th Bomb Group, Archie Old's former command [he now led a wing], not only borrowed planes, but also filled its ranks with replacement crews. Bob O'Hearn, a North Dakota farmer's son, born in 1919, attended a country, one-room schoolhouse for the first eight grades of his education. A high school graduate in the depths of the Depression, O'Hearn joined the Civilian Conservation Corps, one of President Franklin D. Roosevelt's therapies for unemployed youth. He clerked, served as an educational advisor and then quit for a construction job. O'Hearn matriculated at the University of North Dakota, paying his dorm rent through a janitorial job. Unable to hack it in academia, he found a home in civil service as a railway mail clerk. The draft in 1941 reduced his pay from a comfortable $2,400 a year to $21 a month.

"The Air Corps was a cleaner, better-paying life than the infantry and I was selected for the Cadet program in the fall of 1941," remembered O'Hearn, "but due to quotas, my flight instructor at the civilian school had to eliminate two of his students. I did eight frozen hours in an open-cockpit Stearman before I agreed with the instructor that I could kill myself. Without regret I went back through the system and Bombardier School and then was chosen for Navigation School to be dual rated.

"In Walla Walla, Washington, I was assigned as navigator on a crew that would go to England as a replacement in the 96th Bomb Group. I liked them all in my crew—like the E. A. Guest poem: 'Men that are good, men that are bad, as good and as bad as I.' At twenty-six I was the oldest, except for the radioman, Pat Putnam, age thirty, who falsified his age to get into the Air Corps. His language was the most obscene of the crew. He didn't worry about regulations as long as there was a way around them. Si Nettles our pilot did okay, wasn't dictatorial. Jerry LeFors, the copilot, was an ex-civilian pilot and would have made a good crew commander. On passes I went off base with LeFors while Nettles and Bombardier Ed Jones were buddies. Gene Sebeck the engineer, a tough-looking nineteen-year-old, had the look of a man you could rely upon. The assistant engineer, Greg Drobinko, joined us after the assigned man came on duty drunk and was a waist gunner. Marshall Hamer, the ball gunner, was our innocent. Typical expression was 'Geee'! Ken Karlson was the assistant radio op and a waist gunner. Charles Sibert, quiet and solid, manned the tail gun. I don't believe we would trade any of our airmen, if we could. We liked them all."

O'HEARN and his crew would be making only their second mission when they headed for Schweinfurt. Their introduction into aerial combat over Bremen had been anything but reassuring as three ships from the outfit went down and another thirty-two, including their own aircraft, were damaged. In fact, the 96th cadged a B-17 from the 94th in order to send O'Hearn and company to Schweinfurt four days after Bremen. The plane was #453, the ship on which Kuest had worked.

When the intelligence officers at the briefings removed the curtains covering the maps that showed the target and routes a predictable chorus of groans and gallows humor quickly faded to silence. The crews for the 320 planes assigned to Mission 115 of the VIII Bomber Command listened to data on weather, predicted areas of heaviest fighter and flak activity, comments on the importance of success, and the usual ominous prisoner-of-war instruction reminders. All were told to wear dog tags, regulation GI shoes, carry their escape kits which included maps, fake identification as civilians and German currency. They also were reminded to remove any squadron insignia or papers useful to enemy intelligence.

Archie Old, now a wing commander, knew of the destination well ahead of time. "It was another one of those where I was told I would lead and therefore was grounded for probably two or three weeks. Still, there was a very obvious leak. Intelligence was picking up all the damn fighter movements over in Germany and putting them along the most plausible route. We knew we were going the day after tomorrow and then [seemingly aware] they started moving a hell of a lot of fighters into certain areas. We had that kind of intelligence; we had guys there who told us."

Scheduled to fly to Schweinfurt, O'Hearn with the 96th, Bill Fleming with the 303rd, Old, as a wing commander, and more than 3,000 airmen heard a message from Brig. Gen. Frederick L. Anderson, commander of the VIII Bomber Command. "To all leaders and combat crews. The air operation today is the most important air operation yet conducted in this war. The target must be destroyed. It is of vital importance to the enemy. Your friends and comrades that have been lost and that will be lost today are depending on you. Their sacrifices must not be in vain. Good luck, good shooting and good bombing." And at one briefing, supposedly, an anonymous voice responded, "And goodbye!"

The importance of the mission's success placed Archie Old, CO of the Forty-fifth Wing, in the copilot seat of *Fertile Myrtle III* from the 96th Bomb Group, the lead ship for the entire flotilla. Also aboard was Capt. Tom Kenny, operations officer for the 338th Bomb Squadron who occupied the left seat, and group navigator Maj. Robert Hodson, assisted by lead navigator Capt. Bill Jones, were responsible for guiding the armada. Stationed at the Norden was 96th Group bombardier Capt. John Latham, who would sight the target first.

Once again clouds mangled the grand design. Assigned as the low element in the Fortieth Combat Wing with the 92nd and 306th Bomb Groups, the 305th could not find the rest of the formation when it broke through the overcast at the assembly area. In order to participate in the mission, the 305th instead accompanied the First Combat Wing to the target. Unavoidably, the absence of the 305th weakened the combat box formed by the Fortieth Wing. All together, sixty-two Forts dropped out for various reasons. The B-24 bomb groups recently returned from North Africa, failed to add their numbers to the strike force. Swifter than their B-17 cousins, the Liberators had been given a longer route but the thick overcast cut the assembled planes to fewer than half of those dispatched and they executed only a diversionary feint before retreating to England.

Chinks in the entire wall of bombers had opened up even before it advanced over the Continent. Adding to the woe, the P-47s, their fuel capacity although slightly augmented with belly tanks could only convoy the 291 B-17s as far as Aachen, 240 air miles from Britain, well short of Schweinfurt. Even at that, the 4th and 352nd Fighter Groups could not locate their bombers in the murk and barely groped their way back to their bases. The 56th and 353rd Fighter Groups, however, not only chaperoned B-17s but when the enemy showed they quickly engaged him. The Luftwaffe pilots withdrew, bloodied after a series of dogfights at 30,000 feet, prime conditions for the Thunderbolts.

However, as soon as the "Little Friends" regretfully bade farewell to their "Big Friends" the Germans stalked the B-17s unmercifully. Rockets, mortars propelled by rockets, air-to-air bombs and massed attacks by fighters bearing cannons and machine guns poured into the formations.

From his seat in the lead airplane Archie Old recalled, "German fighters came up from every point of the compass after our fighters turned around. Then when we made our turn and were going in, I think the copilot standing there said, 'Look, the damn First Division got ahead of us.' I said, 'First Division, hell! That is flak.' He said, 'Do you mean we have to go through that?' I said, 'Tom, I don't know any way to get to the target without going through it.' He thought the flak was a whole lot of airplanes up there. They were already throwing it at us when we were five to ten minutes away from the target." For all of the fury visited upon the Americans, *Fertile Myrtle III* had gone unscathed until the final moments of the bomb run.

"The fighters were all over us. They really got interested in me," said Old. "Enemy fighters took a bit of a dim view of taking you on and their own flak, too, but some would. I noticed the fighter action dropped off when we started getting into both barrage and tracking flak." The fortunes of the plane and Old now shifted radically. An antiaircraft shell burst just in front of the nose. The blast and fragments ripped into the compartment where bombardier Latham sat, wounding him in his head and legs. "Little Hodson," said Old, "got him under the arms, sat him back on the stool and said, 'Hit that target, you son of a bitch.' The guy [Latham] started thumbing those damn knobs and did a hell of a superb job of bombing. We had it on automatic pilot; that's where you could do the best piloting because the bombardier is flying the airplane. Some of my lead crews, I would have to threaten to court-martial them if they didn't do that because they thought they could fly it better. They couldn't. The equipment was all geared together." With Latham tending to his Norden instrument, the ordnance tumbled an accurate arc to strike the designated factory.

However, the crew had no time to savor its triumph. According to Old, "We maintained our course because we had to catch the bomb impact with our camera. There were other aircraft in the formation, at least three or four, also with cameras in case ours malfunctioned. Soon after we started a turn to the right, about a minute later, Whambo! There were twelve or fifteen fighters in formation, coming back. I could see flak going over, black smoke all over the goddamn place. You didn't worry about it until you could hear it. Then you knew it was damn close. Barrrooom! Barrrooom! A dull explosion. All hell broke loose down in the nose. It could have been either fighters or flak but I think it was both. The explosive 20 mms were coming in the nose and I think we got hit with flak too. Hodson was killed immediately. Bam, he just went down."

The enemy fire struck bombardier Latham, wounded the second navigator Bill Jones and knocked Old out of his chair. "They took out both of my inboard engines, Nos. 2 and 3. Both were burning. I immediately called for feathering. No. 2 would, but No. 3 continued windmilling, acting like a brick wall. All of the other aircraft in this group were in the same turn and we had to pull out and abort, an obvious move to keep from going down. I stayed under my group for as long as I could for whatever protection they could give me as the Germans were extremely adept at getting cripples and they had no scruples about it.

"We knew we had to get down in a hell of a hurry and to hell with how much punishment the airplane could take. We knew a B-17 could take quite a bit. We rolled the stabilizer all the way forward and actually put our feet on the wheel and pushed it to make that son of a bitch go down as quickly as it could, a thousand miles an hour but we didn't give a damn. It would fly apart long before that but we had to get down quick.

"There was 50 percent cloud cover and between 2,000 to 3,000 feet in this particular area. We leveled out, and of course here was a whole bunch of fighters, probably eight or ten. They would get in on the kill. When I got to the cloud cover, we straightened out. Then with two engines running practically full power, No. 2 feathered, No. 3 windmilling, the damned airplane wouldn't fly. It isn't supposed to fly that way but with both engines feathered, it would maintain airspeed because we had dropped our bomb load, a lot of fuel was gone and we were expending quite a bit of ammunition, making it a pretty light airplane.

"We had no option and I told the crew, 'I have a flight plan to get back home,' but when you're taking severe evasive action in those clouds to try to throw the fighters out of the way, it is a little bit hard to follow a ninety-degree course. The airplane would not fly so we had one possibility and all the way along there were two or three members screaming, 'Let's bail out!' But hell, I had an airplane full of wounded people, some so severely injured they couldn't bail out. I wasn't going to go out and leave them in there.

"My bombardier was wounded and so was the pilot but not seriously.

In fact, there was a waist gunner who didn't get wounded. But he was the only man in the damn airplane without a scratch. I got mine in the right wrist, from the explosion of a 20 mm. It bled like a stuck hog all over the place. (Since then, every once in a while I have a piece cut out.)

"To get back, we had to start those bad engines. We would unfeather No. 2 and go through the starting procedures. It would start giving us power and we were doing okay. Then it would begin burning again. We'd cut it off and feather it. Then we'd do the same with No. 3, but there we could forget about feathering. It too would run, produce power, about the same length of time as the others until it too caught fire again. We started, shut off and started those damn engines several times.

"We would go into a cloud and then turn and straighten out. When we would come out and had momentarily thrown those fighters off, I would head for the next cloud. Knowing my course, I would if I could, go left. I didn't want to be doing any circles. If I was supposed to make another turn say thirty minutes after I made one, I might go ahead for maybe forty minutes instead of the thirty because of the turning I'd done. [By this time] the fighters were out of gas too. But the antiaircraft people on the ground were tracking us and any other damn airplane in there. Fortunately, the weather started getting worse.

"We were supposed to hit the English coast just south of the Thames River. The weather got solid and sure looked good to us. We knew we had to be going across the coast when the small caliber ack-ack started getting heavier. It was heavier along the beach. As soon as we knew we were over the water I gave the order to get rid of every damn thing in the airplane. I looked down one time and a guy was about to throw my parachute out. I took a damn dim view of that. I said no. We threw guns, radios, anything we could break down. We were flying in kind of a nose-high position about ninety to 100 miles an hour, squishing through that soupy, solid stuff. Our next worry: we could miss England pretty damn easy. With all this messing around it ain't so damn far from the Thames to Land's End [the western coast]. We had no damn radios so how do you know you are going right? You don't know whether the weather is zero zero all over that damn part of the country.

"All at once, I saw a flicker of light, then another flicker and then it started lighting up. We came into clear sunshine and there was the coast of England. That was lucky. But we didn't know where; it turned out to be about fifty miles farther south than we were supposed to be; farther away from home.

"We had these wounded guys hurting like hell, and most of them were hollering, 'Land at the first damn airport you come to.' But I knew that it was only another 150 miles or a little less to our home base where I knew we would get a lot better care than landing on any one of the many bases." *Fertile Myrtle III,* however, had given the beleaguered crew about all it could and the worsening condition of the engines demanded a landing at the closest base. An RAF fighter installation at Gravesend, with a grassy strip, hove into view.

"We started shooting out a lot of flares, making them damn well aware we were in trouble. We put the gear down. The electrical system was all shot out but we were still able to drop it by its [the gear's] weight. I put the flaps down, depressed ten to fifteen degrees and then started burning on one side, another damn fire. It was from leaking gasoline and a spark or something set it off. I went over the fence at the end of the runway and made a helluva good landing. It didn't bounce, just stuck. It wasn't too far from the fence over yonder. Goosing the No. 1 engine swung a wing around and we sort of paralleled that fence. While we were still moving at about fifty miles an hour, the goddamn firetrucks were running alongside of us, spurting foam. They nearly blinded me but hell, they got the fire out before we stopped." According to pilot Tom Kenny, when Old dropped to the ground through the nose hatch he said, "Save me a pew in church on Sunday."

Aside from the navigator, two other members of the *Fertile Myrtle III* crew lost their lives, the ball gunner and one of the men manning a waist position. "One waist gunner didn't get hit at all," said Old, "but the other one died. It was a matter of luck, where you stand. It was luck that I only got hit in the wrist."

In the B-17 #453, *Wolf Pack,* borrowed from the 94th group, the 96th's Bob O'Hearn, navigator, remembers, "Even before takeoff, optimism faded. Our engines were running rough and using too much fuel. About twenty years later I learned that its original crew in the 94th had refused to fly it. They were shot down that day in another plane.

"German fighters hit us several times. More mechanical problems appeared. Near the I.P. of the bomb run, a vibrating engine had to be shut down. Unable to feather the spinning prop [the turning blades became a drag], we could not keep up with our group. We were taking hits from attackers; two engines started smoking.

"As the target area was not visible, the crew voted not to abort yet. We flew into dark clouds of exploding antiaircraft shells with Luftwaffe fighters attacking through their own flak [the same as Old reported]. Shrapnel rattled off or onto our B-17. We reached the target well behind the rest of the formation. After 'bombs away' in the burning target area, we cut corners and caught the last group in our wing. The wing from behind overtook us and left us over Germany with No. 2 engine on fire, a propeller screaming, oxygen and ammo going fast and more fighters closing in.

"The top gun turret was hit. Engineer Sebeck shot down one of four FW-190s from the damaged turret. With flames streaming out of two engines, Nettles [the pilot] hit the alarm bell as our signal to bail out. We hooked up our chutes. Copilot LeFors came down from the cockpit to check us. Brought up short by his still-connected oxygen hose, he grinned, waved and left. Seconds seemed to be ticking off in slow motion.

"I popped the forward lower escape hatch and looked down. The inboard prop seemed close. With Jones [the bombardier] behind me, I sat at the edge and slid into space, apprehensive, but very glad to be out. Falling with my face to the sky, I watched the B-17 slowly pull away as I moved with it. I should have counted to fifty before opening my chute. After forty, I was unsure of my count. I had been off oxygen for some time. When I pulled the rip cord, nothing happened for three seconds. Finally, the pilot chute came out and drifted slowly up past my face. At an altitude of about 10,000 feet, the main chute burst into a reassuring white blossom.

"In the distance, #453 was in a flat spin with two FW-190s firing at it. A wing came off as it crashed and exploded. A bomb had hung up in the bomb rack. I counted nine chutes in a long uneven line. I was very concerned for my survival. Later, at a lower altitude with warmer air and a sunny fall countryside below, I felt less pessimistic.

"Landing in a plowed field, I congratulated myself on a 'book' landing, then noticed I'd forgotten to collapse the chute which was billowing in the wind, tugging me along. I ran into the canopy, rolled it up and partially hid it. I decided to go to a hedge about a hundred yards away, check my map and see what to do. An elderly couple walked towards me. I pointed to my ears, shook my head and kept on walking. They looked shocked, but made no attempt to stop me. Over the next rise, two young Home Guards met me. Their rifles pointing at me were shaking which seemed amusing. I was supposed to be the shaky one. It seemed that an official surrender required that I raise my hands. I pretended not to understand but the fun ended when they twisted my thumbs and we marched away.

"A score of Germans, mostly women and children with a couple of old men gathered around. A lady said, 'You have had a hard time today.' Another said almost enviously, 'For you the war is over.' We met Jones in a dazed condition under guard. The Germans found our parachutes.

A guard thrust one at me to carry. Feeling more at ease I said, 'No! I am an officer' and pointed to the gold bar on my collar. The teenaged guard consulted with others. I heard, '*Ja, Offitsier.*' A couple of children proudly accepted the task of bringing the parachutes to the village.

"A guard intervened when I offered Dentyne gum to the kids. I showed them how gum was chewed. The kids loved it. The crowd now seemed almost friendly, except for an old man behind me, muttering unpleasantly, who lunged and jabbed my left shoulder blade with a long pole. If I had not moved as I heard the commotion, he could have cracked my spine. The blow hurt more than I admitted. When the guards turned on him, I asked that he be let go, explaining, '*Lose in der Kopf*' (crazy). This was about a third of all the German I knew but if ever there was a time for public relations it seemed now was the time.

"We approached a building where black-shirted SS troops lounged on the steps. Happily, we went on to a jail where an official who resembled German Kaiser Wilhelm of World War I with spiked helmet, old-fashioned uniform and a large mustache drove us in a Mercedes sedan to a town a few miles away. There we met the rest of the crew and were questioned rather kindly by a local official. An old man touched my sheepskin-lined jacket and inquired, '*Varm?*' I agreed. Later we were taken to a military prison at Heidelberg. A German officer with a facial scar delivered a threatening tirade. When he left, a guard quietly said not to worry, do as we were told and we would be treated fairly.

"As we passed a row of cells containing German military prisoners, we heard remarks like, 'Anybody from Detroit?' 'Don't feel bad. I'm a German and look how they treat me!' We were stripped of our flying jackets and personal items, locked in solitary cells with bare board bunks, no bedding. It was now late evening. I hadn't eaten since 5:00 A.M. but was glad to be alive. I slept soundly until transported to the interrogation center at Frankfurt [the same site to which the more abused fighter pilot John McClure had been taken]."

WHILE Billy Southworth, having completed his tour with the 303rd as a command pilot, applied his knowledge and experience to a staff post, and Jon Schueler entered the medical system because of his emotional stress, Bill Fleming served on other B-17s seeking to fill out his quota of missions. Having overcome an inner ear infection that grounded him for several weeks after he shorted out his electrical heating system in his flight suit, Fleming was still with the 303rd on October 14, hoping to complete his tour with the mission to Schweinfurt.

"When we saw the lines on the map that morning at the briefing, it was a horrible feeling. It began funny and ended funny. When we took off that morning, our escort left, and there was no enemy antiaircraft fire or any German fighters that usually would fly alongside giving our direction, speed, altitude and other information back to their bases. Everybody thought it was awful quiet. About 100 miles inside Germany, it was reported that waves of fighters were coming in on us and there were about 200 of them. We expected that; it was not out of the ordinary. Fighters would attack for thirty to forty-five minutes before they had to land and refuel. We knew if we could survive that long, they would have to leave. They hit us, took out several of our planes. As they were leaving, we all kind of relaxed until somebody hollered, 'My God! Here comes another wave!' This continued all the way in to the target and by the time we got there, we'd lost twenty-five airplanes, 250 men. We bombed, turned, came back and on the way out, the same thing, one wave after another.

"We found out later the Germans knew ahead of time we were coming and positioned their planes to attack us in waves. It was one huge fight for six hours. Finally, we ran out of ammunition; there was only one or two guns firing out of the formation. All they had to do was come in and shoot down what was left of us because there was nobody to fire back. Evidently they were just as tired as we were, because they broke off. It wasn't just the number of planes lost over the target that hurt us, sixty in enemy territory, we also had another twenty-seven crash-landed back in England plus the battle damage to other planes, and the wounded. There was more wounded on that day than any previous mission. That was the one time that I got so scared I vomited all over myself. The calamity and disaster of it was learned when an order came down to see how many planes could be mustered for another attack. Only about 15 percent of the crews and planes were available."

As Fleming indicates, the score registered by the enemy buckled the knees of the Eighth Air Force. The 305th, which could only participate by attaching itself to another air division, was heavily punished for its boldness, with thirteen ships shot down, three more than its closest competitor in this dubious category, the 306th. Archie Old's former command, the 96th lost seven; the 92nd, 94th, 379th and 384th mourned half a dozen each from their complement, sixty empty bunks for each one of these groups. The luckless 100th, due to the battering it withstood at Münster and Bremen, only fielded eight B-17s although all made it back to Thorpe Abbotts without human casualties.

The gunners and fighter groups claimed to have downed 199 enemy planes for sure with another ninety-four probables. Post–World War II investigation showed the Luftwaffe recorded only thirty-eight of their craft destroyed. The sixty B-17s shot down, an unsupportable loss of 26.7 percent, meant that no crewman could last even five missions, let alone twenty-five. The official statistics listed seventeen bombers scrapped even after they wobbled back to United Kingdom bases and 121 ships that required the work of repair crews. Pointblank at this moment seemed a disaster and the results of the Schweinfurt expedition clearly stated the bombers were unable to protect themselves on their own. The policy of daylight, precision bombing could not continue unless fighter bands could accompany the Forts and Liberators to and from the objectives.

Still swallowing the bitter truth, the top commanders tried to label the effort a triumph. Gen. Hap Arnold telegraphed Secretary of War Stimson, "All five of the works at Schweinfurt were either completely or almost completely wiped out. Our attack was the most perfect example in history of accurate distribution of bombs over a target. It was an attack that will not have to be repeated for a very long time, if at all."

Gen. Frederick Anderson, bomber commander, said, "The entire works are now inactive. It may be possible for the Germans eventually to restore 25 percent of normal productive capacity, but even that will require some time."

The claims, like those of enemy fighter kills, were vastly exaggerated. Overall damage to the three main plants at Schweinfurt was about 10 percent, with 3.5 percent destroyed, 6.5 percent damaged. Allied intelligence experts did not realize that while the bombs blew off roofs and smashed walls, the vital machinery in the factories could be salvaged. Some plants resumed full production immediately after they dusted off the powder from the machines. Had the B-17s been able to repeat their visit within a few days, the exposed works might well have been destroyed. But VIII Bomber Command could not mount even a minimum effort against Schweinfurt. The scornful Germans boasted, "No equipment held up because of a shortage of bearings."

However, the Nazi leadership recognized the peril. Albert Speer, Hitler's minister of armaments, said, "The raids on the ball-bearings industry at Schweinfurt in August 1943, evoked . . . a crisis the full import of which was made known to the Führer in all its gravity. Here again the delay in development of repetitions of the attack gave us the necessary time to take defensive precautions."

In response to would-be critics, Hap Arnold insisted, "Regardless of our losses, I'm ready to send replacement crews and continue building up our strength. The opposition isn't nearly what it was and we are wearing them down. The loss of sixty American bombers in the Schweinfurt raid was incidental." The statement was preposterous by any form of accounting. A postwar strategic bombing survey noted, "In one raid, the Eighth Air Force had temporarily lost its air superiority over German targets." A few more victories on the scale of Schweinfurt and the Eighth Air Force might well have been forced to switch over to the RAF's night operations. To the airmen of the Eighth, October 14 became known as "Black Thursday."

10

TURNING POINTS

In the immediate aftermath of the Black Thursday debacle, as Bill Fleming noted, the badly battered Eighth could hardly muster any significant forces. Fighter groups carried out sweeps over Dutch islands and northern France with modest results. The only positive aspect lay in the steady increase in men and machines. "We were rushed right into the 388th Bomb Group," says radio operator Larry Goldstein, "because of the heavy losses in the raids on Schweinfurt and Stuttgart." Unlike so many of his compatriots, Goldstein had not chosen the Air Corps and in fact had attempted to enlist in the Marine Corps from his Brooklyn home shortly after Pearl Harbor. "I was told to go home and wait for my draft call which came two weeks later. Most Americans thought the war with Japan would be over in months. How wrong we were.

"I had been interested in aviation by reading and movies and was working as a typographical draftsman with the U.S. Coast and Geodetic Survey when drafted." That background apparently persuaded those assigning draftees to slate Goldstein for the Air Corps. At the basic training center in Miami Beach, classification specialists designated Goldstein for radio operator school which he completed but he then flunked out of radar school. Awaiting new duty, Goldstein volunteered for flight duty. "Several factors entered into my decision—the promise of flight pay, promotions in rank and the glamour of wearing wings on my uniform."

Subsequently placed in a combat crew training in the Northwest, Goldstein underwent the then standard three months of preparation for battle. "Our ground classes were thorough but like everything else at that time, I, like my fellow airmen, took it all lightly. That is except for our pilots. Our [first] pilot, B. J. Kiersted, was a very dedicated and religious man. His demeanor was catching to us as a crew. When we met for the first time, he stressed that some day one of us might be responsible for the lives of the other nine, so he asked us to learn our jobs well and be prepared for any emergency.

"When we reached England, we named the plane assigned to us *Worry Wart* because our copilot Ace Conklin worried about everything. The name was never painted on the plane because it was taken from us after seven missions. On the first day that we were assigned to our B-17 in England, our pilot asked the crew chief, how many crews have you had. When he answered you're my third in three months, that might have shaken a weak man, but B. J. merely said, 'We will be the crew that completes our twenty-five missions.' We were young and impressionable and I distinctly remember my reaction as being certain B. J. meant it. I was naively assured that this is the way it would be.

"We trained for several weeks with the 388th, mostly for the pilots to become oriented to the English weather and flying conditions. Once we began missions, as a radio operator, unless you were a lead or deputy lead, all you did was monitor the radio for weather reports, fighter rendezvous and a possible abort call [for the mission]. When fighters attacked, I manned a gun which fired to the rear. It was not an effective weapon because the field of fire was limited."

While Goldstein and his cohorts acclimated themselves to combat, squadrons of P-47s attached to recently arrived groups reached operational levels and P-38s, absent for several months to serve in North Africa and the invasion of Sicily, roamed the skies unsuccessfuly inviting the enemy to attend their rodeos.

Among the newcomers shipped by sea was Joseph H. Bennett, a former farm boy from Texas. "We had taken a daily newspaper after I learned to read," said Bennett. "Our mail box was 100 yards from the house and when I was not in school, I would get the paper, read Will Rogers's column and the headlines as I walked home. We also bought a radio in 1925 and it kept us better informed about elections in the late 1920s. Newsreels in theaters perked my interest in world events. I thought I was informed but as it turned out I knew very little."

While a college freshman, Bennett heard a former student, now a second lieutenant from Randolph Field, talk at assembly. He could not convince his parents to agree to enlistment at the time but when it seemed apparent to him the U.S. would soon be at war, Bennett, at age twenty-two, with three years of college, applied for cadet status. Once he earned his wings as a fighter pilot in mid-December 1941, Bennett served with a number of units, including a stint as an instructor on P-39s. He then joined the 356th Fighter Group, as a Thunderbolt squadron operations officer.

"We were going to fly our planes over but at the last moment they decided to send some over by the ferry command. We were packed on an old British liner that was equipped to accommodate 1,500 guests; there were 7,500 of us on British rations. Since we went as a unit, we did not get much training. We were at Hull, England, for about one week, flew some but spent most of our time learning procedures for radio, safety and flying among hundreds of planes. When we moved to our permanent station, Lord Haw-Haw [a British traitor who broadcast Nazi propaganda] on German radio greeted us on our first night."

Bennett participated in some of those uneventful mid-October sorties as his indoctrination into aerial combat. "It was not unusual to see people who just did not have the nerve to fly in combat. The group I went over with had two majors in headquarters operations who never made it across the Channel due to engine trouble while I was with the group. A captain in another squadron asked to be grounded. One lieutenant failed to take evasive action when called to do so. When he landed, his P-47 had three unexploded 25 mm bullets in the gas tanks. He said his controls froze."

Bennett transferred to the well-established 56th Fighter Group becoming in effect a replacement. "I saw my first enemy plane on November 29. It was an ME-109. He was some distance away as I gave chase. When I closed to about 400 yards, the group leader called a return to base. I fired two short bursts without results so I put the sight below him, pressed the trigger and slowly pulled up. This time I got several visible strikes and a small flame where the wing joined the fuselage. I had thought we were at the same altitude but he was higher. I knew closer is better but I learned not to rely on tracer bullets as an aid to sighting. I did a fast turn but could not see the group. I set the throttle to conserve fuel and led my flight of four back to base."

Bennett was impressed by the leadership he originally encountered in his outfit. The same professionalism exemplified by commanders and pilots like Zemke and Johnson pervaded the ground service, according to Bennett. "I flew sixty-two individual flights and not once did an engine miss a beat. Not once when I pressed the trigger did my guns fail. Radios worked excellently but could be in situations where they were less than perfect. I believe this related to the instrument and was not a fault of maintenance."

John Truluck, born 1918, in South Carolina, also signed in at the 56th Fighter Group in the fall of 1943. "While in college," says Truluck, "I was in the ROTC program and I ended up with a commission in the infantry reserve. When World War II started, I applied for the Air Corps. I reported to the infantry, first at Camp Joseph T. Robinson in Arkansas, and then Camp Claiborne in Louisiana, still in the infantry. While I was there orders came through transferring me to the Air Corps. I went through pilot training as a second lieutenant in the infantry.

"I was fortunate enough to go into P-47s and I was real fortunate when I went overseas to be assigned to the 56th Fighter Group. Anybody who has any damn sense is scared. I don't think I was scared going on a mission but after. I remember telling about one where I shot down two planes. I was sitting on a table with my feet hanging down and I was shaking so, one pilot caught one leg and another the other leg pushing it down so I'd stop shaking.

"The bombers weren't doing that many missions when I first got there. We kept doing these fighter sweeps, hoping to get the Germans to come up but they didn't. They figured we were just using up gas and airplanes flying around up there. Colonel Zemke got the idea that if we carried a bomb occasionally that would more or less force them to come up and intercept us because they wouldn't know whether we were going to bomb them or not. They finally arranged for a B-24 to go out and lead us and the bombardier would fire a flare to tell us when to drop our bomb. We had never carried a bomb before. On that particular day, the B-24 traveled at about 160 miles an hour while we cruised at 240. It was sloppy flying, barely had flying speed. We dropped our wheels to get a little bit more control. Right after I dropped my bomb, if I hit anything it was a Frenchman or his cow, or tore up a barn two or three miles from the target—we were scattered all over the sky—this burst of flak went off right under the airplane and it felt like a ton of dynamite hit it. If I hadn't been strapped in, I'd 'uv gone out the canopy. The engine started to run rough; the controls were heavy, I didn't think I'd get back to England. I was afraid if I brought them up, I'd never get them down. I flew back with the wheels down. Everyone else had gone off and left me. I called the tower and said I was shot up and said I'd buzz the field and they could tell me if I had anything wrong. They didn't see any damage so I landed. Sergeant Walker as usual jumped up on the wing and asked, 'Well, how'd it go, Lieutenant?' I said what the hell you mean, I got my ass shot off. He jumped down and looked and said I don't see anything. The two of us finally found a place about the size of a quarter where this flak had hit the wheel cover. All the rough engines and heavy control was up in my brains because I was scared. It was also the only time I ever scratched one of the airplanes."

THE exigencies of production and the scarcity of aircraft allowed little room for manufacturers to attend to seemingly small details that could bring disaster. Truluck tinkered with his Thunderbolt to eliminate bugs he discovered. Truluck recalls the crash of a friend and what he eventually deduced. "On an early mission, we were going over to the edge of the Dutch islands, at about 18 to 20,000 feet and Pat Williams peeled off and went straight down into the water. Nobody could contact him or ever knew what happened. Several weeks later I was on a mission and when I got to the edge of France I saw that half of my oxygen was gone. I looked at my oxygen regulator and it was on full rich, really barreling out oxygen into my face. When I got back I checked this out with Sergeant Walker, my crew chief. I asked, 'Didn't I have this oxygen regulator in the automatic lean position?' and he said 'Yes sir.' That puzzled me. Some time after, I was getting ready to start the engine. I reached up to prime it and my elbow hit the oxygen regulator lever. I called Sergeant Walker over and said, 'Watch my elbow,' and I reached up to prime the engine and my elbow came very close to the regulator level. I told him that's what happened to me that other day. I talked to the other pilots saying 'I bet that's what happened to Pat Williams. His oxygen then ran out and he went straight in.' I had Sergeant Walker move the oxygen regulator forward about ten or twelve inches."

Shortly after, to improve the climbing power of the P-47, engineers designed paddle-bladed props with blades the same width almost to the end where they formed a half round circle. To install them, the 56th flew the planes to a depot. When they returned, Truluck noticed his oxygen regulator had been moved to its original site. In addition, the engineering staff filed a report on the unauthorized placement of the regulator. Nevertheless, Sergeant Walker, in accord with Truluck's instructions, reset it forward.

Another improvement in the P-47's performance came through the installation of an injection kit which produced better manifold pressure, and as with the paddle props it required a second trip to the depot. Once again the oxygen regulator was restored to its designated place, a second complaint was filed and Truluck, with his mechanic, doggedly refitted the instrument out of his elbow's way. When an air inspection team visited the 56th and found Truluck's alteration, the base engineering officer chewed him out. "I told him, 'Major, when you're flying that airplane you can put that regulator anywhere you damn please. But as long as my ass is up there being shot at, the oxygen regulator is going to be where I want it. I don't give a damn what you, fighter command or Wright Patterson Field [headquarters for matters on aircraft design and engineering] says about it.'

"A couple days later," recalled Truluck, "Colonel Schilling calls me and says, 'Lucky, what in the hell is this oxygen regulator business all about?' Fighter command had called him. I told him and he said, 'God-damn, why in the hell didn't you tell me? I'm going to have mine moved today.' I wrote a report on the matter, recommending all oxygen regulators be moved forward and it went through channels. When I came back to the States later as an instructor, I found all of the planes had the device where I said it should be.

"At first I flew whatever plane was available. Then they brought in some new ones and I got the newest thing, right off the production line, a P-47 D26. With my crew chief we started cleaning it up and I went into town and I bought seventeen dollars' worth of shoe polish to wax my plane, and painted Lady Jane [while attending flight school, Truluck had fallen in love with a young woman named Jane] in bold white script across the left side. You didn't have very good rear vision in a P-47 and I bought another mirror from a Rolls-Royce agency in London and we put it on the side. I bought a sun visor, we rigged it on the inside of the canopy so I could look into the sun through this smoked-glass sun visor. I had the heating system rejuvenated so I had heat on each foot and each hand. If it hadn't been for that I probably would have frozen to death. I don't have much of a layer of fat on these bones.

"I had a really good crew. I flew seventy-one missions, close to 200 hours. I never did have an aborted mission. I came close once but because the radio wasn't working however, the entire mission was called back. After I landed I nearly jumped down Sergeant Walker's throat about the radio. They examined it and couldn't find anything wrong. Someone said let me see your helmet and there was a broken wire in the headset. It had nothing to do with the airplane. Fighter pilots were the quarterbacks of the war. They got all the publicity but did the smallest amount of work. Ground crews worked their cans off during the night, in freezing cold, rainy weather and got no recognition. We owed our lives to them. The stupidest thing is we never realized it until the war was over. They probably sweated out my missions more than I did. When we came in to land, they were sitting there waiting for us.

"Most of the people felt the way I did, although there may have been a few possibly flying for glory instead of the purpose of defeating the Germans. We had a lot of them made themselves heroes in the eyes of the news media. But there were a helluva lot of heroes that nobody ever heard of."

ANOTHER recuit to the 56th was Joel Popplewell, born in Liberty, Kentucky, in 1921. Popplewell enlisted in the Air Corps as a private in 1940. After six weeks of marching and drilling in Alabama, Popplewell rambled through a series of camps where he helped construct the first buildings. He started flight training in Minnesota, learning to fly Cubs and Aeroncas, briefly studied gliders but upon curtailment of that program he applied for fighter instruction. In Florida he first encountered the P-47. On his maiden excursion Popplewell recalled, "I forgot to switch from main to auxiliary after taking off. I flew around, had a great time but when I came in for a landing, I overshot and had to go around again. She conked on me. I started to bail out over Fort Myers, but something pushed my hand down and I turned on the gas tank. I brought it in and I learned a whole lot. Each time we went out, even in combat we learned something new."

From New York, Popplewell and 122 replacement fighter pilots sailed on the *Île de France* to Scotland. "We flew a little off a base near Atcham before assignment from the RTU [Replacement Training Unit] to the 56th at Horsham Saint Faith. There, we went through a training program second to none. Not comparable to anything we'd learned in the States. We had received a little aerial gunnery instruction before but we got a lot of it with the 56th before they'd allow us to fly a mission. We had good commanders, like Gabreski. He never yelled at anyone. Maybe he had someone else chew a man out but he himself never did.

"Of this replacement group, I guess I was the first one to fly combat, as we escorted some bombers over Calais. It was early in the morning. They dropped bombs, circled and came back and so did we. Some of the fellows asked me how it was. I said, 'Nothing to it. They're not after us; they're after the bombers.'

"That afternoon, on my next mission, we had to go in deep and had wing tanks. I'd never flown with them before. I tried to remember what to do. I didn't: I forgot to switch my wing tanks. The flak got heavy and came between me and my wing but didn't hit me. Somebody told me on the radio to drop my wing tanks but I needed the fuel to get home. I switched them on, alternating to keep the plane balanced.

"On the way back from my first trip to London, my friend C. P. Nail who had gone to school with me said, 'I gotta feeling one of us is goin' to get it.' Two days after that we had a big fight at Bremen over the airdrome. I was flying Colonel Gabreski's wing. Guy by the name of Heineman was the element leader and Nail was Heineman's wing, the Tail-end Charlie. We saw this flight of FWs coming off the airdrome. Gabreski said we should let them get off the ground. On his signal we did a 180-degree turn and went back down after them. They were at about 3,000 feet. Gabreski knew better what to do than the rest of us. I saw him shoot down two. Then I lost track of him because I was trying to get one off C. P. Nail's tail. I was getting some hits but about that time my airplane just nosed up because of 20 mm fire from a Focke Wulf. I kicked right rudder and ended up about treetop level trying to get away from him. Engines and observers were on the field. Soon as I landed, I cut my engine. In the excitement, getting out of the plane I forgot to undo the dinghy [inflatable raft] from my belt. It blew up in the cockpit, but I made it back home by myself; nobody was around to escort or give me any protection.

"At the base after everybody else had landed. They vectored me right in on the runway. They knew I was shot up; fire in the cockpit scared everybody else but not me. I was just so damn glad to be back on the ground. The doctor was there, name of Hornig, a very good friend of mine. He would not let them debrief me until he took me to the clinic. I think he had in mind to give me a shot but back then we were leary of that so I had some Scotch and water. It cured my ills and they could debrief me.

"They shot down two of our planes and damaged two. We shot twelve of theirs. I didn't think it was a very fair margin because my friend got blown up in the sky."

WHILE Eaker sounded a triumphant trumpet for the achievements of Black Thursday, he constantly pleaded for more of everything, particularly bomber groups. To augment the fleet of B-24s, several more Liberator groups with their greater bomb load capacity came to the United Kingdom to beef up what temporarily became known as the Second Bombardment Division. The First and Third Bombardment Divisions flew B-17s.

One of the B-24 arrivals shortly after Black Thursday was the 445th Bomb Group with Hal Turrell who had joined the National Guard in 1937 when he turned eighteen. "This was at the time Neville Chamberlain, the prime minister of Britain, sacrificed Czechoslovakia to Hitler for 'Peace in our time.' Churchill said of this in the House of Commons, 'We have sustained a total and unmitigated defeat. We are in the midst of a disaster of the first magnitude . . . and do not suppose that this is the end. It is only the beginning.' He was shouted down by the House! I was certain that war would come and be long and terrible."

Turrell trained as an infantryman with the 40th Division on the West Coast and upon federalization of the National Guard he became a platoon sergeant for a year in March 1941. "When the draft started we got numbers of Nisei, young Japanese-Americans. The other platoon sergeants did not want them because of prejudice against the Japanese. I took them and was grateful to have them. Naturally, during company maneuvers we were always the enemy.

"One of the platoon sergeant's duties was to give a current events seminar every week. It was late summer of 1941 and war with Japan seemed increasingly certain. I concentrated on that as I knew it was a matter of special concern for them [his Nisei troops]. They were very stimulating and well informed with an enormous blind spot. They could not believe that Japan would go to war against the U.S. The rationale was they did not think the Japanese were foolish enough to think they could prevail against American industrial strength. We had an officer and a sergeant in the company who felt the same way about Germany. When I pointed out the historic inevitability of American involvement on Britain's side, the response was, 'I do not want to hear that.'"

Turrell says he became increasingly disenchanted with his outfit as it started to gear up for the approach of war. "I was doing the job normally assigned to a lieutenant. The National Guard, even though it was in federal service, was still quite political. After it was made clear to me that no Jew would be sent to officer candidate school, I took a reduction to private and transferred to the Army Air Corps, Regular Army."

At Lowry Field, Colorado, he worked on a fabric-covered biplane, hardly conducive to optimism about U.S. preparedness. He volunteered for the flying cadet program but without two years of college he went on a long waiting list to take the equivalency examination. The Pearl Harbor debacle quickened the pace and within three months Turrell reported to Randolph Field, Texas.

"I was qualified for any flying position and selected bombardier, as my ambition was simply to kill Germans. I was introduced to the theory and practice of bombing and the Norden bombsight. The secrecy surrounding this sight was intense. It had to be carried everywhere under armed guard. I have since learned that a German employee of Norden had provided the plans for the bombsight to Germany in 1938! They never did anything with it because they never desired a strategic bomber force.

"The sight had a very simple basis. When a bomb is dropped from high altitudes, it is blown downwind. The bombardier must release upwind from the target. The sight contained a gyroscope in its base. The bombardier would position the vertical crosshair so that it held steady on the target. The bombsight tilted the telescope to bring the airplane the proper distance upwind. The bombsight was hooked up to the automatic pilot of the airplane so that the bombardier would actually turn the plane with the sight. There was also a pilot direction indicator (PDI) that had a needle that moved right or left for the pilot's information. The pilot would endeavor to keep the PDI on center.

"There was a second gyroscope in the bombsight's head. The bombardier then used a double control knob to hold the horizontal crosshair on the target. The double control knobs measured the speed of the airplane and positioned the crosshair on the target. If you had the crosshair on the target and it moved, the speed had been measured incorrectly. The Norden was actually an early mechanical computer. The knobs measured the speed of the airplane over the ground and theoretically the bomb should hit the target when the airplane was directly overhead. This meant the bomb must be released a distance before the plane would travel to the target."

Lining up crosshairs was only part of the system. Every bomb type had different characteristics in the wind and air resistance which dictated its "trail." The bombsight included a dial that could be set for the expected amount of trail based upon prepared tables. Within the bombsight, the system brought together the trail measure and the movement of the airplane. When the two indices met, an electrical impulse triggered the bomb release. There was no button for anyone to push and the bombardier employed both hands manipulating the four control knobs on his Norden.

"After dropping quite a few bombs," says Turrell, "I no longer subscribed to the much-advertised 'pickle-barrel' theory. The plane we flew in was a twin-engine trainer, the AT-11. It was quite stable and our practice bombing was done at 5,000 feet with 100-pound practice bombs that were filled with sand and had a smoke bomb that went off on impact so we could see where we hit. I did not think I was very good, but they graduated me anyway. I gave some thought to the fact that in combat we would probably bomb from 20,000 feet which would reduce our accuracy quite a bit. I was sure that the Air Corps had an answer for that problem.

"After receiving my commission and wings, I was given some leave and went home to show off. I met with a friend of my father who had taken refuge in the U.S. from Nazi Germany. He questioned me about visual bombing and said, 'The weather in Europe is not like Texas. The sky is covered with clouds most of the time. How will you see your target?' In the supreme confidence of my twenty-five years I said, 'Oh, we can handle that.' In truth I had no idea and later found out how right he was. I have always wondered why General [Hap] Arnold never asked Mr. Schamburg about German weather."

Qualified for combat, Turrell, instead of heading for the war, was sent to study navigation, as the Air Corps discovered a critical shortage of men with this skill. Turrell learned how to calculate a good idea of where he was headed and when he would arrive, with an occasional landmark to confirm. He quotes the trade's aphorism, "A navigator never knows where he is. He knows where he has been and where he is going to be, but never where he is."

Completion of this course qualified him for both jobs. "I concluded the navigator worked from before takeoff to after landing and that the bombardier role was a lot less arduous. I joined the 445th Bomb Group, 703rd Squadron. After checking in I was told to see a Captain Stewart, the operations officer. I wore my bombardier wings. As I saluted, I was flabbergasted to see the actor Jimmy Stewart. His first words to me were, 'Great! I am up to my ass in bombardiers, short of navigators, and they send me another bombardier.' I said, 'Sorry, sir,' saluted and turned to leave. He then said, 'Just a moment, lieutenant. Are you one of those dual-rated people?' One does not lie to a commanding officer so I said, 'Yes, sir,' and I was assigned to crew #71 commanded by Lt. Ralph Stimmel."

Shortly thereafter, the crew with Turrell flew a night practice bombing mission in South Dakota. Turrell admits that inexperience with higher altitudes and boredom led to careless use of oxygen, and drunk with anoxia he badly miscalculated their whereabouts. Low on fuel, pilot Stimmel managed to set down in a grass field in Marshalltown, Iowa. A phone call to Jimmy Stewart produced gasoline and the locals, including a crowd of kids atop a billboard, gathered to watch the takeoff from a very short runway that ended with trees.

The blast from the four engines blew down the billboard and the plane itself barely skimmed the treetops. Back at the home field, the navigator says he was told, "Captain Stewart wanted to have some words with Lieutenant Turrell." "My words with Captain Stewart were brief. A second lieutenant can only say three phrases: 'Yes, sir,' 'No, sir,' 'No excuse, sir.' I later learned that Captain Stewart had asked Ralph if he wanted a replacement for me. When Ralph said, 'No, I think he has learned his lesson and he gets along well with the crew,' Stewart smiled and said, 'That's good, there are not any replacements.'"

The 445th readied itself for overseas. "We were given a brand-new B-24, with the latest modifications and named it the *Liberty Belle*. There had been a story in the *Reader's Digest* about a crew that had gotten a new airplane. They found a note under the control column saying, 'God bless this plane and crew.' The story went on to tell how the crew had survived many harrowing experiences. Naturally, we were eager to see if we had a note from the factory workers. We did and it said, 'Fuck you.'"

With the greater range of the B-24s and the onset of North Atlantic weather, the Air Corps had developed a southern route to England. *Liberty Belle* made its last contact with American soil at Puerto Rico, headed first to Georgetown, British Guyana, on the mouth of the Amazon and then to Natal, Brazil. As a navigator Turrell relied on the celestial method, orienting the aircraft according to the heavens. Holding an octant steady while the aircraft bounced through the air, identifying stars, calculating the probable miles traveled between observations using a government-issued chronometer (each error of a second means an error of one mile) taxed his abilities to the utmost. "If it were not for the wind," insists Turrell, "navigating would be easy. The wind can be calculated, if you shoot fixes, star shots or landmarks, but it does not stay the same. The wind calculated an hour ago, 160 miles away, can be totally different now. The airspeed indicator was not the true airspeed, like that of a car." Because this rate was gauged by a Pitot tube which depends upon the volume and pressure of air flowing into it, compensation had to be made for altitude and temperature.

"Everyone on our crew knew how to transfer fuel, a rather tricky exercise," remarks Turrell. "The wingtip tanks [Tokyo tanks] had been added after the airplanes were designed. It was quite easy to think you were pumping gas from the auxiliary tanks into the main ones, when in reality you were doing the reverse. During our crossing, we heard on the radio the crew of one of our group asking for directions on how to transfer fuel from the wingtip tanks into the main tanks. They never did figure it out and crashed in the jungle. Their bones are no doubt still there. I remembered Ralph and I seeing the pilot of that crew at the officers' club in Puerto Rico the evening before, intoxicated. We were shocked and troubled by this." Those aboard *Liberty Belle* went through moments of anxiety, as the route carried them from Natal to Dakar in Senegal, West Africa, and on to Marrakech, Morocco, in North Africa before the last leg to England.

The 445th established its base at Tibenham, an East Anglia hamlet. "The officers were assigned to a Quonset hut shared with the officers of Ralph Metcalfe's crew. The enlisted men were bunked with another crew so their huts slept twelve and ours eight. The toilets were located some distance away and the flush toilet, invented in England by Mr. [Thomas] Crapper had not been installed. We just used buckets. Each hut was 'heated' by a small cast-iron stove in the center. It was every crew for itself when the coal ration arrived. Sometimes it came when we were on a mission. When that happened we just went and took our share. Nobody wanted to argue with a combat crew. The stove was our social club and kitchen. We would heat C rations until they were very nearly edible. Very often after a mission, nobody felt like eating. Sometimes you gave it back in an hour.

"We were photographed wearing European workman's civilian clothing. This was for our escape kit so that the underground could have photos for our forged documents. We later heard the Germans could identify which group we came from by the clothing worn in our escape photos! The kit contained a map of Europe, various currencies and items such as fish hooks and line. To a navigator, the map was ludicrous. The scale was so large it was of more use for a geography class."

Aside from increases in sheer numbers with the arrival of groups such as Turrell's, engineers in the UK added items to enhance performance. A sheet-metal crew chief with the 91st Bomb Group said, "The biggest changes to the B-17s were Tokyo gas tanks in the outboard wings which increased the flight range [planes now coming off the assembly line in the U.S. like Turrell's *Liberty Belle*, brought this innovation built in] and the chin turret under the plastic nose carrying twin .50 caliber machine guns, standard in the B-17G. Before these came about, there was a steel armor-plate kit to be installed in the front of the instrument panel. This added weight to the B-17s and was soon discarded. The crews, however, had our welding shop cut the plates up to fit the seat bottoms. They knew what needed to be protected. There were many Boeing reps in and about the base. They didn't do much in the way of repairs but provided a quick ride into London in their cars."

ASIDE from the personnel and aircraft, the Eighth increasingly relied on new techniques, pathfinders to locate targets and lead bombardiers upon whose drop those following would salvo their loads. Strategists and intelligence experts also attempted to devise ways of outwitting the opposition.

Jack Kidd with the 100th Bomb Group, nominated as command pilot to lead a wing for an operation, participated in one experiment. "We had a mission scheduled not too deep into Germany but a new technique was used. It meant flying out across the North Sea, taking a left-hand turn to the north, making a big rectangle and then penetrating in to the target. The idea was to bring the German fighters up and we'd penetrate after they had to go down to refuel. When we got out to the North Sea area, some stratus clouds got in our way. At the worst of it, we could see maybe 150 feet, one airplane off the wing. Only thing we could do was fly straight ahead until we got out of those clouds. When we broke out we turned to the prescribed route and it was apparent the formation had fragmented. The tail observer, the copilot on the airplane when the command pilot flies, reported airplanes from five different groups identified by the tail markings.

"This presented a problem for me. Did we go in with a motley crew, people who had never flown formation together? We didn't know whether they'd stick with us or not. I made the decision to abort the mission. The planes peeled off to their respective bases.

"A day or so later, General LeMay had a critique on the mission. My heart was in my mouth; aborting a mission was simply not done. Individual pilots did it and we were pretty strict reviewing their decisions. Some of the more senior officers described their predicaments; several up front had gone on in. To my utter relief, General LeMay laid out a new rule that said we would attack targets only when the formations had maintained integrity. That took a heaping load off my mind. I respect General LeMay for that and other decisions he made. I thought he was a tremendous combat leader, strict, stern but always right. He got the loyalty of the airmen who worked under him."

Some accounts suggest that in the wake of Black Thursday, the Eighth Air Force all but abandoned its raids. While the pace certainly fell off—six major expeditions in the first two weeks of October compared to a similar number over the next four weeks, the daylight raids continued. The 44th and 93rd Bomb Groups, back in England, resumed operations under the Eighth Air Force. To fill in for the many lost at Ploesti, the 44th recruited Bill Topping, the bombardier who had participated in a successful operation against some U-boats while working with the RAF on antisubmarine patrol. When the U.S. Navy assumed responsibility for this kind of work, the relieved B-24 crews became members of the Eighth Air Force.

"When the 44th Bomb Group looked at my records on antisubmarine patrol, they credited me with twenty missions. My squadron commander said, 'You've logged more time than anyone, including me. You fly five more missions and then you can go for pilot training. I'll get you a good crew.' But I wasn't happy with any of them. They were young while I'd been with boys from Randolph Field, people who had lots of experience. I was finally assigned to a crew that had been bombing radio stations in Norway.

"Our first mission, November 13, was Bremen and I was glad we got shot down. I would never have made it back. Some idiot gave me an electric flying suit with boots and gloves, except these were gloves which didn't have the little clip to complete the circuit. We had a brand-new B-24. I was up in the nose turret with the navigator. I showed Bill Peck, the navigator, how to open the bomb bay doors and said I'll tell you when to salvo. We dropped our bombs—incendiaries to burn the town up.

"We were getting some flak going in and it got us first. Then the fighters started to peck away at us on the way out. My guns wouldn't fire. They were frozen. I couldn't fire those stupid guns and I was freezing to death. I unzipped my flight suit; the wind was howling through that damned nose turret like forty degrees below. I put my hands beneath my armpits to warm 'em up. I was trying to get to the top plate cover on those .50 calibers, to see if I could get them to feed so I could fire at those planes coming head-on. All I could do was swing around my guns on them so they would think I had something. At least the steel armor plating in front gave me protection—they might only shoot me in the legs or shoulder but they weren't going to get my privates, my belly or chest."

Topping continues, "We started losing engines and began dropping back. We were headed out over the North Sea and the pilot said, 'We'll never make it, we're going to come back.' In that frigid water we wouldn't last forty-five seconds. We were really shot up with one gear down. I got out of the nose turret and up on the flight deck in front of the top turret. We came back over Holland and the pilot dove down over an embankment and sheared that extended gear off. One engine was still going as we went in. I didn't think we'd ever stop, with dirt flying but finally we came to rest. As we got out of the aircraft I said, 'Looks like some other plane's been here. Look at that wreckage.' Someone said, 'That's ours.' We had engines strung out behind us. The plane had been badly torn up. No one was hurt bad. The copilot was bleeding from a head wound. I found out later I had some flak in my leg. When you have the hell scared out of you, you don't realize you have been hurt.

"Some Germans slowly walked over to us. We'd just missed a building that housed some troops. The first words were, 'For you, the vor is over.' I said I'm glad. I swear that if I had gotten back to England and found the sergeant who gave me a flight suit that didn't work and I damn near froze, I'd have shot that sucker."

Housed in a local building, Topping and his crew followed the route through Amsterdam and then to Frankfurt. "We were marched through the station. Civilians, women, men, kids started beating on us. I started slugging them off. I had heard they hung some downed crews. Luftwaffe officers and men took us to the holding camp for interrogation. All I would tell them was my name, rank and serial number. Then they got on me about how did we find those submarines. I said, 'What subs?' They said the ones you got in the Bay of Biscay. They told me they got their information from a newspaper, *Stars and Stripes*. I still didn't give them any information. They sent me to Stalag Luft I at Barth, Germany." Topping, as a member of the 44th Bomb Group, had accrued just one-half of a mission.

HAL Turrell recalls being alerted on December 13 for the 445th first combat experience, an assault on the submarine pens in the Bremen-Kiel region. "We met our first enemy fighters over the North Sea. They came diving in at us from twelve o'clock high. Our combined closing speed was about 550 miles per hour. These Luftwaffe pilots were very aggressive and experienced. They came right through our formations, rolling on their sides to avoid collisions. Collisions did occur, disastrous for both airplanes. Machine gun fire at these speeds is notoriously inaccurate at distances greater than 500 yards. One cannot aim directly at the enemy. You have to lead them, aiming ahead, deflection shooting.

"At this moment, the intercom on our ship quit working. Our only means of communication was screaming over the noise in each other's ear. For some reason, Hollywood movies show the crews shouting and chattering on the intercom constantly. Doing that is the road to disaster.

On every raid I was on, the stickier the situation got, the more intercom discipline [there was]. Mostly silence interrupted by terse calling out of fighter locations and other germane information. Profanity was never heard. I flew a few missions with other crews and it was the same.

"One of the navigator's duties is to keep a log recording enemy planes shot down, sometimes [the number of] our planes shot down and the number of parachutes out, if any. I looked around and all I saw were American planes going down and/or exploding. I remember thinking, Lord, it wasn't like this in the movies. Where is John Wayne? An American P-38 suddenly came diving down past us and I thought, great, the cavalry has arrived. Then I saw a German ME-109 on his tail. About the time he was level with us, the P-38 exploded. So much for the cavalry.

"Sometimes the explosion [of an aircraft] would be caused by bombs going off in the bomb bay and sometimes by the gasoline exploding or both. This produces a spectacular sight. First there is a brief white flash that quickly turns into a giant red fireball. The aircraft splits into hundreds of pieces of metal, some with a slight hint of their previous function such as a wing. If you're looking just right you might see bodies, not ever parachutes.

"Airplanes go down in different ways," Turrell continues. "Sometimes they will slide down tail-first and be completely covered in flames. Some will go into a flatspin; the plane revolves around its nose. Others go into a tailspin; the wings revolve around the fuselage. Sometimes they tumbled end over end with parts breaking off and flying in all directions. Others with no visible damage would circle in a descending pattern. Some dived straight into the ground.

"After an eternity, we turned for the target and started the bomb run. As I had bombardier training, I opened the bomb bay doors. Our poor *Liberty Belle* had been lost with another crew. The plane we had for this mission had been equipped with a nose turret to counter the German tactics of head-on attacks. That changed the navigator's view from the best on the airplane to the worst. I could only see the ground directly in front of me and had two small windows to see to the side. The only person available to handle the chin turret was bombardier Hugh Francis who had been given a couple of hours' crash course in turret gunnery. He was in the turret [with no intercom].

"We were supposed to drop our bombs when the lead aircraft of the formation dropped his. A few minutes into the bomb run, Hugh Francis suddenly opened the turret door and gestured wildly towards the bomb controls. I thought he wanted me to drop the bombs so I hit the salvo handle. What he wanted was for me to open the bomb bay doors. Our bombs went down to do winter plowing on farmland near Bremen. Several other ships in the group, seeing our bombs drop, salvoed theirs also. After all, this was the first combat for the entire group. We were also experiencing our first flak. I thought that every gun the Germans had was shooting at us. Later on I would describe that amount of flak as light.

"We turned off the target and headed home. The fighter attacks stopped and we were away from the flak areas. I looked at my log and realized I had entered very little after the first shot. I now knew what was meant by the shock and fog of battle. There is nothing that can prepare you for it. Suddenly you realize you are mortal. I then felt there was no chance I would survive to complete my tour. Then the chances of a flier living to complete his tour were one in three."

THE December 13 assault on Kiel was supposed to count as radio operator Larry Goldstein's third mission. His ship *Worry Wart* escaped both flak and fighters but almost killed its occupants anyway. "We were forced to abort because of a runaway prop on No. 4 engine about an hour into the flight. The prop could not be feathered so the pilot and copilot had to fight the controls as we turned back to our base. The propeller eventually cracked its shaft and was cutting into the engine nacelle. We had maximum gas and bomb load so the plane was difficult to handle. When we hit the runway, the copilot called the crew on the intercom to abandon the plane as soon as we came to a stop. Those in the rear stood by the door and as soon as we braked to a stop, we took off for the safety of the field as far from the plane as we could. The airplane had gone off the edge of the runway, bogging down in the mud. Our top turret gunner was in the front escape hatch, ready to jump clear, but when the plane lurched to the left, he was thrown to the ground and struck the stopped propeller. He had a fractured skull but survived the war." As Goldstein testifies, accidents could be as threatening as the enemy but he, like almost all airmen, insists the fault was not maintenance. "The cold and the blackout were part of it. But if an airplane aborted it was not because of the ground crew but more like the mechanical factor of an airplane under the stress of combat flight."

Ralph Golubock, a replacement pilot with the 44th, who flew a brand-new B-24D to England in early October had paid attention to world affairs while growing up in St. Louis where he read "the wonderful *Post-Dispatch*." Only a high school graduate when he entered the service, Golubock passed a college education equivalency test to qualify for flight training. "I joined the Air Corps because of Lindbergh, Doolittle, Roscoe Turner [a noted pilot of the 1930s] and Tailspin Tommy [a comic-strip character]. I was one of those kids who was an aviation nut, built model airplanes, some of which even flew. Silver wings were the epitome of the greatest thing I could ever do. I had been in a plane, a five-dollar flight from Lambert Field in an old Travelair. Two of us sat in the front cockpit and it was a wonderful thrill.

"Although I was not looking forward to combat, I did want to get a crack at those lousy Japs. I hated and despised those people who had conducted a sneak attack on us at Pearl Harbor and then continued to humiliate us at Corregidor and throughout the Pacific. I also felt tremendous animosity towards the Germans with their super race beliefs and the horrible things that were being done to my people [he is Jewish]."

In England, before assignment to the 44th, Golubock spent weeks learning the local navigation routines. "The British were far ahead of us in the use of radio for navigation purposes. They had a great system called 'Darky.' The pilot of a lost plane only had to give the proper call sign for the day and say, 'Hello, Darky.' On the ground, the nearest Darky station would respond with an identifying name. The pilot could then locate the station on his chart and know within a few miles his location. If requested, the Darky station would also supply a heading to your destination."

Golubock also received intensive drills in formation flying, largely omitted in the States, the bombardier practiced drops on ranges and the gunners practiced their skills. Finally, the crew flew a number of anti-submarine patrols ["we never saw a sub"] that gave them added hours of air time. "I was alerted for a mission on December 30, 1943," remembered Golubock. "I had a total of 410 hours of flying time, and thought that was quite adequate. The night before the mission, however, I had great difficulty sleeping. What I was feeling was not so much fear but apprehension. Would I perform well? I went over and over in my mind what I was supposed to do as a copilot. How would I be accepted by this experienced crew? [As usual, when possible, pilots in particular went on their first raid with veterans of combat.] After mulling things over in my mind, I realized I would perform well. I had been well trained and felt confident. I fell asleep."

Awakened at 3:00 A.M., and with a hearty breakfast under his belt, Golubock headed for the briefing session. "After a few remarks, the CO turned the briefing over to the briefing officers who opened the curtain which had been covering a large map of Europe. As soon as the target was revealed, by a red ribbon running from England to the target, a loud groan was heard from all of the crews. The target was the I.G. Farben Industries at Ludwigshafen, a very deep penetration into the Third Reich."

Having absorbed what information he could, Golubock went to his locker to dress for the mission. He decided not to carry his standard-issue .45 pistol. "It would be very bulky and I did not think I would be able to shoot my way out of Germany with it. The next problem was whether or not to wear my dog tags. We knew that Hitler had attempted to rid Germany of all Jews and perpetrated all sorts of atrocities to accomplish this. Should I wear my dog tags with the letter H for Hebrew and risk execution if caught? I asked several people about this but did not receive a definitive answer. The decision was to be mine alone. I put them on."

The newcomer garbed himself in the sheepskin jacket and pants. "We did not have any heat on the B-24 and we had not received heated flying suits yet. I took my steel helmet, flak vest, parachute, heavy gloves, sheepskin boots, life preserver, helmet and goggles, oxygen mask and escape kit. I wore or carried all of this out to the trucks which took us to the hard stands. From there we took all of this to the airplane and finally the flight deck. By then I was exhausted."

"The mission proved to be very long and for most of it I was very confused. All of the maneuvering to form up looked a lot like the traffic in Piccadilly Circus. We had to form up into elements, squadrons, groups, wings, divisions and finally into the Eighth Air Force strike force. All of this required about two hours and was extremely difficult. With hundreds of airplanes flying around in a restricted area, there was always the danger of collision.

"We were soon in enemy territory. This was evident by the flak coming up at us. I was fascinated. Flak would suddenly appear in what had been, just moments before, a completely empty sky. It was almost pretty. All of the bursts looked exactly alike. There was a round puff of very black smoke with what appeared to be two legs sticking out underneath. They would usually appear in groups of four. Fortunately none of the planes in our group were hit."

Beyond these flak batteries, Golubock enjoyed a respite from danger and became acutely conscious of the frigid temperatures. Then the Luftwaffe surfaced, snatching his attention from creature comfort. "We could see them queuing up in the distance and soon they started coming in from about twelve o'clock, slightly above our altitude. They would dive straight in at us, firing the whole time until I thought they were going to ram us. Just as it appeared there was no way to avoid a collision, they would roll over on their backs and dive out below us.

"The noise was terrific. All of our guns were firing and the smell of cordite permeated the plane. It was my job as copilot to act as gunnery officer, calling out incoming bogeys. I did my best, but they were coming in from all over and I was overwhelmed. I was also fascinated. The enemy fighters, ME-109s, were really very pretty airplanes and it was sort of like watching an air show. Then mysterious lights seemed to appear off our right wing. They would light up, twinkle and then disappear. What the hell were they? I later found out they were exploding cannon shells!

"As quickly as they appeared, the fighters disappeared. The attack was of very brief duration, maybe two or three minutes but I did see airplanes exploding, or burning and going down, usually in a spin. Both American and German airplanes were lost. I saw many parachutes. The 44th lost only one that day. It had been a short but vicious attack.

"Shortly after the fighters left, we opened our bomb bay doors and we were on our bomb run. It soon became clear why the fighters disappeared. We were in a huge flak attack, and the German fighters did not want to be hit by their own flak. [At Schweinfurt, Archie Old noted that some enemy planes had ignored their own antiaircraft for an opportunity to hit the bombers.] Flak was everywhere. We had no choice except to fly right through it. Again ships were going down. The flak was very accurate."

Unscathed, the B-24 with Golubock as copilot headed for England as part of the 44th's formation. The veteran pilot turned over the controls to the neophyte while he took a breather. "We finally reached Shipdham and safety after eight and a half hours. I did not realize how tired I was until we shut down. It was wonderful to be back on the ground again.

"The crew reported for debriefing and our obligatory bottle of Scotch. At the time I did not drink, so my share was divided among the rest of the crew. In listening to the debriefing, I began to wonder if we were all on the same mission since many of the men described various occurrences that I had not seen. They spoke of 24s going down and fighter attacks I had not witnessed. This was a phenomenon I was to notice on many succeeding occasions. We all saw the mission a little differently."

Blooded, Golubock remained a floater, replacing copilots on crews where needed until assignment as a first pilot with his own crew and ship. For the bulk of the Mighty Eighth, the period between Schweinfurt in October and the first days of the New Year seemed almost like a stalemate. The organization accumulated strength in aircraft and crews for matches against the enemy, particularly the deadly fighters, and both sides came away bloody.

WITHOUT much commotion, however, the Americans introduced another player in mid-December. During 1939–40, the British entered into a contract with North American Aviation for production of a fighter. The RAF accepted the new design of what would become known as the Mustang. Two planes were handed to the U.S. Air Corps for experimental purposes, the P-51 Mustang which initially functioned acceptably at lower altitudes and briefly became a tactical weapon, and a dive bomber designated the A-36 Invader.

According to Jim Goodson, "The American-made Allison engine lacked a supercharger so above 15,000 feet the plane wasn't very good. Ron Harker, a Rolls-Royce test pilot, flew a P-51 at Duxford and when he came down said the plane would be a worldbeater if they put a Rolls-Royce Merlin engine in it. People said it couldn't be done but Ron said it could."

Harker prognosticated correctly. The result of the transplant was even better than anyone could have imagined, producing a plane with the flight characteristics that at least equaled the Spitfire. Maj. Tommy Hitchcock, famous previously as a ten-goal polo star, but serving as assistant air attaché in London, notified his superiors in Washington that the summer tests of the Merlin Mustang identified it as "one of the best, if not the best fighter airframe that has been developed..." Air Marshal Trafford Leigh-Mallory, the RAF fighter boss, and World War I ace Eddie Rickenbacker strongly endorsed Hitchcock's appraisal. On the strength of these reports, in November 1942, the Air Corps ordered 2,200 of what was now officially the P-51B.

The first performances of the P-51 at U.S. test sites revealed a truly superior fighter. It sped fifty miles faster than an FW-190 at 28,000 feet, tacking on another twenty-mile advantage above that height. It could similarly outrun an ME-109. The Mustang outdove either German fighter and turned considerably tighter than the Messerschmitt and marginally better than the Focke Wulf. Only in rate of roll could the FW-190 claim a slight advantage.

The original Mustangs operated over a scant 200-mile combat radius, but with external wing tanks distance extended considerably. On December 11, the first day for the P-51 to see combat as part of the Eighth Air

Force, the 354th Fighter Group ships made only a shallow penetration of France. Two days later, however, the P-51s chaperoned bombers to Kiel and back, a distance of nearly 1,000 miles.

When they recovered from the shock of an Allied fighter that could not only outperform their best but also go prodigious distances with the supplementary fuel equipment, the Germans sought to counter with feints that induced pilots to drop the cumbersome wing tanks to make their ships combat-ready. Then the enemy would withdraw, leaving the P-51s without the wherewithal to continue as escorts. The opposition ploy worked only until the engineers crammed an extra fuel supply in behind the pilot's armor plate. With this system in place, the P-51, now able to travel greater distances, would make a major change in the air war's balance of power.

11

NEW DIRECTIONS

The new year brought profound changes to the Mighty Eighth. The most obvious was the nomination of Lt. Gen. Jimmy Doolittle to replace Ira Eaker on January 6. For months, Hap Arnold had expressed impatience with the progress and achievements of the organization. The Air Corp chief brushed aside excuses, largely legitimate, for the considerable number of aircraft grounded for mechanical defects. He chafed at constant demands for more of everything from Eighth Air Force headquarters. Instead of the enemy air opposition lessening through Pointblank, the Luftwaffe appeared to be growing in power. For all of the devastation visited upon the sources of aircraft, the Germans actually produced more planes per month than were lost during 1943. Although during the final weeks of December, the fleets of bombers packed with more than 500 B-17s and B-24s (a record 649 attacked the northern German coast installations December 13)—far larger than the original magic figure of 300—struck several times, the decision to change commanders was irrevocable. Conceivably, Eaker fell from grace because the appalling toll for the last six months of 1943 demanded a scapegoat. He protested his transfer and Spaatz, now in England also as a key figure in the planning for the invasion of the Continent, sought to intercede but Arnold was adamant.

Compared to the minuscule original force in the United Kingdom, Doolittle inherited a potently puissant outfit with 185,000 men manning 100 bases. In the eyes of Spaatz, however, Doolittle seemed timid during his first days on the job. He canceled several early missions because of weather. Outraged, Spaatz allegedly challenged Doolittle, "I wonder if you've got the guts to lead a big air force. If you haven't, I'll get someone who has." Doolittle then took his superior up in a B-17 to demonstrate his point. When they could not find their way home and landed in a cow pasture, Spaatz supposedly conceded Doolittle's point.

But before he could truly show his approach to strategic bombing, Doolittle made a critical policy decision. During Ira Eaker's reign, under no circumstances could fighters leave the bombers. Even when the enemy appeared vulnerable because of numbers or position, the standing orders dictated that the Little Friends must maintain their place to prevent anyone from attacking the formations of B-17s and B-24s. Doolittle changed the doctrine, allowing the P-38s, P-47s and P-51 groups to attack the Luftwaffe on sight. Maj. Gen. William Kepner, imported from the U.S. to take charge of the Eighth Fighter Command, had reluctantly accepted the dogma that decreed escort duty as the primary function for fighters. On his wall, Kepner reportedly had the motto of his command, "Our mission is to bring the bombers back." When Doolittle visited Kepner's office he ordered the sign removed. "From now on that no longer holds. Your mission is to destroy the German Air Force."

While the fighter groups heartily endorsed the new direction, the bomber people naturally reacted negatively to what they perceived as a policy that would leave them naked to the onslaught of the enemy. Their fears were not allayed by the initial orders that offensive action was conditional upon having enough aircraft to remain with the bombers in case interceptors showed. But as the flow of planes and pilots from the U.S. increased, the Mighty Eighth was able to go after the foe whenever he appeared.

With Doolittle firmly in charge, the bomber command on January 29 dispatched its most massive attack ever in the form of an 806-plane raid upon Frankfurt. Equally impressive, more than 630 fighters roamed the skies in support. With the fighters now encouraged to seek and destroy, between the two forces the gun cameras registered more than 120 enemy ships destroyed and an additional ninety or so probables or damaged.

RALPH Golubock with the 44th Bomb Group had continued to serve as a fill-in copilot on B-24s. He pleaded for a ship of his own but even with eleven missions behind him Golubock was advised to be patient. On February 13, with no activity scheduled, Golubock slept late, passing up breakfast and was at the officers' mess for lunch when an alert sounded, ordering crews to report for briefing immediately.

He was somewhat relieved to find the flight would be relatively short, to bomb a secret installation in northern France. "After studying the map, I felt pretty good. Maybe four hours total with about thirty minutes over enemy territory. Sounded like a milk run. As usual, the Protestant airmen assembled around the Protestant chaplain and the Catholics around the Catholic chaplain for prayers and blessings. Because I was Jewish I had no chaplain to pray for me and it was my custom to alternate between the two. This day I didn't know which to see since I had forgotten which one I had seen on my last mission. Suddenly it seemed important that I report to the proper chaplain but I was torn with indecision. Pondering the question, I became agitated and finally pissed off. Why should I have to make a decision like this. Why wasn't there a Jewish chaplain? Here I was going to lay my ass on the line and the Air Force didn't think it important enough to take care of my spiritual needs."

He calmed down, attended the Catholic group and then headed for his post, seconding senior pilot Lt. Gail W. Larsen. Because he skipped breakfast and the assignment canceled his lunch plans, Golubock's sole sustenance consisted of a GI chocolate bar, a hard, chalky-tasting substitute that was in reality an emergency ration. Unknown to Golubock, the objective housed launching sites for German buzz bombs and was surrounded by a concentration of antiaircraft guns.

"The mission was strictly routine," said Golubock, "until we started our bomb run, but then all hell broke loose. We were taken under flak attack by some of the best gunners in the German army. We had just dropped our bombs when we started taking hits. The first burst was just to our starboard and was loud and very visible. We immediately lost No. 3 engine, which controlled all of the hydraulic operations. There was also damage to No. 4 which kept running but wouldn't put out full power.

"After assessing battle damage, and being able to hold some sort of course, we headed toward England alone. We could not keep up with the rest of the formation and were gradually losing altitude. The gunners in the back began calling in to tell us of casualties. Sgt. John Glenn of Arkansas was badly hurt while at his right-waist position. Several others received minor wounds. On our two and a half engines we had very little altitude left when we crossed the coast of England. We had to find a place to land at once. No thought was given to bailing out because of the wounded. The rest of the crew elected to stay with the ship.

"When we were down to less than 1,000 feet we suddenly saw a small grass fighter base. Gail immediately headed for the field while I attempted to pump the wheels and flaps down. We headed straight for the field at about 200 miles per hour when I spotted an RAF amphibian on the runway preparing to take off. Apparently, he also saw us because he immediately cleared the runway. None too soon. We touched down at high speed and both Gail and I got on the brakes. With No. 3 out, we had only one shot at the brakes so we locked them and eventually came to rest in a revetment used by the base Spitfires.

"We were hurriedly evacuating the aircraft when Gail noticed that No. 4 engine was burning furiously. He grabbed a fire extinguisher as he went out the top hatch. We went on the port wing onto the wall of the revetment and Gail began applying foam to No. 4. About that time the British fire engines arrived and put out the fire. We opened the rear hatch to check on the men in the rear. Unfortunately, Sergeant Glenn was already dead. One of his legs was blown completely off. The others who had sustained slight wounds were treated by RAF medical personnel.

"That evening after a lovely dinner on linen served by the RAF, I went to the bar for a drink. While there I was approached by an RAF flight surgeon who offered a sleeping pill. I refused saying I never had a problem sleeping but the doctor insisted so I put it in my pocket. When I returned to my room and tried to go to sleep, it would not come. I flew the whole mission over again, from briefing until our crash landing. With the lights out, I saw the black flak with fiery centers bursting around our plane and felt it hitting us. I flew the plane back to England, finally saw the body of Sergeant Glenn again. I relived the entire mission. I gave in and took the sleeping pill which worked almost immediately.

"When I awoke and began dressing I realized my GI shoes were gone. I could not imagine what happened to them, but assumed someone had stolen them. What a rotten thing to do, steal a man's shoes when he is asleep. I was furious and started out of the room in my stocking feet when I discovered my shoes just outside my door, all polished and looking new. Then I remembered, the English have the custom of leaving their shoes for their batman to clean and polish. I laughed. Imagine cleaning and polishing a lousy pair of muddy, scuffed GI shoes! I was still laughing when I sat down to an excellent English breakfast. The British really know how to live."

Three days later, Golubock and others from the 44th boarded a train from Shipdham for Cambridge for the burial of the dead waist gunner. "It was a typical February day in England—cold, wet, rainy and miserable. The funeral was very depressing and somehow unreal. I felt like I was in a movie theater, watching all this on the screen. Certainly this could not be me, attending a funeral for one of my crew mates. The somber ceremony came to an end with the playing of Taps, followed by a second bugler, some distance away, repeating the sad refrain. This brought tears to all of us 'tough guys.'"

When Golubock returned to Shipdham after a drunken episode in London he received his long-sought role of first pilot. A crew was assigned to him with the exception of a copilot. Not only did the 44th now believe Golubock had the ability to command one of its Liberators but also he was handed the added responsibility of checking out pilot replacements who would serve as his seconds until they became familiar with the rudiments of combat efforts.

DURING the first days of February, the city of Frankfurt continued to reverberate with the detonations of thousands of tons of American bombs. B-17s from the 306th Bomb Group were among those ranging over the city. Lt. Howard Snyder, a Nebraskan drafted as an infantryman in April 1941, who subsequently won his wings and commission from the Air Corps, was a veteran of the air wars, having come to the group in the preceding October, a few days after Black Thursday. "On February 8, we were briefed to bomb Frankfurt. It was just another raid as far as I was concerned at the time. We had been there before and had an anxious and lonely time of it returning on three engines. But nothing happened to us, and the suspense and anxiety were unnecessary.

"We were to fly the hole, number seven in the lead squadron of the low group. When I saw my name on the formation board, I was a little apprehensive for a moment. I could not help but think of Berry whom we lost flying that position a few days before, bombing that same target. However, I had long ago ceased to be nervous or afraid before a mission and the thought didn't remain with me long.

"The join-up was uneventful and we joked over the interphone about our party the night before. Danny [bombardier Richard L. Daniels], Benny [navigator Robert Benninger], Eike [copilot George W.] and I had been on a little spree at the Falcon with some of the boys and were feeling surprisingly well for the condition we were in a few hours before. There is nothing like oxygen to clear up a fellow's blood.

"We flew at 24,000 feet going in. The day was lovely way up there, with an almost solid layer of billowing, milky white clouds beneath us. The sky was a bright, almost pastel blue. We had a new ship which was performing beautifully, and as we were in the lead squadron, it was easy to fly good formation.

"No enemy fighters or flak were met on the way in. However, the usual intense flak was met over the target. It was barrage flak and fairly accurate. One burst pitted the windshield in front of me and I was thankful we had bulletproof glass in the ship. Several times the flak hitting the ship sounded like hail on a tin roof.

"Daniels couldn't get the bomb bay doors open, so I gave the ship to Eike and proceeded to pull the emergency release when I saw the bombs begin to drop from the lead ship. They released without any trouble and we made a sharp turn to the right and got the hell out of there. Flak continued to break all around us. Flak [didn't] scare me but I could still feel my heart speed up as if it were thrown into high gear. My pulse throbs as if the pressure would burst the veins. The sweat runs down my back and sides in small streams. I feel hot and flushed and all of my actions speed up, making normal movements seem like slow motion. Whenever I left a heavy flak area, I cooled down as if after some sudden violent and heavy physical exertion. I don't think I can actually say I enjoyed the sensation but I didn't dislike it. There is something invigorating and satisfying in knowing one can conquer fear.

"Danny couldn't get the bomb bay doors up, so I had him come up and try to wind them up mechanically, but he couldn't and finally had to give it up. We were running low on gas as we had constantly pulled too much power and now with the added drag I was wondering if we would have enough gas to get us back. I had Eike constantly working on rpm to conserve as much fuel as possible."

Pilot Snyder remembered, "It must have been an hour before I heard one of the gunners call out, 'Two 190s at five o'clock.' We had seen no fighters up to this time and only a few scattered bursts of flak on the way out. There weren't but a few seconds left until we had 'had it.' He called out again, 'Watch 'em! They're coming around to the front!' Then Benny responded, 'I see them. Let 'em come!' Well, they came, and if he had known what was to happen, he wouldn't have been so anxious to receive them.

"Suddenly the nose guns were thumping away. I could hear the dull crackling fire through my headset, as if the guns were a great distance away. The vibrations of the fire shook the ship, and as I looked from one ship to the other above me, I could see the empty cartridges fly out of the nose turrets into the slipstream and whiz past our cockpit.

"The bursting of 20 mm around our ship was the first indication that we had been singled out. Then the celestial dome [a radar installation on some bombers] blew up in front of me. After that I could hear 20 mm striking and exploding as they hit the ship. Pieces of equipment and parts of the ship were flying about, striking my feet and legs.

"When the oxygen cylinders exploded, I didn't realize what had happened. The noise of the explosion was muffled by my helmet and headset, but the concussion stunned me for a few moments. I don't believe fragments from an exploding 20 mm would have caused the escaped oxygen to catch fire. There must have been tracers hitting us as well as the 20 mm. Someone lighting a match in a gas-filled room would cause much the same effect as the explosion. Only, instead of the flames decreasing immediately after the explosion, they seemed to continue all around us with the same intensity.

"As I looked around in a half-dazed state, I became slowly conscious that the entire cockpit was filled with smoke and flames. It was difficult to see through the smoke and flames, but I could see the terrified face of Eike, his eyes almost out of his head, looking crazily around him as he tore frantically at his flaksuit and safety belt. I think Holbert [Sgt. Roy T., engineer] had already jumped as I couldn't see him at all.

"As I looked back at Eike, after trying to see Holbert, he seemed absolutely mad and out of his head. Then, as my mind seemed to clear a little more, I too became absolutely terrified. I had been frightened before but never completely lost my wits from terror. It was horrible. I tried to yell or scream, but the sound died in my throat and my open mouth emitted no sound. I tried to jump out of my seat, but my safety belt held me there. My only thought was to get out of that terrible fire. I couldn't think as I clawed wildly for my safety belt. The fact that I had buckled my safety belt under my flaksuit on this raid, instead of over it in my usual way, was the only reason I was able to regain a semblance of sanity. For as I endeavored to unfasten my safety belt, I could not realize in my terrorized and stupefied mind why I could not find it. It was only with great mental effort that I could figure out why and thus start my thought process again. As I looked down and realized what the trouble was a little of the terror left me. But it wasn't until I had thrown my flaksuit from me and unfastened my safety belt that I regained control of myself."

The explosion that dazed him and ignited the oxygen happened in but a few seconds and while the smoke cleared somewhat, Snyder saw his cockpit a mass of fire with great tongues of flame shooting out between the seats and around his and Eike's head.

"As I left my seat," says Snyder, "Eike had just taken his chute pack from beneath his seat. I hesitated momentarily, not knowing what to do and switched on the auto pilot. Although not as terrified as before, I was still greatly shaken and afraid. I acted more from instinct; I don't recall any thoughts. I grabbed a fire extinguisher, but it had no more effect on the blaze than an eye dropper. Deciding it would be impossible to save the ship, I threw the extinguisher down, climbed back from between the seats where I had been standing, held the emergency switch on and began calling through the interphone for the crew to jump. I don't know how long I continued to call, but not getting any response, I felt they had jumped.

"The fire was getting so hot I could hardly stand it. My neck was burning and I pulled my scarf over the exposed skin. My nose, cheeks, eyebrows, eyelids and lower forehead must have been burned when I was using the extinguisher. I don't recall any pain from my face until I was on the ground. It was impossible to go back through the fire to see if they had jumped from the rear of the ship, and as I couldn't get any response from anyone, I left the cockpit.

"As I crawled down to the escape hatch, I was surprised to see Benny and Dan still in the nose. As I made my way toward them, Benny looked down and saw me. I motioned for him to come. He hit Dan on the arm and they both dived toward their chutes. We went out through the nose hatch.

"It didn't occur to me at the time, but I believe the interphone and auto pilot were shot out. The men in back must have jumped, earlier because of the smoke and fire, and they possibly could have seen Holbert or Eike jump. Because the ship crashed one or two kilometers from where I landed, the auto pilot could not have held level flight for very long. Of course the ship could have exploded soon after we jumped. With the fire so fierce, it would not have been unlikely. But a Belgian lad who saw the ship crash described it coming down and said it didn't explode but rather fell to pieces.

"When I jumped our bomb bay doors were still open. As I crawled through the escape hatch, I recalled the discussion we had about clearing them when jumping and I wondered if I would. I did! I had been a good while without oxygen and was feeling the effects as I fell. We were at 20,000 feet. I was determined to make a delayed jump and as I extended my arms to stop somersaulting, I caught a glimpse of what I thought were eight billowing chutes. I must have counted wrong, for I found out later there were only seven."

On his back, with his feet elevated, Snyder plunged toward the earth. He could hear nothing but roaring wind. "Someone had told me that we would fall about 10,000 feet a minute so I started counting to sixty as I fell through clouds, vapor and then clear air. But after reaching sixty, I still couldn't see the ground. I started counting again but gave it up and watched for the ground. As I came out of a cloud, the earth appeared for a second and then disappeared again as I reached another cloud. I was falling in the country. There were little clusters of white farm buildings, green squares of pasture and dark brown, irregular and leafless woods. Then as the earth appeared again, I waited until I could distinguish objects very clearly and pulled the rip cord.

"It seemed natural to wonder if the chute would open. I knew soon enough as the air caught, filled the chute and the jerk nearly snapped off my neck. The rushing air roaring in my ears stopped suddenly and a most wonderful and peaceful quiet settled over me. It seemed as if I had come out of that hell above into a heaven of peace and rest. Up above, I could now hear the heavy deep sound of the Forts mingled with angry rasps of the fighters. But with the peaceful country coming up to meet me, baked in sunshine, the war and all that had happened only a few seconds before seemed like a bad dream long ago. A light breeze seemed to carry me toward a wood and I reached up to grab the shrouds in order to guide myself into a pasture. I found I was so weak I could hardly lift myself up in the harness. I was too close to the ground to pilot my course. I placed my feet together and resignedly watched the trees rush up at me."

Snyder's chute snagged in some trees, leaving him hanging some twenty feet above the ground. A Belgian farmer and his two sons discovered the hapless American. They told him to remain where he was, to avoid the German patrols prowling the ground with dogs in a hunt for him and the others. Under the cover of darkness, the Belgians rescued Snyder from his perch and hid him in the forest. He was then taken to a farmhouse to begin a seven-month odyssey as an evadee and resistance fighter with the Belgian Maquis.

Two members of Snyder's crew perished with the airplane. German forces captured bombardier Daniels and waist gunner Joseph Musial, both wounded. After they received medical treatment, they were sent to POW camps, as was the engineer Holbert. Tail gunner William O. Slenker, copilot Eike, navigator Benninger and waist gunner John Pindroch, like Snyder became evadees.

EXCEPT for the massive assaults upon Frankfurt, the bombers under Doolittle seemed only to be flexing the Mighty Eighth's muscles until the third week of February. Starting on February 20, the B-17s and B-24s participated in what became known as Big Week. Meteorologists had forecast several days of clear weather over Germany. The Eighth Air Force conspired with British Bomber Command and the U.S. Fifteenth

Air Force operating out of Italy to visit a six-day cycle of destruction upon Third Reich industry, with particular emphasis upon its aircraft factories.

On opening day, 880 B-17s and B-24s from twenty-nine bomb groups and 835 Lightnings, Thunderbolts and Mustangs from fifteen fighter outfits lifted off fields in the United Kingdom, to strike at a series of targets. Despite the predictions of the weathermen, heavy cloud cover obscured some objectives and some raiders resorted to targets of opportunity. Poor visibility may also have hampered the enemy but in any event, the thick swarms of fighters buzzed around the mob of bombers. Their efforts helped limit the four-engine losses to twenty-one aircraft, a ratio of 2.2 percent compared to the horrendous 29 percent downed on Black Thursday.

Unlike earlier days, when a maximum effort left the bomber command supine for days, the Eighth mustered another intensive assault the very next day, penetrating German air space with 762 bombers. Again, the overcast skies shielded the objectives forcing many to focus on alternatives or return with their ordnance unused. On the third day of Big Week, although almost 800 bombers took off, less than one-third could overcome the adverse weather and barely one-tenth found the primary target. Conditions improved for the bombers on their fourth and fifth missions as from 685 to 750 placed tons of explosives on the designated recipients, including two notorious sites, Regensburg and Schweinfurt.

Ralph Golubock flew four missions during Big Week. For the very first of these he learned the targets were Messerschmitt plants at Oschersleben and Helmstedt, a pair of intensely defended sites. When he grabbed a breakfast and attended the briefing, the weather seemed forbidding, thick black clouds, low ceilings, heavy rain. Golubock realized the conditions dictated instrument takeoffs, followed by a long climb to get above the clouds to build the eventual formations. As he and his colleagues prepared they felt certain the brass would scrub the affair, even as they taxied out to their assigned positions.

"The first two planes took the runway and awaited a takeoff flare which we were sure would never come. But it did! Right on time. The lead bomber raced down the runway and took off and was almost immediately enveloped in clouds and disappeared from sight. We all followed in turn, the planes spaced apart by thirty seconds. When my turn came I advanced the throttles and immediately went on instruments. The copilot tried to watch the runway to prevent accidentally drifting off and onto the rain-soaked grass. The engineer stood between the pilot and copilot to carefully monitor the engine instruments. He also called out our airspeeds so I could concentrate on taking a whole lot of airplane off the ground safely.

"Our takeoff was successful. Upon leaving the ground we were immediately immersed in rain and clouds. The tail gunner was back in his position with an Aldis lamp, which he blinked on and off so that following planes would see the light and keep their distance. The climb was long and grinding, and to our horror, we saw a huge flash of light in the sky. We all knew that two planes had collided and exploded."

To his surprise, at 17,000 feet the B-24 broke through into a deep blue sky with the sun a bright ball of fire. Below lay a white cottony carpet. "I turned the plane over to the copilot and just sat back and totally relaxed. I drank in the beauty surrounding me and wondered why I was carrying a load of death to be dropped on people I didn't even know. My meditations were shortlived. There were hundreds of airplanes around us and this was not the time for daydreaming. We had to find our proper spot in the formation. The procedure was to fly a racetrack course around a radio signal called a buncher. The lead plane was constantly firing flares so we could identify him. Each group had their own buncher. Out of all this confusion, we began to form up. First as elements, then as squadrons and groups, finally as wings and divisions. Then the three huge divisions took their correct place in the Eighth Air Force bomber stream.

"The outside air temperature gauge, on the instrument panel, was against the peg at −50 degrees Fahrenheit. The cold was biting and almost unbearable. We did not have heated flying suits or heaters that worked. We only had sheepskins that just could not keep the cold out. It was a numbing and strength-sapping cold that made concentration on flying and staying in proper formation very difficult.

"The ground was completely covered by snow, and as we approached our target, clouds began to form beneath us, making it impossible to bomb visually. We would have to bomb using PFF equipment, which was on board the lead plane. Unfortunately, the PFF equipment failed. We had to seek out a target of opportunity. We were soon on a bomb run to one of the other targets and made our drop. What we hit, I do not know. There were no fighter attacks and flak was moderate. We headed home and all of us except the two that had collided and a third that crashed in England, landed safely.

"What a screwed-up mess! Three aircraft and crews lost. We bombed a secondary target, and probably achieved nothing. All to fly a mission that should have been scrubbed in the first place."

On the following morning, Golubock faced another takeoff in abominable weather and a deep intrusion into enemy turf for a run at aircraft factories at Diepholz. "The Eighth Air Force sustained minimal losses and the 44th returned intact. Enemy losses were reported as heavy, thanks to the fighters; good bombing thanks to the bombers. Finally back in the sack for some much-needed rest after a seven-hour-long, grinding, cold mission."

A chagrined Golubock shook off mental and physical fatigue for a third attack in as many days. The briefing brought the unpleasant news of the destination, Gotha, a heavily defended site for a Messerschmitt plant. For this trip, Golubock reverted to his role as copilot for a Lt. Sam Paulsen [not his actual name]. Golubock knew Paulsen, thought him a pleasant, likable fellow but had never flown with him.

The takeoff passed routinely and while Paulsen controlled the flight Golubock tended to other duties. "About ten minutes into our climb, I began to feel that something was wrong," notes Golubock. "A quick glance at the flight instruments confirmed my fears. We were headed down in a steep spiral to the left and our air speed had increased to about 200 miles per hour. If we continued in this position, we would surely crash in a few seconds. I tapped Sam on the shoulder and pointed to the instrument panel but he did not respond. By this time the engineer was also alarmed and screamed for me to take over. I grabbed the yoke, while the engineer pulled Sam's hands off. I was able to gradually level the airplane and started into a normal climb. Sam then took over control. He seemed okay. He must have just suffered a case of vertigo, as I had, when we were leaving Greenland. Vertigo is one of the reasons that the Air Force always had two pilots on their large planes. Sam had reacted properly by relinquishing control and letting me fly us out."

Having achieved proper altitude, there remained the tricky business of insertion into the right slot in the formation. However, the pilot's vertigo again interfered with his ability to maneuver effectively. Golubock, reluctant to usurp the senior man's prerogatives waited anxiously until Paulsen said, "Ralph, please take over. I am still having vertigo problems." The entire business went almost for naught as the expedition was canceled for bad weather shortly after the fleet broke into enemy territory. But because they had reached this point, the participants received credit for a mission. Whatever the distressed pilot's problems, they did not seem to interfere with him completing his full tour.

After standing down a day, the 44th again threw itself at Gotha. "We were picked up by enemy fighters as soon as we reached Germany and were under attack during most of our run in," says Golubock. "Our gunners were doing their best to hold them off but it was impossible to keep them all out. Many got through and inflicted heavy damage. We could see B-24s and B-17s going down all around us, with parachutes blossoming out of some. There were also fighters, German and American, blowing up and going down in flames. It looked like the end of the world. About all the pilots in the bombers could do was to sit there and fly the airplane. How I wished I were in a fighter; it would be rough, maybe rougher but at least you could fight back.

"Suddenly, as if on signal, all of the fighter attacks ceased. We all knew what that meant. Flak! Close and deadly. We were now on our bomb run so no evasive maneuvers were allowed. We had to fly straight and level for the duration of our run, which lasted about five to ten minutes. The Germans laid on a deadly flak barrage which was directly in front of us and at our exact altitude. We would have to fly directly through this to the point where we would unload on our target. I watched with fascination and gut-wrenching fear as we approached the bursting flak. Surely we could not possibly fly through that hell without taking heavy losses. Suddenly we were right in the middle of the barrage. It was all around us! Black, ugly, crimson when it exploded.

"I heard the bombardier yell 'Bombs away!' and immediately we were through and into a descending left turn which left most of the flak behind us where it would take its toll on the following formation. I could not believe that we had not been hit. A miracle. We made the long trip back to Shipdham. We were all emotionally and physically exhausted. I counted fourteen down and eleven [missions] to go.

"That night at the officers' club after dinner, we were all sitting around drinking wine, which was plentiful, Scotch, which was not. We waited to see whether we were alerted for tomorrow. I was scheduled to fly if a mission was scheduled. The announcement usually came early in the evening so that if you were actually going to fly the next day, you would stop drinking and head back to your quarters. Finally word came; the 44th would stand down tomorrow. There were some signs of relief, a nervous laugh or a quick smile. The room grew noisier as everyone headed to the bar for more drinks. The laughter grew louder. It was like a college fraternity party. Everyone was having a great time. We would all live another day."

And on that next day, the crews gathered for a critique by the group commander and his staff. "As usual we were taken to task for not flying tight formations, using too much fuel and poor bombing results. Actually the bombing results of our last mission were spectacular. We had truly hit the target dead on. The colonel grudgingly admitted we had done 'a hell of a job.' He also told us he had an important announcement. Then he dropped the bomb. Eighth Air Force headquarters had made the decision that our tours were to be extended from twenty-five to thirty missions before rotation home. I could not believe what I had just heard. In the toughest theater of the war where few crews completed twenty-five, we were now told we would have to fly thirty. The colonel advanced several reasons for the extension but in fact the real one was they needed to get more out of the experienced crews because we were losing new ones at an unexpectedly high rate, many of them on their first five missions."

Larry Goldstein in the 388th, by now nearing the home stretch of his combat tour, added all four raids of Big Week. "The last was to Poznan, Poland, the longest raid of the war at the time. General Doolittle, on that day, sent the Third Division, ours, to this target without fighter escort. His reasoning was that it was all over water and there would be no enemy fighters. He was right. The enemy was the distance and the fact that we had to use oxygen sparingly was very trying to our morale and exhausting for the pilots. Several planes realized they did not have the fuel to return to England so they turned toward Sweden to sit out the war."

Big Week demonstrated that the Eighth at last could mount sustained campaigns, thanks in part to the infusion of new bomb groups and replacements for older ones. But the heavyweights could not have continued to operate with such frequency or numbers had it not been for the ability of their guardians to go the distance. While Big Week crimped enemy industrial production, far more significant were the results of the toe-to-toe battles with the German interceptors. The scorecard for the Eighth listed almost 800 in the categories of shot down, probables and damaged. Even with allowances for exaggerated claims, by the end of Big Week, the Luftwaffe was hanging on the ropes.

A relative novice to the European Theater as Big Week began, Tommy Hayes nevertheless brought considerable battle and flight hours to his 357th Fighter Group which earned the classification of "operational" on February 10. Hayes was one of the few veterans of aerial combat against the Japanese during 1942 who completed a torturous odyssey from the Pacific to the Eighth Air Force.

Born in Portland, Oregon, to a middle-class family in 1917, Hayes said he paid mild attention to world affairs although, "The Civil War in Spain had my interest, not because of the political issues but in the air war, the German air support. By the spring of 1940, I was finishing three years at

THE MIGHTY EIGHTH | 219

Oregon State. The situation in Europe was chaotic; the British [fleeing] at Dunkirk, the French surrender. Wisely the military reduced the educational requirement for flight training from four to two years of college [his application had been rejected when he graduated from high school] and I signed up immediately. I had never been in an aircraft before but the interest was there. I was ten when Lindbergh flew solo across the Atlantic. World War I aces and active duty military pilots made fly-ins at air shows. Records were being set one day, broken the next. I was [hearing about] Roscoe Turner, Jimmy Doolittle, Wiley Post, Amelia Earhart.

"Like myself, a large majority of our class had never flown or had a ride in an airplane. The first concern was would I become sick; would this be temporary or chronic? The rate of washouts in Primary and Basic was about 30 percent, although the washouts for academics were very low. Students had frequent check rides by another senior instructor. These evaluated the cadet and to a lesser degree his instructor. All students trained in single-engine planes and upon graduation received assignment based upon the instructors' recommendations and supply and demand [for multi- or single-engine pilots].

"On February 7, 1941, I graduated and pinned the silver wings and gold second lieutenant's bars on my uniform. My orders put me in the 35th Pursuit Group at Hamilton Field, California. It was newly formed and had a small number of P-36 fighters. They were obsolete then although the French flew them against the Germans in 1940. After a few months we started getting P-40s. At Hamilton Field was the 20th Pursuit Group. It had history, status and priority. We got the P-40A when they received the P-40Bs, sort of like my older brother getting a new bicycle while I got his old one. Col. Ira Eaker commanded the 20th. We fighter pilots, all second lieutenants then, used to joke about this bomber pilot trying to make like a fighter pilot. It was part of his experience for the job of a general officer in the future but a fighter pilot he was not."

By December 1941, Hayes had flown considerable hours and now sat in the cockpits of the latest version of the P-40. The crisis of the Pacific in the preceding months had split up his 35th Pursuit Group, with one-third shipped to the Philippines, one-third at sea diverted to Hawaii and the last bunch which included Hayes having sailed to Australia. They flew their P-40s to a new base created at Surabaya, Java. "On board the ship we had a Navy intelligence officer who briefed us on the Japanese air force—a collection of fixed landing gear, biwing aircraft. The P-40 pilots on board were sure we would be home in six months. Yes, they had a few of those obsolete planes but they also had the Mitsubishi Zero and the Betty two-engine bomber. Their navy had better fighters and bombers than their army. And their disregard for human life contributed to their successes over the British, Dutch and the U.S. in initial air battles. The pilots were very good, having gained real experience and training in their war in China from 1937 to 1941. They deployed their equipment quite well against our P-35, P-36 and P-40, Brewster Buffaloes, Hurricanes, etc. Their weakness was a lack of self-sealing fuel tanks."

From the outpost on Java, Hayes with his compatriots fruitlessly tried to halt the swift conquests by the Japanese. The Americans had quickly learned they were not up against paper tigers. "We had ten or twelve fighter pilots from the Philippines and who had a few weeks of war. The majority of us had not even squeezed the triggers of our machine guns. We were up against veterans who had been at war in China for four or five years. We overcame our fears and anxieties, gained experience. The guys from the Philippines emphasized, 'You don't turn with a Zero [the best Japanese fighter].' It was hit and run and the P-40 had speed and was fast in a dive. Learning was costly, however. Our supply lines from Australia were cut on February 20, when the Japanese occupied Bali. I got shot up by a Zero who hit me from the rear. The tail was damaged and the canopy dislodged from its track. On landing, coming in over a coconut plantation and turning for a final, I slowed to land, the tail dropped and the P-40 fell into the trees. It stopped quickly, the tree trunks ripping the wings off. My head hit the gunsight. I was taken to the hospital with a concussion. Then a major landing by the enemy on the northwest coast of Java ended the campaign. All pilots and air crews were evacuated by air. I was still in a hospital and not on flying status so I was taken out on a freighter with about 2,000 Americans and British from Malaysia and Singapore. All of the staterooms were given to badly burned sailors from the sunken cruiser *Houston*."

By mid-1942, Hayes had regained his role as a fighter pilot but now he flew P-39s in New Guinea. "It was still hit and run but the P-39 was less capable than the P-40. The arrival of P-38s in mid-1942 changed things. It was still hit and run but again and again now we had speed, better altitude capability and rate of climb. The tide turned."

For his having survived this long, the brass handed Hayes, credited with downing a pair of Zeros, a month of Rest and Recreation in the States in the form of selling war bonds through public appearances. When he completed that assignment he became a squadron commander of the new 357th Fighter Group, then in its gunnery phase of training with P-39s. "The P-39 was an aircraft you flew with a cerebral sense. It did not warn you how close the 39 was to the edge. Zap! and you're in trouble. We had too many crashes in a short time, evenly spread among the squadron. Maybe we commanders and flight leaders were pressing too hard. It was usually the newer pilots who bought the farm. The result was exit Col. Loring Stetson, who was all fighter pilot and got the 357th off to a great start, picking the initial key officers.

"Our new colonel called his three squadron commanders in and told us this was a good group, that his was a good job and he did not want to lose it. He added if necessary we will fly straight and level to avoid accident. He lost us then and there. He was right that we should pause and ask ourselves are we pushing the newer pilots too hard—too quick?

"But he had too much against what he needed. He lacked a positive, strong appearance or posture. His voice was high-pitched and his mannerisms put people off. But he was an officer, a senior one and I respected his rank and responsibility. But as time went on, my subordinates would question the lack of group integrity and unity. My reply was that we will surely go to the Pacific because we are training in P-39s and they are used there, not in the European Theater. In the Pacific, we almost always flew as a squadron, seldom as a group."

The Air Corps top command obviously held other ideas. Rather than ship the 357th to the Far East where in fact the P-39 was already being phased out, the 357th was ticketed for the Ninth Air Force, a more recently created organization in the United Kingdom. However, movement was delayed because its airfield was not completed. "We marked time in Wyoming and South Dakota, for six weeks, flying in the morning, pheasant hunting in the afternoon," remembered Hayes.

When the 357th sailed on the *Queen Elizabeth* in November 1943, instead of the weakling P-39, their bird of prey became the Mustang. But the Ninth still seemed unprepared to employ it. "We had no aircraft and no date when we might get them," says Hayes. "We studied aircraft recognition, British, German and U.S. After two months of this we were quite good at it. The war went on without us. The 354th, the first to fly P-51s in Europe was already fighting the Luftwaffe. Christmas came and went. The mess hall ran out of turkey and my flight leaders invited me to fried chicken cooked on their potbellied coke stove. They told me it would be rude to ask where the chicken came from. I was not rude but I think some nearby farmers lost some of their hens.

"Toward the end of January or beginning of February we were transferred to the Eighth Air Force which gave the Ninth an operational P-47 group in exchange for the 357th which now had about fifteen P-51s. The Ninth seemed to care less but the Eighth needed the long-range 51s. For a week supply trucks were bumper to bumper entering the gate. By February 5, seventy-four P-51s were on hand.

"This wasn't a problem since the P-51 was such an easy aircraft to check out in. Most pilots had flown the AT-6 in Advance, made by the same manufacturer which provided some familiarity. Compared to the P-39, the pilot could concentrate on instrument flying and or the enemy pilot. I would have preferred that our pilots had more instrument-flying capabilities. Flight leaders were good but wingmen were not as capable. If they lost formation with their leader, some lost reference to their altitude and spun in. On one occasion when the weather was bad, the mission was aborted about an hour after takeoff. The Eighth Fighter Command lost fifty-five fighters and most or all their pilots. The Continent was socked in. No German fighters were scrambled. I'm sure the fifty-five were lost due to the bad weather."

In the few days prior to the 357th's certification as operational, its commander, flight leaders and a handful of others gained valuable experience serving as wingmen of members of the 354th, the first organization to put P-51Bs over Germany. "On my first mission, I flew on Major Howard's wing as he led the 354th," recalled Hayes. "My emotions were high and there were butterflies in my stomach. It was almost a milk run. The flak was of concern but directed at the bombers. We were a comfortable distance from it. I covered Howard and witnessed a beautiful shoot-down of a 109 by him. We went to bed February 10 knowing we were on the board [as a unit] for tomorrow's mission. It was an air orientation into France and a milk run. Our first two victories were on our fourth mission." In fact the 357th scored its kills while participating on the first day of Big Week.

Stetson's successor had brought the 357th to England but never physically led the outfit into battle. Instead, he transferred to the Ninth Air Force. After four missions without a top officer in the air, command of the 357th went to Col. Henry Russell Spicer. He was known as "Hank," "Russ" or "Pappy," depending upon when and where one served with him. Spicer graduated from the advanced flying school in 1934 but had to remain a cadet for another year because in those Depression days the Air Corps lacked the funds to commission new flying officers. When the war erupted, Spicer was at Randolph Field checking out student pilots and treating them to aerobatic demonstrations. He had come to England as executive officer of the 66th Fighter Wing before taking charge of the 357th.

"He was a natural leader, a Pied Piper," said Hayes, "having the qualities absent in his predecessor. Appearance, posture, caring, respect, voice, eyes. His arrival was an example. We were called to a personnel meeting. Spicer took the stage, introduced himself, related that he personally knew Stetson, was familiar with our past, said we were a great group and weather permitting, our mission tomorrow would show just how great the 357th is. That was it—no more, no less. He had physical presence and personality. After seven months we had a group commander again.

"My crew chief was Bob Krull and his assistants were Gene Barsalore and Fred Keiper. They were great. It was really their aircraft and they let me fly it. They generally went to work when we received the mission alert late in the afternoon. Usually, it called for a maximum effort and specified an estimated time of takeoff. They had their orders and worked well into the night, even through it, helping other crews if necessary. They would nap after we were off, but all crews were up and sweating out the return of their aircraft. They had put tape over the gun barrels to keep moisture out and if the tapes were gone when we landed, they knew the guns had been fired. You can imagine the sorrow when a crew's plane did not return. The sweating went on because maybe the pilot returned but landed at another base. That was probably known within an hour or so.

"Before takeoff, after the group briefing, we always held a squadron briefing. If the bomber escort was a milk run, we would hit the deck in sections, eight aircraft or by a flight of 4 aircraft. We were after military targets, transportation, trains and trucks. Airfields were a surprise—only if while at fifty to 100 feet suddenly there is an airplane. We would pick the targets and strafe. There was no second pass.

"My record includes eight and a half Germans, all in the air—six ME-109s, an ME-110, an ME-410 and a shared ME-410. The dogfights were from altitude to the deck. Some were relatively easy and some hairy and difficult and some I felt lucky to get home. I considered myself an above-average pilot but not one of the top guns of the group. The P-51 had a slight advantage over the 109 and 190, but the German pilots varied in ability from fairly inexperienced to veterans who had been around.

"Then there was the matter of weight and wing loading. We could be heavy if the combat was early in the mission. Half of our fuel was external but those two 108-gallon tanks were dropped when a fight was imminent. After takeoff we burned some gasoline out of the fuselage tank immediately behind the pilot. This tank was an add-on to improve the P-51 range but it changed the center of gravity. If the pilot forgot and engaged a 109 or 190 with a full tank behind him, he better hope the

German was on his first flight out of flying school. I forgot once and had an awful time with a 109. Even without the excuse of a full fuselage tank, I thought I was fighting one of their top aces. Even when that was not a problem, the German interceptors would fly several missions against our bomber stream, from about a hundred miles, front to rear. The ME-109 or FW-190 might be low on gas or even ammo because of a short pit stop. Add this to experience and you had a good dogfight.

"We always expected a heavy Luftwaffe reaction. But we never knew when and where. The fighters usually made several large attacks, the last just before the probable target. Flak was fairly constant. It was not moved about. Our fighters had no reason to be along the bomber stream. We flew the same track but off to the side until we rendezvoused with the division we were to escort, usually the last 100 miles before the target. We avoided the large flak concentrations except when over a solid under-cast where we could only fly time and distance and pray. Once when returning from the Munich area with a flight of four our briefed course brought us over a solid undercast. I was concerned about the heavy flak defenses of the industrial Ruhr Valley. On a fudge factor and based on briefed winds, I corrected to my right. Then it began. Flak! [From radar-assisted antiaircraft guns.] The defense must not have had any targets to shoot at for some time as they really opened up on the four of us. We were cruising at about 25,000. I ordered the flight to spread out, far enough to keep in sight and each pilot to change course repeatedly. As I recall, it took an 88 mm shell about twenty seconds to reach 25,000 feet. The flak accuracy falls off at altitude but climbing means slower speed. The four of us gave them four separated targets. It seemed like we were in it forever—probably 15 to 20 minutes. When I landed, I climbed out of the cockpit, got on my hands and knees in the mud to kiss the good earth and thank the Lord. My crew chief asked me if I was okay and what I was doing. Then he got down next to me.

"The P-51 had a good heater and I don't recall any problems. P-38 pilots with the cockpit between the two engines did have difficulty in Europe. Sometimes you flew one to two hours before you began to escort and the P-38 pilots were so cold they could hardly move. I was over-dressed on missions in case I had to evade. Pilots who successfully evaded, mentioned the cold sleeping outdoors in the winter. The roar of the engine smothered other sounds, except for the .50 caliber machine gun fire. On occasion I heard flak explosions but only if the burst was close. Then you felt the jolt and smelled the exploded powder. Otherwise you smelled the usual cockpit odors, the mix of oil, gasoline, solvents, etc."

MOST outfits in the Eighth Air Force, like those in all military organizations included the superb, the competent and a handful of ineffectives. While breaking in new pilots Ralph Golubock, having coped with a pilot with temporary problems, remembers one lieutenant who had just been assigned to the squadron but refused to fly combat missions. For a short time he was assigned as the unit's censor officer but superior officers, cognizant of the investment in his training, ordered him into the air and he agreed to sit beside Golubock.

"Lieutenant X was fine on takeoff," says Golubock, "handling the copilot duties in a very professional manner. He acted completely normal until we took some relatively minor flak hits as we approached the target. At that point he went completely berserk, grabbing the controls and causing a major disturbance on the flight deck. Because we were deep into enemy territory I did not want to call any of the crew away from their positions to help me. Eventually, he quieted down and I was able to take control and regain our proper position. I glanced at him and was shocked to see him as if in a trance. He sat slumped in his seat, staring straight ahead, his arms on the arm rests. My engineer had to take over during the landing procedure, setting the landing gear, flaps, etc. He came alive again when we were on the ground. He told me he just could not fly combat missions and would so inform the squadron commander, Major McAtee."

Several days later, McAtee requested that Lieutenant X have a second opportunity. Golubock refused to take him, exercising the traditional right that one could not be ordered to fly with a person if he had good reason. His superior, however, said that unless X became a member of a crew he faced a court-martial. Under these circumstances Golubock accepted X. "The second mission," says Golubock, "was a repeat of the first, only worse. I had to call the engineer from his position as top turret gunner to restrain Lieutenant X. He was again trying to take control of the aircraft. He had seen German fighters and was terrified. We completed the mission with the engineer flying copilot and Lieutenant X spread out on the flight deck.

"Upon landing, Lieutenant X took me aside and told me he just could not fly combat missions. He felt that he was a menace to himself and the whole crew. I agreed and told him to report to Major McAtee and explain his situation. He did. The next day he was gone. I never saw him again but heard he had been court-martialed. I always regretted having been part of this incident. Lieutenant X was a very likable fellow and a competent pilot. I don't think he was a coward in the truest sense of the word. He was just a mixed-up kid who could not take the pressures of combat. He did the right thing not flying combat because he would have killed himself and perhaps his entire crew if he had continued. Years later I heard that after a court-martial he had been broken to private and sent to the South Pacific as an infantryman."

Of the 354th Fighter Group Tommy Hayes reports, "Some people, who were problems, slipped through, got their wings, insignia of a commissioned officer and flew combat missions. Most could be brought along with special treatment but not all. It is human nature to fear, to be afraid of dying, of being killed. It relates to a lack of confidence or capability to do the job and it is normal to overcome this, as happened in 95 percent of the cases. One of my pilots would always abort the mission before crossing the border heading for Germany with excuses of the aircraft running rough, strange noises, vibrations, etc. Now we had wasted gasoline. He flew an hour out and an hour back. A pilot must test the 'ailing a/c' (aircraft) and it always checks out okay. Then the pilot says he is not at ease in the P-51 and needs more training. It ends when I call our higher headquarters. *Voilà*, he's gone, today. The truth is he was afraid to die. I say yellow is a better word. The top pilots are mission oriented and will give their lives to carry out the duty.

"In another instance, after a fight, both the Luftwaffe and 357th elements broke up. A pilot from one of our other squadrons was by himself when he spotted another lone P-51. He joined him, flying wing and noticed the other plane had *Frenesi* on the nose. He assumed that I am the pilot. [Hayes had named his Mustang after a popular song of the day.] Wrong. I was not on the mission that day. Then the lead pilot started a descent. The wingman assumed, 'Tom Hayes sees a bogey' and he fell back in a covering position. But the dive steepened. Concerned, he leveled off and watched *Frenesi* hit the ground and explode. Too late, we find this guy has told his buddies he can't do the job and that sometime over Germany he feels like diving an aircraft into the ground. And so a good a/c was lost. He should have aborted over the North Sea but didn't. No pilot is going to rat on a buddy. The commander will be the last to know. I depended upon my flight surgeon to mix with the pilots, to be part of a group of several of them and hope that he would hear of a pending problem. People could be saved and we did save some."

HAYES enthusiastically approved the removal of Eaker in favor of Doolittle. "The difference between the early days in the Pacific, Java and New Guinea in 1942, was that you had very little to work with and so you tried to get the best out of what you had. In the Eighth Air Force, it became a question of how you handled vast resources, how to *effectively* use what you had. Under Eaker, bombers were sent east into Germany while as a diversion fighters went south into France on a sweep. The result? The Luftwaffe feasted on the bombers and our fighters saw no German aircraft. Even the effectiveness of escort was limited by demands for extremely close cover, actually making the fighters targets themselves. And the escort could not seek and pursue—could not descend below 18,000 feet."

Hayes credits the troika of Spaatz, Doolittle and Kepner for waging a successful campaign to gain air superiority. Certainly, Eaker's bomber-protection orientation restricted the contribution of the P-47s and P-51s. As a bomber advocate he had been a member of the school that originally believed high-flying, heavily-armed bombers could cope with whatever came at them from the air. The bloody encounters and horrific losses in the first fifteen months of Eighth Air Force operations had converted him to the need for escorts, to the point where he would allow the fighters no freedom of action. Eaker also seemed unable to shake off the mistaken presumption, derived from the ideas of Billy Mitchell and Douhet, that the explosives and incendiaries dropped on enemy factories would render the foe unable to defend against his B-17s and B-24s. In fairness, until 1943, with the advent of enhanced fuel supplies for P-47s and P-51s, the American fighters lacked an essential ingredient for all-out war on the enemy interceptors. But to those on the scene, with the longer-range Thunderbolts and Mustangs on hand, Eaker never seemed to grasp the need to change his strategy.

12

JOURNEYS TO BIG B

Beginning with Big Week, the Eighth Air Force carried the battle to the Third Reich with an intensity previously unseen. Whereas the sacking of cities and factories had earlier been spaced by intervals of days or even weeks, the Forts and Liberators sortied almost daily and with them came coveys of fighters prepared not only to protect their big friends but also to seek, pursue and destroy any enemy planes that ventured aloft. For the first time in the war, the German aircraft industry could not match or surpass their losses of fighters. That deficiency was temporary as manufacturing installations pushed up their pace of production. But the Luftwaffe could not churn out capable pilots fast enough to offset the loss of experienced and skilled hands in the cockpits.

Bob Johnson, the veteran fighter pilot from the 56th, says, "As time went on, we were knocking the best boys the Germans had out of the air. We were knocking off some of the best German pilots, primarily because we didn't know any better. We didn't know we were supposed to be afraid of these guys and that they were so much better than we were. We went after them and we got them. As time went on, they moved back out of our range, and finally ended up back around Dummer Lake at Brunswick, Germany—that was as far back as they could go."

At the same time, a number of American fighter pilots using P-38s and P-47s quickly saw the virtues of the latest entry, the P-51. "We all wanted the P-51," said Jim Goodson. "It was the most remarkable plane of the war. It had as much range as a B-17, was about the size of a Hurricane and only slightly larger than a Spit." His boss, Col. Don Blakeslee, commander of the 4th Fighter Group which had started out with Spitfires and then Thunderbolts, pleaded with Kepner for Mustangs. Kepner balked, noting that the Eighth in the midst of its huge offensive could not afford to stand down a fighter group while the pilots accustomed themselves to the new ships. Blakeslee supposedly pledged, "Give me those Mustangs and I give you my word—I'll have them in combat in twenty-four hours. I promise—twenty-four hours." His guaranty persuaded Kepner.

When the first P-51s arrived at the Debden airdrome, Blakeslee informed his subordinates of his promise to Kepner. "You can learn to fly them on the way to the target." In fact, the 4th's pilots squeezed in about forty minutes of flight time to familiarize themselves with their new equipment before heading out on a mission at the end of Big Week. Within a matter of weeks, group after group in the Eighth converted from the dependable but less agile P-47, and from P-38s, which continued to develop problems in the frigid climes of upper altitudes over Europe. Only the 56th Fighter Group, led by Hub Zemke retained the Jugs; all fourteen other groups in the Eighth eventually manned Mustangs, although the Ninth Air Force with heavier air-to-ground tactical responsibilities continued to operate a number of P-47 outfits.

Little more than a week after Blakeslee's outfit adopted the P-51, the 352nd Fighter Group with Punchy Powell switched. "I flew the P-47," says Powell, "for about half my eighty-three missions—all with the Thunderbolt were shorter than those in P-51s. I loved both airplanes for different reasons. The 47 was a flying tank, most durable, more firepower and absolutely the greatest for strafing attacks and excellent at the higher altitudes for air-to-air combat. However, it lost a lot in aerial combat at lower altitudes. Its number-one weakness was its limited range. It was a big sweat returning from almost any penetration of the Continent because of lack of fuel, particularly if you got into a fight or misjudged your time over the Continent. The Mustang doubled our range and eliminated this problem, except on a few extra-long missions to which we were assigned. It had range and firepower, particularly the D models with six guns instead of the four in the Bs and Cs." Actually, the ability of the P-51 to travel greater distances stimulated the devotees of the P-47 to enlarge its combat radius and while never quite the marathon performer of the Mustang, Thunderbolts eventually journeyed ever deeper into enemy territory.

The 357th, which went into combat flying P-51s on February 11, was jolted by the loss of their commander less than three weeks later. Even as the Luftwaffe tottered under the weight of firepower poured out by the tidal wave of bombers and fighters and the Third Reich earth shook from the thunderous rain of explosives, the Germans continued to draw blood. Henry Spicer, who in the eyes of Tommy Hayes transformed the 357th Fighter Group into an effective instrument, had led fourteen missions and been credited with three enemy aircraft destroyed when a burst of flak struck his P-51 on March 3. He bailed out over the English Channel, and hauled himself from the frigid waters into his inflatable dinghy. But search-and-rescue units failed to find him before, after two days, he drifted onto the beach near Cherbourg. There he lay on the sand, with frostbitten hands and feet until German soldiers discovered him. After medical treatment and interrogation, the Germans lodged him in Stalag Luft I, a growing encampment of downed aviators.

ON March 4 the VIII Bomber Command dispatched 238 B-17s for a run at Berlin, the first strike by the Air Corps at the German capital. As the navigator for *Spirit of New Mexico,* 95th Bomb Group, housed at Horgham, Lt. Vincent Fox, remembered, "If Berlin could be attacked in daylight, then all of Germany would become accessible to the full weight of American bombs. For us, the bomber crews who were assigned the mission, Berlin was a giant mental hazard, the toughest of all missions, for which we had little genuine enthusiasm. However, the briefing officer, Maj. Jiggs Donohue, the silver-tongued lawyer from Washington, D.C., had the ability to make it sound like a gallant adventure into the wild blue yonder to be cherished.

"But the procedure wasn't new to us. We were on our twenty-fourth mission. We'd been briefed for Berlin on five previous occasions, but each time the adverse European winter weather had forced us to abandon the mission short of 'Big B.' The previous day we'd climbed to 30,000 feet over the Danish peninsula only to be confronted by a solid bank of swirling, turbulent clouds. The meteorology officer glibly promised better weather for today's mission but our faith in his predictions had suffered numerous setbacks before.

"At our takeoff time of 0730 hours, scattered snow squalls limited visibility down to a scant 300 yards as we peered apprehensively into the eerie predawn light while we spiraled up to group-assembly altitude. During the tension-filled climb, the English countryside was visible only momentarily through multilayered clouds."

The 95th formed successfully but other groups were defeated early on by the towering overcast in their assembly areas. Shortly after Fox and associates crossed into Germany, Eighth Air Force headquarters supposedly sent out a recall signal. However, the mission commander of the 95th, Col. H. Griffin Mumford, leading a wing, resolutely droned toward Berlin. Puzzled by the failure to turn back, one pilot broke radio silence to advise Mumford there had been a recall. Still the 95th's B-17s continued on the pathway that carried them over the Rhine River. Unhappy crewmen watched other groups turn back with a volley of radio comments to the 95th, "You'll be sorry."

Grif Mumford, however, had been advised by his superiors that combat wing leaders could use their own discretion, continuing to the target, hitting targets of opportunity or simply heading home. Subsequently, it appeared that the recall attributed to the Eighth Air Force headquarters came from an enemy transmitter. The colonel, relying on the word from Curtis LeMay's Third Bomb Division, decided he and his aircraft were already in too deep to simply reverse course and escape enemy fighters lurking along the pathway. Instead, he reasoned that the poor visibility might hide them until they struck Berlin. Then if they flew a different course back to England they might escape unhurt. He was obviously aware of the morale and propaganda value of a hit upon Big B and perhaps the glory that might accrue to his command if he successfully pulled off the raid.

Navigator Fox said, "We soon had the chilling realization that we were alone in our undertaking. Our ball-turret gunner could identify squadrons with the 95th 'Square-B' tail markings and elements with the 'Square D' of the 100th Group [part of the wing led by Mumford] still maintaining the integrity of the formation. It seemed incredible that our token force was still bearing east toward the German capital. We got a brief glimpse of the ground near the city of Brunswick and were greeted by a barrage of enemy flak bursts."

Indeed, the ground fire had begun to exact a toll. Lt. "Doc" Thayer, a copilot, said, "I could see the vivid red flashes of flame from the gun barrels and then for the first time ever, I saw the 88 mm flak shells themselves, distinct against the white snowing background, coming all the way up as if in slow motion, then rapidly accelerating the closer they got. Fortunately the flak barrage burst above us. Then another flak shell came up through the bomb bay doors, knocked the fuse off one of our bombs and kept on going, completely through the top of the fuselage.

"Our bomb ended up on the catwalk between the two bomb bays, making a noise like a volcano-type sparkler and spewing out what looked like small shiny pieces of aluminum. How we got the bomb bay doors open and that smoldering bomb out of our aircraft in less than ten seconds I will never really understand. Apparently, there was another B-17 almost

directly below us which the falling bomb missed by a matter of inches."
A further hit from antiaircraft punched a hole in the wing of Thayer's
B-17 and damaged the engines.

Aboard another 95th Fort, a shell smashed through the bottom of
the ship, concussing the ball-turretman without a single piece of shrapnel striking him, but blasted a waist gunner in the face and chest as it
threw him from the plane. Flak ripped into the engine of a third ship
which erupted in flames. The crew continued to man their machine guns
but the wound was fatal. Eventually, they bailed out, leaving a pair of
dead waist gunners to go down with the aircraft.

Leader of the assault, Grif Mumford, in a stream of consciousness
after the fact noted, "4 March 1944, 28,000 feet over Berlin. The first
of many. God, it's cold at that outside air temperature gauge—minus 65
degrees and it isn't designed to indicate anything lower. [On at least one
B-17, the bomb doors froze.] Forget the temperature. Look at that flak.
The bastards must have all 2,500 guns operational today. This has to
be the longest bomb run yet. Krumph . . . boy that was close and listen
to the spent shrapnel hitting the airplane. Look at the gaping hole in the
left wing of number three low element . . . an 88 must have gone right
through without detonating.

"Wow, look at our little friends. Love those long-range drop-tanks!
That old 'escort you across the Channel' crap just wouldn't get the job
done. Not to worry in the target area today about the ME-109s and
FW-190s. [Others on the scene counted a dozen P-51s which apparently
drove off the enemy fighters.]

"I wonder if they realize the significance of this mission, that it could
be the turning point of the war. Stinking weather, fighter attacks and
flak over Berlin so heavy it could be walked upon is enough to make us
anxious to get out of this wieners-and-krautland and back to Jolly
Old . . . We made it. Wonder what old 'Iron Ass' LeMay will think of
the show his boys put on today."

At the end of the month, LeMay issued a commendation to the 95th
that paid tribute for completing 100 heavy bombardment missions and
specifically stated, "On 4 March 1944, this intrepid group led the first
daylight bombardment of Berlin by American heavy bombers, a feat for
which it has already won world renown."

While perhaps scoring a propaganda victory for the folks in the
States, the raid barely laid a glove on the city. Only thirty aircraft from
the 95th and 100th reached the objective as the remainder of the 502
planes assigned, thwarted by the weather or mechanical breakdowns,

brought their ordnance back to base. John Regan with the 306th Bomb Group led one flight that was forced to turn around. Shorn of a full complement necessary for mutual protection, the Americans lost five Forts. Actually, British heavyweights had been hammering Berlin for months but from this day on the Americans also called upon Berlin regularly and with far more weight. What's more, to the dismay of the Luftwaffe, they came accompanied by fighters. Hitler allegedly scoffed that they must have benefitted from favorable wind currents but Goering later admitted that when he saw American fighters in the skies over Berlin he realized the air war was lost.

"As of March 6," says Tommy Hayes, "we were not experienced veterans. We were still learning. Up to that date we had thirty victories with seven our high for a mission. The weather en route to Berlin on that day was bad. The bombers flew a dogleg north of us while we flew a straight line to our rendezvous point west of Berlin. Colonel Graham [elevated to group commander upon the downing of Spicer], had to abort over the North Sea and passed the baton to me. We were flying time and distance because of a solid overcast below. A cloud obscured our left as we passed the rendezvous time. Were we early or the bombers late? Or was I south of the rendezvous point? Geez, I screwed up. A little later, someone called out 'bombers nine o'clock.' There they were, B-17s coming out of the poor visibility. *But* we were to escort B-24s of the Second Bomb Division. It entered my mind to look for our 24s but then someone called out, 'Bogeys at two o'clock.' When they appeared, it was fight now.

"I called, 'Let's fight. Drop tanks.' The 109s, 110s, 410s and FW-190s were estimated at 120–150. They were going head-on for the bombers. We turned left onto their rear. Some turned into us. Some continued for the bombers. Then a top cover of thirty or so 109s entered the fight. My high squadron, up-sun, engaged the top cover. The score was twenty kills and no losses. It was important for us because it was our first big fight against a large force. And we kicked ass. We were still learning. It was good timing, good for morale. But it wasn't the best work. We didn't escort our assigned bombers. We lucked out, getting a distinguished unit citation."

"I was on three of the first Berlin raids," remembers Bob Johnson of the 56th Fighter Group. "I was the lead airplane on March 6. I had only eight airplanes to protect 180 bombers; the 62nd Squadron had dropped off to take up battle over the Zuider Zee. Gabreski had moved off the top and south to try to find some enemy. [A freelance hunt not permitted under the pre-Doolittle regime.] I was circling overhead. As I got to the front of the bomber line and made my orbit to turn left, I saw a gaggle, not any particular formation, just a group of airplanes, coming in from the north. At first I thought they were P-47s, a new group had just gotten over there and was flying all over the sky. As I came up to them, I said, 'Christ, they're Focke Wulf 190s.'

"We were line abreast, all eight of us and we just opened fire and went right through some sixty or so 190s and 109s. As we turned to get on their tails, we saw another sixty or so above and another sixty or so to their left. Probably 175–180 German aircraft. Eight of us.

"We followed the first gaggle through our bombers, head-on. We had no idea how many we hit. We were firing, airplanes were falling out of the sky all over, from bomber gunfire, from their gunfire to our bombers, from them ramming into our bombers. Burning bombers and fighters and parachutes filled the sky. There was no space; they weren't ramming purposely. You never saw such a sight in your life. Bombers falling, parachutes falling, fighters falling.

"I didn't have to think about the situation, it was there. I thought only of survival, and hitting the enemy. If there are crosses, shoot at them. So much damage was being done in the air there, at that moment; it took place in seconds. We lost sixty-nine bombers, and I was right in the middle of it. How many of the bombers were shooting at me and my buddies, I don't know. But they were shooting at airplanes. That's all they cared about. And I don't blame them.

"A heck of a lot of those [bomber crewmen] were out in parachutes and in burning airplanes that were falling with flames two thousand feet deep. The bombers scattered all over the sky trying to get home. We went after the 109s and 190s who were still attacking. We did not have radio contact with the bombers but we got a lot of waves from waist windows as we crossed the North Sea and a lot of free drinks in London when we ran into some of those bomber crews. I lost one guy out of the eight. I think our boy ended up a POW. We got sixteen or seventeen Germans."

Two days later, Johnson immersed himself in what started out as a replica of his first trip to Berlin. But this time as he headed into the enemy fighters with eight planes abreast in formation, he says, "All the time I was calling over various buttons [frequencies], slowly and distinctly calling our exact location on all the different channels, even the bomber channels, so they could call other fighters and get them there. When we hit them, our eight little guys scattered their fighters all over the sky. Other batches of our fighters came down to help and confused the Germans. In just that few minutes we had brought in P-38s and P-47s all over the sky. That was one hell of a battle. We stopped the Germans at least two miles away from the bombers."

Joseph Bennett plunged into the maelstrom. "The 56th Group was awarded the Presidential Unit Citation for destroying thirty planes in the air [twenty-eight by official records]. Possibly the three I destroyed were significant in that instance. However, they would have received the citation at some date for another reason. I made claims of ten destroyed, two probably destroyed and three damaged. Three were in dogfights, four tried evasive action and the others let me slip behind them."

Paul Ellington, an Eagle Squadron recruit now in the cockpit of a P-47 was on his way home from Berlin when a burst of flak forced him to belly in his ship in a Belgian field. "I burned it, stuffed my parachute in the fuel tank and used it as a wick." He wandered about for a few hours before German soldiers apprehended him and he started the journey that would end at Stalag I, in Barth.

Although the loss ratio of heavyweights fell from about 10 percent during the previous attack on Berlin to less than seven, that still meant close to 400 Americans were MIA, KIA or WIA. The Eighth insisted it had destroyed or damaged as many as 400 enemy fighters in these two encounters. During the March 4 foray against Big B, assembly problems thwarted a number of groups including the 388th. Larry Goldstein's crew already had finished twenty-four raids and had hoped for a milk run. Berlin hardly seemed like a soft touch but now that they were on the verge of ending their time in combat, the men were willing to take dangerous chances. "Our crew elected to fall out of formation, pick out a target in Germany, drop our bombs, climb back into the formation and all would be okay.

"We did drop out, we did bomb a railroad yard and when we attempted to climb back to the group, we were attacked by a FW-190 who hit us several times with 20 mm shells. We were able to escape by diving into the clouds. My pilot asked me for an emergency radio fix from the British rescue net. Despite German jamming, I was able to get a position report, pass it on to the navigator. He plotted a course for England and when we broke out of the clouds, we were over the English Channel. When we landed we had no brakes and went off the end of the runway, ending up in a plowed field. When we left the plane, we saw the extensive damage and realized how lucky we had been to escape disaster, especially when I saw a hole in the radio room just above where my head had been. This was twenty-five and we all kissed the ground when we realized that our flying combat was over." Pilot Kiersted's boast to the crew chief that they would complete a tour had been correct.

Jack Kidd, as a command pilot for the 100th led the entire 3rd Air Division, about 300 aircraft, on another crack at Berlin. "It was an almost idyllic mission," recalls Kidd. "The weather people had forecast some low clouds and a 120-mile-an-hour tailwind, which would have whizzed us across the twenty miles or so of Berlin. We got in there and we were bombing on radar a target somewhere near the center of Berlin. The RAF did a great service by flying their reconnaissance Mosquitos in, and ejecting chaff, the bundles of foil which fooled radar into thinking they were planes. We headed in over the target, instead of 120-mph tailwind, it was almost opposite, so our groundspeed was down to about 100 mph. Here we were inching across the target but all the antiaircraft fire was going off beneath us at the chaff. There were no bursts anywhere near my formation while we went across. There was only one aircraft lost when we bombed Berlin that day."

EVEN as the P-51 forged ahead as the weapon of choice for the bulk of the Eighth Fighter Command, the 364th Fighter Group continued to operate with P-38s. Among those in Lightning cockpits was Max J. Woolley, the Montana-born son of a lawman. He had attended the state university. "I didn't like hearing Hitler and Mussolini ranting and raving to their own people and eventually to those they overran with their war machines. The 'rape of Nanking' by the Japanese irritated, scared and concerned me about them. I knew that the United States was big and had great potential but I was afraid because I sensed that we were not ready for war.

"I had never flown, but in 1927 Charles Lindbergh, already famous for his flight across the Atlantic, made a brief stop in Helena. To see his plane was a thrill." But when drafted into the Army, Woolley received a more earthly assignment, motorcycle mechanic in the Quartermaster Corps. "I didn't like working on those dirty, greasy machines. I had never been on one, around one nor had anything to do with one. A fellow soldier who shared my viewpoint suggested we take the Air Corps examination for pilot training. By the time we did there were a total of eight disgruntled mechanics like us who took the test. After several more examinations and physicals, I was the only one selected for pilot training."

At the end of the third phase of flight instruction, Woolley and his class of cadets were given a chance to choose the type of tactical aircraft they would prefer. "Most of the cadets who wanted fighters wanted the P-38.

Too many bad stories about the P-39 being a 'killer coffin' turned cadets away from it. Some wanted the P-40 as it was supposed to be doing a remarkable job in the Pacific. Stories circulated that the P-47 was a sluggish, heavy machine that couldn't perform well in combat. That was untrue. One need only look at the kills it attained to know the rumors were unfounded. I chose the P-38. I liked the two engines, probably for safety, the speed of the aircraft, the firepower, and I red-lined [to push or pass the manufacturer's speed limit] a number of times. With four fifties and a 20 mm cannon up front, the Jerries knew that you could hurt them."

Placed in the 384th Fighter Squadron, one of the three operational units that composed the 364th Fighter Group, Woolley practiced flying techniques and tactics while stationed in California until a troop train bore everyone east for a voyage to England on the *Queen Elizabeth*. Established at Honington in the United Kingdom, the 364th began operations on March 2, 1944.

"I had about four or five hours of training in England before I went 'active.' A pilot learns combat by being in combat," notes Woolley. "None of my flight instructors had been in combat so they had no first-hand experience to pass on. No one can tell you about the feeling, the tenseness and your grinding guts. You have to have been there and felt it first hand. Although I had quite a bit of target shooting in stateside training, nothing takes the place of shooting at an ME-109 or FW-190 while it's moving better than 400 miles per hour for a split second across your gunsight.

"My first encounter with the enemy was on my first mission [March 15]. From the Allied viewpoint, historians have classified this particular battle as one of the five greatest air battles of the European War over Germany. It wasn't great because I happened to be over Europe that day, but because of the great effort that Hermann Goering put forth with his air force to break the back of the Allied fighters. Our group was near Hanover, Germany, around 23,000 feet and heading east. A gaggle of German fighters were below us around 18 to 19,000 feet, set there as a decoy. Several thousand feet above us was a much larger group. Undoubtedly, this was the main strike force intent on reclaiming the skies for the Fatherland.

"The signal was given to drop belly tanks, close flight to our tactical position, increase rpms and manifold pressure as we headed down to intercept the Jerries below. This being my first mission, I was assigned the flight's most protected position—number two on my flight leader's wing. The enemy above us came down for the attack as we knew they would. Within seconds there was one massive hornet's nest stirred up in the German skies. I immediately knew that I was in a battle for my life. Planes were going everywhere, red flashes streaked the sky, puffs of black smoke started to curl upward as Orville Myers, my flight leader, called, 'Red Two. Tighten your turn. Jerry on your tail.' At that moment, streaks shot past my canopy. In my mirror was a 109 which appeared inches behind me, and tightened his turn to put me in the 'has been column.' I had everything forward exceeding the red line, hit the flap handle again and stood her on a point, desperately trying to save my skin. A 109 slid in front of me, intent on taking Myers. He crossed my gun sight. I hit the trigger button as four fifties and a 20 mm cannon belched their hate for a fair-haired Superman. Part of his tail swished past my wing, only a superficial nick but enough for him to wing over and head below.

"P-47s in the area heard the chatter and came rushing to the fray. Friend and foe now were desperately trying to annihilate one another. 'Red Two. Tighten your turn.' Again I hit the flap handle, kicked left rudder, fought the control wheel to shake him with all needles vibrating beyond their safety zone. Soon it was over. What seemed like an hour lasted only minutes.

"They saw, they came, but they didn't conquer. The sky was now void of the Reich defenders. Only white-streaked contrails left by the angry hornets seeking their adversaries fluttered in the brilliant blue. Down below a few broken machines jabbed back and forth amid the rising acrid smoke, soon to take their place in the graveyard of broken dreams. Both friend and foe paid dearly for this exercise in self-determination. The fight was a great lesson. Classroom instruction can never take the place of flak and live ammunition trying to separate a man from his inner soul.

"I had heard the weather in England was bad," Woolley continues, "but having spent my early growing-up days in Montana where the sun shines almost every day, and having trained in California, to see and experience the cold, clammy, foggy weather was not so much of a shock as it was depressing. It added to the sense of foresakenness, loneliness, bad meals, being tired, the inevitable colds, sinus problems, plus flu and diarrhea.

"One morning the flight surgeon was checking every pilot trying to get enough to make up a flight. He looked at everyone and most were in bad shape. He asked me, 'How do you feel?' I spent about a minute telling him of my severe case of diarrhea. He responded, 'Stick a cork up your ass and enjoy the flight.' We had a long cold flight to Berlin that day. About an hour after takeoff we encountered some twenty 190s, all sporting the famed Hermann Goering yellow jacket nose. They hit us from three o'clock high out of the bright morning sun, going through our group with guns blazing. Just at that moment, my diarrhea kicked in, but I was forced to concentrate on self-preservation, not body control. I emptied the contents of the lower colon at 20,000 feet over Steinhuder Lake, spending the rest of the drive to Berlin and the return sitting on an icicle of excrement.

"After my first mission, my crew chief and crew had asked me about a name for our plane. I turned the question around and asked them what they would like. One answered, 'The Homesick Angel. We'd all like to go home and after hearing today's mission on the PA system we didn't know for sure if you were coming back or if you were an angel.' I thought it a pretty good name and that's what we called my P-38. My ground crew was undoubtedly the best in the group; I'm sure most pilots will say the same. My guys worked their butts off keeping my plane airworthy. They missed meals, put up with the cold, the fog, lack of parts, no time off, terrible housing, few commendations, continual jawing from the ground engineer as well as me to hurry and get the plane ready so that I could take it up and probably bring it back full of holes, a burnt-up engine, frayed cables or any number of other problems. The only rewards were burnt fingers from a hot engine. I aborted a couple of times due to mechanical failure but my plane was the oldest in the squadron and overdue for another set of engine changes."

Woolley attempted to shield himself against the impact of losses. "I tried not to become emotionally attached to any one person as a pilot never knew when his name would be called by his maker. It was tough seeing your friends taking the worst of things, but so much harder if you were extremely close to them. Most of the pilots from our original group in California were outstanding fliers. Some had personalities I didn't care for but I never questioned any of their technical flying ability."

WHILE fighter pilots by the nature of the job could perhaps wall themselves off from others in the squadron, it was more difficult for the bomber crews which not only lived together but also worked side by side. Golubock in the 44th Bomb Group had bonded with navigator Bob Bauman, a member of his replacement crew that broke up in England. Although they now flew in different planes the pair roomed together, usually managed to take leaves together. On April 7, after a trip to London, Golubock learned he was not scheduled to fly the following day but his friend was. "I woke up while he dressed and we exchanged the usual banter and kidding. I said, 'Hope you have a milk run.' Then I went back to sleep.

"The first indication I had that something was very wrong was when the group began arriving back at the base. As they circled, preparing to land, it was obvious that we had taken some losses. In addition to holes in the formation, there were many airplanes firing flares indicating an emergency or wounded. As they continued in their landing procedures, I began counting and was horrified. The group had taken a terrible beating. Our losses were enormous. I searched in vain for some sign of Bob or his crew. I asked many of the returning airmen if they knew anything about Bob's plane but they were unable to help me. There had been so much confusion that it was impossible to identify any single aircraft that might have been lost. I waited in the debriefing room, but didn't get any definitive answers. Eventually, all of the crews had been debriefed and I was waiting alone. It suddenly hit me. Bob was not coming back."

Dazed, Golubock says he walked to the officers' club and drank himself into a stupor. "I could not accept the fact that my buddy was not coming home. Much later some guys came over and woke me up. It was now dark and I had missed dinner. I slowly walked back to my quarters with tears in my eyes. When I arrived I was stunned. There were six or seven guys in the room, all going through Bob's possessions.

"'What the hell is going on!' I yelled. 'Get the hell out of here.'

"'Take it easy,' was the reply. 'He won't be needing any of this.' I went berserk. I grabbed my gun, which I kept hanging over my bunk, and pointed it at them. 'Get the hell out of here, you bastards, or I will blow your fucking heads off.' They could see that I wasn't kidding and almost broke their necks going through the door. I have never been more ashamed of a group of men. And they were all officers in the U.S. Army. All bastards. Later that night some of the guys from my old crew came in and sat with me. They had heard what had happened and wanted to settle me down. One of them gently took my gun and put it back in the holster. We all spoke of Bob and hoped he was a POW." Indeed, some time later, the 44th learned that although badly wounded, Bauman had survived and was a prisoner. Unfortunately, the swift appearance of scavengers bent on looting the possessions of the downed airman was not unique and frequently friends of those lost engaged in a frantic race against others intent on plunder.

An accident forced Joseph Bennett, from the holdout 56th Fighter

Group, to splash down in the Channel in his P-47. On April 15 he was briefed for a mission that might last six hours. "I had always flown with my seat belt tight and on one long trip, the bottle for inflating the rubber dinghy that was packed with our parachute cut off blood circulation, causing numbness from the knees down. To prevent this, I loosened my safety belt, giving me room to change my position and be more comfortable. We took off with a man flying his first mission on my right wing; the other two of the flight were on my left wing. We went into a cloud soon after takeoff and flew on instruments. At 21,000 feet, my supercharger cut in and I pulled the throttle back to maintain a constant airspeed. The wingman's wing made light contact with my canopy and it popped off.

"I jammed the stick forward unconsciously and in seconds I was vertical. The loose seat belt allowed me to slip up until my head was sticking out of the plane. My little and second fingers were still on the stick at the last knuckle but when they slipped off, I was sucked out through the harness or else the belt broke. When I left the plane I was falling so fast I could not breathe so I pulled on the rip cord and it slipped out of my hand. I grabbed it again and pulled so hard that when my arm extended past my body, the wind jerked it straight upward. The chute opened with quite a jerk and I was sitting on air.

"It suddenly came to my attention that I could not see. I put my hand to my face and couldn't see it. It was quite unlike anything I had ever known. Something warned me to prepare for landing. I uncoupled one leg strap and twisted the connector on the other when I hit the water. When my head came out of the water, my eyesight had returned and the parachute was folding upon the water beside me. I unbuckled the chute waist connector and reached for the dinghy but it wasn't in the pack. Part of the plane was floating about fifty yards away so I started swimming toward it. My left shoulder was hurting, the water was cold, and the swimming pretty slow.

"After about thirty feet I found the dinghy, less than a foot under the surface. I got it in position and pulled the pin for inflation, then tried to roll it under my body but it slipped out of my cold hands as it was inflating, which would make it more difficult to mount. Grabbing the dinghy I gave another roll with all the strength I had and got a part of it under my back but didn't make it to the center. Finally, I could feel it inflating where my hand was gripping and I began to rise out of the water. I slid to the center and began to put the hood on and fasten the windbreaker. I was so cold I began to shake and my teeth were clattering so hard I thought they might break. I was having trouble breathing and started to blow my nose only to discover that more than half of it was almost severed. My upper body began to warm up, but my butt and feet ached and were cold.

"Opening the windbreaker, I discovered about four inches of water in the bottom of the dinghy. I took off one of my GI shoes and bailed until it was almost dry, then fastened the wind-breaker. I had been there about an hour when I heard a plane go by. The clouds had lifted to another 300 feet. On the third or fourth circle he spotted me and stayed around for about an hour. It was McKennon, from another squadron in our group. That perked me up. However, I knew chances of being picked up by air-sea rescue were slim. A slight breeze had started and if I could live through the night, I'd possibly drift to Belgium.

"I fell asleep to be awakened by a seagull standing on my head with my nose in his beak, shaking his head from side to side quite violently. I don't know how long before I fell asleep again, but the noise from a rescue-boat engine woke me. It was about seventy-five yards away, headed toward me. A native of Norway, named English, was in command of the vessel in the service of British Air-Sea Rescue. I never did know how they got me aboard but they wrapped me in blankets, gave me two cups of hot buttered rum and I drifted off into a sound sleep. I awakened hours later as I was carried up a gangplank on a litter. I learned later that the boy on my right wing had called in a distress May Day." Bennett, unlike the unfortunate Henry Spicer, would fly again.

Some three weeks after Spicer went down, another squadron commander in the 357th was KIA and the musical chairs of replacement elevated Tommy Hayes who says he now perceived the effects of the incessant pummeling of the enemy. "The all-out air war in February and March paid dividends by April. Hitting their oil was serious enough so that pilot training was reduced drastically. At the same time they were losing their most experienced people. During the period of March 2 to May 29 I shot down several who were still green. I also had engagements with the 109 and 190 where it was a tossup. Some flew the 109 like it was a P-51. Then there was an FW-190 which outran my flight of four, all of us with the throttle against the wall gave up after five minutes. This pilot outflew me from 22,000 feet to the deck as he slipped, and skidded, power off, power on. Sometimes our pilots on the tail of a 109 or 190 saw them release the canopy and bail out, some without ever firing a burst. A victory is a victory. Some 190 pilots couldn't really handle their fighter. The 190 had a high wing loading, but when on the deck, if they pulled it too tight, they stalled and went in. Again, a victory without firing the guns."

The diminution of the Luftwaffe notwithstanding, spring 1944 for the Mighty Eighth hardly ended its bloodshed. Even as the aviators mourned and coped, they absorbed hordes of newcomers, fresh from flight training in the U.S. And now the UK-based airmen took their cues from the strategists who scripted new and critical assignments in support of the coming Allied landings in France.

13

READYING FOR D-DAY

As 1944 rounded into spring, the United States' production of the accoutrements of war and trained personnel accelerated into high gear. President Roosevelt's promise of 50,000 airplanes a year was being fulfilled while flight schools taught thousands of pilots, bombardiers, navigators, gunners and mechanics how to use them. What had been a plane-poor, crew-short Eighth Air Force now bulged with new assets, enhanced further by the extension of tours for already experienced and qualified airmen.

Punchy Powell, the P-51 pilot with the 352nd Fighter Group says, "When we went into combat in September 1943, there was a general policy that fighter pilots would be relieved from duty after 200 'combat hours.' However, when D-Day approached, the powers that be realized that most of the early pilots like myself would be reaching that mark at about the time D-Day would probably happen. Whoa! The word came down that 'those pilots who had completed 180 combat hours' had two options. 1. To return to the U.S. on R & R after completing 200 and then return to the group to be there for D-Day and fly a second full tour. 2. To complete their 200 hours and stay on board for an extra 100 hours and then return to the U.S. after that for a permanent change of station (or at least until needed in the Pacific). I opted to stay on for the 'long and short tours' as did many others. We were there for D-Day. Those who went home on R & R did not make it back until about D-Day plus ten."

Bomber crews who had hardly adjusted to the increase from twenty-five to thirty missions before relief now learned they would have to complete thirty-five before going home. (Some extra credit accrued to those who served as lead pilots, navigators or bombardiers and their gunners.) The explanation given to the unhappy fliers was that the advent of more fighter groups capable of ushering the bombers to and from the target had so increased the chances of survival it was reasonable to tack on the additional number.

Even with the change from twenty-five to thirty and subsequently thirty-five punches on a mission card to qualify for rotation home or transfer to noncombat duty, some early air warriors left the scene. The crew of 91st Bomb Group's *Memphis Belle,* the first to go the full twenty-five without losing a man had gone home in 1943 to sell war bonds. Billy Southworth, who had flown his final mission for the 303rd in the summer of 1943, hung around in a staff position until early in 1944 when he too chose to return to the States. His first navigator, Jon Schueler, a casualty of emotional stress, had been invalided to a military hospital in the U.S. before receiving an honorable discharge in February 1944. Their former gunner, Bill Fleming, remained in England as a gunnery instructor.

John Regan, a green second lieutenant when he started to fly B-17s with the 306th in 1942 and by April 1944 a twenty-four-year-old lieutenant colonel commanding a squadron, made no less than five attempts to round out his tour [he flew actually twenty-five but received credit for thirty under a system where flight leaders were awarded a premium] before he achieved the goal in a raid near Brussels. Feted by his associates with boozy parties, Regan admits, "I had extreme difficulty unwinding when I came home. When I got to the U.S. and after I had been with my family for a while I just about had a nervous breakdown. I was in a train station and felt I wanted to stand there and scream. Nowadays, this would be called post-traumatic stress syndrome."

The ordeals that drove Regan to the breaking point and Schueler beyond it were only partly mitigated by the living conditions of the Eighth Air Force flight personnel. "When not flying," says Regan, "my life was quite relaxed. My associates and I lived in barracks with about thirty-two men. Eventually as squadron CO I had my own place with its potbellied stove to keep me warm."

Some airbases provided separate accommodations for officers and enlisted men. At the 96th Bomb Group home, Archie Old said, "We kept the crews integrated, the whole damn ten-man crew sleeps and lives in the same quarters." Old stressed the value of noncombat support. "If you feed them better, pay them better, clothe them better, house them better, transport them, this sort of stuff, the better this part is, the more relaxed they are. There will never be another war fought like that one we had over there. We lived as good or better over there than we did at home." In point of fact, there was a great disparity in the accommodations with some men housed in splendid castles, regular beds with sheets and convenient bathing and toilet facilities. Others froze in tent cities, slept on cots under mountains of blankets and hiked through the mud to latrines and showers.

Almost without exception, airmen speak fondly of the host nation. Says John Regan, "The British treated us wonderfully. When we had time off, we'd jump into our Jeeps, tear off into the countryside firing flares, feeling no pain, having a big time, probably go to the town of Luton, fairly close to our base. We'd go to the same pub and people would see us, really greet us, cheer, sing songs. We got to know everybody there. We enjoyed it so much that one time I got all my men together and we called the fellow that owned the place up in front. I presented him with stripes and made him an honorary sergeant in our squadron.

"I spent quite a bit of time in London when it was being bombed. Instead of going down in the subways like most of the British did, we were like typical, crazy Americans, young, full of ginger and we would stand outside and watch the antiaircraft. The bomb damage didn't make me think about what we were doing. We were engaged in daylight bombing and trying to be pinpoint accurate and I think most of the time we were."

W. O. "Ollie" Joiner, with a high school education scored highly on the standard intelligence tests on entering the service and went to the Air Corps. He had an option of auditioning for the Army Air Force band but passed up the opportunity to study radio. When he completed school he and a bunch of fellow graduates were assigned to the 364th Fighter Group for shipment to England.

"My main job was CNS—Control Net System. We had three radio stations near but off the base. One was a receiver station, one a transmitter and one a D/F direction finder station. A pilot would call for a 'homing' and we would give him the direction to fly to get back to the base. My other job at Honington [the 364th's home] was being the arranger, first trumpet vocalist leader of the base dance orchestra, 'The Goldbricks.' We played eighty-six gigs which does not include all of the beer busts we played. We were never paid for the beer busts but at some of our dances each man would receive ten shillings [about $2.40] and a share of usually one bottle of Scotch. Once in a great while we would receive a pound [$4.86]. Other times we might receive two bottles of Scotch, but not very often. You can see that musicians did not play for the money."

Red Komarek, among the early American airmen ensconced in the

United Kingdom says, "We were told by the brass that a formal introduction would be necessary in order to meet English girls and that the English were more strait-laced than us broad-minded Yanks. We found both to be untrue. Whoever researched this information must have seen a lot of old British movies. It was obvious from our first visit to town (Huntington) that boy-meets-girl routines were not very different from those back home."

Tommy Hayes recharged himself with excursions to London. "My trips, the so-called forty-eight-hour pass, was a break from the war and the opportunity to relax, to again be an officer and gentleman. For me that meant a comfortable hotel, a nice dining room, sleeping on sheets that might have been silk and a bath in a tub, the length of which exceeded my height. It happened often enough that you remained a member of the human race, although always eager to get back and fight.

"Seeing London and the damage reminded one of the war at ground level. We had almost none at our base. The most amazing aspect was the spirit of the British and the total war they fought. With almost all men in uniform, I would see elderly, old women working at menial jobs, for example in train stations, pulling and pushing four-wheel baggage wagons."

Southworth's diaries contain numerous references to fun-filled excursions to London and partying in the vicinity of the base. On a number of occasions he speaks of awakening for a mission after only an hour or two of sleep. Although numerous survivors speak of the carousing between missions, Archie Old, however, insisted, "Our boys learned real quick that you didn't get drunk every night and fly a mission the next day. In spite of all the heroic things you read about the great drinkers going out and having a hell of a good time, dating and everything, and then they go out and fly the mission, that ain't the way it works." But, despite Old's contention, as Howard Snyder indicated, oxygen cleared many a hangover.

On the other hand many of the visitors in residence pursued less exuberant activities. Fighter pilot Joe Bennett says, "After the evening meal I would go to the bar for a couple of beers and listen to the radio or get in conversation with others. I wrote two or more letters each week and always had a book to read to pass the time. I would be in bed by nine o'clock most nights."

Ball gunner Wil Richardson was another who eschewed carousing. "I was never a drinker and only took the 'shots' after two missions. I gave the drinks usually to Gil or Bruton [fellow crewmen]. I became acquainted with the chaplain. Along with the left waist gunner, Ken

Rasco, I liked classical music. A small bunch of us, officers as well as enlisted men, would meet with the chaplain and have mini concerts. Each of us would pick something to play [on a phonograph] and tell why we chose it. It was a great way to help cope."

East Anglia, where many American air bases were located, was then largely rural. "The largest city," says Hal Turrell, "was Norwich. It was a poor area with a hard-working population, scratching out a living from farming. Few of the homes had modern conveniences. Quite like our own rural South of the time, and it furnished many of the volunteers for its country's wars.

"The relationship between the Yanks and the Brits was at first wary, then cordial and in the end close. They had been fighting alone for a long time," notes Turrell. "Universal service was the norm, their country a battlefield and here came the Americans. We were better dressed, better paid and quite cocky. Life in that time for young women was very bewildering. For long periods there would be only women around and a few very old men. Suddenly there would be a situation where they were surrounded by hundreds of young men. The American air bases would put on dance parties. They would send some trucks into the nearest town, announce the party, and the girls would climb on board. At the end of the party, the trucks would take them back. Although usually there would be one or two girls turning up a few days later.

"While we were on combat status, the girls would not get too involved with us. The reason was that when they grew to like someone and they were shot down it was too hard. So everything was kept on a casual basis. Many of the ground personnel did marry British girls. I think 60,000 brides went to America after the war. The Army actively discouraged marriage and made it quite difficult. I never did understand the rationale for this stupid policy."

As Turrell remarked, ground crewmen like Whit Hill had the most opportunity to mingle with their hosts although Hill indicates some culture shock. "Life in the English economy was austere—food was rationed, there were few automobiles and the drinking habits confused us. The tea rooms and pubs had screwy hours. Pubs opened at 10:00 A.M. then closed at 2:00 P.M. They opened again at six and closed at ten. It took a bit of doing to get accustomed to the pub hours, but in the end they were a godsend. If one didn't meet up with a girl by 10:00 P.M., he could go home and get a good night's sleep. On the other hand, if he did, he didn't have to sit up at the bar until the wee hours of the morning just to shake her hand goodnight.

"All the young men I traveled around with had bicycles. As a result, we mostly frequented outlying towns and pubs where our brother Yanks didn't go. Doing so, we met and made friends with many of the local people in such little towns and villages as Bassingbourn, Kneesworth Hall, Litlington, Ashworth, Ashwell, Arrington, Orwell and Biggleswade. To be assured of a whisky drink back then, one had to know the delivery date the various pubs received their ration of beer, wine and spirits.

"On occasions we would take the GI 'Liberty Run,' recreation trucks to Cambridge or Royston; or the trains to Baldock, Cambridge, Hitchin, Letchworth, Luton and of course London, the place we called the 'Ancient City.' The local pubs were night rides, but with a forty-eight-hour pass, it was off to London. Coming from Philadelphia I was right at home there. On a first visit to the Hammersmith Palais dance hall in 1942, doing a lively fox trot, I changed to jitterbugging. Shortly there was a tap on my shoulder and a gentleman advised that 'We don't do that kind of dancing here, Yank.' Time soon changed that policy.

"I eventually met and married Dorothy Dixon from Litlington, whose family had moved away from the bombings of the industrial areas of Manchester, Liverpool and Stockport. As more and more of my friends married English girls, American women wanted to know what the English girls had that they didn't. The answer usually was 'Nothing, but it's over here.' Of course one has to consider we were all getting to the marrying age and barracks life had left lots to be desired. Our first son, Carl, was born in Royston."

Before his friend Bob Bauman was shot down, Ralph Golubock and the navigator explored London. "Bob and I were staying at the Reindeer Officers Club. An elderly Englishman approached me and asked if I would like to have a guide to show us around. Thinking that he was trying to sell his service, I politely turned him down. He smiled and said, 'See here, Yank. There is no charge. This is just my way of doing my bit. Please let me show you around.'

"The old gentleman seemed to be quite a nice chap so we cheerfully accepted his kind offer. We wanted to see Westminster Abbey and he took us there first. For two young, unsophisticated Americans, Westminster was a marvel. We looked at it from top to bottom, with our English gentleman happily pointing out all of its treasures. We visited all of the famous authors, poets and royalty [entombed there] that we had read about. We were thrilled and overwhelmed. Then our friend took us to the 'best part.' He showed us the cornerstone which had been laid in 1066. 'Imagine,' he said, 'this was the very beginning and it was laid during the time of the Norman invasion.' To him this was sacred territory and to me this man epitomized the wonderful English people. They were unbelievably cordial. In Norwich we had a cab driver who took us out, stayed with us, brought us back to the base and wouldn't take a penny."

REPLACEMENTS and completely new groups far outnumbered the rotated airmen like Regan and Southworth or those shot down like Marshall Draper, Lu Cox, John McClure, Howard Snyder and others. For the Mighty Eighth was now committed to what Winston Churchill designated "the mighty endeavor," Operation Overlord. In spite of the fanciful beliefs of the RAF's Sir Arthur "Bomber" Harris that the enemy could be knocked out through the ministrations of his forces and the Air Corps, few others in strategic planning believed anything short of a full-scale deployment of ground armies on the Continent could destroy the Third Reich. As early as March 1942, the War Department began work on an outline for an invasion of Europe the following year. In January 1943, at the Casablanca meeting wherein Bill Fleming had the privilege of serving on the B-17 that bore Ira Eaker to the North Africa summit session, more realistic appraisals of what could be accomplished over the coming months pushed the schedule for a massive cross-channel assault into spring 1944.

Experts from the major Allied branches of military service had accumulated intelligence with gathering intensity, wrestled with logistical matters and plotted strategy and tactics. Considerable debate involved the role of the air arms. Those with Harris's point of view, or at least a faith that the strongest blows from the air should concentrate on the means for the Wehrmacht to wage war, argued the bombers and fighters of the Eighth Air Force should be devoted to demolishing the sources of weaponry and fuel. Some advocated that the Ninth Air Force, reconstituted in the UK in October 1943, and a tactical outfit dedicated to battlefield support rather than the concept of strategic bombing, should, along with various units in the RAF, participate directly in Overlord, while the heavyweights of the Eighth could continue to pound away at installations inside Germany. Equipped with eleven medium bomber groups and eighteen fighter groups, the Ninth may have had some of the tools suited for close-in support of ground troops but it possessed neither the quantity of operational aircraft nor the range to cripple German efforts to reinforce coastal defenses. Spaatz, as head of the U.S. Strategic

Air Forces in Europe, working directly under Eisenhower, agreed that the Eighth would have to devote some, if not all, of its resources to Overlord.

Even within a general agreement on responsibilities, opinions on the precise use of the B-17s and B-24s differed. Originally, Allied intelligence drew up a proposal for an onslaught against seventeen selected rail routes immediately before D-Day. Air Marshal Sir Trafford Leigh-Mallory of the RAF, the air commander for Overlord, pointed out that a spate of bad weather could ground the planes, leaving the enemy railroads able to deploy troops and guns where needed. Prof. Solly Zuckerman, a British scientist advising the Allied Expeditionary Air Force (AEAF), drafted a blueprint based on an analysis of the destruction of the Italian train system. Rail transportation there had been virtually paralyzed by attacks on the marshaling yards, the service and repair facilities, locomotives, rolling stock and track. To achieve similar results by D-Day in France required an all-out, three-month campaign. Eisenhower and his staff were committed to this plan, and the Eighth Air Force's bombers and fighters hewed to the strategy bible, chapter and verse.

According to Hayes, "Choo-choo missions dispatched as many as 700–800 fighters, each assigned a separate sector, to ravage the locomotives, rolling stock, depots and airfields at deck level in a time-synchronized assault. On our first choo-choo, our sector was north of Berlin, along the Baltic. We did a job on two trains in a suburban station. There were no white crosses on them but that night, Lord Haw-Haw said the Yoxford Boys showed no consideration for women and children as we strafed trains carrying many bombed-out residents from Berlin to emergency housing along the Baltic. We saw military trying to flee from the cars but *no* women or children. A few nights later, Haw-Haw said, 'Today, the military was able to rescue a Yoxford Boy from enraged civilians armed with pitchforks. The pilot had crash-landed his red and yellow checkerboard fighter.'

"Higher headquarters—the 66th Fighter Wing—called and wanted to know if we wanted a new color. Our reply was, No! The Yoxford Boys are a proud lot. If the Germans think we are a 'bloodthirsty lot'— Haw-Haw's words—they haven't seen anything yet. But we did order all pilots to bail out and not belly it in." Hayes notes that the P-51 outfits engaged in comparatively few choo-choos because the Mustang's best use lay in aerial combat. The P-47, on the other hand, with its heavier firepower and less vulnerability to ground fire—a single bullet through the cooling system of a Mustang was enough to disable it—excelled at this kind of work.

Shooting up locomotives was regarded as an acceptable sport but there was a mild controversy over the destruction of aircraft while on the ground. Fighter pilots whose gun cameras or associates confirmed the damage done to a parked airplane received the same credit awarded for a kill in a dogfight. That registered poorly with men who believed only a win in a *mano-a-mano* duel worthy of the ultimate recognition. F. Michael Rogers, a P-51 man who shot down six ME-109s and six FW-190s with the 353rd Fighter Group, remarked, "The 4th Fighter Group went strafe-happy. An awful lot of their kills were on the ground, which I never thought was the way to count a kill."

Joe Bennett, recovering from his dip in the English Channel, had missed out on the choo-choo period. "Destroying planes on the ground was as good as destroying them anywhere but it could not be considered an aerial victory. The first two or three to make a pass would get the planes and those that followed would get shot [by airfield antiaircraft emplacements]." Indeed, the risks in ground strafing often surpassed those of combat with enemy aircraft.

The source of much of the contretemps lay in achievement of "ace" status. During World War I, the figure that conferred the title had been arbitrarily set at five and it remained so for World War II. German pilots, involved in combat since the Spanish Civil War in 1936 and with years on the eastern front tucked under their flight jackets, counted their victories in the hundreds and their very best rated as *expertens*. The top figure in Europe for Americans was that of the 56th Fighter Group's Francis Gabreski at twenty-eight; Bob Johnson was runner-up at twenty-seven.

"Scores were sometimes made with a pencil," says Bennett, himself an ace. "I heard that I lost one-half of a plane to my squadron commander; he did not fire a shot that day."

PUB crawling and racking up victories were not on the minds of some Eighth Air Force airmen. Knocked out of the air over enemy territory, a number evaded in hopes of repatriation, a small portion fought with the underground, most coped with the rigors and uncertainties of prisoner-of-war camps and some met a cruel fate. Having plunged from his burning B-17 on February 8, pilot Howard Snyder had found refuge with the Belgian guerrilla resistance forces. To the farmhouse where Snyder was temporarily hidden, Paul Tilquin, a member of the underground, brought the uniform of a border patrolman, including a khaki cape and the peculiar square cap worn by the gendarmes.

"It was rainy and in the dark of evening when we left," recalls Snyder. "We left riding a tandem bicycle which I could only pedal with my right leg. My left had been injured during the attack so I could only wait until the right pedal came around for me to step on it. We were both pushing the bicycle up a hill at one point, since Paul was unable to pedal both of us to the top. There was a tavern at the crest. When we reached it, two German officers came out with their girlfriends. All of them appeared to be drunk.

"One of the officers came up to my side, put an arm around me and proceeded to jabber some drunken German. I was scared. I spoke no German and did not know what to do. Fortunately, Paul interceded and told the German we had to get going. He argued that it was a rainy night and we had a long way to go. The German was persuaded to return to his girlfriend and we were able to leave the area."

Even though Snyder had been seen descending in a parachute and required assistance to the ground after dangling in the trees, he was not immediately accepted as an American airman and drafted for service with the resistance. "The German military often dressed their own men in various Allied uniforms and bailed them out over territory they held. The purpose was so these men who spoke whatever language was necessary for the ruse might be picked up by underground members and thus later be able to give away the identities and locations of underground participants and residences to the Gestapo."

Once accepted, Snyder was given a forged identity card that stated he was deaf and dumb. Wherever he traveled, another guerrilla stayed with him. "Nobody ever bothered to ask me for my card." For the next few months, Snyder, in the company of resisters, remained in German occupied territory.

Marshall Draper, the bombardier on an A-20 shot down July 4, 1942, the first raid under Eighth Air Force auspices, had endured a lengthy train trip from an Amsterdam hospital to another medical facility at Oberursel, near Frankfurt where doctors tended further to his wounds. He believes he received good treatment, given the limitations before antibiotics. When the authorities decided he was fit enough, they incarcerated him at Stalag Luft III.

"Military discipline prevailed in the camps," says Draper. "Except for the restricted movement, the crowded environment, the bad sanitation and the lousy food it could have been an army post complete with the night and morning roll calls. Morale was governed by the progress of the war as announced by the BBC and received on various clandestine radios in the camp and the relative abundance of food. We regularly got the German newspapers but these were not introduced primarily for propaganda purposes. They were German versions of Charmin. Col. Charles G. Goodrich and Lt. Col. A. P. Clark [who retired as a lieutenant general] were outstanding in organizing the camp and maintaining discipline and morale in a difficult situation."

Draper and his fellow captives quickly developed slang for their surroundings. Germans were "goons," prisoners of course known as *kriegies,* guards "ferrets" and OKW stood for *Das Oberkommando der Wehrmacht,* the enemy high command. In an example of the common parlance, says Draper, "All kriegies will be pleased to learn that the OKW has admitted that the goons have bought it at Stalingrad. The ferrets are very gloomy." Indeed, his general impression of the local soldiers was that they seemed terrified, caught up in something they didn't understand but were afraid to complain about.

"I got interested in math and studied calculus; we had a couple of math books. Most of the stuff supplied by the American Red Cross [for reading] was garbage but the Brits had some good books. A colleague in the camp who had studied to be a priest undertook to teach me Latin, but this palled because we only had one Latin grammar for practice. Stalag Luft III had both a Catholic and a Protestant chaplain. The Catholic priest had been on a steamer sunk by a German U-boat and the Protestant had been a paratrooper. I don't know how they ended up in an Air Force POW camp [the Luftwaffe operated facilities separate from the Wehrmacht]. They regularly conducted services and the POWs seemed to be a fairly religious group, a consequence I suppose of surviving being shot down."

Behind the boredom and apparent lack of activities the kriegies gathered and forwarded intelligence and schemed to escape. "I was a code writer, transmitting intelligence. Under the Geneva Convention, a POW was allowed three letters and four postcards home per month. I used most of my allotment. I regularly received letters from a correspondent named 'Hilda' on mauve stationery which tended to be a little mushy. Still the system was quite effective and I didn't get caught. An Englishman, who was using a code based on words in a Bible was apprehended and disappeared.

"I was part of a small group that conveyed information on strategic targets, aircraft equipment failures or malfunctions, information on concentration camps, requests for escape supplies and other equipment. The Brits kept track of all the rail traffic which went through Sagan, a rail center for traffic to and from the Russian front, including supply shipments and hospital trains. The last one I sent before the camp was evacuated was a two-parter about a tank factory hidden in a forest. Information of this kind was elicited by 'goon sprechers,' individuals designated to cultivate (and blackmail) 'pet goons,' usually interior guards or ferrets. The internal organization of the camps was remarkably efficient. Every individual had a job aimed at furthering the war effort in one way or another. Equally amazing were the number of latent skills possessed by the POWs, a relatively young group of men. No matter what the required task, there was always somebody who had experience in that particular line of endeavor, from building clandestine radios, forging fake papers, preparing 'escape food' (a highly concentrated ration designed to enable escapees to survive in the open), tailoring phony civilian clothes or German uniforms, to metal fabricating and tunnel engineering.

"Most of the activities of the camp revolved around escaping. The accounts I have read or seen about tunneling or other escape efforts at Stalag Luft III seem to indicate that these were primarily activities of men from the RAF. As a matter of fact, the Americans were heavily involved and supplied a good deal of labor and technical expertise for such enterprises. I was number 101 on the priority list to go through a tunnel if and when it was completed. I contracted diphtheria in the summer of 1943 and was quarantined in the sick bay for a couple of weeks, during which time one of the tunnels was discovered. A few days later, the Americans were separated from the RAF and moved to a different compound, away from the two other partially built tunnels.

"Of these two, one was discovered by the Germans, but the other, closed down for the winter, was successfully completed the following spring and resulted in the exit from the North Compound of seventy-six RAF men. Three of these, two Norwegians and a Dutchman, made it home. Fifty of the recaptured men were shot by the Gestapo, fifteen returned to the camp and eight were sent to the Oranienberg concentration camp.

"I met English, Canadians, Australians, South Africans, New Zealanders, Rhodesians, Poles, Czechs, Dutch, French, Norwegians and even a couple of Russians. For the most part they were fine people, courageous and trustworthy, and I think they felt the same about our side, with the possible exception of a couple of Russian officers at the hospital in Oberursel. These guys told me they were going to wipe out the Americans. They were both little fellows and I said, 'Sure you will!' But I don't think they got it since their English wasn't too good."

Lu Cox, the 93rd Bomb Group navigator who nearly drowned in the Mediterranean after enemy fighters off the coast of North Africa blasted his B-24 *Double Trouble,* endured a long haul before reaching the same Stalag Luft III about eighty miles southeast of Berlin. "Stalag Luft III," says Cox, "contained only aircrew flying personnel. It was divided into sections called compounds and the usual number of POWs in each compound was about 2,500. The strength of Stalag Luft III, as we arrived, [March 1943] was about 8,000 of which approximately 350 were American flying officers. There were two compounds that held only British and there was one, our new one, which held both Americans and British.

"The barracks were new and were all wood. Each building was about forty-five feet wide and eighty-five feet long. There were about fifteen rooms including a washroom and an indoor toilet which could be used only after lock-up time at night. My room, which I initially shared with three other American prisoners was sixteen feet by sixteen feet. There were two double-decker bunk beds and a small wooden table with four wooden stools. In one corner was a little stove to heat the room. Each building had a little kitchen also."

Cox reports a steady influx of new prisoners, including friends from his old squadron. "As soon as any new prisoners entered our compound, they proved their identity to us. They did this by telling one of the old POWs where he lived and comparing notes on the way of life in those areas. They were questioned on small but relevant things about that part of the USA or England. Questions about professional sports were always used—the Yankees, football, cricket."

Cox was assigned the duty of medical officer for nearly 400 Americans in his compound. His medical supplies amounted to a few rolls of gauze, some antiseptic, aspirins and tape. Two British doctors ran a small makeshift hospital for serious cases. It was Cox's job to initially evaluate the seriousness of an ailment before recommending treatment from the professionals. On hot summer days, the men stripped off all clothing whenever not attending a roll call where the Germans insisted upon propriety. To cool off, they swam in a fire pool. For recreation they played softball, featuring all-star teams drawn from the Americans and Canadians familiar with the game.

By September 1943, the Americans, now segregated in their own area, as Draper indicated, numbered close to 1,000. As the primary-care medic, Cox was assigned assistants and even given additional items that came through the British Red Cross. Some special diet packages, largely milk products and custards, from the same source went to the most undernourished and wounded.

"My cases varied greatly," says Cox, "flak and shrapnel wounds, bullet wounds, fractures, torn and strained muscles and ligaments. Skin diseases and burns were a constant challenge. Several of my patients had such severe facial burns that their faces were no longer human in appearance: slits for a mouth, no nose, no ears, and eyes that stayed open all of the time. When these men laid down to rest, their roommates would place a cool wet cloth over their eyes and would try to keep flies away from them. Some were repatriated and faced many years of facial surgery back in the States."

The conditions at Stalag Luft III, as Draper remarks, while unpleasant, make POW life seem like that of an army post, but in fact the Germans with an almost stereotypical punctiliousness, provided better for the officers. Cox notes that in the fall of 1943, a number of enlisted men who volunteered for the duty, came to the compound to work as orderlies, mainly preparing food. "This was quite a break for them," observes Cox, "as it placed them in a better camp and they were under the protection of a large body of American officers which influenced the treatment they got from the Germans. Here they were pretty sure where their next meal was coming from and they had a reasonably good place to sleep. The food in our camp was the best they had had since they became prisoners of war. We were on FULL PARCELS (one Red Cross package per man per week) and the Germans were bringing in a few fresh vegetables such as turnips, potatoes and cabbage.

"The Geneva Convention stated that officers (POWs) would not be made to do forced labor; however, they could and did make the enlisted men do some pretty nasty jobs. Many times, POW's were responsible for cleaning up U.S. and British bomb damage, placing them in very dangerous locales. It was an operational habit of our bomber and fighter crews to come back from time to time and flatten and shoot up a target area they had previously handled." Indeed, aside from such perilous tasks as that, enlisted men taken prisoner, whether from the Air Corps or ground forces, have described their incarceration as one marked by near-starvation rations, louse-ridden, disease-racked living conditions.

Navigator/bombardier, Bob O'Hearn, on only his second mission, Schweinfurt on Black Thursday, had seen the entire crew of the borrowed B-17 *Wolf Pack* in parachutes after flak and enemy aircraft hit the ship as it ran for home. He endured the first terrifying moments of uncertainty upon capture but nevertheless resolved to supply only name, rank and serial number. "I was accused of being unreasonable. The Germans told me, 'After all you see we must get this information [date and place of birth, religion, hometown, various innocent-sounding queries that could only lead to real intelligence] so the Red Cross can let your parents know you are alive. You are making it difficult for your comrades. We only want to get done with you and get you in your permanent camp [described as an officers' club].'"

On another day of questioning, O'Hearn, first in line, not only refused to give more than name, rank and serial number but added that no one else in his group, which included members of his crew would talk either. "A guard prodded me in my rear with a bayonet and took me to the cellar of a large house. Later I was taken to join my comrades. A sergeant from Amarillo said, 'We didn't tell them a damn thing, Lieutenant!'" O'Hearn's pilot, Si Nettles, confided to him they thought he was "gone" when they heard some rifle shots.

En route to a prison camp, O'Hearn reports a female streetcar conductor refused to accept the prisoners under guard as passengers. A one-legged worker on a loading dock cursed them and shook his clenched fist. A POW retaliated in kind. At a holding camp, an Afrika Korps noncom told the Americans that Germany was *"kaput."* During a final train ride, two prisoners sawed an opening in the barred windows with a hacksaw blade. They escaped but were captured within hours.

O'Hearn went behind barbed wire at Stalag Luft III while the NCOs who had been part of his contingent headed to another camp in Austria. "I eventually moved into a room with B-25 and fighter pilots who were shot down in the Africa-Italy area. Monotony was relieved by discussions on everything from farming to philosophy. We had knowledgeable men from many fields. We avoided talk about women. Our senior officer, Col. Charles Goodrich, had been shot down in Africa in 1942. As the buffer between the prisoners and the Germans, he was well respected and liked by all.

"Two roommates were engaged in 'X' work, escape activity. I sometimes did lookout duty while they were in the tunnels, or I recited the 'Gin,' the BBC news reports received in another part of the camp. Our competent escape committee made maps, identification and escape clothing for escapees. Tunnels were dug but discovered before we could use them. Lieutenant Colonel Clark, a tall West Pointer, was in charge of escape activities. Another key man, Maj. Jerry Sage, a huge Army paratrooper (he was really an OSS agent) conducted judo classes. We had a 'last resort' plan for a mass escape—storming the fence while an expert crew under Major Sage would disable the guards. The plan was hairy but seemed better than getting exterminated. At least some might survive."

John McClure, the downed pilot from the 56th Fighter Group, had undergone intensive grilling at the Oberursel interrogation center that included solitary confinement, exposure to cold by turning off the heat and then reversing the duress by raising the steam heat temperature to high levels. McClure obdurately refused to even say what kind of airplane he had been flying but after perhaps ten days of his efforts, the chief inquisitor pulled out a book and read out his résumé, beginning with where he was born, his father's occupation, what college he attended and his chief subject of study although the dossier was blank on his early military period. However, the German officer knew the roster and top officers in the 56th.

In the company of a group of RAF officers, McClure boarded a boxcar bound for Sagan, Stalag Luft III. "There were relatively few Americans, and it was known as Allied Airman's camp. When I came in, here was one of my classmates from flight training, he'd been with a bomber group. If somebody in there can actually recognize you and vouch for you then you're not a slip-in. Some of these Germans, like one I knew later on, spent a lot of time in New York City, spoke English like anyone from Brooklyn, knew all the American slang and you would never be able to tell that he wasn't an American. We found out later he was an impostor because nobody knew him and he had a story that couldn't be proved. We'd been warned ahead of time. I knew one guy to look for, Albert P. Clark, tall redheaded guy who got hit by ack-ack while flying with the RAF over LeHavre in a Spitfire. He was a West Pointer, well known, easily identified. He had a little series of questions he could ask, and if you had the right answer you were okay.

"They opened up an additional lager [South African word for camp] on the south side as more Americans came in. You had to have a place for a tunnel and one of them was the stove. You dug it out of the cement around it, so you could lift the stove out, then fake the cement around it with sand, so it would not be noticeable, and then we dug a hole straight down underneath. We found out you needed to go down about twenty feet deep before you start your tunnel out. We'd build a reception sector, you dropped straight down into the antechamber before starting work on the tunnel. At the depth you needed in that kind of location, you had to have an air pump. From milk cans, we devised a ventilating pump to put air down there and pump it out, a circulating system with a hand-operated bellows.

"What do you do with the dirt? We wound up with a system to dispose of it. You can't just throw it down because that's obvious. Its moisture content is different than what's around and it's a cinch they'll notice it, and know you're digging. We devised a means to get rid of it without it being noticed. In our favor, we had as much time as we needed to work things out so we didn't compromise matters. We had a security system to protect anyone digging. We kept a surface system and kept a tab on every German guard that came in the camp. We usually had a team watching them. Some guy sitting outside, reading a book if he could find one or piddling at something but what he was doing was watching the gate. Teams were assigned to certain guards and anytime he showed up, you followed that one. Could be a dozen teams working on this at any one time. They would pass a signal on to those guys working down in the tunnel, to get that thing closed up."

Confirming Marshall Draper's account, McClure notes, "We had people in the camp, a guy raised in Chicago who'd been born in Germany who was fluent in the language, to keep our ears and eyes open. You get a bunch of Americans in a place like this, you can find an expert in almost anything. The talent you'll find in there is amazing. And they'll try most anything, the ingenuity kinda threw the Germans. We would bribe Germans with Red Cross coffee to get a tube or something for the clandestine radios. It was for reception only, usually, because if you transmitted, they'd know almost instantly."

According to McClure, the high command was aware of the breaches of security within Stalag Luft III, and even sent the SS in to investigate. As a lieutenant general from that organization walked through the camp, two Americans chased after an errant baseball, collided with the officer and the trio fell to the ground. The captives apologized profusely, dusted off the general who continued his stroll. As he was about to leave the lager, another American approached him. "This is not a hostile gesture," he announced to the SS general. He then reached inside his clothing and handed to the officer a pistol artfully removed from the man's holster during that seemingly innocent encounter with the baseball players.

While evadee pilot Howard Snyder added his infantry-training experience to the work of the Belgian Maquis, other members of his crews also hid out with local people. On the morning of April 22, eight American airmen, including George Eike, Snyder's copilot, his navigator Robert Benninger and gunner John Pindroch ate breakfast in a hut owned by a Belgian farmer. Plans had been set for the evadees to seek safety. They were given money, some received civilian clothing. Suddenly, a party of as many as 1,500 soldiers, Gestapo and Belgian collaborators, descended on the area and seized the Americans along with those who harbored them.

The captives were taken to a nearby schoolhouse for interrogation. All of them still had their dog tags which identified them as military personnel except for Eike and Benninger who were out of uniform. Around 2:30 in the afternoon the Americans were loaded into a truck, and under guard driven to a nearby woods. Lined up in single file, with a pair of soldiers behind each one, they were marched into the forest. Some 500 feet from the road, each airman was moved in a separate direction, still accompanied by his two Germans carrying pistols. Upon a prearranged signal, the soldiers shot the captives in the back three or four times and left them for dead. Sometime later, the bodies were buried in a common grave. A pair of Belgians who had been acting as hosts to the evadees disappeared into concentration camps.

The savagery against the hideouts may have been a reaction to the relentless battery of German-controlled turf. The rain of bombs that killed, maimed and destroyed must have generated increasing hostility towards those responsible, and as D-Day approached the raids struck ever harder.

FEARSOME as had been the losses sustained by the Eighth Air Force, particularly among bomber crews, the ranks of U.S. airmen lodged in the United Kingdom continued to swell with replacements. The 385th Bomb Group, which went operational in the summer of 1943, welcomed a B-17 crew in the spring of 1944 that included gunner Bob Andrews, a few months shy of his twentieth birthday.

A graduate of high school in Moultrie, Georgia, Andrews in the summer of 1942 worked in construction for the War Department Engineers. "During this time we had air raid wardens appointed to spot enemy aircraft if and when the foreign devils should decide that Moultrie could be a priority target. During this time several friends and I spotted many Japanese Zeros leisurely flying over our little town. To our later embarrassment, we learned they were AT-6s [U.S. trainers]." But Andrews also tried to learn to fly.

Lured by a promise that recruits could volunteer and choose a place to serve, Andrews enlisted and was sent to Spence Field, three miles from his home. "I was bored with perfunctory duties and disappointed with the rather mundane chores to which I was assigned. One night, I saw a movie where John Wayne shot down three-fourths of the Japanese Air Force. I was thrilled and immediately recognized my calling. I requested flight training but was told nothing was open except gunnery school. I volunteered and was assigned to a crew training for combat. Good ole John Wayne. What an inspiration!

"I can truthfully say that my training was totally inadequate for the events to come. During phase training, gunners generally just went along for the ride. Occasionally, we were permitted to shoot at a large sock towed by an obsolete plane which was piloted by a boy who was not very well liked. During training I was given instruction on how to live in the jungle, how to use bayonets to kill for food and how to cope with the disease-infested areas of the South Pacific."

Shortly after this training period, Andrews and his colleagues sailed to England where they were remanded to the 385th. "We were anxious to show what we could do. For my first mission, I was assigned to fly in the tail with a veteran crew. True to my Southern upbringing, I searched out the pilot, introduced myself, and with patriotic zeal professed my determination with God's help to slap the Axis. He looked at me kinda funny, but agreed we all had a job to do.

"My first mission was a 'Noball' [a designation for the sites used to launch V-1 and V-2 rockets] raid, we encountered no fighters, no flak, no nothing but I still had a really great feeling to be in combat at last. Upon our return, I adopted a veteran's attitude with the appropriate swagger. Two days later, April 22, 1944, I flew with our crew to Hamm, Germany. This was an aging experience, tons of flak and many German fighters, one of which attacked our plane. I was in the tail; he was attacking our tail. He shot at us; I shot at him. To my total amazement he did not go down. As he barrel-rolled by, I had an almost uncontrollable urge to pee. I observed other planes, some with engines out or smoking, others out of formation. I wondered if everyone was experiencing the same subdued terror that was racing through my mind. On the way home I decided that it wouldn't be a bad idea to pray a little, which I did."

Andrews had flown seven missions before he notes, "as Walter Cronkite might say, a day 'filled with those events that alter and illuminate our time.'" His ship had aborted on its first start towards Berlin because of a faulty oxygen system but a day later, in the same plane, *Quittin' Time*, he was bound for Big B. For a second time, the oxygen system malfunctioned. "We were too proud to abort again," remembers Andrews. "We went on with the full knowledge that we would have to leave the formation after 'bombs away' and come back alone, because by that time our oxygen supply would be depleted. [The ship would be unable to fly at the altitude assigned to the group.]"

Over the target *Quittin' Time* suffered a flak hit that cost an engine. With the bomb load gone, the B-17 left the group and dropped to a lesser altitude. Two British P-38s stayed with the plane as it sought to find its way home. "We didn't have a navigator with us. We had a togglier and our regular bombardier was acting as navigator. He had difficulty in locating the direction of the earth so naturally we were lost. Suddenly, the British left and we were attacked by six ME-109s. They attacked our tail in pairs. I fired at them until my guns jammed. Their first pass shot our ball-turret gunner in the leg. He left his position for the radio room just in time to get shot in the face by the second pass. This also shot up the radio operator. He had numerous holes in him, but he survived. On one of the attacks, the top-turret gunner was hit in the neck and he also lost an eye.

"During all this melee, I was frantically trying to get my guns unjammed. One of the 109s apparently thought the tail gunner to be dead for he came in real close, pumping cannon shells into us. My guns were still jammed. My heart was pounding with the certainty that I was about to die. I shouted to God for help and my guns immediately unjammed. The rest was simple. The next time that fighter came in I fired on him point blank. The fighter didn't explode; it just came apart. We claimed and confirmed the destruction of three of the 109s.

"What a price! We had lost another engine during the attack and were lost. We knew that to the west was England, so that was our course. I left my position to see if I could help those I knew were hurt. When I got to the waist, I found the ball-turret gunner on the floor with his hands over his face and what looked like an eye between his fingers. The radio operator was crying and bleeding profusely. The top-turret gunner was bleeding on his face and neck. A waist gunner was trying to wind around the ball turret so we could ditch. Though we were wracked with fear and exhaustion, we had confidence in our pilot. As we prepared to ditch, suddenly, we saw Manston [an air base]. We hit the tarmac with great force, without brakes and out of control. When we finally stopped, the ambulances caught up with us and I assisted in removing the wounded. I examined the plane. It was full of holes in the wings, fuselage and props. *Quittin' Time,* how appropriate.

"When we returned to our base, I learned our regular navigator, flying with a different crew, had been shot down over Berlin that day. Later, our bombardier was shot down and taken prisoner. I was to fly twenty-seven more missions, thirty-four in all, with a different crew each time. They included Karlsruhe, two missions on D-Day, Hamburg, Merseburg, Hanover and three more trips to Berlin. They were all frightening, but none compared to the terror of May 8."

In January 1944, ten men who had completed their preliminary training met at a Florida air base to become a family rooted to a B-17. They represented a generous sampling of the American spectrum, a credit and collection worker, an employee of an aircraft firm, a corset firm clerk, a mechanic, a riveter for an automotive plant, a truck driver, a farmer, an assistant boilermaker, a baked-goods salesman. Geographically they hailed from Brooklyn, Albuquerque, Cleveland, Trenton, Pilot Mount [Iowa] and other diverse locations.

For three months, while they flew as a crew, they honed their specialties, classroom work on gunnery, navigation, radio codes, instrument flight, bomb-drop mechanics, ditching procedures, POW rights, first aid, enemy tactics. Having passed muster for overseas duty, they shipped out for the United Kingdom to join the 385th Bomb Group. Five days after being greeted by their new boss, Col. Elliott Vandevanter, a B-17 pilot with the ill-fated Air Corps units stationed in the Philippines, they started their war, although for this first effort two traveled as spares and one gunner replaced a man grounded from another ship. From then on, however, they flew as the crew of a Fort they named *Joker*.

"It was [always] the same old routine," says left-waist gunner and assistant radio operator John Hibbard. "We would lie awake at night and sweat out the battle orders. If we were listed on them we would spend the rest of the night discussing the prospects of the bombing mission, venturing guesses as to where the target would be or we would catnap until briefing time. We were always too excited and tense for sound sleep. We didn't have any exceptional battle experiences. The *Joker* was just an ordinary member in the Eighth Air Force. We bombed factories and other objectives in Berlin, Zwickau, Leipzig, Hamm, Munich, Merseburg and a lot of other cities in Europe whose names we couldn't even begin to pronounce."

While *Joker* visited Berlin no less than five times, it was hit only the first time by enemy fighters, on April 29, further indication of the decline of the Luftwaffe. According to Hibbard, that experience explained why the faces of the older men blanched when Big B was revealed as the objective.

"Due to strong crosswinds we were blown sixty miles off course and were late in reaching our rendezvous with our fighter escort which was to be our protective umbrella into the target area. This made all of us jittery; we felt naked and conspicuous without our 'little friends' riding herd on us. Nevertheless, we had to go on to the target area without them. We flew deep into Germany and could not turn back. The Eighth Air Force had a proud boast that it had never been turned away from its objective by the enemy.

"All went well for us until after 'bombs away.' Then we sighted enemy fighters. There were between sixty and seventy ME-109s and FW-190s out there in a jumbled mass, milling around like a swarm of mad bees that someone had just stirred up. They flew ahead of our formation, just out of range of our guns and formed a long line, three or four deep to attack. Over the ship's interphone, I heard Lester Esterman, our bombardier shout, 'Here they come, one o'clock high!' The other waist gunner, Myron Sanchez (Snatch) swung around on the right waist gun and started hammering away hot and heavy at the enemy fighters. That was Snatch; he was scared silly until he started to shoot, then he was all business on the friendly end of his .50 caliber machine gun. It is the same with everyone. When you can fight back, to feel the gun bucking in your fists, you aren't afraid. It's a cool business of estimation, sighting and firing on a target as it flashed by. The first attack, or pass, that was made on our formation and was concentrated on our right side. The 'luftgang' came in, flying like demons possessed and so began the game of cat and mouse [Pilot James La Penna's favorite expression].

"This was *Joker*'s first battle with the 'dead' German air force. Frankly, they didn't look very dead to us. Those enemy planes seemed healthy and very *deadly*. Nothing is dead until all of it is destroyed and ceases to exist or operate.

"As the enemy planes poured in on us, our pilot James La Penna and copilot Lt. Arthur F. Cousemaker, automatically began flying evasive action so the Jerries wouldn't have a sitting duck to shoot at. The *Joker* bobbed up and down like an express elevator on a rampage. While this is happening one seems to experience the sensation of floating, but actually it is the movement of the ship. It is like placing some marbles in a cigar box and then shaking the box like hell! It was due mostly to the evasive action Jim and Art took, rough as it was, that saved all of us. We had two damn good white-collar workers up front in the 'office' of our ship.

"I heard the deep throated 'brup, brup' of Donald Ryan's top-turret guns from up front, mingled with the chatter of navigator Edward Lipsky's and bombardier Lester Esterman's guns. Then as some of the attacking fighters zoomed close under our plane to get at those that were beneath us, Sgt. Thomas J. (Pappy) Pappas, our ball-turret gunner opened up. His guns sounded as if they were belching thunder in an empty barrel. Hurtling fighters rushed by, almost colliding with each other and with ships in our formation, some trailing back streamers of smoke, some seeming to trip and stagger as if they had struck an invisible brick wall, stopped cold by some Fort's guns, while some just seemed to disintegrate into a black puff of smoke.

"The whole scene was a picture of madness and wild disorder. At that moment we couldn't absorb and digest all of the horror and sudden death that we witnessed because we didn't have time to think of anything but doing what could be done to survive. All during the attack, John (Curly) Wells, the *Joker*'s radio operator, dashed madly from the radio room, from the right window to the left window, then to his gun, all the while trying to see where the fighters were, and hoping to get in at least one wee burst at one of them. He looked and acted like an excited squirrel in a cage in the sense that his antics in the radio room were something out of a Charlie Chaplin comedy.

"It is hell to have to just look on and trust in others to take care of things when the battle rages all about you, not even able to fire one single round of ammunition at the enemy that is doing his best to destroy you. I know how Curly Wells felt because I was in the same fix. Of all the attacking fighters that passed through my sights, not one could I fire on without hitting another one of our own Forts in our formation. There was nothing I could do but stand at my left waist gun and watch for an opening which never came. I didn't have the chance to fire a single shot. Snatch, however, fired enough ammunition for the whole crew from the right waist gun.

"As the fighters passed our ship, Kenneth Long, our tail gunner, had his choice of the fleeing targets and really salted some Jerry tails as they slithered through the rest of the formation. A tail gunner has a funny job. He rides backwards wherever his ship goes. An enemy plane, making a frontal attack on his ship, approaches from his rear, as if from nowhere and sails right on by. He had to do some fast thinking and damn good shooting. The tail is a tough spot to ride.

"After the first pass on our formation, the surviving 'Luftpack' regrouped and made two more such attacks before our guardian angels and saviors, the escort fighters arrived and drove the enemy off. When the jaunt was over and we were back at our base in England, we made the *Joker*'s claims for enemy fighters destroyed. Lieutenant Lipsky received credit for one destroyed and Lieutenant Esterman was credited with one probable." The 385th counted seven B-17s downed, giving Hibbard an understanding of why veterans paled at designation of the target as Berlin.

"Later that night, we felt the complete revulsion and horror of the battle as we lay alone in the darkness and our memories revived all that had taken place."

The severe attrition of the Luftwaffe's skilled hands limited its reaction to the Eighth Air Force appearances. But some targets were so vital for continued resistance that the Germans felt forced to respond. To the bomber command that meant strikes, for example, at the natural and synthetic oil facilities which not only denied the enemy essential materials but also brought enemy fighters out where the accompanying P-51s and P-47s could further reduce the potential for interference with D-Day. Unfortunately, human error sometimes led the best laid plans astray.

IT was this sort of mission, May 12, that launched the 94th Bomb Group, with Wil Richardson in a ball turret, at Brüx, Czechoslovakia. "What we didn't know," says Richardson, "was that 061, the B-17F we were assigned, was a weary one. It had been shot up, repaired, crash landed and repaired again. This queen had seen her best days. It just didn't fly that well. This became apparent as we started our roll down the runway. We were at max load and 061 barely got off. I usually sat on the doorsill into the bomb bay in the radio room so I could get out of the open hatch above quickly if necessary. I would look down through the large crack of the bay door to watch the runway drop away as we left the earth. Today it was nervous time as we used up all of the runway and I saw green grass as we lifted off just in time.

"Another ominous happening: upon forming the usual way we headed for the coast but because of some SNAFU, the bunch we were with missed the fighter escort. We weren't long into the Belgian air space when the yellow-nosed 'Abbeville Kids,' Goering's crack group, rose to the occasion. In our area there were only six P-51s, not much help with such odds. I watched a 51 and 109 collide head-on. It happened so quickly and no chutes were to be seen. Devoid of friendly fighter support, the battle line of B-17s drew German a/c attention full measure.

"The heavies continued on a prescribed course, south of the Ruhr, then skirted highly defended cities and flew east toward our target area, fighting upwards of 400 enemy aircraft all the way. They came from all directions; the tail as well as the effective nose-on attacks. In some cases there were twenty-five to thirty abreast and even attempts at ramming by using a wing so the pilot could bail out [the Germans were pilot poor, not short of aircraft].

"As the upper and lower turrets could fire in all directions, Jim Bruton and I were kept busy twisting and turning constantly. From the navigator or the bombardier, in the nose, we would hear, 'Bandits ten o'clock low' or 'straight in at twelve o'clock' and if I wasn't shooting to the rear assisting the tail gunner, Gilbert Gabriel, or in some other direction, I'd swing forward ready to follow through those attacking from the nose. It was a busy time.

"We were hit in No. 1 and lost much oil so we had to feather it prior to the target. It was a struggle to keep up with the group with bombs still aboard. The flak over the target was moderate, which I almost welcomed because we had a brief respite from the fighters. We received some flak damage including loss of oxygen in my ball as well as some on the left side.

"Soon after bombs away the second half of the attack came. Twin-engined fighters joined the 109s and 190s. These would sit out behind the bomber boxes in groups of ten to twenty to fire rockets and cannon, just out of effective range of our .50s. There they joined the single-engine fighters to attack close in. It was unusual, memorable."

With the loss of oxygen, 061 could not maintain a position with the group and dropped quickly to a lower altitude. Inevitably, the wounded beast attracted would-be matadors, 109s and 190s zeroing in for the kill. The ship rocked from many hits.

Richardson says, "As I was looking to the rear, firing at one below, another one hit the top turret with cannon fire. I saw the plexiglass and Jim Bruton's empty, special leather flak helmet go over the right horizontal stabilizer. I thought he had had it. Later I learned he lost consciousness for a few moments and came to on the deck. Jim wasn't hurt, just highly put out and using four letter words as he couldn't vent his anger by returning their fire. The shells that knocked him out of the turret damaged both .50s beyond repair."

A cannon shell that smashed through the right elevator severely limited its range of movement. To help keep the nose up, Lt. Leo C. Riley, the copilot, locked his left arm and right hand around the control column while jamming his feet against the rudder bar and applied heavy back pressure on the column. Another missile tore through the elevator, passed through the right waist window before it exploded against the left waist gun. The gunner, Ken Rasco, was uninjured but his weapon no longer worked.

The battered B-17 managed to seek some mutual protection with another group returning from Brüx, but crossing the Channel it continued to sink ever lower. "We seemed to have enough altitude to make just one attempt to land. Being alone and late, we were able to make a straight-in approach. This was fortunate because we lost No. 3 from fuel starvation as the B-17 nosed down and lined up with the runway. We had spent a gruelling eleven and three-quarter hours in the air, and I spent ten and a half in the ball.

"Because we were late and crews at debriefing reported seeing us go down in trouble with fighters after us, we were listed as MIAs. After our debriefing we returned to the barracks, just in time to stop our personal belongings from being picked up by the first sergeant." In fact a telegram had already been sent to Riley's wife listing him as MIA and a correction quickly followed.

At the debriefing, the crew from 061 reported an unmarked B-17 that shadowed their formation from a safe distance. It accompanied them inbound from the Rhine to near Brüx and others mentioned the mystery plane on their way out. The Germans operated several such captured American planes, using them both for reconnaissance and to train their own people. During their interrogation, Bruton claimed he shot down one plane; Gabriel said he got another and Richardson put in for two himself. None of them received credit since no independent witness could verify their claims. In fact, none of the 814 bombers that participated on May 12 were officially recognized for knocking down an enemy although American fighters confirmed sixty-six shot-down defenders. Richardson's group lost a pair of bombers and overall the B-17s and 24s for the day counted forty-six lost plus another nine like 061 that never flew again. The latter became a "hangar queen" whose parts kept others in the air.

One week after the Brüx adventure, the 94th Bomb Group along with about 500 other heavyweights struck at Berlin and Wil Richardson in his ball turret witnessed the awful consequences of error amid a tight formation engaged in its bomb run. "The ship above us just missed us with his load. One of the thousand-pounders fell behind No. 3 [engine] and I saw this one go by my turret. I quickly followed it down only to see it hit the left stabilizer of *Miss Donna Mae* that was out of position below us, drifting from left to right. Apparently it jammed the elevator [of *Miss Donna Mae*] in a down position. It lost altitude rapidly and began a steep dive. I watched in vain for chutes. None appeared. Others indicated that the plane started to break up. I can still remember the top turret telling our pilot to move left as the a/c above was directly over us."

By accident, the camera aimed through the bomb bay doors of the upper plane for recording the effects on the ground was set to begin when the bombs were released. It captured on film the fatal injury to *Miss Donna Mae.*

Accidents like what befell *Miss Donna Mae,* flak and the still malevolent enemy fighters cost many Americans their lives or freedom. Joe Bennett, having recovered from his dip into the North Sea, on May 25 was once again on duty over the Continent. "It was about 9:00 A.M. after an encounter with sixteen FW-190s and twenty ME-109s and I was climbing for altitude while looking for my wingman. Pain reminded me that I had not been to the bathroom since 10:00 P.M. the night before. We had gone through a quick briefing without time to do the usual routine, like empty pockets, strap on a .45 automatic, visit the bathroom and I don't believe we had breakfast. I turned to the left and looked up, down and all around then to the right and decided it was all clear. I unzipped my flying suit, then the pants, clawed through the longjohns, then the shorts, picked up the funnel with the rubber hose attached, wrapped my right leg around the stick to control the plane, got the funnel in my right hand, and flying along with one wing low, proceeded to marvel at what man can do when he puts his mind to it.

"My eyes had ceased watering, my seat belt was not so tight. I felt a calming relief when all hell broke loose. There was this noise and my controls went limp. It started to spin a flat position. I pulled on the canopy but it was jammed. I butted it with my head three times before it flew off, whacking me on the top of the head. I stood in the seat, then sat down and removed my oxygen mask and unhooked the radio connector. I stood in the seat and went over the side. I pulled the rip cord and began my descent. The plane came spinning past me with the motor running like a top. As it passed me I could see the gas tank that fit under and behind the seat."

Although Bennett had scanned the sky for any planes seconds before he began the maneuvers required to relieve his protesting bladder, a youthful German pilot, Hubert Heckmann, on only his second combat effort had slid in behind him. Before Heckmann could open fire, however, his machine guns jammed. In hot pursuit of the P-51, Heckmann unintentionally guided his ME-109 into the rear of Bennett's, shearing off the tail section and opening a hole through which the American was able to see his fuel tank.

"I landed about one hundred yards from the nearest house," says Bennett, "which my plane damaged when it crashed." Farmers armed with pitchforks, hoes and clubs surrounded Bennett even as his feet touched the earth. They led him off to a jail in the nearby town of Brackenheim. Meanwhile Heckmann glided his crippled fighter toward a nearby field. "I was impeded by your tail unit," he later told Bennett, "which was situated on my nose." Nevertheless, Heckmann managed to belly in without injury.

About an hour after they met in midair, Heckmann arranged for a more formal introduction. He walked to the jail where Bennett was held and introduced himself. The pair shook hands, exchanged a few words. Then Bennett began his journey to a stalag while Heckmann returned to his unit.

RALPH Golubock with the 44th Bomb Group, now in command of his own crew, had racked up nine missions during the first twelve days of May, including a pair to Berlin. "I was exhausted. I didn't even want to eat. I was physically and emotionally drained. Double daylight saving time [which made for extra hours of light at night] and contemplating the end of my tour were making it difficult for me to sleep."

He celebrated the unexpected award of a Distinguished Flying Cross at the officers' club when his squadron leader suddenly announced that Golubock and his crew were to take a week's leave, at a "Flak Shack," special Red Cross–operated resorts for rest and recreation. Although Golubock protested he was only one mission short of completing his tour, his superior was adamant. The others from his plane, also nearing the end of their combat assignment, also objected but to no avail. The enlisted men separated from the officers and Golubock with three others entrained for their Flak Shack.

"[Our train was] met by a young lady, a Red Cross worker. She drove us to the home. Upon arriving we were truly surprised. The house was like no other I had ever seen. It was a beautiful mansion with magnificent grounds. There were tennis courts, croquet courts, and a lovely hothouse where exotic plants were grown. We were told it was owned by a nobleman and he had donated it to the Americans for the duration of the war. There were about fifteen of us and everyone was congenial. We were supplied with civilian clothes which we were to wear for the length of our stay. The only exception to the rule was dinner time when we were required to wear our uniforms. We had cocktails for dinner and the food was wonderful. We were also given bikes to use and the Red Cross people were very kind and helpful. They did everything in their power to make us happy and forget the war for a week. Everything was perfect, too perfect. I stayed two days and took the train back to London and spent the rest of my leave there. I didn't get much rest in London, but I had fun and returned to the base after my week was over.

"We were not scheduled to fly for the next few days so I spent my time sleeping and hanging around the officers' club. The squadron was a very lonely place for me. Due to our recent heavy losses I did not know anyone. We had been inundated with a large number of replacement crews, all waiting to fly their first missions. They were all curious and anxious. I was then the oldest pilot in the squadron and many sought me out for questions. It was all very flattering but I knew there was no way I could tell them what it felt like. They would know soon enough.

"We were finally scheduled to fly on May 29, my thirtieth and last mission. I was hoping for a milk run to France. No such luck! The target was a synthetic oil refinery in Pölitz, which was once in Poland. I was to lead an element in the low squadron."

His aged B-24 that had borne three names—*Prince-ass, Prince, Princ-ess*—carried some extra equipment, a radar-jamming device, and three neophytes, a pilot, navigator and the radar jammer on their first missions. Over the target, the aircraft experienced very little accurate flak which may or may not be attributed to the radar jammer. Having dropped the bombs and seen a good deal of smoke rise from the target, Golubock guided the Liberator out over the Baltic Sea for the voyage back.

"Soon after breaking the coast," recalls Golubock, "we were hit by a lone ME-410 or ME-210. It was difficult to identify because he came slashing through. I don't think he was aiming at my aircraft. He was just spraying the formation and he luckily hit me. Our No. 1 engine was knocked out immediately and the fuel cells of the left wing were also hit. Fuel was flowing out in huge amounts. Had any of it hit our hot superchargers, I'm sure we would have gone up immediately."

Golubock could not feather the prop on the damaged engine because the motor for that task had been shot up. He struggled to right the airplane which seemed to want to flip over. When he got the ship under control it was in a dive with tremendous drag from the windmilling propeller.

"Shortly after being hit," he recalls, "I rang the bell one time to alert the crew to buckle on their chutes and prepared to bail out. I didn't ring the bell the second time because it appeared the airplane was flyable and we would be able to get somewhere. However, our tail gunner, Sgt. Zeke Jones, having seen what happened and seeing the gasoline flowing off the port wing, decided it was time to part company and bailed out. He was the only one to leave the ship. He had made headlines earlier in the year when he got two ME-109s with one burst. It seemed he hit the top one, who fell into the lower one. He got credit for both of them. After he bailed out, he was picked up at sea by the Germans and remained a POW until the end of the war.

"I called the navigator, who was inexperienced [it was his first mission] and asked him for a heading either back to England or to Sweden. Unfortunately, he did not have any charts that showed him how to get to Sweden. I contacted our engineer, Sergeant Dunlop, to determine our fuel situation and to transfer the fuel he could from the port to starboard wing. He was able to salvage enough fuel that I felt we could make Sweden. The chance of getting back to England was zero!

"I ordered the crew to dump everything overboard. All the ammunition, machine guns, even the Norden bombsight which Lieutenant Fitzsimmons took a great deal of pleasure in tossing out. This allowed us to maintain altitude near 10,000 feet." To his horror Golubock saw a coven of German fighters approaching and he felt certain they would shoot the crippled B-24 down. But they never attacked, perhaps reasoning there was no need to waste any ammunition on a wreck bound to crash.

Princ-ess stumbled on, eventually entering Swedish airspace. Airplanes Golubock recognized as early American P-35s picked them up and escorted the bomber to the city of Malmo. "When we were hit, our bomb bay doors were knocked open and couldn't be closed. One Swedish fighter tried to fly under us, presumably to check for bombs. When he did, he hit our left wing with his radio antenna which tore off. We then made an excellent landing on their grass field and were immediately surrounded by Swedes armed with submachine guns."

The Americans were taken to Swedish Air Force Headquarters to be questioned by a colonel. "He spoke perfect English and the first thing he wanted to know was why one of his pilots had torn the antenna off of his airplane. When I explained what had happened, he went ballistic, shouting something in Swedish. Later, one of the Swedish officers told me that the colonel had the errant pilot thrown in the brig for destroying government property."

Their hosts interned Golubock at a rustic summer resort located on a large lake. Assigned to two-man rooms, the men slowly became accustomed to the leisurely pace. With their loved ones assured of their safety, the Americans settled in to a comfortable life as tourists, restricted only by the borders of the country.

Aside from Sweden, Eighth Air Force planes with mechanical trouble or battle damage could also resort to the other neutral turf, Switzerland. Whether or not it was necessary to take refuge rather than try to make it home to fight another day was a matter of some controversy. Archie Old, at first a group and then a wing commander growled about seeing aircraft head for the two countries, "It happened a small amount of times. I sat in the cockpit and cussed those sons of bitches when I would see them leaving. I didn't really know whether they were crippled or not."

14

D-DAY AND BEYOND

During the spring months before the scheduled invasion the first week of June, the Eighth Air Force labored to carry out its vital responsibilities for lower-altitude hits at the infrastructure of ground defenses while coping with a heavy turnover in personnel as men completed their tours and casualties continued to mount. Hal Turrell, who had done the requisite number of operations with the 445th Bomb Group on April 29, offered to hang about and contribute to the coming landings, but his group commander responded that only if he volunteered for a full tour could he continue. Turrell sailed for the U.S. on a nearly empty troop ship, June 3.

Ramsay Potts, who had bounced back and forth from the UK to North Africa several times and survived the ill-fated Ploesti raid, had ascended the staff ladder to the post of operations officer for the 93rd Bomb Group, then chief of staff for a combat wing and finally took over the 453rd Bomb Group. "Their commander had been shot down on one of their first missions. My chief job was to give them confidence and straighten out some of their operational procedures. They were not flying very well together as a group. They had a considerable number of individually skilled pilots and crews, pretty good maintenance but very poor organization.

"I got permission from the division commander to stand down from flying combat missions and immediately started training operations, which was very irksome to the crews but we ironed out some problems and troubles. We started to fly against German airfields, V-1, V-2 sites, some oil targets, marshaling and transportation objectives in preparation for the invasion. I flew an occasional mission myself, but I was trying to develop the organizational skills and get the group to function as a cohesive unit. I don't believe I got more than five hours of sleep a night for the three and a half months leading up to D-Day."

With D-Day imminent, the capacity to rotate experienced hands like Turrell home and still mount ever larger, sustained efforts bespeaks the wealth of manpower available as newcomers not only replaced those who completed their tours but also boosted the bomber and fighter group complements far beyond that which marked the early days. Among the additions was Wil Richardson, a ball-turret gunner who arrived in April. By June 1, he had flown fifteen missions, including the one where bombs from one B-17 struck another. He recalled that at the 94th Bomb Group in Bury St. Edmunds, on May 25, "Something occurred that made everybody really start talking about this invasion that should be coming up soon. All crew members had to carry their sidearms, .45s, at all times on the base. The ground crews were given various kinds of shoulder weapons to carry with them as they worked on the airplanes. We were told to do this because they expected German paratroopers to come in to louse up any invasion plans that were being put together." Farfetched as this possibility may sound, the Air Corps thought it necessary to issue an official memorandum on May 15 to all personnel warning that the enemy was capable of an airborne gambit and how to defend against it.

D-Day was kind of an anniversary for Richardson. He notes, "I had been attending Long Beach [California] Junior College day classes while working a night shift at a local Douglas Aircraft plant. I saw the first B-17 go out the door of that plant in 1942. The date was June 6, 1942."

His route to the Eighth Air Force had started with the Civilian Air Patrol. "I joined because one selling point was you would certainly be able to get into the Air Force after some time at the CAP. I was drafted late in 1942 and began my army career in the Signal Corps. As promised, I was given the written test for the cadet program and I was one of the few who passed it. I transferred to the Air Corps, was sent to radio school and then gunnery school. This training was excellent and fun. I enjoyed the skeet ranges and my first time ever shooting a shotgun, and I was very adept. We had ample time shooting at moving targets and air-to-air practice. Around Christmas of 1943 I was sent to Tampa, Florida, to join a B-17 crew for phase training."

Originally detailed as a tail gunner, Richardson, at 5'11" went into the ball by default as the original candidate opted out and two other possible alternatives, the waist gunners, both stood well over six feet, beyond the maximum for the under-the-fuselage cocoon. "The ball is about forty-three inches in diameter," observes Richardson. "You have to double up, on your back most of the time, with your knees up to your eyeballs so to speak. You looked between your knees and feet through the side and through the round window down at your feet. It was a very tight fit. The ball contained 1,200 rounds of ammo, the electric motor and two hydraulic pumps that drove the turret in each direction of elevation and azimuth. There was no room for your clip-on parachute and while the rest of the crew could wear flak suits, I couldn't. It was cold because the wind would blast through the shell case ejection chute, and the clips were supposed to also eject, but seldom did. If you were busy shooting at a bunch of airplanes, you'd be busy with one hand getting rid of the clips and then firing your guns with the other hand on the control handles and the firing button."

When their brand-new B-17Gs were grounded temporarily to fix landing gears, Richardson and a batch of replacement crews rode the rails to New York, boarded the *Queen Elizabeth* and sailed to Scotland. A total of eleven new crews were assigned to the 94th where all practiced for two or three weeks before their first mission, Brunswick. "You would enter the first one as a youngster, but would grow up rather quickly upon being shot at and see all these black and gray puffs coming up your way. You realized it was for real. They were out to knock you down. You would see one or two go down. When will it be your turn? We lost our closest training crew on our fourth mission, Berlin. We aborted and the standby crew, led by Lieutenant Chism, took our place. They failed to return. The ball gunner, Gene Powell, was killed by civilians, the rest POWs. We knew them quite well. We were very sick about it and didn't get acquainted with anyone else for that reason."

Called out on June 2 for a target on the shoreline of the French coast, Richardson says the invasion talk was rampant before, during and after. Summoned to fly again in the very early hours of June 5, the group bombed up and down the coast in different places to prevent the enemy from guessing the actual landing sites. On the following evening, they breakfasted before midnight on powdered eggs fixed into a nog, bacon, toast and coffee. "The briefing officer said, yes, this was the day. The invasion was going to begin and we had to be over the target and gone by 6:30. That meant the last of the airplanes had to be gone by then, so some of us would fly earlier. Because this was the invasion day, nothing was going to keep crews down. Those that usually hated to go to the regular targets, even the ones that normally might bitch and complain, this day they wanted to go. We were told in briefing that the airplanes over the target area would be all allies, and they didn't expect any German aircraft at all. Flak would be very light, and it turned out that way. There was so much animated talking going on, shouting, hurrays and all that kind of stuff, hey, the war's going to be over earlier. It took a while to get everybody calmed down before they could tell us exactly what we were going to do and where. What a different climate.

"We were off the ground I think around 3:00 A.M. and we flew for an hour and a half, two hours in darkness. As I did the night before, I sat in the tail. I volunteered because the tail gunner didn't want to do it. I sat there with an Aldis lamp, flashing the letter 'A'—de da—indicating this was the 94th Bomb Group [its aircraft carried a big square A atop the rudder]. The target's conditions were as we were told. The Germans were not around. We came back and sat on the ground after about seven and a half hours up. I had a bite to eat. We quickly refueled the aircraft with the bombs and while that was going on, I was interviewed by the press.

"The second mission of the day was a little farther in because of the action on the beach below. The weather had broken up a bit more; the clouds had more breaks in them. We got a real good look at the action down there. Hundreds and hundreds of boats still coming across the Channel, and all those that were lined up along the beach. I saw the battleship *Texas* firing her big guns across the water to the target areas just beyond the invasion forces. I watched those 2,000-pound shells as they left the muzzles of those rifles and went into their targets and exploded. The crews were very tired after the second mission and the day before we had a long one and didn't get any sleep for two nights. But we weren't really sleepy. We were all keyed up, wondering what was going to happen."

"My log book for June 2nd," says Martin Garren, a copilot in the 94th Bomb Group, "notes we went to Conches Airdrome, twenty or thirty miles behind what would be the beachhead although we did not know at the time when and where the landings would take place. We were neutralizing enemy planes that might interfere with the invasion. My next entry is for June 4th, Le Bourget, the field near Paris where Lindbergh had landed in 1927 but was now a German base." Garren was certainly among the youngest to sit at the controls of a B-17. Born in 1925 in New York City and raised in the suburbs, he had just passed his nineteenth birthday as D-Day approached. "I graduated from White Plains High School in 1942," says Garren, "and immediately enlisted. I had changed my birth certificate from 1925 to 1923 by altering the horizontal bar at the top of the last number. It was extremely important that I go to war before I started the rest of my life. We were exposed to a lot of propaganda, radio, newspapers, magazines and in the movies. A lot of it glorified war but my motivation was my family values. You do what you're supposed to do, maybe it was my parochial school background; honor and duty, these were basic things to me. In the long run I felt I was defending my mother and my sister from invasion by our enemies. There was tremendous patriotism in those times. Everybody, even if he or she was not in uniform, knew someone, had a brother, father, uncle, friend in service."

Having taken some flight instruction even before he became a cadet, Garren easily handled the early stages of training, although later instrument flying and formation work increased the degree of difficulty. He requested multiengine duty because he thought it suited his personality and perhaps might aid him in a career after the war. However, his choice had been the A-20, light bomber, the type that had made the first Eighth Air Force operation against the Continent July 4, 1942, but he believes his obvious youth influenced a selection board to post him for a copilot's job in a B-17.

Once he achieved combat status, Garren says, "I was afraid, like everybody flying with me, but I never wanted to turn back. I knew that would be the worst thing in the world for me for the rest of my life."

Garren already had chalked up ten missions when slightly before midnight of June 5/6, an orderly advised the officers of the three crews with whom he shared a hut they were to be briefed about 1:00 A.M. for a mission. He took the mandated shower, a matter of protection against infection in the event of a wound, dressed in clean underwear for the same reason and shaved, a necessary act since any stubble might interfere with the fit of the oxygen mask. After breakfast, he joined everyone in the flight crews, roughly 360 men at the briefing. The invasion had been scheduled for June 5, but Eisenhower postponed it because of the bad weather. Garren says he knew this was it as soon as he sat down in the briefing room. At most the airmen had seen maybe a single one-star general and a couple of colonels at a briefing, but now visiting high brass packed the place.

"We were to hit the defenses in the Utah Beach area [the westernmost of the proposed two U.S. beachheads], maybe fifteen minutes or so before the landing barges came ashore around 7:00 A.M. That meant taking off around three o'clock and assembling in the dark, which was very hazardous, and there was a lot of apprehension since we had never practiced that kind of thing although we all had experience flying at night. We got off all right and began to form up. The tail gunner had an Aldis lamp, a very bright lamp, which he kept flashing to indicate this is the tail of a B-17 here and don't bump into it. We also flew with wing lights, which would have been of great help to German fighters or antiaircraft.

"Soon after we took off, the sun was in the sky, although not on the ground. We could see each other and we turned off our lights. Things were normal. We assembled into our thirty-six-ship formation, then the 108-plane combat box of our wing and headed for Utah Beach to bomb the concrete fortifications the Germans had built. I kept looking out and all I could see was our wing, close to 108 planes and I thought now they've really screwed up. Then a minute before we were to bomb, I looked to the right and to the left and out of the high-altitude haze I suddenly saw what looked like the entire Eighth Air Force, maybe 1,500 planes almost in a line abreast like the kickoff of a football game. We went on and dropped our bombs. We had expected the Luftwaffe to put up everything they had since once we got our men ashore—we had two million in England waiting to invade—it would be all over. We did not see a single enemy plane or a burst of flak.

"To make sure that nobody mistook who we were when we returned to England, we had a specific course to fly over France and then make a big, wide U-turn. We came over Ste. Mère Église, where a few hours earlier our paratroopers had dropped. As we were passing over Ste. Mère Église, I was thinking of what might be happening to the paratroopers— anyone who came swinging down in a parachute was likely to be shot at. Suddenly, we developed a fire in our control panel. Si, our navigator, and Tim, our bombardier, started tearing away insulation. Barehanded they pulled some wires loose and stopped the fire. We all thought, 'My god, what a place to have to bail out.' We returned to base without further incident. Actually we were scheduled for a tactical mission later on D-Day. But they had time lines and you couldn't attack a certain area after a specific hour because our guys might now be there. So after we took off we were called back and landed with our bombs."

Joker, the B-17 assigned to the 385th Bomb Group, according to left waist gunner and assistant radio operator John Hibbard, brought its crew back to Great Ashfield on June 5, after a sally along the French coastline. "We [found] the usual alert waiting for us," recalls Hibbard, "meaning we were to fly again the next day. There was something unusual about this alert, though. All of us felt it. At briefing time the next morning, June 6, 1944, we found out! Colonel Vandevanter [the 385th CO] addressed us. Everyone was tense with excitement, trying to catch every word. 'Gentlemen, you are about to embark upon a very important mission, the success of which will greatly affect the outcome of this war. Today is the day we've all been waiting for—D-Day.'

"A cheer went up. This was it! Everyone was bursting with excitement and pride because we were all to be there to help those doughboys assault the enemy beaches. We made two successful operations that day. One to bomb gun installations at Caen and one to bomb road junctions and railroad bridges. It was a great day. The Luftwaffe didn't dare show itself. We were all out, both the Eighth and Ninth Air Forces as well as the British RAF. It was a day we will remember as long as we live."

Harry Reynolds, dual-rated as a bombardier/navigator was a comparatively old twenty-eight when he started his tour for the Eighth Air Force. Born in Ossining, New York, and having attended New York University, Reynolds was swept up by the Selective Service in January 1941. Reynolds says, "After Pearl Harbor I decided the infantry was no place for me and transferred to the Army Air Cadets. I took pilot training but had difficulty with landings and was told that eventually I would kill myself." He switched to bombardier school and then qualified as a navigator. That led to assignment with a B-25 antisubmarine patrol operation.

Reynolds changed affiliation and aircraft as he and some associates helped create the 491st Bomb Group with B-24s. Upon completion of crew training, the 491st shipped to England in March 1944 but not until June 2 did the outfit see action. "Our first mission," says Reynolds, "we were briefed to bomb an airdrome, Bretigny, southeast of Paris and then a secondary airdrome north of Paris. Bombing results were good, especially on the secondary. We blew the fuel dump, flames shooting up about 1,000 feet. On the entire trip, from the coast to the target area and five miles out into the Channel, we experienced heavy flak. We lost one plane in our group. Flak hit the No. 3 engine of Evans, from Rochester, New York. He went down and was never seen again. I had a lump in my throat and stomach the whole trip."

For D-Day itself, Reynolds's ship, *The Hot Rock*, aimed at Coutances, a small town in the Cherbourg area that held a communications center. "The area was covered with an overcast to about 13,000 feet. We did not want to drop the bombs because we were afraid of hitting our own troops who had advanced in from the beachhead which was well established." In fact, the Eighth Air Force, after consultation with Eisenhower and other top brass arranged to bomb farther inland rather than near the shore where they would run the risk of smiting the landing craft and troops headed for the beach.

Irwin Stovroff, a Buffalo, New York, son of a liquor distributor hit hard by Prohibition, was enrolled in the University of Illinois, having transferred from Purdue when the Japanese attacked the U.S. "Just about everybody I knew was ready to enlist, to be a part of a program. Very few didn't feel we had a responsibility for ourselves and our country. I started out volunteering for the Navy air cadets but I was advised to go back to school [since I was color blind]. I went to the draft board, told them I was in college and considering joining the Air Force. They told me I was far from being drafted and could spend at least another six months in college. I wasn't back a month when I got drafted. At Fort Niagara, I asked how to get into the Air Corps. That worked so well I wound up in Arkansas as a combat engineer with the 13th Armored Division. I was the youngest and most frightened guy in the whole organization. Even my sergeant knew I was totally misplaced.

"When I heard the AF was desperately looking for people to fly, I went to the doctor who did the examinations and asked if there was any way I could get to the Air Corps. He said he'd test me physically and mentally and said if you pass you'll be there. I passed all the examinations and my CO was so mad he had me cleaning guns for everybody instead of getting a leave and going home after basic training. But it was worth it, I was getting into the branch I wanted.

"Like everyone else, I wanted to be a pilot, and particularly thought I'd enjoy being a fighter pilot. After standing in line, taking all of the tests, I learned no pilots were needed but bombardiers and navigators were. It was one way to become an officer. If I didn't choose one of those positions, I would probably wash out and end up as a gunner. I chose bombardier." With Stovroff's brother Morton a volunteer for submarine duty, their father Max remarked, "I raised two sons. One nut went up; one nut went down."

Upon graduation from the program at Midland, Texas, Lieutenant Stovroff traveled to Davis Montham Field in Tucson. There he trained with the actual crew that would go into combat together, as replacements in the 44th Bomb Group. "John Milliken, our pilot, was pretty good; he slid right into the formation slots and he had no fear about flying combat. My copilot, Bill Manierre, and I were very close friends. He had a brother, Cy, a West Point graduate and the last we heard was that Cy was working with the French Maquis, underground."

Like thousands of ground troops splashing ashore on June 6, Stovroff marked that date as his baptism of fire. From his point of view, it was uneventful with no enemy opposition. The story was the same down the line. The 487th Bomb Group tried to carry out three missions on June 6 in its B-24s but the adverse conditions aborted two of the drops.

"The 352nd Fighter Group," says Punchy Powell, "flew several missions on D-Day but these were probably some of the easiest we flew. Our job, like most of the Eighth's fighter groups, was to provide a wall of aircraft from the deck to 30,000 feet in a semicircle about fifty miles south of the beaches to make sure no enemy aircraft reached the shoreline. In this we were successful (Hollywood be damned for indicating otherwise). No German aircraft reached the beaches that day."

According to James Goodson, leader of the 336th Fighter Squadron, in his role as supreme Allied commander for Europe, General Eisenhower visited the 4th Fighter Group at Debdem Airfield just before the invasion and asked, "whether we could prevent German armor and trucks coming up on the beachhead. The Germans had kept most of their forces back, but as soon as the Allies landed they could bring them up. I replied to Eisenhower that I thought during the daytime we could stop anything that was moving on the roads but couldn't do it at night. I thought we could create enough havoc on the roads so we could jam them, preventing reinforcements from getting through. I was pretty sure we could prevent the Luftwaffe from attacking the beachhead, spraying machine gun and cannon fire on landing troops. On D-Day, only two German fighter planes got through. After the war I talked to one of the pilots who did penetrate and asked how they did it. He said, 'We were right down among the weeds and when I got back the tips of my propeller were bent where they struck the ground. Only my wingman and I got through. We got over the beachhead and saw several thousand troops on the beach, several thousand ships at sea and looked up above at several thousand aircraft above. My wingman asked what do we shoot at and I said, just spray and we'll go home.'"

Herbert Holfmeier, a wintertime recruit for the 56th Fighter Group, recalls, "We expected D-Day to happen but didn't know when. We just crawled out of bed, got into the briefing room in the early morning, maybe two or three A.M. There on the big board in big soft letters it said, THIS IS IT. We had a briefing from Hub Zemke. Meanwhile, we hadn't realized it but the ground crew had spent all night painting these white stripes under the wings to avoid friendly fire from the ground. Around 4:00 A.M. we took off, just going back and forth, shooting at anything that moved toward the beachhead. We kept coming back, eating an egg sandwich, waiting around the ready room while they gassed up your plane. I had four missions over France that day."

Joel Popplewell recalls D-Day as, "A very dreary day, very bad day for flying. We flew two missions giving top cover for the ships. They [Allied naval vessels] shot down some American planes that weren't supposed to be in the area but the pilots were all rescued."

Tommy Hayes and his gang from the 357th Fighter Group never flew over the landings or the beaches. "I believe we had as many as five or six missions but all were area support 200 miles south against any German intrusion."

The German who spoke with James Goodson mentioned "several thousand aircraft" and on June 6, according to historian Roger Freeman, "an estimated 11,000 aircraft were in the air over southern England." The fortieth and final regular bomb group assigned to the Mighty Eighth, the 493rd broke its maiden on D-Day. All together, the high command dispatched almost 2,600 B-17s and B-24s [aircraft flew more than a single mission that day] and close to 2,200 fighters. Only a single bomber went down because of enemy fire; two others collided and another crashed and exploded at his home field on takeoff. Losses among fighters added up to twenty-five.

Postwar studies indicate that the Air Corps, pounding the enemy from both the United Kingdom and Italy with bombers plus the interdiction and choo-choo tactics of the fighter groups during the weeks before D-Day effectively hamstrung road and rail traffic that might have brought immediate reinforcements to the coastal defenses. The air strikes and the miserable flying weather also combined to restrict the Luftwaffe to no more than a token appearance on June 6. But the poor visibility also significantly reduced the tactical effectiveness of both the Eighth and Ninth Air Forces that were expected to smash blockhouses and emplacements guarding the Normandy beaches. While Navy support vessels pounded portions of Omaha Beach, the eastern American sector, the Air Corps drops fell well inland, behind the enemy lines. Utah Beach also largely escaped any significant blows from the skies.

WITH beachheads established in Normandy by the Allies along a broad front, the Eighth continued to serve in the unfamiliar role of ground support even as the organization resumed its strategic assaults. Fresh bodies and machines enabled the groups to fulfill their dual obligations. Joel Popplewell with the 56th Fighter Group on June 7 remembers he flew two missions. "The first was with Gabreski, just ground support. That afternoon, I led the group with Zemke. It wasn't too large a group and we established like a traffic pattern when you come in to land, to strafe these columns of tanks, horse-drawn vehicles, ambulances. It was kind of sad to see dead horses lying there in their blood but they were part of the enemy. I don't want to call any names on who shot up an ambulance parked under a tree but it was obviously loaded with ammunition because it blew up with a lot of smoke.

"During the course of the strafings, Zemke called on radio and said, 'Somebody get those P-51s out of our traffic pattern.' A little squeaky voice came on the air, 'Colonel, they're not 51s, they're ME-109s,' which somewhat resembled the 51s. One just kinda scooted in front of me. All I had to do was pull the trigger. That was the second time I got to shoot at an enemy in the air and was my only kill."

While the flow of men and machines to the United Kingdom by D-Day seemed smooth, the appropriate assignment of personnel and their equipment depended upon decisions made many months earlier. To fill a pilot's slot at the 91st Bomb Group, Howard Donahue, a 1922 Malone, New York, baby, took a detour from his original assignment as a B-26 Martin Marauder crewman. "The catastrophic run of casualties from raids like Schweinfurt took me off the B-26; I even met a P-38 pilot who was yanked out to fly B-17s." Donahue had completed two years at the University of Maryland when he enlisted, thinking of himself as a fighter pilot. He remembers his attitude at the time was, "'Who wouldn't want to be in the Air Corps?' That was the glamour organization. Couldn't you imagine yourself sitting in a P-51 or P-38, mounting a slashing attack on the enemy? Everyone wanted to be fighter pilot. But we were selected as far as need was concerned. I graduated to go to twin-engine school." From there he transitioned into the Forts.

"We had about ten hours of practice in England before our first mission and learned fairly well on the job. Flying formation in a B-17 is not the most fun thing in the world. We'd practiced a very little bit of that in the U.S. They used to teach us cloud penetration; as we'd approach a deck of clouds, people would peel off, do a circle and come back in line. In combat with the 91st when you'd approach a heavy cloud formation we heard Colonel Klette [Immanuel or 'Manny,' the squadron CO] in his gravelly voice, 'Flock her in tight, boys. We're going right through,' and that's what we did.

"By the time we got there they were flying so many missions you flew all different planes and I can't remember their names. I think everybody there damn near flew or took off with a hangover and they didn't really worry about the weather. We had to take off many times strictly on instruments; all you could see was the line down the runway in front of you. We were probably lost a couple of times particularly when flying at low levels over Holland and Germany.

"My first encounter with enemy occurred shortly after D-Day, on a carpet bombing raid ahead of the troops near Aachen or St.-Lô. The first time we got flak, like an idiot, I said, gee isn't that pretty, I wish it would be closer. I never said that again. Carpet bombing was at 18,000 feet or lower. The flak at 12,000 to 18,000 was incredibly accurate with 88 mm guns, but fortunately they didn't have many firing. They did shoot down some. Unfortunately, one time we dropped short, because the smoke [the signal of the drop zone] drifted back over our own positions."

J. C. Wilson, a Johnson City, Texas, son of an oil-field worker and farmer, was infatuated with the airplane like so many youngsters of the 1930s. "I can remember running outside just to watch one fly over south Texas, and if you ever saw one flying at night that was really something. You could hear the engine and see the navigation lights, and that was all. The doctor in the oil-field section of Texas had a Beechcraft twin-wing plane and if he had a case he couldn't handle, he would put the patient in the plane and fly him to San Antonio. All the kids would watch the plane until it was out of sight. We all built model planes and some of them even flew. When the Air Corps started increasing training, the planes would fly over our oat patch and I knew this was what I wanted to do if we ever went to war.

"Then on December 7, 1941 [he was 17 by then], the Japanese bombed Pearl Harbor, a place I had never heard of. I was real excited. The United States had been attacked and now we would have to show them Japs they couldn't do that to us. I had no idea of why the Japanese would want to bomb us. I had no idea of world affairs. I was aware that Germany was harassing the Jews but I didn't know they were trying to eliminate the race. I only thought they wanted them to leave Germany."

Drafted in early 1943, Wilson requested pilot training but was told he did not qualify. "I liked guns as well as airplanes so I said how about gunnery." After six weeks of Air Corps basic training—learning to salute, march, drill with wooden rifles (with no time on a firing range), Wilson entrained to Las Vegas to learn aerial gunnery.

"We had classroom instruction for operation, maintenance, and nomenclature of the Browning .50 caliber machine gun, mounted and flexible. We trained on the Sperry electrohydraulic gun turret, both upper and lower ball, and the Emerson electric turrets. The Sperry was used in both the B-17 and B-24 and the Emerson in some B-24s and lighter bombers. Afternoons were hands-on operations. We fired at skeet from the range and from weapons' carriers [trucks about the size of a modern pickup] with a flexible-mount shotgun. We would fire .50 caliber machine guns from stationary mounted turrets while scale models of German aircraft were carried on railcars around a set course. We fired flexible machine guns at both mobile and fixed targets. We had some air-operated machine guns and thousand-inch ranges that used wooden machine guns to learn how to aim.

"One device, the Jam Handy trainer, was in an enclosed building. One wall was a large hemisphere, like half a ball set on its edge, the concave side facing the trainee. He sat in a turret in the direct center, facing the sphere. Behind him were five movie projectors, each one focused on one-fifth of the sphere. Synchronized together, they covered the entire hemisphere. An image of an aircraft would appear on the outer edge of the screen and seem to fly toward the trainee. As it crossed his field of view, it passed out of the first projector and the second one would show it moving along the same course. It would appear to come closer to the trainee and then go by him, seeming to fly away. The images would come from all parts of the screen and you really learned the curve of pursuit."

Subsequently, Wilson and those in his class practiced using machine guns in a series of different types of aircraft. He was schooled in other bomber aspects, the ordnance, the shackles that held the bombs, the mechanics and electrical aspects of turrets. "Me and electricity didn't get along at all. I failed in this part of the course and had to take it over, which put me back one class." His entry into the shooting war was further delayed when the Air Corps misplaced his records and for two months he served in a limbo that included kitchen police duty. "Even though I was a sergeant, the Air Corps had to use noncommissioned officers for KP because they had so many of them."

Ultimately committed as a waist gunner for a replacement crew, Wilson sailed to Liverpool from New York in mid-May, assigned to the 351st Bomb Group at Polebrook in the United Kingdom. After two familiarization flights that did not add up to six hours, Wilson learned he and his mates would be supernumeraries for a raid upon Le Bourget near Paris. As was customary, Wilson's regular first pilot, Lt. Einer Peterson, moved into the copilot's seat while an experienced aviator commanded the ship. That bumped copilot Lt. James Tebel to another plane. When one of those scheduled for the operation reported engine trouble and turned back, Wilson's B-17 moved into place.

"As we crossed the coast into France," says Wilson of his introduction to the shooting war, "I observed some airplanes approaching our formation. I reported them and all of us started watching. They turned out to be our own P-47s, the fighter escort. A few minutes later, another flight of planes showed up and they were P-38s. Then we had P-51s, all kinds of escorts and no German planes. We arrived at the target and started our bomb run. It was easier making history than it was studying it in school.

There was sporadic antiaircraft fire but not too much and none close to us. We finished our mission and as we crossed over the English Channel again we could see it was still full of ships going both ways. We landed back at Polebrook, removed our guns and reported back to the debriefing room. They gave every man a shot of Scotch whisky. I didn't drink so I gave mine to another crew member. I drank a Coke instead. We then cleaned our guns and stored them in the armory. We had completed our first mission. We were combat veterans."

Navigator Jim Hill was a member of a mid-May replacement crew in the 305th Bomb Group. Son of a Pennsylvania college professor, Hill had quit high school two months before graduation in 1943 to enlist in the Air Corps. "I wanted to choose the best option open as opposed to the draft. I chose navigation because I thought it best matched my capabilities. In my last semester of high school I bought a book on the subject and studied under my trigonometry teacher."

Rather than plunge Hill and his associates into the maelstrom of the massive D-Day enterprise, the 305th leaders chose to hold them out of combat until two weeks after the landings. That some groups had the luxury to delay use of reinforcements further testifies to the growing abundance of people and aircraft. At that, Hill benefitted from an almost benign introduction to the war. "The first mission was short and easy, no fighters and no flak. I found the whole experience interesting. There was no early trauma but gradually I learned not to expect to survive."

Another new recruit was Russell Strong, also a navigator, who was posted to the 306th Bomb Group where he developed a more affirmative attitude. Born in Kalamazoo into an education-oriented family, Strong already had a semester in Kalamazoo College when he enlisted. "I was given my choice but I picked navigation instead of pilot training. I had read a lot about flying and thought I'd become a pilot. But then after ten hours in a Piper Cub I felt acrobatics was not my cup of tea.

"Celestial navigation was interesting and even enjoyable but I never used any of it in combat. [Daylight raids restricted the potential for guidance through the stars.] It was all DR [dead reckoning, which relies on map reading, compass headings, charting progress on a blank Mercator chart] and pilotage [navigation by means of visible landmarks, such as railroads, bodies of water, etc.]. In England I learned much more about pilotage and we were introduced to the British Gee system [a radar method that utilized a number of stations to obtain a fix on one's location].

"I arrived at the 306th on June 7, and a week elapsed before my first mission. It was pretty normal, a run south over the Channel, down into

France, a turn back north and drop the bombs. I flew the first few missions, knowing that I wouldn't complete a tour. But by ten, I knew I'd make it if I wore a flak suit and helmet, carried my parachute on the bomb runs, and was prepared. We had some close calls, but I always felt I had a superb pilot who 'knew' his aircraft. On my fourth mission we were shot out of formation over Berlin, with a couple of external wing fires. The pilot extinguished those. My navigation was good enough to get us out of Germany without overrunning Hamburg or Berlin and out over the North Sea. Then 'Darky' [a network of low-power radio stations that advised airmen of their approximate location] made the navigation easy and we made an emergency landing, with only one good engine remaining, on the coast."

Although the Allies now held a firm grip on the edge of the Continent, for both veterans and neophytes the struggle in the skies flared as hot as ever.

15

SHOOTDOWNS AND SHUTTLES

D uring the winters of the early 1930s, Dick Bowman, as a boy in Moab, Utah, wore a cloth helmet with tiny goggles and the inscription LUCKY LINDY on the side. When a major fire enveloped Yellowstone Park, Bowman convinced his father, a forestry service worker, to allow him to go along in a Ford trimotor that would drop camp kitchens, extra clothes and other supplies to young men from the Civilian Conservation Corps, fighting the inferno. "It took quite a while to get from Idaho Falls to Yellowstone Park, over the Great Divide and I was really hooked."

Bowman pursued an aviation career through the Civilian Pilot Training program, an operation designed to prime candidates for the Air Corps. "I had a little problem with air sickness in the CPT when we took our primary and soloed in Piper Cubs. My father had come over from England and been very seasick. He knew of pills for the condition and when I told him I was becoming airsick he told me to get some Mothersills Seasick Pills. The local pharmacy in Pocatello said they never heard of such a thing but miraculously found some in Salt Lake City. I took a few and once I got over air sickness I was never bothered again, even in rough weather."

Once in the service, however, Bowman's dreams of becoming a pilot foundered on the Air Corps' surplus of candidates for that job and after a brief period learning to handle a glider, he attended radio schools while learning gunnery. "When we were put together as a crew at Peyote, Texas, I was the smallest, weighing 120 pounds and standing 5'5". The pilot selected me to be a ball-turret gunner and I was quite happy with it.

"I got to England three days before D-Day and we were assigned to the 96th Bomb Group at Snetterton Heath [another East Anglia base]. They took us up to the Wash [a shallow water area of the North Sea about seventy miles north of London set aside for training] and let us fire at targets on the ground. We had experienced gunners who finished their tour of duty to clue us in on what we would face. Our crew also flew training missions."

On June 18, for the first time since D-Day, the Eighth Air Force committed itself to a series of major assaults on strategic targets. A week later Dick Bowman tasted the air war. "On our first mission, we had a very old, war-weary airplane. We had flown a new airplane over but they took it away from us to put the latest modifications on it and debug it of any problems. Meanwhile, as newcomers you flew the oldest standby on the base, which in our case was called *Bad Penny* and belonged to another group.

"Above 25,000 feet as we were coming up on our target [Bremen], a piece of flak apparently disabled the vacuum pump which runs the gyros. The bombardier with the bombsight was basically in control of the plane, but because of the lack of the pump, the gyros came uncaged and the airplane heeled over. We headed down at a steep angle towards the ground. By the time they gained control of the airplane we were down around 16,000 feet and all alone. We still had the bombs but they decided to keep them since we were by ourselves. We went home alone, at under 10,000 feet and dropped the bombs in the North Sea.

"Two of the original crew members came forward after that first mission and said this was not for them. Both went to work for the armament section on the ground. No one made anything of it. If you couldn't hack flying there was no stigma attached to it. Maybe you were even smarter than the rest of us. Their replacements, a tail gunner and a waist gunner, shot down over France in the same plane, had escaped back to England through the French underground."

The 305th Bomb Group, formerly led by Curtis LeMay, who now supervised B-29s destined to scourge the Japanese mainland, added a crew that included David Nagel as engineer/turret gunner. The son of a New York City garment-industry entrepreneur who had gone to France with the artillery in the 77th Infantry Division as part of the American Expeditionary Force during World War I, Nagel hoped for a Navy chief petty-officer rating because of his time with the Sea Scouts. "I bugged my parents to let me enlist," says Nagel, "but when they finally gave me permission it was too late. All the ratings had been given out."

Subsequently, Nagel sought to follow his father's footsteps to the artillery but while on line to sign up was convinced to switch to the Air Corps by an acquaintance who argued, "In the artillery you gotta clean horses, and the guns blow your ears out." Given a choice of technical school, Nagel opted for mechanics. He did his gunnery work in Texas and then received assignments to a series of bomber plants and airfields before actually entering mechanics school.

During this period, Nagel remembers a crew chief telling him to put sparkplugs in a plane used for aerial gunnery practice. "I got up on the scaffolding, looked at the engines, then went to the supply room which issued the plugs. I went back to the plane, removed the furring, looked at the tech orders on the tools and tensions to use. I got them out, opened up the boxes of plugs when some brass rings fell out. I figured, 'Gee, I'll take these back to the guys and they can use them when they take girls out.' Luckily, the sergeant came up on the scaffolding and he saw the rings in a heap on the side. He says, 'What the hell are you doing with those?' I said I'm going to give them to the fellows in the barracks. 'You crazy?' he says. 'If you don't put those rings in on the bottom with those plugs, that plane would be in the gulf or not even get off the ground before it crashed.' That's when I started to make sure I checked everything I did." Subsequently, Nagel received his formal instruction in aircraft mechanics and then was made a member of a replacement combat crew.

They flew their B-17 to the UK over the northern route through Bangor, Maine, to Newfoundland and then to Nutts Corner in Ireland. "We were sent to the 422nd Squadron," recalls Nagel. "It had been acting as a night-drop outfit, food, ammunition, radios from B-17s painted black. My pilot, Dale Malloy knew how to do two things, drive a tractor and fly an airplane. He was a damn good pilot. He would go up to the barracks and have dinner, go to the officers' club, buy a fifth, go back to his room and finish it. If we had a mission the next day I would always make sure he had an oxygen bottle he could whiff in the tent by the plane. He wasn't an alcoholic but he drank after every mission." Two weeks after their commitment to the 305th, the crew of *One Man's Family,* named for a radio soap opera of the day by Nagel, went on its first combat mission, Leipzig.

Like Nagel, ball-turret gunner Harry Wolff with the 305th Bomb Group was another new participant in the air war. A precocious youngster from New York City, Wolff graduated from Bordentown Military Academy in New Jersey at age sixteen in 1942. While attending the University of Virginia he informed his father he wanted to enlist in the marines. Rather than see his son quit school for the life of a leatherneck, his father made a proposal, "If you can pass the test for an air cadet, I'll say you're seventeen." Wolff made the grade and in October 1943, entered military service.

"We were at Randolph Field, Texas," remembers Wolff, "and one day, after three months of instruction in pilot training, we were told, 'Gentlemen, we seem to be winning the war. Your services are no longer required in the capacity of a pilot.' We were informed that the other positions open to us were military police, cook, baker, clerk or aerial gunner. I wanted to go on a plane so I went to gunnery school."

With the 305th, Wolff went into combat after a few weeks of training in England. He discovered that no matter what anyone taught, the possibility for friendly-fire casualties was almost equal to that of potential damage to the enemy. "The turret never turned fast enough when they came through a formation. You had to watch what you were doing and hope he'd fly through your bullets. They got very annoyed at you if you hit the next B-17. But by the time I got there, the worst was over. The P-51s had destroyed the Luftwaffe. They were running out of pilots and they had no fuel."

As fewer enemy aircraft challenged the Americans in the sky, the fighter pilots with their mandate from Doolittle sought them on the ground, which most fliers conceded was more dangerous than dogfights.

Max Woolley, manning a P-38 for the 364th Fighter Group, was one victim claimed by antiaircraft fire while inflicting heavy damage on ground personnel and enemy equipment. "After my plane was hit [June 27 near Charleroi, Belgium] by enemy ground fire, I was forced to abandon ship near the 18,000-foot level. As I neared the ground, German troops opened up with small-arms fire, slicing a four-foot cut into the canopy of my parachute, causing me to free fall at the rate of about fifty feet per second. Several bullets struck me."

Despite Woolley's proximity to soldiers, a Belgian family took him in. "I spent a lot of time, reclining on a hardwood floor in a home in Belgium, with no medical help except the kind people who hated the despised Boche. They sacrificed their safety and gave me the best they had to offer, a place to rest, food from their sparse pantry, wet towels to subdue the stifling heat from being crammed into an eighteen-inch high enclosure and to wipe the blood and infected pus that oozed from my wounds for almost two months.

"I've often asked myself, 'Could I befriend a bloody, dirty, wounded man whom I had never before seen, share my scant supply of food, jeopardize the safety and welfare of myself and family?' I had a lot of time to think about what I had done now that I was shot down, wounded, and suffered like the enemy troops must have suffered. At the time I looked upon it as a job, a challenge at first, but later had remorse from the many days and nights I spent wanting to scream because of the pain, the loss of my loved ones who didn't know my location or condition, and the dejection and depression that comes from being isolated, left alone in a foreign land not knowing whether or not I would ever see the country that I loved, a family and beautiful fiancée wanting me home. Prayer was the greatest source of inspiration for me in dealing with the stress of combat and especially after I was shot down, listed as Missing in Action. It gave me strength, consolation and a way to talk, to plead for help and life itself."

The underground preserved Woolley from a prison camp with fake papers, a phony identification card and an employment certificate listing him as "Auguste Lamarre." Woolley would remain an evadee for about ninety days.

Among those also engaged in air-to-ground warfare was Jim Goodson, squadron commander of the 4th Fighter Group's 336th Squadron. He had achieved excellent results strafing enemy airfields; as May ended, his crew chief had painted fifteen swastikas alongside the cockpit of Goodson's P-51 for confirmed kills on the ground. But on June 20, while spraying an enemy airfield, Goodson was forced to belly in his Mustang and became a prisoner.

"After I got shot down," said Goodson, "I was taken prisoner by the Gestapo [Nazi secret police]. I persuaded them to get in touch with the Luftwaffe which sent a party to take me in handcuffs to the interrogation center near Frankfurt. Going there, we had to change trains in Berlin. I asked the officer in charge of me where we were going. He said the Frie-derichstrasse Banhof. I asked the date and then remembered that 1,000 planes were scheduled to hit Berlin with the main aiming point that rail-road station about noon. What time did we get there? About noon!

"We took refuge in bomb shelters. Because I had taken part in planning the raid, I knew who would be leading the different boxes of bombers and my own fighters would be escorting. It's a very different view of the war, when you're up there at 30,000 feet and you see only little flashes and puffs of smoke. You don't think of people. Sitting in an air raid shelter with Germans all around you, and the crashing, deafening noise above you is something else. About halfway through, the all-clear sounded and everyone was about to leave the shelter. I said, 'No, no! It's not finished yet. The second wave is going to come in.' They looked at me peculiarly but the officer with me said, 'He knows.' Sure enough, another devastating wave of bombers came over. I saw devastation a hundred times worse than the London Blitz which I went through. There were hundreds of bodies of people who had not been able to get into the shelters. It brought home a war pilots very seldom see. Digging women and babies out of the rubble we had caused was profoundly affecting."

Goodson was caught in Berlin by a raid with an added wrinkle to it. While the main bomber stream headed for the German capital, two wings of the Third Bomb Division, accompanied by their P-51 shadows, hammered the oil refinery complex at Ruhland, then continued east with the intention of landing in the Soviet Union at Poltava and Mirgorod. Harry Crosby, as a navigator in the 100th Bomb Group, described the first part of the venture to Ruhland, "not a milk run but a lot safer than Berlin." As they proceeded east after the drop, the fighter pilots could be heard complaining that the Berlin contingent got all the action. That changed with the sighting of enemy fighters. According to Crosby, the would-be interceptors never came near the 100th as the Mustangs shot down seven and the remainder ran away. All together, during the journey beyond Ruhland, P-51s shot down fourteen enemy aircraft in a matter of minutes with no losses to themselves.

The success of the Mustangs notwithstanding, one B-17 from the 452nd Bomb Group caught fire and on board was an unlucky passenger. Rather than rely on the Red Army to supply knowledgeable ground crews, the shuttle bombers had packed aboard extra hands from England, some of whom having been given gunnery instruction, occupied waist positions.

Jim Goodson's own crew chief, S. Sgt. Robert L. Gilbert, detailed to service P-51s on this mission, happened to be on the burning Fort. He parachuted out and landed hard but intact. Polish partisans quickly hid him from the Germans. For five weeks he lived among the guerrilla fighters before being handed over to forces from the Soviet Union. Eventually, he flew from there to North Africa and then back to his home field at Debdem.

Meanwhile, the bulk of the two wings reached the Soviet Union. On the ground in Soviet territory, Crosby with the 100th, slept on a hard bench covered with hay, the guest accommodations for the visiting firemen. "That afternoon," he remembers, "a problem developed. German reconnaissance planes droned over the field looking at us. The Russians had no antiaircraft. Russian pilots in American Airacobras went up, and the Germans, apparently Stukas [an obsolete dive-bomber by 1944], went away. Colonel Jeff [Tom Jeffrey, the 100th's CO] was uncomfortable. 'We're naked in front of those guys.'"

He was not the only one disturbed by the sight. On the ground at Mirgorod, Col. Joseph Moller, the 95th Bomb Group leader for the expedition, also became alarmed by the appearance of a German photo reconnaissance plane overhead. Before leaving the United Kingdom, the Americans had been instructed that while at the Soviet airfields, they would be under the command of the Soviets. Moller and the 13th Wing commander, through an interpreter, requested permission from the ranking officer for some of their P-51 shepherds to knock the intruder out of the sky. Moller saw a few meager flak bursts that hardly disturbed the spy plane.

"After a lengthy discussion with another Russian, he refused. I asked him why. He replied that if we did shoot down the German plane, it would always be said that we had to defend ourselves on Russian bases. I then asked how he proposed to defend us and our parked aircraft against a probable air attack. He had no answer, except merely to shrug and turn away."

The two American officers tried to contact the Forty-fifth Bomb Wing led by Archie Old in Poltava by telephone and by radio without success. While walking along the field past a small clump of houses, Moller says his radio operator called his attention to a series of violet-blue flashes from behind the curtain of one building, which he was certain indicated radio transmissions. Moller and the wing commander persuaded their hosts to allow them to fly to a different location. Moller also informed the Soviet officer of their suspicions of radio signals emanating from the house bordering the airfield.

Using a road map supplied by the base commander, the Americans took off from Mirgorod by the light of the moon and fled to other airfields. For several days, Moller and his people then waited for bombs and fuel required to fulfill their second shuttle leg. Crosby and the other airmen circulated among the Soviet soldiers, male and female, admired the prominent bosoms of the latter, heard tales of the vicious battles endured and the murderous behavior of the German occupation troops. They swapped souvenirs, partied briefly and saw nothing of the enemy.

The story at Poltava was quite different. Archie Old brought to that airfield about seventy-five bombers from his Forty-fifth Bomb Wing. "When we landed there," said Old, "most of the aircraft had practically empty tanks. We knew we were going to have problems with refueling before we left. The fuel there was in fifty-gallon drums and you would pump it directly from the drums into the airplanes. You could quickly see that you couldn't do that very fast, even if they had an almost unlimited number of men and machines.

"We hadn't much more than gotten on the ground before we were met by a General Permanov, the Russian commander at Poltava, and a General [Robert] Walsh, I believe his name was, from our Embassy at Moscow [Walsh's assignment had been to arrange resupply and refueling]. I noticed this aircraft that looked like it was up 10,000 to 12,000 feet, not more than that and I was pretty sure it was an ME-210. I mentioned to the American general and General Permanov through his lady interpreter that the plane could signal trouble. But there wasn't a helluva lot we could do about it. We had empty tanks down there, and there was no way, if we started to work then, that we could fill those things up and go to some other base. We had been told this was the only base readily available. I questioned that it couldn't be done but I had no authority to challenge any Russian decisions there. It was their country and their bases. But they said [the Germans] wouldn't come in and bomb or anything like that. But it looked like an awfully juicy target to me, sitting down there with these silver airplanes. It was a moot question. We could never have gotten the aircraft refueled, I don't think, until hours after the first Germans arrived.

"We were having a pretty big dinner in honor of myself and some of my key staff people from the 96th Bomb Group, the 388th and the 452nd at General Permanov's mess. The dinner was progressing pretty well with frequent toasts to toss off some vodka. They would make a toast, 'Long live Stalin.' and you were supposed to chugalug, toss it off. Then someone else would [say] 'Long live Roosevelt.' I got the impression the Russians wouldn't be too disappointed if I happened to partake of a little too much of it because they looked like they were trying to get us intoxicated. I'd always heard that eating butter would help you a bit when drinking so I ate about a pound of butter.

"We got a report that there were some aircraft coming in, generally from the west. They were bringing reports into General Permanov. Finally, it was pretty obvious that these were German bombers coming in to bomb at Poltava and Mirgorod. Dinner immediately ceased and [people] went down into a bomb shelter.

"The first German aircraft over the field was a pathfinder, dropping flares. Those silver airplanes stood out like a sore toe. Then the Germans proceeded to bomb; they did a superb job. Of course those silver airplanes sitting out on the ground with those silver wings and silver bodies was like shooting fish in a barrel. It was rather insulting. They were using some of the oldest damn equipment that they had available. They wouldn't have dared, I don't think, to go over England with anything like that.

"I could have done something about it but I had been thoroughly briefed that we would cooperate fully with the Russians. I had somewhere around seventy-five P-51s sitting over there at either Mirgorod or Piryatin [another field] and they had been refueled. It was my understanding we could have put them up and shot down every one of those German bombers before they did as much damage as they did.

"However, when I discussed this with General Permanov, he said he would have to get in touch with Moscow. I can only presume he did try but we were unable to get permission to put our fighters up. I was not about to put the airplanes up to shoot down aircraft over Russian territory when they had told me I would have to get permission from Moscow to do that. I didn't go into the bomb shelter but walked to the edge of the field. There was no danger as long as you stayed off the field. I stood there watching. My people, the crews, were in an area adjacent to the airfields. We had two or three casualties."

While very few Americans were injured, the devastation wreaked upon the Forty-fifth Bomb Wing was enormous. When the last of the unmolested enemy planes departed, little more than half a dozen of the seventy-five that had arrived were in condition to fly. At Mirgorod, the Luftwaffe flares illuminated only an empty airdrome as the Thirteenth Bomb Wing had flown the coop.

For the return lap, the two bomb wings met at a location within sight of the Black Sea where Old tacked on his six surviving B-17s to the formation of the Thirteenth and together they blasted an oil refinery and rail yard at Drogobych, Poland. From there they flew to Foggia, Italy, for a stopover en route back to the United Kingdom. The Eighth Air Force ran a few more shuttles between the UK and the Soviet Union but no one could generate much enthusiasm for such operations after the disaster at Poltava.

BY the early summer of 1944, a series of reports to the U.S. embassy in Switzerland, to agencies such as the International Red Cross and to both London and Washington confirmed the worst fears of the Nazi policy towards Jews and others incarcerated in concentration camps. Escaped prisoners from Auschwitz described in detail the systematized mass murders carried out there. Underground operators in Eastern Europe detailed the movement of the victims by railroad to the camps from Hungary now in the process of funneling hundreds of thousands of people towards the gas chambers. Attached to these accounts of the growing holocaust came pleas to use the Air Force to bomb the murder apparatus and the tracks that bore the hapless to their doom.

The Auschwitz location was closer to the airfields operated by the Fifteenth Air Force in Italy. Indeed, on two occasions, planes from the Fifteenth, obviously passing over the rail lines that led to the site, struck at the slave-labor factories in Auschwitz, a mere five miles from the gas chambers. And although the target was more convenient for the Fifteenth, the shuttles by the Eighth put its planes within reach of Auschwitz and carried its planes over Hungary and the transportation to Poland.

The policy makers rejected all requests to use Air Force assets to halt implementation of "the final solution." It is true there were antiaircraft batteries in residence and fighters to ward off attacks upon the slave-labor plants. But the defenses were hardly as formidable as elsewhere. Naysayers claimed attacks directly on the camp would feed the German propaganda mills with stories about the slaughter of "resettled people." Furthermore, they argued that the rapidity with which the enemy could restore its tracks meant that the raids would only provide a short delay. That consideration did not prevent the employment of the bombers against railroads elsewhere. On the other hand, suggestions that it would have been an easy matter to simply divert two or three bombers to smash the rail lines ignores the harsh lesson learned by the Eighth Air Force. The surest way to attract enemy fighters with disastrous consequences for the bombers was to dispatch them in small numbers. Security depended upon a combat box of size.

The U.S. War Department said such missions would divert airpower from "decisive operations elsewhere." And while the decision ultimately rested with the top civilian officials, it is unlikely that any generals, including those directly responsible for Eighth Air Force, who, even if apprised of the situation, would have been eager to employ their weapons for any purpose other than the destruction of the enemy. Auschwitz remained basically untouched because of political reasons in a behind-the-scenes debate where even some Jewish organizations failed to make vigorous representation of the need to destroy the genocidal machinery.

The controversy over the possibility of bombing Auschwitz was tangential to the Eighth Air Force's operations. With the range of both bombers and fighters boosted by installation of extra tanks, there was very little reason for shuttles. The American big and small aircraft could penetrate into the heart of Nazi Germany and just as well make it back to England as to continue for several hundred miles to a secure Soviet site. For example, Harry Reynolds participated in a major operation that included 939 effective B-17s and B-24s beamed at central German oil, bearing and aircraft plants. The 491st's particular objective was a factory at Aschersleben.

"We were introduced to the Luftwaffe," says Reynolds, "as soon as we hit the Dutch coast. At the I.P. we saw two P-47s going down in tight spins, smoking. On the start of the bomb run, four ME-109s passed 200 feet below us, dark blue-black crosses plainly visible. Two P-51s were on their tails and all four German planes were shot down. We finally came to the target, the bombs of the lead squadron hit smack on the factory, saw explosions, fire, smoke in the target area. We high-tailed for home, glad to reach the Channel. Thank God for our fighter coverage; they were good friends." The 491st and 489th Groups lost a plane apiece but a single squadron in the 492nd counted eleven bombers downed. "We were told this was the biggest sky battle since D-Day," recalls Reynolds. Overall, big and little friends officially destroyed almost 120 enemy fighters.

MUNICH, the Bavarian city of southern Germany that spawned the Nazi movement, and another deep target, drew a thousand-plane raid on July 11. The experience of Herb Shanker, an engineer/top-turret gunner indicates shifts in the background of personnel and procedures. Manning the top turret of a B-17 in this assault was Shanker. Born in the Bronx, New York, the son of immigrants who might well have been consigned to a concentration camp, he grew up as an aviation enthusiast although he had never been in the vicinity of an airplane. "I don't recall any airports in the Bronx." However, after being drafted in January 1943, he filled out a questionnaire in which he indicated he would like to become "a flying mechanic."

In the earlier days of the Eighth Air Force, a pool of men with mechanical experience or knowledge had supplied the need for flying engineers, but manpower demands now drafted even those like Herb Shanker who had no background in the specialty. Granted his wish, Shanker attended a B-17 mechanic's school and learned gunnery. "In general our training was more than adequate, but you are never completely prepared to enter combat. You learn by *experience*. I had no mechanical knowledge or experience prior to the service. Luckily, I had some buddies who were very well versed in aspects of aviation that helped fill in the voids. One buddy, who did not survive the war, was an engine expert. He could answer any of my questions. I often wondered why I had to keep copious records while we were flying. This involved continuous recording of various instrument readings. I eventually realized it taught us to 'sweep the board' which enabled us to look at the instrument panel and detect any abnormal reading."

A further case in point, one of Shanker's classmates during the training course was another New York City boy, Harry Serotta. "To this day, I don't know why I was chosen to be an engineer." With a year of college, and a dream of a career in advertising, Serotta gained some knowledge of the Air Corps as a civilian clerk for a depot near Harrisburg, Pennsylvania. That affiliation drew him assignment to the Air Corps after his induction. "The idea of flying and the glamour appealed to me," says Serotta, "even though I hate heights." He managed to retain his enthusiasm even after his first flight from Kingman, Arizona. "The pilot flew through the Grand Canyon, even skimming the water and then going into a steep climb. I gave back my last couple of meals but still I think I enjoyed it.

"It seems to me that we had lots of air-to-air gunnery training and after forming our crew, we practiced, practiced, and then practiced some more. I feel we were more than adequately trained and it probably helped us survive."

When Serotta reached England and the 379th stationed at Kimbolton, he was gratified to discover the place formerly housed the RAF. "It was well established and considering the war and our distance from home, the food wasn't bad. And before our first mission, we attended a final five-day course at an advanced school."

Assigned with a replacement crew to the 303rd Bomb Group in mid-June, the outfit that had included Billy Southworth and company some months earlier, Herb Shanker and his associates underwent an intensive ten-day course of gunnery and ground school. "There were some advances in instrumentation that we had not heard about before. Some procedures we had not learned in the States had been instituted overseas. We had not experienced real high-altitude flying till we got to England. We had flown old wrecks in training, never higher than 16,000 feet or longer than six hours. We never had carried fuel in our Tokyo tanks or more than 1,000 pounds of bombs. Now, on our first mission to Munich, it would be nine-plus hours at 25,000 feet, a temperature of thirty to forty degrees below zero, with a full fuel load of 2,700 gallons and 5,000 pounds of bombs from a 6,000-foot runway it took a bit of acclimatization. Takeoffs were always hair-raising. At least half the time we couldn't see 100 yards down the runway because of the fog. The length of the runway gave us about a 1 percent safety factor. On our third mission, we had to abort our takeoff because of an inoperative airspeed indicator. We stopped just in time but ran off the runway and were just ten feet from a drainage ditch when we stopped. Had our pilot not acted immediately when informed the instrument wasn't working, it would have been a disaster.

"For Munich, we were assigned a togglier—our bombardier had been taken from us in the States and sent to radar school—who had about twelve missions at the time. He, Joe Cappucci, of Croton Falls, New York, completed his tour with us for which we were extremely grateful. A togglier was an enlisted man who toggled the bombs out when the lead plane dropped. His functions included setting up the intervalometer and whatever other instruments were involved and also to call for an oxygen check every five minutes to make sure everyone was conscious. He was more competent than 98 percent of the bombardiers we had. He also helped our navigator by doing pilotage, which I'm not sure other bombardiers were happy to do. The use of lead bombardiers eliminated the need for a commissioned specialist aboard every ship as the toggliers set up their intervalometers and salvoed upon the leader's drop. Whether the results were less precise than if each aircraft employed its own Norden expert gave way to the recognition by bomb-damage assessors that under combat conditions, no method guaranteed direct hits on an objective."

The same mass visit to Munich described by Herb Shanker included Harry Serotta on his first mission. "I didn't know what to expect. I was most certainly frightened but I steeled myself and did what I had to do. The flak was heavy but the crew performed well. Jim Spratt our pilot was cool and calm. Formation flying for a first mission must be difficult under optimum circumstances, but on this and following missions, he was up to it."

Two days after Shanker and Serotta traveled to Munich, another huge effort brought Wil Richardson and the crew of *Kismet* from the 94th Bomb Group to the city. "Over the target," says Richardson, "I was seriously wounded by 155 mm flak. There was one very small hole in the wing and a very large one in my turret and in me. I stayed in the turret to count the bombs away. I thought I could stick it out longer but was losing too much blood. So I reported to the pilot and he said to get out and the left waist (6'2") could take my place. As bandits were reported in the area, the radio operator Bernard Jeffers and the right waist, Milo Johnson, stripped off my flight clothes, the new pants and shirt I had just purchased. I was treated and placed in an electric survival blanket. A short time later, we were hit with fighters. I jumped up at the sound of shooting and grabbed the radio gun.

"I didn't have any intercom so wasn't sure what the action was. I saw only one I could shoot at from that position. After a bit I realized I had nothing on but a T-shirt and shorts and at minus fifty or sixty degrees, I was getting awfully cold. I hit the blanket to get warm. It was three and a half hours back to the base and I was still losing precious blood. We left the formation to get back as soon as possible and another ship with a wounded waist gunner joined us. Upon landing I was strapped on a stretcher, placed in an ambulance for a ride to a hospital. I didn't get back to the base for over four weeks." Rather than accept a post as head of the base armament section, Richardson rotated to the States. He returned to flight status there after completing a B-29 engineer-mechanic's school.

THE fighters, particularly the P-51, also roamed far from home. On June 29, Tommy Hayes went along with the bombers to the hitherto infrequently targeted environs of Leipzig. "The bomber stream was about 100 miles from end to end," remembers Hayes. "We were assigned the lead B-17s with our rendezvous about ninety miles from Leipzig. The weather was clear and we met on schedule. We proceeded ahead, sweeping. I was leading the 364th Squadron with the 362nd on my left about 1,000 feet above and the 363rd on the sun side, to the right about 2,000 to 3,000 feet higher against a German top cover. We ranged about forty miles ahead; you can get back quicker than get ahead. I was about to make a 180-degree turn with the group and fly a racetrack pattern bringing us just ahead of the bombers to repeat the sweep. I may even have called and started the turn.

"I think it was Bud Anderson who called, 'Bogies at two o'clock level.' It was the usual approach, like a swarm of bees with one leader. The main thrust was comprised equally of 109s and 190s and a lesser number of 110s and 410s. Their leader had a tough decision—continue course head-on to the bombers or to engage the P-51s. He also said, 'Let's fight.' I picked out a gaggle of seven or eight 109s with my flight of four, taking on what looked like the lead 109. Meanwhile, their top cover of thirty or so 109s started down but the 363rd had good position on them. We were credited with twenty-one against one loss, my wingman Richard Smith."

The performance near Leipzig brought an encomium from Gen. William Kepner, VIII, Fighter Command chief, which read, "I wish to commend all groups and particularly the 357th and 361st for the most outstanding escort job ever performed on June 29, 1944. No bombers were lost to enemy aircraft. In providing protection you destroyed forty-eight Huns and damaged others. You made the enemy pay dearly for his attempt to intercept our bombers. We strive for perfection and on yesterday's mission you made the closest approach to it under difficult conditions ever recorded. I am proud to be the 'the old man' of you who carry the fight to the Hun wherever you find him." Hayes's outfit also was awarded a Distinguished Unit Citation. But he remarks, "I celebrated less than anyone because the only loss was my wingman."

Despite some losses, the Allied fighters continued to increase their dominance over their opposite numbers in the Luftwaffe. The Germans started the war with aircraft superior to that of the Allies, but first the Spitfire, then the P-38, P-47 and P-51 with all of their innovations equaled if not surpassed the Messerschmitts and Focke Wulfs, although these also improved over the course of the war. The Germans stepped out front toward the summer of 1944 with the earliest versions of jet fighters. Dave Nagel on his fifth mission, July 18, to Peenemünde, the home of the buzz bombs, saw this latest weapon engage the P-51s and P-47s. Wil Richardson gaped at a pair of ME-262s while over France. "They came from the front, attacking the group ahead of us, knocking down two. They came by our group on the left and passed by us a little low, and very fast. We had been briefed on the propellerless aircraft, but it was astonishing. I fired at them but I'm sure I missed. The turret was a little slow."

Herb Shanker remarks, "We were briefed that the ME-262 was around. That scared hell out of me. One of our missions was to bomb an advanced training school for jet pilots at Halle. That was fine with me, as maybe we could do a little preventive work."

The ME-262 shocked and even frightened many Allied airmen. Some historians insist that the German jet might have turned the tides of the war if it had appeared in sufficient numbers. Development of the first jet fighters was detoured by Hitler's desire for modifications that would transform the airplane into a swift bomber that could exact revenge upon the forces battering his kingdom. The ill-advised effort in this direction not only produced a worthless version but held up the manufacture of the ultimate and highly dangerous ME-262. However, as the war headed into its third summer for the Americans, the problem for the Luftwaffe was not a shortage of competitive aircraft. Even without the ME-262, the German air force could mount the latest versions of the 109 and 190 in sufficient quantities [the Luftwaffe counted as many planes in its inventory as from the previous years] to have battled the Allies, except that the severe attrition that began with Big Week had robbed it of proficient pilots and created a scarcity of oil and its products. No matter how many jets rolled off the assembly lines in the summer of 1944 there were nowhere near enough adequate individuals to fill the cockpits nor fuel to fire up the rockets.

The growing successes notwithstanding, summertime hardly eased the discomfort of the Eighth Air Force crews. Life at 25,000 feet for seven to ten hours in an unpressurized, unheated bomber transformed simple bodily functions into painful moments. Bob Andrews complains, "Now, movies romanticizing the B-17 combat role tug at my heart. However, they never show the blisters you get on your joints and fingers from the heated suit and gloves. They cannot possibly depict the discomfort of a snot-filled oxygen mask or the feeling of futility you have when trying to use a frozen relief tube."

Hal Turrell notes, "On one mission we had been delayed for hours on the takeoff. I had made the mistake of drinking quite a bit of coffee. As I was always busy I postponed doing anything about it. A B-24 does not have the niceties of a 747. So about the time of the bomb run, when I had little to do except observe, I decided to relieve myself. For this reason we had a little rubber funnel attached to a hose that led outside the ship. At forty below zero with long underwear, wool pants, heated suit, fleece-lined suit, parachute harness and flak suit, getting it out or even finding it was a struggle. As I was blissfully emptying my bladder, an 88 mm shell jolted the ship. This caused me to touch the lip of the funnel that was also forty degrees below zero and my member stuck fast! What to do? If I left it out, it would freeze and need amputation. I wrenched it free and stuck it inside my suit where it could bleed freely and did. When we landed I made my way quietly with the wounded to the hospital. There, instead of sympathy, I got many bad jokes. After I was sewn up I asked the flight surgeon if I qualified for a Purple Heart. He said no, this was a self-inflicted wound."

A ball gunner in the 303rd Bomb Group reports a similar disaster after he tried to provide himself with a relief system using a metal can inside the ball, where ordinarily no facility existed. The system for disposing of waste posed a problem for many ball gunners. Not only did they have to come out of their position but the emptied urine frequently splattered against the outside of the turret, covering it with a yellow ice. "If anyone used the relief tube for the crew in the bomb bay," says ball gunner Wil Richardson, "my turret would get neatly iced up and I couldn't see. I kept the plane supplied with bomb-fuze cans to be used and tossed out over the target, frozen, of course. For myself, I went to the boneyard, and cut a relief tube with about three feet of hose. When I needed it, I pushed the tube out of the clip chute [that discarded empty cartridges] with the guns straight down. Much later, a tube was installed at the factory. At the same time, they put them in the waist and tail positions."

Some crewmen brought an empty pail along for unexpected demands made by their bowels or in an emergency used a flak helmet. There are numerous anecdotes that describe the consequences of a sudden maneuver by the airplane or an unexpected enemy assault. The bulky garments and equipment in the heat of combat or in those cases where diarrhea struck, forced some to soil themselves.

"The top turret was unique," says Herb Shanker, "in that your head was exposed to the sun and was hot while the rest of your body was freezing. On rare days, we might fly under an overcast which meant that your entire body was frozen. On a mission to Cologne, the thermometer hit the bottom, which was fifty-five below and I assume it was between sixty and seventy below. I never wore the so-called heated shoes and it took my feet six hours to thaw out with commensurate pain all the while."

Waist-gunner J. C. Wilson in the 351st Bomb Group, like many crewmen, devised his own methods to preserve body heat. "There were two types of electric suits, the English and the American. The English model, called the millie watt glow, was a quilted type with resistance wire in the body of it, down the back of the silk gloves and across the top of the feet. The gloves and the boots were plugged into the suit proper. The American model, made of blue wool felt was wired the same. Mine was the English version. I found that if I wore the right boot on my left foot and vice versa, my feet would stay warmer. The flak suit consisted of four aprons of two-inch platelets, overlapping like fish scales. Two of the aprons were for the front and two for the back. The flak jacket fastened at the shoulder with four snaps and had an emergency release where, if needed, you could pull a strap and they'd fall off. The top half of the apron would cover the chest and the bottom the thighs and crotch. They weighed between fifteen and twenty pounds. They were not bulletproof but would stop low-velocity projectiles such as flak shrapnel or pistol bullets. They'd been known to help men survive 20 mm shell hits.

"I found that while flying at altitude, my wearing of the flak suit held the electric suit closer to my body and made it even warmer, to say nothing of feeling safer from harm. They issued the regular steel helmets, but everyone took them, hit them on the cement sidewalk to make a flat spot on the top so it would sit on the table, and used it as a wash basin. They took the regular helmet [designed for airmen] and cut the ear protection out, then fastened with a hinge a large saucer-shaped ear piece over the ears. This fitted over the leather flying helmet with earphones without causing any discomfort."

Typically, while welcomed, replacements endured a mild form of hazing from their predecessors. Ira O'Kennon, a student at Virginia Polytechnic Institute until drafted in 1943, recalls, "Before our first mission we were not only briefed on what to expect but were well indoctrinated by seasoned crews in our barracks who tried to scare our pants off and nearly succeeded. As we entered, one jumped from the top bunk, arm stretched out as a wing and imitated a stricken bomber. Others 'limped' towards us, some with makeshift arm slings, head bandages, etc. We swallowed the whole routine and later practiced it on others."

O'Kennon, a June arrival with the 385th in the capacity of radio operator, says that although he enrolled in an ROTC program at VPI, "I was neither aggressive nor ambitious. I did not comprehend the consequences of war nor did I have any particular vision of anything—pay, career or comfort. In those days our primary motivator was patriotism. I was simply a country boy from a family made poor by the Depression. FDR was our idol and America our heaven. I had a wonderful boyhood in a poor family on a fifty-acre farm which offered everything a boy could desire: animals, vegetables, copious fruits from multiple orchards, playmates, church and mostly family."

Unlike so many others he seems to have come to the Air Corps by someone else's choice. "I was drafted, reported to Fort Lee, Virginia, where we were tested and screened. My IQ and ROTC may have been influential in my assignment to the Air Corps. We had thorough training, flying numerous practice missions, not to mention radio school and gunnery school that preceded it. Our crew flew over alone and remained as a replacement crew, reduced to nine men when they eliminated the right waist gunner. The radio gun was removed so I fired his gun." In August, O'Kennon's crew saw its first action, a hit upon Saarbrucken.

It had been macabre fun and games when the old timers greeted them but O'Kennon and his colleagues quickly grasped the precarious hold on life by Eighth Air Force airmen. "Other crews were associates; we rarely made lasting friends except our crew. It was not usual to lose someone from your barracks but you didn't dwell on it. On one occasion, the man who slept in the next bunk was flying left waist in the plane on our right wing. His plane was hit by flak and exploded, tossing him out of the window without a chute, arms and legs outstretched. Flying right waist in our plane, it is an image I'll never forget. That night, his locker was raided by others in the barracks. His bed remained empty until the replacement arrived."

16

CADILLAC, COBRA AND
TACTICAL STRIKES

In the six weeks after D-Day, the Allied armies, in a war of the hedge-rows, supported by the Air Corps, slowly enlarged their hold upon Normandy against stiffening German resistance. But by mid-July, the advance hit a stone wall. To the east in the vicinity of Caen, the British bucked up against German Panzers, the bulk of armor available to defend against the armies that had waded ashore on June 6. Field Marshal Sir Bernard Montgomery who had plotted the capture of Caen on D-Day called in the RAF. An armada of 450 Wellingtons crossed the Channel shortly before midnight on the evening of July 7 and laid a carpet of bombs 4,000 yards wide and 1,500 deep in front of Montgomery's forces. At dawn, tankers, infantrymen, engineers and other ground troops slugged their way into the shattered ancient university town. It fell almost five weeks behind schedule and now it was up to the Americans to push ahead to maintain the line.

For the twelve divisions of the U.S. First Army, bogged down in front of the town of St.-Lô, Gen. Omar Bradley scripted a plan named Cobra. The strategy envisioned an opening gambit of intensive bombing across a patch of ground three and a half miles wide and one and a half miles deep, starting with a road that ran from Periers to St.-Lô. In his memoirs, Bradley wrote, "Indeed, it was this thought of saturation bombing that attracted me to the Periers road. Easily recognizable from the air, the road described a long straight line that would separate our position from that of the German. *The bombers, I reasoned, could fly parallel to it without danger of mistaking our front line.*" (Italics Bradley.)

Until drafted for a role in Overlord, the invasion and conquest of

Normandy, the Eighth Air Force had pursued its own objectives, the strategic goals designed to knock the enemy out of the war by demolishing the inventory, production and distribution of the tools of combat. The preparations for D-Day and the missions flown on June 6 had been the first tentative attempts of the Air Corps and the American ground forces to focus on the same objective: the German forces in the field. Even here, the airmen were not engaged in direct support of ground forces but in a more general collaboration. For the bombers particularly, the responsibility to play a tactical role in a specific campaign like Cobra was something new. Unlike the Navy, the Air Corps had neither trained nor practiced for this sort of function.

Cobra was born July 10, but not put into effect until two weeks later when Bradley and his subordinates had maneuvered into position the units expected to reap the advantages of the massive carpet bombing of the enemy. Meanwhile, the U.S. sought to exploit the presence of the underground resistance fighters who increasingly engaged in overt confrontations with the enemy as well as sabotage and intelligence gathering operations. Operation Cadillac appropriately furnished the Maquis with tons of guns and ammunition on July 14, Bastille Day, an annual national fête for the French.

Dick Bowman, ball-turret gunner on *Bachelors' Lair,* recalls, "They loaded little canisters, fourteen to sixteen inches long, each with a little Sten gun, its handle folded in, and a couple of clips of ammo. We had hundreds of these canisters laid out on a piece of plywood in the bomb bay. It turned out to be a very long mission because we flew without radio contact between some bonfires on different headings. We flew at night with the drop time just at dawn. When we dropped the canisters, one of the waist gunners, the radio man and the engineer lifted up the piece of plywood to dump them out. Each one had a little red, white or blue parachute."

Ellis B. Scripture, who served as lead navigator for the 95th Bomb Group and later guided the entire Third Air Division, recalled an ad lib to the carefully packed canisters. "As they were being packed, the American airmen wanted to show their admiration for the French resistance fighters. We scattered packages of cigarettes into the canisters and later that night when the coded acknowledgment came over the radio to notify us the arms and supplies had been received safely, the message read, 'Daylight drop successful. Cigarettes also received. Many thanks.'"

Early on the morning of July 24, Cobra started in earnest. The most forward of the Nazi troops noticed that the Americans, for no obvious reason, had withdrawn from the field to positions behind the line of the

Periers highway. Shortly thereafter, the German infantry heard aircraft, overhead hidden by a thick ground haze.

The poor visibility—the operation had already been postponed three days because of overcast—prevented almost two-thirds of the 903 planes dispatched from ever reaching the target. Some held their ordnance because they could not see the target and the others obeyed a recall. Nevertheless, 343 B-17s and B-24s struck the zone outlined by Bradley. The bombs fell mostly in a no-man's land between the opposing armies although by error some exploded in the area occupied by U.S. troops, killing twenty-five soldiers and wounding more than sixty.

On July 25, with the skies clear, the Eighth Air Force, preceded by fighter groups of the Ninth Air Force carrying high explosives, fragmentation bombs and napalm, struck with the full fury of more than 1,500 heavyweights. When they departed the field, Ninth Air Force medium bombers and fighters rained down tons more of ordnance. For the German soldiers it was an awesome demonstration of what bombers could achieve in a tactical situation. Lt. Gen. Fritz Bayerlein, commander of the crack Panzer Lehr Division reportedly said, " . . . back and forth the carpets were laid, artillery positions were wiped out, tanks overturned and buried, infantry positions flattened and all roads and tracks destroyed. By midday the entire area resembled a moon landscape, with the bomb craters touching rim to rim . . . All signal communications had been cut and no command was possible. The shock effect on the troops was indescribable. Several of my men went mad and rushed round in the open until they were cut down by splinters. Simultaneously with the storm from the air, innumerable guns of the American artillery poured drumfire into our field positions." Bayerlein remarked that 70 percent of his soldiers were "either dead, wounded, crazed or dazed."

The ferocity of the saturation bombing literally blew open the gateway to the American advance and the ground troops poured through the shattered German lines for what would become known as the St.-Lô breakout. The U.S. Third Army under Lt. Gen. George S. Patton Jr. seized the advantage to streak south to the Loire River where he hooked a left to plunge deep into France.

Heath Carriker, a young man raised on a North Carolina farm and drafted at age twenty-two before Pearl Harbor, did his peacetime service as a member of an armored unit at Fort Knox, Kentucky. "I felt pleased and happy about being part of what I considered a necessary activity, meeting new people, learning new things, a welcome change from my life to that time. Until then I had never had any contact with Jews, Italians,

Polish or Yankees. Although I took a lot of teasing about my accent and 'southernness,' I ate up this expansion of my world."

Carriker had nourished a dream to fly and when the Air Corps announced it would now accept applicants without a college degree if they passed an equivalency test he approached his commanding officer. Not only did the officer encourage Carriker, he assigned two men to coach him in math, English grammar and other academic areas. The tutors and Carriker were relieved of some duties to allow sufficient time for his studies and the captain even sat in on some sessions.

Thus armed, Carriker got through the examinations and entered the training program for pilots. Having successfully soloed, he became somewhat overconfident and on a routine trip landed too hard and too fast, smashing up an airplane and a shoulder bone. A "wash-out" board convened for the formality of dismissing cadet Carriker. "The colonel asked if I had anything to say. Thinking this was the end anyway, I put all my eggs in one statement, 'I realize that crashing an airplane usually washes out a cadet but I believe that if I am washed out, the Army will lose a good pilot; I know I can do the job.'" The board relented and Carriker struggled through ground school and earned his wings and commission. When given a choice he opted for bombers and flew a B-25 first, then a B-17 and finally B-24s.

He started to train with a complete crew and they underwent special instruction in a radar-equipped craft. After four months the crew was ordered to pick up a new airplane and fly it to England. Named the *Liberty Belle*, it had a huge bell painted on its nose but like its namesake in Philadelphia, it had a flaw. "It was difficult to trim," says Carriker. "The left wing tended to be heavy. At Newfoundland, the engineers were not able to find any 'problem.' The next morning we headed toward Ireland with extra equipment, extra men and a full load of fuel. Before we reached the point of no return, we had used more than half our fuel and had to turn back. The next day, with better tail winds we made landfall in Ireland. There the *Liberty Belle* was taken from us. My crew was disbanded and sent to various groups.

"I was assigned to the 466th Bomb Group stationed at Attlebridge Air Base. The first plane I saw after arriving at the base was the beautiful and hard to trim *Liberty Belle* that I felt close to, despite its serious flaw. About a week later, a lead crew of eleven men took her off for her maiden flight, got 100 or more feet in the air, went into the ground and the crash killed all eleven men aboard. I turned so sick after the crash that I just doubled over and vomited and vomited and cried. Today, fifty-two years later, I still feel guilty that my complaints to the engineers were not specific enough or not clear enough to cause a major testing program to find the difficulty."

As a newcomer about to enter battle, Carriker had to cope, not just with the fear of death or injury but that of the terrifying unknown. "Of course I was afraid, a gut-wrenching and never-ending fear accompanied me even when walking around base, or on a trip to London or Cambridge. We simply had to face and deal with these feelings or else fail our responsibilities and give up. After serious discussions with crew members over a period of years, I believe the fear of letting down the crew and failing to measure up to my responsibilities to crew and country were more important than fear of death or dismemberment." To help him through his anxieties, Carriker relied on religion, prayer. "I used the Catholic priest although I am Protestant. The local pub, trips to London and Cambridge also helped."

His initial testing came with Cobra. "According to my best memory, the Army [ground troops] would outline an area four miles by one mile astride the German front lines, by firing different colored smoke shells one mile apart showing the beginning of the bomb drop. An all-out effort by the Eighth Air Force heavy bombers and medium bombers [from the Ninth Air Force] would bomb in squadron formations beginning at the smoke line and ending one mile deep. Two hundred fifty pound antipersonnel bombs were used so that great craters would not result in hindrance to Army equipment [e.g., armor] and secondly to kill and demoralize enemy troops. It was reported to us that the bomber stream was to be about eighty miles long.

"The next morning at the group meeting for briefing for another mission, the map showed the American armor and troops many miles past the starting point. The breakthrough was successful. This was a very satisfying and proud moment for me and the beginning of a feeling of power and eagerness for more of the same. Later, we were told that our bombs had killed American soldiers, including General [Lesley] McNair; very sad and a dampener of our spirits."

Successful as it had appeared, the first close-in support by the big bombers to the ground troops was, as Carriker recalls, a disaster for some U.S. units, specifically the 9th and 30th Divisions. Several hundred men were killed or wounded and among the dead was Lt. Gen. Lesley McNair, chief of the U.S. Army Ground Forces and the most senior man with the forces astride St.-Lô.

The painful friendly fire results at St.-Lô are traceable to blunders,

ignorance and perhaps bad luck. The blueprints drafted by Omar Bradley, as he indicates, specifically directed that the attack pathway follow
a horizontal route centered on the Periers road. Disturbed when he
learned of the slaughter of Americans on July 24, Bradley had demanded
an explanation. To his outrage, he was informed that instead of following the generally east-west line of the battlefield, the raiders flew north
to south, perpendicular to the front.

The American First Army commander had contacted Air Chief Marshal Sir Trafford Leigh-Mallory, head of the Allied Expeditionary Air
Force for further explication. In Bradley's account, Leigh-Mallory said,
"I've checked this thing with the Eighth [Air Force] and they tell me the
course they flew today was not accidental. They were planning to make
it a perpendicular approach over the heads of your troops."

"But why," Bradley asked, "when they specifically promised us they
would fly parallel to the Periers road? That road was one of the reasons
we picked this spot for the breakout." Leigh-Mallory had responded that
it would require two and one half hours to funnel 1,500 heavy bombers
down a narrow path like the road, to say nothing of the time demanded
if one included the hundreds of fighters and medium bombers. And if
Bradley insisted on his approach, the mission for the 25th would need
to be scrubbed in order to brief crews of the Eighth that perpendicular
was now out and horizontal in. Bradley says he was "shocked and
angered" by the answers for they seemed a breach of good faith on the
agreed-upon plan. Against his better judgment, he consented to the
north-south vector rather than postpone Cobra further.

With the bomber stream operating along a perpendicular axis, the
1,500 planes now indeed could dump within a far shorter period of time
than if they had had to come in almost single file to the designated zone.
Bradley reasoned that the road provided a clear marker to guide the bombardiers from dropping on the friendlies but somehow, no one had ever
pointed out to him that such a path would weaken the effect of the bombs
since it would lessen the concentration over a period of time. On the other
hand, given the vagaries of the European weather, dependence upon a
landmark seen from 12,000 to 18,000 feet up—altitudes described by
some participants as their positions—would also seem rather chancy. Nor
does anyone seem to have considered what the wind might do to the colored smoke shells, particularly over a period of time, as squadron after
squadron from the eighty-mile-long bomber stream queued up for its shot.

At the time, as Carriker notes, those in the airplanes knew nothing of
the carnage inflicted upon the enemy and the GIs below. Only later would

they be apprised of the shortcomings of their efforts. Post mortems suggest other factors that contributed to the mishap. Irwin Stovroff, with the 44th Bomb Group recalls, "We did drop some bombs on the Allies' position when the lead plane dropped smoke and it drifted back. We came in behind the lead group and followed to the smoke to let our bombs go."

Herb Shanker, the engineer/top turret gunner with the 303rd Bomb Group agreed that the decision to fly perpendicular to the front line enhanced the opportunity for error. He also reports, "We carried cluster bombs which opened and released twenty-pound bombs after leaving the plane. The prop wash from the planes scattered those twenty-pounders all over the place. We also had three hit our wings."

Other airmen who were present spoke of the effect of the wind on the smoke bombs and that the dust and smoke generated by the first bombs obscured visibility, which further increased the margin for mistakes. Still, most participants like navigator Jim Hill of the 305th Bomb Group who went on strategic raids on oil centers, aircraft plants and the rocket sites, draw great satisfaction from this tactical effort. "The carpet bombing near St.-Lô was the most effective mission of all because it made the breakthrough possible."

For one crew, a mechanical mishap created a near catastrophic situation. The navigator of a B-24 for the 392nd Bomb Group at St.-Lô, Manny Abrams from the Boston suburb of Brookline, Massachusetts, had been midway through his sophomore year at Harvard when he entered the service as a nineteen-year-old in 1943. "My father was a rabbi of a Reform temple and all through the thirties and into the forties, our home had often been visited by German refugees seeking help in establishing themselves in the Boston area. Realizing how their lives were being uprooted and altered, and hearing their stories, I couldn't help feeling antipathy (a mild word) towards the Germans."

Abrams signed up to become a meteorological officer. Told the program was filled, he had accepted an offer of flying cadet school. "After taking the Air Corps test," says Abrams, "I was found qualified for all three flight officer positions—pilot, navigator or bombardier. I chose navigation but that was filled so I said OK to pilot training. After breaking a spar on the left wing of the Stearman on which I had just soloed, everyone agreed that maybe navigation school would be a good solution for us all."

Assigned to a replacement crew, Abrams and his colleagues were en route to New Hampshire, first leg of the trip to the United Kingdom when he was informed by the pilot that the Allies had begun landing operations in Normandy. About six weeks later, Abrams himself was high over the Continent on his first mission. "I expected flak and enemy fighters over France all the way in and out. I got three flak jackets—one to wear, the others to stand on! We did have flak, but not fighters."

On July 24, the 392nd took off as part of Cobra. "I remember," says Abrams, "that we did reach the peninsula but we were recalled due to a solid undercast [blotting out the earth below the aircraft]. Although we frequently bombed through such a cloud cover, the possibility of any bombing error in close proximity to the Allied line prohibited such a gamble. All planes [from his group] returned to bases without accomplishing the mission. It would have to wait until another day."

The next morning the enormous fleet of U.S. planes roared off towards St.-Lô. "The target," explains Abrams, "was a few square miles of Norman hedgerow country. The boundary was marked by white sheets laid out in a line [other accounts speak of orange panels and smoke pots]. South [was] the target; north the Allies. The German troops were dug in just to the south. Whereas our normal bombing altitude for a mission was 20,000 to 26,000 feet, this one was set for 10,000 feet. The day was sparkling sunshine, not a cloud in the sky.

"A bomb group in combat usually had four squadrons. Each put as many as twelve planes in the air. One plane in each squadron flew in a lead position, with the other eleven assigned to a particular slot aside or below it. Defensive firepower was the first gain through flying in a tight formation.

"The other key objective was to release a compact pattern of bombs. Each bomb group functioned as an entity. The group lead plane did the actual target aiming. When the lead plane released its bombs, that act simultaneously sent out a radio signal to the other forty-seven or so group bombers, triggering the release of all the bomb loads [via the intervalometer]. Therefore the tightness of the formation, coupled with the attitude of each plane at the moment of release determined the compactness of the bomb run.

"St.-Lô was our sixth mission. We had not yet been made into a lead crew. We were flying in the mass of 392nd Bomb Group planes, all with the bomb bay doors open. The mission had turned into a true milk run—no flak or enemy fighters, not much danger. It was a lazy, lovely summer day, two miles up over Normandy.

"Soon after our group crossed over the white line, all planes released their bomb loads by signal. Well, correction—all planes but one. Ours. For reasons unknown, our bombs remained neatly hung up on their individual racks in our bomb bay. Some malfunction had occurred in our release mechanism.

"When bombs fail to eject, only a few paths of action are left. In this case, the bombs would have their safety wires replaced. This prevents them from exploding if there were a subsequent accidental release. Landing with armed bombs was against the Code of Continued Living. The radio bomb release mechanism was alongside the navigator's table in the nose of the plane and when the group dropped their bombs over the target zone, I tried jiggling and joggling for several seconds to get a release, but to no avail.

"The bomb bay doors were now closed. The bombs had been rewired for safety. The bombardier left the nose and I was still puzzled by the failure. Our bomber stream had now taken up a heading back to our air base. We were just crossing the coast of Normandy. Below was still a heavy scene of Allied landing craft, destroyers, support vessels, etc.

"I had been playing with the bomb-release mechanism for some moments trying to determine what had been the problem. [Suddenly] the release system complied with its role and produced that hapless and now least desired of all actions! There was a sudden lifting of the plane as the full bomb tonnage salvoed—taking the bomb bay doors with them [the doors were designed so that if by accident the ordnance was loosed with them closed, they broke away]. I recall a sudden exclamation from the pilot on the intercom—no worse than 'What the hell?' Needless to say, I was shocked and appalled by this sudden event, and not about to stand up to be counted. No one accused me of causing this badly timed salvo. I found, to my amazement, that I could portray innocence quite convincingly.

"Between the uplift of the plane and my other reactions, I knew what had happened and pressed my face into the concave plexiglass window on the right side near my desk. I could just see the dark clump of falling bombs, and was relieved to see them plunge into the Channel, *very close* to a medium-sized ship. There may have been some surprised Allied sailors who might have trouble believing in the pinpoint bombing technique of the Eighth Air Force. But I am quite certain no damage was done but to the aluminum bomb bay doors."

While Abrams and those whom he later took into his confidence could find some comfort in their own serio-comic moment, not even the phenomenon of the Third Army's spectacular burst through the enemy positions persuaded the top generals to plot more closely coordinated ventures with the Air Corps. According to Bradley, Eisenhower confided to an aide he would no longer countenance use of heavy bombers in tactical situations. "I don't believe they can be used in support of ground forces. That's a job for artillery. I gave them a green light this time. But I promise you it's the last." And it would be until the ground forces needed them again.

The bombers carrying out the mandates of Cobra encountered no enemy aircraft, further evidence of the decline of the Luftwaffe. The onslaught of the extended range, constantly increasing flocks of the latest U.S. fighters destroyed not only German pilots and planes but also shot down morale. One Luftwaffe squadron commander wrote in his diary, "Every day seems an eternity. There is nothing now—only our operations, which are hell, and then more waiting—that nerve-wracking waiting for the blow which inevitably must fall, sooner or later. Every time I close the canopy before taking off, I feel that I am closing the lid of my own coffin."

Even before Cobra, with dogfight foes scarcer, the American fighter pilots, perhaps spurred by competition to boost scores, intensified their strafing attacks upon German airfields. They rampaged over parked would-be interceptors and in their zeal some cut the margin of safety below the utmost. On July 20, Francis Gabreski of the 56th Fighter Group led all Americans with twenty-eight kills. Joel Popplewell remembers, "Colonel Gabreski saw on the bulletin board in the briefing hut a mission he decided he'd like to take. He was our squadron commander but his clothes were already packed for a trip back to the States on R & R. He thought it was going to be a pretty hot mission [to Koblenz]. We didn't contact any planes in the air but we saw some on the ground, about seven sitting at this grass airfield. I was in the first flight of four to go down and strafe. We were hitting but nothing was lighting up. In disgust, Gabreski said, 'My flight's going down.' He strafed and barely got the fabric on one to burn. The other three didn't get anything so he said, 'I'm going down again.'

"This time he went down, I thought I saw bullets hitting the ground but it wasn't that. It was his propeller." With the prop blades bent, the P-47 lacked enough power to lift and Popplewell believes he belly-landed on a railroad track but others report Gabreski plowed a deep furrow in a meadow. In any event, Gabreski scrambled out of the cockpit and dashed into a nearby woods. A fellow pilot then shot up the airplane. "This was a new bubble canopy P-47, one of the first of its kind," says Popplewell. "We lost two great things, the airplane and our commanding officer. I felt like he might get out of the place. He spoke several languages but he became a POW [after hiding out for several days]."

WITH the supreme commander of the Allied Expeditionary Forces in Europe opposed to further use of the heavyweights for ground support, and because the tide of battle now appeared not to require tactical efforts from the B-17s and B-24s, the Eighth concentrated fully upon its original strategic objectives. A major and dreaded target was the heavily defended synthetic oil complex at Merseburg, well over 300 miles east of the coastline. Bill Ruffin, from a broken family in a tiny Kentucky coal mining town, saw Merseburg from the air on four occasions and of all his destinations came to fear it most.

"Although I had only a high school diploma," says Ruffin, "I was able to pass the test for the cadet program. Like all of my cadet friends, I knew I was destined to become a P-38 pilot. Throughout pilot training, due to my limited education, I was motivated to study extra hard, even to study by flashlight under my blanket after 'lights out.'" He was successful enough to be chosen for an experimental class that sped up the training process, but instead of the P-38, he drew first the B-25 and the rank of flight officer. Subsequently transferred to B-17s, he united with a crew and upon completion of instruction in formation flying, navigation, bombardment and instrument work, he pinned on his gold bars as a lieutenant.

At age twenty-two, Ruffin brought his crew to the Eighth Air Force and the 306th Bomb Group. "We left the U.S.A. with ten crew members but when we arrived at our base, they decided we only needed one waist gunner. My original ball-turret gunner exercised his option to relinquish his rank and accept a position not in combat. He was replaced. My tail gunner studied hard and upgraded himself to flight engineer with another crew and was killed in a midair collision.

"My first mission, July 28, was to Merseburg. As they say, 'the flak was heavy enough to get out and walk on.' I did not realize the danger. I didn't know that these little black clouds that suddenly appeared around our plane were there to destroy me until we returned to base and counted the holes in our plane. I soon learned that if I could see the red center of those little black clouds, I could count on some damage. On very rare occasions, I could hear and feel the explosion of those shells and knew we had suffered some major damage. On one such occasion, three feet of nose section was blown away, wounding our navigator and bombardier. They were dragged up into the pilot compartment where, after being attended to, the navigator had to sit on the hatch to stop the air being forced through. The German 88 was a remarkably accurate antiaircraft weapon, particularly at 25,000 feet where the B-24s were normally assigned, while we in B-17s drew 29,000 to 31,000 feet."

Ruffin, like so many of those who entered the war in its final year, speaks more of flak than he does of the enemy fighters. Although the latter appeared sporadically and in lesser numbers than the former, the casualties among Eighth Air Force crews continued to be substantial as the enemy invested heavily in antiaircraft batteries, both fixed and mobile. The percentage of losses had fallen well below the double digits of Black Thursday to 2 or 3 percent and occasionally less than 1. But with thousand-plane raids now commonplace, hundreds of young men died, disappeared or were maimed each week. The Air Corps hoped to balance its payments in blood with a shutdown of the enemy war power. Indirectly, the savage exchanges aided the Soviets because even before D-Day the mammoth aerial attacks on the Fatherland had forced the Germans to deploy guns, ammunition and troops away from the eastern front.

The sprint through the German lines at St.-Lô by Patton's armor, coupled with the advances achieved by First Army now commanded by Lt. Gen. Courtney Hodges, pinched the already retreating Wehrmacht between the Second British Army and the First Canadian driving from the east pincers. The only route for escape or reinforcement lay in a corridor less than thirteen miles wide between Falaise and Argentan.

Although Eisenhower dismissed the use of the heavy bombers for ground support only a few weeks before, the strategists called upon the big planes to stop German traffic in both directions, trapping the tens of thousands enemy soldiers enveloped in the Falaise Pocket and blocking off any attempt to relieve the pressure on the beleaguered troops. While not quite flying at the same close-in level as at St.-Lô, the mission for the Eighth again had a tactical purpose rather than the long-range strategic one.

Irwin Stovroff, having bombed every major target, from D-Day through Munich, Hanover and Peenemünde, had completed thirty-four missions on August 13 when his 44th Bomb Group was posted for his last operation, a road junction near Rouen, a choke point for enemy movement in either direction. "It was supposed to be a milk run—easy in, easy out," says Stovroff. "Hell, we'd never been out of sight of the English Channel. I'd already packed my footlocker that morning at the base. I was supposed to go to Northern Ireland to be an instructor when I came back."

Stovroff belonged to the crew of the *Passion Pit,* a B-24 given that name in honor of the basement bar at the Santa Rita Hotel in Tucson, where the men training together under pilot Lt. John Milliken relaxed when on pass. They had been given their plane on June 14, a week after they had become operational.

Bombardier Stovroff describes the trip to the Rouen target as "a long, straight bomb run, no evasive action. We never dreamed there would be antiaircraft like that that day. But by the time they hit us, we were at about 18,000 feet. Our No. 1 and 2 engines were on fire. I toggled the bombs through the bomb bay doors so they wouldn't explode. We all saw the flames and it wasn't long before we got the word to bail out. The bomb bay doors were still open so everyone could get out there.

"I put my chest chute on. We didn't wear chutes when flying because we had so damn much clothing and heavy equipment that you couldn't move around if you had a back chute on. We did wear a harness to which we hooked our chest chutes. We had practiced on the ground how to put it on. But I'd never jumped before.

"I had a dear friend of mine who told me he was standing at the bomb bay when they had to bail out. There were four guys standing there and he said to them, 'Come on, come on, jump!' Then he did but they never jumped. There was no hesitation on my part or the others in my plane."

In a Liberator in the squadron behind, John McLane Jr. saw the heavy and accurate flak burst within the formation that included *Passion Pit*. "I was looking directly at it when one of their planes [*Passion Pit*] started to burn. The plane fell out of formation. As I looked directly at it, there was a monstrous explosion and the plane disintegrated before my eyes. The motors were torn from the wings and went tumbling through the sky with their props windmilling as they fell. The wing, fuselage and tail were torn to shreds. As the pieces of aluminum drifted and twisted while they fell, with each turn the sun reflected off their surfaces back to my eyes as if they were mirrors. The most spectacular sight was the tanks which had been torn from the wings. The gasoline did not explode but rather burned in huge orange flames streaming out behind the tanks as they fell in wavy fans to the earth below."

Stovroff remarks that no one anticipated the intensity of antiaircraft in the area. Russell Strong, a navigator with the 306th and historian of the outfit confirms his statement. "The mission of the 13th was ahead of the front lines in the Rouen area. Turning east at Flers, the group came under fire from German army mobile 88 mms which had been elevated to shoot at the planes at 21,000 feet. Six aircraft were severely damaged." In fact, Strong's own ship lost its No. 4 engine and shrapnel in his hip incapacitated the bombardier. Strong immediately assumed his duties and toggled the ordnance. Then he turned his attention to his stricken comrade. "I got him out of his seat and stretched him out on the floor, turned up his heat suit and kept him comfortable for the forty-five-minute ride home from the target to base." The aircraft managed to limp home on two engines.

McClane assumed all of the occupants perished in the fiery detonation of the *Passion Pit* over the Rouen area but in fact, unseen by him, everyone including Stovroff had already exited when *Passion Pit* blew apart. "I landed right in the front lines," says Stovroff. "I hit a fence coming down, got up and got out of my parachute. Germans were coming in all directions. I threw away my dogtags which had an H [for Hebrew as his religion] and I threw away my .45 pistol. I put up my hands and surrendered.

"We were taken to a cemetery and there were holes in it and there were bodies in them, Germans. When you see something like that you might figure this is it. I never did really think that. But coming down I wondered how the hell did this happen, what am I doing here? Am I going to get out of here alive? You always think something good will happen, I had to think that way.

"The German officer in charge came along, and all he had to do was look at us, standing near open graves and he immediately said, 'Nein, nein. We do not kill our prisoners.' We began to feel good for a couple of minutes but we knew we were captured. Within thirty or forty minutes they had us all together; there was just nowhere to go. They took us to a farmyard and we were plenty scared. They kept us near the front for a while. After things quieted down—the American fighter pilots were shooting up anything that moved on the road—they put us in trucks and took us back several miles to a big farmhouse where we stayed for several days.

"I had an opportunity, I thought, to escape. With Bill Manierre, I walked out, casually, quietly, and we were out for about ten or fifteen minutes. Before we knew it, we were surrounded by soldiers and warned don't ever try that again. Then we traveled in trucks to Paris. Somehow, John Milliken had kept a knife hidden. We were sitting in this truck with a canvas cover. I don't know how he did it but he slit the canvas beside us, not at the end of the truck but more toward the front. He rolled back and forth and just rolled right out of the truck and was gone." After the war, Stovroff learned Milliken had lain among cows in fields for days on end until the British broke through, rescued him and he returned to England.

Interrogated briefly in Paris while housed in a former girls' school, Stovroff rode a boxcar to Frankfurt, the main center for questioning downed airmen. He fended off a German intelligence officer, offering only name, rank and serial number. To Stovroff's astonishment, the Luftwaffe specialist announced, "Since you won't tell me about yourself, let me tell you about you." "He told me that my father's name was Max, my mother's Bertha and my brother's Morton and that I had a sister

Irma. He said I had gone to Public School 56 and Lafayette High School in Buffalo and even named a girl whom I had taken out. At this point, he informed me that he too had lived in Buffalo, on Ashland Avenue right around the corner and I had been his newspaper boy. The story we heard was that when he had visited Germany, he had been conscripted."

A second bizarre incident marked Stovroff's stay in Frankfurt. Both he and Manierre were unshaven, wearing rumpled, dirty clothes looking as grimy as veteran infantrymen. "Bill and I were sitting there and he said to me 'Russian'—my nickname—'look over there. There's a guy staring at me and you. Do you know him? Were we in some camp with him? Did we fly with him somewhere?' I looked at the man, a gaunt guy, deep-sunk eyes, thin as a rail and mustache. I said, 'Bill, I don't know the guy. I don't think I've ever seen him before in my life.'

"'But he keeps looking at us,' said Bill. 'Oh my God! That's my brother!' It was unbelievable when the two of them got together and they seemed to recognize one another at the same moment, and began hugging. Cy Manierre had been dropped by parachute and was leading French underground Maquis in underground operations, blowing up trains. He'd been caught and actually could have been shot as a spy. Cy told us they'd line him up with half a dozen Frenchmen, then 'brrrmm' with a machine gun and stop at him for more interrogation. Finally, they gave up on questioning him and for some reason sent him to this center where they worked primarily with the Air Force. When the Germans found out they had two brothers there, they made a big thing of it. Bill's mother had received a telegram in the morning and then one in the afternoon about her two missing sons and she flipped out. Because of the relationship, the Germans sent Cy with us to Stalag Luft I at Barth."

Cy Manierre, a West Point grad, was among a handful of Americans to drop behind the enemy lines for liaison with the French guerrillas. Hopeful that these irregulars could seriously harass the German army the Allies arranged to supply weapons to the Maquis from the air. Ball-turret gunner Wil Richardson in the B-17 *Kismet* with the 94th Bomb Group participated in the first of the massive supply missions for partisans late in June. "This gave me more satisfaction than any trip except maybe D-Day," says Richardson. "Prior to D-Day the drops were by one or two planes at night. This was the first of three massive day-drops. All together we had 176 planes to cover five zones spread out over a very wide area. We flew across all of France to near the Swiss–Italian border at the normal 25,000-foot altitude.

"Near our zone we made a fast descent to about 300 feet which was very unusual and dangerous for us. We were in a mountainous area and would drop the canisters in a valley. We passed low over red-roofed French villages and sometimes it seemed the wingtips almost scraped the jagged edges of the mountains as we headed for the Rendezvous Point. We split into threes and from my ball turret I had an excellent view, a grandstand seat in my plexiglass-aluminum globe as we swooped low through the valley. The resistance fighters would dash out quickly to pick up canisters. Sometimes a cart would be used. Then they rushed back to the woods. Some would wave or make a large Vee sign with their arms to show thankfulness.

"I was sure glad that the enemy fighters had shown up early on while we were at altitude. We lost one a/c to the persistent attackers. But our small group battled through and they left before our descent. I dread to think what might have happened had the 'Bandits' caught us in the valley. The 94th and 100th Bomb Groups received the croix de guerre avec palme for this mission."

Martin Garren flew one of the later missions of this sort which took his B-17 to southern France where the Allies had invaded along the Mediterranean coast with airborne troops and conventional landings. "On a plateau were these young FFIs [French Forces of the Interior] kids, teenagers or in their early twenties. They were hopping up and down, waving their hands at us and they had set signal fires in a triangular arrangement which was the code. We dropped medical supplies, food and ammunition. They were some enthusiastic people and we were so proud to have been able to go down there and save them. They were surrounded by Germans. Many, many years later I learned they were completely annihilated shortly after we left."

WALTER Konantz, whose father had run both a music store and an undertaking business in Lamar, Missouri, had owned his own airplane since his high school senior year and entered the Air Corps with 250 hours of flying time. "The Air Corps was the only choice for me. It would have been a catastrophe had I been drafted and ended up in the Navy or the infantry." In spite of his background, he dutifully passed through the standard phases of flight instruction.

"The selection process to determine whether a cadet goes to multiengine or single-engine advanced training is usually determined during Basic Flight School, just after Primary and before Advanced. I made it clear to my Basic instructor that I wanted single-engine advanced and he helped me get there.

Usually, the top 25 percent of the cadets make it to single-engine advanced and the rest go to bombers, transports, etc. Occasionally the needs of the service at the particular time preclude this and if there is a shortage of bomber, transport, etc., pilots, then *all* the Basic cadets would go to multiengine training regardless of their wishes. I was selected for single-engine Advanced School because I made it very clear that I wanted to go there and kept up my academic studies and flying ability well up in the upper 10 percent of the class. Bomber pilots were generally those who were unfit to be fighter pilots either by temperament or lack of ability. I am not belittling them as persons but it was well known that only the best got into fighters. Of course there were some mistakes both ways." A number of Eighth Air Force veterans take exception to Konantz's assertions on who got to fly in what kind of cockpit for which reason.

At a Replacement Training Unit (RTU) in northern England, Konantz practiced formation, tactics and a ground-strafing sortie before he shipped out to the 55th Fighter Group. "They had changed from P-38s to P-51s only a few days before my arrival. At the 55th we had another ten hours of tactics, formation and strafing practice before our first combat mission. At no time during my training did I feel I had not gotten enough instruction. Most of the time I felt I was ready for the next step well before they let me take it."

The log of Konantz's early sorties suggests the still-prominent role for fighters in aid of the campaign through France during August. On the eighth of the month, his first time on the aerial battlefield, he served as one of the chaperones for B-17s hammering the Romilly-sur-Seine airfield south of Paris. He described the affair as "uneventful."

On August 12, he participated in a pair of ground-strafing and dive-bombing ventures. Of the first he noted at the time: "Southern France. Destroyed one locomotive and damaged several boxcars—lost two pilots due to flak. Time logged: 3:15." He wrote of the second mission in the Verdun-Nancy area: "Destroyed fifteen ammunition rail cars and a city water tower. Aircraft badly damaged by flying debris from exploding ammo cars but made it back to base. Dented the leading edges of the wings and tail as well as knocking off the propeller spinner. Lieutenant Gilmore shot down by flak. Time logged: 3:15." August 13 he reported, "Dive bombing and strafing south of Paris—Hit a railroad station with my two 500-pound bombs and strafed a German staff car. Time logged: 3:00."

Interspersed with the rampages against railroad traffic and installations, Konantz added several more sorties in which he covered for bombers. He watched one flak-struck B-17 explode with its bomb load. "Saw only the four engines falling out of the fireball." Over the Ruhr Valley Konantz observed another B-17 blow up, "men jumping out of it with their chutes on fire."

By the end of the month he was strafing in Germany just over the French border. "Shot up three trains, one of which was a long troop train. Train was moving fast when I raked it from the rear to the front and saw soldiers jumping out the windows while it was still moving thirty to forty miles per hour." It is a measure of the Allied domination of the skies that not until September 11, more than one month after he first flew a mission, did Konantz see his first enemy fighters.

While they poured shot and shell on anything that might be connected with the enemy war effort, the Allies employed their bombers for propaganda leaflet drops. Crews given the assignment were mordantly known as "newsboys" and such duty was often as hazardous as that of those who bore lethal materials.

The Allies never refined their propaganda operations to the level of the Germans who could call not only upon a former resident of Buffalo to gather intelligence but also skilled broadcasters like the redoubtable Lord Haw-Haw and Axis Sally. Some measure of the weakness of the American program is exemplifed by the experience of Harry Serotta. "I spent two days in London under orders to make some broadcasts in German. I had been a German major and high school medal winner in the subject. I hadn't used the language for several years. The interviewer, a beautiful, non-Jewish anti-Nazi, was very patient and helped me with the words I couldn't recall or didn't know. The broadcasts were of my combat experiences, entirely uncensored." How that could have influenced the German people only the creator of the program might know.

17

MILK RUNS AND MARKET GARDEN

They were known as the "Newman Crew" in the fashion of listing the men in a particular aircraft under the name of the ship's first pilot, in this case Lt. Herb Newman. Along with fifteen other sets of replacements they had been inducted into the 398th Bomb Group in July, and like all crews were made up of men from disparate backgrounds. The leader, Herb Newman, in his mid-twenties, who already held a lieutenant's commission in the infantry, transferred to the Air Corps while an officer to qualify as a pilot. He told his associates he "didn't like walking." His original navigator, Bill Frankhouser recalls, "Herb Newman was a dedicated person. He looked out for his crew. He had learned some of that responsibility in the infantry. He was older than the rest of us and we got guidance from him. When there was a disruptive person in the crew, he got rid of him."

Frankhouser, a native of the Pennsylvania-Dutch Country says his sense of world affairs was "essentially nil" even when he turned seventeen and the United States went to war in 1941. "I had no idea that the Japanese attack would affect my life. I had started as a Penn State student in the fall of 1941. I suppose the Air Corps sounded more glamorous than the Army and Navy but I signed up in the Army Air Corps program at Penn State and was told that I could finish my college degree before call-up. That was changed soon to 'we need you now.'"

The Penn State Army Air Corps group left campus as a unit on May 17, 1943, and although Frankhouser's copy of the orders list 240 names, he believes there were even more on the train that carried them to basic training on the boardwalk at Atlantic City where they were housed in a premier hotel. Subsequently they dispersed to various stations, and Frankhouser went through ten hours of instruction in a Piper Cub. He was approved for navigation instruction, his first choice over pilot training. "I did not feel confident that I could make the plane do what it was supposed to do." Although, like many others, Frankhouser frequently suffered from air sickness during flights in the twin-engine training planes, so long as the cadets performed their navigation duties, the instructors passed them. Later Frankhouser was relieved to find that he was free of the ailment while in B-17s.

"I had no gunnery training because they were filling the heavy-bomber crew pipeline, which was fast being depleted. The navigation training with a crew in B-17s [in the U.S.] was rather sketchy and in England was at best minimal. Too many crews were being lost or finished their tour of duty. I never had a precombat furlough. My mother wrote to the Air Corps about that and caused me some embarrassment."

Paul Deininger, the copilot, was seven years older than Frankhouser, having been a seminarian for five years until he says he dropped out because of "the rigid life and grueling curriculum." He enlisted a few days after the bombing of Pearl Harbor, hoping to attend a photographic school in the Air Corps. Obliged to pick another skill he chose airplane mechanics. "I did so well in mechanics school they kept me for instrument specialist instruction. Then I worked on the flight line at Jefferson Barracks, Missouri, where I flew constantly as a crew chief. Having been an enlisted man for almost two years, and since I was flying almost every day I got the idea I would like to become a pilot and make some money."

Accepted for pilot training, Deininger proceeded through the stages that led to a commission and pilot's wings. "The training was excellent and very strict. If for any reason you didn't shape up you washed out. Because of my background as a seminarian, I almost washed out due to the fact they were uncertain how I felt about killing innocent people. In advanced flying school, we were asked what aircraft we'd like to fly. I requested the B-17 but was told I was too short. Then I asked for the B-25 but true to Air Force tactics I was assigned to the B-17. We received 90 percent of our flying skills in the States and I really thought that we were adequately prepared [a viewpoint quite opposite of Frankhouser's]."

Californian Dean Whitaker signed up for the Air Corps in 1943 with two high school buddies, both of whom were killed in combat. Appointed an aviation cadet, Whitaker qualified as a gunner while awaiting an opening in the classes for navigator/bombardier training. Still only an eighteen-year-old, he relished the instruction, simulated bomb runs on the Douglas

Aircraft plant in Long Beach, mock attacks on small towns in the Mojave Desert. "Most fun was the low-level bombing where we would skim over the desert floor, sometimes scaring up a coyote or jack rabbit."

Having graduated in March 1944, Whitaker became a member of the Newman crew at Rapid City, South Dakota. "For four months we trained together in a B-17, flying missions in formation, learning what to do when attacked by enemy planes and stuff like that. Our crew became very close during this time. I will never forget the picnic with the entire crew and some special guests that included Paul Deininger's fiancée, Herb Newman's mother and sister."

The Newman crew sailed to Europe on a captured Italian liner converted to a troop transport. "Being an officer," says Whitaker, "really paid off now because we had good accommodations, a stateroom with just four guys in it, sat at a dining table and had waiters serve us, had freedom of the ship and could go on the top deck and lay in the sun. Our voyage ended at Liverpool where we landed on a typical English day, fog covering everything like a wet blanket.

"On first driving up to our base [Nuthampstead] in the GI truck I was kind of disappointed. There were some permanent buildings but mostly there were tents. My crew was assigned to one of the half-tents, the bottom four feet were wood."

During the brief training period before combat, the Newman crew barely escaped destruction. "We were taking off from the short runway," says Whitaker. "I was at my usual position in the nose, watching out in front and I saw this farmer running his tractor. I thought, 'Man, we are going to scare hell out of him when he sees us coming.' When I saw him jump off his tractor I knew we were in trouble. Sure enough one wheel hit sending us scooting along the ground and into a grove of trees just beyond the runway. Leaves and branches were flying through the nose because the plexiglass had disintegrated upon impact with the first tree. I had no trouble exiting; just crawled out of the nose. I could smell the plane burning and looked around to see the pilot and copilot coming out of the nose also. As soon as the fire reached the .50 caliber ammunition, all hell broke loose, with the bullets going in every direction. Luckily everyone got out, although MacKenzie, the waist gunner, was badly burnt and spent the rest of the war in the hospital."

While other replacement crews in the 398th were involved in Cobra, because of the accident, the entry of the Newman crew into the shooting war was delayed a few days. "Our crew," recalls Frankhouser, "was first assigned to *Witka Tanka Ton* ['The bird that lays big eggs' in the Sioux language]. The plane had been given to the colonel and just before he left the States an Indian chief had come to the base in Rapid City and 'anointed' it. When we were assigned to it, the plane was aged.

"On the sunny morning of August 8, the operations officer came to our tent and said we were to go that day on our first mission, which would be a milk run to Caen to support ground troops. We were collectively relieved because other recent 398th missions had been to targets with massive flak defenses like Munich and Merseburg. Someone even said, 'Well, we won't need flak jackets or helmets today.' Our copilot [Deininger] was assigned to another crew and an experienced copilot named to fly with us.

"As we approached the target area at about 14,000 feet, I saw multitudinous tracers reaching toward us and many small flashes and shell-bursts, all below our formation. I thought they were shooting only small caliber weapons that can't touch us. Suddenly the picture changed. I now noticed larger bursts from shells directly within our squadron formation, and I could smell the acrid smoke from the burning powder of explosives.

"Several things happened in quick succession. I noticed a one- to two-inch-diameter hole as it opened in the aluminum hull close to my right-side gun, and small metallic shavings were propelled inward. This was my first realization that we really were in combat. The Germans were shooting big guns and the plane's hull offered no protection! The copilot yelled when a piece of flak struck and lodged in his flying boot. I suddenly was blinded, unable to see through my goggles. I wiped my hand over the goggles and saw a red smear. My God, I thought, blood! Realizing that I was still able to move, I looked around and determined that the hydraulic lines on the bulkhead below the pilot's compartment had been severed and red fluid was spewing all over the plane. Next I heard the pilots discussing how to feather No. 3 engine which had been disabled by flak. Meanwhile our bombardier [Whitaker] had opened the bomb bay doors and I was watching the lead ship for the bomb drop. That ship suddenly heeled-over as the bombs came out, and it disappeared from the formation. As the bombs exited our plane, it lurched upward—my first experience of the comforting leap in the flight path.

"Then I learned that we were not able to stay with the group for the return journey because of the feathered engine. I now would have to find the base at Nuthampstead by myself. Thank heavens for a clear day. Although the weather had benefitted the German flak batteries, it also made pilotage navigation easy for me. I sighed in relief when we saw the large water tower near Nuthampstead. Landing without brakes, because of the loss of hydraulic fluid, was sort of anticlimactic after those other experiences.

"When we cut engines at our hardstand, Gino Franceschini, a navigator friend of mine, who had already flown three or four missions, came strolling over to congratulate us on the first one. He said, 'Well, that was another easy one.' I was too dumbfounded to respond. Then he smiled and said, 'No, that was rough and much worse than my other missions.' After examining the many holes in our fuselage and a shattered windshield, I was comforted somewhat to learn that this mission indeed had been a rough one. The 398th lost three planes that day, including the lead with our squadron commander."

"For a first mission," recalls Dean Whitaker, "it made quite an impression being able to see the flash of guns firing at us. One of the worst sights that fliers can witness is an airplane flying next to them explode after being hit by gunfire. Our crew experienced that on this first mission. I got a face full of plexiglass and hydraulic fluid when the nose was shot out."

PATTON'S Third Army, upon its breakout through the battered and befuddled enemy around St.-Lô after the Eighth Air Force bombing, raced through the French heartland at such a breathtaking pace that it far outdistanced its supply lines. A shortage of gasoline threatened to halt the advance of the tanks and other armored vehicles. In a desperate and innovative gambit, the Air Corps transformed B-24s into flying tank cars. Assigned to haul the gasoline was the Ninety-sixth Bomb Wing, whose three outfits included the 466th Bomb Group, pilot Heath Carriker's outfit.

Barkev Hovsepian, son of a machinist at Colt Firearms in Hartford, Connecticut, volunteered as an aviation cadet because, "I wanted to be a pilot and emulate my heroes, [Eddie] Rickenbacker, [Frank] Luke [World War I heroes], Lindbergh, Turner, Eaker, Doolittle and Clarence Chamberlain. I flew once with Chamberlain for a few minutes over Boston Airport and Boston Harbor. It took all my savings and extra money from Mom, which she couldn't afford."

In spite of his overweening desire, Hovsepian washed out of flight school. "Night landings were my downfall. A temperature inversion misled me with the smoke from oil pots outlining the landing strip. I found it difficult to land. I was a 'Wash out for insufficient progress.' I was bitterly disappointed."

Although examination qualified Hovsepian for instruction as a navigator or bombardier, his facility in communications ticketed him as a radio operator. Put together in a replacement crew, Hovsepian spent a month at Langley Field, Virginia. "We were selected to learn H2X, the radar navigation system for a lead crew and given a new airplane. We flew it to England, getting there right after D-Day and they took the ship away from us because it had to be modified—the altimeter was obsolete. We flew as deputy leads but we realized that we were going out only once or twice a month and it would take forever for us to complete our tour. We gave up the right to lead and settled down to be a regular crew.

"Morale was not good for the period when we hauled gasoline. A skeleton crew of five was used; the bombardier and four gunners were left at home. Combat crews resented being wasted and the active crews received no recognition or credit for a mission. Maj. John Jacobowitz [Carriker's commander] was in charge of fourteen ships from the 466th and twelve from the 458th. He was one of the first to fly his plane with 218 GI cans [five gallon containers] to Clastres for the tanks. Later, the war-weary rejects were fitted with four 400-gallon fabricated tanks to fit the large bomb bays in order to carry more gas. Additional low-octane fuel was filled into the Tokyo wing tanks which were isolated from the aircraft's 100-octane fuel tanks. Also there were several five-gallon GI cans or wingtip (fighter) tanks strapped down in the forward waist section. That gave us approximately 2,000 gallons per load on each flight.

"We had no special problems with the gas-haul missions. It was very dangerous since we were unarmed with a skeleton crew and landed at the former Luftwaffe fighter bases that were bombed by our Air Forces. Landing on these previously bombed strips was an extreme challenge for our pilots. The heavy load in war-weary rejects was unnerving when you dared not stray from the cleared strips or taxiways. In addition, we had no oxygen for we stayed under 12,000 feet. No smoking was allowed for the fumes were volatile.

"If we arrived late in the afternoon, we did not attempt to fly back after the Army engineers offloaded our gas. We took turns guarding our ship until the following morning. In all this time we hadn't eaten since we left our base the previous day. The ground boys would not feed us. Our group," says Hovsepian, "lost twelve flying personnel and one ground man while acting as tankers. The ground men were volunteers helping with various mechanical needs when we landed on the Continent." When the two-week period as flying tankers ended, total casualties for the Ninety-sixth Bomb Wing were thirty men. But the supply effort enabled the armies of Patton and Montgomery to extend their gains even further.

WALTER Konantz in the cockpit of a P-51 with the 55th Fighter Group had completed sixteen missions by mid-September and neither in his train-busting expeditions nor his bird-dog efforts on behalf of the bombers had he seen a German fighter in the air. On the eleventh of the month during a major attack on the synthetic oil plants, the three squadrons of the 55th approached the rendezvous point with Forts targeting Ruhland. "I had noticed a bunch of tiny specks up ahead but without a closer look had dismissed them as P-51 escorts from another group," says Konantz. "I had drunk a second cup of coffee at the mess hall some three hours before and the urge to get rid of some of it had become painful.

"The P-51 has a relief tube stored in a clip under the seat. It is a plastic cone with a rubber tube running out the bottom of the airplane. In order to use this appliance, it is necessary to undo the seatbelt and shoulder harness as well as the leg straps on the parachute/dinghy combination and scoot well forward on the seat in order for the relief tube to connect with the proper part of your anatomy. I was in this position when I heard a voice over the radio calling, 'ME-109s, here they come!'

"I looked up just in time to see fifty or sixty ME-109s streaming through our formation in a forty-five-degree dive with their guns firing. Fortunately, none had picked me as a target but one crossed right in front of me firing at a Mustang below and to my left. These were the first enemy airplanes I had ever laid eyes on and buck fever and instinct caused me to roll over in a dive after the ME-109. He saw me coming and steepened his dive to the vertical. We were both now headed straight down from 24,000 feet on a wide-open power dive. Both airplanes were very skittish from the extremely high speed and since I was not strapped in, the slightest movement of the stick caused me to leave the seat and hit the canopy above. I was in a neutral-G situation, just floating inside the cockpit.

"We passed through a layer of slight turbulence and I felt like a basketball being dribbled down the court. The ME-109 was having as much trouble as me, his plane was bucking and skidding as both of us were nearing compressibility, the limiting speed at which the plane no longer responds to the controls. At 10,000 feet, I initiated a steady four-G pullout and the ME-109 started to pull out about the same time. But before he had raised his nose more than thirty degrees, his right wing ripped off through the wheel well and he spun into the ground in a matter of seconds. He had no time to get out and was still aboard when the 109 impacted and exploded in a wooded area. Just before I started my pull-out, I glanced at the airspeed indicator and saw the needle on 600 miles per hour, ninety-five per hour over the red-line speed of 505.

"After parking my plane, I had climbed out on the wing ready to jump down when my crew chief said, 'Hey, Lieutenant, better zip up your pants before you go in to debriefing.' One of our pilots counted the fires on the ground after this huge, fifteen-minute dogfight and reported to the debriefing intelligence officer that he had counted thirty fires on the ground. Our squadron had claimed twenty-eight ME-109s versus the loss of two P-51s. My claim for one ME-109 was allowed, even though I had no gun camera film of the victory or even a witness."

A day later, Konantz again accompanied the bomber stream over central Germany. A pair of enemy fighters appeared and the P-51s raced after them. Konantz guessed correctly the evasive maneuvers of the prey and quickly reached a firing position on the Messerschmitt's tail. "I moved up to perhaps 100 yards and with the vibration of my first few rounds fired, my gun sight bulb burned out. I started moving up to point-blank range where I could just use the center of the windshield as a gun sight.

"I was about ready to try another burst from about fifty yards when I saw some tracers come close over my wings from behind. I looked around and saw another Mustang firing right through my position at the ME-109. This guy seemed very determined to get this victory while hoping he would not hit me. His stream of bullets were coming uncomfortably close so I moved out of his line of fire to the right and was flying formation with the 109, about fifty feet off his right wing. I could see the pilot clearly, looking wildly behind as the bullets of the second Mustang began to pepper him. Then his canopy flew off and he stood up in the cockpit to bail out, but the 280-mile-an-hour slipstream jerked him out of the cockpit and rolled him back down the top of the fuselage until he hit the vertical fin and rudder. He then bounced at least ten feet higher than his plane and fell away.

"I expected that he would have been killed or badly injured so I watched him fall and fall, over 15,000 feet, until I could no longer see his body, then watched the area he was aimed at to see a puff of dust or his chute spilling when he struck the ground. However, at an estimated 600–800 feet above the ground, his chute opened and he survived. I know who was in the other Mustang, but he denied it."

IN mid-September, the Eighth Air Force served Operation Market Garden, an airborne operation in the Netherlands and for the first time since the fiasco (in terms of friendly-fire casualties) at St.-Lô, provided direct support to ground troops. Pilot Bill Lindley of the 95th Bomb Group chauffeured Gen. Matthew Ridgway, the commander of the Americans in what was an Allied enterprise, to a front row seat. Recalled Lindley, "He [Ridgway] asked what we could expect to see from 20,000 feet. I replied, 'Not a hell of a lot.' This got his attention and he asked, 'What height would you recommend?' The only thing that made any sense was to go in with the C-47 Dakotas and the gliders and stay in their immediate area, at their altitude. The heavy flak we could dodge, and with all the planes in the air for the Germans to shoot at, one more wouldn't make that much difference. He bought the whole package."

Lindley guided his B-17 into position, slowing down to accommodate the slower-moving transports and gliders at about 2,000 to 3,000 feet up. The enemy threw up some antiaircraft fire, from machine guns and 20 mm cannons to the standard 88s but concentrated upon the vulnerable C-46s, C-47s and gliders of the Ninth Air Force with their human cargo. A vast array of chutes, the ones containing equipment in various hues for identification of their cargo, floated down and dappled the ground. In close proximity to the Americans, British paratroopers also tumbled from the sky. Orange smoke bombs delineated the front lines. According to Lindley, Ridgway and his aide in the nose compartment manned machine guns to pepper anything that moved beyond the airborne GIs scrambling for their equipment and cover as they touched down.

Unlike the chaotic night operations of the airborne for D-Day and Southern France, the daylight parachute drops and glider landings of Market Garden went off smoothly and accurately for the most part in the vicinity of Eindhoven and Nijmegen, but the reception for the invaders at Arnhem was much more hostile. Dick Bowman, as a ball-turret gunner with the 96th Bomb Group says his B-17 was one of six assigned to strike at an airfield near Arnhem. "Intelligence on probable enemy fighters sometimes was not accurate and what we were told about this mission didn't pan out. We got all sorts of surprises. They had antiaircraft guns on barges and why intelligence didn't know they were there through air reconnaissance puzzles me. But a lot of heavy flak from AA 88s from the ground did a tremendous amount of damage to the C-47s and gliders. We attacked gun emplacements from a couple of thousand feet, dropped fragmentation bombs to try to keep any fighter aircraft from the air while the C-47s with gliders and paratroopers were to come in. We got there before everyone, saw C-47s being shot down. One with a glider still in tow, unable to break loose, was over the water without any possibility of landing on dry ground."

The German defenders massed their troops and applied extreme pressure upon the Allied forces who counted on ground troops from Field Marshal Sir Bernard Montgomery's command to break through and join the besieged paratroopers and glidermen. As the situation for the airborne of Market Garden worsened, the Eighth Air Force pitched in for supply and tactical support. Manny Abrams, as a B-24 navigator, says his mission card for September 18 carries only the designation Holland, but the objective for his 392nd Bomb Group was the town of Eindhoven. "Our mission was to fly 'on the deck,' at treetop level with an altitude of 500 feet or so to be attained only at the time of the drop of supplies to British paratroopers. This would make each of us targets to ground fire for the least amount of time, it was hoped.

"The mission truly required clear weather, and the actual use of a road map of Holland rather than our aeronautical chart. There would be no way for a navigational wind to be computed when you flew that close to the ground. The mission depended upon the lead plane's perfect navigation coupled with the stream of planes visually following.

"We flew on the deck immediately after leaving the British coast and held our altitude fifty feet above the North Sea. We should be below German radar surveillance at this height and have the element of surprise. We actually had to climb a bit to clear the coastal dikes. Just before we did so, we passed Dutch fishing boats a few miles offshore, all hands staring at the stream of bombers. On the land side of the dikes were Dutch cattle and they ran about frantically in all directions as we thundered by. Their exposure to us was a thoroughly new experience; our usual altitude was 20,000 to 32,000 feet [for B-17s]. The cows must have produced a lot of butter that day.

"As we continued on at 200-plus mph, we passed small Dutch villages, each with a church and steeple in the center. I saw German soldiers with submachine guns crouching on the ground, kneeling in the belfries, all firing away at the bomber stream. In turn our tail and waist gunners were returning fire with their .50 calibers. The plane would shudder a bit, either with recoil from our guns, or from the spattering impact of the ground fire hitting some part of our fuselage. We were lucky to have no injuries on board.

"The paratroopers outlined the drop area with white sheets around the perimeter. Before we reached the area, we gained several hundred feet so the chutes could take effect. After our drop, we climbed to about 10,000 feet and flew out over the coastline. I think all air crews heaved a sigh of relief, leaving this kind of personal war behind."

For those in Abrams's section, the risky expedition was carried out with relatively few injuries. For Harry Reynolds, bombardier/navigator on *The Hot Rock,* a B-24 with the 491st Bomb Group, the Market Garden support, his thirty-first mission, was scheduled to be his last. "Plans were to fly in at 1,500 feet, and for the first time heavy bombers would drop supplies at low level. The crew and I thought it a big mistake to use slow heavy bombers to fly at such a low altitude. We were briefed to drop supplies to British and American troops encircled outside of Arnhem. Instead of carrying bombs, our bomb bays were filled with medical supplies, communications equipment, food, etc. Each plane was supplied with a drop master supervising the drop by chute."

The Hot Rock lifted off a few minutes after 1:00 P.M. but not until 3:23 had the group assembled. The circling over the Channel, believes Reynolds, alerted German radar. "We flew over the Dutch coast a few minutes before 4:00 P.M. and immediately caught small-arms fire. We were quite concerned as we were at only 700 feet. I saw smashed gliders and supplies in fields below us, dropped by the previous group. I also saw German troops and tanks bogged down on country roads.

"We arrived at the target area and immediately our leader, Jim Hunter, was hit, went down in flames. The plane crashed into a wooded area and blew up, no chutes out of a crew of ten, one survivor. Being deputy leader, we immediately took over and instructed our group to follow at 400 feet. Reached our designated drop zone, dropped supplies and moved to higher altitude, 2,500 feet, climbing to 7,000 feet. Several of the paratrooper carriers and our planes were in trouble, a Twentieth Combat Wing plane ditched in the Channel, turned upside down; a C-47 went down in the water." *The Hot Rock* had its own troubles, with one engine shut down and another throwing oil but Reynolds and company made it back to base. "The mission was certainly no milk run [a hoped-for but often denied prospect for one's final mission]. Really felt bad about our friends that did not make it back."

It was all for naught. The Nazi armies overwhelmed the most forward Allied troopers who either died or surrendered as Market Garden, a bridge too far, collapsed. The Eighth Bomber Command wrote off seventeen bombers shot down or too badly damaged to restore and almost 300 in urgent need of repairs. Fighter command's responsibilities were to perform low-level attacks to deter the enemy stretching over six days, but the bombers participated only on September 17 and 18, losing nearly 100 aircraft.

WHILE Market Garden faded into a bad memory, the Eighth Air Force resumed its strategic role as the bombers, accompanied by the organization's fighters, mounted heavier and heavier raids. Tactical responsibility and ground support devolved to the Ninth Air Force whose twin-engine mediums, aided and abetted by its fighters, worked with the ground forces.

As a fourteen-year-old plowing Kansas fields near the town of Olivet in 1936, Charles McCauley recalls a white biplane overhead. "I pulled on the reins of Tom and Jack and let go of the plow handle. The mules stopped quickly, glad for a breather. I admired the plane and envied whoever was piloting it." The boy who gaped at that rare sight often dreamt of piloting a plane, with a desire so strong that while still on the farm in Olivet he enrolled in a correspondence course on aviation and aircraft engines. Although hard times on the farm forced McCauley to end his formal education with only a single year of high school, his avid curiosity led him not only to learn about aircraft but also to pursue knowledge in a wide range of subjects. Still a teenager, he was among the first to obtain the latest scientifically developed hybrid seed that produced a bumper corn crop in a dry season. When the Rural Electrification Administration brought power to the area during the Great Depression McCauley attended meetings that instructed him in the workings of electricity. To compete in the 4-H program, McCauley developed a project that involved the new process of artificial insemination of cattle.

As his call-up through the Selective Service became imminent in 1942, McCauley convinced his father to sign an application for him to enlist in the Air Corps. Requested to take the cadet examination on September 25, 1942, McCauley received orders to report for induction on the same day. A relative with connections to the draft board arranged a delay of enough hours for McCauley to take the test and then report to the Army.

McCauley, who traveled to the site of the examination on a train for the first time in his life, recalls, "There were twenty-three applicants and most had a college degree or at least two years of college. I wondered what I was doing there, having had only one year of high school. Some of the test was mathematical problems, some was multiple choice and others covered mechanical questions. The engine mechanics course taken from Lincoln Aeronautical Institute really helped. I at least knew terms and some vocabulary in mechanics."

With no clue as to how well he scored, McCauley became a private in the Army, assigned to a medical unit. Two months later, while stationed in California, his father wrote that the Air Corps was looking for him. In January, he was notified to appear for a "mental test," obliged to obtain a pass from his unit and then pay his own way to the site, 200 miles away. Ultimately, at the end of March, the Air Corps accepted him and to his delight paid him the costs of the trip to preflight school and threw in five dollars for meals along the way.

As a cadet in preflight at Santa Ana, California, McCauley immersed himself in a curriculum of navigation, code, communications, recognition, weather and instruments. With a minimal academic background, McCauley studied hard, and welcomed aid from friendly cadets who had attended college. "Each Sunday there was a parade where the entire group passed in review . . . over 25,000 cadets! We learned that our base has a number of big names in baseball as enlisted men. They were not cadets but members of a baseball team representing our base to keep up morale. Joe DiMaggio and Red Ruffing of the New York Yankees are the ones that I had heard of. Joe DiMaggio also had been my calisthenics instructor. He did the exercises right along with us too!"

Upon completion of school at Santa Ana, McCauley began flight training. The home study course on engines paid off in classes on that subject while McCauley learned the rudiments of aerial maneuvers. After nine hours in the air, he soloed. "Until you soloed," says McCauley, "you had to wear a tape across the top of your helmet that carried your name and serial number. A student wearing a tape was called a 'dodo.' I was sure glad to have that tape off!" As a child of the Depression, Mac McCauley marveled, "Just imagine what I was getting for free. It cost the government seventeen dollars an hour for a plane to be in the air. I also got my living quarters, food and pay of seventy-five dollars per month!"

The Basic program introduced McCauley to swifter, more sophisticated aircraft, cross-country jaunts, night trips, aerobatics, navigation problems, and an unpleasant hint of dire possibilities. "I had to climb to the top of a 100-foot tower . . . which itself brought out a cold sweat . . . wriggle into a parachute harness and be ready to jump. They checked your weight and placed counterweights which caught you before hitting the ground. This was to give you the feel of the real thing, when and if you had to bail out. One jump was enough."

At the end of Basic, McCauley received assignment to a twin-engine program in New Mexico. He studied meteorology in depth, navigation began a major concern and radio communications replaced the visual signals of his earlier training. On February 8, 1944, he graduated, with the status of a lieutenant and slated to fly a B-17. "A very pleasant shock! I must have done well to be considered worthy of flying one of those great planes!

"February 28 was my first flight in the B-17 [a stripped-down version with no armor plate or guns and able to use 91-octane gas]. I could not believe the mass of instruments . . . 146 switches, gauges, indicators and warning lights. Use was made of a 'check list' card wherein the copilot called off checkpoints while the pilot had to reply that the item was in order. This included fifty-seven checks before takeoff during flight, and after landing. There were thirty-eight checks for 'end of mission.' A lot to learn, and we had only nine weeks to complete the job."

The economics of his military career continued to bemuse McCauley. "Each flight lasted about five hours at a cost to the government of $500 per hour to operate those planes. . . . I have been told that I will need to pay ninety dollars in income tax for 1944. This is the first time I have ever heard of this tax. I guess I am making too much money now. We draw $246 per month, pay for food at thirty-five dollars, insurance is six dollars and fifty cents and my War Bond is seventy-five dollars, leaving $129. I still think Uncle Sam has been pretty good to me."

At Lincoln, Nebraska, McCauley awaited the assemblage of a crew. "We were among the first to take the psychological test to sort out men into compatible crews. The crew was to be a family circle. Men with similar views of religion and other phases of life were matched up. But among the questions we were asked—many made no sense at the time— was 'If you bailed out of a plane and found your parachute wouldn't open, would you prefer to bail out at 10,000 or 7,000 feet?' Staff officers at Lincoln emphasized that we pilots were not 'just one of the guys.' We were to be commanders of the plane and crew and were responsible for them. If a crewman got out of line, it was the pilot's job to straighten him out. Also the pilot must take the blame for any trouble in his plane or crew. The pilot has authority to break a crewman, and he also recommends promotions."

The McCauley crew met in Tennessee where they practiced formation flying, bomb runs, high-altitude performance and flew to the Gulf of Mexico where a B-26 towed a target. "This was the first and only time our gunners got a chance to use their guns in the air."

During the last week of August, the McCauley crew headed to the Eighth Air Force in England in a brand-new B-17G. Packed with a cargo of mail and K rations, they followed the route from New Hampshire to Labrador, then to Iceland as the last stop before reaching the United

Kingdom. Ordered to the 385th Bomb Group at Great Ashfield, the crew flew several practice assignments before September 22, when McCauley was ordered to serve as copilot on a mission to Kassel. Five days later he again occupied the right seat on a different Fort with the destination of Ludwigshafen. Neither of these ventures brought serious damage to his aircraft and with two successful trips he qualified now to take his own crew out.

THE infusion of bomber personnel was matched by the debut of fighter pilots. As a member of the 364th Fighter Group, Max Woolley had piloted a P-38 when flak had knocked him down toward the end of June. A few weeks later the outfit switched to P-51s, amid some grumbling from men who remarked they had learned their trade in two-engine aircraft and staggered back to base after losing one. But a few hours in the cockpit of a Mustang converted even the most obdurate naysayers. Replacement pilots, like Jim McCubbin of Kansas City, arrived at the 364th's Honington home already schooled in the P-51.

"On this typical damp English morning of September 1944," recalls McCubbin, "as I sat in the cockpit of my beautiful 'D' Model P-51, waiting for the 'start engines' command, I could hardly believe that finally I was going on my first combat mission. This dream about to be fulfilled, started at the age of twelve.

"During my early teen years," says McCubbin, "we spent a considerable time constructing paper-covered, balsa-wood frame, rubber-band-powered model airplanes. Some would even fly more than fifteen feet. My record was almost one minute of flight. We even devised a bomb, consisting of a small firecracker tied to a kitchen match that could be ignited when the match tip struck the pavement. My first flight training was in a government program called Civilian Pilot Training. This was in June 1940 after graduation from Kansas City Junior College."

Working as a draftsman for a refrigeration company, McCubbin acquired a number of hours of flight time before he entered an Air Corps reserve program that guaranteed he could complete his engineering degree at the University of Missouri. However, six months before earning his diploma he says he was told, in January 1943, "'We need you now.' Our first training started with 'preflight,' two months of ground school. And what a lot of shit we had to take. For example, I carried a letter from home for one whole week before I could find the time to read it. We were not permitted to walk or talk. We had to run to each successive event. Eating was even a discipline experience. We had to keep our eyes fixed on an imaginary spot straight ahead while selecting and lifting food to our mouths. But the worst part, the most difficult to take was the hazing— harassment by the upper classmen. They were the ones on their second month of preflight. Surely the purpose of this misguided system was to weed out all but the ones who were willing to do almost anything to fly. I definitely qualified."

Having endured the early foolishness and focused on earning his wings, McCubbin had come to the 364th in the waning days of the summer of 1944. Lined up on a morning in late September were forty-eight fighters of the three squadrons in the outfit, along with several spares standing by in case anyone aborted. Remembers McCubbin, "Then came the long awaited radio call. 'Gentlemen, start your engines!' The memory of the emotions at that particular moment, even after fifty years is still strong enough to bring tears to my eyes. The thrill of fifty Rolls-Royce, twelve-cylinder, 1,600-horsepower engines, coughing and struggling to catch enough fuel to start. The first deep-throated roar as one caught, quickly reinforced by an ever increasing thunder until the whole field shook and vibrated. These feelings never diminished, even after forty-four missions, almost 200 combat hours.

"Taxiing a P-51 is not easy. Being a tail dragger it puts the long engine cowling sloping up front, blocking your view. To compensate, you have to weave down the taxiway to maintain forward view through the side of the canopy. But to keep the engine from loading up, you need about a thousand rpms which will translate to some thirty miles per hour. Therefore, you need a lot of brake action. But this can cause burnout or worse, a locking of the wheels when the cool air of flight hits, meaning a rigid gear upon landing. Sometimes the brakes even catch fire. Trying to push fifty airplanes through takeoff in the least amount of time doesn't help.

"To gain formation with a minimum use of time and fuel, the first ones off made a calculated wide climbing turn with each following plane making an ever tighter, and steeper climb. It was a difficult maneuver and often left the last men really struggling to catch the group using full power and a vertical bank from takeoff."

Fulfillment of his dream verged toward nightmare. "As we approached the Channel, my engine began to exhibit unusual signs. When I was over the water all sorts of things went wrong. Among other problems: the left magneto, the oil pressure seemed low; the coolant temperature was climbing. Flying over friendly territory with engine problems is one thing, but this was another. However, as soon as we were over land, on the other side, somehow all the problems disappeared. Strangely, I had the same engine problems over water on every mission.

"For some, the need to abort was so strong it couldn't be resisted. When this happened more than two times, the pilot was reduced to being a 'ground pounder,' the worst insult. One pilot claimed to lose oil pressure while approaching the Channel. The problem could not be duplicated when checked by others. After two such occurrences, he was given a warning. On the next try he had to bail out over the water, but fortunately near shore. Problem was, it was the enemy shore—good news, bad news.

"My roommate reported a defect in his propeller governor, which sometimes caused the engine to overspeed. Each time this was reported, the base engineer was unable to duplicate the fault. After several such occurrences, he was suspected of having the problem of 'overreacting.' When he was given his last chance, I volunteered to trade planes with him. Sure enough, on some engagement requiring a steep dive, the engine rpm started climbing. In spite of cutting the power, pulling up into a climb, putting the prop control into manual, the engine continued to speed past 3,000 rpm. Finally, after I earned a few gray hairs, it returned to normal for no obvious reason. The proof vindicated my friend."

But on his first combat mission, as McCubbin noted, he flew through the apparent malfunctions and headed into enemy territory. "The 364th had a procedure which required each new member to fly his first mission on the wing of 'Outshine' (the group commander [Col. Roy W. Osborn]), and this was my place. As we approached landfall, large black puffs of fire and smoke appeared in our midst. What a shock! We were hardly over the shoreline and they were shooting at us already. If it's this bad at the beginning of enemy territory, what must it be like farther inland? It was later explained that 'ol' one-eye' with only a single antiaircraft battery gun, perched on a small island off the Dutch coast, had never hit anyone yet.

"Our assignment was to guard a maximum-effort bomber run on the right side and at the same level. The sight of that endless string of boxes of bright, shiny B-17s [400 plus] was incredible. I didn't know we had so many planes. They stretched out of sight in both directions. And they looked so invincible in their tight formation, with interprotective gun patterns. At least that was what the newspapers told us.

"The sky was so clear, and everything so peaceful that we failed to notice a thin cloud layer over the bomber train. We had to continuously follow an 'S' pattern to reduce our speed to that of the bombers. All was clear when I took my eyes off the bombers and we started to weave outward. But, when we swung back towards them, an indescribable sight met my eyes. What had been a beautiful formation was turned into a junk pile—burning planes, pieces of falling aircraft, parachutes, damaged planes wandering out of formation. How could this happen so quickly?

"As we approached what was left of the formation, I noted a lone FW-190, still firing on a crippled B-17. Outshine fired on the German, but due to his speed was unable to concentrate his fire over a few seconds. Due to my better position behind and to the outside of the curve toward the target, I was able to swing farther out to kill my speed and thus could hold my fire on the target until the pilot bailed out. Whether Outshine's bullets had the most effect or mine was controversial.

"It later became obvious that the Germans had been hiding in that thin overcast and made one pass through the formation when we turned on our outboard path. At this point I had lost contact with the group and I reasoned that if anywhere, the Germans would have gone for the deck. I spent the rest of my flying time hunting for those FW-190s to no avail. At the last possible moment I headed for base alone, my first time over Germany. I was the last of the entire group to return. I must admit that the feeling of being alone, over enemy territory, felt good and somehow reminded me of hunting experiences from an earlier life.

"I made a low pass over the field, followed by a climbing slow roll, the victory signal. How presumptuous I was, but oh, how elated. It turned out that this was Outshine's first victory and he was near the end of his tour. He offered to share the credit, but I thought that if it was this easy, why not be more generous. I could bag more tomorrow. Ha! Little did I know the Germans were running short of good fighter pilots."

Nevertheless, the Luftwaffe could still draw blood and on October 6 hit the 385th Bomb Group over Berlin hard. For their first effort together the McCauley crew had drawn the dreaded Big B. "The early morning skies were filling with bombers that eventually numbered 1,250. The armada would separate later to strike oil, aircraft and ordnance production facilities in various parts of Berlin [other industrial sites of northern Germany were also targeted and roughly 400 struck the enemy capital]. Almost 1,000 Thunderbolt and Mustang fighters were the escort along the way [the Berlin-bound contingent numbered more than 360 P-51s]. They were not always in sight but generally had to be called by the group leader when bombers were in trouble.

"We flew off the right wing of Lieutenant Foss, who was section leader. Just before we got to the I.P., the squadron leader had to turn back because of engine trouble. Lieutenant Foss moved up to squadron lead and we had to move up to section lead. This was all new to me except for practice in our training missions. Foss's bombardier was the lead man as we went in over the target, and we dropped our incendiaries as he used the bombsight to drop his. Flak was really heavy, but we hunched down and rode it through. Foss banked hard to the right and we followed.

"At the rally point, we looked back and saw the target exploding in flames. We had scored direct hits. Nearly all the bombs in our squadron landed in the thousand-foot 'bull's-eye' circle. Before we had a chance to congratulate each other, Click [copilot Robert B.] hollered over the intercom, 'Look at those bombers and fighters going down!' The high squadron from the group following ours had overshot the turn at the I.P., putting them out in unprotected space about fifteen miles behind us. One ship had aborted earlier. This left eleven out there alone.

"All eleven bombers [the official record lists ten planes] were knocked down by a mass attack of nearly seventy-five enemy fighters. Wave after wave of the German fighters were diving on the one group. The entire squadron was being shot out of the sky. This brought our crew to a sudden alert, but we were never attacked.

"They had scored a great victory but we thought little of it since the planes weren't among us [from the 385th Bomb Group]." McCauley and his mates were appalled to learn the truth upon their return. "The squadron of planes shot down had been the 549th squadron [part of the 385th] flying with another group. This was hard on morale as many friends were lost." All together, the visit to Berlin counted fourteen B-17s missing in action.

Bill Frankhouser, as a navigator with the 398th Bomb Group, remarks, "When I got to Europe, flak was a worse problem than fighters. However, when fighters did attack, they were deadly because our gunners were inexperienced."

Ira O'Kennon was a radio operator in the same group menaced by the fighters. However, he says, "Our nemesis, flak, was the only hit we took. Losing power rapidly, we fell behind the formation. By the time we reached France we had only two engines left. Ultimately, we landed in Chantilly, a small town about forty kilometers north of Paris. That night we got our first look at one result of the previous German occupation: girls with shaved heads at a dance we attended. That was their punishment by locals who resented their fraternization with Nazis."

The resort to landing at an airstrip on the Continent by O'Kennon's pilot signifies how much the Allied ground advance had added to the Eighth Air Force resources. The retreat of the enemy also brought the return of some evadees. Howard Snyder, shot down in the *Susan Ruth* on

February 8 over Belgium, had lived and fought with the Maquis ever since a farmer hid him from the German patrols. While several of his crew who escaped capture for almost two months subsequently had been executed by the enemy, Snyder, with the identity card that described him as a deaf mute, avoided friendly fire as well as capture. He emerged unhurt after American B-25s smashed a railroad marshaling yard while he stayed in an adjacent building. When enemy soldiers conducted a search on another occasion, Snyder climbed onto the roof of a house to escape detection.

As both the Gestapo and the soldiers hunted for airmen and their saviors, Snyder crossed the border into France where he joined a group of about twenty people. "We received our orders by radio from England to harass and destroy German military targets. British planes dropped arms, ammunition and explosives to us. We blew up portions of motorized military columns and troops."

In place of the hit-and-run tactics before D-Day, after the invasion, the Maquis engaged in operations that coordinated with the Allied ground forces. The irregulars that included Snyder heard that American troops were in the village of Trélon and set up a barricade that could detain fleeing Germans. When the enemy failed to show, the guerrillas met the Americans at Trélon where Snyder quickly established his identity. On September 10, he wired his wife Ruth that he was alive and well; her first news of him since she received word he was missing in action almost seven months earlier.

Keeping the pipeline filled with the manpower to handle the swelling number of planes frequently brought in some airmen with only rudimentary knowledge of their tasks. Al Greenberg, a would-be commercial artist taking night courses at Cooper Union in Manhattan and the offspring of a Bronx, New York, cab driver, volunteered for the Air Corps even though he'd never flown because "the infantry did not sound particularly exciting. I thought the Air Corps seemed like a class act and the nice uniform with wings wouldn't hurt with girls either."

Summoned to active duty in January 1943, Greenberg enjoyed a rather easy six weeks of basic training at Atlantic City before being shipped to the University of Pittsburgh. "There were not a lot of soldiers in town and we were treated royally by the city. We went on long marches singing the Air Corps song and were always invited to parties on the weekend. I learned to fly while I was at Pittsburgh, with ten lessons in a Piper Cub but I wasn't very good at it."

At the classification center in Nashville, where they separated cadets into specialties, Greenberg was designated a future bombardier. His first instruction was in gunnery and then he received the official cadet's "sharp uniform and hat" as he began to learn the secrets of the Norden bombsight. Having absorbed the ground instruction and performed proficiently on the practice range, Greenberg looked ahead a few weeks to graduation and toward that end, he and his contemporaries had been photographed in uniforms with the lieutenant's gold bars affixed. Then on one of the final exercises, he became unstrung. "I have no idea of why it was but all the bombs I dropped, instead of falling in New Mexico, dropped someplace in Texas." A classmate, routinely assigned to report another cadet's performance, "accurately wrote down how badly I had done. Soon after I was called in and told I was one of the 20 or 25 percent to be washed out. I was to be a gunner on a B-17 and because I had already passed that test, I was automatically made one."

As a member of a unit assembled in Tennessee, Greenberg spent three months in the role of a waist gunner before the crew picked up a new B-17 in Lincoln, Nebraska, and then ferried it to England to enter the 96th Bomb Group. "As soon as we got to the base," says Greenberg, "the captain of my plane said he had just found out that instead of a ten-man crew they were now flying nine-man crews and one gunner was now being eliminated from each plane. He told me he had looked at my record and found out I had been three weeks from being a bombardier and getting a commission. It was felt that I could do better as a bombardier than as a gunner."

The decision ignored the absence of any bombardier-crew training for Greenberg, because with the system of a lead and deputy lead bombardier, other planes in the groups relied on toggliers who released their loads when the lead dropped his, or if he were shot down, on the cue of the deputy. The role of a bombardier and the skills required had certainly been downgraded, and Greenberg's superiors seem to have believed that all he needed to know was how to flick the toggle switch at the appropriate moment. "As a tech sergeant," says Greenberg, "I was now doing exactly what I had been trained for, without having the commission. I sat in the nose, with the chin turret. I had the same duties and problems of bombardiers."

Greenberg unexpectedly flew his first assignment, Bremen, September 26, and shortly afterwards he began keeping a journal. "At 7:00 A.M., crew was called for a mission. I got up, ate, went back, handed in laundry, swept the floor and was helping the new guy make a fire when the CQ [charge of quarters] opens the door and says, 'Greenberg, up to the orderly room. There's a Jeep waiting for you. You're flying.' I grabbed my long johns and my parachute scarf that Pop [a nearly fifty-year-old

Portuguese gunner who had just about finished his missions] had given me. The Jeep took me to the 413th Squadron where a sergeant told me I was flying as togglier. The bombardier on ship #952 was flying lead and it needed a bombardier, I was him.

"I cleaned the chin guns the best I could with the help of the engineer on the crew and put them in the turret. I introduced myself to the copilot and he told me the navigator would help in case I had trouble. The crew bombardier showed up and took the time to explain all the switches and settings, which I understood. The navigator came in and we talked about home and cadets. We finally took off about 11:50.

"The navigator pulled on Mae West and parachute, so I did same, only to have leg straps much too short. After about fifteen minutes of violent pulling it was on. I plugged in the heated suit and waited. After a while the gunners called for a test fire. I tried to hand-charge the chin turret but the damn thing was screwed up and the navigator seemed P.O.'d. He called the armorer and after a while he too gave up and the navigator was really P.O.'d.

"About this time, the navigator noticed the light was on and the bomb doors open. I immediately closed them but the crew noticed and bitched. The navigator now helped me on with the flak suit. As the I.P. approached, I switched on the intervalometer and the navigator put the flak hat on my head. I opened the doors as soon as I saw the lead ship open theirs, and immediately everyone started yelling that I was losing some bombs. I still don't know what was wrong. I don't think I pushed the toggle switch, but it's possible. At any rate, this P.O.'d everybody. I lost five bombs and dropped the rest over Bremen. I didn't shut the salvo switch for a while and the crew started to shout, 'Close the f——g doors.' I finally learned the secret and closed them hurriedly.

"Flak was bursting way in front of us, but it didn't seem close at all. There was an oxygen leak in an extra outlet in the nose of the ship and oxygen was very low. The navigator amazed me by saying I was completely out at the I.P. I don't remember a thing about it, but my emergency valve was on so he must have used it.

"On landing, everyone wanted to know what the trouble was and I didn't know. They all kidded me but said as long as we got back, it was okay. I had to fill out a bombardier's report and get briefed by S-2 [intelligence] and the group bombardier. All in all, it wasn't too bad except for my mistakes. I hope I can stay on as togglier. The nose is warm and I can drop bombs. I hear we knocked hell out of Bremen and I must have hit some farm houses with my first incendiaries."

Some two weeks later, Greenberg again acted as a togglier. Still unfamiliar with the chin turret, he needed assistance from a ground armorer to install the guns because in this aircraft the switches were electrical instead of manual. He struggled with his parachute harness until the navigator lent a hand.

Over the target, Cologne's railroad yards, Greenberg says, "I pushed the toggle switch but only twelve bombs dropped [out of eighteen]. Flak was coming up and nothing would get the bombs out, not even the salvo [switch]. The armorer and the engineer went into the open bomb bay to kick them out but couldn't. Finally after what seemed like an eternity, I set the switches again, and dropped the remaining six. I don't think I made any mistakes, but for the second time in a row, something went snafu." Apparently those in charge did not hold him responsible for the problems because for the duration of his missions, Greenberg continued as a bomb dropper, serving with a number of different crews.

18

MERSEBURG AND MURDER

As Ira O'Kennon's forced landing at Chantilly demonstrated, the liberation of France opened up emergency airfields for the Allies' bigger planes. It also provided bases closer to Germany for dispatching fighters and eliminating ground fire as aircraft crossed the coastline. On the other hand it enabled the Germans to concentrate their antiaircraft weapons inside the Third Reich. Outwitting the ground fire preoccupied the minds of some tacticians. According to Dave Nagel, the flight commander from his squadron would make a slight adjustment to help protect the crews. "When headquarters designated you gotta go in at 25,000 feet," says Nagel, "he would send us in at 25,350 feet. He would never send us in at the exact altitude which we were assigned. The flak gunners knew where everybody was, from where those in front had been. Management didn't know their ass from their elbow when it came to certain decisions. They went by the book, and pure inexperience."

A day after the ill-fated 385th met the Luftwaffe over Berlin, the defenders showed just how awesome their flak could be at Pölitz, home to a synthetic oil complex near Stettin on the Baltic. Waist gunner Jim Wilson with the 351st Bomb Group calls this, his twenty-eighth mission, "the worst of my flying in Europe and it was all the fault of the leadership in my opinion. On this mission, my old crew was separated and on different aircraft. Lt. Einer Peterson, my first pilot, was flying with a new crew and one of our gunners, Sgt. Paul Waxler, was a gunner in the lead plane. The group started the bomb run and for some reason had to turn off. The leaders decided to make a 360-degree turn and make a second run. You don't do things like that with the Germans."

According to official statements, the enemy mustered 270 105 mm and 88 mm guns to meet air attacks at Pölitz. Aware of this stiff reception awaiting the aircraft, the strategists' plot scripted an eight-minute bomb run and exit for the more than 140 B-17s over the target. Unfortunately, the Air Corps later reported, for some reason the formations broke down and subsequent maneuvers to rectify the error brought two groups, including the 351st over the objective within such a short space of time that the concentrated fire from below shot down seventeen B-17s or so badly crippled them they could not get back to England. Another thirty incurred major damage. Most worrisome to the Eighth Air Force was the deadly effect of the batteries upon lead ships and their deputies. Unknown to U.S. intelligence, the H2X radar emissions from the lead ships now could be tracked by German ground radar, greatly facilitating accurate shelling.

Whatever the technical aspects, Wilson agonized over his former associates. "Paul Waxler's plane was beside me and I could see the holes in the wing and the fuel coming out. Even though he couldn't see or hear me, I kept telling him to jump. I guess maybe it was better he couldn't hear because they reached Sweden, were interned and then sent home.

"Lieutenant Peterson lost two engines over the target and had his fuel system holed, and was losing gasoline. He started for Sweden. He was attempting to make an emergency landing when he lost one of his remaining engines as he made an approach and saw people working in the field. He tried to apply power on the only engine he had. He crashed; the tail gunner and one other survived. I hated to hear of his death because I really cared for the man.

"While we returned to the airfield, everything was nice and smooth until we touched down and found our left main wheel was flat. Lieutenant Underhill had to make an emergency turn off the runway and stopped in the grass. I walked under the left wing and removed a piece of flak hanging from it while the mechanics counted over 200 holes in the plane.

"I was assigned to assemble Lieutenant Peterson's gear and get it ready to ship home to his family. I wouldn't let the supply men steal any of his stuff. They seem to think that if you were dead, they could have anything they wanted."

STILL, as the enemy coped with its dearth of fliers, raw new talent from the States, perhaps even more naive than McCauley, flooded the fields of the United Kingdom. Wayne C. Gatlin, an eighteen-year-old Duluth,

Minnesota, youth, like his predecessors in the fighters, thirsted with an irrepressible lust to fly. A faithful correspondent to his parents beginning with his entry into the Army, February 1, 1943, Gatlin recorded his passages from basic training through flight training and then his stint with the 356th Fighter Group.

By the time Gatlin put on a uniform, the Air Corps could no longer expect to recruit young men with a college background. To the folks back home, Gatlin wrote, "I guess the outfit I'm in is more or less a 'guinea pig' squadron. I'm in Squadron A of the first bunch to be sent to a college program like this [at the University of Missouri]. The purpose of this schooling is to better equip us to make the grade when we get farther along. They are trying to prevent the high number of washouts that come at Primary and Basic." Gatlin noted that the would-be aviators studied English, history, geography, physics, the usual curriculum for freshmen rather than subjects directly applicable to their expected responsibilities.

The University of Missouri sojourn lasted just one month. On April 15, he reported, "I've got my first hour of flying under my belt. Oh man! Is it ever fun! As soon as we got up and out of traffic he'd [the instructor] demonstrate something and then say, 'Now you do it.' We did glides, climbing, left and right turns and gliding turns. We were flying in pretty rough air—those light Cubs pop up and down and all over. When he said, 'Take over,' then it started something tingling inside me, I didn't do too bad for the first time up and he seemed like he thought it wasn't so bad. I feel more at home in the air than if I were in a boat. Some of the guys heaved up their dinners, but I didn't feel airsick at all. Don't worry about me, Mom. I have to wear a parachute always and the instructor said he could land it, even if the wings fell off—so that shows how dangerous it *isn't*. As for myself, I love it."

During the following week or so, Gatlin described in detail the maneuvers he performed, counted the hours he logged and proudly announced, "My instructor . . . said he knew darn well that I could make the grade. Gosh, did I beam all over." A little less bravado followed his check-flight after more than ten hours but Gatlin still brimmed with a naive enthusiasm. "I want to be a (fighter) pilot but I'd even take gunner as a second choice. If you can't fly and fire your own gun, you sure could have a picnic if someone else flew it and you could concentrate on knocking the enemy down. Bombardier or navigator are good deals too. They both handle guns. Whatever it is, it'll be the best for me because there won't be any mistakes about it at classification—they know."

Shipped to San Antonio, Gatlin entered a different regimen. "More discipline, upperclassmen, lots of drill and studies . . . We'll get math, physics, aircraft and naval identification. Morse code, liquid-cooled engines and stuff like that, nine weeks of it should really fly by." Then, a week later he announced, "Hi, I'm classified as *PILOT*—sure am glad."

Nine weeks later, having completed a ground-school program in San Antonio, Gatlin reported to Grider Field, Pine Bluffs, Arkansas, to begin the Primary Flight course. The training intensified, "It's all work and no play," he reported, and he seems to have become accustomed to "getting chewed by the instructor."

Gatlin turned nineteen toward the end of August 1943, but his big day was September 21. He wrote to his sister, "Well, it happened today. At 11:33 A.M. to be exact. After three trips around the field, I taxied up to where we were taking off and stopped to clear the area. Bang! Mr. Smith popped the hand brakes on, unfastened his safety belt and climbed out. He gave me some instructions and said, 'Good luck, she's all yours.' Then he waved me off. I hit the throttle and in a minute, there I was, up in the air with $12,000 worth of airplane under my control. I had a funny feeling in me and I smiled all the way around. I even tried singing. My throat was kinda dry though. I had all the confidence in the world during those few minutes. Then I was on my base leg, so I popped the throttle forward and started my glide in for a landing. I actually hated to land because I was having so much fun, but I had to do it, according to the book. I rolled out of my upwind turn and hit the flaps and pointed her down. As I got down, I started back ever so slow on the stick, back, back. I was just a few feet off now and losing flying speed so I kept back, back. Then I heard the wheels spinning and there I was with a three-pointer. Not a bounce. Boy, talk about glorious feelings. I had one!"

A series of minor health problems with his teeth and a persistent cold dampened Gatlin's ardor and for the first time he expressed serious doubts about his future. Early on October 12, he declared, "What a lousy ride I gave Smith yesterday. It was terrible. If I can't do better than that I'd better go GDO (Ground Duty Only) and save the government a lot of wasted expense. I'm sincere about that too. Mr. Smith said he was willing to keep working with me because he thinks I can do it. But I can't satisfy myself. I try, but the way it has been going, I've lost that alertness or eagerness, or whatever it is and it doesn't mean much to me now."

But that evening, his spirits soaring, he dashed off another missive. "Hello again. I had my ride and I made my decision. I'm going to keep on slugging away and fly the pants off of these planes. I went up with Mr. Smith today and started right in expecting the worst. For some reason, I was on the ball and really flew that plane like I wanted. After a while of this unexpected flying, Mr. Smith said, 'Goddammit, Gatlin, how come you're doing everything right?' . . . I was awful close to giving up but something kept egging me on and now I'm in the groove again. Gee, but I feel good about it."

Gatlin easily rode out the remainder of Primary and in the final days he noted, "The five of us under Mr. Smith chipped in and bought him a flying suit and scarf to show how much we appreciated his patience and teaching ability. He was a hard man to please but by being just so, I think he helped us a heck of a lot more. We had a washout percentage of about 11.5 percent. It was the lowest rate in the history of the school. When we left preflight, one of our tactical officers told us that 44-C was a horse-shit class and he'd bet 90 percent would wash out. I think a lot of boys stuck it out just to make that son of a b—— eat his words."

At Independence, Kansas, Gatlin began the Basic phase, at the controls of faster, more complicated airplanes. He learned instrument and night flying, practiced acrobatics and did some cross-country traveling. Friends from the early days washed out even while Gatlin renewed his desire for fighters. "There was a P-51 in here today. Boy, that's the kind of ship I want to fly. It really moves, four cannon make it a deadly job too. It buzzed the field a couple of times and chandelled up a few thousand feet. Boy, what a beautiful sight! . . . We had to state our choice today for what we want to fly. Mine went—1st Pursuit; 2nd Observation; 3rd Bombardment. I'm built for pursuit so I think that is what I will get. I don't like bombardment because it's like driving a truck and sitting up like a clay pigeon over the target. Pursuit—you can go in and fight or you can run for home. Observation—you don't have guns but your plane is lighter and faster so you can run."

Shortly after New Year's Day, 1944, Gatlin arrived at Moore Field in southern Texas, for advanced instruction. He and a friend walked around the post after supper and looked at the next generation of machines for them, AT-6s and P-40s. Gatlin wrote, "I climbed into the P-40, boy, what a hunk of airplane. The cockpit is tiny and really compact. Man-oh-man I can't picture myself flying one of those babies but I'm gonna try darn hard. Golly they're beautiful. . . . We were issued our flying equipment today. We really got some nifty leather jackets. Class! They're light and really smooth."

At Moore Field, he completed the last of his ground-school courses, shot skeet as an introduction to gunnery, fired a 20 mm cannon before practicing with tow targets in the air, used the Link Trainer to enhance his knowledge of instruments and of course piled up more hours in the air. He ordered a uniform to suit his coming elevation to the ranks of the commissioned although uncertain whether he would be a lieutenant or mere flight officer. Subsequently he learned he would need the gold bars.

Freshly minted Lieutenant Gatlin had hardly acclimated himself to a P-40 before assignment to Camp Springs, Maryland, and P-47s. "I'd rather have P-51s but there's not a thing wrong with the 47. It's a giant, weighs seven tons and has an engine of over 2,000 hp. It is the safest plane there is to fly in combat as the pilot is protected completely and it flies above the altitude of antiaircraft fire." Gatlin obviously ignored the role of the Thunderbolt as a train-buster and low-level tactical scourge. He quickly developed a fondness for his new vehicle. "I was down on the line today, looking over the P-47 and it is sure a beauty. I guess I'm pretty lucky to get to fly it. I'm sure I'm destined to be a P-47 man."

Impatiently awaiting the first flight in his ship of destiny, Gatlin and his fellow pilots attended a session at a local swimming pool to try out their Mae Wests and learned the technique of inflating the dinghy. On D-Day as Allied troops waded ashore on the Normandy beaches and fighter planes searched and strafed the enemy Gatlin took his first trip in a P-47. After a few more hours of familiarization he wrote, "I sure like this ship. Some of the fellows don't like it but here's one lad that's dang thankful for being able to fly it." On Father's Day, after expressing his appreciation for "a swell family" Gatlin said, "Boy, Pop, they've put your kid into a really swell fighting ship. The more I fly it, the more I see it and the more I hear of it, the better I like it."

During the summer of 1944, in this final phase of stateside preparation, Gatlin reported gunnery work, mock dogfights, instrument flights and meeting the men who would be closest to him overseas, replacements consigned to the same squadron. On September 2, he advised his folks he was in England but not until the middle of the month could he say, "Today, I got back up into the blue and it sure was wonderful. It has been six weeks since my last flight in the States. I felt like I was going up on my first solo ride. After a few minutes, she felt right again and I was happy. I had a nice ship and really enjoyed viewing England from the air. Great stuff this flying, yea, man!"

Posted to the 356th Fighter Group, he wrote, "It's a really good outfit and I consider myself lucky as Hell. Nick, Rags, and Dunn and I are all in the same outfit. We live in a nice old castle—yup, there's a moat filled with water around it and all. It's quite a distance from the field and I'm gonna like it fine. We have our mess right in the castle and a lounge and all. I've a nice sack, a big bed and sheets."

On the eve of entry into combat he reassured his family, "Golly, when you sit down and think it over, I've got a doggone good job. I'm doing what I want (flying) and leading a dang nice life. Eating good chow, seeing a lot of country I'd probably never have gotten to see. Meeting a heck of a lot of swell fellows and most important of all, I've learned to appreciate what a wonderful family I have . . . I won't have any regrets when I get back to being a civilian. The Army Air Corps was and always will be a pretty well-spent part of my life."

On October 24, the 356th escorted B-17s to Hanover and Gatlin flew his first mission over Germany. Obedient to the restrictions of censorship, Gatlin said nothing about the time in enemy territory but described his worst moment which occurred upon his return. "I had a little trouble landing today. The left wheel was locked and then the tire blew. I really started sweating because if I got off the runway I'd probably nose up as the ground is awful wet and the wheels bog down easily. When the tire blew, I didn't have a snowball's chance in Hades of staying on the runway and visions of ole Gat nosing up a nice new ship was really prominent in my brain. So I poured the coal to her, and bent the stick back in my lap and prayed. The slipstream over the stabilizer was enough to keep the tail down and I scooted over muck. I got her stopped okay and then proceeded to swallow a time or two to return my heart to its original encasement. Both the Group and Squadron COs said I did a good job, but had I pranged it, well what they'd have had to say wouldn't be fit to print.

"I've been almost two years in the Army now and I've finally done what I've always been wanting to do—that is, to be classed as a fighter pilot and fly overseas."

Another faithful diarist was Lewis A. Smith. Born in 1924 at Wichita, Kansas, where his father held a sales manager post with a flour mill, Smith, who had never been in a plane, says he opted for the Air Corps because of the "glamour of flying." He found ground school somewhat difficult, "because I put so much pressure on myself. I had an all-consuming passion to succeed and not wash out." He has no idea why the selectors classified him for multiengine duty but the choice suited him fine.

On September 18, as the first pilot for a crew that had been assembled and commenced working together at Rapid City, South Dakota, Smith and his gang took off on the first leg of a northern Atlantic crossing. They reached the UK five days later and after a month of ground school, orientation, practice and two weeks with the 385th Bomb Group, were pronounced fit for missions.

Smith, on October 22, received his baptism of flak over Münster. "It was an easy mission," he confided to his diary. "I flew as copilot in *Stork Club*. It was rough flying formation from the right seat. There was very little flak over the target. Only counted about ten bursts but you can bet your life I had on my flak suit and helmet. Saw about six enemy fighters but they didn't attack. Plenty of P-51s escorted us all the way. Our group put up forty-one planes and all returned."

Three days later, bombing an oil refinery at Hamburg he noted, "It was pretty rough. Flak was intense over target and Jerry wasn't kidding. Two holes in glass in nose, half a dozen in the chin turret. Saw one ship go down. He peeled off four times and pulled out three. I didn't see any chutes open before he went into the clouds. Threw out all kinds of chaff but in spite of that lots of guys lost engines."

As the missions began to pile up, the glamour and the eagerness faded and Smith's record of events began to include more mundane reflections. "Gee, is it ever rough to get up at 3:30. You're just in the midst of your sleep and dreams and just getting warmed up finally. Some guy comes along and says, 'Briefing at 4:30. You roll over and say, OK, and want to go right on dreamin' but you know one minute late means no two-day pass." During these off-duty intervals he toured, where along with the typical sightseeing, he gaped at the bomb damage done by the V-2 rockets. After several trips he remarked, "London is getting kinda boring now. We've seen all of it and probably won't go back again. Besides, it's getting dangerous there!!! You can't hear those damn rockets coming and they're deadly as heck!!!" As a resident of Great Ashfield, he frequently saw them overhead: "They rightfully call this tract of land between here and London, 'Buzz Bomb Alley.'"

Occasionally he savored the scenery from the cockpit. "Clouds were really beautiful. You never know how beautiful the world can look . . . a world of sun, clouds, sky and green earth below. If I ever get a chance I'm going to take Naomi up. She would really enjoy it." Numerous entries record his joy when a batch of letters from Naomi arrived.

Such raptures in the skies were few. Says Smith, "The weather in Europe was horrible. Clouds and rain on the ground and often rain above the clouds. The contrails from hundreds of planes was like soup. We were lost most of the time. Couldn't see the ground. Couldn't see the stars. Fortunately coming back from missions we always had a radio beam to home in on and could usually find the field even though we couldn't see it."

By the time of his seventh mission, he had impressed his superiors enough for them to suggest he attend school to be a squadron lead. Smith remarked, "It would be nice to get a captaincy out of this deal but to be a squadron lead takes lots longer to finish up, and then [you must] stay over several months after you finish your missions as a squadron operations officer. I'm afraid that's not for me 'cause I'm too hot for getting home!"

Along with rural recruits, like McCauley and Gatlin, the Air Corps attracted city boys, like Chicagoan Charles W. Halper who enlisted in November 1942. "I was a 'hot pilot,'" says Halper recalling his cadet days. "We would shoot touch and go night landings in a BT-13, nicknamed the 'Vultee [the manufacturer] Vibrator' or 'Washing Machine' for the number of cadets who washed out trying to fly her. Every landing I did was a 'grease' job [smooth], one after another perfect. I would casually light up a cigarette. The BT-13s all leaked oil and fuel which sloshed around in the bottom of the fuselage about three feet below the seat and so smoking was strictly prohibited; prohibited applied to all except the hot pilots, like me. On one of my landings, I caught some prop wash and between controlling the stick, the throttle and the manual flap control, I dropped the cigarette. It stuck on a cross member in the bottom of the fuselage where it glowed bright red in the draft.

"I flew in a wide, exaggerated pattern and I spit down on that cigarette until my mouth went dry and I could spit no more. Realizing that the next landing might jar it loose and bring on a fire I was near panic. On the extended final approach, the solution came to me in a flash. I simply unzipped, took out Wilbur and wet down the entire bottom of the fuselage, putting out the cigarette and diluting the fuel oil as well."

Halper moved on to the B-17 Transition School at Hendricks Field in Sebring, Florida. He was bemused to come across a captain and a first lieutenant swapping punches in the ready room. He learned the cause of the fight. During the long triangulation flights over the Gulf of Mexico, with just two pilots as crew, a pair of women, trained as radio operators, would handle communications. The pilots ordinarily arranged for one man to take on cockpit duties while the other would be free to go to the radio compartment and attempt to entertain one or both women. The pair battling in the ready room were contesting which would get an opportunity with a particularly good looking blonde scheduled for the flight. When peace was declared, the women were both removed and male radio operators substituted.

A replacement with the 385th Bomb Group, Chuck Halper flew his first mission against Münster late in October of 1944. As the missions piled up, he coped with the loss of two of his crew to injuries, and four officers with whom he shared quarters were shot down. Halper continued to play the role of hot pilot. "Every now and again, to lighten things up in the cockpit, I would take a deep lung full of pure oxygen off the 'full rich' position on my regulator. Then I'd put a lit cigarette in my mouth, tap my co-pilot on the shoulder and when he turned toward me, I would exhale and the flame would shoot within inches of his nose.

"I happened to tell Captain Hunter, our medical officer, what I was doing. He said, 'Idiot,' a nickname he had given me sometime before, 'if you had inhaled instead of exhaled you could have blown your lungs out.' I still thought it was a great joke, because sanity was slipping away quickly."

Halper and his crew were also diverted by the behavior of their navigator. "He had a nervous stomach. Regardless of the food, prepared for us, no beans or sauerkraut, he would be in distress about every fifth or sixth mission. He carried big paper containers with lids which he picked up from the mess hall. And despite layers of clothing, parachute harness, Mae West, heated suit, trousers, long johns, etc., he would make his contribution in the containers, slap the lid on and get dressed. Later, when the bombardier took over on the bomb run, the navigator would hook up to a portable oxygen bottle, pick up the carton and go back and stand in the bomb bay. When the first bomb fell free, he would throw the container out. We were all somewhat flak happy and each of us accepted his behavior as perfectly normal. We named his special bomb *flieger sheit*, German for flying shit. We joked about the Germans saying, 'It's not bad enough they drop bombs on us, but now they're shitting on us.' It helped to be able to joke about things like this during the long flight back to base."

Like Jim McCubbin and Wayne Gatlin, Earl Pate Jr. had been infatuated with airplanes from an early age. Growing up in Tennessee, Pate, born in 1923, says, "I never missed any movies with an aviation plot— *Hell's Angels, The Dawn Patrol, Hell Divers*. I pleaded to be taken to the local airport on Sunday to watch planes. I built models of World

War I aircraft, drew pictures in my school notebook, and was well aware of World War I aces, Luftberry, Rickenbacker, Luke, von Richthofen. I could identify planes, the Spad, DH4, Nieuport, Fokker. Although my father did not want me to fly and gave me no assistance or encouragement, I earned two dollars and twenty cents each Saturday working in a grocery store for sixteen hours to pay for lessons. I soloed at sixteen. No solo, even in jets or as a mach buster [sound barrier breakthrough] ever came close to that thrill on that snowy day in 1940."

Entering the Army at age nineteen, Pate brought a half year at Vanderbilt University and a private pilot's license with him. Accepted as a cadet, he quickly progressed through the phases of training. Assigned as a B-17 pilot, Pate describes the ground school on the Fortress as "at best casual. We had no printed check lists. Everything was verbal. There were no schematics on the various systems of the aircraft. Power setting, fuel consumption, three-engine performance and 'hands-on' experience was it." Casual also marked the preferred ambience for bomber crew relationships, the intimate team composed of both enlisted men and commissioned officers. Pate and several colleagues received a hurried assignment to crews preparing for overseas, because he says, "Eight West Point graduate pilots were relieved of crew training since their attitude was not conducive to crew bonding. They insisted upon shoeshine inspections, always 'sir' on the radio, and generally rigid rank distinctions. These 'future generals' were sent to navigator and bombardier training units. There they could pull their rank to their hearts' content."

Pate and his crew sailed to England. "It was the luck of the draw whether you flew a plane over or went by ship." His was one of five replacement units forwarded to the 91st Bomb Group at Bassingbourn. "We had very little squadron training, merely formation flying. When it was discovered you could hold a tight wing position, you were assigned a mission. During the first two or three of these, my crew and I all flew in their various positions, with experienced crews. No two of my crew were in the same plane. I saw my first aircraft shot down. I pointed it out to the 'instructor' pilot whose only comment was 'I bet he thinks this is a rough mission.' The aircraft was not from our group and one had a tendency to take a detached attitude, perhaps a kind of insulation.

"The flak reminded me of black barbells in appearances. When you were taking hits, it reminded me of throwing gravel on a tin roof. When you could taste the cordite, see the flame, hear loud crunches, feel the concussion like turbulent air and see things like holes in our wings where there had been none, it got your attention. Funny stuff, flak. You could see the group ahead of you getting shot to pieces and, by the time you got there, nothing. At other times, the sky would be clear and then suddenly the sky was black with it all around you. Once, it was rather quiet, we were off the target on withdrawal. I saw only a couple of bursts, yet, part of it went through my right wing and severed all the cables to the throttles and rpm controls for the No. 3 and 4 engines. The most I ever saw of flak damage was in a group ahead of us. I counted seven B-17s going down while the first had not hit the ground. I bet they thought it was a rough mission."

While the men in the bombers worried over the ever heavier concentrations of flak, fighter pilots like Wayne Gatlin regarded it more as an annoyance than a genuine threat. After his second mission, he remarked, "One of the fellows is quoted as saying, 'why the flak was so thick, even the automatic pilots in the bombers were bailing out.' That's what's nice about fighters—you can dodge flak easily whereas the bomber boys can't do it very well, especially on the bomb run."

Earl Pate coped with other problems. "I learned the hard way that our training had been inadequate. There should have been practice bomb runs because from the I.P. to the target, the squadron formation pattern changed. I had no knowledge of this. During the first couple of missions, the planes I was in were not affected. But during the first mission with my own crew this created a problem and messed up the whole squadron bomb pattern. No briefing or instruction was given to me on this and when I did not move into [the correct position], plus the fact that only half of my bombs got away because the switch for bomb release was not in the armed position on the left side, all hell broke loose. Between trying to talk to the togglier and correct the matter, release the rest of my load, stay in position during the turn off the target and the squadron CO yelling at me, I was ready to shoot the whole bunch down and join the Germans!

"By the time I came to the squadron I was a twenty-year-old with a responsibility that neither I, and I am sure very few others understood. We were only vaguely familiar with the aircraft's performance, its limitations and emergency procedures. Looking back, I realize how little we knew of four-engine minimum-control speed, two- or even three-engine minimum-control speed. We had no de-ice alcohol for the props. Nor did I know how to operate the de-icer boots on the wings. Why bother; the wing de-icer boots were removed. Patching a hole in those things was an impossible task. This wasn't the fault of those in command. It was the expedience of the times. Aircraft losses were expected and if any accident investigations were conducted it was lip service at best."

In terms of living quarters, Pate admits he was lucky in his assignment to Bassingbourn. "It was a permanent RAF installation and was known as the Savoy of the Eighth Air Force. No duck boards, Quonset huts, coal stoves, mud and two blocks to a latrine, thank you very much. It [the base] was in a beautiful Georgian style. All quarters were of brick, two stories, tiled baths, paved roads. Officers' quarters were two men to a room. About every six weeks the whole group would stand down and there would be a party/dance that started about dark and lasted until the next morning. The entire nursing staff from a general military hospital up the road would be invited. To supplement them, about four in the afternoon of the party, GI trucks would go to the several villages in the area and all the English girls would be invited. Crowds would gather at the base HQ as the trucks returned. If none of the ladies accepted your offer to be her escort for the evening, you simply waited a few minutes until the next truck arrived. During the party, the usual drinks were boilermakers—a water tumbler half-full of Scotch and half-full of beer. Very effective for a festive mood."

It was a far different atmosphere before a mission. "A list was posted that listed the crews for each squadron and the next morning's mission. For some reason, alert time was usually at 2:00 A.M. I got to the point where I would automatically wake up about ten minutes before and wait to hear the squeal of the Jeep stopping out front and hear the CQ [charge of quarters] coming up the steps, followed by the rap on the door and the call, 'Alert, lieutenant. Briefing at three.' That gave you an hour to pull on your clothes, walk about one-quarter mile to breakfast and then back to the briefing. For breakfast we either had square eggs [powdered], toast, cereal or stove lids they called pancakes. I hit on the idea that on my one day stand down [customary but not always given after three missions] to stop at the various farms and buy eggs. I quickly learned to bring one for the cook or chances were yours would get accidentally dropped.

"During the briefing, every eye would follow the long, half-inch-wide red ribbon that led from our base to the target. A graph of the squadron showed the position each crew would be flying, time to start engines, taxi and takeoff. There would be a point on the east coast, Felixstowe, where the bomber stream would depart the UK. [We would be told] the weather over the target and on return, the flak expected by some intelligence officer who would never see any himself and always got it wrong."

Having shaved closely to avoid discomfort with a sweaty oxygen mask, gathered his crew and with them gone through the preflight procedures, Pate says, "It was always eerie quiet just before engine start with everyone in position and waiting. Then one or two engines started; then the whole roar of all 140 engines of the thirty-six aircraft soon to depart. You watched the tower for the flare (green) signal to taxi. Red flare shut down and wait—white—mission scrubbed. Daylight joinups were easy. A predawn joinup, a low overcast that you had to climb until you were on top, sometimes 18,000 to 20,000 feet and then try to join up was terrible. Scary! Imagine a thousand airplanes trying to line up in groups of thirty-six, spaced two minutes apart in pitch-black darkness and over an exact spot on the English Channel at a precise time, make the orderly, perfect formation envisioned by the men behind armor-plated desks, you get a feeling for the high risk of collision.

"Early in my tour when I was back in the pack and after we had a predawn 'demolition derby' I would go straight to Felixstowe and when the group or what part of it was together crossed at the designated time, I'd slide into position. The Krauts were doing their best to kill us. I didn't see any need of helping them by letting some silly SOB going the wrong way run into me. There were midair collisions but if you consider the hundreds of bombers without radar-control milling around in darkness trying to join up in tight formations, the number of these accidents were surprisingly few. When it did happen, two 65,000-pound, four-engine aircraft loaded with bombs and 2,780 gallons of high octane made a very untidy mess. The horrible crashes I have seen over the years still fill me with wonder at the human animal who has such a morbid fascination with violent death and will rush to any kind of accident. If ever you have smelled that nauseating sweet stink of burning human flesh scattered in unrecognizable chunks of meat among equally unrecognizable pieces of metal, it will fill you with a horrible memory you never escape."

While Pate learned on the job and developed his own techniques to enhance his chances of survival, Wayne Gatlin, who had barely seen action in P-47s, began the transition to new equipment. He wrote home. "I was up in the Peter-51 today and she's sure a sweet flying ship. Seems so tiny after Dumbo" [like "Jug" another affectionate nickname for the Thunderbolts]. He had created a code expression, "up in the blue" to signify a combat mission to his parents. In late November he wrote, "I was up in the blue today for a long spell again. We had quite a time too. Say, Pops, you can tell Noah Rawn [a next-door neighbor and railroad engineer] that I'm sure glad he wasn't at the controls of three jobs I messed up. Nope, it wouldn't have been healthy for him, if you get what

I mean. I worked 'em over in good shape and what a thrill it was. Sure is satisfying to know that you are doing some good now and then."

During the summer of 1944, U.S. fighter pilots had begun to experiment with primitive versions of a pressure suit, an aid for preventing loss of consciousness during sudden maneuvers at high speeds that sharply increased the gravitational forces. By the time Gatlin made the transition to the P-51, all U.S. fighter pilots were wearing a pressure suit, inflatable pads around the torso and legs. On October 30, Hub Zemke, returning to the wars after a stateside sojourn, led a group of fighters shepherding B-24s bound for Hamburg. His flight encountered savage turbulence which hurled the Mustangs into violent spins. The G-suit enabled Zemke to retain consciousness long enough to bail out even as his plane broke apart. Captured by the Germans, Zemke disappeared into Stalag Luft I at Barth, joining there, among others, Henry Spicer, Francis Gabreski and Irwin Stovroff.

THE G-suit that enabled Zemke to survive had been issued to Gatlin's group after they checked into P-51s. "The suit reminded one of cowboy chaps as it fit over the legs and wrapped around the waist," recalls Gatlin. "As you pulled Gs [One G equals the gravitational pull equal to one's weight] the bladders in each leg filled and then moved on up to the bladder around the waist. The tighter you pulled, the more the pressure exerted on the legs and stomach. It prevented you from 'graying' or 'blacking' out as it maintained a good supply of blood out of the extremities to feed the brain. One of our flight leaders didn't like the legs of the suit and elected to remove them and use only the stomach portion. After tangling with an FW-190 one day and having the bladder kick him in the stomach 'like a mule,' he reattached the legs."

Gatlin, like Pate, regarded the gathering of the flock among the more dangerous phases of an operation. "A typical mission for the group called for three squadrons of sixteen birds each. There would also be a couple of spares per unit so usually about fifty-four birds took to the sky on a normal effort. Spares would usually return early if not needed. To get this mass of aircraft airborne, joined up and on course with minimum delay and loss of petrol was a sight to behold.

"The lead squadron would take the active [runway] and move as far down as possible to ensure getting safely airborne. Lead would take one side of the runway and the wingmen would take the opposite side. We would jam as many birds on the active as possible and as the second hand hit 'Takeoff' a flag officer would send the first two racing down the runway. As soon as the first birds lifted their tailwheels off the runway, the flag man would send the next two and so on until the entire group was airborne. Lead would go straight out for a bit and then commence a turn and each succeeding element would cut the turn and slide into proper position. Individual flights would join up in a tight fingertip and succeeding flights would slide into a tight string formation. Subsequent squadrons would pull up almost abreast of the group lead, with one on each side.

"If there was an overcast to penetrate and joinup was underneath, the group lead would wait until everyone was in formation. He'd then climb out on a set heading with the left and right squadrons trying to maintain visual contact with the lead squadron. Everyone caged and set their directional gyros on the climb-out heading, and one always hoped precession [a potential distortion that could occur in the process] wouldn't do you in if you lost contact. Some of those climb-outs were hairy and times when contact was lost and you dearly hoped that once you broke out on top you could reestablish contact and get on with the mission.

"There were times when the mission was a 'go' however, while the prevailing ceilings and visibility precluded a joinup underneath. You would then take off by element, climb on course and join up on top. I remember being number four in a flight and watching the lead element roll ahead of us. Next I was on the wing, in the soup and climbing out. Breaking out on top there was only the lead ship ahead of us. We flew the mission as planned; the spare moved into number two's slot. Not until hours later did we learn that number two had crashed shortly after takeoff and was killed. He apparently got vertigo, fell off his lead's wing and the war was over for him, victim of another enemy.

"Six hours at altitude without cockpit pressurization was rigorous," says Gatlin. "You had to battle fatigue, the cold and that insidious foe, hypoxia [oxygen deprivation]. I came close to becoming a casualty on my second mission. We were on our way home and I was told that I pulled ahead of my flight, and then peeled off back toward Germany, all by myself. My flight leader, Hank Laviolette, repeatedly called me but got no response. When I did come to I was all by myself, had lost a lot of altitude and was scared as hell. I imagined the sky filling with ME-109s and having at me. Fortunately, the bombers were conning very heavily [exuding thick contrails], and I tightened my mask, cobbed the engine and climbed up into the con train until over friendly territory. I got a new mask when I got home.

"Along with several others I watched hypoxia claim another victim on a later mission. We were stooging along at 35,000 feet, trying to make a rendezvous with some chaff-dropping Mustangs, somewhere in that bottomless miasma of clouds. We had been at altitude for quite some time, just barely skimming the tops of the cirrus. I noticed a ship in the flight off to my right behaving erratically. He was weaving back and forth and suddenly stalled and flipped over on his back in a death spiral down through the cirrus. You could see the corkscrew of his spin [from his contrail] a long way down through the stuff. His flight lead was calling, 'Blue 2, pull out.' 'Blue 2, pull out.' After a moment or two of silence the group lead, realizing the futility of the mission said, 'Let's go home.' We were to learn later that the pilot lived. He apparently came to at a lower altitude and bailed out before the bird crashed. Another victory [or defeat] without a shot being fired."

FIGHTERS, flak, human errors, mechanical malfunctions and weather combined to strike the Eighth as the war ground on. Because of the heavy casualties in his squadron, Bill Frankhouser from the 398th Bomb Group left the Herb Newman crew to serve as a lead navigator aboard another ship for the outfit. Bombardier Dean Whitaker now took his slot under Newman with tail gunner Arnold Money assuming the role of togg, lier. Another member of the Newman crew begged off further combat duty following a trip to Cologne where the lead navigator missed the target and forced the section to make a 180-degree turn in order to drop the bombs. The delay enabled the flak gunners to zero in and put 110 holes in the horizontal stabilizer, although Newman and copilot Paul Deininger nursed the B-17 back to base.

For the Newman crew's navigator, Dean Whitaker, the wakeup call on November 2, presaged his twentieth mission. "The first thought was whether this would be a short run to the front lines or a deep penetration into Germany. Deep silence prevailed when the operations officer walked up to the eight-foot by eight-foot wall map covered with a white sheet and with a sweep of his arm revealed the mission for today. It was not going to be an easy trip, as attested by the moans and groans of some crew members. The red yarn from our base to the target stretched to the center of Germany, an eight-hour mission.

"Our crew met outside the briefing room and exchanged a few greetings. The tail gunner, Bill Jones, always complained about being disturbed from a dream he never completes. Our leader was the pilot, Herb Newman, who at twenty-nine was the oldest. Paul [Deininger] the copilot was also in the old category at twenty-five. I was the navigator and having just turned nineteen was the youngest. Loaded down with all the gear we needed, we gathered around the silver flying machine. Herb always got us together and said a little prayer before we climbed into the plane."

Upon the flare signal, Herb Newman and Deininger lifted *Knockout,* a B-17, off the Nuthampstead runway and guided the plane into its slot as lead ship of the Tail-end Charlie element for the 603rd Squadron as it droned towards Merseburg. The specific objective was the Leuna refinery, an objective fiercely guarded because oil had become the major resource in short supply.

From his post in the nose, Whitaker says, "Every time I looked back to see the coast of England vanishing from sight under the bright aluminum belly of our B-17 I wondered if we would see it again. Being a positive thinker, I thought someone has to come back; they can't shoot us all down. Flying across the Channel was just a short hop and [we] were busy checking our guns, radio equipment, oxygen masks, etc. Checking the guns was always hold-the-breath time. When the group leader gave the word, thirty-six planes started to test-fire their guns; this amounted to 300 .50 caliber machine guns being fired at one time. Some of the fresh-from-the-States gunners would be so anxious they forgot to look where they were aiming. We might have lost a few planes to the careless gunners.

"Approaching the coast of Holland we could see the beautiful countryside that the farmers had created through their unplanned yet symmetric placement of different crops to create a pattern any modern artist would envy. Farther into the Continent we approached the shaky, uncertain lines of German defenses. This was always marked by a few bursts of flak to wake up the crew. Today was no exception; the few shots that came up at us were like a roadsign telling us where we were, about thirty minutes from our target.

"Straining our eyes to catch the first glimpses of our target we witnessed a maximum effort by the Eighth Air Force as streams of bombers and a protective cover of fighter planes converged on the synthetic oil refinery. The sightseeing was soon over when a huge black cloud became visible ahead of us. It was made by hundreds of 88 mm guns; the Germans must have moved every gun in Germany there to protect this refinery. Being the last group over the target was no blessing. The Germans were getting more accurate with their guns as demonstrated by the B-17s going down ahead of us. Some would be on fire and others would be missing vital parts, like a wing or tail. Knowing it would soon be our turn to run the gauntlet made blood pressure rise.

"On approaching the turning point to the target, the bomb run started. Lowering the bomb bay doors seemed to stop the plane in mid-air when actually we only lost about ten mph. Wishing the plane could do 600 mph instead of the 150 we were now at, the bomb run began. Flak was everywhere, to the right, left, overhead, ahead, sometimes so close you could hear the dull thud of it exploding. Smelling burning metal I knew we had been hit. All I could hope was that it was not something important. All of a sudden the black cloud of a shell explod-ing directly in front of us, sent bits of steel through the nose. Luckily nothing major was hit, although some noisy holes marked the plexiglass.

"This brought a big distraction to the job of dropping our bombs. Finally, the bombs away signal was given. The sudden release of a belly full of bombs gave the B-17 a new surge of life. It shot up a few feet and increased its speed about ten knots which was great with us. The sooner we got out of the flak area, the better. As suddenly as we had entered it, we left, exposing a beautiful, clear sky with no ugly scars from dark clouds of gunfire.

"No sooner had we cleared the flak area," Whitaker remembers, "when a cry of 'Bandits' erupted over the intercom. After surviving all that flak it seems we should at least get a break from the German fight-ers but no such luck. Looking up at the planes in our group, I could see the tail guns of those ahead and above us moving about, seeking a target. Flying in the last group of planes over the target was not the best place to be at this time but who do you complain to.

"In a few minutes, the fight was on. The German planes hit us first with their 20 mm cannons which had a longer range than our .50 caliber guns. The tail gunner was giving us a blow-by-blow account of what was going on. Being in the nose and the attack coming from the rear, all I could do was watch and listen. Smelling the familiar smell of hot, burning metal I knew we had been hit again.

"Crying out over the intercom was the voice of the tail gunner saying he had been hit. Sending the waist gunner back to check him out, we waited for the next attack which came very suddenly. There was no sitting back and lobbing 20 mm shells at us this time. They made a direct pass at our tail. Apparently the waist gunner had taken over the tail guns because he was shouting that he had hit one. Sure enough I looked down below us and saw an FW-190 going down trailing black smoke. About this time all hell broke loose, apparently our tail got shot off because the plane was going every way but straight and the odor of burning airplane was very apparent."

Copilot Deininger recalls, "We had dropped our bombs on the target and were heading home when we encountered fighters. We had P-51s and P-47s for escort, but they were at the head of the formation and we were flying Tail-end Charlie. We called for fighter support but before they reached us, we had suffered a hit in the astrodome and the tail gunner Bill Jones [the interrupted dreamer] had a direct hit which killed him.

"After the hit in the astrodome, some of the instruments in the cockpit popped out of the panel and we went into a dive. There was very little, if any, control with the stick or wheel and we couldn't keep up with the formation. Additionally, we were losing altitude at a terrific rate. I said to Newman, 'Goose the throttles some more and see if we can't get up under the formation so we can get some protection from the tail gunners ahead of us.' Newman replied, 'I'm afraid if I do that the engines might explode.'

"I then asked him if I should give the order to bail out, to which he replied, 'Yes.' I lowered the landing gear so that the Germans knew that we were totally disabled and engaged the automatic pilot, hoping that it would level off the aircraft to enable us to jump. I gave the order to bail out, dropped down between the two seats and headed for the exits. Before I jumped, I yelled to Newman, 'Let's get the hell out of here,' because he was still sitting in his seat. He replied, 'I'll be right there.'

"We wore chest packs and because it didn't interfere with our flying, we only hooked up one side of the pack and let the other dangle between the seats. Because of all of the excitement, I forgot to hook up the other side of my chute and I came all the way down on one riser from an altitude of about 22,000 feet. To avoid getting tangled in the aircraft, I fell free for about 1,000 feet before I pulled the rip cord. There was complete cloud cover below me and by this time our fighter escort reached the scene and engaged the German fighters in an air battle. I could hear the bullets passing by my ear and never thought I would make it to the ground in one piece," notes Deininger.

Before leaping out, Whitaker, who also buckled only one side of his chest pack, tried to remove his flak jacket through an emergency release, but when he pulled the tab, nothing happened. He abandoned his efforts and dove out the nose escape hatch. "As soon as I hit the slipstream going by at 160 knots, the flak suit ripped off. I was free now to put the rest of my chute on but the only problem was that due to the lack of oxygen and the force of the wind I could not get the other side of the chute fastened. Trying to accomplish this while falling toward the ground was like attempting to get out of the way of a train but being unable to move. As soon as I entered a layer of low stratus clouds, I knew it was now or never time to pull the rip cord. Being half-dazed by the lack of oxygen, it seemed as if I was floating through the air without a worry in the world. This abruptly was broken by the sound of rifle fire and bullets zinging by me. Looking down, I could see a couple of Germans shooting at me. Also there was some kind of camp to one side of the field I was heading for. Before I hit the ground, a soldier came running out of this camp. He stopped the civilians from shooting me. At this time I noticed my chute was buckled on both sides. Sometime during the struggle to hook it, I must have made it. Hitting the ground hard dazed me for a few minutes, but when I looked up the German soldier was standing over me with his rifle pointed at me, arguing with the civilians not to shoot me."

Deininger remembers, "My bombardier [S. Sgt Arnold Money acting as togglier] and I landed about 1,000 feet apart and were picked up by the Landwacht [home guard]. I had come down in a plowed field and before I could get out of my chute, he had a rifle at my head shouting, 'Pistol! Pistol!' Having had five years of German, I replied, 'Ich habe kein Pistol.' This was the wrong thing to say, because later they took me to Luftwaffe headquarters for interrogation, thinking I might be a spy. At the interrogation a German enlisted man stood behind me with a rifle and threatened to hit me with his rifle butt when I refused to answer questions."

This grilling, because of his acquaintance with the German language, occurred some hours later. More immediately, Deininger recalled, "They rounded us up and I would say there may have been forty or fifty men. We must have lost five or six planes in the group. [Officially the 398th listed three B-17s missing in action but nine more from other groups attacking Merseburg also went down.] All the men on our crew got out safely, except the tail gunner who was already dead. We knew this because one of the waist gunners checked on him and reported back to me while still in the plane. Four of our men landed in one area and were spotted in our chutes by a German officer on the roadway. He stopped the civilians from harming us. The rest of the crew landed in a different area and were picked up by civilians alone."

According to Whitaker, "We were at a POW camp that held British soldiers. Being the first one out of the plane I was the first captured.

Within a few minutes three other members of the crew [Deininger, S. Sgt. Arnold Money and S. Sgt. Cornelius Harrington] were brought in to the camp. No one was injured except Sergeant Money who had caught some 20 mm flak in one foot. He could still walk and the British soldiers cleaned it up for him. Although we were glad to see each other, we wondered where the rest of our crew was."

Like the quartet that included Whitaker, the other four in the Newman crew including the pilot, parachuted to earth safely in the vicinity of Polleben, a small town northwest of Merseburg. Unfortunately, there were no German soldiers around when a band of Nazi party members, which included the local leader, the Polleben police chief and several cohorts, set upon them. Herb Newman, radio operator Melvin Cohen, gunners Leroy Kucharski and Anthony Perry were murdered, either clubbed, shot or stabbed according to different investigators, then buried in paper bags along with the corpse of Bill Jones, the tail gunner whose remains were found in the wreckage of *Knockout*.

Still ignorant of the fate of their comrades, the four survivors, after their interviews with Luftwaffe intelligence specialists, became residents of Stalag Luft III. Deininger notes, "The enlisted men were kept separate from the officers [in a different section of the same camp] because they had to go out on work detail helping to clean up some of the bombing mess."

Togglier Al Greenberg in the 96th Bomb Group made the journey to Merseburg that same November 2, and he declares that at the I.P., "I saw the first flak—much more than I'd ever seen before or hope to see again. It made a complete carpet and the sky was black with it. Finally, they dropped their bombs and I did likewise. Flak was still something awful, but the evasive action was good. Most of it went to either side. Then something popped in front of me and I had pieces of plexiglass all over my flak suit. Right in front of me was a hole about as big as a quarter and a cold draft rushed in. Otherwise the trip home was uneventful. I slept most of the way, and my escape kit covered the hole. Everyone along today said they saw more flak than all the other missions put together."

Merseburg on November 2, the fifth mission for 96th Bomb Group pilot Al Ganyu, added a bizarre quality to the intense ground fire. The son of Hungarian émigrés, Ganyu notes, "My father was urged to come to McKeesport, Pennsylvania, by U.S. Steel recruiters." With a diploma from McKeesport Technical High School in 1941, Ganyu enrolled at a state teachers college while working during his summers. He volunteered for the Air Corps in December 1942, to beat both the draft and the closing of enlistments.

His replacement crew made its combat debut over Cologne. "I remember the briefing specifically telling us to avoid bombing the cathedral. On this mission our bomb bay doors would not open, not even with the salvo switch which flings the doors open and also drops the airplane. We flew the same airplane on our third mission and the same thing happened. We had to crank the doors open and closed by hand which meant that the engineer, McNeil, had to go back to the bomb bay, stand on the narrow catwalk, leaning to the side and crank the doors. Since we were at high altitude, McNeil used a walk-around oxygen bottle. It was made of metal with fifteen to twenty minutes' supply of oxygen. It was very dangerous because the bottle clipped onto the flight suit or parachute harness and easily came apart with all that movement. When all this was new, who keeps track of time?

"We had a lot of problems on the Merseburg mission of November 2, none of which seem to have been reported. After we dropped our bombs, we increased our speed to get off the target and away from the intense flak. The next thing we knew we were over Leipzig where we turned around for home. But there was a strange wind phenomenon. I think we encountered the jet stream which we didn't know about then. It blew us over Leipzig and it took forever to get away from there. Not only did we have to fly through the Merseburg flak but also the Leipzig flak, and it was intense and interminable. Our ground speed must have been about fifty miles an hour when we were up against a jet stream of 100 or more miles per hour. We didn't talk about it because I guess we didn't want to be labeled as goofy or crazy.

"Our group CO, Col. Robert Warren, kept us in formation and at 24,000 feet. As we were flying home, some crews began to be concerned with having enough fuel to get home. An occasional request came over the radio to let down, reduce altitude to save fuel, but the colonel was adamant about staying in formation and staying off the air. He denied all such requests. Finally, ships started to leave the formation as we neared the coast. The colonel's ship did not make it back to Snetterton Heath that day. I believe nine of us made it back to our base and I was the first to land. All nine of us should have received the DFC for this mission. The ground personnel told us we all made picture-perfect textbook landings with each plane in the exact position to have three planes on the runway at one time. My crew chief told me I had twenty gallons of fuel left which would not have been enough for a go-around. Alas no DFC, no commendation and nothing in the stories about the wind and Leipzig."

Arthur Prager, a New Yorker whose father owned a drug store, also saw Merseburg on November 2 from his navigator's post in a 92nd Bomb Group B-17. "I volunteered for the Air Force because it was an elite and I had never belonged to an elite, nor was I likely to have an opportunity to join one. I did have heroic vision stimulated by films like *The Dawn Patrol* and *Hell's Angels*. The novels of Alexandre Dumas helped too. It seemed to me that fortunes and glittering careers could be made from battlefield service. And I desperately wanted to be an officer.

"I felt that if there was a war one ought to do some actual fighting. Too many of my friends were scurrying about looking for safe berths in the Army Finance Corps in Kansas City or in the Coast Guard. I had nothing but contempt for them. The comfort did help. I didn't look forward to muddy trenches and foxholes. I later learned that eight hours a day in an unpressurized plane at sixty degrees below zero was in no way more comfortable than trenches."

With three years of college, Prager easily qualified for the cadet program and breezed through the academic portion of his program. "When I had passed the primary Air Corps schools I had a hard decision to make. Although I wanted to be a fighter pilot, the washout rate was high. Navigation, however, was mostly classroom stuff based on simple mathematics. I knew I could become a navigator easily but becoming a pilot was risky, with the danger of washing out and being returned to the ranks."

Having opted for the sure thing, Prager won his wings and commission. "After being placed on a crew and flying around Oklahoma and Nebraska with them a few times we were shipped overseas. The training between the end of advanced navigator training and overseas assignment was totally inadequate. When we got to England we got practically no instruction but were promptly tacked on to the tail end of a squadron formation and sent out on bombing missions.

"After we got over Germany and saw our first flak, I ceased to be apprehensive. Like all twenty-two-year-olds, I had a strong feeling of immortality. When the first shells didn't hit me I felt that none ever would. I was worried at first about measuring up. Suppose I was a coward and the others weren't. Could I ever hold my head up again. To us superannuated teenagers the war and the missions were like a series of high school football games. We wanted to win and show ourselves as stars. Few of us were afraid of death, but we were all terrified of mutilation, loss of organs and parts, blindness and the like. On that first mission, everyone behaved very well. We were all terrified of the dangerous unknown but we didn't show it. One of the crew threw up in his oxygen mask, but no one knew it until we were back down on the ground again. He flew the whole mission with a mask full of vomit rather than let the others see that he had shown fear.

"The worst missions I ever flew were four to Merseburg in November 1944, to the Leuna Synthetic Oil plants. [The raids cost the Eighth at least seventy-five bombers and more than 750 men.] From the I.P. to target, about thirty miles at 126–130 miles per hour, was the worst part of a mission, because there was no possibility of a change of route or evasive action. For important targets, the Germans had figured out long before the bomb run where we were going and brought in extra flak on trucks and railway flatcars. They laid a huge carpet of exploding shells at our altitude over the target, hoping for random kills rather than aiming at the planes. As we went down the bomb run we could see that great black cloud ahead of us but there wasn't anything we could do but keep on going. The worst was when we didn't complete the drop because of some bomb-sight or bomb-release malfunction. We then had to make a 360-degree turn and do the whole bomb run a second time with the deputy lead plane taking lead position. That gave the German gunners ample time to correct the sighting or altitude errors made during the first run."

Al Greenberg was assigned to loose the bombs for Ganyu during a November 9 attack on Saarbrucken that was marked by extreme temperatures. Greenberg recalls it as the coldest day since he had arrived. "My hands went numb trying to put the guns in and I had to call an armorer to finally install them. The cold [at altitude] was terrific. Finally it was bombs away. The bomb doors wouldn't close electrically and the pilot was having a fit, as he couldn't keep airspeed. After about fifteen minutes, the engineer cranked them up. "The trouble was," says Greenberg, "that at 30,000 feet, half the devices which worked on the ground didn't function." He would be vexed by mechanical problems throughout his thirty-five missions.

The omnipresent peril in tight formation flying came home to the 385th Bomb Group while en route to Wetzlar on November 21. Myron "Frenchie" Loyat, drafted in 1942, and a volunteer for cadet training after a stint as a medical records clerk, was the bombardier on a B-17. As a member of a crew under the pilot, Lieutenant Foss, Loyat had come to England in June 1944, and was now well into his tour.

"We were flying squadron lead. Fighters were always looking for the loose formation in the bomber stream which necessitated tucking aircraft in as close as possible [for mutual protection]. The low echelon lead under us came too close. The pilot must have miscalculated and his high vertical stabilizer clipped the ball turret of our aircraft and flipped his ship up to our port side.

"The impact of the collision bent both props on our No. 1 and 2 engines, necessitating feathering them. The plexiglass nose shattered and disappeared. Our pilot never issued a bailout but the bombardier could see disaster and jumped out after impact, followed by the engineer. They used the escape hatch on the left side of the nose. The opening created a strong wind tunnel, with a temperature at minus fifty-five Fahrenheit. Anything loose, maps, dividers, etc., went out the hatch slipstream.

"We had been at the bombing altitude of approximately 25,000 feet and we were in a dive. The pilot knew the bombardier had bailed and said over the intercom, 'Frenchie, salvo the bombs.' I did and that helped in the dive recovery, we recovered at about 18,000 feet. I had been ready to bail out myself. Fortunately, the last item for me to unplug was my headset. After I executed salvo, I felt things must be somewhat under control. I grabbed an oxygen walk-around bottle, which promptly disappeared out of the hatch with my heated gloves.

"The copilot came down from the flight deck and grabbed me, to keep me from being sucked through the escape hatch and out the door. I then flew in the left seat while the pilot went back to pry the ball-turret gunner out. His intercom and oxygen were cut off when the collision spun the ball in its mounts. We had to descend to about 12,000 feet for him to live while they were extracting him from the ball. When he was pulled out, he was in a confused state due to his lack of oxygen. A cigarette dangled from one corner of his mouth and he said, 'I thought you SOBs had all bailed out and I was having one last cigarette.'

"The pilot stayed in the waist and assisted in tossing everything out that had come loose so we could maintain altitude on two engines. We were coming back alone to England and crossed the Ruhr Valley above cloud cover. When flak appeared around us, having had pilot training, I assisted in evasive action. We noticed for the first time that our air speed indicator read 150 mph no matter what we did, up or down, veering right or left. The impact had knocked off the Pitot tube [exterior device used for airspeed calculation] and we were flying by the seat of our pants. We could easily have stalled the bird.

"Crossing the Channel, the pilot took over and we landed without hydraulics, as was anticipated. Later we got a letter through the Red Cross that our bombardier was a POW. He wrote that when I salvoed the bombs they came down around him. One had grazed his leg as he sat in his chute. Our props apparently cut up the other ship so badly that it went down and we heard that three of the ten men jumped and survived.

"The whole thing, from impact until we pulled out of the dive, took maybe twenty seconds. It was nobody's fault. The pilots were twenty to twenty-one years old, the ink hardly dry on their car drivers' licenses. They had not a lot of air hours, not a lot of formation training in flying a four-engine aircraft."

19

WOES OF WINTER

The swift strides across France and through the lowland countries, the devastating march of the Soviet armies towards Germany and the ever larger raids upon the battered cities and industrial complexes of the Third Reich by the air forces that crushed Hitler's dwindling empire generated hopes that it might all end by Christmas 1944, or the New Year. Having come through the worst episode of his combat career on his twenty-eighth mission, J. C. Wilson, as a waist gunner on a B-17 in the 351st Bomb Group, had completed his tour and been assigned to a fighter group base. "The bomb bay of a B-17 had been modified and radiomen were carried there along with our regular operator. We would be sent to Belgium and fly a set course, then relay radio messages from the fighters back to base. It was fine duty because people stationed at the base wanted to come with us and nothing ever happened to us. From reading about the First World War, I figured our war was about over." Some others who accumulated the requisite missions or combat hours [for fighter pilots], chose the dangerous work of "Buckeye Red," aircraft that preceded the bombers to a target for the purpose of transmitting information on weather and other possible problems.

While Wilson was finishing out his overseas duty in a noncombat situation, others like P-51 pilot Wayne Gatlin settled in, seemingly fully at home in their roles. By mid-1944, newcomers flew whatever plane was available and as more and more airmen arrived, many never became affiliated with a single aircraft. But Gatlin had achieved a pilot's prime status symbol, his own P-51. He wrote home: "Me and my honey (my ship) went up into the blue for a little fun today. We worked on battle formation for a while and then we started fooling around. There were some beautiful white cumulus clouds building up and boy, what sport it was in them. I spent a long time just diving, rolling and zooming thru those clouds.

"You know how some fellas are just crazy to get a car of their own. Well, I never did get that crazy, but I really know how these fellas feel because that's how I feel about my plane, only more so. It is about as wonderful a feeling as there is. It puts an added touch to flying that was never my privilege to feel until November 27. Gee, every time I even look at it, I breathe deep, put my chest out and say, 'There's the best plane on the field,' and I believe it too. Every time I start out across the North Sea, I give her a kiss and as I start back across to England, I kiss her again. She sings to me all during the mission and listens intently when I speak to her, as I often do. Not even any back talk. She agrees with me all the time. When something looks interesting, I just say, 'Let's go, baby,' and away we go."

The stubborn defenses of the Wehrmacht at the Huertgen Forest on the edge of Germany persuaded ground-troop commanders that perhaps the war was far from over. And while the newspapers spoke of almost daily thousand-plane attacks, the Eighth Air Force bled freely and required steady transfusions of fresh plasma in the form of replacements.

David Ferguson, a minister's son halfway through college when called up in 1943, started out as a cadet for pilot training but "95 percent of my class washed out and were tested and assigned as crewmen. I tested highest in radio-gunnery and was sent to Sioux Falls, South Dakota, to take courses." Subsequently posted to a B-17 crew he flew to England in August to become a member of the 94th Bomb Group.

"My first mission, to Wiesbaden, as a radio-gunner was with an experienced crew. My pilot flew copilot and I flew as a gunner. We were hit by flak which knocked out two engines and the prop ran away and came off the third engine. We made a long glide back across the battle lines with one engine, knocking over a row of trees during a belly landing in a Belgian turnip field. We were all MIA for about ten days, since it took us that long to catch a ride back across the Channel to England and our home base.

"We found our names had been scratched off the flying board and a telegram was to be mailed to my wife the next day. The crew with which I took my 'buddy ride' was killed within a few days of our landing back at the base when they collided with another bomber on final approach."

As an eleven-year-old growing up in rural Ohio, Willard Richards attended the annual "Homeday" celebration which featured seventy-five-cent airplane rides for children. Although warned by his parents to "stay away from the airplane," Richards entered a series of contests for boys his age to earn the fee. He picked up fifty cents as winner of the fifty-yard dash and then staggered home in second place in the three-legged race with a classmate for a quarter prize. Impatiently, he waited out the line for rides.

"Finally, it was my turn; all fear was gone. After all, I knew the pilot, Kenny Hoyt. He was a senior at our school. I remembered all the talk about how he had hung around the local airfield and that some experienced pilot had taught him to fly. It didn't occur to me that he had borrowed the open-cockpit, 1928-model Waco GEX biplane, and that he was flying it out of Bert Boyd's hayfield that was bounded on one side by tall towers supporting lines carrying high voltage electricity.

"Kenny helped me into the front cockpit and yelled for me to hang on or something. The engine was really noisy and the propwash drowned out whatever he said. But who cared? Taxiing for takeoff was really bumpy, but as we lifted off the ground it became unbelievably smooth.

"There I was, getting a view of my whole world from a new angle. The big shale pile by the abandoned coal mine, the outline of an old racetrack, the ponds where we skated and fished all came into view. There was the local cemetery and the steel mill where Father worked. The sandstone quarry and the new hospital on the edge of town all looked like blocks on a Monopoly board [the game hadn't been invented yet]. My grandfather's farm looked like a postage stamp and our house on the edge of the farm was so small. We descended over the high-tension wires and came in for a really rough landing. The whole flight took about ten minutes, but it changed my outlook on life."

On the ground again, Richards reached home in time for supper and no one gave him away for disobeying his parents' dictum about the airplane. But, while playing with his younger brother he made the mistake of describing what he had seen from the sky and his mother overheard him.

"She didn't say a word to me. However, just before my bedtime, Father called me out to the kitchen. There he stood, looking very stern, with razor strop in hand. He wasn't a loud or brutal man. I'm sure he doubled the strap more for the sound effect than to hurt me. He quietly told me to turn around and to drop my trousers. Then it hit me . . . flying can be hazardous to your health!"

The bottom side of his first flight failed to dampen Richards's enthusiasm for airplanes. He still rushed outdoors when he heard the sound of a motor in the sky, built models and even discovered a new hobby in photography as he tried to take pictures of his flying creations. He graduated from high school, married a young woman he met at a church-sponsored summer camp and as the war started in Europe earned nearly a dollar an hour as a clerical supervisor in a steel mill. The entry of the U.S. into World War II brought substantial overtime and uneasiness.

"My employer had arranged a series of deferments for me as an essential employee in the war effort. I felt increasingly uncomfortable sitting safely at a desk as many of my young co-workers and friends were in combat or training for it." With the agreement of his wife, Richards refused his next deferment and on July 7, 1943, volunteered for induction into the Army Corps of Engineers, where he thought he could best use his work experience.

His high scores in both the intelligence and mechanical-aptitude tests brought Richards an exemption from his commitment to the engineers. Now given a choice, he quickly asked for the Air Corps, especially after the thrill of seeing a flight of B-17s. Qualified for cadet training, a cocky Richards after some delay entered the preflight college training period and then started the first phase of pilot training. But in early April 1944, the entire officer-candidate unit designed to produce pilots, navigators and bombardiers was eliminated. Richards along with others began gunnery training.

In July, at the Lincoln, Nebraska, base, Richards became a waist gunner and a member of a crew. "I was the only one over twenty-one. When they discovered I was twenty-five, they began calling me 'Pop.' That didn't last long, however, and they settled for 'Rich.' After the requisite practice exercises, Richards and company took their B-17 across the U.S. then over the Atlantic to become replacements with the 385th. During his training period, Richards had become friendly with Dave Ferguson.

After several operations were scrubbed, Richards was awakened early on November 25 for his first mission. "After they announced our target, all of the experienced crews greeted it with loud moans. It was to be Merseburg. Some of the guys had been on two previous missions to the same target. I could tell by their reactions that it would be a rough one.

"I was in charge of the machine guns and the flak-protection clothing for the entire crew. It was my responsibility to take the equipment on a truck from the gun shack to the plane. I unloaded it, put each gun in its place and distributed the flak suits and helmets. We had practiced this phase so often it was almost automatic." Other groups were assigned duties of this nature on a different basis.

"About an hour before takeoff, Bill Poorbaugh [tail gunner], Dick

Ward [ball gunner] and I got out of the plane to wait for Bob's [pilot Robert Bensing] signal to pull the engines through. This was done by all of us grabbing hold of the same propeller blade and pulling to rotate it. The object was to loosen the oil in the engine to aid it starting up. We did this to each engine in sequence. With the aid of a portable generator hooked up to the electrical system, the engines would slowly come alive."

As a waist gunner, Richards was the one crew member able to walk freely around the aircraft, *Honky Tonk Sal*, a veteran already of eighty-seven raids. Because of his hobby of photography, he had been assigned an official camera and he packed his own personal one in his pocket, even though orders forbade shots of combat with personal equipment.

Nearing Merseburg, the enemy abundantly baptized *Honky Tonk Sal* and her companions with a concentration of flak. "The whole plane shook and one of the starboard engines appeared to be on fire," says Richards. "We had taken a solid hit, and gasoline, streaming from a ruptured tank, was ignited by the hot exhaust. We were also receiving many small fragments of flak all over the plane.

"Bob called over the intercom for a crew check. Starting with Bill in the tail, we were to report in sequence. Bill answered affirmatively as did Dick in the ball. I did the same. However, when it was Joe's [radio operator Joe Kolasinsky] turn to respond there was silence. Bob called for him to answer but there was no response. He then ordered me to go forward to check on Joe.

"I disconnected my heated suit and oxygen hose, and plugged in a walk-around bottle. As I opened the door I saw Joe on the floor, flopping around and gasping. His main oxygen hose had been shot through by flak. He was semiconscious. I grabbed the hose from the other side of the plane and hooked it up to his mask. In what seemed like a long time, his body quieted. I can still see his eyes coming back into focus and his forefinger-to-thumb OK signal.

"We were within a minute or so of dropping our bombs, flying through very heavy flak. As I watched Joe give me the OK sign, my supply of oxygen in the walk-around must have been depleted. Joe and Jerry [Mangan] said that I fell backwards, through the open radio-room door into the A-frame of the ball turret. Dick was in the act of rotating the turret that entangled me and forced my flak jacket to wedge into the plane's floorboards.

"Joe said he struggled to free me as our bombs were being dropped. He warned Dick to hold the ball turret still and called to Jerry for help. Jerry, in his excitement, forgot to hook up to a walk-around bottle. He came back across the catwalk of the open bomb bay door without oxygen, grabbed one of the two main lines in the waist and hooked up. They reconnected me to my regular hose but could not free me where I was caught. They tore up a couple of floorboards and dragged me free of the A-frame. Joe said after they had me free and lying on the floor, my face was ashen and colorless. They had just about given up on me when I showed signs of reviving. I recovered as well as Joe and was fully conscious and alert for the balance of the mission."

On reaching their home base, the crew found that *Honky Tonk Sal* had absorbed one of her worst beatings, surviving an 88 shell that had smashed all the way through the right wing to rupture a main gas tank and some ninety other holes from fist-sized to small punctures. But none of those aboard were wounded.

Richards flew his next two missions while suffering from a severe case of hemorrhoids and he bled so profusely that Bob Bensing ordered him to be taken by an ambulance to the infirmary. Hospitalized, Richards met soldiers from ground combat. "I thought I knew what war was all about after only three combat missions until I observed the wounded infantrymen and tank crewmen in that hospital. There were wards full of young men whose feet and legs were black with gangrene. They had been pinned down by enemy fire in cold, wet foxholes, unable to move for so long that circulation of blood had been cut off [rather than gangrene the GIs probably were afflicted with trenchfoot]. What seemed even worse were the fellows who had been inside a tank when a direct hit by the enemy had set the whole interior afire. Most of the men who were burned over 35 percent of their bodies were given excellent care but had little chance of survival."

Another washout from pilot training "at the convenience of the government" was John Morris, a waist gunner from New York City, who originally enlisted in the cadet program thinking this his destiny and preferable to slogging across Europe. Converted into a gunner, Morris completed his stateside training in mid-1944. "We had each been to appropriate individual specialist schools and we flew a lot of practice missions 'attacking' Atlanta or Memphis. We dropped dummy bombs on targets inside bombing ranges. We fired our guns at target sleeves towed through the skies by training planes with very courageous pilots. We flew long distances at night to sharpen navigation skills. Perhaps most important, we got to know and like each other.

"We learned what each of us was good at, and what his limitations were. Aside from being waist gunner, I was assistant engineer—backing up our chief engineer who was also our top-turret gunner. He was a full-blooded Cherokee who was a brilliant bridge and poker player. He was also totally unreliable, being frequently shacked up and hung over when he should have been on the flight line. He was supposed to be teaching me all about B-17 engineering but he didn't. He couldn't teach me much because he didn't know that much about the subject. How did he get away with it? First, he was one of the cleverest people I've ever met. He had deep insight into and understanding of the way the army worked and could play it like a virtuoso violinist. And we all covered for him—including our pilot who frequently chewed him out but never turned him in. Second, that untutored Cherokee was a brilliant improviser who frequently reasoned things that he had not learned in school. And our pilot was a real engineer by prewar training and from that background had absorbed vast B-17 lore in the course of his pilot instruction. Unlike the Cherokee he was always on hand with his backup knowledge."

In September 1944, Morris's crew turned in their tired old B-17 on which they had trained for a brand-new one. "It was gorgeous with all the newest bells and whistles. We flew it around Savannah for about a week and checked out all the systems. We discovered that it would maintain altitude with just one of its four engines. Being brand-new, it had not been named, but we saw that the last three digits of its serial number were 568 and we began to refer to it by those numbers."

After a mishap in which the chief engineer and Morris burned out an engine while warming up the airplane, 568 bore them all to England where they mournfully relinquished the plane to the Eighth Air Force staging personnel. A train and bus delivered the replacements to the 91st Bomb Group at Bassingbourn.

"As luck would have it, 568 was assigned to the 91st and specifically our squadron, the 324th. Our pilot pleaded with the brass to give her to us to fly, pointing out the obvious power of the omens. Not too surprisingly since all Eighth Air Force fliers were highly superstitious, they agreed." During the first years of Eighth Air Force operations, with aircraft and men in short supply, bomber crews usually flew the same airplane unless it were damaged or they were recent arrivals. Under these circumstances, the 91st's *Memphis Belle* and its crew had become the first to complete a twenty-five-mission tour in early 1943.

By late 1944, with enough men and machines on hand for both to regularly stand down, the opportunities for a permanent affiliation between aircraft and crew had become less frequent. There were exceptions, however, and for Morris and his associates the connection with

568 was truly fortunate. "From the beginning of November until the end of April, we flew 568 for twenty-four missions [only on the first mission did they use another aircraft] and suffered only two German-made bullet/flak holes. A remarkable record. In contrast, none of the ten replacement crews that came on the base with us completed as many as five missions. They were all gone before Thanksgiving. And when we were finished, we turned 568 over to a new crew who were hit over Dresden on their first mission and went down, never to be heard from again."

When Morris referred to the grip of superstition, he could have been talking about himself. When the duty noncom came around to awaken him and his companions for the first mission at around 3:00 A.M., the waist gunner burrowed under his blankets for a few more minutes of sleep. Only at the third summons did he finally roll out. "I had about ten minutes to make briefing. I got dressed in and out in two minutes and discovered how dark it was. You couldn't see more than ten feet. The briefing hut which I could find easily in the daytime became hidden. I took my bicycle by the handlebars and started to stumble down the squadron streets and eventually by a very circuitous route, came upon the briefing hut. It was empty. Next I tried for the mess hall; same result. By the time I found it, the chow line had closed down and everyone was heading for the flight line. Out at the hardstand, we loaded guns and ammunition and turned the engines over; the bombs had been loaded during the night. Just before takeoff the adjutant buzzed up in a Jeep and gave each of us two candy bars and a pack of gum. And off we went into the wild blue yonder.

"I survived the mission, but just barely. I was so impressed with my survival that I resolved to repeat the preparatory routine precisely in all future missions. And I did; up late, circuitous route, no briefing or breakfast, twenty-four more times. I lost a lot of weight—about fifty pounds—but it worked."

This first confrontation with the enemy was expected to be a milk run, just over the German lines. "Since this was our first time, we had a veteran combat pilot flying with us to keep us from screwing up," says Morris. "The Luftwaffe picked this day to try out a new tactic. They massed about 150 fighters behind our formation, just out of range of our .50 caliber machine guns, and let fly with a barrage from their 20 mm cannon. It wasn't too effective in knocking down B-17s, but it sure created a lot of excitement, especially for our veteran combat pilot who was supposed to be keeping us cool, but apparently didn't want to die with all us rookies.

"He grabbed the control column and pumped it up and down to get out of the barrage. In the back of the plane this created the effect of a seesaw gone wild. The only thing I had to hold on to was my gun which was anchored to the fuselage by a pivot mount designed to let me shoot the gun in any direction. I clung to it like it was the tail of a tiger, slamming first off the deck, then the ceiling, then the deck again. Exertion and fright had me breathing heavily by now. My hot breath escaped my badly fitting oxygen mask into my goggles and immediately condensed into ice on the inside of the lenses. I couldn't unstrap my flak helmet to lift the goggles so I couldn't see anything. A blinded gunner! Once or twice I let go of the gun with one hand to scrape a hole in the goggle ice and peek out to see, up close, German fighters, which had begun to fly through our formation, shooting. But the ice would start to form right away again, so I didn't see much and had to quickly grab the gun with both hands to stay attached.

"In my wild thrashing around, hanging on to the gun, I apparently sometimes squeezed the trigger 'cause I shot six feet off the horizontal stabilizer of my own plane! There was no question; the bullet holes traced right to my gun. The ground crew chief was furious since he had to change the stabilizer instead of going to London on a pass. I was just relieved to be on the ground again. In subsequent missions, I got better—more expert at shooting Germans while dodging their bullets and flak. That was the normal pattern; most Eighth Air Force casualties were suffered in the early missions of a tour of duty."

The drain upon manpower allowed little time to improve obvious deficiencies in training for combat. Mike Dascoli, the son of a Connecticut cobbler who had managed to build a ten-room house during the Depression, chose to be a bombardier after he entered the Air Corps. He graduated four days after the Normandy landings. "Bombardier training was adequate for one going into combat," he remarks, "but gunnery school did not provide enough time in the air for firing on targets. It had to be on-the-job training." And while instructors and veterans spoke of how difficult missions could be, no one could appreciate battle until exposed.

His replacement crew went to the 305th Bomb Group where perhaps a month elapsed before their first mission, to Merseburg on November 25, 1944. "I was amazed at the amount of 'black clouds' [flak] from the I.P. to the target. There was no way around it. One simply had to fly through it and hope for the best. I now knew what I had been told; the Germans could really put up the flak. It was probably my roughest mission.

We took flak hits, lost parts of the electrical and hydraulic systems. Two gunners suffered anoxia but were revived by the radio operator. I dropped my bombs on the leader [salvoed the load].

"Going home was worse. Cloud coverage built up to 10/10ths solid [visibility was sometimes calibrated on a basis of tenths with 10/10ths meaning none]. As we hit the Channel, we let down through the overcast. It was every aircraft for itself. We flew blind, not knowing where we were or when we passed the English coast. We were down to 800 feet and still in solid cloud. Going lower, we determined we were over English soil but didn't know where. We got down to about 500 feet, now fearful of running into those English radio towers that were higher than we were flying. Still socked in, I was blinking the Aldis lamp in the nose while the tail gunner did the same at his end. With other aircraft in the clouds, and in the same predicament, our immediate concern was ramming another aircraft. We came close to doing that several times.

"We must have flown around two hours this way. Then the pilot spotted a hole in the undercast, dove for it, and we quickly saw an airfield below. We didn't know whose base and we didn't care. The pilot made one pass, the wrong way and put down. We had landed on an inoperative runway at an RAF base but we were down. Other planes from other groups also were forced to use this field as an alternative. I learned the next morning we had about twenty minutes of fuel left.

"During my first few missions, I sensed fear. I wondered how one could survive from the I.P. to the target, flying straight and level. Later it never fazed me. I maintained some of my religious beliefs. Occasionally I took Holy Communion before a mission. I wore a religious medallion a nun from home had sent me for safe keeping."

Merseburg, a continuing curse to those dispatched there, during one excursion mixed farce with terror for John Morris. As had become his custom, he skipped the briefing but says, "When I caught up with the crew after breakfast and the briefing, I got the bad news and instantly got as tense as everyone else. The tension mounted further. Our navigator was missing. We wondered if he had advance word that the target was Merseburg. Whatever, we learned his place would be taken by a totally green navigator who had just arrived at the base. He was to supply our pilot with escape headings if our plane should happen to be knocked out of our squadron formation but still able to maintain some altitude. Since the target was Merseburg, this was a distinct possibility! It was a pretty grim bunch that climbed aboard 568.

"As we passed through 10,000 feet we all began to pull on our

high-altitude garb, electrically heated coveralls and boots over our regular fatigue uniforms, and then the fleece-lined leather suits on top of
that. But not the green navigator. He hadn't been checked out on the
equipment and didn't know how. We were all treated to the disgusted
and profane instructions of the bombardier who shared the nose compartment with the navigator as he coached the rookie until he was all
suited up. Then he was told to stay the hell out of the way."

When they reached the level to go on oxygen, the bombardier again
spewed expletives, explaining to the navigator how to fit his mask and
hose properly. At the German border, the crew donned steel helmets and
flak jackets and the harried bombardier erupted with further profanity
as he assisted the newcomer.

"We had our usual welcoming salvos from front-line batteries on the
Rhine but had gotten so used to those that we hardly noticed," says
Morris. "A short time later and deeper in Germany, we encountered a
whole bunch of unexpected flak and took more notice. But it was still
no big deal; we knew it'd be much more intense at Merseburg, just over
an hour away.

"But whereas we knew we hadn't seen anything yet, our green navigator was already impressed with the harsh reaction from the ground.
More accurately, he was quickly getting downright frazzled. The tension
had quickened some of his nervous functioning, which he announced
over the intercom, was giving him an urgent call of nature. Deep in his
cocoon of armor, oxygen, fleece, electrically heated insulation and
Class-A uniform—he came formally dressed—there was one of those
unexpected battle developments which great generals might dread. But
our bombardier was not fazed. He instructed our greenhorn to stay in
his corner and let nature take its course. From other crew stations on
the intercom came suggestions mostly to the effect that the German
batteries at Merseburg would solve all of his problems one way or
another. At length, our pilot objected to all the unauthorized noise on
the intercom. Then, being the kindly soul that he was, gave orders that
our neophyte be allowed to perform that certain function before we
arrived over the target. Off came the armor, oxygen, fleece, electric suit
and Class As, accompanied by increasingly profane instructions from
the bombardier and titillating hints and comments from all over the
plane. Soon the deed was done, in the navigator's own steel flak helmet.
By the time he finished we were almost at the I.P. for the bomb run and
the flak barrage was beginning in earnest. It was all we expected and
worse. But we hit the target well and were relatively unscathed.

"Once past the target we left the flak behind and began our long return flight to England. After the Rhine we surrendered our altitude and over the English Channel were low enough to unplug from oxygen to light cigarettes and congratulate ourselves on having survived Merseburg. Another hour and we were on the ground at Bassingbourn and piling out of the plane. The last one out was our navigator-for-a-day. He had brown streaks running down his face and light blond hair. Apparently in the heat of battle over the target he found it imperative to jam his helmet on his head. Of course the contents quickly thawed but this did not persuade him to remove the helmet. I don't blame him. Merseburg was no place to take off your flak helmet in late 1944. I remember him quite fondly in hindsight. Were it not for the entertainment he provided on our intercom that day, I'd have been a nervous wreck flying to Merseburg."

Serving as navigator in the same ship as Mike Dascoli was Frank Aldrich, a banker's son from Jackson, Michigan, and a Dartmouth College student when World War II began. "Returning to the Dartmouth campus in the fall of 1942 to begin my sophomore year," says Aldrich, "I found all services represented by recruiting teams. It seemed wise to hedge one's possible future in the military by making a selection while the option was available. I had never flown in an aircraft nor had any particular craving to do so, but the sea interested me even less and I held no desire whatsoever to crawl about on the ground as an infantryman. Accordingly, I stopped by the Army Air Corps station to take the multiple-choice exam. The future role of navigator was chosen for me based on the result of that test and subsequent ones employed at the classification center in Nashville, Tennessee."

Aldrich passed through preflight school and then flexible gunnery school before starting the courses in navigation. "Ground school was intense, but not all that difficult if one paid close attention. The quality of instruction both on the ground and in the air was superb. We were already graduates of flexible gunnery school endowing us with professional competency as aerial gunners [a viewpoint which contrasts sharply with that expressed by his planemate, Dascoli]." Aldrich entered into an Operational Training Unit (OTU) to become a member of a crew and first met Dascoli as well as others with whom he would fly. "I fail to see how anything further could have been done to better prepare us to face up to combat conditions. These can be simulated only up to a point; the real thing being a unique experience."

In the United Kingdom, Aldrich came to appreciate the immensity of operations under difficult conditions. "For the first time we encountered the English weather and had to absorb quickly the techniques of assembling in combat formation within a 1,500-plane bomber stream employing the British short-range Loran system or G Box. Having been adequately briefed on what to expect and where, the actual confrontation with the weather in Europe cannot be described as shocking, but clouds and heavy turbulence up to 35,000 feet with winds of 125 mph were factors to be coped with the first time. Thanks to equipment and training we never found ourselves lost over Europe."

Following the standard procedure, Aldrich, like Dascoli and all other replacements flew the introduction to combat with an experienced hand at the controls. "Pilot Willy Basler was on his thirty-fifth and last mission which took us into the stalement area around Aachen [the edge of the Huertgen Forest line]. Ample rations of flak were served up to us and Basler's calm demeanor and encouraging words over the interphone did much to bolster the confidence of a neophyte like myself. Heavy fog over Britain upon our return caused us to put down at an English base where I think I was terribly amusing to RAF personnel listening to my description of the rigors of aerial warfare; these people had been at this sort of thing since 1940."

Another winter arrival, but more dubious of his readiness than Aldrich was John Greenwood, a native of Indiana who entered the service with three years of Field Artillery ROTC at West Virginia University and Cornell. At Fort Sill, Oklahoma, when the Air Corps advertised for volunteers due to heavy losses, Greenwood transferred to the cadet program, choosing to learn navigation. The crew, of which he became a member, assembled in Avon Park, Florida. "We had just enough training in navigation missions, day and night gunnery missions (.50 caliber, hand-held, flexible mount). I didn't fire over thirty rounds and this wasn't enough to become proficient. We had no chin-turret training till we arrived in England where in place of the B-17F we had a B-17G."

On the roster of the 351st Bomb Group at Polebrook, Greenwood and his confederates underwent a one-month program to instruct them in the flight-control system that was almost entirely governed by the RAF and its systems. "Most of the Eighth Air Force control towers had a permanent RAF representative stationed with the U.S. complement. The navigation was very difficult due to having over 110 airfields in this relatively small country. Some of the fields were only five miles apart. The British weather was very difficult for aerial ops. We would take off in the morning with perfect flying weather, and when returning after an eight-hour mission, we might have a solid cloud cover with a 200-foot ceiling and 1,000 four-engined B-17s and B-24s would be milling around, trying to get down and with very little fuel remaining.

"The 351st BG had many special people, particularly in a leadership role. Our COs were noted for going out on missions and leading, rather than flying a desk. Col. Clinton Ball, a West Point graduate, was unique. He had a small daughter named Linda Ball, so all the B-17s in his squadron had the word ball in the aircraft's name, *Screw Ball, Foul Ball,* even one called *No Balls At All.*"

P-51 pilot Jim McCubbin with the 364th Fighter Group, closing in on his third month with the outfit says, "December 5 was my best day. This was another maximum effort to bomb Berlin. As usual the weather was lousy. We were flying between heavy cloud layers on a low left of a bomber train segment. We were the last flight, spaced out so we could barely keep track of the flight ahead of us. Wilson led the flight; without a wingman I was the element leader. A dream came true when a box formation of some fifty FW-190s appeared from our two o'clock position, crossing between ourselves and the flight ahead, some 2,000 feet below. Wilson called the squadron leader as we turned in behind the large group of Germans.

"As we dropped our wing tanks, my wingman called to tell me he had to abort because one of his tanks would not release. Wilson then lined up on the left side of the enemy group and I on the right. Due to the weather conditions, each plane had a huge contrail, so that only the wing tips protruded from the ball of vapor.

"Their box formation was something like seven or eight planes wide and seven or eight planes deep. After firing a short burst into the rear corner plane, I was surprised to see how quickly he burst into flame. I only damaged the next plane forward in the same line, causing him to roll and dive for the earth. As I exploded the next, I noticed that I was almost in their formation, so I dropped back to the next row over. Only then were a few Germans starting to drop their external tanks and leaving the formation. Our intelligence had told us that German fighter pilots were instructed to avoid our fighters and concentrate on our bombers. Further, they were putting pilots into combat with minimum training. And German discipline is world renowned. I can't imagine any American pilot following orders to stay in formation, while being shot at. [McCubbin is speaking only of fighters, not bombers, which did hold position during their run from the I.P. to the target.]

"Before closing on the next FW in line I looked behind me and saw several P-51s approaching from the rear. I realized that to them, we looked the same as the enemy because of the contrails. So when I damaged the next FW, I followed it down. Apparently, due to the damage I had inflicted, his horizontal stabilizer tore loose during the dive, for which I received credit since my wing camera was on at the time.

"My other reason for following this plane down was that I expected many of the German pilots would try to escape via the deck. Unfortunately, I could not find a single target. I should have stayed and taken my chances with my fellow pilots. I did see one lone airman land from a parachute. I assumed him to be German and turned to make a strafing run. As I was taking the slack out of the trigger, I asked myself, 'Do you really know if that is an enemy?' Since some doubt surfaced, I held my fire and passed so close to him that I could see every feature. He was German, but after looking into the man's face, I could not bring myself to return to the attack. Shooting machines is a lot easier. I'm glad I didn't strafe that airman."

By December 16, the Allied armies had paused at the border of Germany, stalled by stiff German opposition and in part also to rest some combat-weary infantrymen while adding reinforcements who had shipped out from the States a few weeks earlier. American intelligence experts failed to detect the stealthy buildup of an enemy force led by armor. Early that Saturday, Panzer units smashed into the advanced positions of U.S. troops in the rugged terrain of the Ardennes. Backed by thin reserves and in some instances poorly led, the surprised GIs fell back. Within two days a salient some forty miles deep and sixty miles wide marked the maps, creating an ominous bulge into the line that ran through Belgium and Luxembourg. A key element in the breakthrough lay in the absence of either the Eighth or Ninth Air Forces to observe or attack the enemy. Both were grounded by a spate of unusually bad weather during what would go on record as one of the worst winters in European history.

"The next day [December 17]," says Mac McCauley of the 385th Bomb Group, "fog rolled in over the battlefield and airpower was grounded. We read the news, knowing that bombers could be rushed in to change the flow of German ground forces. The fog was so heavy we couldn't see fifty feet. Ice was forming on all bushes, etc. Day after day went by and still the fog hung thickly over the land."

ALTHOUGH the heavyweights were unable to perform over the Ardennes, some 600 bombers called on Cologne on December 18, 1944, while a handful of fighters from the Ninth Air Force helped to slow the spearhead of the Nazi advance. Several P-47s from the Ninth swooped down upon the SS Panzer column led by Lt. Col. Jochen Peiper which was responsible for the massacre of surrendered U.S. soldiers around Malmédy, near the village of Trois Ponts, to bomb and strafe. The Thunderbolts inflicted sufficient damage to impede or block the armor advance. The slowdown enabled GIs to defend several key bridges and commanders to truck reinforcements into the breach.

In his diary for that day, Sgt. Leroy Kuest, with the 94th Bomb Group ground crew, wrote "39 Forts went out target Mainz." Kuest made no entries for several days and then scribbled for December 23, "It has been foggy all this while and today is the first time we sent any out. It was an ME [Maximum Effort] and we sent out all we had to stop [Field Marshal Karl von] Rundstedt's breakthrough in the Ardennes."

Lewis Smith, as a B-17 pilot in the 385th, did not mention the German breakthrough in his diary until December 19. "Boy, what a fog there is this morning. We were going to bomb a marshaling yard right behind the lines to try to stop the Nazi drive back into Belgium. I guess they're really driving the boys back. We could have done them a lot of good, if we could have taken off today." On the following days he reported a succession of scrubbed operations.

In the first frantic scramble to plug the gap in the Ardennes, the demands for manpower temporarily transferred barracks orderlies from their duties to assist in more essential work. "We had to make our own beds, mop our own floors and start fires in the little pot bellied stoves set in the middle of each Quonset hut," recalls Chuck Halper from the 385th. "When we returned from a mission and were debriefed, we routinely went to the mess hall where a long table with dozens of shot glasses filled with bonded whisky were available. Back in the barracks, one of the officers who had downed a number of drinks turned his attention to getting some heat in his quarters. He made a fire in the stove and to speed up the process, along with the kindling wood, tossed in some flares from his Very pistol. It worked fine until the door blew off the stove, the stack came down and filled the room with soot. When they poured water on the stove, it cracked and the fire fell on the floor. By the time everything was brought under control, beds, walls, floors and all else were covered with soot, dirt and debris. A petition to the colonel asked for the return of the barracks orderly and to execute the man with the flares."

The 385th's quarters, according to Halper, were almost as dangerous as the skies over Germany. "It was common practice to wash down the latrines with 110-octane aviation gasoline and it was only a matter of time until someone walked in with a lit cigarette and boom! The roof blew off from the brick walls but the smoker luckily escaped with some singed hair from various places on his body."

The Battle of the Bulge raged for a full week before the Eighth Air Force could buttress the determined effort of the ground forces to flatten the salient. In the interim, the paratroopers of the 101st Airborne, supplemented with scattered units from other outfits, held firm while surrounded at the town of Bastogne. Air drops from the Ninth Air Force brought in some supplies to the beleaguered. On December 23, as Kuest indicated, the Eighth sought to prevent the enemy from moving up reserves and supplies with strikes at railroad yards and communications centers but the weather continued to hamper effectiveness.

During the night of December 23, a high-pressure area sifted over the Continent and McCauley recalls, "When the fog lifted, everyone gave a sigh of relief. It was time to help the ground forces being pushed around by the enemy. The next morning [Christmas Eve day] an armada of fifty-seven bombers rose from Great Ashfield. Each was carrying a full load of bombs. It was announced at briefing that we were to help pave the way for General Patton's Third Army to rescue the U.S. 101st Airborne Division surrounded at Bastogne."

All together the Eighth mustered almost 2,000 bombers and more than 800 fighters to batter airfields, communications centers and other key military installations behind the bulge. Even though the skies were clear, the Fourth Combat Wing, led by Brig. Frederick Castle, encountered problems in forming over the Channel. As a consequence, the B-17s, with Castle in the copilot's seat of the lead ship, reached the rendezvous point some fifteen minutes late. That seemed no cause for undue alarm, since the German fighters ordinarily did not intercept over territory occupied by the Allies. But from out of the sun, a flock of ME-109s suddenly fell upon the bombers.

Castle's aircraft, already having some difficulty with one engine, took a hit and drifted toward the rear of the formation and then the enemy pounced on what was an obviously wounded bird. Their guns bloodied the radar operator aboard and the plane's usual copilot now in the tail gunner's post. Two engines started to burn and over the intercom, Castle declared, "Okay, men, we've been hit—get out." As the crewmen scrambled to bail out, the B-17 heeled over into a dive before it leveled out. Castle lowered his undercarriage to reduce speed and facilitate exit by the crew. He ordered the pilot to leave. The men jumping from the nose hatch saw the pilot going for his parachute. Everyone except for Castle and the pilot had left the stricken Fortress when the right wing tank exploded. The burning bomber, still loaded with its explosives, spun into the ground. The crash killed Castle and the pilot, who never managed to buckle on his chute and leave. Among the dead were the copilot who succumbed to his wounds and the radar operator whose body was found without a parachute. It was believed that Castle stuck at the controls to give the others an opportunity to save their lives and retained his bomb load rather than risk dumping it on civilians or troops in the vicinity.

Waist gunner Willard Richards from the 385th, in the same bomb wing, says, "Our P-51 escorts were scheduled to meet us as we crossed the front lines, minutes later. This was a surprise attack. We watched in disbelief as the lead group was riddled. At least nine planes were shot down or forced to leave the formation." The 385th's bombers and other groups which in Richards's words "stretched to the horizon and beyond" continued on to the targets.

Lewis Smith told his diary, "About twenty minutes before we got to the German border, Jerry fighters hit us. They hit the first group in the bomber stream and knocked down eight ships, including the lead one in which General Castle was flying. Three ME-109s started to come in on our group and our fighter escort was on them in a second. They came shooting down in front of our squadron with four P-51s right behind them and when they got at about eleven o'clock low, one ME-109 was blown to bits. We could see dogfights going on all around. A P-51 and ME-109 collided. Both pilots bailed out. One P-51 pilot bailed out and we saw a Jerry machine gun him. That makes you pretty mad."

"I never saw a German pilot strafe an airman in his chute," says Tommy Hayes. "But Pete Peterson, one of my flight leaders caught one doing it, strafing crewmen from a bomber. The ME-109 made several passes at the parachutes when Pete saw him. Pete overtook the 109, setting on his tail and kept nipping him until he threw off the canopy and bailed out. Then Pete made several passes, firing six guns until 'he looked like a sack of potatoes hanging from the parachute shrouds.' It was a house rule in the 357th that when you saw a German strafing an airman in his chute, you had to kill him, even if you ran out of gas trying.

"On the whole I think the German fighter pilots were humane and Christian. The bad guys were handpicked for the SS and Gestapo. Pete Peterson also told me about the time he shot down a fighter. Off went the canopy and as the pilot bailed out, and went by Pete, he saluted his adversary as the victor for this day."

In fact Walter Konantz of the 55th Fighter Group says, "I personally never saw any German pilots shoot any Americans in their parachutes. One of our pilots gloated that he had one hell of a dogfight with a 109 and eventually caused him to bail out. He said he shot him in his chute because he was so good that he didn't want to meet him in the air again at a later time. I gave him hell as I pointed out that the Germans had far more opportunity to shoot descending Americans in their chutes than we had to shoot Germans and I would hate to see this practice started. At times over heavily defended German targets it looked like a snowstorm with so many B-17 crewmen floating down. My trust in the humanity of the German pilots was reinforced when a 109 pilot I had just shot down after climbing out of his bellied-in plane saluted me as I flew by on a low pass."

During the Battle of Britain, some RAF fliers who bailed out were machine gunned, much to the outrage of their comrades and the press. Logically, Germans could say that to allow an enemy to float to the ground, unharmed, allowed him an opportunity to fight another day. The same argument could be made by Allied airmen confronted with Luftwaffe pilots who bailed out over their own turf. Bob Johnson, who by December 1944 was back in the States teaching what he had learned from experience and selling War Bonds, says, "I saw them [the enemy] go after crippled airplanes and they had a right to. But when they went after parachutes, I was going to get them and I did, a couple of them. I drove them right into the ground. I had them before that but I stayed with them until they splattered." But there is no evidence that shooting up a man in a chute was a regular practice for either side, although it happened.

Al Greenberg, the 96th Bomb Group togglier, remembers December 24 as "supposedly the biggest operation of the Eighth Air Force. I took my stuff out to the ship and returned to briefing which was packed to the gills. General Olds was there and a couple of civilians, probably correspondents. The whole Eighth Air Force was going after airfields right back of the lines to help the boys.

"We were flying 140, the oldest ship in the squadron. We assembled at 7,000 feet and Kramer and Nehls helped me take out the pins [safety devices on bombs]. We wrote Merry Christmas on one bomb with a piece of fudge and then I went to the nose. Over the lines flak started coming up and I felt the bottom of our ship peppered with it. Ships kept aborting right and left [about 150 of the original 2,046 quit before reaching the targets]. Rockets kept coming up all the way.

"It took an awful long time to reach the I.P. but we finally did. The leader opened his bomb doors and so did I. I called Nehls in the ball to ask him if they were open but he didn't answer. Red had passed out from lack of oxygen in the waist and both Nehls and Roy were helping him. I pushed the toggle but only the inside racks dropped. I had to wait a while before I found out about it, and when I salvoed the bombs they all dropped in the river. Two patches in the nose blew out and I had to stuff my clothes in them to keep from freezing. One of these days I'll have a mission without a malfunction."

For this Christmas Eve expedition, Leroy Kuest of the 94th Bomb Group groundcrew noted, " . . . when they returned all West England was fogged in so eighty-seven Forts from other bases landed here. It was quite a sight to see them all flying formation with their landing lights on. It took two solid hours for all of them to land. We worked all night and had most all of the ships ready to go in the morning but the fog was so bad that the mission was scrubbed."

Lt. Jim McCubbin was in his P-51 on December 24 at 2:00 P.M. meandering about as wingman for the operations officer, Capt. Bill Crombie. With nothing on their agenda or worthy of their hostile efforts, Crombie suggested a visit to a French P-47 field where he had a friend. "The three of us retired to the officers' club where conversation could be lubricated," recalls McCubbin. "We cut the time so short that we arrived at our planes some five minutes till four. We discovered that the ground crew had failed to refuel our planes and we had to make a decision of crossing with barely sufficient fuel, no reserve or facing disciplinary action. We chose to take the chance [flying home]."

Shortly after they reached a convenient altitude, McCubbin and Crombie heard the discomforting news that the weather over England had turned, making it impossible to land at their base or anywhere else in the United Kingdom. The pair reversed course and now sought refuge in France. "But with our limited radio channels, we were unable to contact any airfields. As we worked our way southwest, it began to dawn on us that we didn't know where we were. As the sun was setting, a rising ground fog was beginning to block our view of the landscape." In the dimming light, McCubbin and Crombie thought they glimpsed the configuration of an airfield. McCubbin dropped back to give Crombie sufficient clearance for a landing approach and on his radio he heard the operations officer advise he was on the ground.

Now it was McCubbin's turn, but the fog had thickened during the interval. "I dropped down and when I saw the perimeter track [encircling the field] flash under my wing, I cut the power and hit the ground hard, but under control. Just as I was getting ready to stand on the brakes, a

B-17 appeared like an apparition out of the fog. I pushed the throttle to emergency full and staggered at a stall just over the bomber. At low speed, flaps must be retracted slowly and carefully to avoid loss of altitude, of which I had none. As I was hanging by the prop, I noted treetops and once a cathedral spire pass my wing at a frighteningly close distance."

McCubbin now tried a second time but realized he had erred in his approach and once again resorted to emergency measures to lift the ship up, dragging through the town at treetop level and by the same church spire. He considered bailing out as the visibility decreased further after his third pass missed. Finally, on his fourth try he had barely touched down and applied the brakes, "when I felt the plane lurch into space and then drop to a crunching stop. I discovered I had landed in a bomb crater and the wings spanned the hole to support the plane."

In fact, the two Americans had set down at an abandoned Luftwaffe strip full of wrecked aircraft. A French citizen directed them to a nearby military installation and from there the pair moved on to a local boîte with women and wine. In the morning, Crombie, whose ship was undamaged, took off, but McCubbin had to wait for other transport as his P-51 became part of the junkpile. "I feared that the squadron commander would really chew me out over this foolishness to say nothing of the loss of a combat aircraft. To my great surprise, nothing was ever mentioned to me. I'm sure they took it out on Bill, which is one advantage for not being in charge."

As the Americans slowly pushed the Nazi armies backward in the last weeks of the Battle of the Bulge, the fierce winter storms left many U.S. ground troops cut off from the rear echelons. Bombers replaced bogged-down supply trucks. Dave Nagel, as an engineer/gunner with the 305th recalls, "We went through all the camps, took galoshes, a set of long underwear from each man and then dropped them haphazardly to the guys on the ground, hoping they'd get some of it." With the 385th, McCauley says, "We'd come in low, over the flaps and lower the wheels to slow down the B-17. Canisters attached to parachutes were released through the bomb bay. The canisters contained food, medicine and ammunition."

THE pace of the war, the enormous numbers of men, machines and the accoutrements plus the rapid turnover in skilled hands meant quick elevation to new responsibilities. Yesterday's neophyte became an element, squadron, section, group, wing and even division lead pilot, bombardier or navigator. Bill Frankhouser's life may have been saved when he was taken from the ill-fated Newman crew to serve as a leader for the group. Mac McCauley, from the 385th Bomb Group, with a mere nine missions on his card, had drawn a month-long assignment to Command Pilot Training returning just before the affair of the Ardennes. "This was to lead up to my leading a section, a squadron or even the entire group," says McCauley. "Many hours were spent in the lecture room where we were taught the planning that went into a mission. The main selection and detail of the target was handed down from the wing. Our job was to study our level of readiness based on yesterday's losses, select the layout of crews and assignment of aircraft. Certain persons determined fuel loading and we had to confirm their findings. We learned how intelligence officers selected our targets. I flew several observer flights while the group was making the assembly [to study each squadron for timing and formation quality]. I had an additional assignment to fly as instructor pilot to check out copilots who had been recommended for first pilot. This was possible when the copilot had completed about thirty missions."

Arthur Prager, with the 92nd Bomb Group, was made a lead navigator. "It meant that I had a room of my own and flew a little less frequently. I was made a lead navigator due to seniority combined with mathematical skills and abilities. We were rated by senior officers on the ground whose only source of information was the detailed logs we kept in flight. Mine apparently impressed the squadron and group navigators. Also I seemed to impress the pilots I flew with, not as much because I was good but because I gave them nothing to complain of."

Frank Aldrich advanced to the role of lead navigator for the 305th Bomb Group. Mike Dascoli, his former associate, attended classes to learn dead reckoning to qualify as a navigator for his crew. There was to be no letup; in fact the bomb tonnage would reach new heights.

While Aldrich pronounces himself satisfied with the preparation for battle, others seem less certain of the efficiency of their precombat exercises. Saul Levine, another recruit to the 305th, a Brooklyn-born son of immigrants who fled Czarist Russia in 1905, had two years of night engineering school at Cooper Union in New York City before he entered the Air Corps. Although Levine had never flown previously, he volunteered for the branch because of his engineering background "and the challenge and the adventurous aspects of the 'wild blue yonder.'" Selected to train as a pilot, Levine says, "I had no desire to become a buzz boy and asked to fly twin-engine aircraft." He attributes his nomination as a B-17 pilot, after undergoing instruction in smaller planes, because "I was good at precision flying and maneuvers, in addition to being method-ical and well coordinated. They regarded my judgments as well thought out and responsible, according to my training records.

"The tactical aspects of the job of flying a bomber were minimal in the States since tactics varied from theater to theater. There was no training on high-altitude formations in the States since this put lots of stress on the training aircraft. Many missions over Germany were at 30,000 feet. Plane response at that height was sluggish, making close formation dangerous. Training at the various bomb groups [in England] varied." (That explains the contrasting opinions of their preparedness voiced by men who reached the United Kingdom at the same time.) "I was given several indoctrination flights before my first combat mission, December 28.

"I did my first one as a copilot, my second as first pilot with an expe-rienced crew. From the third on you picked up your own crew." Echoing Lewis Smith, Levine remarks, "The weather in England during my tour was dismal [European meteorological conditions during the winter of 1944–45 have been described as unusually bad]. I took off on instru-ments and very often landed being guided by runway flare pots. The fog even made bicycling hazardous with open ditches. I did not see the countryside during my first eight missions.

"Most losses were on the early missions. Survival rates improved with experience. Learning how to fly high-altitude close formation, hoarding your gas supply, being particularly watchful during assemblies, all con-tribute to better survival chances. Keeping rested and laying off the booze before flights also mattered."

20

NEW YEAR MOVES

On New Year's Eve, ten of the Eighth's four-engine bombers took off at dusk for a leaflet operation. "They were never heard from again," says Dave Nagel. "They sent them without fighter escort and were all lost." To add to the chagrin of the commanders, the celebratory activities of the holiday allowed a sneak assault by enemy fighters on American planes sitting on the ground in Belgium. As many as 100 U.S. planes were destroyed or damaged.

Leroy Kuest at the 94th Bomb Group opens 1945 with entries for the first few days, "Jan. 1—thirty Forts went out. Target were troops near Bastogne. Jan. 2—twenty-eight Forts went out. Target front lines. Jan. 3—thirty Forts went out. Target marshaling yards." Then came words of still more ghastly accidents. "Jan 5—thirty Forts went out, target front lines. Lieutenant Slaff accidentally hit the alarm bell and three gunners bailed out. One was killed—chute failed to open. Two Forts and a P-51 collided in midair. Only three chutes came out. Pieces landed all over the countryside. Jan. 6—thirty-three Forts took off. One ship failed to take off and crashed on end of runway. It caught fire, burned for a few minutes and then the bomb load exploded. Four men got out and the rest were scattered all about. It blew the door open on our Nissen hut which is two miles away. Flames flew about 100 feet in the air."

Willard Richards recalled a mission on the final day of 1944, when on approach to the target, "we spotted a single-engine German bat-winged observation plane, flying at least 10,000 feet above us. We identified it as an ME-163-B Comet. Rocket-propelled, it could reach speeds of 590 mph but it had very limited combat range, about fifty miles. The only threat it posed to us was its ability to observe and report its findings to ground stations.

"As we were looking up at the 163, we saw our own P-51 escort planes flying about 2,000 feet above us. They gave us a very secure feeling, just knowing that they were there. Suddenly, as if out of nowhere, an ME-262 Swallow came up from behind two of them. Both P-51s exploded and fell as we watched helplessly. The 262 was jet propelled, with a maximum speed of 540 mph.

"After downing our fighter escort, he did a climbing turn, then dove with guns firing right down through our squadron formation. Its speed was unbelievable. There was no way we could fire at it because of the danger of hitting our own bombers. He apparently did no damage, but we all expressed the helplessness and fear we experienced as he dove through us.

"The pilot must have been success-happy or insanely eager. We watched him level out, then gain altitude behind us. He made his fatal mistake, a run at us from the rear. Every top, ball and tail gunner opened up on him. Evidently he flew into a wall of .50 caliber slugs. All we saw was a bright flash and a puff of smoke."

But as missions continued, Richards's crew began to worry about Dick Ward, their ball-turret man, about whom they had been uneasy even as they formed a unit in the States. They had become more suspicious after the initial mission when he disconnected his oxygen supply and fell unconscious. A few days into the New Year, aboard the *Golden Goose* while running a solo mission to dump chaff over large concentrations of 88s banging away at the ground forces nearing Kaiserlauten, what was supposed to be a milk run quickly became terrifying as flak hit them hard. A piece ripped away the waist door, missing Richards by six inches. "As Bob [pilot Kiersted] turned to head for friendly territory, he called for a routine crew check. Once more Dick Ward didn't answer. Joe and I went to investigate and found that he had disconnected his heated suit and was in shock from the cold. We dragged him up out of the turret, attached his suit and worked with him until he revived." When the *Golden Goose* returned to Great Ashfield, the frostbitten Ward was grounded, a status that became permanent after a few weeks.

John Greenwood, new to the 351st Bomb Group, had spent a somewhat lonely Christmas at the Polebrook base. Most of the veteran crews who had taken off on the Christmas Eve day support missions for the embattled GIs in the Ardennes had been diverted to landing fields elsewhere because of the weather. The old timers hardly reassured him when they were about. "They would sit around the barracks and 'flak us up,' telling us combat stories." The novitiates were jolted by hard evidence of imminent danger. "Just before we started missions, one of the crews flying *Buckeye Babe,* a ship with 103 missions to its credit, was last seen going down over Germany with two engines out. The empty bunks in the barracks were very noticeable."

Greenwood began his combat tour over Euskirchen ten days into the new year. "This was the big day because for over a year we had been training for this very thing, fighting a war." He and the pilot went out with experienced crews before the rest of their companions. "The crew I was with flew the mission without any trouble. Naturally, everything was new to me and I was always one step behind everyone else. At the briefing and throughout the mission there were butterflies in my stomach and a feeling of tension all around—the sort of thing that is prevalent when you don't know what is coming off next. We made a visual run on the target [an airfield just beyond the front]. We landed back at Polebrook after an uneventful mission. This combat business seemed a snap."

A few days later, with his original crew working as a unit, Greenwood readjusted his thinking. "Our target was the Hohenzollern Bridge at Cologne, the main bridge across the Rhine River. Everything went fine until we ran into some unexpected flak. It was light but accurate. The second burst hit us in the nose. It knocked out the oxygen system on the right side leading to the togglier. The flak ripped the soundproofing material on the side of the ship and it is something like chicken feathers. The combination of escaping oxygen under pressure and chicken feathers made the inside of the nose look like a heavy snowstorm was raging. We didn't diagnose the situation immediately because we couldn't see too well and we didn't know whether to bail out, light a cigarette or what. We finally cleared the feathers away and hooked the togglier onto my oxygen system. I can't describe the look of fear that came into his face when that flak hit, but no one was hurt. We landed back at Polebrook. My outlook on combat flying changed a little. Maybe it wasn't that easy. Our squadron missed the bridge by 1,000 yards."

WHILE the outcome of World War II seemed inevitable, one small element of the Luftwaffe continued to hurt the Eighth. The emergence of the jet-powered ME-262 as a substantial threat in the air made destruction of the swifter enemy fighter on the ground all the higher a priority. In mid-January, Walter Konantz with the 55th Fighter Group went on a sweep over central Germany. "We strafed Geibelstadt airfield again [a week earlier, a raid on the site destroyed thirteen aircraft, including a two-engine Junkers 88 ignited by Konantz]. I caught an ME-262 shortly after takeoff and clobbered him with over forty hits. After downing the jet I made a strafing pass on a parked plane but it was a burned-out hulk from our January 6 strafing so I held my fire. As I went across the field at ten feet and 400 miles per hour, I picked up a single .30 caliber bullet through the cockpit that cut a groove in my leather jacket sleeve and knocked out my radio. Strafed some ammo sheds and exploded a few.

"There were no other P-51s in sight so I started home alone. I searched for any Allied planes headed for England as the weather was bad and without a radio I could not call for a steer to my home base. I found a lone P-47, joined up in close formation with him and signaled my radio was out and I wanted to land with him. I followed him and landed at the 9th AF base at St.-Trond, Belgium. I spent the night there, had my radio replaced and came home the next day. When I walked into the barracks, my mates were dividing up my belongings. They had seen the fiery crash of the ME-262, heard nothing more from me on the radio and when I failed to return that night they figured my stuff no longer had an owner."

Like Konantz, Jim McCubbin hunted for quarry on the ground. During one sweep while he led a three-plane flight, his radio chattered with sounds of an encounter by other planes from his group but his element could not locate the battle. "As we searched for the source," says McCubbin, "we passed near a German airfield. As our frustration grew, the temptation of hitting that German field became overwhelming. My reluctance was due to knowledge that every man with a gun on the field was daring someone to try a strafing run. But we agreed it had to be done. I instructed the flight that we had to hit the field line abreast rather than freelance. My reasoning was based on the experience that inevitably, gunners under-led the first planes but the next in line really get it. Striking line abreast is difficult for the wingmen because they have to watch the leader.

"The field was loaded with JU-88s, a medium-size, two-engine bomber or nightfighter. The flak was so intense that if any one view could be frozen, you could walk on the bursts all across the field. Due to the flak, our aim was not the best. I did manage to burn two planes, but my wingmen didn't do as well. The good news was no one was hit."

Hungry for prey, he and pilot Robert McKibben vowed that if ever they became separated from their group, they'd do their own sweep. And when the 364th, working with a new radar system, milled about chasing figments reported by the radar, McCubbin and McKibben "escaped" for their own sortie in southern France. "We flew line abreast some 2,500 feet apart to maximize our field of view," says McCubbin. "Shortly, a bogie appeared on Mac's side that became an ME-109. They made a frontal attack on one another, followed by a tight 'luftberry,' a chase around a circle." The maneuvers brought the German fighter within range of McCubbin who began tracking the foe with his gyroscope-controlled gunsight designed to automatically compensate for lead. "Since I had never had time to use this sight in the prescribed way, I thought this was my best opportunity. While Mac was screaming for me to hurry, I was taking my time to make my first perfect gunnery pass at his opponent. The shot was beautiful, all bullets poured directly into the enemy's cockpit." What neither of the two Americans realized was that the Germans were listening to their radio transmissions and the conversation would come back to haunt McCubbin later.

THE need to attack an objective over and over frustrated the strategists and led them to experiment, sometimes disastrously. Eighth Air Corps headquarters, miffed at unsatisfactory results from a number of forays, attributed the errors to a shortage of time for bombardiers to set their sights once they began the run from the I.P. To afford more minutes, the tactical experts ordered approaches be made upwind, which slowed the speed of the heavyweights. As the B-17s of the 305th lumbered toward the Cologne area, their vulnerability increased sharply with the failure of the lead aircraft to release its ordnance. Unknown to the crew, the plane, borrowed from another bomb group, had its cargo wired differently and the release mechanism did not function. "Had the bombs gotten away on schedule," says Frank Aldrich, "we would have all gone home, having chalked up another one. The second go-around was another matter entirely. We all moved into it with a great deal of apprehension. We expected hell and caught it." Horrified, Aldrich saw a Fort that included close friends, four men from his original crew, lurch upward, then plunge towards the ground. None of his pals survived. "Aircraft were dropping out of formation all over the place, and when the bombs failed to tumble out of the lead aircraft for the second time, we wheeled around to form for a third run. We all knew we were in deep trouble." The group leader quickly realized he had few capable aircraft left and abandoned the mission.

In the interim, the flak gunners, tracking the slow-moving planes bucking the wind for a third time, scored many hits. Among those crippled was Aldrich's ship which lost an engine. When they broke out underneath the cloud cover, the pilot spotted a runway. He tried to line up his ship but he lacked enough power to maneuver into position and Aldrich braced himself for a crash landing.

"We were coming in fast, so all I could do was withdraw to the catwalk behind the nose compartment, directly underneath the pilots. I hung on, as we bounced across the runway at an angle and plowed through the field, coming to rest gently in a large bomb crater. The wings suspended the plane from the edges of the crater and we sat there like a huge moth caught in a web. Fear of fire caused me to move quickly in dropping through the lower escape door. I found myself at the bottom of the crater with the plane hanging above me in perfect suspension.

"I scrambled up the rather steep side of the crater in record time and was on the rim, staring down at the plane by the time the first base personnel arrived. As yet, no one else had emerged from our ship and the base people found it difficult to believe that I had come out of that airplane. Things sifted out quickly and we were driven in Jeeps to the farmhouse which served as headquarters of the P-47 fighter group which occupied this former Luftwaffe base. It turned out that my brother, Lt. William Aldrich, was one of the pilots attached here and we were treated to a reunion. I had not been aware that he was in the European theater. I also was advised that had the bomb crater not halted our wild dash across the airfield, we would have encountered the squadron's main bomb dump, some 150 yards beyond and perhaps blown up half of eastern Belgium." The experiment to approach upwind was quietly discarded.

Saul Levine flying a B-17 with the 305th recalls disasters due to experiments with ordnance. "We lost two planes on takeoff, carrying a pair of 4,000-pound, rocket-propelled bombs externally. This configuration was particularly hard to handle because higher speeds were required for a safe takeoff. After these two successive accidents the arrangement was scrubbed."

Such faults did not lie with the ground crews who in the eyes of their clients continued to provide quality service. "Mine were super," says Levine. "Not only did they maintain the aircraft well but they did things like supplying additional steel plates for sitting. *Idiot's Delight* never aborted because of mechanical problems."

That does not mean that the equipment never broke down. "As a spare ship," says Levine, "we became lost over Holland in the heavy clouds while trying to intercept my squadron after a late takeoff. We blew two engines trying to get above the cloud layer. The navigator, airsick, couldn't function. Fortunately, England responded to our May-day call. We were given our choice to bail out, heading for England over water or let down at an emergency field in France.

"France was the better option, if we decided a bailout was necessary because one engine was on fire. The crew had their chutes on, ready to go, on command. We were on instruments until we broke out of the clouds at 800 feet, with the field dead ahead, greased it in and then ran like hell."

Undoubtedly, highly discouraging to the defenders of the Third Reich was the mounting number of aircraft and airmen in the skies despite the thousands of planes knocked down and the tens of thousands of men killed or captured. German fighter defenses seemed reduced to almost token appearances in spite of the redoubtable jet. Howard Donahue, completing his thirty-five-mission tour toward the spring of 1945, says he never saw an enemy plane make an attack on his ship, although some of his gunners spotted them once or twice. Where once Ira Eaker had argued that if he could field as many as 300 bombers the Germans would be blasted into submission, it was not uncommon for a thousand or so heavyweights, accompanied by 700–800 fighters, many of which also bore explosives, to assault the Fatherland. The Germans remained able to throw up heavy concentrations of antiaircraft fire but bomber losses often were confined to single digits, although certain targets, like Berlin, resulted in heavier casualties.

As the Third Reich crumbled, the pipeline from the U.S. training bases disgorged an abundance of newcomers to administer the *coup de grâce*. Dan Villani, a Greenfield, Massachusetts, son of an immigrant shoemaker, as a boy helped his father in the shop repairing footwear while modeling airplanes from broom handles and pieces of wood found in the street. "I devoured pulp magazine air stories in *G-8 and His Battle Aces*. By age eighteen I could identify just about every aircraft in existence."

Two weeks after that birthday, Villani convinced his mother to sign enlistment papers before the draft could snap him up in 1943. "I can't say I had any sense of world affairs. I cannot remember ever having conversations with my male friends in high school about the war. It was just something happening elsewhere and we were not concerned until Pearl Harbor. I don't even remember teachers ever talking about the war. It was a case of being swept up by events after Pearl Harbor. From then on, as the draft took hold, we all talked about what branch of the military we wanted to enter. For me my dream of joining the air force had come true. I was going to be a flier."

After six weeks of basic training, Villani entered the cadet program at Michigan State. "This was a grueling academic, physical and discipline regimen. Physics lecture and lab three hours a day, five days a week. Civil air regulations, mathematics, composition, speech, geography, European history, drill flight alert and physical training. No free time and a demerit meant walking a tour with rifle in full dress. My happiest moments were ten hours of flying instruction on Piper Cubs under civilian instructors contracted by the Air Corps."

At the classification center in Texas, Villani says he faced a moment of truth. "Either I was going to make it as an air cadet or GDO, ground duty only—infantryman." Two weeks of written and physical examinations weeded out and designated the aspiring cadets. "When I wasn't taking a test of some sort I was on KP duty. Scuttlebutt was that the air force had met their quotas for the year and most everybody was being GDO'd. They needed a lot of infantrymen for the coming invasion of Europe. On the final day, a long list of names was posted. I pushed through the crowd to see it and all I could see was GDO one after another, all down the list. As I got to the bottom, I spotted a B [for bombardier] after what I thought was my name. I took off a shoelace from my boot and stretched it across the paper to connect my name with the B. It was me. I screamed with joy. Most everyone turned away in silence and I had to temper my behavior because I knew what they were feeling." Throughout his cadet period, Villani fretted over the disappearance of classmates and friends who did not make the grade.

Summoned before a three-officer board the following day, Villani learned he qualified for all three categories—pilot, navigator and bombardier—but had scored highest in the last skill. "This is where they thought I should go, if it was all right with me. All right with me? I couldn't believe they were asking me. Getting into the cadets was the sole focus of my life and I would have kissed their feet if they had asked me. I thanked them profusely and said bombardier/navigator school was just fine." The joy of entering flight programs had not diminished since Jim Goodson, fresh off the sunken *Athenia,* almost six years before, had been willing to pay for the privilege of an RAF berth.

During the next stage of instruction, Villani's boyhood fixation on aircraft identification stood him in good stead for what was considered the toughest subject. In fact he was so skilled in it that from his rear corner seat he passed answers to the final exam to others. "I put in a few wrong ones so as not to arouse any suspicion but the instructor was proud as a peacock that his was the highest-scoring class. It was the only dishonest thing I ever did in the air force. I just did not want to see any more washouts, although I trembled at the thought of what would have happened if I had been discovered."

After Villani earned his wings as a bombardier and dead-reckoning navigator, he joined a B-17 crew being formed at MacDill Field, Tampa. "We turned out to be the youngest crew in the Eighth Air Force, average age a little more than nineteen. The oldest was a waist gunner age twenty-one."

Working with the Norden bombsight on a B-17 was not easy. "The B-17," notes Villani, "had no power assists. All the control surfaces were operated by cables connected directly to the pilot's hand controls. Maneuvering meant applying force to a control surface and waiting for the plane to react. This little inertia [during the brief interval between manipulating a control and effect] was what made it tough. The pilot, for example, was always inching the throttles back and forth in order to hold position and not crash into somebody." For weeks Villani practiced lining up the crosshairs of the bombsight, rotating the knobs on the Norden to fly the B-17 and even during clear weather with no enemy guns booming away he found precision no easy task.

The crew developed good rapport, although off base enlisted men and officers separated. "Paul Wagner, our pilot, was a confident and very competent pilot with an aggressive personality," says Villani. "He demanded good performance and was very hot-tempered when things did not go his way. On one occasion when our ball-turret gunner dozed off at his station, Wagner made him crank the landing gear up and down by hand on our way home from a flight. On another occasion, I observed him verbally abuse our copilot, Walter Thumbler, for being sloppy and inattentive while in flight. I didn't object to any of this. I always felt there should be no nonsense after we left the ground. I have been accused of being too much of a perfectionist but I most liked Paul because he had the same attention to detail and desire to do a job well.

"Our copilot, Walter Thumbler, was a good ole boy and quite different. Sleepy-eyed and laid back, he resented being a copilot according to Paul Wagner. I believe he was a good pilot but didn't have the same confidence in him as a first pilot as I did with Paul. Ellis O'Neal, our flight engineer, I believe was a Mormon, very handsome, didn't drink, smoke or chase girls. I never heard him swear. I never knew what he did in his free time, but I was very confident that he understood the mechanical aspects of a B-17. Our tail gunner, William Stegall, was everything

Ellis O'Neal was not. He was all personality, very likable with a winning smile. He picked up girls very easily, drank and swore. He married his sweetheart from Texas just before we left for England. Guy Mattana, the ball-turret gunner and Douglas Mann our waist gunner were more reserved. I could never understand how Mattana could stand being inside the ball turret for hours at a stretch. You stepped into the turret, the hatch was closed and you laid back in it like a closed-up hammock. I tried it once and decided I'd rather die up front hunched over my maps. Our navigator was Lawrence Croker from Brewster, Massachusetts, and Larry and I became the closest of friends. He showed his skills on our flight to England from Gander. He handled the celestial while I did dead reckoning as a backup."

At the 398th Bomb Group at Nuthampstead, Villani settled in for a miserable English winter living in a badly heated Quonset with other officers. For about a week, they performed random flights in the area, breaking in a new engine for a ship or transporting a Fort needed at another base. He learned that the easy pilotage navigation in the States with clearly defined landmarks would not suffice for England where the ground often became obscured by clouds and the similarity of towns with the patchwork of airfields defied recognition. Villani did not get any additional training with the bombsight because under the system of lead bombardiers he was essentially a togglier, salvoing upon cue from the lead ship's drop.

"Our first mission, Neuss, Germany, January 23," says Villani, "was an eye-opener. This was a fairly short mission, just over the border into Germany close to Düsseldorf. Our group, the 398th, was the lead one taking the Eighth Air Force into Germany. Our base commander, Col. Frank Hunter, who was very popular, was in the lead plane with two navigators and a bombardier. For our first mission, our copilot was assigned to another crew with some experience and their copilot assigned to us. We got an old B-17G, *Leapin' Lizzie,* with a lot of missions.

"Things started to go wrong right away. As we taxied out, a B-17 in front of us slipped off the icy runway into the mud, blocking all the following planes. By the time it was towed out of the way, we were late trying to join our squadron at 20,000 feet. We never did reach them. Engine trouble forced us to shut it down and another had a supercharger failure. We were over enemy territory so rather than risk losing any more power, our pilot ordered me to drop the bombs and we turned for home alone. Stragglers were prime targets for German fighter planes and I worried about this all the way back. We got to our base just as our group was returning. They had been badly mauled. Our commander, Colonel Hunter, leading the strike force and [with one exception] his crew were killed. The plane carrying our copilot had crash-landed in Belgium but the entire crew survived." By the time he had finished his third mission, Villani was enough of a veteran to say, "I now had reasonable control of my bowels. We were allowed to stand down and have a few days' rest. We went to London by train. We couldn't wait to see the action at Piccadilly Circus. Prostitutes were a dime a dozen and a pack of cigarettes [American] would get you anything you wanted."

Villani was just one of thousands who were added for the final months of the war. The German capital was the first port of call for newcomer Bill Powers, a top-turret gunner with the 381st Bomb Group. Drafted after completing high school in Rochester, New York, Powers says, "We were told we were handpicked for the Air Corps. I went to airplane mechanic school at Keesler Field, Mississippi, and then to factory school at Willow Run, Michigan. I volunteered for aerial gunner school and with these three schools behind me qualified to be a flight engineer and operate the top turret."

Placed in a fifty-crew replacement pool, Powers was among the half sent by troopship while the others flew the Atlantic. "We arrived in England in December 1944, but we were a B-24 crew with all our training on 24s and we had to learn to fly and operate turrets in a B-17. A veteran crew taught us and after ten days we were put on combat flying status."

Scheduled raids on Berlin at the end of January were scrubbed for poor weather but on February 1, ship No. 100, *Old Century Note,* carried Powers to Mannheim. "We were a little jumpy, it being our first mission," says Powers. "The navigator passed out and I had to climb down and slap him around to revive him. His oxygen mask froze up. The flak was meager but accurate, no enemy fighters. What I remember most is, I was up in my top turret, waving to my friends, the crew that trained us, and they were motioning for me to get down. Flak was bursting all around us. I didn't realize what it was all about but I soon learned." On February 3, after three cancellations because of miserable flying conditions, *Old Century Note* headed for Berlin. "Moderate flak, but accurate," noted Powers, "we had seventeen holes. Two ships collided, another got a direct hit in No. 2 engine and went down. Some of the crew bailed out. I saw a friend get blown out of a ship when they received a direct flak hit."

Although Arthur Prager complains of inadequate preparation for combat, as for most participants, war either taught or it destroyed. Promoted to the role of a lead navigator, without any increase in rank, Prager held the slot of First Air Division deputy lead, on February 9, as more than 300 B-17s set out toward the heartland of the enemy. "The lead plane had a malfunction and we moved up into the lead. I don't remember the target but as we passed into central Germany the weather was so bad at such high altitude that I was ordered to cancel the original target and select and plan the navigation for a new mission right there in the plane over enemy territory. I did so with all possible speed, with the entire First Air Division droning on behind me.

"The new target was railroad marshaling yards in the vicinity of Lützkendorf. [After the bombing] we had spent considerable time and fuel flying around avoiding flak areas and thunderclouds and were ordered to come back to England over northern France so we could join up with fighters stationed there. A small calculation showed me that if we did this, the whole 92nd Bomb Group would run out of fuel over mid-Channel. I pointed this out to the lead pilot who radioed division headquarters. They repeated their order. I repeated my calculation. 'You better be right,' the pilot said to me and we countermanded the order of the division commander (a major general) and went home directly over Germany and the North Sea with no fighter coverage but enough fuel.

"A pilot in flight on a mission had the authority to make this kind of decision regardless of the rank of the commanding officer back on the ground. I was later to get the Distinguished Flying Cross for this event. There was another navigator aboard, as was usual in wing and division leads and deputies and we worked together on the mission revision, though the fuel decision was mine. I don't know if he was decorated too."

Even when conditions forced a crew to abort, the plane often still ran a gauntlet. Filling in as a spare after others abandoned the formation because of mechanical problems, the 351st Bomb Group crew with John Greenwood as navigator were ten minutes from the I.P. for Merseburg and 150 miles inside enemy territory, when the gears on an engine sheared. "It was impossible to feather the prop and oil was streaming out into the slipstream covering the rear portion of the ship," remembers Greenwood. "We decided to leave the formation and go back to England. We turned around and jettisoned our bombs to lighten the load."

Now, with a 10/10 undercast, as navigator, Greenwood could not rely on pilotage. Because of their engine malfunction, the plane's maximum altitude was reduced to 17,000 feet, the prime height for the radar-controlled flak gunners. Using dead reckoning, Greenwood advised the pilot to dogleg over northern Germany to avoid the heaviest flak areas.

"We broke out into the clear about five miles from a very heavy flak concentration at Emden. They opened up with the 88s. From our altitude, the safe open water of the North Sea looked not too far away to Walt, our pilot. He decided to make a run for it. It was actually twenty miles away and in terms of time, about eight minutes from us.

"Our course took us over the very center of Emden and the boys on the ground had plenty of sleep the night before because every shot was accurate. The tail gunner was hit first by flak on the fourth burst. About a minute later the waist gunner was hit. The flak was bursting so close we could hear it explode above the roar of the engines. It would burst under the plane and we could feel the ship quiver and rise. All this time Walt was doing some beautiful evasive action but they would track us on every turn. The tail gunner, even though he was hit stood by his guns, because supposedly there were fighters in the area. The waist gunner, hit more badly, was moaning over the interphone, since he had fallen on the mike button."

When the plane at last traveled beyond the reach of its tormentors, it had lost another engine and the holes in the fuselage ventilated the interior. Still, another 200 miles of North Sea had to be crossed and a third engine produced reduced power. They staggered through a rainstorm while issuing an SOS and an alert to the air-sea rescue units. When the wounded plane touched down, it bounced, swerving off the runway and drawing dead aim on the waiting ambulances. The pilot took it up again, barely missing a parked B-24 and then a hangar. On his second try, the pilot set it down successfully but Greenwood notes, "We went into the interrogation room where the medics broke out the (medicinal) whiskey bottle. We all had two double shots. There were two guys on our crew who didn't drink usually, but this time they made an exception." Both of the wounded gunners survived.

While others found the skies highly dangerous, Jim McCubbin and his fellow fighter pilots chafed at the boredom of accompanying bombers without fighter opposition or opportunities to strafe. When a briefing officer announced a deep penetration effort McCubbin and his flight [with a total of four operational P-51s] volunteered to fly, even though they were unscheduled. It was an event where McCubbin's penchant for freelancing would finally do him in.

"Because all of our missions were long-range," remembers McCubbin, "our planes carried two drop tanks of 110 gallons each. We often lamented

THE MIGHTY EIGHTH | 413

the waste in dropping those tanks indiscriminately—that is, wouldn't it be great if we could drop them on some kraut's head?—better defined as a target. A crude plan evolved where if the lead plane would jettison his tanks on a target, the following plane would ignite the fuel by firing his armor-piercing incendiary ammunition. This bit of phosphorus was so effective that it would flash whatever it struck. Then the second plane would add his tanks as he overflew the same target. The whole idea was rather juvenile since the tanks would not fly like bombs and were difficult to place. Also, it was hard to concentrate on firing one's guns while trying to determine when to let go of his tanks.

"Due to heavy thick clouds, we were almost to Berlin before we could find a break to go down to the deck. Shortly thereafter, the squadron encountered three trains within a small area. I directed Berry, my element leader to hit the train first so that I could set off his tanks on my run and drop mine for Kenworthy on his run. I saw numerous hits on the locomotive on my pass, but didn't notice any flames.

"As I pulled up from my run, I noticed that Berry continued straight away from the target at low altitude. When I called him on the radio he informed me he had been hit. It was later that I noticed a flak car toward the end of the train—a flatcar with an antiaircraft gun mounted there and camouflaged. I caught up with Berry and after examining his plane could not detect any damage. I asked if he could make it back to the base and he responded, 'No!' I asked if he planned to bail out, and he said, 'Yes.' Shortly after, he jettisoned his canopy, the plane rolled over and crashed into the ground. I concluded that he must have been badly injured and when he got rid of the canopy, the edge hit his head. We were instructed to duck while jettisoning to avoid this possibility."

The weather actually was not propitious for this type of operation, explains McCubbin. Low clouds obstructed the field of vision when greater clearance permitted a wider aspect for target selection and maneuvers. With one man lost and the prospects unpromising the squadron leader decided to pack it in. "I disagreed for several reasons," says McCubbin, "not the least of which was that Berry could not return with us. He was my roommate. So I conveniently became lost and unable to rejoin the group. I followed the main tracks west as most likely to provide targets. My ceiling was gradually dropping but I did find a large railroad marshaling area. A good pilot avoids such areas because that is where the guns are.

"Because of my poor forward vision, I had little choice but to shoot and go. I reasoned that a 180-degree turn would offer too much target for the gunners, who undoubtedly had been notified of this 'nut' coming 'down the line.' The targets were so numerous that I had difficulty concentrating my fire. The other problem was due to the low altitude I had to porpoise, climb to 100 feet, so I could point the aircraft at the ground target on the next shallow dive and repeat. The altitude had to be limited because each gain allowed more gunners a shot.

"I had almost made it across. On one of my 'jump ups' a shell opened up a two-foot-diameter hole in my right wing, just outside of the right machine gun. As I zoomed up into the overcast, I noted that my airspeed and artificial horizon instruments were not functioning. As I was trying to compensate for this I acquired vertigo, I didn't know which way was up—literally. Instead of breaking out on top of the first layer of overcast, I broke out at the bottom, heading for the ground.

"Reentering the overcast, I began to check my engine instruments. All of the things a pilot never wants to see, were happening. The coolant temperature was climbing, oil pressure was dropping, and oil temperature was going up. As I shifted the coolant doors from auto to manual open, I knew the engine was going to burn up soon. And then I broke out on top of the bottom overcast. Because of the wing damage, I could manage the plane only by holding the control stick to the extreme left side of the cockpit. By now I was flying about 100 feet above the clouds, some 3,000 feet above the ground. As the engine began to lose power, I called my squadron leader to say, 'hasta luego, I hope.'

"Bailing out was tricky because when I released pressure on the control stick, the plane would start a snap roll. Therefore, I elected to jump straight up from a crouching position on the seat, instead of the normal procedure of diving for the right wing. I had always wanted to make a parachute jump. Imagine the peace and calm of no engine noise, or vibration, of peacefully enjoying the view as you lazily float down. What a contrast! By the time I could pull the rip cord I was in the clouds. But I had lost valuable altitude because the parachute wouldn't deploy until my second try. As I cleared the clouds, I could see several groups of people gathered, obviously waiting for something—like me. I realized that my engine must have sounded so bad, in its death throes, that it alerted many local citizens in its path.

"Because of the loss of time [until the chute opened], I only made one complete oscillation before hitting the ground—hard! Fortunately it was marshy which saved me from breaking something. But I would limp for several days. Realizing that escape was unlikely I walked to the nearest group of some fifteen old men and women. They encircled me. Being the center of attraction, I felt compelled to say something. All I could think of was to approach one of the more kindly looking old ladies and ask if they could help me escape. With this bit of English, the whole mood of the group changed drastically. Up to that point they didn't realize what they had. A teenage boy who could speak some broken English [talked] about how bad the Americans were and particularly President Roosevelt.

"Shortly after, several members of the Volksturm [people's army made up of older men and disabled former soldiers] appeared on bicycles to escort me to the road and nearest town. Our group quickly became a parade, followed by an ever increasing number of local citizens. At one point an approaching cyclist held up the 'V-for-Victory' sign. The mob immediately swarmed over him. Later two large trucks came. The drivers stepped out of their vehicles and immediately began to beat me with their fists. My adrenaline level was so high I didn't feel a thing.

"The Volksturm turned me over to an army major at the jail in town. His first inquiry in perfect English was 'Do you know the Arkansas Conservatory of Music?' He said he had received his music degree there before the war."

McCubbin passed through the system for downed airmen, traveling by rail, under guard of course, to the main interrogation center at Oberursel. An intelligence officer explained he would be kept until the authorities felt certain he was simply a prisoner of war rather than a spy. After recovering the wreckage of his plane they would be able to determine his squadron and group. During his stay in a tiny cell he discovered a friend from primary training occupied the one two doors away.

After several days, during which meals consisted of a piece of bread in a bowl of hot water with a handful of peas floating on the surface, the German interrogator announced, "We now know that you are from the 364th Fighter Group and 385th Fighter Squadron. We also note that your plane is credited with nine victories." He told McCubbin the name of his roommate and then to the chagrin of the American played a recording of the radio talk between him and McKibben during which they excitedly discussed their sweep and the shootdown of an ME-109. McCubbin parried a series of questions about his outfit until he was finally moved to a distribution center. There he relished his most substantial meal since being shot down, "two prunes, two sardines and one whole slice of bread."

21

FINAL BLOWS

With the last vestiges of the Ardennes bulge wiped out, the Allied ground forces drove toward the final geographic obstacle, the Rhine River. Overhead, the bombers and fighters continued to pound anything that might be construed as sustaining the ebbing strength of the enemy. Arriving for the last few months was George Odenwaller, birthed at home in 1925, and who grew up in Cliffside Park, New Jersey, just across the Hudson River from New York City. His father owned a hay and feed business located across from what is now the entrance to the Lincoln Tunnel. "Dad supplied the Fort Lee [New Jersey] studios with hay and feed for the horses, when the first cowboy movies were made. Tom Mix [a star of the silent days] still owes him money." The family also dabbled in show business with Odenwaller's sister working on Broadway as a singer-dancer with "her buddies, Alice Faye, Marilyn Miller, Kate Smith, Cesar Romero and Van Johnson" and young George even had bit parts in two films.

"Just about every male wanted to be drafted or join up when Pearl Harbor was attacked. We wanted to get those Jap bastards and stop that Nazi SOB. We all found out just how patriotic we really were. We all wanted to serve our country somehow. I think we felt we were invincible."

Drafted while still in high school, but awarded a diploma nevertheless, Odenwaller had been hooked on airplanes after his first flight at age six. He qualified for flight training but washed out of cadet training in February 1944 "because of a gunner shortage." Still determined to fly he accepted the opportunity for gunner instruction and in the summer of 1944 entered an Overseas Training Unit where crews formed. Originally slotted for the tail gunner post, Odenwaller says, "When the ball gunner, Walter Linberger (Lindy), and I looked at each other, we knew right away he was too cramped and too big for the ball, so we traded positions.

"Our pilot, Joe Harvy, was somewhat of a special guy. When Joe applied for flight training, he was already a second lieutenant, a tank commander. He obtained his wings and upon graduation gained the rank of first lieutenant. Being trained in the ways of the ground forces left much to be desired for the rest of the crew including the other officers. We considered having Joe replaced because of his chicken-shit ways and as a combat crew we could vote him out. By chance our engineer Neil Jorgenson met Joe in a pub and while totally drunk told Joe of our plans to vote him out if it was to be 'Lieutenant Harvy,' 'Yes, sir,' 'No, sir,' and the rest of the ways we didn't like.

"At our next crew meeting with him the following day, Joe said he had something to tell us. He apologized to all of us for keeping a broad line between himself as an officer and us as enlisted personnel. From this meeting on, we became unusually tight. Off hours we began to socialize, although in a military manner. After all, we were still stateside. I think we spent as much time in the officers' quarters as they spent in ours. Also at this time, Joe decided we all should have stick time to fly each other's position since we were flying every day doing slow time [tuning an engine] and cross-country."

With the 91st Bomb Group, Odenwaller's crew was assigned the B-17 named *Outhouse Mouse* and for its first mission February 14, 1945, the target was Dresden. Odenwaller says, "All of us were uptight. I was scared stiff and had some trouble installing my guns. However, we lost No. 3 engine and could not keep up with the group so we aborted and salvoed. Just before the engine loss, as we approached the I.P., a lone silver P-51 came right up into our formation surrounded by B-17s. Showing off the big black crosses, he just sat there. No one fired a shot. Then all of a sudden down he went and was gone. G-2 [intelligence] could not understand why no one pulled a trigger. I learned later that the P-51 was a captured aircraft used by German pilots for orientation."

Frank Aldrich as a lead navigator for his squadron in the 305th Bomb Group participated in the raid on Dresden that day, but his aircraft too did not strike the city. "As we approached the target," says Aldrich, "the sky was filled with planes as far as one could see. From the Initial Point we turned onto the bomb run in routine fashion, but at the point of the drop, the bombardier sighted one of our own formations passing through his bombsight directly below us. Accordingly, our bombs were withheld as were those of the rest of our lead element. As I recall, the elements following us were ordered to make the drop, while we crossed over the city retaining our load of 500-pounders.

"At this juncture, a decision was made for the five aircraft still holding bomb loads to seek a target of opportunity while those which had emptied their bomb bays were to join the homeward-bound formations. I was asked to select such a target and opted for the synthetic oil refinery at Brüx in Czechoslovakia to the southeast of us. Selecting this target was not an act of courage but made simply out of convenience since I had Brüx plotted on my map and it would be the first candidate to appear beneath us on our wide sweep southward for the return to England. The wind was in the 120-mph range, pushing us rapidly eastward so that when we came around we found ourselves moving upwind toward Brüx."

For Aldrich, the scene implied a dreadful *déjà vu,* the bloody upwind approach mandated for Cologne a month earlier. However, at least there was no question of a faulty bomb-release mechanism.

"Nothing was spared in the defense of synthetic oil facilities. Thus it must have been baffling to the personnel of the thickly clustered flak batteries around Brüx to spot a force of a mere five bombers approaching them on a course upwind, slowing their ground speed to less than 100 mph. We were probably the smallest formation to attack a major target during the entire course of the war. Nonetheless, they threw everything they had at us during our run which we calculated at a full twenty-one minutes. Coming out with more holes than a sieve, we hobbled across Germany—the Luftwaffe mercifully leaving us alone—to land near Lille. That was as far as the old bird could make it." For this venture and another subsequently, Aldrich was awarded a DFC.

ON February 15, American bombers again struck Dresden, and waist gunner John Morris with the 91st Bomb Group was there. "It was an easy mission. No fighters attacked us. Since Dresden had never been attacked before, the Germans may have thought we would never hit it. So there were no antiaircraft guns on the ground in the vicinity. Viewed from 35,000 feet there was nothing dramatic to report."

The Dresden raids in mid-February, which Odenwaller and company had aborted and where Aldrich had led his five B-17s to an alternate target, were part of a massive three-day assault that created a firestorm estimated to have killed 60,000, wiped out the center of the city and became a *cause célèbre.* Dresden itself appeared to have no substantial military objectives within it, although a network of rail lines lay on the outskirts. Bomber pilot Saul Levine of the 305th Bomb Group believes the purpose was to drive civilians out onto the roads, clogging the transport system, already burdened with the retreat of men and supplies from the eastern front. The bulk of critics blame the RAF, which did most of the damage at night, for targeting a civilian site, and many Germans accuse Winston Churchill of having approved what they consider an atrocity.

At the time, most of the air crewmen had little sympathy for those on the receiving end of their bombs. Dave Nagel says, "If you saw London, like I saw it, you wouldn't have any remorse. I don't know anyone who was remorseful. We didn't know whether an area was populated or not. We were supposed to be over a target, normally a factory when we let the bombs go, but we assumed it was surrounded by civilians. I didn't hate anyone, but near the end [of their combat tour] we were nervous, uptight. German fliers did go after stricken planes. They were unmerciful and it took the heart out of us to see these guys just trying to stay alive and this bastard would let 'em have it. There were instances where planes made passes at men in chutes. As time went on, for me a dead German was the best German. To this day, I won't buy German goods, if I can help it. I am prejudiced."

John Morris says, "I'm hardly ashamed of having gone to Dresden that day. It was sound strategy to prevent [the Wehrmacht] from falling back to regroup and be lethal again. So we bombed the hell out of the railroad marshaling yards and road hubs along the Wehrmacht's line of retreat, up and down Germany's eastern border. I don't rejoice at the 35,000 Germans killed there [other estimates range from 60,000 to 100,000 killed]. I doubt there were many Jews in that number. The good burghers of Dresden had shipped them all off to Auschwitz. It is true that the RAF purposely started a firestorm, causing many of the casualties. It was a tactic they frequently tried. But they, and we, killed more people in other cities, on other days. So did the Russians. So did the Japanese. So did the Germans. Dresden was not unique."

By the time of Dresden and probably much earlier, the airmen knew their destruction was not limited to strategic targets. The vagaries of weather and wind, the fierce, deadly opposition and the imperfect systems for laying bombs in a confined area all combined to spread the devastation well beyond the stated target. Furthermore, the desperate desire for self-preservation, particularly as the missions stretched out, often led to drops off the mark. During one mission, the crew with Dan Villani from the 398th Bomb Group became separated from their companions because of thick clouds. When the plane broke into the clear, they found them-selves temporarily alone. Spotting another flight of B-17s they decided to attach themselves to it rather than lose credit for a mission. The naviga-tors for what was the 91st Bomb Group took them over Schweinfurt [en route to Berlin] where the usual concentration of antiaircraft pockmarked the sky. "Most of the formation spread out to avoid the flak," notes Vil-lani, "and in so doing ruined the accuracy of the drop. I'm sure many of the pilots didn't give a damn. They just wanted out of a target area as fast as possible. This is the only time I remember dropping bombs one by one in a train, instead of all at once. The aiming point was the center of Berlin and I don't think this was bombing a military target. But I personally felt no remorse. They brought Hitler to power and supported him and sealed their fate."

With the armies of the Third Reich seemingly in their death throes, the Eighth Air Force sought to knock out the last vestiges of resistance. Dave Ferguson, the radio operator in the 94th Bomb Group recalls flying eight consecutive days between February 19 and 28. "I still remember how tired we were. The Germans were closely grouped and putting up a fierce flak barrage. We lost a lot of bomber crews. The German air force was up again and I saw them machine gun our men as they jumped from bombers with parachutes. A helpless feeling for us."

Willard Richards as a gunner with the 385th Bomb Group says that within the space of fifteen days he flew eleven missions. "Evidently, the strain was beginning to show as we were issued a forty-eight-hour pass. To supplement the departure of recent veterans like Ferguson and Rich-ards came the latest graduates of stateside curricula. W. W. Varnadoe, a former Georgia Tech student bounced from ROTC in the coast artillery to the Army Specialized Training Program [ASTP], was back at Tech until he signed up for the Air Corps. Like Odenwaller he entered the cadet school in February 1944 to learn the trade of navigator. He com-pleted his courses in October, receiving wings and a commission.

Varnadoe became a member of a crew led by Lt. George H. Crow Jr. "One of the first things we did was just to fly about the Florida skies to get familiar with the B-17 and each other. On one of these trips at night, George called me up to the cockpit. The copilot, Don Black, had gone off somewhere and George asked me to sit in the right seat. He asked me, 'Have you ever flown an airplane?' 'No,' I answered. 'Well, do you know what the controls are?' I had read as many comic books as anyone, so I said yes. Actually I did know the rudder pedals and the movements of the control column, but nothing else. The artificial horizon with the little airplane on it seemed sort of obvious.

"George next said, 'You've got it.' At once I began to overcontrol, so we began to hop across the sky. It was my very first time ever at the controls of an airplane and it was a big four-engine monster. It was night without a natural horizon in sight. I really wasn't sure I had things under control and gripped the wheel as though it were holding me in the plane. At this point, George announced, 'You're doing fine.' Then he got up and left me alone on the flight deck! Thus I learned to at least keep the plane straight and level and to point it in a given direction. I never did get the hang of flying in formation, and, of course, never took off or landed."

By January the Crow crew was equipped with the latest model B-17 and traveled to Scotland, a fourteen-hour trip across the Atlantic. Bomber command took away their brand-new Fortress and shipped them to the 385th Bomb Group at Great Ashfield. Varnadoe received instruction in the use of the local navigation aids and the pilots practiced working in tight formation. A three-day pass enabled them to visit London. "We were impressed by the darkness at night during the blackout. One could stand at Piccadilly Circus and see absolutely nothing, just hear the incessant clacking of wooden heels as people walked about. One could barely make out the features of the Piccadilly Commandoes [whores]. We hired a disabled British soldier to act as a guide and show us the sights. We witnessed the changing of the guard at Buckingham Palace. Although the fancy dress uniforms had given way to wartime khaki, the ceremony was still impressive. We also toured the Tower of London, Westminster Abbey and at night we saw the girlie shows at the Windmill Theatre."

Their first raid was the railroad yard for a tank factory at Kassel. "There were 10/10 [ground completely obscured] clouds at the target," notes Varnadoe. "We bombed by PFF, sometimes called 'Mickey' or H2X. This was an early-type ground-image radar. It showed a clear contrast between land and water but was difficult to interpret over land. The lead Fort had a radar dome in place of the ball turret.

"Over the target there was light flak but no fighters. We jammed the German's radar with 'window': the strips of metal foil which the radio operator threw out in bundles. On some missions a British Mosquito would fly ahead of us and lay a blanket of window below our formation. Also, occasionally, a jammer B-17 would accompany us. This Fort had a radio room filled with transmitters. The radio operator would scan the frequency board and when he picked up a radar, he'd fire up a transmitter on that exact frequency. All that jamming seemed to work well. On the mission to Kassel, the 385th lost no planes."

Varnadoe's second mission, the first in which his original crew performed as a unit, again demonstrated the slim margin for error in formation flying. "We were left wing off Rusecki's crew who was in the lead of the low element of the lead squadron. The left wing of the lead element was Armbruster's crew in a B-17 named *Mr. Lucky*. There was a cloud deck just below the group. It was mostly flat and smooth on top, except there were occasional humps of cloud here and there.

"Just as we reached the Belgian coast, the low element and Rusecki passed into one of these humps. Suddenly, Rusecki came up out of it in a steep climb. He came up just over us and into Armbruster. *Mr. Lucky* was hit by the No. 1 and 2 engines of Rusecki's B-17, which cut into *Mr. Lucky* about the rear of the radio room. Rusecki slid back chewing up the waist section of Armbruster's plane which was now in two pieces. I lost sight of Rusecki's Fort and the tail of *Mr. Lucky* as I focused on the front half, which was sliding to the left and dropping, mighty close to us.

"I could clearly see Chuck Armbruster looking back over his shoulder trying to see what was happening. As he continued to slide towards us, Crow pulled us out of formation or there would have been three planes in the collision. Armbruster's front half went into a flat spin and disappeared into the clouds. We then edged back into the lead slot, where Rusecki had been moments before. The whole thing was over in less than fifteen seconds.

"It was eerie seeing all that metal ripping apart only yards away, without making a sound as if in a silent movie. Of course it was making noise, but the constant deafening roar of our own engines drowned out everything. We were so used to our engines that the impression was one of silence. Another lasting image was the sight of the radio operator falling out of Armbruster's plane, without his parachute. On B-17s, crew members generally wore a parachute harness, but not the chute itself. These chest packs had clips which could quickly be attached to our harness. However, after this incident, and seeing that tumbling crewman, several of us wore our parachutes all the time while in the air, cumbersome or not. Later, we learned there were only two survivors. The waist gunner of Rusecki's crew who bailed out and the tail gunner of Armbruster's."

Joe Jones was on his twenty-second mission as tail gunner in *Mr. Lucky* when he knew something was terribly wrong. According to Jones, he heard his pilot over the intercom tell his substitute copilot, "'Pull over! We don't want that guy's wing in our lap.' Right after I felt a terrific jolt and looked up through my tail section plexiglass. I was horrified to be looking right at the bomb bay section of the B-17 in the number two position of the element above us. I thought 'My God! We've collided' and immediately felt what I thought was the entire plane falling away. I hit the radio toggle switch, 'Tail to pilot,' no reply. Again, 'Tail to pilot' still no answer. 'Tail to pilot, dammit, answer me!' Dead silence. I clawed my way to the escape hatch in the tail of the plane; it was jammed. Then I thought if I could get my parachute through the tail window, I could bail out, but the window was too small. My next thought was one of confidence in the pilot. Our crew thought we had the best of them all in Chuck Armbruster and I remember thinking that if anybody could get us out of this mess, he could. I had no idea at all that the collision sheared off the plane's tail section and that I was free-falling. For lack of more brilliant thoughts, I sat back in the gunner's seat and waited."

The tail of *Mr. Lucky* with Jones still in it smashed into a Belgian cow pasture. A farmer and friends found the gunner, cut him out of the tail with an axe and took him to a British hospital where he recovered fully after a week in a coma.

Varnadoe remarks, "Nobody knows why that Fortress came up abruptly like that. Perhaps that cloud hump had an updraft, or perhaps Rusecki flying formation, concentrating on the plane he was flying off, didn't see the cloud coming, then suddenly losing visibility, got vertigo."

Not only was collision within the tightly packed formations of a squadron or group an omnipresent danger, but with hundreds upon hundreds of aircraft threatening gridlock in the sky, midair crashes resulted from other outfits intent on their own destination. Bill Powers recalls scary moments after a raid on Plauen. "We flew in intense haze most of the day and had to bomb by radar. I thought I saw spots of oil on my plexiglass dome on the turret and they got larger. Here was another formation of B-17s turning directly in our path, heading right for us. All at once my pilot broke silence and said, 'Looks like every man for himself,' and pushed down on the stick and pulled back, using evasive action. When he pulled up, I fell out of my turret and was pinned to the floor with my oxygen line stretched to the limit. I saw the tail end of a B-17 fly by. When I returned to my turret and looked around, planes were everywhere and some going down due to collision. I saw *Old Century Note* in a flat spin, and they said that once in a flat spin that was it. Later when the remaining ships returned to the formation I spotted *Old Century Note* coming back. We had flown in her and had a certain feeling for her."

The poor visibility and the crowded skies also added to navigational confusion. Barky Hovsepian, as a radio operator in the 466th Bomb Group remembers his outfit trying to form up over southern France. "While flying to the target through dense clouds, a B-17 group flew through our twenty-eight a/c formation, scattering us. We took evasive action to avoid collisions with them. Despite a call from the leader to abandon the mission, nine planes put together a reasonable formation and decided to bomb a target of opportunity. There was some uncertainty whether it was Freiburg, Germany, or Basel, Switzerland. Both towns were on either side of the border and had similar marshaling yards. We didn't drop our bombs for our navigator had very strong reservations. But the ones that did were within a thousand-foot circle with 100 percent results. The rolling stock in the yards had contained ammunition and the secondary explosions so indicated. When we returned to base, an extensive critique was made at our debriefing session. We were all ordered not to discuss this incident. It was Switzerland we had hit, and the U.S. Government diplomatically paid $70 million in reparation (despite my personal skepticism about where that ammunition was headed)."

Walt Konantz of the 55th Fighter Group had scored his fourth kill on January 29, his last opportunity to encounter the enemy in a dogfight. He sortied nine times during the following month, engaged in escort duties to Berlin, Frankfurt, Dessau and other targets without ever coming across a German fighter. He strafed a number of locomotives, trucks, a horse-drawn wagon—"I didn't see the horse until too late"—a tractor, and even a soldier on a motorcycle. But he logged out as a combat pilot still shy of the magic number for an ace.

Konantz was only one of thousands now completing their battle service. Dave Ferguson and his crew realized that while others were getting time off, their proficiency kept them scheduled. "After our thirtieth mission, the flight surgeon talked to us all and we came out on orders to go to the 'flak house' [rest and recreation center] for a few days. We came back, flew another five and happy day, ended up with thirty-five."

Mac McCauley, elevated to deputy lead for his squadron in the 385th Bomb Group, noted, "Many crews were finishing their tours now and it was difficult to train new crews with the shortage of men. Also, Great Ashfield had only fifty-nine aircraft on the base. Trying to put up thirty-six or thirty-eight planes each day left no planes for training. Eleven were pathfinders and couldn't be used for instructing regular crews. With those down for battle damage and maintenance, few were left for training."

One change designed to provide enough people cut the number of gunners on B-17s. Lewis Smith, as a first pilot, chose the man to transfer. "It was easy," he says. "I had a number of problems with my ball-turret gunner, going all the way back to Rapid City during combat crew training. He had not properly locked the ball turret. Upon landing, it came down, dragging the twin .50 caliber gun barrels on the runway and grinding off about three inches of barrel."

The traditional system of putting an experienced hand aboard with a replacement gang took Smith's right-hand aide, copilot Bill Chaney, to another ship with a first pilot named Cocke, for a mission to Berlin on March 18. "The weather broke over the target and we bombed visual," Smith informed his diary. "However, contrails were still very bad, just like flying in soup. Flak was very intense and accurate. Jets attacked us over the target. Just after the target we went into some heavy contrail and when we came out, Cocke who had been on my left wing was gone. According to several guys who saw it, a burst of flak knocked out their No. 2 engine and set it on fire. They did a wing-over out of formation and dove to put out the fire. They apparently succeeded and leveled out, quite a way below the formation, while headed for Russia.

A mournful Smith scribbled, "We lost three other ships to flak and fighters and sustained quite a bit of battle damage. It's getting rougher all the time. Cocke and his crew were from our barracks. We have numerous empty beds again. That's nine men we've lost out of sixteen, six in the last month. They took Chaney's clothes out tonight. What a feeling that gave us. One ship exploded over the target but we don't think it was Chaney's. If he's in Russia, we should know in several weeks. If he's in Germany, we should know in several months. Naturally the boys are pretty broken up about it. They all figure if he would have been with us, he would be OK. He only had two more missions to go." Lost on the same raid upon Berlin was the ball gunner transferred out by Smith. However, Chaney and his crew did make it to the Soviet lines, only to be treated, according to Smith, "almost like prisoners."

For Dan Villani, that assault on Berlin was his worst. "The Russians were closing in on one side and on the other General Bradley was poised on the Elbe River," remembers the navigator with the 398th Bomb Group. "The Germans had everything concentrated for the defense of the city. I thought I was in hell. The sky was literally dark from flak bursts. Every time a piece of flak hit the plane it sounded like a piece of coal going down a metal chute. I was busy with nose pressed against the plexiglass, straining to see the lead plane. Just before bomb release, a burst of flak hit the plane.

"We called around the intercom to see if everyone was OK. No answer from our tail gunner. After we peeled away from the target area, Paul [Wagner, the pilot] asked me to go back and see about our tail gunner, William Stegall. With a portable oxygen mask I crawled back and saw the stricken look on our waist gunner's face. Stegall was hit with a piece of shrapnel in the back of the head and it stopped just behind his nose, pushing it out a little. He died instantly in position, straddling his banana seat at the tail gun. We pulled him back to the center of the plane and laid him on the floor.

"I was certain of his death and so informed our pilot. He asked for a heading to the nearest field for a landing. I think I convinced him that there was no sense to that and we should try to make it home alone. We knew the war would be over soon. If we were interned by the Russians, we might not get home for a long time. We were now flying by ourselves. The formations were in disarray. [In the past] many bombardiers and navigators were goofing off on the job by sandbagging it and letting the lead plane do the navigating. Not me, not after the fiasco in getting lost when we first got to England. We were all alone and we navigated back across northern Germany and the Netherlands and down to the English Channel, actually with the help of German AA guns.

"The maps given to me at briefing had crayon markings drawn around the cities or towns where we could expect to see flak. S-2 intelligence was great [others report the information often was erroneous, and rarely accounted for mobile antiaircraft units]. If I was unsure of my exact position I asked Paul to fly so many degrees to the right or left toward the flak markings and as soon as the flak started I changed position to another flak position. When the flak started again I could pinpoint my position and figure a wind direction.

"The same burst of flak that killed Stegall also cut some control cables so we could not land. Our resourceful flight engineer came to the rescue, found the break, tied it together with a piece of heater cord and then held it under tension by twisting it with a .50 caliber shell while Paul landed the plane. Stegall was buried at Maddenly, the USAAC cemetery just outside Cambridge. We all attended his funeral. It was the lowest point in our lives as a crew."

Wayne Gatlin, who retained his boyish enthusiasm, at least in his letters home, was now a senior pilot in his squadron. "I don't know what this outfit is coming to nowadays," he somewhat ingenuously informed his parents. "When they start letting guys like me lead flights, well it sort of makes you wonder. I led Blue and Green flights as we covered our box of bombers. All in all, ten ships were flying off of me and I was pretty busy keeping with and covering the bombers. The dang bombers made three circles around the target before they finally bombed and we were getting pretty 'browned off' at them. I guess they were waiting for the smoke to clear as a number of bombers had bombed before us, shrouding the target in smoke. It felt good to see home and it was a pretty nice feeling to know that you hadn't screwed up the detail."

For all the production capacity in the States, the Eighth still had to scrounge for enough airworthy ships to fill the mission orders. To achieve the requisite numbers, some that should probably have been retired stayed on. For that reason and as a public-relations ploy, the 385th kept an aging queen, *Rum Dum,* in service. "They wanted her to be the first B-17 in the European theater of operations to make 100 missions, without having an abort," says Lewis Smith. With his own steady *Gypsy Princess* temporarily down for repairs, Smith piloted *Rum Dum* on its ninety-seventh, ninety-ninth, 100th and 101st trips. "It wasn't easy because often when she got up to around 20,000 to 25,000 feet, her superchargers would cut out and we would start to lag behind, unable to keep up with the formation. Then they would kick in again. They [the mechanics] were never able to figure out why. It was never reported, but on her last few missions before the 100th, we understood we were to complete the mission or go down trying."

The milestone for *Rum Dum* came on Smith's thirty-first mission, on the final day of March. He noted, "[David] Schanke [bombardier] was the only one of the original crew with me." And as in the past, *Rum Dum* behaved erratically. "At altitude, over the middle of Germany, all four of the turbos cut out for a few minutes. I thought we had had it. They finally came back on. Anyway, they took our pictures when we came down." *Rum Dum*'s career ended a few missions later with a crash landing in France.

Much of the impetus to set a record with *Rum Dum* may have stemmed from the esprit of the ground crew who serviced it. They, more than the different air crews that flew *Rum Dum,* had a continuing relationship with the plane. Ball-turret gunner George Odenwaller, of the 91st Bomb Group, notes the rather unique, proprietary attitude of ground crews. "We never became too friendly with the ground crew. They could not do enough for us, but always let us know that the airplane we just brought back broken was theirs."

That did not prevent them from going to great lengths to please those who "borrowed" their machines for a few hours. "One time," says

Odenwaller, "our a/c was shot up a bit and couldn't be used. We were told at the briefing to use 909 for our mission. We were trucked out to it in the dark and to check out my turret, I opened the escape hatch and put on a few lights. Lo and behold, I realized I was looking at a ball turret fully upholstered in old fleece jackets, a virtual cocoon, all fuzzy and inviting. I called to Lindy, my tail gunner, and his tail position was also fleece-lined.

"After we landed [from the mission] our ground crew asked if everything was okay. We raved about the fleece. Would you believe, the next mission, our own a/c had a fleece-lined ball turret and tail position. These guys had worked through the night and part of the next day putting fleece into our *Outhouse Mouse*."

Relationships occasionally struck shoals. Bill Powers on a mission climbed into his top turret and squeezed into position. "While doing so, my parachute harness snapped over a cable which came from the electronic sight. I struggled to get loose but couldn't. If the ship went down, I'd have to go with her. I finally managed to touch my push-to-talk button and called the copilot who came and released me. He said to tell the ground-crew chief to get the cable out of the way. I did and the next day, just as I squirmed into the turret, I heard and felt a 'snap.' I was too embarrassed to call for help again. I struggled while flak was all around us. Finally I gave up and called the copilot to release me again.

"'Dammit,' he said, 'get on that crew chief's butt and get that cable out of the way.' After the mission, everyone stood around and watched me chew out the crew chief. He was about six foot six, and I a short five foot seven, standing there, chewing him out. He could have squashed me. Bottom line, next day I checked out the cable before doing anything and it was secure and out of the way."

Togglier Al Greenberg continued to be vexed by breakdowns with his devices. Over Nürnberg, on his thirtieth mission, communications with the lead ship were out. Pluto, the system that salvoed on the lead bombardier, malfunctioned and the bombs dropped without regard to location of the target. "I didn't report the malfunction," says Greenberg. "I didn't want to do any explaining. But even with different airplanes, Pluto refused to perform properly during several more raids but for my final effort all systems worked." In his journal he noted, "On the way back, there was no flak but one ship was on fire. We watched it all the way until it turned around and blew up. We came out over the Zuider Zee and buzzed the field and shot flares [his pilot was also completing his combat runs]. It was an easy mission and my tour of operation is completed, thirty-five missions as an enlisted bombardier without a scratch. New York, here I come."

Some airmen from the Eighth who went operational toward the end of 1944 or the start of 1945 saw hardly any enemy fighters, but the ME-262 remained a deadly if infrequent threat. *Outhouse Mouse* with Odenwaller aboard encountered several during one flight. "Two came around from six o'clock level," says the ball-turret gunner, "and at about 600 yards out, I fired at the one on the left who blew out black smoke, then at about 300 yards out, the a/c on the right belched black smoke and fire in his port engine. He flew right under me while looking up and I saw his face. As I wheeled the turret to the left to follow them, both broke left and dived away. When I came back around right, I got a look at the a/c flying on our starboard. It was *Blood 'N Guts* from the 401st Bomb Squadron. The tail gunner's guns were pointing in two different directions; the rear window was blown in and no tail gunner to be seen. Then I saw the ball turret. The two-inch-thick glass plate was apparently blown into the gunner who was then blown out the back of the turret, empty with headset, heated suit, electrical cable lines trailing out the front of the ball. To track these 600-mph a/c was difficult. The turrets were engineered for three-four-hundred-mph a/c. The turret could not traverse fast enough."

Even though the P-51s spotted the 262 at as much as 200 mph, the Americans did not shrink from dogfights with them. Winding up his required number of combat hours in early April, Wayne Gatlin led a flight escorting bombers striking some ten miles north of Berlin. Just as the planes dropped their explosives, Gatlin saw jets attacking a bomb group ahead of the one he was supposed to protect. "I was on the right-hand side of the bombers going toward the tail-end of our box when I saw an ME-262 making a pass from six o'clock high. He appeared to be hitting two stragglers and then continued in a dive right on down through the box. I made a 180-degree diving turn—a split S—to the right and was able to cut him off very easily. I slid in on his tail as he continued his dive and opened fire at zero degrees deflection and 200-yards range. I observed hits all over the jet and continued firing as he started smoking. I kept on him until his dive became almost vertical and I had to break off in order to pull out. After leveling a bit, I cocked my wing and saw where he hit and burned. The pilot did not get out." To the folks back home, the triumphant fighter pilot wrote, "He was in a dive and as I poured lead into him, his dive became steeper until he reached the vertical and plowed into the ground. He was a jet-job and one of the Germans' best, so I feel kinda good about it."

Gatlin's joy over his victory was tempered by the loss of his close friend, Raleigh "Rags" Ragsdale who occupied the bed next to him in the base quarters. "He had engine problems, over friendly territory," says Gatlin, "and was going to bail out. He had unstrapped but his aircraft entered an overcast and he waited until he was under the clouds. He was then too low to bail out when he came out of the clouds and attempted to land in a stubble field. His Mustang flipped over on impact and threw him from the plane with fatal results."

There were empty beds in Lewis Smith's 385th Bomb Group barracks also, not only because of the collision he described, but from a mission the following day that saw six more unaccounted for. Smith, however, missed that calamitous occasion because he had been given the day off. "Every time our losses are big, I'm on pass," he told his diary. "Everybody was feeling pretty lousy so the barracks (what's left) went over to the club en masse and proceeded to tie one on!!! We started in the barracks with two quarts of bourbon, willed to the barracks by Chuck Armbruster's crew and finished in the club on wine, Scotch, gin and brandy. What a party we had. Numerous flares were set off in the barracks. Numerous holes were made in the barracks by .45s. Numerous guys slept outside because they found their beds there. Numerous people were out in the field chasing horses at 2:00 A.M. We all threw one because there was a Group Stand Down for tomorrow."

The 466th Bomb Group organized a fête upon completion of its 200th mission. "With the cooperation of the Red Cross women and Special Services," says Barky Hovsepian, "truckloads of women and girls came for a prolonged celebration. It was turnabout—GIs were off duty and the officers did all the details. They were cooking and washing dishes like GIs on KP. At night they acted as bartenders, dispensing the beverages. There was a Pub Race, drinking beer, bicycling to bases and home plate. Winners who made it were awarded a quart of Scotch whisky. Then there was an air circus, a dance, a floor-show and a movie." The affair lasted for two days.

The longest entry in the memoir of Lewis Smith covers the date of April 7, his thirty-fifth and last trip. It was not a milk run. "As soon as we got into German territory, we got the report of bandits in the area. Fifteen or twenty minutes after that they were on us, ME-109s, FW-190s and ME-262s—jets. They had been ranging up and down the battle stream. We had good fighter support, lots of P-51s but they would always take off and chase some bandits and then four or five others would attack our formation. First we saw them hit the group behind and a couple of planes went down. Then they hit the group in front and one guy began to straggle so they really poured it on him. After about five passes, he blew up—just a red flash, black smoke was all that was left.

"There were numerous dogfights going on all over, especially up higher. You could see lots of jet trails. Five ME-109s came in on our tail. One was right behind us, really blazing away. The tail gunner said, 'his wings were winking like mad.' It looks kinda pretty at first but when you feel the slugs start hitting the ship, it's a different story. The tail, top and ball turrets opened up on them, but they kept right on coming and four of them went right through the formation. The one right behind us broke into flames at about 200 yards and dove into our number-four man flying right beneath us. Both blew up. Who was sweating like mad was me! It gave us quite a jolt when they exploded.

"About that time, the nose, ball and top-turret gunners opened up and I saw four FW-190s peeling through the formation right in front of the nose. Everyone really cut loose. One disappeared in a red flash and two others were smoking as they dove away. After that, two or three planes would come in from different angles every two or three minutes. We were pretty busy for about forty-five minutes. When we were about halfway down the bomb run, three jets directly above us dove straight down through the formation, knocking one guy out. He got the ship under control and seven or eight chutes were seen before the plane hit the ground. It lit in a wooded area and covered about a mile with flame and bombs. After bombs away, things quieted down and the trip home wasn't bad. We had quite a few bullet holes but nothing serious.

"Since I was a 'Happy Warrior' I left the formation at the Belgian coast and put the old nose down and flew 210 mph to the base. We crossed the Channel at 500 feet and scared the heck out of numerous ships. Who was glad to set the *Gypsy Princess* on the ground was me!!!"

Among the last to enter the aerial arena was Paul Krup, nearing his twenty-eighth birthday when he reached the United Kingdom. Born in Cleveland, Krup had completed three years at Ohio State during the Depression and gone to work for General Motors. Even as the plant switched from automotive to aeronautic production upon the advent of the war, Krup became concerned about his future if drafted. "I took the civil service exams for policeman and fireman with the city. I passed both and the first opening was with the police. As I expected, I was drafted in April 1943, and sent to the army finance school. While there I had the urge to fly and joined the Air Corps. At the processing center,

I was told my age, then twenty-six, was against me and they also had surpassed their quota of candidates for OCS. I was given the option of training as a radio operator or flight engineer and chose radio."

Upon completion of training and insertion into a replacement crew, Krup, with his colleagues, reported to the 398th Bomb Group early in 1945. On April 10, as a member of a crew headed by pilot Jim McAfee, Krup was on his way to Oranienburg, an airfield and army base near Berlin. "We were on our bomb run when we were attacked by an ME-262. His cannon shells hit us in the left waist, opening a hole big enough to drive a truck through. Felix Tichenor, our waist gunner got his left leg and arm blown off by the explosions. The oxygen and electrical systems were both shot out. I made my way to the cockpit to tell our pilot what happened in the waist. I tried to arrange an emergency intercom but it didn't work. I started back to the radio room.

"While I was still on the catwalk in the bomb bay, we were hit again. No. 3 engine was on fire and flames were pouring into the bomb bay. When I got into the radio room there was another explosion and the ship went into a dive. The walls caved in, the floor gave way and I was underneath it all. I thought 'this is it,' and started to pray. I couldn't move. Then all of a sudden, the plane leveled off and I got up and found my chute. I ripped off my flak suit and put the chute on. I noticed Haskell Boyes, our ball-turret gunner, diving out the waist door. I learned later that Max Paxton, a replacement for our tail gunner who had gone sick after a bad experience the day before, was the first to bail out. Haskell, whose left arm was blown off at the elbow had beckoned for me to follow him, but dazed from anoxia, I kept looking for a spare chute for Felix Tichenor who was lying there, badly wounded, unable to move. Felix waved me away to bail out, which I did and none too soon because the ship exploded about a moment later.

"When my chute opened, I looked up and could see four chutes dangling in the distance behind me. As I floated down, I seemed to regain my composure as the anoxia slowly lessened. The other four would have belonged to our spot jammer Robert Engard, Haskell Boyes, our togglier Frank Lewis and Max Paxton. The pilots, Tichenor and our engineer Art Roit never got out before the plane blew up."

On the ground, Krup was lucky enough to run into a German lieutenant from the Wehrmacht. "Then a lot of angry civilians came at me, but this lieutenant chased them away. He took me to a first-aid station where my face was bandaged. The left side of my face, forehead, nose, lips and eyebrows were burned. At the aid station I ran across Boyes.

His left arm was blown off above the elbow. He couldn't be moved [to a stalag] because he was so weak from loss of blood. I believe Paxton was killed on the ground." Krup in the company of some other recent prisoners entered a POW camp, for what proved to be a very short time.

On April 25, the Eighth Air Force delivered its last bangs, with its final bombing mission, hammering the munitions works at Pilsen and other targets. With only two weeks to go to V-E Day, six B-17s went down; another 180 absorbed flak damage from the still-virulent ground batteries. But there were no more targets and bombs would now endanger friendly forces, the tens of thousands of displaced persons and an increasing number of prisoners liberated from the camps.

Radio operator Paul Krup, who parachuted after his aircraft was shot down April 9, had been incarcerated at Stalag III A, the camp nearest to where he was captured. Subsisting largely on the meager food contained in Red Cross parcels, the Americans were separated from the Soviet prisoners by a barbed-wire fence. The latter, not participants in the Red Cross, bartered and begged for something to eat. "The guards were older, handicapped soldiers and ex-soldiers," says Krup. When news that liberation by the Russians was imminent, the guards quickly abandoned the camp, disappearing in fear of retribution. Confusion and disorder reigned.

"A small group of Americans including me decided to leave the camp and head for the Elbe River with hopes of meeting American troops. Being the sixth of seven siblings born of Russian immigrants, and growing up in a multiethnic environment, I was able to communicate with the Russian soldiers even though I didn't speak fluently. They recognized that we were Americans, treated us cordially and we traveled through Wittenberg until we made contact with an American scouting party at Torgau, by the bridge crossing the Elbe.

"We traveled with the scouting party, on wheels, and rounded up wandering German soldiers, many of whom were running towards us and away from the Russians who were shooting up Wittenberg. We disarmed the Germans and detained them until backup troops arrived. They knew the war was just about over. Our small party was delivered to Halle, then Merseburg by truck and finally flown out."

AMERICANS, like Ralph Golubock, who had been forced to land in Sweden, endured a pleasant sojourn while awaiting the end of the war. Golubock even spent the Jewish High Holidays with a local Jewish family. During one excursion to Stockholm the Air Corps men noticed another group of young men surrounded by Swedes as they were. Someone who spoke English informed Golubock and his colleagues that the others were all German Luftwaffe pilots.

"We were dumbfounded. What to do now? Finally, one of our guys started laughing and waved at the Germans. They in turn began waving and we all began laughing. Then they walked away and so did we. We felt no hatred toward them. We were all airmen and felt a certain kinship. Sure our countries were at war and if we were in the air we would all be trying to kill one another. Here in a neutral country, none of us had any desire to fight."

Pleasant as life had become, Golubock yearned to leave his limbo and get on with his life. In November 1944, word came that the Americans would be quietly repatriated. From the U.S. legation in Stockholm, he and some companions departed for the airport in the dead of a cold, rainy night. "When we arrived at the airport, I was pleased to see that the plane was a C-87, a transport version of the B-24," says Golubock. "I also noted without much pleasure that a JU-52 transport was parked close to the C-87. Maybe it was there to repatriate German airmen."

Eventually flown to the United States, Golubock and the others received a stern warning at the Pentagon. "We were not to tell anyone, and he [the officer] emphasized *anyone,* where we had been for the last six months or how we got out. He explained the delicate nature of negotiations with a foreign country which must not be jeopardized because of Americans still being held." Golubock would finish the war flying airmen on training missions.

Although Golubock had been unhappy about his internment, he recognized how much better off he was than those held in the prisoner of war camps. Henry Spicer, the senior officer in the camp until the arrival of Hub Zemke, became a sharp thorn to his captors. Interviewing newcomers Spicer heard tales of mistreatment by civilians and soldiers. He may also have had an opportunity to witness the brutality meted out to Soviet captives. In any event, Spicer soon became the instigator of resistance to the camp routine as the captives harassed guards, mucked up their roll-call counts and challenged any behavior proscribed by the Geneva Convention. When Zemke came to the camp and became the prisoner leader, he supported Spicer's campaign. On a frigid November morning with the entire population rousted from the barracks to stand shivering in the open air the guards exacted their own revenge as they stretched out the count from the normal fifteen minutes to two interminable hours.

At this point, according to Lt. Philip Robertson, "Colonel Spicer dismissed us, over the loud protestations of the German guards. He then called us over to his barracks, and we gathered around him, as he stood on the steps about three feet above us and began to talk loud enough for the guards to hear."

Capt. Mozart Kaufman, in the audience, and who later reconstructed with others Spicer's speech, said the outspoken fighter pilot first recounted an incident in the stalag. "Yesterday an officer was put in the 'cooler' for two weeks. He had two counts against him. The first was failure to obey an order of a German officer. That is beside the point. The second was failure to salute a German officer of lower rank.

"The Articles of the Geneva Convention say to salute all officers of equal or higher rank. The Germans in this camp have put out an order that we must salute all German officers, whether of lower or higher rank. My order to you is salute all German officers of equal or higher rank." Spicer then shifted to other matters. "I have noticed that many of you are becoming too buddy-buddy with the Germans. [Irwin Stovroff says he too saw some officers, including ones of higher rank, cozy up to their captors in return for small favors, such as an egg.] Remember we are still at war with the Germans. They are still our enemies and are doing everything they can to win this war. Don't let them fool you around this camp, because they are dirty, lying sneaks and can't be trusted.

"As an example of the type of enemy you have to deal with, the British were forced to retreat in the Arnhem area. They had to leave the wounded in the hospital. The Germans took the hospital and machine-gunned all those British in their beds. In Holland, behind the German lines, a woman with a baby in her arms was walking along the road, evacuating the battle zone. Some prisoners were passing her. She gave them the Vee sign. A German soldier saw her and without hesitation swung his gun around and shot her on the spot. They are a bunch of murderous, no-good liars, and if we have to stay here for fifteen years to see all the Germans killed, then it will be worth it."

The prisoners cheered loudly and a German major, outraged at the tirade, ordered Spicer into the "cooler," a small cell about six by eight feet. The camp authorities held a court-martial, charging him with inciting a riot. The initial sentence was six months in the cooler and then death by firing squad. When the men happened to be led past Spicer's cell they yelled encouragement and Spicer would reply with words like, "Keep fighting! Don't give in to the bastards." After he had endured a number of months in solitary, his gaolers relented, canceling the orders for execution and returning him to the general population.

Conditions in the prison camps had begun to deteriorate further as the Soviet armies to the east and the Americans and British to the west squeezed the area controlled by the Germans and food supplies shrank. Bombardier Irwin Stovroff, shot down in August while aboard *Passion Pit*, had taken the precaution to toss away his dogtags which identified him as Jewish. But on January 19, 1945, with the entire compound population drawn up for the usual roll call and count, the commandant ordered all Jewish prisoners to take one step forward. Before anyone could respond, Henry Spicer, backed by Zemke, shouted for all of the Americans to step out. None of those present hesitated and all obeyed. The solidarity shown by his comrades in incarceration heartened Stovroff but to his dismay, he and the others of his faith were soon segregated. Luftwaffe intelligence apparently already knew the background of most of their captives.

Paul Ellington recalls, "The commandant, von Mueller, went to Hub Zemke and asked him for a roster of the Jews. Zemke told him, 'We're all Jews.' I guess von Mueller thought he'd make his job easier. But they knew who the Jews were and put them in some buildings separated from us by a fence. At night, we cut up the fence so people could move back and forth and they never repaired it. Some of the Jews had been treated badly. There was a fellow named Goldstein, from the 56th Fighter Group, and he had been cut badly on his shin when shot down. He was picked up by the Gestapo and they kept kicking him with their steel-pointed boots in that shin. When he got to the camp, his shin was a terrible mess, all scarred. Somehow, they didn't have his name when they separated out the Jews. He went to Zemke and said, 'I feel I ought to go with my people.' Zemke said, 'You've had enough trouble already. Keep your mouth shut.'"

For the next four months, Stovroff and those with him feared the worst. Spicer, who once again had annoyed the authorities, drew no extra punishment for his attempt to shield the Jewish prisoners. Apparently, the camp officials accepted him as a hard case.

Bill Topping, who had completed only one-half of a mission after he transferred from antisubmarine patrol to the 44th Bomb Group, was on hand when the roundup of Jews occurred. "We thought, uh oh, they're going to execute these guys. They didn't but they put them in a special barracks and treated them nicely. They knew the war was going to be over and wanted to get on the good side."

Perhaps the most dangerous status of the prisoners was to be in transit. Jim McCubbin said, "A German army sergeant told a group of us, consisting of about one hundred, that we were to be transported by train to a prisoner of war camp in Nürnberg. He [said] he had taken this trip with other prisoners twenty-six times and had been strafed by our fighters twenty-five times.

"The train was an ordinary passenger one with three boxcars attached to the end with a flak car between. Half of the car was roped off for the guards, and some thirty prisoners shared the other half. There was only room for a few to sit. The remainder had to stand. There were two openings high up on the side walls through which one could gain a limited view. We had only been traveling several hours when the 'lookouts' shouted that two Mustangs were strafing the locomotive. The two lookouts dived for the floor, allowing several others and myself to then gain access to the view. I was just in time to see the fighters starting a run down the length of the train. As I turned to join the heap on the floor, the only opening was on the top. I shall never forget the sound of those .50 caliber bullets crashing through the wood and bodies. It reminded me of the game played in bars where you shake five dice in a wooden cup for drinks. There were two passes, but I didn't hear the second. That time I was thankful for the German flak car. If it hadn't been for them, I know the planes would have made several more passes." McCubbin adds, "I should know. I had done this frequently.

"In all there were about sixteen prisoners killed, about the same number of civilians, and many wounded. Later, after the bodies were laid out and the wounded identified, a German medical officer and several orderlies began to attend to those in need. I was impressed to witness how the wounded were attended without regard for nationality." Marched to another rail line to resume the journey, McCubbin endured a dive-bomb attack from P-47s. Watching the bombs leave the wings, he says, "I remembered that you were supposed to lie down but to keep your stomach off the ground. The bombs landed so far away I hardly noticed them. But that gave me a feeling of life in the infantry. I was much more scared than I had ever been in the air."

He entered the prison camp at Nürnberg on his twenty-fourth birthday. "The good news here was that the soup had more peas. The bad news was that over half the peas had worms in them. We soon eliminated the foolishness of discarding the worst ones, to just squeezing out the worms, to finally just enjoying the badly needed protein. We slept on a hard floor in groups to conserve body heat and to share the one five-square-foot blanket issued each. When one person's pain became unbearable, we would all roll to the other side in unison. We became so weak that we rationed trips to the latrine. You had to be careful rising to the standing position to avoid blacking out."

Indeed, at the date McCubbin entered the ranks of the *kriegies*, the stalag conditions had deteriorated greatly. Lu Cox, the 93rd Bomb Group navigator shot down over the Mediterranean in January 1943, had languished in Stalag Luft III in Sagan, Germany, near the Polish border since the spring of that year. Late in January 1945 he could clearly hear the heavy artillery along the eastern front as the Soviet armies inexorably neared the camp. Within a week, he became a member of a lead column of 1,800 officers and enlisted men setting out in a driving snowstorm on a march south away from the oncoming Red troops. "It was so cold that our bread and margarine froze. Our clothes froze. Worst of all our shoes froze. To start up again after a ten or fifteen minute rest was sheer agony. I felt as though I was wearing iron shoes with loose gravel inside. My shoes had frozen so solidly that both of them broke in half at the balls of my feet." The only heart the men could take was that their guards were also in bad shape and some had discarded helmets, packs and rifles; a number even deserted.

It became a death march as weakened *kriegies* collapsed from unhealed wounds, disease or hunger and either froze to death or else guards murdered them. In some instances, the prisoners carried a sick man to the door of a house and after knocking left him there, hoping for mercy from the inhabitants.

As medical officer, Cox tried to tend to the sick and injured but his supplies were so limited he could mostly offer only Band-Aids for blisters. The torturous hike in the worst snowstorm Cox had ever seen covered 100 miles and all along the way they saw a vast caravan of German refugees, old men and women, small children and babies, in farm wagons pulled by oxen or on foot, also fleeing the oncoming Soviets. At the end of a nearly six-day journey, the surviving prisoners crowded into boxcars that carried them to their new home, a huge camp that eventually held more than 100,000 Allied prisoners. In his compound Cox says, "A thousand men were flat on their backs suffering from advanced stages of diarrhea, flu, pneumonia, dysentery, malnutrition, exposure, frostbite, frozen feet and irritated and reopened wounds. There were no doctors, next to no medical supplies, not even a place fit to lie down. After appealing time after time for medical help from the Germans, the worst patients were taken out of the camp and given showers and deloused and moved into another compound. The most serious were removed to the hospital." Cox and the others in better condition now coped with the omnipresent frigid temperatures, sanitation problems and a diet he describes as "unfit for pigs to eat, for it contained bits of wire, wood, worms, bugs and sometimes a dead mouse."

Paul Deininger, the copilot of the Newman plane and several of whose crewmates had been murdered after they parachuted from their B-17, was another resident of Stalag III marched out at ten o'clock at night in two feet of snow. "While on the march, several times we were forced into ditches because of raids by our own fighter planes. I was totally exhausted and my bombardier, Dean Whitaker, helped me reach our destination after the second day." After the forced march, Deininger and Dean Whitaker were packed into freight cars. "The Germans crammed us in like sardines. We had to take turns sitting and standing. In three days, they never let us out more than once to relieve ourselves."

Joe Bennett, the 56th Fighter Group pilot, captured after an ME-109 rammed his plane like Spicer, had been somewhat discomfited by certain associates in the POW compound. "The conduct of some senior officers was shameful." The last moment transport of POWs was brutal. "Walking thirty-three hours with three hours of rest [along the way] ahead of the Russian troops was tough. When you and another man have half-carried and dragged a man along for two hours and bullets start flying and the man you had been carrying beats you to the ditch, you wonder if you should ever help another man."

The situation at Barth, Stalag Luft I, was somewhat better because there was no evacuation. Bill Topping says, "Every day around noon we got barley. It had worms in it but they laughed, 'that's your meat ration.' We ate it worms and all. We were supposed to get Red Cross parcels once a month but on many occasions didn't get any. The Germans told us every time a train would move with our parcels, our fighter planes shot them up.

"I tried five times to escape, digging tunnels. Hell, the Germans knew we were digging them. They'd let us alone and by the time we were ready to pop out, they'd swoop in and catch us. It gave us something to do and kept us busy. I played so much bridge in the camp that I became sick of it. I played solitaire, listened to stories that got bigger and longer as you stayed there.

"Some of the guards treated you decently. We had one officer who tried to sneak food to us. We caught some cats and ate them. The Germans put up signs saying it's *verboten* to eat the Pomeranian long-tailed rabbits. They didn't have to worry because we'd already eaten all of their cats and were trying to catch their dogs next. We all lost weight, with starving conditions. We didn't have to work since we were officers but I volunteered to work in the German kitchen. We were grinding up horsemeat, making hamburgers for the German troops. I stole some of the meat, packed it around my stomach and sides, patted it down underneath my shirt. When I'd come home from work detail, I'd unbutton my shirt, pull out all the meat and the eighteen guys in my room would eat pretty good with what I was stealing. If they'd have caught me, they would have shot me."

Although Irwin Stovroff had been fearful of his future once the officials separated the Jewish prisoners, he experienced no ill treatment. Stovroff recalls a brief visit to camp by Max Schmeling, the former world heavyweight boxing champion, who said, "I wish you all luck and hope to see you in the States." He handed out photographs. "We put them in the urinals," says Stovroff who relieved his mental stress by reading every book supplied through the Red Cross and by trying to write poetry. Parcels through the Red Cross periodically supplemented the meager rations of the camp. "I certainly feel I owe the Red Cross a helluva lot, and part of my life.

"There came a period," said Stovroff, "when we could hear the guns and we knew our liberation was nearby, if the Germans didn't shoot us. At the end of April, the Germans began to burn as much of their records as they could, including papers and equipment from a flak school outside the base. They were going to turn the camp over to Zemke and we were given orders to start digging slit trenches, just in case there was a battle. Major Steinauer and Captain von Mueller, the camp commanders, actually surrendered to the Americans before the Russians got in, hoping they would receive protection. It didn't do them any good. The Russians wanted them and got them. Colonel Zemke began negotiating with the Russians, after our liberation. They wanted all American prisoners to be sent back through the Black Sea. Zemke was adamant that there was no way we were leaving this camp and going into Russia. The American troops would soon arrive and we would be taken out. It was touch and go; they did have us packed for Russia.

"But the great day finally arrived with an arrangement that allowed Americans to come in with all kinds of equipment. We had a certain period of daylight hours to evacuate the entire camp. There was a complete armada of airplanes. In turns, we were taken to the airstrip and as soon as a plane would land, we'd start running to it. The plane stayed on the ground just long enough to get the bodies aboard and then take off because another plane was coming in. Our pilot was great. He gave us a tour of some of the cities so we could see what we had done and then we went to Camp Lucky Strike [near LeHavre]."

Bill Topping remembers a chaotic scene. "You never saw such a sight in your life. The Russians came in, tore the gates down, drove cattle in.

The guys went crazy; there was a training school for girls nearby and all the guys wanted to go over and see the girls but they'd been moved out. Some men just took off, trying to get to the British and American lines. I rode a little distance with Russians in a tank who said they were going to go to Berlin. I'd been taught a little bit of Russian. There were women in the tank as part of the crew and I decided, this is crazy. Let's get out and get back to camp." He too was flown out to France for the trip home.

At the Moosburg prison camp, Bob O'Hearn, shot down over Schweinfurt and having spent nineteen months as a *kriegie,* awaited deliverance. "Rumors were that Hitler ordered that American officers be killed if liberation seemed probable. April 28, 1945, was a BEAUTIFUL day in my imprisonment. The 14th Armored Division, with a flurry of bullets whizzing through the camp, liberated us. The war was still going on, but for us, as the German lady said the day I was captured, *'der var iss over.'* While awaiting transportation out of Germany, many became sick from the rich rations brought by our troops. Finally, after being deloused with the 'miracle' product, DDT, we were flown to Camp Lucky Strike at LeHavre, France. We got hot baths, new uniforms and a high-calorie diet. Our crew had a happy reunion."

Marshall Draper, a prisoner since the July 4, 1942, attack by A-20s, remembers that after the tanks of Patton's 3rd Army freed the Moosburg captives, he waited for two weeks while the GIs shelled enemy holdouts across the Moos River. Able to move about the immediate environs of the camp he dealt with displaced persons, agricultural and factory workers imported by the Germans. "They appeared to be in good physical condition but anxious to get home. After liberation, three of us drifted to the town of Au near Moosburg where the *bürgermeister* offered us food, nonalcoholic beer and lodging if we would stay in town and fend off a large group of marauding, liberated Russian soldiers. We did; the advancing army had left a lone GI in Au to occupy the place and he was very glad to see us."

As the prisoners gained their release and headed for home, the Mighty Eighth now finished its European war days performing mercy missions. Bill Varnadoe recalls, "They placed plywood doors inside the bomb bay, rigged to the bomb-release shackles. The bomb bays were then loaded with food packages. We flew in, very low over an airfield marked by white crosses and dropped the food. Our drop point was Schiphol, the main airport for Amsterdam. Many Hollanders were out waving at us and we wagged our wings back at them." Later some ships from the 385th Bomb Group served as passenger planes, carrying displaced Frenchmen from Germany back to their home country.

Even as these relief runs were conducted, plans were made to transfer the entire operation to the Pacific, but V-J Day ended World War II before the Eighth could bring its planes and men to bear upon Japan. The Mighty Eighth, born and blooded in 1942 like the rest of the American war machine, now stood down.

22

DEBRIEFING

A total of 350,000 airmen served with the Eighth Air Force in England, and of this number, 26,000 were killed, or 7.42 percent. Compared to the percentages of the other military branches—U.S. Marines, 3.29 percent, the U.S. Army, 2.25 percent and the Navy .41 percent—the Air Corps sustained the heaviest losses. More airmen with the Eighth Air Force lost their lives than in the entire Marine Corps, whose enrollment included 250,000 more people. Strictly measuring the mortality rate for the 210,000 air crewmen the casualty figure soars to 12.38 percent and in addition, 21,000 from the Eighth Air Force wound up in POW camps. Of those who flew the original twenty-five-mission bomber tour in 1942–43, just 35 percent survived; the twenty-five to thirty-mission requirements of 1944 saw 66 percent completed, and by 1945, 81 percent of the combatants flew their full thirty-five engagements.

The planes themselves averaged a shorter period of survival than their occupants, with the typical bomber listed in service for only 147 days. All together the Eighth logged 6,537 B-17s and B-24s lost and another 3,337 fighters destroyed.

With such devastating numbers for men and machines, the obvious question is what did the Eighth Air Force accomplish. Postwar investigation by the United States Strategic Bombing Survey indicates that in spite of the enormous amount of explosives rained down upon the military-industrial complex of the Third Reich, not only by the Eighth but also the other U.S. outfits and the RAF, the belief in victory through strategic warfare which began with Billy Mitchell, was not vindicated. German armament production rose over 300 percent between January 1942, and July 1944. Even in

November 1944, as strategic bombing crescendoed to a peak, the output of the armaments industries still rose to 260 percent above the first days of 1942.

The researchers allowed that at best, the assaults slowed the rates of increase. That of course does not take into account what might have come off the production lines had there not been a strategic bombing campaign.

Right up to V-E Day, however, the German ground forces never seemed seriously hampered by a shortage of weapons, bullets, shells or armor. Even the intensified efforts to pulverize the key ball-bearing plants, with the awful costs from the Schweinfurt raids, brought only a moderate return upon the investment of men and aircraft as the Nazi supply *meisters* cobbled together sufficient quantities from outside sources and from their own well-dispersed factories.

The effect upon overall production facilities aside, the Eighth Air Force and its compatriots, however, struck two vital blows. While the rain of bombs upon industry could not obliterate it, the Luftwaffe was obliged to commit all of its resources to the protection of the manufacturing and transportation sites along with the workers and nearby residents. That brought the German planes up against superior numbers and overwhelming firepower. Another effect of the bombing was to mandate withdrawal of resources from the armies of men and guns on both the eastern and western fronts to fight off the overhead hordes. An estimated two million people, soldiers and civilians, engaged either in antiaircraft defenses or in the cleanup and repairs after the bombers.

Although the pinpointed attacks on the essential ball-bearing industry did not keep the war machine from functioning, the concentrated assaults upon the fuel complexes, first at places like Ploesti and then the synthetics plants, critically weakened the German forces. According to Albert Speer, the mastermind of Nazi war production, the May 1944 attacks on the *ersatz* oil-production facilities signified doom. "On that day the technological war was decided. Until then we had managed to produce approximately as many weapons as the armed forces needed, despite their considerable losses. But with the attack of 935 daylight bombers of the American Eighth Air Force on several fuel plants in central and eastern Germany, a new era in the air war began." Mechanized units on the ground lost their freedom of movement as oil and gasoline became scarce. Vulnerable and slower-moving animal-drawn vehicles moved vital reinforcements and supplies. Part of the scenario for the breakthrough in the Ardennes during the winter of 1944–45 depended upon the capture of Allied fuel dumps. When the spearhead seized only a small amount of these supplies, it creaked to a halt, affording the Allies precious time to regroup and counterattack.

Overmatched against the Allied bombers and the fighters, the Luftwaffe was defeated in the air. While the Germans still had a considerable number of first-line fighter planes to the end of the war, they began running out of men to fly them. The massive American fighter sweeps, the posses of P-51s and P-47s seeking out "bandits" overwhelmed the enemy. Even on a one-for-one basis, and the Luftwaffe incurred ever higher ratios of casualties, it could not afford the losses of men in the cockpits while trying to fend off attacks on urban and production centers. There were many more Americans in the flight-training pipeline than the Germans could hope to match. With bombers constantly ranging overhead, there was no safe training facility, and there was always a shortage of fuel. Student fliers in the Luftwaffe could only fly one hour a week in training in the latter stages of the war, not nearly enough to meet their foes with equal proficiency.

Winning the war in the air protected Allied ground forces from being savaged by German aircraft and certainly assisted greatly in the conquest of the Third Reich. Furthermore, by taking control of the skies, bombers and fighters could freely wreck the enemy transport system, demolish readily available supply dumps and prevent reinforcements from plugging gaps in the lines. Thus, the direct, intended results of strategic bombing, while not accomplishing their avowed purpose of snuffing out the power to make war, nevertheless struck a mighty blow for victory.

But behind the strategy, tactics and the performance of the Eighth Air Force were the people who actually fought the war. As much as any military organization fielded by the U.S. during World War II, the Air Corps drew a patchwork quilt of Americans. The Air Corps brass decided that its expensive and complicated flying machines, and the systems that guided them and enabled them to unleash their destructive power, required a certain level of intelligence and education. They established a minimum of two years of college as a prerequisite for working the front of the bus, the pilots' seats, navigator and bombardier slots. And the first in these positions were men who'd attended institutions of higher learning, albeit no distinction seems to have been made between Harvard [Manny Abrams], Dartmouth [Frank Aldrich], Notre Dame [Francis Gabreski], UCLA [Marshall Draper], West Point [Howard Adams], and Kansas City Junior College [Jim McCubbin], University of North Dakota [Bob O'Hearn], Friends [Lewis Smith], to mention a few. To fill all the positions that would be needed, however, forced acceptance of anyone who could pass the examination. Clothing salesmen like St. Louisan Ralph Golubock, Kansas and North Carolina farmboys like Charles McCauley and Heath Carriker, high-school lads like Wayne Gatlin and Earl Pate qualified. The roles of gunners, flight engineers and radio operators had always been open to any volunteer who could read the 20/20 line of the eye chart. That brought in New York City draftsman Larry Goldstein, textile worker David Nagel, high-school graduate Red Komarek, part-time actor George Odenwaller, Kentucky coal miner Bill Fleming, Washington service-station attendant Leroy Kuest, Cleveland cop Paul Krup, Harrisburg, Pennsylvania clerk Harry Serotta, California junior-college student Wil Richardson. The mix included minor-league ballplayer Billy Southworth Jr., English teacher Jon Schueler, civil engineer Archie Old, former seminarian Paul Deininger, son of a rabbi—Manny Abrams—and the offspring of a Protestant minister, Dave Ferguson.

Geographically and ethnically, they were, like the rest of the U.S. armed forces, a sampling of the melting pot with the notable exception of African Americans. [The military was rigidly segregated during World War II, with nonwhites largely restricted to noncombat organizations and the only men permitted flight duty assigned to a few all-black units in the Fifteenth Air Force.] Induction into the Army brought the disparate parts of America together. Heath Carriker, the North Carolina farm youth, says, "Up to this time I had never had any contact with Jews, Italians, Poles and Yankees. Although I took a lot of teasing about my accent and Southernness, I ate up this expansion of my world." It is safe to say that few men from these ethnic backgrounds had much previous contact with a man who could say, "There is not a more satisfying work than turning land in the spring with a good pair of black, 1,200-pound mules."

It is a measure of the U.S. during World War II, that Jews were viewed as a novelty to many from areas away from the urban centers. In a number of anecdotes, the storytellers feel obligated to describe an individual as Jewish, although there is no pejorative element to the tale. (Because of the high premium Jewish culture placed upon education, it would also seem, at least anecdotally, that more Jews volunteered and qualified for the Air Corps.)

Frequently, discord rather than unity marked the beginnings of a crew. Billy Southworth and Jon Schueler, so different in their upbringings, mutually detested one another at the start of their association but over time became fond and respectful of each other. Even those who seemingly had similar roots differed. Bomber pilot Ralph Golubock recalls, "Our left waist position was manned by Wallace Kirschner of the Bronx, New York. He was the only other Jewish member on the crew. He was brought up in a very tough section of New York and was what we used to call a typical New Yorker. He looked tough and talked tough. It was difficult for me, a Midwesterner, to understand him."

The discoveries of Carriker and Golubock were typical, but nothing bonds individuals like a common purpose and confrontation with a common threat. This was particularly true of the bomber crews whose survival depended upon one another and who physically were together far more than the fighter pilots. "We adhered to military discipline when that was necessary," says Barky Hovsepian, radio operator. "Otherwise, we were very close, cared for each other, real pals." The notorious informality of the Air Corps fostered the tight bonding. George Odenwaller recalls, "To be in proper uniform on the field was a rarity. Saluting was out except for a staff car. No exceptions. Usually, I stopped at the officers' quarters to see how Lt. Paul Katz was doing with his model airplanes sent by his wife. Once, I met a general there who said he thought that 'These enlisted men should not be allowed in here.' The general's son, a pilot, had Joe Harvy [Odenwaller's pilot] introduce each one of us by handshake as his crew members. The general of course was from the ground forces. Oh yes, we were also all out of uniform."

"I liked them all," declares navigator Bob O'Hearn of his crew. Red Komarek says, "I loved these guys." Irwin Stovroff remarks, "They were all good kids in our crew. We became very compatible."

But these were also men who brought with them the baggage of their era and upbringing, attitudes and culture passed on to them, which meant relationships were not always close. Manny Abrams as a navigator recalls standing with his pilot, copilot and bombardier just before the 'start engine' time arrived. "Suddenly, without warning, my bombardier grabbed hold of my jacket and swung me around, jabbering some loathsome anti-Semitic catch phrases. We had never been close or really friendly. From our first meeting I sensed a negative flow toward me. I think he came from a really prejudiced upbringing in Brooklyn. I recall being stunned, shocked by this unprovoked and irrational verbal onslaught with physical component. My copilot, a solidly constructed individual, about 6'3" and later an all-American football player very quickly intervened, as did my pilot. I think they suggested that we had enough to do in fighting the German military and that we must hang together as a team. The attack quickly dissolved, but had a disturbing effect on all of us. I think the incident brought the two pilots into closer contact with me."

Heath Carriker, assigned "pickup" crews for fourteen straight missions, became somewhat depressed at constantly working with strangers. "Not knowing which crew members could be depended upon in routine work or especially during crisis times of heavy flak or fighter attacks began to weigh on me. My luck changed when my squadron commander stood me down in order to put together a lead crew and start flying radar planes. I felt a heavy load was lifted from my shoulders."

In his new post, Carriker trained the rest of his plane's crew. None of them had ever flown in England or faced enemy fire. Only two were twenty; the rest only nineteen. "My experience with pickup crews determined my treatment of these new men. Before each practice mission, I checked everyone, their clothes, their equipment, the safety rules, oxygen equipment, flak vest, etc. I feel sure they were checking me out also, but not quite so overtly. Later, I learned my name had been changed to 'asshole' when I was not present. However, I quickly learned that I was associating with a remarkable group of men, both as individuals and as a team. Eventually, I felt very comfortable and loose with all the crew. Some even made the joke that I was the only man who moved from mules to a B-24 in one year. I pointed out that keeping a stubborn pair of 1200-pound mules synchronized was more difficult than keeping four engines in sync. We jelled, we respected each other."

The youth of Carriker's crew was not unique. War is reserved for the young and the physical requirements for flight duty, which placed a premium on vision and reflexes, insured that those only a few years beyond puberty, before age exacted a toll upon eyesight and slowed responses to stimuli, would provide the greatest number of recruits. Their humor and their language, scatological and sexual in character, reflects their recent childhood where taboo bodily functions fascinate. Freed by distance and circumstance from the restrictions on behavior usually enforced by the elders of society, they could not only explore pleasures of the flesh, but were actually encouraged by peers and the 1940s sense of masculinity.

The informality that developed in the Air Corps bothered some officers who came from the more highly structured ground forces, as Odenwaller pointed out about his pilot, a former infantry lieutenant. It seems to have been a particularly difficult adjustment for those who attended the United States Military Academy with its emphasis upon the separation of the commissioned from the enlisted.

What brought these disparate Americans to the Eighth Air Force to build such an effective team was, of course, World War II, but other factors drew them to flight duty. As they came of age, aviation had barely shed its swaddling clothes. They grew up while the airplane was still a novelty. During an early 1930s World Series, New York Yankee pitcher Vernon "Lefty" Gomez stepped off the mound at a critical moment to gaze at an airplane meandering above. [Nowadays, sports events try to persuade airlines to shift the flight patterns away from the arenas because the planes annoy players and fans.] Authors and filmmakers too were captivated by the airplane, separating it from the grim horrors of World War I trench warfare to paint combat in the skies as a replica of chivalric duels. Boys who rode in the open cockpit of a rickety jenny, even those who only saw a plane on the ground or in the air became infatuated with flight. These fantasies were fueled by the sharp uniforms with the glamorous silver wings that helped encourage volunteers.

But the willingness to serve, the enlistment ahead of the draft, the waiver of the right to be deferred, the eagerness to see combat, was motivated by another powerful force. Pilot Martin Garren, one of the youngest to earn his wings says, "It was a matter of honor, duty, family. We were exposed to a lot of propaganda. I was defending my mother, my sister, from invasion. I never felt I was a hero. I did what I was supposed to do." Walt Kelly "fiercely wanted to help defeat Hitler." It was a time when patriotism among Americans rose to its zenith and as Irwin Stovroff says, "After Pearl Harbor, just about everybody I knew was ready to enlist, be drafted, be part of a program. Very few people didn't feel we had a responsibility for ourselves and our country."

What did change for these young men when they won their wings and particularly after they went operational was the notion that what happened in battle resembled that of the knightly joust depicted by pulp magazines, books and movies. Wil Richardson speaks for all when he says, "You would enter the first [mission] as a youngster but would grow up rather quickly upon being shot at and see all those black and gray puffs coming your way. You realized it was for real. They're out to knock you down."

All of them speak of fear. "Suddenly you realize you are mortal," notes Hal Turrell. "There is nothing that can prepare you for it." Because of their youth, most began combat duty with perhaps a vestigial sense of adolescent omnipotence—someone else might be killed, but not themselves. Concerned for various organs of the body rather than life itself, they tried to shield these precious parts with extra flak jackets, pieces of steel plate. But even the most intrepid could not escape a nameless dread, what in another context President Franklin D. Roosevelt pronounced as, "Fear of fear itself." They were anxious about their ability to perform, to properly protect a wingman or the big friends, to fly the bomber even when badly damaged, to man the guns, know where the ship was and how to find the target or home, to effectively place the bomb load. It was a matter of doing one's part. "Would I perform well?" Ralph Golubock asked himself on the eve of his introduction to war. What irks a Walter Konantz so much about a reluctant colleague, or so disgusted Archie Old when he spied B-17s headed for the safety of Switzerland is the failure to support those who shared the life and the danger.

The Air Corps had the reputation for freely handing out medals. Anyone who completed five missions almost automatically picked up an Air Medal, and subsequent clusters to add if he survived further. But the bravery of many went unnoticed. Navigator Frank Aldrich recalls what he believes is an example of true courage. "A bombardier in our group was gripped by an uncontrollable phobia whenever a mission approached. In the early hours of the morning, before wakeup call, he would crawl from his bunk and conceal himself in a bomb shelter or some corner where he might not be readily found. But before retiring, he would exhort his crewmates to seek him out from his hiding place and forcibly conduct him to briefing. Once seated among his fellow bombardiers, he regained his composure and went on to fly the mission. He completed a full tour."

"We had," says Bob Johnson, the American with the second-highest number of aerial victories in Europe, "three guys out of 105 who got what we called '109 jitters.' Two were useless. The third was the bravest guy I ever knew. He was a Jewish boy and built like the Liberty Bell, narrow shoulders but a hell of a big butt. He fit the P-47 beautifully. He was absolutely scared to death of flying combat, but he forced himself to and he did. He flew missions when he was absolutely trembling when we left the briefing room. But he did his job. He flew. He never became an ace but was certainly there and helped out."

"Fighter pilots got a lot of attention," says Joe Bennett, who occupied the cockpits of P-47s and P-51s. "But my hat is off to the bomber crews. It takes grit and guts to crawl in a bomber day after day after you saw the hits they took."

Bob Johnson, who frequently describes himself as a coward at heart, says, "I think back to the days when I used to run around in the hills of Oklahoma with the rattlesnakes. You would hear a rattle and a lot of my friends would freeze. I would get out of there. When I was frightened, I would react. I react rather than freeze, the same as when I was boxing and somebody would throw a punch at me. We were a very determined bunch of super pilots," adds Johnson, "who were eager to get to the enemy and stop their killing our boys. We were afraid. We were terrified every time we went into combat. When I get scared, I move, I take action. You just have to make sure it's the right type of action."

A handful were unable to face the challenge. Joe Bennett mentions four fliers among his replacement bunch who balked when faced with combat. Walter Konantz, with the 55th Fighter Group, recalls a comrade from his squadron who completed a tour and bragged he had never fired his guns in combat. "I could hardly believe his statement," says Konantz. "He should have been a bomber pilot."

"We all suffered from battle fatigue," says navigator Bill Frankhouser. "You had to live through it. A few persons, mostly enlisted men (gunners) asked to be relieved of flying duty and were assigned to ground work."

Whether one became "flak happy" or not depended to some degree on individual personality but it was also a matter of luck, for miraculously there were crews who flew the requisite missions to the most hotly defended areas and came away totally unscathed. Pilot Earl Pate says, "I was truly blessed or fortunate, in that *not one* of my crew was ever wounded!! A classmate, also flying B-17s, lost two of his gunners and another wounded. The impact and trauma of that mission has had a lifelong effect upon him. He finished his tour and when he came home, he went off flying status and has never flown again.

"I believe there was a kind of subconscious insulation, a detached feeling in most us when we saw an aircraft explode or spin out of control that prevented a grasp of the reality that lives were being snuffed out before our eyes. Only when it happened to one of us did the reality come into focus." Although he did not falter, Pate has some awful scenes stored in his memory bank. "I saw crashes happen, been the first on the scene, hoping there had been a bailout only to find a great smoking hole with pieces of jagged metal mixed in with chunks of flesh, undistinguishable except for a hand, foot, pieces of guts hanging from trees. The stinking, nauseating smell of burning flesh stays with you the rest of your life."

According to navigator Arthur Prager and others, those who could no longer take the pressure of combat would not be court-martialed or ostracized. "He would simply be assigned ground duties and relieved of his flying pay. We had one man like that in the 92nd and nobody scoffed at him or treated him with contempt. We didn't pal around with him (flight crews stuck pretty much together) but we didn't make life miserable for him. We understood his feelings and perhaps some of us envied him a little."

Some managed to bury the stress of their experiences until after they departed from the scene. John Regan, after eighteen months with the 306th Bomb Group came back to the U.S. "I had extreme difficulty unwinding. I had been so tight with the conditions I suffered while in England. When I got to the train depot after I had been with my family for a while, to go to a rest station, I just wanted to stand there and scream. It was just about a total nervous breakdown. Nowadays they would call it Post-Traumatic Syndrome."

The attitudes toward superiors is mixed. For example, Prager remarks, "For the most part we disliked our superiors and tolerated them without much respect for them. Many of them had been promoted into rank-bearing slots because others ahead of them had been killed. Except for survival, they had little to qualify them for positions of leadership. Some achieved rank they didn't deserve because they had been at West Point."

Joe Bennett credited sound leadership to, "Good military training to the extent that one can demand discipline in a way that brings respect to his command. Slightly aloof, but not unapproachable. Be a leader but assign others leadership roles. Tone of voice when under pressure is important. L. F. Stetson Jr., William Elder and Hub Zemke had these qualities and it was an honor to have served with them. If a group commander was in control and knew his business then it seemed the squadron commanders followed. When Colonel Zemke [boss of the 56th Fighter Group] went back to the States, Gabreski and Schilling [squadron leaders] were disruptive when another colonel was placed in command. [Joel Popplewell thought Gabreski provided superior leadership.] He was a thirty-eight-year-old graduate of West Point, not a hot pilot but flew missions and made rendezvous without a flaw. He flew every mission he could and had trouble with the bends and would sometimes have to climb back to high altitude and descend slowly.

"There were [group commanders] who were good leaders in the air but their administrative work was not up to par. The group then did not measure up as a military unit. They had high losses due to lack of discipline, among other factors."

"Our group commander," says Jim Hill of the 305th Bomb Group, "was Colonel MacDonald. He was younger, very personable and mixed with the guys. Our squadron CO Major Greybeal called me in once and said, 'Hill, if you promise to wear a necktie, I'll make you a lead navigator and a first lieutenant.' I said, 'Yes, sir,' and I did, for the next day only. Our only bad officer was a West Pointer, a pilot captain who put his ground crew in a brace and told them that he didn't want anyone touching 'his' aircraft without his permission. They didn't and he was later lost—no tears for him."

To Howard Donahue, a pilot with the 91st Bomb Group, Col. Immanuel "Manny" Klette personified excellence in command. "A leader must have courage, a willingness to lead and know how to interpret a situation. Klette flew constantly, ninety-nine missions, led us and always knew what was going on. He designed the breakaway after the bomb run. Somebody thought you just go in, drop your bombs and fly straight out. But Klette after the bomb drop, would make a diving turn to the right or left to screw up the flak gunners. The technique was adopted throughout the Eighth Air Force."

Hal Turrell praises his squadron commander, Maj. Jimmy Stewart. "He was a wonderful human being and excelled as a command pilot. He was always relaxed with crews but rarely visited off the base because of his celebrity status and famous face, he would be mobbed by civilians. He never grandstanded by picking missions. If our group led the wing, he flew. If it did not, he stayed on the ground."

Saul Levine remarks, "Some of our squadron brass were good, some stinko. My personal experience with West Pointers was negative but as a group I'm sure they varied greatly. I believe some of them graduated in three years. Most of us believed that the fact they received flight training and flight pay was too much of a perk. As expected the West Point ring was an asset to early promotion and opportunity. The one specific instance I consider poor judgment was a three-go-around ordered by a command pilot, a West Point graduate and three ships were lost at the last pass. In my view some of them were pushed too fast, beyond their capability and this individual committed suicide upon returning to the States."

Fighter pilot Walter Konantz describes two of his four squadron commanders as "mediocre" and one as far less, a man "whose primary purpose was to survive and not to risk life and limb. He often aborted a tough mission claiming a rough engine or who knows what." On the other hand Konantz refers to his second group commander, Lt. Col. Elwyn Righetti as "a true fighter pilot, risking life, limb and aircraft in wild abandon. He was the top ground-strafer of enemy aircraft with twenty-seven to his credit. He was killed only a few days before the group's last mission of the war. He was hit by ground fire while strafing a German airfield. He was streaming coolant from a radiator puncture and knew he had about five more minutes before his engine seized up but instead of heading west as far as he could get, he announced he still had some ammo and made another pass on the field, destroying one more enemy plane before his engine froze up. He bellied in at the field he had been strafing and was killed by German civilians as he announced on his radio at that time he had a broken nose but otherwise was okay."

"The most effective leader," believes Levine, "is one who gains the respect of his men. This is achieved by them knowing he will go all out for them. The superficialities, such as bearing, tone of voice and so forth, didn't amount to much in my experience. You were dealing with a special group of men in the Air Corps, during combat, where you were judged by action and deeds, not b.s. A leader must also be fair to his men. I flew fifteen to twenty missions as Tail-end Charlie because of differences with my operations officer—a West Pointer. I was always moved to another slot when the assistant ops officer set up the formation. He was a fair man and well respected."

Carriker has his own criteria for effective command. "Major Jacobowitz, my squadron commander, is my pick as a true leader. He was not a talker but a doer and led by example. He was a Jew and I mention that only to point up his bravery. We all knew that the Germans could be especially brutal towards the Jews."

Tommy Hayes speaking from the command point of view says, "I figured my example as more effective than my voice. I was older than my men, twenty-six to twenty-seven in Europe while the pilots were five or six years younger. Some were only a year or so out of high school. But I had no problems. The guys were professional. The job was discussed, decided, then carried out."

Verdicts on the top brass vary based on experience or lack of it. Joe Bennett had an opportunity to meet some decision makers and notes, "Wing Commander Jesse Austen and General Doolittle liked to mix and talk with pilots. Doolittle had a good sense of humor, would tell stories and joke and both were great to be around." Says Prager, "We were too remote from the top brass to think about them one way or another. They were dim figures seen in newsreels like movie stars. Their names sometimes appeared on directives, but we knew we would never meet or see them."

Punchy Powell, like all fighter pilots, praises Doolittle. "In retrospect," remarks Powell, "some missions were foolhardy. General Doolittle admitted that to me one time in discussing a low-level one he assigned to the 352nd over the Pas de Calais area. His words were, 'I owe you and your fellow pilots an apology for planning that mission. It was one of my dumb mistakes.' I loved him for having the guts to admit it."

That sort of behavior was highly unlikely in Curtis LeMay, "Iron Ass" in the vernacular of his men, "Iron Eagle" in more favorable accounts. Nevertheless he receives high marks from those who served with him in the Eighth Air Force on the basis of his contributions to effective use of bombers. Jack Kidd, whose postwar attitudes ran counter to those held by

LeMay, regards him as having been a very effective commander in World War II. But to some, LeMay would come to exemplify the notion that generals tend to fight a current war based upon the past one. Earl Pate who continued his career in what would become the independent Air Force and did not serve under LeMay at the Eighth Air Force but did subsequently, says, "He did not lead; he ruled the Strategic Air Command [a post–World War II LeMay position]. The creed for the SAC was blind allegiance which led to a cover-your-ass in SAC. Never, never, never vary from the regulation or directive. He left no room for decision based on existing conditions."

While the Big Friends loved the close attentions paid by their Little Friends, they occasionally disputed who was a superior pilot. Konantz had no doubts; not only can one cite his remarks about the selection process but his sneer at the unaggressive fighter pilot—"he should have been a bomber pilot"—amply testifies to his attitude.

Tommy Hayes says, "There is a difference and it lies in the mission, the job and the equipment to carry it out. The bomber pilot knows what he is going to do. It is, to a degree, programmed and practiced. He and the airline or transport pilot are the same—only the load or cargo varies. He will fly from A to B, maybe several courses from A to B to C. But he has a target or stop and checkpoints along the way. He has a responsibility to get something, bombs, supplies or passengers from A to B. And he is assisted by others, navigator, engineers, bombardier and a copilot. The fighter does not know where or when. His job is based upon reaction. The fighter pilot is loose. His reactions are quick. He must have great eye-hand-foot coordination." Those in the cockpits of the four-engine behemoths, battered by flak and cannon or machine-gun fire, overloaded and at extreme altitudes with sluggish controls yet obliged to remain within yards of other bomb-laden, gas-filled heavyweights undoubtedly needed quick, forceful eye-hand-foot coordination particularly since their craft responded so much more slowly than fighters.

Regardless of the talent and skills demanded, Hayes recognizes the awesome responsibility of the multiengine crews. "I wonder how I would have stood up in 1944. From the I.P. to the bomb release, straight and level without wavering and flak going off all around, seeing your buddies hit. And after the mission there were the personal matters of those lost. The fighter pilot could always exert some control over his fate." Indeed, there was always the ten to twenty minutes when those at the helm of a B-17 or B-24 lacked even the right to control their ships; they were in the hands of a bombardier oblivious to what was going on outside as he manipulated the knobs of his Norden.

Punchy Powell also professes respect for the men in the big planes. "I have great admiration for the bombers and their crews. It is hard to imagine the balls those guys had sitting in those B-17s and B-24s, tooling along at 150 mph on a straight-in bomb run—no variations allowed—as the flak pounded the hell out of them, and if they survived that, taking the beating they did from German fighters on the way in and out, particularly those that were battle damaged."

According to Bob Johnson, "The spirit of the guy, primarily the spirit in a combat situation, determines where a pilot is best suited. Some of the best precision pilots I know, and some of the best test pilots were some of the first to be shot down in combat. They were not necessarily good combat pilots just because they were great aerobatic pilots. There is a makeup in the combat pilot. You have to have the aggressiveness and determination. You have to be able to put the gun where you want it, when you want it, no matter what the situation. You do not necessarily fly precision, except in heavy clouds and close tight formation."

Frank Aldrich, as a lead navigator comments, "The prototype of the fighter pilot as flamboyant, perhaps somewhat reckless in manner, continues to persist and not without some merit. A fighter pilot has more freedom of expression in maneuvering as contrasted to the often-called truck drivers of bombers. I suspect the devil-may-care attitude which seemed to characterize the fighter pilot was often affected to conform with the politically correct image of the time. Quite likely, the selection of those who were to go to fighters and those to bombers was dictated by the exigencies of the moment. We had more than our share of extroverts among bomber pilots."

The job shaped some personalities. Recognition that one was responsible for the lives of eight or nine other human beings in the back of the bus, to say nothing of the hundreds in the entire formation, undoubtedly helped sober some to their position. Fighter groups counted their human losses by ones, bomber groups by tens.

The exigencies of the times also changed behavior towards other people and not necessarily for the better. "We were an endangered species," says Prager, "and we had to cram in every kind of pleasure possible before a leave or three-day pass was over. We had unlimited money (by British standards) and we were able to spend a month's pay on one three-day pass in London. The girls loved us because we were not only young, superbly healthy, and unusually horny, but we could take them to night clubs, restaurants and other haunts they normally could not have hoped to see. We had never run into girls like the English where even the ghetto poor were blonde, blue-eyed and pretty. Brought up on American high school and college girls—'Don't you dare touch me there, you dirty pig!'—English girls would say, 'Hey, that feels good! A little more to the left.' At twenty-two I didn't know girls like that existed." Judging by the adventures implied in the memoirs of both Billy Southworth and Jon Schueler there may have been less difference between the American and British women than Prager believes.

Along with sexual release, many airmen pursued the oblivion granted by the period's drug of choice, alcohol. There was little concern about alcoholism during the World War II era. While no one approved of obvious drunks in the cockpits, few recognized the impairment in those who appeared "man enough" to hold their liquor. Drinking was encouraged with shots issued as rewards after missions. Prager notes, "When we weren't flying, we were either dead drunk—I'd never been drunk before the war—or in bed with some girl, any girl. Each of us had his own girl in the local village, and we were welcome there because we had access to booze, coffee, butter, and if you wrote home to a friend in the U.S., nylon stockings. The girl selection in London was unlimited. Thus we found the women in England to be hospitable, the men grudgingly so because it was hard for them to compete."

His description of life suggests some means for coping with the pressure. Many obtained surcease by different means. "Some of us, right after briefing," says George Odenwaller, "saw their ministers, rabbis or priests for prayer. Actually, these three sky pilots stood two-thirds of the way down the runway holding up a horseshoe as we sped past on takeoffs, even in the dark rain and cold." Tommy Hayes says, "When I left the States for Europe, I left my wife and daughter of sixteen months. We each had a job to do and we talked about that. I know the stress was greater for her than for me. She wrote me a letter every day. We lived our lives together by our letters. It helped when I shot down a plane and the local paper or radio had a story or a few words on the local boy, Major Hayes. If she hadn't had a letter for a week or more, at least on this date she knew I was okay. I was not a drinking man. We both trusted in prayer."

Like Hayes, others such as Joe Bennett and Saul Levine had wives and passed their evenings reporting to their loved ones. "Writing letters home helped to relieve stress a great deal," says Levine, "and getting letters from my wife was a way of looking to better days. I didn't believe in lucky hats from the time a tail gunner's lucky hat didn't protect him from losing most of his head. Doing your job well and knowing your crew would do theirs relieved stress."

Many, like Earl Pate, Leroy Kuest, and Ralph Golubock soaked themselves in the British countryside and culture. Whether exploring for knowledge, spiritual uplift or pure pleasure, almost all report the sights of
bombed-out cities and the resilience of the British people motivated them
to carry the war to Germany. Fifty years later, few express regrets for what
they did and most believe the German people of that time should recognize
that their failure to resist the Nazi leaders justifies the devastation that
befell their country. Airmen, working tens of thousands of feet above their
targets, indicate they had little idea of what the explosions below meant
in terms of human beings. Separation of the instruments of destruction
from personal contact with those on the receiving end, whether the weapon
is a B-17, long-range artillery or today's long-range missile inevitably insu-
lates those unleashing them from a human context.

Fighter pilot Jim McCubbin recalls an intelligence briefing in January
1945, that said the Germans used every type of vehicle, including trucks
marked with a Red Cross and horse-drawn wagons to move troops and
supplies. "On the next mission I saw a string of horse-drawn vehicles.
As we approached, the figures on the front of the wagons began to look
like men and women dressed in rough farm clothes. At the last possible
second, I gave the order to hold fire and we swooped over the wagons
with fear-struck faces looking up. I often think of how glad I am today
that I don't have a guilty conscience over destroying these people."
McCubbin had no hesitation over shooting down an enemy plane but
was glad he restrained himself from firing on a pilot, who became a
person after he fled his downed aircraft.

Tommy Hayes remarks, "I had no feelings of guilt or remorse. After
General Doolittle assumed command, our mission was to destroy the
Luftwaffe. Doing the job was both thrilling and rewarding. Destroying
an aircraft and maybe the pilot in the process, was a matter of him or
me. I regarded the Germans as soldiers doing their job. Like the knights
of old, who won the joust when he unhorsed his adversary, you didn't
have to kill him."

The perspective changed somewhat for the Americans who were
unhorsed. Not until Jim Goodson, Max Woolley and Jim McCubbin were
shot down and saw not only the carnage but personally came under the
hammer of bombs dropped in their vicinity or experienced fighters strafing
their trains did they come to have feelings about the effect of their efforts.

In all likelihood, the world will never see another organization like the
Mighty Eighth, which at its zenith nearly blotted out the sky with aircraft.
Like all great enterprises, particularly when operating under the demands

of war, it was hardly a smoothly running machine. It nearly broke down on several occasions. Theories and practices held by the Air Corps before the Mighty Eighth came to England proved mistaken in many respects. The quantity, quality and endurance of the enemy was stronger than anticipated. The learning curve on European weather was disastrously off the mark. The machines and the training of the men to use them frequently fell short of what was required. Still, linked to all the other military organizations of the Allies, the Eighth shared a great triumph. But the saga of the Air Corps, like that of all units who fought in World War II is a cautionary one; that the conduct of war defies rational planning, that actual combat rarely squares with abstract assumptions and there is no military equivalent to the simple surgical stroke.

War, if it comes in the twenty-first century, will be fought with different kinds of weapons. The kinship of those who served with the Eighth will not be replicated and indeed, it is not the same for them anymore. The intimacy of the bonds among those who lived together and faced death together comes only in the maw of war. But nevertheless, for many that time continues to burn brightly in their memories. And they can still draw satisfaction that they did end one terrible threat to our way of life. The generations born since can hardly appreciate what their fathers and grandfathers experienced, but it would seem appropriate for them to realize what was achieved by the airmen, along with all others who stood for their country. Perhaps for an epitaph, the veterans of the Eighth might ask those who came after them to recall the words of Ira Eaker addressing his British hosts, "We hope that after we're gone, you'll be glad we came."

ROLL CALL

Abrams, Manny. Navigator, 392nd Bomb Group. "When things got sticky on a mission, I would probably say to God that if he would get me through this one, I'd be a good boy and go to temple. I'd try anything at such times, but I never meant to go through with them, and never did." A consultant for corporate growth, Abrams lives in Natick, Massachusetts.

Adams, Howard. Pilot, 44th Bomb Group. A 1941 graduate of West Point, he was killed in action February 26, 1943.

Aldrich, Frank. Bombardier/navigator, 305th Bomb Group. "If you wish to see how it really was, watch *Twelve O'Clock High*. If you simply wish entertainment and can accept how it wasn't, go to see *Memphis Belle* [the fictional account rather than the documentary]." Aldrich remained in the reserves while following a career as a banker and now makes his home in Dover, Massachusetts.

Andrews, Robert E. Gunner, 385th Bomb Group. "I do not know why I was spared injury—I was not better or worse than any other crew member. Perhaps I was spared to testify to the horror of war and to the criminal ignorance of those who would sacrifice the cream of a generation for political purposes, lest we forget." After leaving the Air Corps, Andrews became an attorney, served in the Georgia House of Representatives and until recently piloted his own plane. He lives in Gainesville, Georgia.

Bennett, Joseph. Pilot, 56th Fighter Group. After his liberation from a prisoner of war camp, Bennett farmed for ten years, operated a fishing lodge, worked at oil production and then for the U.S. Army Corps of Engineers before retirement. In 1990, he began corresponding with Hubert Heckmann, the Luftwaffe pilot who knocked him out of the sky, and briefly visited him when first taken prisoner. They met face to face in 1991. Bennett's home is in Clifton, Texas.

Bowman, Dick. Gunner, 96th Bomb Group. "As a citizen airman I did my thirty-five missions and came home to the States in December 1944. I had a tremendous feeling of guilt that I came home without a Purple Heart, without a scratch, when so many others were less fortunate. I think I carried that around with me for twenty-five years before it passed." Bowman lives in Diamond Bar, California.

Carriker, Heath. Pilot, 466th Bomb Group. Following the war, he taught and served as a supervisor in public schools. He resides in Ellerbe, North Carolina.

Ciarimboli, Alfred. Ground crew, 91st Bomb Group, he spent thirty-three months in England. "The first year there was the roughest for all. Mostly, of course, the combat men whose losses were very high. There were few replacements of men and materials. Even tools were scarce along with jeeps." He lives in New Windsor, New York.

Cox, Luther. Navigator, 93rd Bomb Group. Remaining in the Air Corps after his release from a POW camp, he retired as a colonel. He lives in Orlando, Florida.

Crosby, Harry. Navigator, 100th Bomb Group. He taught writing at several universities before retiring to a farm in Maine.

Dascoli, Mike. Navigator/bombardier, 305th Bomb Group. Attending college after his discharge, as a reserve he was recalled for the war in Korea and flew fifty-five missions in B-26s. Upon leaving the Air Force he worked in sales and makes his home in Hamden, Connecticut.

Deininger, Paul. Pilot, 398th Bomb Group. "After returning to the States for my ninety-day recuperation leave, I married the girl whom I dated before the war and returned to my job at a book manufacturing plant." He is a resident of Scranton, Pennsylvania.

Donahue, Howard. Pilot, 91st Bomb Group. Following his separation from the Air Corps, he owned a gun shop, then became an expert on forensic ballistics. He lives in Towson, Maryland.

Draper, Marshall. Navigator/bombardier, 15th Bomb Squadron. Repatriated to the States, he returned to UCLA to secure a degree in chemistry. "I never heard any American express doubt about the ultimate outcome of the war. There was a unanimity of opinion lacking in later conflicts: We would do what was necessary to win. I believe that the touchy-feely approach to war simply doesn't work. Winning takes a certain amount of fortitude and ruthlessness, as in the Hiroshima bombing." He lives in Woodland Hills, California.

Ellington, Paul. Pilot, 56th Fighter Group. "I weighed 135 pounds when shot down and 100 by the time I was liberated. In spite of everything, I thought I'd like to make the Air Force a career. But when I saw the conditions with the military stateside, it was horrible and I wanted out." He became an instructor for the school that taught him to fly and helped set up a small Oklahoma airline. He is deceased.

Ferguson, David. Radio operator, 94th Bomb Group. He worked as an occupational counselor after the war and lives in Traverse City, Michigan.

Fleming, Bill. Gunner, 303rd Bomb Group. Upon leaving the Air Corps, he returned to the coalfields but after seventeen years in the Kentucky mines he contracted black lung disease. He then worked in factories and for a meat packing firm until retirement. His home is in Lakeland, Florida.

Frankhouser, Bill. Navigator, 398th Bomb Group. After the war, he pursued the fate of the missing members of the Newman plane, his original crew. Through his U.S. senator, he obtained documents about war crimes investigations and sought to spark further efforts by the German government to determine if others contributed to the murders and to punish those responsible. As a civilian, he helped develop new fuel and associated materials for all of the first-of-a-kind commercial and military nuclear power plants. His home is in Bedford, Virginia.

Ganyu, Al. Pilot, 96th Bomb Group. "We had to have a lot of luck to survive. Why a flak-burst missed us and hit somebody else is unexplainable. Why we didn't run into each other on takeoffs and climbing to altitude also involved somebody watching over us. I never crash-landed nor had any wounded. When I read those war stories today I wonder if I was in the same war." After his exit from the military, he graduated from California State Teachers College, earned a master's degree from the University of Maryland and taught industrial arts in Barton, Maryland. He retired to New Castle, Pennsylvania.

Garren, Martin. Pilot, 94th Bomb Group. His plan to become an airline pilot did not work out and he embarked on a lifelong career in sales. Now retired, he lives in Friday Harbor, Washington.

Gatlin, Wayne. Pilot, 356th Fighter Group. "Rags's cousin's husband located the place where he crashed and his remains were returned to Rotan, Texas, about 200 miles west of Dallas in 1948 or 1949. My wife and I were able to attend the funeral. We stayed at the Ragsdales' and I got a tremendous shock for there in the living room was Rags's casket. I had a hard time sleeping that night knowing that I was alive and well and yet in the next room was a friend of mine whose last night on earth had been in the bed next to me in the Annex [their quarters with the 356th]." His fondness for flight enabled him to rejoin the Air Corps through a National Guard program and he retired as a major general. He lives in Duluth, Minnesota.

Goldstein, Larry. Radio operator, 388th Bomb Group. "As a Jew I never gave much thought to the enemy and religion. Our navigator was also Jewish and also from Brooklyn. We never discussed the fact that we might be shot down. Most men will tell you that they never expected to be shot down or have to bail out. Even those who did [parachute] acted on impulse. A burning airplane about to blow up was incentive enough to take that leap." Upon discharge, he began a career in the life insurance field, which was interrupted by recall through the Air Force Reserve during the Korean War, but instead of flying worked as a communications chief in Japan. He returned to the life insurance business until his retirement to his home in Ridgewood, New York.

Golubock, Ralph. Pilot, 44th Bomb Group. "I didn't envy the people who flew a B-17. It's a bunch of BS that we pulled off fighters because we were easier targets. B-17s could fly higher, but they were slower. The Second Air Division [composed of B-24 Bomb Groups] would be leading the Eighth Air Force and we would have to fly an S approach, slow down so the B-17s could stay with us. We would be on the ground at briefings and the B-17s would be gone because they were slower and it took them longer to get to the target. I've always been unhappy when someone says the B-17s won the war." After repatriation from internment in Sweden, Golubock went into sales and marketing. His home is in St. Louis.

Goodson, Jim. Pilot, 4th Fighter Group. Freed from prison camp, he says, "When I started out, flying was an adventure. By the end of the war I had had enough of it. I went to work for international corporations and built plants overseas. I had learned to speak a number of languages while in the prisoner of war camp." He makes his home in Duxbury, Massachusetts.

Greenberg, Al. Togglier, 96th Bomb Group. He attended Cooper Union and Parsons School of Design in New York City, taught and worked as an art director. He lives in a carriage house designed by Stanford White, which he and his wife restored, in Hyde Park, New York.

Greenwood, John. Navigator, 351st Bomb Group. He took a degree in Business and Public Administration from the University of Missouri, then studied to be a stockbroker and after passing the New York Stock Exchange exams, entered the securities field. He has been president of the Eighth Air Force Memorial Museum Foundation, Inc., for eleven years and lives in Alton, Illinois.

Halper, Chuck. Pilot, 385th Bomb Group. He lives in Lakewood, California.

Hayes, Thomas. Pilot, 354th Fighter Group. "Meeting the German interceptors was the greatest moment of the war for me. You've made the rendezvous and assumed your escort duty. You knew there has been an attack elsewhere through monitoring the bomber frequency [radio]. Will our mission be a milk run? Then the silence is broken by 'Bogies, two o'clock level, high or low.' And then there they are. First like a load of buckshot, tiny specks, then aircraft, then ME-109s, etc. And so there they are, plus or minus a hundred and there are only forty of us. Suddenly a mixing bowl from 25,000 to 30,000 and down to the deck. Then it is over, not a plane to be seen except for the bombers. There by ones, twos, etcetera, the squadrons get together. It's the moment before the actual engagement that I will never forget." Remaining in the Air Force, he retired as a colonel and lives in Spotsylvania, Virginia.

Hill, Frank. Pilot, 31st Fighter Group. Stayed in the service, retiring in 1969 as a colonel.

Hill, Jim. Navigator, 305th Bomb Group. With a master's degree in Management and Engineering from Carnegie Mellon, he worked for thirty years for major corporations and taught at Penn State. He edits the Eighth Air Force Historical Society newsletter and lives in Pennsylvania Furnace, Pennsylvania.

Hill, Whit. Ground crew, 91st Bomb Group. Brought back to the U.S. just before the end of the war in Europe, the aircraft maintenance people received a furlough before reporting to Drew Field, Florida. Under the point system for discharging people Hill and his contemporaries had far more than many of those already returning to civilian life. At the base theater in July the men were addressed by their former 91st Bomb Group commander, now a general. "He congratulated us for our outstanding maintenance accomplishments, and then announced that he would like to take us as a group to the still warring Pacific Theater. Breaking the silence, one grizzled old sergeant stood up and said, 'General, you took us to England in 1942 but you left us in '43 and returned to the States. I say, if you want to go to the Pacific, then you go right ahead by yourself.' After a short silence, the general dismissed the meeting." Hill accepted a discharge, and plied his skills in industry but enlisted in the Air Force, changing his career to meteorology. He retired after twenty years, then worked another two decades for the Central Intelligence Agency before retirement to Alexandria, Virginia.

Holfmeier, Herbert. Pilot, 56th Fighter Group. He is deceased.

Hovsepian, Barky. Radio operator, 466th Bomb Group. "I came home unsure of what to do with my life. For a long time my family was worried that something was wrong. I would sit for hours wondering. I slowly adapted back to civilian life and decided I would get more education and learn to make a living at what I was exposed to in the service." He studied industrial electronics and then earned degrees in the field becoming a civilian employee involved in various contracts with the Air Force, Navy and the Army. Active in the Eighth Air Force Historical Society, he resides in Needham Heights, Massachusetts.

Johnson, Robert. Pilot, 56th Fighter Group. Retiring from the Air Force as a lieutenant colonel, he worked for aviation manufacturers. He lives in Lake Wylie, South Carolina.

Joiner, Ollie. Ground control, 364th Fighter Group. He pursued his interest in music along with school administration in college, taught the former for some years before becoming a school superintendent in Iowa. His home is in Monroe, Iowa.

Kelly, Walter. Pilot, 97th Bomb Group. In North Africa, during 1943, Kelly piloted General Doolittle on his command trips before he resumed bombing operations against Sicily and Italy. With fifty-two official missions he was told to pack for home and carry his promotion orders with him to Algiers. "At headquarters there, I had the good luck to bump into General Doolittle and he said, 'What the hell are you doing here, Kelly?' I said, 'Sir, I have my promotion orders here.' Jimmy turned to an aide and said, 'See that Kelly gets promoted immediately.' I was a captain in twenty minutes." Little more than a year after the 97th Bomb Group reached England, Kelly was on his way home. He shifted to the Pacific and put in another thirty-eight missions against Japan. He made the Air Force his career and after retirement as a colonel in 1967 worked in industry for almost twenty more years. He lives in Alexandria, Virginia.

Kidd, Jack. Pilot, 100th Bomb Group. Kidd tried the life of a commercial airlines pilot after the war but found the work boring and low paying. When he attempted to improve conditions for the cockpit crew he once again drew flak. He rejoined the Air Corps and had a distinguished career, retiring as a major general. Convinced from his own experiences that war is unacceptable, he, along with other former high-ranking military men, formed the Center for Defense Information which seeks to counter the arguments of those whose policies are ultimately based upon military solutions. He has written numerous articles on his point of view and a book, *The Strategic Cooperation Initiative*. Written before *detente* and the dissolution of the Soviet Union he urged an end to the arms race, elimination of nuclear weapons and efforts to preserve the world environment. He continues to labor on behalf of peaceful solutions while living in Earlysville, Virginia.

Komarek, W. J. (Red). Gunner, 93rd Bomb Group. Upon leaving the service, he enrolled at New York University's Center for Safety Education and subsequently worked as a safety engineer until retirement. He resides in Hewitt, New Jersey.

Konantz, Walter. Pilot, 55th Fighter Group. "After the war I got married and worked as a civilian flight instructor for about two years, and then went to embalming school, became an embalmer and funeral director and worked for my father until March 1951, when I was recalled to active duty." He stayed in the Air Force until 1969 and then went back to the funeral home. Still flying a 1940 Aeronca, he has written articles about his experiences and makes his home in Lamar, Missouri.

Krup, Paul. Radio operator, 398th Bomb Group. After his brief spell in a prison camp and then roaming about with advancing U.S. troops, he was shipped home. "I kissed the ground when we debarked (as did other guys) in Boston." Discharged upon the Japanese surrender, he rejoined the Cleveland police and completed more than thirty-three years with the department. On retirement he worked as a security technician for the state government and renewed competitive swimming and participates in meets sponsored by the U.S. Masters Swimmers in the seventy-five to seventy-nine-year-old bracket while living in South Euclid, Ohio.

Kuest, Leroy. Ground crew, 94th Bomb Group. He operated service stations before becoming a distributor for oil companies and then owning an ice cream drive-in. He retired to a home in Spokane, Washington.

Levine, Saul. Pilot, 305th Bomb Group. "The B-24s could not hold a candle to the B-17s. Of course this is a B-17 pilot's view but it had a much higher ceiling, handled easier, took much more punishment. The B-24s carried a larger bomb-load, were slightly faster and were easier to land." He completed his college training in mechanical engineering and worked in a business involved in space reconnaissance before embarking on a second career through studies in geology. His home is in Atherton, California.

Loyat, Myron. Navigator, 385th Bomb Group. He lives in Whittier, California.

Lyons, Bob. Ground crew, 352nd Fighter Group. Unable to find work in commercial aviation after his discharge he became a firefighter in Newark, New Jersey, retiring after thirty-two years on the job. He resides in South Plainfield, New Jersey.

McCauley, Charles. Pilot, 385th Bomb Group. A high school dropout, he crammed in a series of home-study English courses which together with his record as a captain, trainer of pilots and service schools attended earned him admission to the University of Oklahoma on a probationary basis. He graduated with a degree in chemical engineering and was employed by a number of companies and after retirement served as mayor of Timberville, Virginia, where he lives.

McClure, John. Pilot, 56th Fighter Group. For eight years he held a position in administration at the University of New Mexico before moving to Atlanta where he went into business and still makes his home.

McCubbin, Jim. Pilot, 364th Fighter Group. As a private citizen he had a career in engineering and management and in retirement from his home in Gerberville, California, has been putting together his memoirs.

Morris, John. Gunner, 91st Bomb Group. "My experiences in the Air Corps grew me up a lot. My prior life had been pretty sheltered but in the service I was suddenly exposed to a greater variety of experience and people. And the vivid events and close relationships that I shared in the Eighth Air Force completed the process. It was there that I learned the value of what I had previously been overlooking or taking for granted. Perhaps I was just lucky in the crew I flew with; we were very close. I cherish the memory of them." After graduating from the University of Pennsylvania he entered the advertising business in New York City and put in thirty-three years before he and his wife retired to Medomak, on the mid-coast of Maine.

Nagel, David. Engineer, gunner, 305th Bomb Group. "Any time our guys go over, they make sure to go to the cemetery. We have seventy-six of our guys there. I say *kaddish* [Jewish prayer for the dead], put flowers at a *Mogen David* [Jewish star] planted in the cemetery by the cousin of a man. I was such a gung-ho flag-waver and I have become very disillusioned with our government, even if it is the best. I would still reenlist. It is so corrupt, it isn't funny. A lot of stuff got to me over the years, even in my own life insurance company, there was politics and graft." After starting a career selling insurance, he built up his own company and then sold it to another concern, retiring to Clifton, New Jersey.

Odell, Bill. Pilot, 15th Bombardment Squadron. After his unit was transferred to the Twelfth Air Force in North Africa, he completed forty-four missions with it by December 30, 1942, and continued his combat service with another fifty-four while assigned to other organizations. He remained in the service, and held various commands and directorships until retirement as a colonel. He resides in Colorado Springs, Colorado.

Odenwaller, George. Gunner, 91st Bomb Group. Upon leaving the service he held a variety of jobs but eventually earned his livelihood through his continuing interest in model airplanes. He became a professional, retired only recently "under protest" and lives in Hillsdale, New Jersey.

O'Hearn, Bob. Bombardier/navigator, 96th Bomb Group. Shot down on only his second mission on Black Thursday at Schweinfurt, he was working as a railway postal clerk when recalled to participate in seventeen missions over Korea for the Strategic Air Command. Mustered out again, he served with the Federal Aviation Administration in Air Traffic Control, put in time with a police department, acted as a deputy coroner, worked on mosquito abatement and other short-term activities. "I plan to retire in another year at age 80." He makes his home in Bakersfield, California.

O'Kennon, Ira. Radio operator, 385th Bomb Group. "When I returned [to the U.S.] got married and went to college, I found that with an incentive I could excel. I had grown up. Without much effort and a new motivation I was consistently on the Dean's list. My confidence soared. Upon graduation I joined a Fortune 500 company and produced. I then set goals of the next position and achieved them. When I retired at fifty-seven in 1981, I was among the elite in the organization. The service did not parallel this leadership but ambition played a part. Air Force commissions generally related to a performance skill—bombardier, navigator, pilot. Ours were nice guys whom we admired because we gave them credit for their position, not their leadership. Eisenhower, Spaatz, Doolittle led through their actions, without regard to their popularity. They earned their position by doing, not by passing IQ tests." An accounting major in college, he worked for a business machine company in sales until he retired to his home in Bon Air, Virginia.

Old, Archie. Pilot, 96th Bomb Group, group and wing commander. He continued his Air Force career, retiring as a lieutenant general in 1965 and died in 1984.

Pate, Earl G. Jr. Pilot, 91st Bomb Group. Serving with the Strategic Air Command during the Cold War, he has nothing but disdain for Curtis LeMay. "He did *not* lead but he *ruled* SAC. LeMay was much like Ole Blood and Guts Patton in his egotistical, total control, demanding blind obedience based on fear. Yet, he was worse. General Patton admired officers and men who could and would use initiative on their own when the situation so dictated. LeMay was on flying status until the day he retired but passed himself on physical disability the day of retirement. Who can forget he ran as vice-presidential candidate with George Wallace on the American ticket? He probably caused more hysteria among the average Americans during the Cold War than any propaganda." He retired as a brigadier general and makes his home in Hendersonville, Tennessee.

Popplewell, Joel. Pilot, 56th Fighter Group. He is deceased.

Potts, Ramsay. Pilot, 93rd Bomb Group. After continuing his Air Force career until retirement as a major general, he became an attorney practicing in Washington, D.C.

Powell, Robert (Punchy). Pilot, 352nd Fighter Group. He obtained a degree in journalism at the University of West Virginia, but after a brief stint in civilian employ, spent four years flying for the Air Force because of the Korean War. "I got out of the USAF in 1954 because I was not flying enough." He then worked in the magazine publishing field until retirement in 1987 and lives in Atlanta, Georgia.

Powers, Bill. Engineer/gunner, 381st Bomb Group. He attended a tool and die apprentice school, spent thirty-eight years in factory positions before moving to Florida to be a machinist at the Kennedy Space Center. His home is in Titusville, Florida.

Prager, Arthur. Navigator, 92nd Bomb Group. He became a civil servant in the office of the mayor of New York City for twenty years, then served as director of the Royal Oak Foundation and later the Irish Georgian Society. He also wrote books, magazine articles and a children's TV program. He lives in Sag Harbor, New York.

Regan, John. Pilot, 306th Bomb Group. "I think the fighters were great. I had many good friends among them. I didn't envy them their freedom and ability to rely mainly on themselves. Perhaps I may have resented this occasionally, but when I did see them [in the sky] I was awfully happy to see them. They did a very good job for us. My biggest objection was that they were so highly decorated. A fighter pilot who shot down five German fighters got the DFC and I knew several pilots who had three or four DFCs. I don't know anybody from our bomb group who got this award, yet we suffered so very much, went through such hectic combat and had such severe losses." He decided to become a regular officer in the Army Air Corps and had a thirty-year career as a command pilot. "I retired as a colonel; it was a wonderful life and I thoroughly enjoyed it." His home is in San Mateo, California.

Reynolds, Harry. Bombardier/navigator, 491st Bomb Group. "It was with great relief that I lived through this war. Afterwards, any civilian crises were easily overcome, compared to a combat situation with all the tension. After surviving World War II, I have been thankful and considerate of others." Having worked in sales for an airline before the war, he returned to the company but then started selling textile piece goods before his ultimate job, selling ad space for magazines to the manufacturers of fibers and textiles. He currently lives in Daytona Beach, Florida.

Richards, Willard. Gunner, 385th Bomb Group. He served in middle-management after his return from Europe and lives in Girard, Ohio.

Richardson, Wilbur. Gunner, 94th Bomb Group. The day after receiving his discharge he entered college, taking both a bachelor and master's degrees to embark on a thirty-three-year teaching career in the subjects of music and history. He is retired and resides in Chino Hills, California.

Ruffin, William A. Pilot, 306th Bomb Group. "I am certain that the war years were responsible for pointing me in the right direction for whatever success I enjoyed throughout the last fifty-plus years." Active in the Reserve after the war he went on the retired list as a colonel. He was employed by the telephone company for thirty-five years and now lives in Diamondhead, Mississippi.

Sanchez, Myron. Gunner, 385th Bomb Group. A railroad worker before enlistment, he returned to the Atcheson, Topeka and Santa Fe until he became a plumber, starting out with his father-in-law. He retired in 1985 and lives in Albuquerque.

Schueler, Jon. Navigator, 303rd Bomb Group. Discharged before the war ended, he became an artist. He worked on the West Coast, New York, France and Scotland and his paintings were exhibited internationally. He died in 1992.

Serotta, Harry. Engineer/gunner, 379th Bomb Group. He owned a supermarket, then a snack-food business before retiring in Hewlett, New York.

Shanker, Herb. Engineer/gunner, 303rd Bomb Group. After separation from the service he went to college on the GI bill and then became an accountant, first in the public sector and then for corporations. His home is in Mashpee, Massachusetts.

Smith, Lewis A. Pilot, 385th Bomb Group. "My war experiences greatly influenced my life. They rapidly matured me—made a man out of a boy—and they taught me the value of an education. I have been grateful for and proud of the experiences." He earned a degree as a doctor of optometry and practiced for forty-eight years. He lives in Wichita, Kansas.

Snyder, Howard. Pilot, 306th Bomb Group. Shipped back to the U.S. after his seven months with the underground, he remained in contact with other survivors as well as the family of his copilot, George Eike, murdered by German soldiers. Derwood Eike, the father of George, invoked the aid of Sen. James Mead to get a full investigation of the deaths. The bereaved father then advised the living crewmen and the families of the slain of the details. In his letter to all he wrote, "As you know, we lost both of our boys in the war. Our son Richard was a pilot of a Fortress and was shot down near Aachen, September 28, 1944, and was killed when the plane exploded. Knowing the facts does not help the deep sorrow that has come to all of us, but it does help to know that they did not suffer long and the mental agony they might have had was of short duration. We pray that they did not die in vain and that generations to come will never forget their great sacrifice." Snyder's home is in Sedona, Arizona.

Southworth, Billy. Pilot, 303rd Bomb Group. Rotated home and promoted to major, he became a B-29 pilot but was killed while attempting an emergency landing at New York's La Guardia Airport in February 1945.

Spicer, Henry. Pilot, 357th Fighter Group. He remained in the Air Force, becoming a major general before his death in 1978.

Stovroff, Irwin. Bombardier, 44th Bomb Group. "I was a C student when I went into the military and an A student after I got back with a whole new attitude about life. How we got out of there, being Jews, we just had to be lucky. That day in January [when the commandant asked all Jewish prisoners to step forward and Spicer thwarted him] I'll never forget." He went into the furniture business and now lives in Boca Raton, Florida.

Strong, Russell. Navigator, 306th Bomb Group. "My World War II experiences, up close and facing death, have had an impact on my life. I don't regret having gone through the experience at all, and feel that I was favored by being in a good combat outfit with good leadership and an interesting group of men. My association with the 306th, including the present, has been almost all joy for me. I rather liked the thrill of flying combat, although I was with the large group who dreaded some targets such as Berlin and Merseburg." He returned to college following separation, worked for a few years on a newspaper before a career in university administration. He lives in Charlotte, North Carolina.

Topping, Bill. Bombardier, 44th Bomb Group. He tried college after his discharge but an overload of academic work drove him to quit school. He was working in construction when recalled for Korea and he decided to make the service a career, retiring as a lieutenant colonel to live in Fenton, Missouri.

Truluck, John Jr. He became an architect and lives in Walterboro, South Carolina.

Turrell, Hal. Bombardier/navigator, 445th Bomb Group. He started a furniture business but was recalled for the Korean War. After seventeen months, he resumed his civilian business and now lives in Arizona.

Varnadoe, Bill. Navigator, 385th Bomb Group. He worked in the space program, until his retirement, at Huntsville, Alabama, where he continues to live.

Villani, Dan. Navigator, 398th Bomb Group. "After leaving the Air Force, I never flew in an aircraft again until some twenty years later. I felt I was lucky to be alive. In the commercial flights of my later years, that landed through cloud cover or bad weather with such ease through the high-tech systems now used, I always remember trying to get back to the 398th. I still do not like flying in bad weather." He is a dentist and lives in Agawam, Massachusetts.

Whitaker, Dean. Navigator/bombardier, 398th Bomb Group. Retired, he lives in Las Vegas, Nevada.

Wilson, J. C. Gunner, 351st Bomb Group. He lives in San Antonio, Texas.

Wolff, Harry. Gunner, 305th Bomb Group. "We had a mission where we dropped the bombs and we could see they were falling in the woods. We said, 'They [the intelligence people] did it again.' But suddenly there was a tremendous explosion. They *did* know what they were doing. We didn't have any problems in dropping bombs on Germany. That's what we were getting paid for, killing people and wrecking things. We were only sorry if we missed them." He reenlisted after discharge and served with a weather squadron. But he eventually went into the book manufacturing business and now lives in New York City.

Woolley, Max. Pilot, 364th Fighter Group. He studied art after his return to the U.S. and became a commercial artist and painter. He resides in Richfield, Utah.

BIBLIOGRAPHY AND SOURCES

Boyne, Walter J. *Clash of Wings* (New York: Simon & Schuster, 1994).

Caidin, Martin. *Black Thursday* (New York: E. P. Dutton, 1960).

Comer, John. *Combat Crew* (New York: William Morrow, 1988).

Craven, Wesley Frank, and Cate, James Lea. *The Army Air Force in World War II*, vol. I, vol. VI (Chicago: U.S. Air Force History Office, University of Chicago Press, 1948).

Crosby, Harry H. *A Wing and a Prayer* (New York: Harper, 1993).

Cox, Luther C. *Always Fighting the Enemy* (Baltimore: Gateway, 1990).

Ellington, Paul. Oral history. American Air Power Heritage Museum, 1991.

Emerson, William R. *Operation Pointblank* (Harmon Memorial Lectures in Military History, 1962).

Freeman, Roger A., with Alan Crouchman and Vic Maslen. *The Mighty Eighth War Diary* (London: Motorbooks International, 1990).

Gatlin, Wayne. "I Was Up in the Blue Again Today" (unpublished manuscript).

Glines, Carroll Jr. *The Compact History of the United States Air Force* (New York: Hawthorne, 1963).

Golubock, Ralph. "Hello Pathway: A Bomber Pilot's Memories of Love and War" (unpublished manuscript).

Goodson, James. Oral history. American Air Power Heritage Museum, 1991.

Greenwood, John. Mission diary (unpublished).

Gulley, Thomas F., Hicks, Edmund, McClintock, William, Blackmer, Jerry, Karas, Christopher J. *The Hour Has Come* (Dallas: Taylor, 1993).

Hammel, Eric. *Aces Against Germany* (New York: Pocket Books, 1993).

Hawkins, Ian L. *B-17s over Berlin* (Washington, D.C.: Brassey's, 1990).

Hibbard, John J. "Joker" (unpublished manuscript).

Holfmeier, Herbert. Oral history. American Air Power Heritage Museum, 1991.

Jablonski, Edward. *America in the Air War* (Alexandria, Va.: Time-Life Books, 1982).

Jackson, Robert. *Bomber* (London: Arthur Barker, 1980).

Johnson, Robert S. Oral history. American Air Power Heritage Museum, 1977.

Joiner, O. W. *The History of the 364th Fighter Group* (Marceline, Mo.: 364th Fighter Group Association, 1991).

Komarek, W. J. *All the Best* (Baltimore: Gateway, 1995).

Kuest, Leroy. Diary (unpublished).

Lucas, Laddie. *Wings of War* (New York: Macmillan, 1983).

McCauley, Charles, with Graham Berry. "The Three Trees" (unpublished manuscript, 1995).

McClure, John. Oral history. American Air Power Heritage Museum, 1991.

McCubbin, James. Memoirs (unpublished).

Maurer, Maurer. *Air Force Combat Units of World War II* (Washington, D.C.: United States Air Force, 1961).

Mets, David. *Master of Air Power* (Novato, Calif.: Presidio, 1988).

Morrison, William H. *Fortress Without a Roof* (New York: St. Martin's, 1982).

Old, Archie Jr. Oral history. Historical Research Center, Air University, Maxwell Field, Alabama, 1982.

Overy, R. J. *The Air War 1939–1945* (New York: Stein and Day, 1980).

———. *Why the Allies Won* (New York: W.W. Norton, 1995).

Popplewell, Joel. Oral history. American Air Power Heritage Museum, 1991.

Potts, Ramsay. Oral history. Historical Research Center, Air University, Maxwell Field, Alabama, 1980.

Richards, Willard. *Fear, Faith, Courage* (Strasburg, Ohio: Willard Richards, 1993).

Rooney, Andy. *My War* (New York: Random House, 1996).

Saward, Dudley. *Victory Denied* (New York: Franklin Watts, 1987).

Schaffer, Ronald. *Wings of Judgement: American Bombing in World War II* (New York: Oxford University Press, 1985).

Schueler, Jon. "The Sound of Sleat" (unpublished manuscript).

Smith, Lewis. Diary (unpublished).

Southworth, Billy. Diaries, 1942–43 (unpublished).

Strong, Russell A. *First over Germany* (Winston-Salem, N.C.: Russell A. Strong, 1990).

Truluck, John Jr. Oral history. American Air Power Heritage Museum, 1991.

Turrell, Hal. "The Price of Air Supremacy" (unpublished manuscript).

Varnadoe, W. W. Jr. "One Man Remembers World War II as a Navigator on a B-17" (unpublished manuscript, 1995).

INDEX